THE JUDICIAL ADMINISTRATION SERIES

PUBLISHED UNDER THE AUSPICES OF

THE NATIONAL CONFERENCE OF JUDICIAL COUNCILS

CRIMINAL PROCEDURE FROM ARREST TO APPEAL

THE NATIONAL CONFERENCE OF JUDICIAL COUNCILS

OFFICERS

Chairman

HON. JAMES P. ALEXANDER

Chief Justice of the Supreme Court of Texas

Vice-Chairman

HON. JOHN J. PARKER

Senior Judge of the United States Circuit Court of Appeals for the Fourth Circuit

Treasurer

FRANK T. BOESEL

Member of the Judicial Council of Wisconsin

Secretary

PAUL B. DE WITT

Executive Secretary of the Association of the Bar of the City of New York

Director

ROSCOE POUND

Dean Emeritus of the Harvard Law School

EXECUTIVE COMMITTEE

Chairman

ARTHUR T. VANDERBILT

Dean of the School of Law of New York University

HON. EDWARD R. FINCH

Formerly Judge of the Court of Appeals of New York

HON. JAMES W. MC CLENDON

Chief Justice of the Court of Civil Appeals of Texas

EDSON R. SUNDERLAND

Secretary of the Judicial Council of Michigan

HON. LAURANCE M. HYDE

Justice of the Supreme Court of Missouri

HON. GEORGE ROSSMAN

Justice of the Supreme Court of Oregon

HON. CARL V. WEYGANDT

Chief Justice of the Supreme Court of Ohio

CRIMINAL PROCEDURE FROM ARREST TO APPEAL

Lester Bernhardt Orfield
Professor of Law, Temple University

GREENWOOD PRESS, PUBLISHERS
WESTPORT, CONNECTICUT

Library of Congress Cataloging in Publication Data

Orfield, Lester Bernhardt, 1904-
Criminal procedure from arrest to appeal.

Original ed. issued as no. 6 of Judicial administration series.
Includes bibliographical references.
1. Criminal procedure--United States. I. Title.
II. Series: Judicial administration series, 6.
KF9619.O695 1972 345'.73'05 73-170605
ISBN 0-8371-6251-3

Originally published in 1947
by New York University Press, New York

Reprinted with the permission of New York University Press

Reprinted by Greenwood Press,
a division of Williamhouse-Regency Inc.

First Greenwood Reprinting 1972
Second Greenwood Reprinting 1973

Library of Congress Catalogue Card Number 73-170605

ISBN 0-8371-6251-3

Printed in the United States of America

To
Roscoe Pound and Arthur T. Vanderbilt
Great Lawyers and Great Friends

FOREWORD

ARTHUR T. VANDERBILT

THIS volume is the sixth in the Judicial Administration Series published under the auspices of the National Conference of Judicial Councils. The preceding volumes have been *Organization of Courts, Appellate Procedure in Civil Cases,* both by Dean Roscoe Pound, *Criminal Appeals in America* by Professor Orfield, *Traffic Courts* by George Warren, and *Selection and Tenure of Judges* by Dean Evan Haynes. Subsequent volumes will deal with "Civil Trial Practice" and a "Survey of Judicial Administration in the United States."

Each volume in the series aims to trace the history of its subject, to sketch the law as it now is and then to set up sound standards of practical reform for the guidance of the judicial councils of the several states and such other groups, official or private, as may interest themselves in the vital problems of the administration of justice.

It is truly remarkable how few lawyers are concerned with the basic problems of judicial administration, even though all know that it is to the courts and to judicial procedure that we must look in the last analysis for the vindication of our fundamental rights. Numerous reasons may be assigned for this strange aversion. Fewer and fewer lawyers go to court; for such work the majority rely, especially in the larger cities, on the services of a relatively small group of advocates, who in turn seem inclined to accept uncritically the rules of the game as they find them. It is easier to float downstream, even though its course is tortuous, than it is to straighten it. The distaste for procedure on the part of most members of the bar dates back to their first days in law school. How many students were enthusiastic over the forms of action, even though Maitland has assured us that though dead they rule us from their graves and even though their story, properly told, has all the thrill of drama? How many find delight in the mysteries of *absque hoc* and *et non* and the replication *de injuria?* Student interest, wisely or not, has concentrated on substantive law, private substantive law—the law of our modern business civilization—to the relative neglect not only of procedure but of public law except where fear of the bar examiners has induced a modicum of attention to public law. In the field of criminal procedure the indifference is even greater than in respect to civil practice. Criminal procedure tends to be neglected, first, because it is adjective law, which law students wrongly interpret to mean subordinate law, and, second, because it is part of public law, which they think less important than private law.

In this attitude lawyers and law students alike merely reflect the general public attitude. Do we not generally pay the judges of our criminal courts lower salaries than the judges of civil courts? And do we not regard them as officially of a lower grade? And are not criminal lawyers in this country as a class rated in lower esteem than civil lawyers? The English courts afford interesting contrasts. There the Lord Chief Justice hears cases for a considerable part of the year at the Old Bailey and the leaders of the bar are just as much at home in criminal litigation as in civil matters.

Whatever the reasons may be, interest in criminal procedure has lagged behind our concern over civil procedure and far behind our interest in private substantive law, notwithstanding the fact that the most elementary analysis of our system of jurisprudence would disclose that, without the criminal law and criminal procedure and criminal law enforcement, our civil rights would be quite worthless. Any victim of mugging or other modern crimes does not require an exegesis of this fundamental proposition. Criminal procedure, moreover, involves vital questions of constitutional law, particularly as to individual rights safeguarded by the Bill of Rights, each phase of which reflects hard-fought conflicts in the courts, in the legislature, or in the field of battle. Indeed, this aspect of criminal procedure has increasingly engaged the attention of the Supreme Court of the United States in recent years in a wide variety of cases. For citizens concerned with the preservation of civil rights and for lawyers interested in the modern growth of the law, criminal law is a subject which cannot be neglected. To illustrate how continuous is the struggle for a fair trial, Professor Orfield quotes on page 493 the rule recommended in 1944 by the Advisory Committee of the Supreme Court against either party submitting a "confidential brief" to the trial court (*i.e.*, a brief handed to the court by a party to a criminal proceeding without simultaneously supplying the opposite party with a copy) and comments on the fact that the Supreme Court did not transmit this rule to Congress. But that did not end the matter for, some months after Professor Orfield's manuscript had been put in preparation for publication, we find recorded in the Report of the Judicial Conference of Senior Circuit Judges, held in October 1946, the following:

The Use of Trial Memoranda in Criminal Cases.—The Conference, after consideration of the report of the Committee appointed to study the subject matter, disapproved the practice, prevalent in some districts, of trial judges in criminal cases receiving from the attorney on one side a brief or trial memorandum that has not been furnished to the attorney on the other side, and recommended the immediate discontinuance of such practice.

The Judicial Conference has enunciated a sound rule for the guidance of the trial courts in criminal matters. Another battle for a fair trial has been won.

Despite the fact that our most treasured liberties may be intimately affected by rules of criminal procedure the disagreeable fact remains that there has been no great interest among lawyers generally either in criminal law or criminal procedure. There has been no really influential American textbook in the field since Bishop's work, first published in 1856. True, there have been many valuable studies and a considerable number of surveys. These Professor Orfield has carefully weighed along with the case and statutory law on the subject. These he has likewise compared with English and Continental experience. Through many years of sustained study, he has succeeded in distilling the wisdom of all of this experience—judicial, statutory, and investigative—and in presenting his synthesis of the subject in simple, scholarly fashion, so that lawyers and judges, legislators and law professors the country over may have the benefit in succinct form of all the learning in this vital, though neglected, field of law. This volume, with the author's earlier work, *Criminal Appeals in America,* furnishes a safe guide for the work of improving the administration of justice in the realm of the criminal law.

More than ever there is a need for this scholarly yet practical exposition of sound principles of criminal procedure. The war has brought in its wake wide disrespect for law, especially for the criminal law. Juvenile delinquency has become a nationwide problem. The Director of the Federal Bureau of Investigation has declared that there is more organized crime in the country than there was a year after the First World War. The only way to induce effective respect for law is to make the law worthy of respect. Professor Orfield points the way in the important sphere of criminal procedure.

CONTENTS

INTRODUCTION

ACCORDING to Professor Gifford the term "procedure" is one "that may be made to include more or less, according to the fancy of the particular author in preparing his book." [1] Professor Mikell has used it in its widest sense in his handbook as including the whole of criminal adjective law—process, pleading, trial, evidence, and habeas corpus.[2] Limitations of time and space have precluded consideration in the present volume of all the topics of criminal procedure. The subject of evidence has not been dealt with except with respect to certain phases closely related to practice and pleading. Neither the American Law Institute Code of Criminal Procedure nor the Federal Rules of Criminal Procedure attempts to cover the subject any more fully. Happily there are available the American Law Institute Model Code of Evidence and Wigmore's monumental treatise. No attempt has been made to cover the law of search and seizure, much of which involves rules of constitutional law or statutes. Procedure in petty cases has not been covered. Much of it is very simple, and based on statutes which vary from state to state. Interstate rendition and international extradition are not covered as they do not occur in the normal criminal proceeding. While venue is covered, jurisdiction is not. The former topic is more clearly one of procedure, while jurisdiction conceivably falls under the heading of substantive law. Habeas corpus is not covered. Technically it is a civil proceeding. Former jeopardy is not covered as doctrines of constitutional law play such great

[1] Gifford, Book Review, Clark, Handbook of Criminal Procedure (1918) 18 Col.L.Rev. 620.

[2] Clark, Handbook of Criminal Procedure (2d ed. by Mikell, 1918).

roles. Coroner's inquests are not covered because of their rarity and increasing obsolescence. Parole and pardon are omitted because the proceedings are usually administrative and not judicial. The Attorney General's Survey of Release Procedures has covered these topics adequately.

Today it is scarcely necessary to argue the importance of criminal procedure. No one would subscribe to the following statement made by the reviewer of a book forty years ago: "Criminal practice, which not one student in a thousand will ever have occasion to use in the federal courts, has as much or more space than practice in equity, which is the subject upon which he requires the most assistance." [3]

Roscoe Pound has stated in an address on "The Problems of the Law" that "First among the problems of the law by general consent, is the administration of criminal justice." [4] Yet as the same authority has stated: "Our standard work on criminal law in the United States is still Bishop. Indeed, Bishop's is still the only original and in some degree creative, complete treatise which we have on the subject. Certainly it is the only American book which has conspicuously influenced our criminal law." [5] He also states: "So far as treatises go, the contribution of our law schools to American criminal law has been in substance nil. Even for students' introductions we have had to look outside the schools." The first American casebook on criminal law from the law schools, that by Professor Beale, goes back only to 1894, whereas the first casebook on civil subjects from the schools goes back to 1871.

[3] Book Review, Hughes, Handbook of Jurisdiction and Procedure in United States Courts (1905) 5 Col.L.Rev. 410.

[4] (1926) 12 A.B.A.J. 81, 85.

[5] Pound, "Toward a Better Criminal Law" (1935) 21 A.B.A.J. 499, 500-501.

The author of a recent casebook on criminal procedure has pointed out that not infrequently the "youthful, or even the more seasoned, advocate trying a charge of crime is gravely embarrassed by the exiguity and vagueness of his knowledge in one of the most multifarious and most exact branches of his profession, one of which it may well be said that 'the study is abstruse and difficult, the occasion sudden and the practice dangerous.' "[6] He adds that an "occasional ill fortune of this nature, and some observation, have produced the persuasion that Criminal Procedure is, by reason of its large scope and infinite variety of incidents, entitled to the dignity of an independent subject in the academic curriculum."

Chief Justice Taft once stated that "our Anglo-Saxon ancestors hammered out their civil liberty by securing from their would-be royal oppressors not general declarations of principles of freedom like a French Constitution, but distinct and definite promises that certain rules, not of substantive, but of adjective law should obtain."[7] Among these rules of adjective law are habeas corpus, jury trial, the right to be informed of the accusation against him, confrontation of witnesses, immunity from self-incrimination, two witnesses in treason cases, no unreasonable searches, and freedom from double jeopardy.

The Wickersham Crime Commission concludes in its report on criminal procedure: "Indeed as one studies American criminal justice in operation, it becomes clear that the three factors, personnel, administration, and procedure, must rank in the order named when judged with respect to their influence upon the results achieved."[8]

[6] Keigwin, Cases in Criminal Procedure (1939) iii.

[7] Taft, C. J., "The Administration of the Criminal Law" (1905) 15 Yale L.J. 3.

[8] National Commission on Law Observance and Enforcement, Report

It goes on, however, to state: "Yet reform of American criminal procedure is by no means to be neglected. If good results have been obtained in spite of an archaic procedure through strong administration, we may be confident of obtaining the best results when there is strong administration of a modern procedure."

Roscoe Pound states: "As one studies American criminal justice in action, it is evident that the four chief factors, personnel, administration, procedure, and substantive law, must be ranked in that order in measuring their influence upon the results."[9] He goes on to state, however, that the "judges, courts, prosecutors, enforcement officers and administrative officials will be guided by the authoritatively prescribed criminal procedure and will be giving effect to the authoritative criminal law"; and that "a satisfactory administration of criminal justice must rest ultimately upon a satisfactory criminal law."

Many persons who pride themselves on their hardheadedness and realistic view of things are likely to stress only the importance of the police and of correctional institutions and to give little weight to matters of procedure. A salutary corrective may be found in the statement of a writer:

> Offenses having been defined the police can then move only to the threshold of the temple of justice. Beyond are the legal profession, the prosecutors, the courts, the correctional institutions, and those who have power to parole and pardon. Each of these sets of authorities or institutions is, as a rule, practically independent of the others. Between the police and the correctional institutions stretches an area where the law and the legal profession hold almost undisputed sway, where problems are numerous, technical,

---

on Criminal Procedure (1931) 3. See also Illinois Crime Survey (1929) 16; Note, "Reform in Criminal Procedure" (1940) 50 Yale L.J. 107.

[9] Pound, "Toward a Better Criminal Law" (1935) 22 A.B.A.J. 499.

complicated, little known, and well-nigh incomprehensible to the average layman, and where change is very slow.[10]

Mr. George Z. Medalie, late United States District Attorney for the Southern District of New York, has well stated the case for emphasis on the reform of criminal procedure:

> The argument is sometimes made that procedural reform, in general, is comparatively unimportant; that the inefficiency and corruption which is frequently found in our law enforcement personnel will destroy whatever effect these reforms might otherwise have. It is persuasive, nevertheless, that an efficient personnel should not be ham-strung by an archaic and antiquated criminal procedure. The movement for improvement in our enforcement personnel is important; but it is equally important that courageous and efficient law enforcing officials should be implemented with effective weapons, adequate to cope with increasing criminal resourcefulness.[11]

The writer would, however, be the last to maintain that criminal procedural reform offers the most important method of crime prevention and control. He heartily agrees with Professor Wechsler that the "most satisfactory method of crime prevention is the solution of the basic problems of government—the production and distribution of external goods, education and recreation." [12]

Back in 1931 the Wickersham Crime Commission referred to the "voluminous literature of reform of criminal procedure which has appeared in the past 30 years." [13] The writer has endeavored to examine this literature. He has found that there have been few full and well inte-

[10] Millspaugh, Crime Control by the National Government (1937) 7.

[11] Medalie, "Making Criminal Prosecution More Effective" (1935) 21 A.B.A.J. 504, 505.

[12] Wechsler, "A Caveat on Crime Control" (1937) 27 J.Crim.L. 629, 637.

[13] Nat. Com. on Law Obs. and Enf., Rep. on Crim. Proc. (1931) 2.

grated programs offered. All too often the literature deals with but one or two phases of criminal procedure and often with phases of relative unimportance.

As an Arkansas judge has said: "There has not been what can fairly be called a revolution in Criminal Law and Procedure since 1789. The criminal law of the various states is still a reflection of the fourth volume of Blackstone's Commentaries on the Law of England." [14] A noted French writer has said: "English criminal procedure has remained, in the 1800s and the 1900s, substantially as it was in the 1700s." [15]

Maitland stated in 1885 that in England "criminal procedure is much more antique than civil procedure." [16] The Wickersham Crime Commission points out: "In the United States civil procedure has been overhauled completely. Criminal procedure has never had any such thorough going revision." [17] As Roscoe Pound states: "Criminal law, whether in English law or in civil law, never attained the systematic perfection that marks the civil side of the law in the one system, at least in the modern world, and is beginning to be found on the civil side of the law in the other also." [18]

The writer has gone to considerable trouble to state the history of each stage in a criminal proceeding. As Mr. Justice Holmes once stated: "The law embodies the story of a nation's development through many centuries, and it cannot be dealt with as if it contained only the axioms and corollaries of a book of mathematics. In order

[14] Folk, J., "Uniform Code of Criminal Law and Procedure," Forty-Second Ann. Proc. Bar Assoc. of Ark. (1939) 303, 304.

[15] Esmein, A History of Continental Criminal Procedure (Simpson's trans. 1913) 347.

[16] Maitland, Police and Justice (1885) 164, n.

[17] Nat. Com. on Law Obs. and Enf., Rep. on Crim. Proc. (1931) 5.

[18] Pound, "The Future of the Criminal Law" (1921) 21 Col.L.Rev. 1, 2.

to know what it is, we must know what it has been, and what it tends to become. We must ultimately consult history and existing theories of legislation." [19]

Professor P. H. Winfield states that "law reform is apt to be ill-considered unless the history of the law is taken into account. I should not say that reforms can never be sound unless the history of the law has been studied, but there is no doubt that, without such study, attempted amendments of the law may be one-sided or even positively mischievous." [20] Moreover as one writer states: "Procedural and substantive elements in the criminal law are intimately intermingled and a small change in the conduct of procedure may have, and frequently in the past has had, most important and far-reaching effects upon our positive institutions." [21]

As the leading historian of the English criminal law has pointed out, to be complete a study of criminal procedure should include its history, a statement of it as an existing system, and a critical discussion of its component parts with a view to its improvement.[22] These three parts will correspond to its past, present, and future condition.

The writer of a book on criminal procedure may seek to state the existing law of the subject. Or he may attempt a criticism of existing law with a statement of needed reforms. The writer is in accord with Dean William G. Hale: "It is believed in this day lawbooks should be of one character or the other and preferably of the latter character. Moreover, the need for the latter type of book

[19] Holmes, The Common Law (1881) 1.

[20] "Some Sources of Modern English Criminal Legislation" (1943) 8 Camb.L.J. 180.

[21] Auld, "The Comparative Jurisprudence of Criminal Process" (1935) 1 U. of Toronto L.J. 82, 83.

[22] 1 Stephen, A History of the Criminal Law of England (1883) 1.

is especially great in a branch of the law which is going through a process of change and in which the reform kettle is boiling so vigorously."[23]

> An ideal system of law should draw its postulates and its legislative justification from science. As it is now, we rely upon tradition, or vague sentiment, or the fact that we never thought of any other way of doing things, as our only warrant for rules which we enforce with as much confidence as if they embodied revealed wisdom. Who here can give reasons of any different kind for believing that half the criminal law does not do more harm than good?[24]

What has been said of teaching criminal procedure in the law schools is equally applicable to the writing of this book: "A law school which seeks merely to give a knowledge of the law as it is fails to perform an important function. In teaching criminal law and procedure the object should be, not only to familiarize the student with the existing law and practice, but also to arouse his interest in remolding the law to meet modern conditions and in improving methods of practice."[25]

The writer has resorted to the comparative method in making this study. He has compared American procedure with English and to a lesser extent with Continental procedure. As one writer says: "The problem of crime and its suppression is a world problem. . . . More and more our social agencies come to be international in their scope. In these circumstances the duty of the law reformer is plain. He must analyze the evils of his system of laws with a view to their correction; and a de-

[23] Hale, Book Review, Clark, Handbook of Criminal Procedure (1918) 27 Yale L.J. 975, 976.

[24] Speeches by Oliver Wendell Holmes (1934) 68.

[25] Report of the Joint Committee on the Improvement of Criminal Justice (1931) 56 A.B.A.Rep. 513, 518.

pendable step in any thoroughgoing analysis is that of comparison. He must see how other systems of laws have dealt with these common problems. He will learn thereby wherein his own system is sound and will learn to cherish and retain what is wholesome; he will learn, by the experience of others, wherein his own system is weak, and knowledge of wrongs to be righted will make plain the path of betterment."[26]

An Arkansas judge has pointed out: "As a rule, a majority of the lawyers in every Legislature are the sworn enemies of any attempt at reform in our methods of criminal procedure. This assertion may not be relished by the profession, but it is none the less true for all that."[27]

Justice Justin Miller has pointed out: "Not only is the maladministration of criminal justice largely attributable to the ignorance of lawyers and their resulting indifference; but it is contributed to also, very greatly, by the antagonism of lawyers to new procedures; of the reason for which they are ignorant, and being ignorant are fearful and being fearful are contemptuous."[28]

The initiation of criminal procedural reforms is primarily the function and duty of lawyers.

[26] Auld, "The Comparative Jurisprudence of Criminal Process" (1935) 1 U. of Toronto L.J. 82, 83. Another writer states: "Good precedent exists for examining the methods of other countries in dealing with problems of the criminal procedure which are essentially the same as our own. Nor would it be an abdication of national intelligence to ascertain the superior features of other procedures and seriously to consider the wisdom of adopting them." Ploscowe, "The Development of Present-Day Criminal Procedures in Europe and America" (1935) 48 Harv.L.Rev. 433, 471. See also Radzinowicz and Turner, The Modern Approach to Criminal Law (1945) c.21.

[27] Grace, J., "The Law's Delays" (1910) 13 Rep. Proc. Bar Assoc. of Ark. 111, 116.

[28] Miller, J., "Lawyers and the Administration of Criminal Justice" (1934) 20 A.B.A.J. 77, 79.

> The specialized information of the lawyer group relates to a system of substantive criminal law, criminal procedure and administration into which the specialized information of all other groups fits at various points. This cannot be said of the specialized information of any other interested group. No other group can set up a system which will be inclusive and into which the specialized information of the lawyer and all other groups can fit. . . . Responsibility for continued failure to attack the problem and to improve the situation, then, is properly chargeable to the lawyer group.[29]

> Members of the bar, as prominent citizens, have a responsibility for the "crime problem". The public's derogation of lawyers because of general mishandling of crime gives the bar special incentives towards improvement of criminal administration. Lawyers can assume a central position as public officials, as voluntary defenders, as vigilant and informed critics and reformers of criminal law, procedure, and administration, and as professional protectors of civil liberties.[30]

The American Bar Association has of course long been interested in the reform of criminal procedure. The American Law Institute drafted its comprehensive Code of Criminal Procedure. Many other agencies have participated. "The American Judicature Society, The American Institute of Criminal Law and Criminology, The American Prison Association, The National Probation Association, The National Municipal Research Council, The Social Science Research Council, the National Crime Commission, federal and state commissions, judicial coun-

29 Report of the Joint Committee on the Improvement of Criminal Justice (1931) 56 A.B.A.Rep. 513, 514-515. The joint committee was made up of representatives of the American Bar Association, the American Law Institute, and the Association of American Law Schools.

30 Riesman, "Law and Social Science: A Report on Michael and Wechsler's Casebook on Criminal Law and Administration" (1941) 50 Yale L.J. 636, 641.

cils and various other public and private organizations, especially those carrying on crime surveys, have made and are making valuable contributions." [31]

While lawyers must take the lead in the reform of criminal procedure, the layman must also play a significant and continuing part. In the words of President Woodrow Wilson when he welcomed the American Bar Association to Washington: "I have in my life dealt with all sorts and conditions of men, and I have found that the flame of moral judgment burned just as bright in the man of humble life and limited experience as in the scholar and the man of affairs. And I would like his voice always to be heard, not as a witness, not as speaking in his own case, but as if it were the voice of man in general, in our courts of justice, as well as the voice of the lawyers remembering what the law has been." [32]

What of the First World War and criminal procedure? A former federal district attorney pointed out: "During the winter of 1920-21 the newspapers throughout the country declared that crime in American cities was at high tide. They repeatedly asserted that a wave of crime was sweeping the country with a deluge of murders, burglaries and robberies and that every kind of violence and lawlessness was rife." [33]

During the World War of 1914-1918 adult crime in England actually diminished.[34] In 1918 the number of offenders tried by jury was 5,904 compared with 12,511 in 1913. In 1918 the number of those tried at Petty Sessions

[31] Report of the Joint Committee on the Improvement of Criminal Justice (1931) 56 A.B.A.Rep. 513, 525.

[32] Wilson, Address of the President of the United States (1914) 39 A.B.A.Rep. 6, 8.

[33] Sims, "Speedy Justice in Criminal Cases" (1921) 46 A.B.A.Rep. 596.

[34] Kenny, Outlines of Criminal Law (13th ed.1929) 527.

was 427,572 compared with 731,048 in 1913. But the number of juvenile offenders increased in a marked degree. Thus while in 1913 the number of boys and girls sent to reformatories was 1,250, in 1918 the number was 1,685 and would have been greater if accommodations had been available. The increase in juvenile crime was due to the absence of fathers and schoolmasters at war, and the ease of obtaining employment at high wages. The decrease in adult crime was due to the same ease of obtaining employment, the absence in the armed forces of many persons of weak or uncontrolled natures, the patriotic public spirit, and restrictions on the sale of alcoholic liquors. The single exception was an increase in bigamy arising out of weakened matrimonial ties.

The coming of peace is likely to produce, for a time at any rate, a higher crime rate. In England after the last war tramps who had gone into the army resumed their habits of vagrancy and many habitual offenders resumed the commission of crimes. Children who had become juvenile delinquents continued the course of their conduct and sometimes became hardened adult criminals. Some men of previously good habits returned home shaken and craving abnormal excitement. "The drafting of the 18- and 19-year-olds makes it probable that a host of youth, schooled to violence under a strict yet paternal discipline, will suddenly be released to make their individual adjustments to civilian life as best they may. That more will fail than do under normal conditions is a certainty." [35] Many workers who had grown accustomed to high wages failed to adjust themselves to lowered wage rates after the First World War.

Not only in England, but also in Germany, where

[35] (1943) 27 J. Am. Jud. Soc. 28.

people are accustomed to obey without question, crime increased after the First World War and even during it. "The social and economic upheaval of war and the fatal economic crisis after the collapse of the German currency, resulted in an unprecedented rise in crime with two marked peaks in 1917-18 and 1923. As compared with pre-war standards, thefts increased two-fold during the War and receiving of stolen property three-fold among that part of the population which was not eligible for military service. The same occurred, but in a more acute form, during the inflation crisis." [36]

A writer in *Harper's Magazine* for March 1944 points out: "Never before has so large a percentage of our citizens been in the military services. Never before have our soldiers and sailors had to serve so long. If you train ten million men in violence, destruction, and the negation of all law, how many are you conditioning permanently?" [37]

President Hoover stated on April 22, 1929, that every "student of our law enforcement mechanism knows full well . . . that its procedure unduly favors the criminal" and that in "our desire to be merciful the pendulum has swung in favor of the prisoner and far away from the protection of society." [38] The Minnesota Crime Commission of 1927 concluded that Minnesota's criminal procedure "gives too great advantage to the accused and too great disadvantage to the state and entails too great delays." [39]

[36] Grünhut, "The Development of the German Penal System 1920-1932" (1944) 22 Can.B.Rev. 198, 206-207.

[37] P.344, at 346.

[38] Quoted in Nat. Com. on Law Obs. and Enf., Rep. on Crim. Proc. (1931) 1.

[39] Minnesota Crime Commission Report (1927) 73.

But, as Roscoe Pound states, "one may well pause to inquire whether we in America shall necessarily be so much better off under the more efficient criminal justice that we seem determined to fasten upon ourselves in the twentieth century." [40] He further states: "The over-technical tenderness for the offender in the nineteenth century is giving way to an over-callousness, to violation of the constitutional rights of accused persons in the supposed interest of efficient enforcement of the penal laws."

One of the drafters of the American Law Institute Code of Criminal Procedure has pointed out: "The twentieth-century advocates of criminal procedural reform tend to divide themselves into two groups. The first group, generally thinking about professional criminals, emphasizes the importance of speeding up prosecution and making it somewhat rougher than it formerly was on the defendants. The second group, concerned mostly with casual criminals or innocent persons, is earnest in seeking to preserve and to strengthen traditional civil liberties." [41] The writer has endeavored to present both positions.

The writing of this book was commenced in February 1944. The writer is deeply indebted to the University of Nebraska for an appointment as a research professor to undertake the work. Gratitude is due to the University of Chicago Law School for the use of its library. Acting Dean Sheldon Tefft was most generous in obtaining all the necessary research materials. No small appreciation of their classes is due to Justin Miller, Sheldon Glueck, and Sam Bass Warner. The writer is deeply indebted to

[40] Pound, "The Future of the Criminal Law" (1921) 21 Col.L.Rev. 1, 9.

[41] Williams, Book Review, Federal Rules of Criminal Procedure, Preliminary Draft (1943) 92 U. of Pa.L.Rev. 221, 223.

Professor Roscoe Pound for editing the manuscript. Grateful acknowledgment is made to Arthur T. Vanderbilt for encouragement in the publication of this book and for writing the Foreword. Sincere appreciation is felt to Miss Jean B. Barr for editing the manuscript in its final form. The study upon which this report is based was made possible by a grant from the Carnegie Corporation of New York; it is not, however, the author, owner, publisher, or proprietor of this publication, and it is not to be understood as approving by virtue of its grants any of the statements made or views expressed therein.

LESTER BERNHARDT ORFIELD

Chicago, Illinois
September 2, 1946

Criminal Procedure from Arrest to Appeal

CHAPTER I

ARREST

1. Stage in Proceedings

A SCHOLAR of the highest distinction has concluded, with respect to criminal procedure: "The two major procedural problems are those of apprehension and trial of suspected persons." [1] The Wickersham Crime Commission states: "Reduced to its lowest terms, the essentials of a criminal proceeding are: (1) to bring the accused before or within the power of the tribunal, (2) a preliminary investigation to insure that the crime is one which should be prosecuted, (3) notice to the accused of the offense charged, (4) opportunity to prepare for trial, procure witnesses, and make needed investigations, (5) a speedy trial, (6) a fair trial before an impartial tribunal, and (7) one review of the case as a whole by a suitable appellate tribunal. Criminal procedure should be as simple and direct as is consistent with these requirements." [2]

According to one of the reporters of the American Law Institute Code of Criminal Procedure, "When a crime has

[1] Wechsler, "A Caveat on Crime Control" (1937) 27 J.Crim.L. 629, 634. According to Holdsworth, "in primitive times the most important of all the topics in the law of procedure" was perhaps that of process. 3 History of English Law (3d ed.1923) 597.

[2] Nat. Com. on Law Obs. and Enf., Rep. on Crim. Proc. (1931) 16. As to the origin of the term "procedure," see Millar, "The Lineage of Some Procedural Words" (1939) 25 A.B.A.J. 1023. Until the nineteenth century it was more usual to use the trichotomy, "pleading, practice and evidence." Evidence is usually viewed as a phase of procedure, although there are some opposing views. See Green, "To What Extent May Courts Under the Rule-Making Power Prescribe Rules of Evidence" (1940) 26 A.B.A.J. 482; (1925) 3 Proc. Am.L.Inst. 506-507. As to meaning of "proceeding," see United States v. Auerbach, 68 F.Supp. 776, 780-781 (S.D. Calif. 1946).

been committed, the first step, ordinarily, in the prosecution of a guilty person, is to secure his body so that he may be forthcoming for his trial, or in other words, to arrest him." [3] Or, as Bishop states: "In general, when a crime has been committed, the first step against the doer is to arrest him." [4]

In England in jury cases, which are tried in the common-law manner, says Professor Kenny, "there are ten possible stages which call for explanation. These are:—(1) Information; (2) Arrest; (3) Commitment for trial; (4) Prosecution, i.e., Accusation; (5) Arraignment; (6) Plea and issue; (7) Trial and verdict; (8) Judgment; (9) Reversal of judgment; (10) Reprieve or pardon." [5]

In some cases the arrest will occur before any judicial proceedings have begun, as where the arrest is for a felony committed in the presence of the person arresting.[6] In other cases, where a complaint is made or an in-

[3] Clark, Handbook of Criminal Procedure (2d ed. by Mikell, 1918) 24. See also Harris and Wilshere, Principles and Practice of the Criminal Law (17th ed.1943) 392. Arrest may also be made for a criminal or a civil contempt. A.L.I. Restatement of Torts (1934) § 112, comment c. With respect to arrest of a defendant on mesne process in a civil proceeding, see Note (1926) 26 Col.L.Rev. 1007.

[4] Bishop, New Criminal Procedure (4th ed.1895) § 30, p.12. See Nat. Com. on Law Obs. and Enf., Rep. on Crim. Proc. (1931) 16.

[5] Kenny, Outlines of Criminal Law (15th ed.1942) 523. The various stages of a Canadian criminal proceeding are described in Riddell, "Criminal Law in Canada" (1926) 10 Minn.L.Rev. 557. The various stages of an American state court criminal proceeding are set forth in 1 Bishop, New Criminal Procedure (4th ed.1895) §§ 30-43, pp.13-20; Smith, Criminal Law in the United States, Prison Reform and Criminal Law (1910) 94-103; Nat. Com. on Law Obs. and Enf., Rep. on Crim. Proc. (1931) 16-18; Black, J., Seven Lectures on Legal Topics (1929) 348-359. The stages in a federal criminal proceeding are summarized in 15 Hughes, Federal Practice, Jurisdiction and Procedure (1932) 642, 832, 911.

[6] Warner and Cabot, Judges and Law Reform (1936) 96. See §§ 21 and 22 of the American Law Institute Code of Criminal Procedure (1930).

dictment found before the accused person is arrested, the court ordinarily issues a warrant for the arrest.[7] Since most arrests are without a warrant it seems correct to say that ordinarily criminal proceedings are commenced by an arrest.

It has been pointed out that, while the topic "arrest" is included in authoritative analyses of criminal procedure from Hale to the Code of the American Law Institute, nevertheless from some points of view it is a matter of substantive law.[8] It is true that, looked at from the point of view of punishment, the accused must be brought in the physical power of the court, and arrest is merely incidental thereto. On the other hand, if the end is judicial decision, the presence of the defendant is not a prerequisite. According to Salmond, procedure is limited to "that branch of the law which governs the process of litigation."[9] This would seem to exclude the law of arrest. Moreover in tort law, arrest has a widely different significance: under prescribed conditions an officer is privi-

---

Arguably no question of procedure is then involved, since there is no judicial or clerical action. Orfield, "The Preliminary Draft of the Federal Rules of Criminal Procedure" (1943) 22 Tex.L.Rev. 37, 44.

[7] Wharton, Criminal Pleading and Practice (9th ed.1889) § 1, p.2. See §§ 1, 2, and 195 of the A.L.I. Code of Crim. Proc. (1930). Professor Kenny states that in England "in ordinary procedure, just as in summary, the first step usually is to lay an 'information' before a justice of the peace." Outlines of Criminal Law (15th ed.1942) 525. In federal criminal procedure a complaint is one of the legally accepted modes of instituting a criminal proceeding. United States v. Simon, 248 Fed.980 (E.D.Pa., 1916). The Federal Rules of Civil Procedure, Rule 3, provides: "A civil action is commenced by filing a complaint with the court." See also Report, Crime Surveys Committee, Law Association of Philadelphia (1926) 108, 167.

[8] Hall, "Objectives of Federal Criminal Procedural Revision" (1942) 51 Yale L.J. 723, 737.

[9] Jurisprudence (7th ed.1924) 495-496.

leged to apprehend; that is to say, he is excepted from the general duty to refrain from conduct designated "assault" and "imprisonment."

2. Time Interval from Crime to Arrest

It is repeatedly asserted that criminal proceedings involve numerous long delays. It therefore seems desirable to examine the time intervals between each stage in a criminal proceeding. The interval between the commission of a crime and arrest of the defendant is usually very short. In Oregon a study of felony cases occurring in 1927 and 1928 indicated that the median interval between the commission of the crime and arrest was three days.[10] During the years 1927 to 1930 arrests for federal crimes in Connecticut occurred within less than a month in almost 90 per cent of the cases.[11] An examination of larceny prosecutions in Boston, Massachusetts, in 1933 revealed that arrests occurred within fifteen days in 72 per cent, within a month in 84 per cent, and within two months in 90 per cent.[12] A year or more elapsed between the offense and the arrest of the defendant in only two per cent of the cases. Delay at this stage does not appear to be excessive.

3. Problems of Arrest

Virtually all the problems of the law of arrest arise under the following headings: (1) definition of arrest; (2) restrictions upon the right to arrest depending upon

[10] Morse and Beattie, "Survey of the Administration of Criminal Justice in Oregon" (1932) 11 Ore.L.Rev. (Supp.) 188.

[11] Nat. Com. on Law Obs. and Enf., Progress Report on the Study of the Federal Courts (1931) 49.

[12] Warner and Cabot, Judges and Law Reform (1936) 95.

whether or not the arresting party is a police officer or a private person, whether or not the arrest is with or without a warrant, and the time of the arrest; (3) the issuance of warrants; (4) duties of the arresting party after the arrest; and (5) the effects of illegal arrest and of violations of duties after arrest.[13] The Uniform Arrest Act, drafted by the Interstate Commission on Crime deals only with arrest by peace officers and covers nine topics:[14] (1) questioning and detaining suspects; (2) searching suspects for weapons; (3) the force permissible in making an arrest; (4) the right to resist an illegal arrest; (5) arrest without a warrant; (6) summons instead of arrest; (7) release of persons arrested; (8) permissible delay in bringing before a magistrate; and (9) identification of witnesses.

4. Arrest by Private Person

At common law, arrests might be made either by a private person or by a police officer. Arrest by a private person has been referred to as "a modified survival from the middle ages." [15] It is seldom employed today. It would appear that existing law provides adequately for arrests

[13] Hall, "Legal and Social Aspects of Arrest Without a Warrant" (1936) 49 Harv.L.Rev. 566. For the most complete treatments of the law of arrest see Voorhees, The Law of Arrest (2d ed.1915); Perkins, "The Law of Arrest" (1940) 25 Iowa L.Rev. 201-289; A.L.I., Code of Crim. Proc. (1930) c.1 and commentaries, pp.173-265; 6 C.J.S., Arrest, pp.570-628; 22 C.J.S., Criminal Law, pp.455-483; 4 Am.Jur., Arrest, §§ 1-133.

[14] Warner, "The Uniform Arrest Act" (1942) 28 Va.L.Rev. 315, 317. The uniform act has been adopted in New Hampshire and Rhode Island. N.H.Laws 1941, c.982; R.I.Pub.Laws 1941, c.163.

[15] Nat. Com. on Law Obs. and Enf., Rep. on Crim. Proc. (1931) 19. There are very few federal precedents. Fraenkel, "From Suspicion to Accusation" (1942) 51 Yale L.J. 748, 755. Modern statutes often do not provide for arrest under a warrant by a private person. Perkins, "The Law of Arrest" (1940) 25 Iowa L.Rev. 201, 215.

by private persons.[16] While the writer does not advocate its extension, he does not favor its complete abolition. There are doubtless situations in which its continuance is in the public interest, as where a dangerous felon might otherwise escape.

5. History of Warrants in England

Between the fourteenth and seventeenth centuries, summonses and warrants developed and took the place formerly occupied by the hue and cry.[17] Justices of the peace were first instituted in 1326. Early statutes empowered them to arrest. Such early statutes did not, however, enable them directly to take any information as to the commission of the crime and issue a summons or warrant for the apprehension of the suspected person. At first they had no more authority to apprehend offenders than did constables or private persons. But gradually the practice of issuing warrants came into use. The general authority of justices of peace as to criminal matters and as to internal government was finally established by numerous statutes. It was thus only natural that their directions should be taken when a crime was committed. Likewise

[16] Warner, "The Uniform Arrest Act" (1942) 28 Va.L.Rev. 315, 317. See A.L.I. Code of Crim. Proc. (1930) § 22 and commentaries, pp.238, 242; A.L.I., Restatement of Torts (1934) § 119. As to the English law, see Kenny, Outlines of Criminal Law (15th ed.1942) 528-529, 531; Archbold, Criminal Pleading, Evidence and Practice (30th ed.1938) 1021. Modern English statutes are so highly complicated and technical that there are few arrests by private persons. Howard, Criminal Justice in England (1931) 300-301.

[17] 1 Stephen, A History of the Criminal Law of England (1883) 189-190. The present English law of arrest is set forth in Kenny, Outlines of Criminal Law (15th ed.1942) 525-531; Archbold, Criminal Pleading, Evidence and Practice (30th ed.1938) 1020-1024; Stephen, A Digest of the Law of Criminal Procedure (1883) 63-68; Harris and Wilshere, Principles and Practice of the Criminal Law (17th ed.1943) 392-401.

it was more natural for the justice to authorize the constable to perform the arrest than to do it himself. Finally, if a suspected person was to be searched for in several places, it was convenient to give written authority to several persons for the purpose, especially in the case of a hue and cry. Without any statute, warrants were frequently granted in the seventeenth century. Consequently various statutes recognized the granting of warrants, and this was done indisputably in 1848.[18] The power of justices to issue such process had previously been disputed for centuries. Of course, there can be no question that it was highly expedient that justices of the peace act judicially in issuing warrants. But Stephen regards it as unlikely that it was intended that they do so when the statutes under which they were first appointed were enacted.[19]

6. Arrest with Warrant in the United States

When arrest is with a warrant, the court issuing the warrant must have jurisdiction and the warrant must not reveal upon its face any defect so serious as to make it void.[20] It is seldom that there is lack of jurisdiction and, with the standardization of legal forms, seriously defective warrants are not often drawn. The remedies for improper arrest here usually lie against the complainant rather than against the arresting party. It is clear there-

[18] 1 Stephen, A History of the Criminal Law of England (1883) 190. See 11 & 12 Vict., c.42, §§ 1, 2, 8.

[19] 1 Stephen, A History of the Criminal Law of England (1883) 192.

[20] Perkins, "The Law of Arrest" (1940) 25 Iowa L.Rev. 201, 212-228. As to the English law, see Kenny, Outlines of Criminal Law (15th ed.1942) 525; Archbold, Criminal Pleading, Evidence and Practice (30th ed.1938) 1020; as to tort liability of the officer, see Prosser, Handbook of the Law of Torts (1941) 154-159; A.L.I. Restatement of Torts (1934) §§ 122-126.

fore that it is arrest without a warrant that presents the most difficult problems. It involves the greatest exercise of discretion and accordingly involves the greatest grant of right. Today the great majority of arrests are made without a warrant.[21]

One feature about arrest by warrant deserves mention. A prerequisite to the issuance of a warrant is the filing of a complaint on oath or affirmation showing that a crime has been committed and that there is probable cause to suspect the accused.[22] The federal and state constitutions provide that no warrants shall issue but upon probable cause, supported by oath or affirmation, and particularly describing the person to be seized.[23] At common law no writing is necessary. Rule 3 of the Federal Rules of Criminal Procedure requires that the complaint be in writing. By the weight of authority it is not enough merely to aver suspicion, or belief on information received from others, but there must be an averment of personal knowledge and be-

[21] Warner, "Investigating the Law of Arrest" (1940) 26 A.B.A.J. 151, 152. Compare the statement in Housel and Walser, Defending and Prosecuting Federal Criminal Cases (1938) ¶49, p.72 that "most arrests are and should be made under a warrant." In England, of persons appearing for preliminary examination before the magistrate upon charges of indictable crime, about thirty per cent come in obedience to a summons. The others are brought up in custody, about ten per cent under a warrant and about ninety per cent without a warrant. Kenny, Outlines of Criminal Law (15th ed.1942) 532. "The law of arrest with a warrant may have been suited to the common-law condition of a comparatively policeless society in which time was not of the essence and the prosecution of most misdemeanors was not very important." Warner, "Modern Trends in the American Law of Arrest" (1943) 21 Can.B.Rev. 192, 197.

[22] A.L.I. Code of Crim. Proc. (1930) §§1 and 2; Kenny states that the first stage in a criminal proceeding is laying an "information," *i.e.*, a complaint before the magistrate, the second being arrest. Outlines of Criminal Law (15th ed.1942) 525. See also Baker and DeLong "The Prosecuting Attorney: The Process of Prosecution" (1935) 26 J.Crim.L. 3.

[23] United States Constitution, Fourth Amendment.

lief. The federal rule leaves it up to local requirements with respect to hearing the complaint either on information and belief or on personal knowledge. Personal knowledge may be more essential when the complaint is filed by a private person rather than an officer.

The First Preliminary Draft of the Federal Rules of Criminal Procedure, Rule 4(b)(1), provided that the warrant "shall have attached to it a certified copy of the complaint." This rule was criticized as creating additional expense and serving no useful purpose. The accused has ample time to prepare his defense before trial, and may be supplied with a copy of the complaint after he has been apprehended. All later drafts omitted the provision.

The Wickersham Crime Commission suggested that one of the major topics requiring further research was present methods of the administration of the issuance of warrants of arrest and of the determination to institute prosecution.[24] Who should be responsible for the issuance of warrants and the institution of prosecution? The problem is important since the issuance of a warrant constitutes a determination to institute a prosecution. If poor judgment is used in issuing warrants, obviously the percentage of cases dropped at the preliminary examination will increase. In Missouri the warrant must receive the approval of the prosecuting attorney.[25] The Illinois Crime

[24] Nat. Com. on Law Obs. and Enf., Report on Prosecution (1931) 86-89, 182. "The power to issue warrants is a tremendous power, capable of abuse in the exercise and in the failure to exercise. Compared with this one function there is nothing complained of in the whole book of criminal procedure of comparable importance." "Detroit Court Solves Bail Problem" (1933) 16 J.Am.Jud.Soc. 143, 145, n.4.

[25] The Missouri Crime Survey (1926) 121-125; Moley, Politics and Criminal Prosecution (1929) 50. "Often magistrates will not issue warrants without the approval of the prosecuting attorney." Nat. Com. on Law Obs. and Enf., Report on Prosecution (1931) 20.

Survey recommended that no warrants be issued in felony cases without the approval of the prosecuting attorney.[26] If the prosecuting attorney be defined to include the municipal prosecuting attorney, a similar system prevails in Cleveland. But the crime surveys have shown that merely to locate the function in the prosecuting attorney does not necessarily produce efficient administrative methods or a careful sifting out of the cases at that stage. It is by no means clear whether it should be the clerk of court using clerical methods, or the prosecuting attorney using the methods appropriate to that office, or the magistrate using methods of a judicial character.[27] Nor is it clear what part, if any, the accused should play in the procedure.

The granting of a summons or of a warrant need not be done in open court. In the case of warrants for arrest "it would often be unwise to advertise that steps are being taken." [28]

At common law a warrant issued by a judge of the King's Bench extended all over the kingdom. But a warrant issued by the justice of the peace was good only in his county unless it was indorsed by the justice of another county, whereupon it could be executed in the second

[26] The Illinois Crime Survey (1929) 258; see Report of the Minnesota Crime Commission (1934) Appendix III, 137.

[27] "One of the big elements in law enforcement lies in the issuing of warrants, and this is commonly overlooked. Should not a responsible judge pass upon every application for a warrant, rather than a deputy clerk or police sergeant? The warrant bureau, supervised by a member of a strong bench, should exist in every city of any size, as it did in the Detroit Recorder's Court as first constituted. It is in the responsible exercise of the power to issue warrants that the police are to be held to their duty and civil rights protected." "Light on Grand Jury Procedure" (1931) 15 J.Am. Jud.Soc. 120, 122. In Massachusetts a "suggestion has been made that clerks alone issue warrants returnable in a district court." Warner and Cabot, Judges and Law Reform (1936) 25.

[28] Jackson, The Machinery of Justice in England (1940) 115.

county. Today any warrant lawfully issued by a justice, whether for an offense punishable on indictment or summarily, may be executed in any place in England or Wales.[29] Section 4 of the American Law Institute Code of Criminal Procedure is equally broad. The statutes of the states vary, some still applying the common law.[30] Under the former federal law a warrant issued in one district did not run in another district. There was considerable debate, with respect to the proposed federal rules of criminal procedure, whether or not they should allow execution all over the United States or within the territorial limits of the state.[31]

When a peace officer receives a warrant for execution, the usual practice is for him to keep it until he succeeds in performing that duty. Ordinarily no record is made of the issuance of the warrant or of its execution, or of the failure to execute it. The same is true of bench warrants. Unless the person should follow up the matter, there is nothing to call for further action, since no record is required or kept. The Minnesota Crime Commission in its report of 1927 recommended that each state have a central state authority prescribing and inspecting the keeping of records by local and state enforcement officers.[32]

Any officer arresting with a warrant must have the war-

[29] Criminal Justice Act, 1925, § 31(3); Kenny, Outlines of Criminal Law (15th ed.1942) 526; Archbold, Criminal Pleading, Evidence and Practice (30th ed.1938) 1020. As to Canadian practice, see Martin, J., "The Preliminary Hearing: Canadian Practice" (1937) 1 J.Crim.L. (Eng.) 107, 110.

[30] Perkins, "The Law of Arrest" (1940) 25 Iowa L.Rev. 201, 222.

[31] The First Preliminary Draft, Rule 4(c)(2), submitted to the court provided for service within the territorial limits of the state; all later drafts anywhere within the United States.

[32] Minnesota Crime Commission Report (1927) 66, 68, 76. The New Jersey Judicial Council proposes that the sheriff should be required to report periodically on the status of all unserved criminal writs. Sixth Report of Judicial Council of New Jersey (1940) 40.

rant with him.[33] This was workable in England in the seventeenth century, but it is not suitable to a city like Chicago, where orders to pick up a man for whose arrest a warrant has been issued may go to more than six thousand police officers.[34] The American Law Institute Code of Criminal Procedure would abolish this requirement,[35] as would Section 8 of the Uniform Arrest Act, and Rule 4(c)(3) of the Federal Rules of Criminal Procedure. Rule 4(a) of the Federal Rules also provides for the issuance of additional warrants and summonses for the same defendant; existing federal statutes did not expressly so provide. The provision for the issuance of several warrants makes less necessary a rule dispensing with the requirement that the officer have the warrant in his possession at the time of the arrest.

7. Arrest Without a Warrant

The common law governing arrest without a warrant may be briefly stated as follows: [36] With respect to misde-

[33] Bohlen and Shulman, "Arrest With and Without a Warrant" (1927) 75 U. of Pa.L.Rev. 485, 492-494.

[34] Warner, "Investigating the Law of Arrest" (1940) 26 A.B.A.J. 151, 152-153; Waite, "Some Inadequacies in the Law of Arrest" (1931) 29 Mich.L.Rev. 448, 459; Note (1936) 5 Fordham L.Rev. 338, 343.

[35] (1930) § 24, pp.29 and 244-247. In England under the Criminal Justice Act, 1925, § 44, he need not have the warrant with him. Kenny, Outlines of Criminal Law (15th ed.1942) 526; Archbold, Criminal Pleading, Evidence and Practice (30th ed.1938) 1020.

[36] Kenny, Outlines of Criminal Law (15th ed.1942) 528-531; Archbold, Criminal Pleading, Evidence and Practice (30th ed.1938) 1020-1024; 9 Halsbury, Laws of England (2d ed.1933) 84-98; Note (1941) 32 J.Crim.L. 439; Nat. Com. on Law Obs. and Enf., Rep. on Crim. Proc. (1931) 19; Wilgus, "Arrest Without a Warrant" (1924) 22 Mich.L.Rev. 673-674. As to tort liability, see Prosser, Handbook of the Law of Torts (1941) 160-166. For an account of the common-law rules of arrest without a warrant, see 1 Stephen, A History of the Common Law of England

meanors in general, neither an officer nor a private person may arrest. With respect to a breach of the peace, an officer or a private person may arrest to prevent or put a stop to the crime, or immediately after its commission. With respect to treason or felony,[37] an officer may arrest if he has reasonable belief both in the commission of the crime and in the guilt of the arrested party; a private person may arrest if the crime has been committed in actual fact, and if he has a reasonable belief in the guilt of the arrested party.[38] The right of a private person is less than that of a police officer only in arrest for felony where no felony has been committed.

Historically as late as 1765 the distinction between the right of a private person and of a police officer to arrest where no felony has been committed is not suggested.[39] The change came about in the case of Samuel v. Payne.[40] Prior thereto, it does not seem clear that a police officer could, without a warrant, arrest for felony even though

---

(1883) 193. The right to arrest without a warrant is much broader in the United States and England than on the Continent. Ploscowe, "Measures of Constraint in European and Anglo-American Criminal Procedure" (1935) 23 Geo.L.J. 762, 767.

[37] It may often be difficult for an officer to determine whether or not a felony, or a lesser crime, has been committed. Nat. Com. on Law Obs. and Enf., Rep. on Crim. Proc. (1931) 20. But the same difficulty exists in European procedure. Ploscowe, "Measures of Constraint in European and Anglo-American Criminal Procedure" (1935) 23 Geo.L.J. 762, 771.

[38] The rule is narrower in some states, such as New York, which requires that a felony must have been committed. Fraenkel, "From Suspicion to Accusation" (1942) 51 Yale L.J. 748, 755; Note (1936) 5 Fordham L.Rev. 338.

[39] Hall, "'Legal and Social Aspects of Arrest Without a Warrant" (1936) 49 Harv.L.Rev. 566, 570. When the modern police were first created, they were given no powers beyond those of private persons. Warner, "Investigating the Law of Arrest" (1940) 26 A.B.A.J. 151-152.

[40] 1 Doug. 359 (K.B.1780). See also Beckwith v. Philby (K.B.1827) 6 B.&C. 635.

no felony had been committed.[41] The change seems to have occurred because of the rise of professional police during the latter half of the eighteenth and the beginning of the nineteenth century.[42] At the same time this limitation was laid down upon the officer's rights within the enlarged area of arrest without a warrant: he must make out a reasonable ground of suspicion.[43] It seems never to have been contended that private persons could arrest upon reasonable suspicion of guilt. It was with respect to the requisite that a felony must have been committed that the common law placed the most important limitations upon arrests for felony by private persons. Not only must a felony have been committed, but the felony for which he made the arrest.[44] The rule in many American states is broader, it being sufficient if a felony has been committed, not necessarily the one for which the arrest was made.[45] In England, extension of the right of officers to arrest has usually been accompanied by limitation of such rights with respect to private persons. Furthermore, extension of the right of officers has been accompanied by restrictions aimed to compel reasonable conduct within the enlarged area. Such has been the resolution of the conflict between the interest expressed by the employment of a trained and professional force on the one hand and the political value known as "individual liberty" on the other hand.

From six to eight states have extended the privilege of the private person to include arrest on reasonable suspi-

[41] Compare 1 Stephen, A History of the Criminal Law (1883) 193.

[42] Hall "Legal and Social Aspects of Arrest Without a Warrant" (1936) 49 Harv.L.Rev. 566, 578.

[43] Beckwith v. Philby (K.B.1827) 6 B.&C. 635, 638.

[44] Walters v. Smith (1914) 1 K.B. 595.

[45] A.L.I. Code of Crim. Proc. (1930) commentaries 240-242.

cion of a felony not committed in his presence, although no felony was in fact committed.[46] Virtually, the same number have narrowed the privilege and require not only the fact of felony but its actual commission by the very person arrested.[47] But almost three fourths of the states adopt the intermediate view that, although the privilege is limited to cases in which a felony was in fact committed by someone, it is broad enough to protect the private person if he believed upon reasonable grounds that the arrestee was the felon even though this happens not to be true.[48]

At common law a mere guess that an arrested person has committed a felony is not enough even though it turns out that he has.[49] A man unable to satisfy the judge that, at the time he made the arrest he had reasonable cause to believe that the person he was arresting had committed the felony for which the arrest was made, cannot justify his action by proving the actual guilt of the person arrested or that he has committed other felonies or even that he is the worst criminal at large. In nineteen states statutes permit an officer to defend on that ground that the person arrested is in fact guilty, though he did not have reasonable cause so to believe at the time of the arrest.[50] This avoids the present paradoxical situation under which an officer may lawfully arrest even an innocent per-

[46] Kentucky, Mississippi, Ohio, and South Carolina. The statutes of Alabama, Virginia, California, and Oklahoma seem equally broad.

[47] Connecticut, Illinois, Maine, Massachusetts, Missouri, New Mexico, and New York.

[48] A.L.I. Code of Crim. Proc. (1930) commentaries, 240-241.

[49] Waite, Criminal Law in Action (1934) 44.

[50] Waite, "Some Inadequacies in the Law of Arrest" (1931) 29 Mich.L.Rev. 448, 453; Waite, "Public Policy and the Arrest of Felons" (1933) 31 Mich.L.Rev. 749, 751; Warner, "Modern Trends in the American Law of Arrest" (1943) 21 Can.B.Rev. 192, 198-200; A.L.I. Code of Crim. Proc. (1930) § 21(b), pp.28 and 234.

son on reasonable suspicion of a felony, but may not arrest a guilty person whom he suspects of a felony, if he has no reasonable ground of suspicion. It also avoids the effect of the rule of the federal courts and of several states that evidence obtained by a search founded on an arrest is not admissible on the offender's trial unless the arrest was legal. The usual basis for contending that the arrest is illegal is that it was made without any reasonable belief by the officer in the guilt of the party arrested. The American Law Institute Code protects the officer [51] but not a private person so arresting.[52] It is not clear why only the officer should be so protected,[53] though he is perhaps less liable to abuse his right.

An officer could at common law arrest for certain misdemeanors committed in his presence. A more doubtful question was: What are the officer's rights if he reasonably, but mistakenly, believed that the person had committed a misdemeanor in his presence? The commentators considered only the arrest of misdemeanants in fact guilty.[54] The American cases are divided, some protecting the officer and others holding that he acts at his peril.[55] It would seem that an officer ought to have the right to arrest when he has reason to believe that a crime is being committed in his presence, irrespective of whether such crime is a felony or a misdemeanor.

Recent statutes have considerably enlarged the right of

[51] Sec. 21(b).

[52] Sec. 22(b).

[53] Waite, "Some Inadequacies in the Law of Arrest" (1931) 29 Mich.L.Rev. 448, 458.

[54] Warner, "Modern Trends in the American Law of Arrest" (1943) 21 Can.B.Rev. 192, 200.

[55] Stone, "Arrest Without a Warrant" (1939) Wis.L.Rev. 385, 387; Note (1941) 32 J.Crim.L. 439, 441. See Bursach v. Davis, 199 Wis. 115, 225 N.W. 738 (1929). But cf. Price v. Tehan, 84 Conn. 164, 79 Att. 68.

officers to arrest without a warrant. The principal change has been to permit such arrest with respect to all or a large number of misdemeanors which were not breaches of the peace at common law and, hence, not subject to arrest without warrant even though committed in the presence of an officer.[56] Even without a statute, courts have sometimes called an offense a felony in order to make valid arrest without a warrant, in spite of prior interpretation of the same offense as a misdemeanor.[57] Today, in thirty-eight states, police officers have been given the right to arrest for any misdemeanor committed in their presence.[58] Furthermore, the phrase "in his presence" is being given an expanded construction by the courts.[59] Illinois has gone even further and permits an officer to arrest when a misdemeanor has in fact been committed and he has reasonable cause to believe that the person to be arrested committed it.[60] Illinois officials, however, believe that the public sharply distinguishes felonies from misdemeanors. If a felony has been committed, the witnesses will usually stick to their stories and see the prosecution through.[61]

[56] Nat. Com. on Law Obs. and Enf., Rep. on Crim. Proc. (1931) 19. See A.L.I. Code of Crim. Proc. (1930) § 21(a).

[57] Drennan v. the People, 10 Mich. 169 (1862).

[58] Warner, "Investigating the Law of Arrest" (1940) 26 A.B.A.J. 151, 152; Nat. Com. on Law Obs. and Enf., Rep. on Crim. Proc. (1931) 19. In a majority of states, private persons may also so arrest. Perkins, "The Law of Arrest" (1940) 20 Iowa L.Rev. 201, 230.

[59] A.L.I. Code of Crim. Proc. (1930) 232 etc. In the past, decisions have been somewhat technical. Nat. Com. on Law Obs. and Enf., Rep. on Crim. Proc. (1931) 20.

[60] Ill. Rev. Stat. 1939, c.38, § 657. See also Wilgus, "Arrest Without Warrant" (1924) 22 Mich.L.Rev. 673, 706. There seems to be no exception in this country to the rule that a private person may not arrest without a warrant for a misdemeanor not committed in his presence. A.L.I. Code of Crim. Proc. (1930) commentaries, 238.

[61] Warner, "Investigating the Law of Arrest" (1940) 26 A.B.A.J. 151,

But if the crime is only a misdemeanor, the parties are likely to patch up their differences. The complainant may not even appear in court, or if the officer brings him in, he may tell an entirely different story.

On the whole there has been but little criticism of allowing police officers to arrest for any misdemeanors committed in their presence.[62] Professors Bohlen and Shulman have, however, contended that such a rule "will undoubtedly lead to officers taking into custody persons for offenses which, though actually committed and in the presence of the officer, are subsequently deemed too insignificant to warrant prosecution. Unless there is some reason to suppose that the offender will escape unless he is immediately arrested, the delay incident to obtaining a warrant will not injure the interest of the state in punishing him." [63] A fortiori this is true with respect to breaches of municipal ordinances and statutory misdemeanors.[64]

The American Law Institute Code does not permit a private person to arrest for a misdemeanor committed in his presence unless it amounts to a breach of the peace.[65] Perhaps this is too narrow, as where the misdemeanor is a theft but not a breach of the peace.[66] The Code gives a greater right to officers, it not being required that the mis-

154. It has been concluded that the Illinois Act has not had any bad consequences. Warner, "Modern Trends in the American Law of Arrest" (1943) 21 Can.B.Rev. 192, 204.

62 It is strongly urged by Warner, "Modern Trends in the American Law of Arrest" (1943) 21 Can.B.Rev. 192, 201-202.

63 Bohlen and Shulman, "Arrest With and Without a Warrant" (1927) 75 U. of Pa.L.Rev. 485, 490.

64 Bohlen and Shulman, "Arrest With and Without a Warrant" (1927) 75 U. of Pa.L.Rev. 491.

65 Sec. 22(a).

66 Waite, "Some Inadequacies in the Law of Arrest" (1931) 29 Mich.L.Rev. 448, 452.

demeanors constitute a breach of the peace.[67] It will not help to call an officer since an officer cannot, without a warrant, arrest for a misdemeanor not committed in his presence. Thus, at common law, both the victim and the policeman called in may have to stand by inactive while an admitted criminal leaves the jurisdiction. Possibly the solution is to authorize a peace officer to arrest when he has reasonable ground to believe that the person to be arrested has committed a misdemeanor and reasonable ground to believe that he will evade arrest if not immediately apprehended.[68]

The common-law rule against arrest without a warrant for a misdemeanor occurring out of the view of a police officer is not always satisfactory or workable. An example is an automobile traffic misdemeanor resulting in a collision but not occurring within the view of an officer.[69] It may be that the collision is reported to the officer by the victim promptly after the collision and that demand is made for the immediate arrest of the wrongdoer, before he leaves the scene of the collision. The officer has no warrant and cannot go to a magistrate's office for a warrant and return before the offender leaves the scene. Yet the officer is not authorized to arrest for a past misdemeanor upon information or suspicion.

[67] Sec. 21(a).

[68] Waite, "Some Inadequacies in the Law of Arrest" (1931) 29 Mich.L.Rev. 448, 453.

[69] 5 Berry, The Law of Automobiles (1935) 498. No such defect exists in the Continental law. Ploscowe, "Measures of Constraint in European and Anglo-American Criminal Procedure" (1935) 23 Geo.L.J. 762, 770. That law permits arrest without a warrant by both private individuals and police officers in many offenses in which the accused is caught in the act. As to English law, see Kenny, Outlines of Criminal Law (15th ed.1942) 530-531; Archbold, Criminal Pleading, Evidence and Practice (30th ed.1938) 1021-1022; Harris and Wilshere, Principles and Practice of the Common Law (17th ed.1943) 398-400.

There are at least three important differences between the right of an officer to arrest without a warrant for a misdemeanor and the right to arrest for a felony. An officer may not arrest for a misdemeanor not committed in his presence, but may for a felony. He may arrest only misdemeanants who are actually guilty, but may arrest one whom he reasonably suspects has committed a felony. He may arrest a misdemeanant only when the crime was committed or on hot pursuit, while felons may be arrested at any time. A leading authority has recently stated, however: "It certainly would greatly simplify the law of arrest and prevent misunderstandings if the historic distinctions between the right to arrest for felonies and misdemeanors were abolished." [70]

There is substantial uniformity of agreement that an officer should be authorized to arrest without a warrant for any misdemeanor, rather than only for misdemeanors likely to lead to breaches of the peace, committed in his presence. There is no such agreement as to arrest for misdemeanors not committed in his presence. The argument in favor of permitting such arrest is that they could always do so as to felonies not committed in their presence and that the distinctions between felony and misdemeanor were arbitrary and purely historical. On the other hand it is contended that the lesser disgrace of arrest for a misdemeanor would lead to arrests without careful checking of the charge of crime. While these opposing arguments are rather closely balanced, it would seem that it should be possible to arrest petty thieves and other misdemeanants who will otherwise escape.[71] In view of these con-

[70] Warner, "Modern Trends in the American Law of Arrest" (1943) 21 Can.B.Rev. 192, 204.

[71] Warner concedes, however, that "there is no pressing social need to permit officers to arrest for misdemeanors not committed in their

siderations, Section 6 of the Uniform Arrest Act allows arrest for misdemeanors not committed in the presence of the officer if the officer believes that the offender will not be apprehended unless immediately arrested.[72] It also makes it immaterial whether the misdemeanor was in fact committed by the person arrested. Section 6 restates the law as to felonies by allowing an officer to arrest any person he reasonably believes has committed a felony, and extends the common law by allowing an officer to arrest any person who in fact has committed a felony irrespective of whether or not the officer had reasonable suspicions.[73] This broadening of the common law, already in effect in fifteen states, will permit pistols, narcotic drugs, and other contraband articles found on the arrested person to be admitted in evidence even in states following the federal rule on the admissibility of evidence obtained by unlawful searches. It would appear that such provision is not unconstitutional as authorizing an unreasonable seizure.

8. Detention Versus Arrest

It has been quite a common practice deliberately to detain persons to facilitate investigation.[74] The practice has

---

presence." "Modern Trends in the American Law of Arrest" (1943) 21 Can.B.Rev. 192, 204.

[72] Warner, "The Uniform Arrest Act" (1942) 28 Va.L.Rev. 315, 331-334; Bohlen and Shulman, "Arrest With and Without a Warrant" (1927) 75 U. of Pa.L.Rev. 485, 490-491.

[73] This is provided in the A.L.I. Code of Crim. Proc. (1930) § 21(b). It is favored by Waite, "Public Policy and the Arrest of Felons" (1933) 31 Mich.L.Rev. 749, 750; Bruce and Rosmarin, "The Gunman and His Gun" (1934) 24 J.Crim.L. 521; Warner, "Modern Trends in the American Law of Arrest" (1943) 21 Can.B.Rev. 192, 198-200.

[74] Beeley, The Bail System in Chicago (1927) 24-26; Report of the American Bar Association Committee on Lawless Enforcement of Law (1930); (1934) 48 Harv.L.Rev. 131.

frequently occurred, even in England.[75] It has existed there because the police have often to work very rapidly. It has been argued that there is a sharp distinction between detention and arrest, since a person detained "is not treated as a prisoner; he is not put in any cell; he waits in a waiting room . . . he has a room and bed there; . . . the police . . . treat them well, they feed them well." [76] But the Royal Commission in its report of 1929 rejected the contention that detention differed from arrest; a person "requested" to accompany an officer to a station to be "detained" there always acceded to the request. Although placed in a waiting room, a detained person would not be permitted to leave the station.[77] On the Continent, however, a distinction has long been taken between arrest and detention, there being no need of any charge nor of a reasonable ground of suspicion for the latter.[78]

Section 2 of the Uniform Arrest Act provides for questioning and detention of suspects.[79] A peace officer may stop any person abroad whom he reasonably suspects of committing a crime, and may demand his name, address, business abroad, and where he is going. Any person so questioned making unsatisfactory answers may be de-

[75] Report of the Royal Commission on Police Powers and Procedure (1929) 56-57; Hall, "The Law of Arrest in Relation to Contemporary Social Problems" (1936) 3 U. of Chi.L.Rev. 345, 370.

[76] Minutes of Evidence Taken Before the Royal Commission on Police Powers and Procedure (1928) 1385, 1389, 1390.

[77] In this country no separate quarters are kept for those merely detained, and there is no different treatment of any kind, except that persons "detained" are more frequently subjected to abuse.

[78] Fosdick, European Police Systems (1915) 17.

[79] See discussion, Warner, "The Uniform Arrest Act" (1942) 28 Va.L.Rev. 315, 317-324. As to the history of the drafting of the Act, see (1942) 33 J.Crim.L. 186. The act is set out in (1941) 32 J.Crim.L. 207-209; and (1942) 28 Va.L.Rev. 344-347.

tained and further questioned and investigated for not over two hours. Such detention is not an arrest and shall not be so recorded. At the end of the detention, the person so detained shall be released or arrested and charged with a crime. The need for such a statute to harmonize the law and the practice seems clear. Large numbers of people are questioned every day by police officers. This questioning, unaccompanied by an immediate arrest, seems essential to proper policing. Of course, making questioning legal imposes upon the person questioned no duty to reply, for that would be unconstitutional.

Is detention a sound practice? It is true that the police have great difficulties in collecting evidence. Hence, if adequate guarantees against abuse are or can be made available, much might be said in defense of detention pending investigation. Arguably, such detention conflicts with the traditional political ideal to the effect that individuals who have committed no wrong shall be absolutely unmolested.[80] The limitation is, however, very slight; it seems to be in the public interest; and it causes the law to be in conformity with the practice.

9. Frisking

At common law an officer has no right to search a suspect before arresting him. But this rule antedated criminals with four-inch pistols. A statute making "frisking" legal in certain cases would be helpful.[81] Moreover, "frisking" should not be regarded as arresting, as the latter requires that the prisoner be brought before a magistrate.

[80] Hall, "The Law of Arrest in Relation to Contemporary Social Problems" (1936) 3 U. of Chi.L.Rev. 345, 371.

[81] Warner, "Investigating the Law of Arrest" (1940) 26 A.B.A.J. 151, 153. By "frisking" is meant passing one's hands over the outer clothing of a suspect to ascertain whether he is carrying any deadly weapon.

If "frisking" reveals that the person is innocent, he should be cleared at once. Section 3 of the Uniform Arrest Act would legalize "frisking." [82] Under this section, a peace officer may search for a dangerous weapon any person whom he has stopped, whenever he has reasonable ground to believe that he is in danger if the person possesses a dangerous weapon. If he finds a weapon, he may keep it until the completion of the questioning, when he shall either return it or arrest the person. An officer has authority, incidental to a lawful arrest, to search the prisoner after the arrest. The justification is the officer's safety, and that seems as applicable to "frisking."

10. Force Permissible

A peace officer should not use unreasonable force in making an arrest, nor desist because of threatened resistance. This statement of the present law [83] is embodied in Section 4 of the Uniform Arrest Act.[84] A provision requiring the officer to make every reasonable effort to advise the person to be arrested that he is a peace officer is more restrictive of the officer than the present law. A provision justifying the use of force dangerous to human life in making an arrest for any felony follows the common law and the existing law of most states.[85] Some would ex-

[82] See discussion, Warner, "The Uniform Arrest Act" (1942) 28 Va. L.Rev. 315, 324-327.

[83] State v. Paschall, 197 Wash. 582, 85 P. (2d) 1046 (1939); A.L.I. Code of Crim. Proc. (1930) § 19, pp.27, 228; Perkins, "Law of Arrest" (1940) 25 Iowa L.Rev. 201, 265; Notes (1932) 23 J.Crim.L. 654, (1941) 31 J.Crim.L. 601; as to tort liability, see Prosser, Handbook of the Law of Torts (1941) 163-166; A.L.I. Restatement of Torts (1934) §§ 131-136.

[84] See discussion, Warner, "The Uniform Arrest Act" (1942) 28 Va.L. Rev. 315, 328-330; Warner, "Modern Trends in the American Law of Arrest" (1943) 21 Can.B.Rev. 192, 206-208.

[85] Stinnett v. Virginia, 55F. (2d) 644, 646-7 (C.C.A. 4th, 1932); Scar-

tend the rule to misdemeanors on the basis that submission to known officers is essential to the safety of the community, and that the present rule breeds contempt for the law. On the other hand, others would limit the right to cases of arrest for felonies committed with violence, and would not include arrests for grand larceny. The adopted rule is a compromise between these two extremes. The writer prefers this compromise to a rule which would extend the present right to kill to all offenses, although he favors even more a rule limiting the right to violent felonies or attempts at them.

11. Resisting Arrest

It has always been the rule that it is illegal to resist a lawful arrest. But if the arrest is illegal, the victim may use force similar to a peace officer arresting for a misdemeanor.[86] That is to say, he should not kill to avoid arrest, but he may oppose force with force and kill if necessary to protect his own life or limb. Historically, this rule was doubtless sound, since a prisoner often could not ob-

borough v. State, 168 Tenn. 106, 76 S.W. (2d) 106 (1934); Pearson, "The Right to Kill in Making Arrests" (1930) 28 Mich.L.Rev. 957, 974. Private persons, however, should be authorized to kill only with respect to dangerous felonies. A.L.I. Restatement of Torts (1934) § 131; Perkins, "The Law of Arrest" (1940) 25 Iowa L.Rev. 201, 274-276. An officer's right to kill was limited to specific dangerous offenses in A.L.I. Administration of the Criminal Law, Tentative Draft, no. 1 (1931) 21. See discussion of the draft 9 Proc. Am. L. Inst. (1931) 179 *et seq.;* Bohlen and Shulman, "Arrest With and Without a Warrant" (1927) 75 U. of Pa.L.Rev. 485, 494-504. One writer states: "The rules governing arrest might be improved if the definitions of crime were more closely related to the dangerousness of the offender." Gausewitz, "Considerations Basic to a New Penal Code: Part II" (1936) 11 Wis.L.Rev. 480, 492.

86 Waite, Criminal Law in Action (1934) 46. For English law, see Archbold, Pleading, Evidence and Practice (30th ed.1938) 910-918. As to tort liability, see Prosser, Handbook of the Law of Torts (1941) 165-166.

tain bail, might die from jail conditions, might be kept in jail for years prior to trial, and might be tortured. Today these conditions do not exist and resistance is likely to be by shooting, with great danger to the peace officers. Resistance is likely to come only from real criminals. Section 6 of the Uniform Arrest Act therefore abolishes the right to resist an illegal arrest by a known officer.[87] The arrested person can no longer defend a prosecution for murder, manslaughter, or felonious assault on the ground that the resistance was legal.

12. Flaws in Remedies for Illegal Arrest

The victim of an illegal arrest has seemingly several remedies available. There is the policeman, there are his superior officers, and there is the municipality or state. Suit against the policeman may be fruitless because of his financial condition, hence few such suits are brought.[88] Furthermore, in the great majority of states garnishment does not lie because of "public policy." [89] The municipality is not liable because of distinctions taken between corporate and governmental functions,[90] and exceptions made

[87] See the discussion, Warner, "The Uniform Arrest Act" (1942) 28 Va. L.Rev. 315, 330-331; Warner, "Modern Trends in the American Law of Arrest" (1943) 21 Can.B.Rev. 192, 208-210. See also Dickey, "Culpable Homicides in Resisting Arrest" (1933) 18 Corn.L.Q. 373, 379-387. The Canadian Criminal Code, § 261 (4), provides: "The illegality of an arrest does not necessarily reduce an offense of culpable homicide from murder to manslaughter, but if the illegality was known to the offender it may be evidence of provocation."

[88] Hall, "The Law of Arrest in Relation to Contemporary Social Problems" (1936) 3 U. of Chi.L.Rev. 345, 346; Train, The Prisoner at the Bar (1923) 48.

[89] 6 McQuillin, The Law of Municipal Corporations (2d ed.1928) § 2681.

[90] Jones v. City of New Orleans, 143 La. 1074, 79 So. 865 (1918).

to the rule of *respondeat superior*.[91] Thus where there is liability, as in the case of a policeman, financial irresponsibility prevents recovery; while where financial responsibility exists, as in the case of a city, there is no legal liability. The most significant step toward relief thus far attempted is provision for the filing of official bonds.[92] Unfortunately, such statutes usually cover the village constable and the county sheriff, rather than the city policeman. Moreover, the applicable law of suretyship results in paralyzing limitations. For example, there is a very narrow interpretation as to whether the principal on the bond, the officer, was acting within the scope of his authority when he committed the tort.[93] There has been a tendency to find that the officer was acting *colore officii* rather than *virtute officii* and thus no liability. Another group of cases hold that action lies "only by the obligee named in the bond," namely, the city.[94] It should be borne in mind that the surety is usually a great corporation while the plaintiff is an individual whose resources are slight. An injunction will not be granted to restrain a threatened illegal arrest.[95] This is because the threat of an irreparable loss to property is one essential condition of such relief. The non-availability of the above reme-

[91] Borchard, "Government Liability in Tort" (1925) 34 Yale L.J. 240; Note (1925) 11 Va.L.Rev. 315. For subsequent developments, see Borchard, "State and Municipal Liability in Tort" (1934) 20 A.B.A.J. 747.

[92] 6 McQuillan, The Law of Municipal Corporations (2d ed.1928) § 2591, pp.409-410.

[93] Hall, "The Law of Arrest in Relation to Contemporary Social Problems" (1936) 3 U. of Chi.L.Rev. 345, 349-352; State, for the use of Brooks v. Fidelity and Deposit Co., 147 Md. 194, 127 Atl. 758 (1925); Taylor v. Shielder, 183 Ky. 669, 210 S.W. 168 (1919).

[94] Sumter v. Fraser, 194 Calif. 337, 340, 228, Pac. 660, 661 (1924).

[95] Burch v. Cavanaugh, 12 Abb. Pr. (N.S.) (N.Y.) 411 (1872). Compare, however, American Steel and Wire Co. v. Davis, 261 Fed. 800 (1919).

dies, it should be noted, does not arise out of the law of arrest or of torts, but rather from the law of municipal corporations, suretyship, and injunctions. It should be noted that habeas corpus lies in certain cases of illegal arrest or detention in custody.[96]

Anglo-American law has not provided public compensation to innocent persons wrongfully convicted. A fortiori it has not provided such compensation to innocent persons who have been arrested. Possibly such a reform is too sweeping and too expensive. Danish law makes such provision with respect to first offenders and a Danish professor of law has written: "Strict regulations should also be enacted with regard to arrest in the case of persons of hitherto blameless character—and should arrest have been ordered in the case of an innocent person wrongfully accused, he ought, in the most comprehensive way possible, to receive full and complete compensation and rehabilitation." [97]

Illegal arrest of a defendant does not affect the jurisdiction of the court trying him. The defendant cannot object to the jurisdiction of the court. He should sue for false imprisonment.[98] While authority is divided as to the admission of evidence illegally acquired, the rule is clear that it is immaterial whether the defendant has been arrested legally or illegally, or arrested at all.[99] It is true

[96] Clark, Handbook of Criminal Procedure (2d ed. by Mikell, 1918) 653; Report of the Crimes Survey Committee, Law Association of Philadelphia (1926) 175. Compare as to defective warrant, A.L.I. Code of Crim. Proc. (1930) § 5.

[97] Munch-Petersen, "The Social Aspect of Procedure from a European Point of View" (1927) 11 Minn.L.Rev. 624, 630; see also Beeley, The Bail System in Chicago (1927) 169.

[98] Ker v. Illinois, 119 U.S. 436 (1886); People v. Park, 156 N.Y.S. 816, 92 Misc. 369 (1915).

[99] Commonwealth v. Conlin, 184 Mass. 195, 68 N.E. 207 (1903). Even a

that the defendant may raise objection prior to trial. But it will do him no real good to object since he can be re-arrested immediately upon his release.[100] Defects in the papers upon which the warrant of arrest was granted may be attacked by a motion to quash the warrant before the defect has been cured.[101]

It has been said "that the accused is in court is sufficient to require him to answer the indictment against him." [102] The fact that he has been kidnapped from another jurisdiction in violation of the territorial rights of a foreign sovereign, by a private person,[103] or by an officer of the indicting state,[104] does not entitle him to release on a writ of habeas corpus,[105] and gives him no defense to an indictment.[106]

13. Summons

Section 12 of the American Law Institute Code provides for wide use of the summons instead of arrest,

---

seasonable objection may not help. Commonwealth v. Gorman, 268 Mass. 294, 192 N.E. 618, 96 A.L.R. 977 (1934). There is jurisdiction to hold a preliminary examination. Martin, J., "The Preliminary Hearing: Canadian Practice" (1937) 1 J.Crim.L. (Eng.) 107, 116.

100 Notes (1924) 38 Harv.L.Rev. 114, (1925) 24 Mich.L.Rev. 192, (1926) 25 Mich.L.Rev. 193. See also A.L.I. Code of Crim. Proc. (1930) § 5.

101 Albrecht v. United States, 273 U.S. 1, 47 Sup.Ct. 250, 71 L.Ed. 505 (1927). The court there stated that the motion to quash may be made after the giving of bail, although technically he is then held under the bond rather than the warrant. See Note (1918) 1 Ill.L.Bull. 175, 178.

102 Ex parte Davis, 51 Tex.Crim.R. 608, 609 (1907). One of the few exceptions is that a defendant who has been brought into the jurisdiction by extradition is immune from indictment for any crime other than that for which he was extradited, until he has had a reasonable time to leave the jurisdiction. United States v. Rauscher, 119 U.S. 407 (1886). See (1923) 36 Harv.L.Rev. 609, 611.

103 Dow's Case, 18 Pa. St. 37 (1851).

104 Ex parte Scott, 9 B.&C. 446 (1829).

105 Ex parte Scott, 9 B.&C. 446 (1829).

106 Ker v. Illinois, 110 Ill. 627 (1884), aff'd. 119 U.S. 436 (1886).

though, unfortunately, it does not cover felonies.[107] In the case of a misdemeanor which the magistrate is not empowered to try summarily, the warrant of arrest is replaced by a summons if the magistrate has reason to believe that the defendant will appear to answer the summons. In the case of a misdemeanor which the magistrate is empowered to try summarily, a summons issues unless the magistrate has reason to believe that the defendant will not appear thereon. In the words of the Wickersham Crime Commission: "Indiscriminate exercise of the power of arrest is one of the most reprehensible features of American criminal justice." [108] Section 9 of the Uniform Arrest Act provides that in any case where it is lawful for a peace officer to arrest without a warrant for a misdemeanor, he may, but need not, give him a written summons.[109] Under Rule 4(a) of the Federal Rules of Criminal Procedure a summons instead of a warrant may be

[107] For pleas in favor of this reform, see Beeley, The Bail System in Chicago (1927) 13-22; Warner and Cabot, Judges and Law Reform (1936) 148-151; Burdick, "Criminal Justice in America" (1925) 11 A.B.A.J. 510, 512; Cleveland Foundation Survey of Criminal Justice in Cleveland (1922) 202-203, 291-292; Puttkammer, "Criminal Law Enforcement," University of Chicago Magazine (Dec. 1940); Chaplin, "Reform in Criminal Procedure" (1893) 7 Harv.L.Rev. 189, 198; Report of the Crimes Survey Committee, Law Association of Philadelphia (1926) 468.

[108] Nat. Com. on Law Obs. and Enf., Rep. on Crim. Proc. (1931) 14. See also p. 47. Bohlen and Shulman state: "Indeed, the interest of the citizen in not being arrested unnecessarily is the inspiration for the tendency of modern criminal laws to provide that the alleged offender shall be brought into court by a summons and not by arrest." See their article, "Arrest With and Without a Warrant" (1927) 75 U. of Pa.L.Rev. 485, 490.

[109] See discussion, Warner, "The Uniform Arrest Act" (1942) 28 Va.L.Rev. 315, 334-336. "Though few felonies are today punished by death, their punishment is usually sufficiently severe to make the substitution of summons for arrest inexpedient." Warner, "Modern Trends in the Law of Arrest" (1943) 21 Can.B.Rev. 192, 211.

issued upon the request of the attorney for the government. Only a minority of states today allow a summons to be substituted for a warrant of arrest. Wider use of the summons seems sound.[110] For example, the arrest of a motorist may greatly inconvenience innocent passengers in his car. The arrest of an intoxicated woman may be undesirable if no one can be found to care for her infant. It will be noted that the Uniform Act does not require that the summons be issued by a judge or clerk of court.[111] Consequently, a peace officer who witnesses a misdemeanor need not apply to the court for a summons and then return to serve it. Under the opposite rule if the officer decides not to arrest, he is likely to feel that applying for a summons is too much trouble. He may threaten the offender and then do nothing. Where the suspected person is likely to leave the jurisdiction, it may prove as troublesome to have to apply to a magistrate for a summons as it would be to have to apply to him for a warrant.

[110] It is widely used in Canada: "The Preliminary Hearing: Canadian Practice" (1937) 1 J.Crim.L. (Eng.) 107, 110. It is much more widely used in England and even more so in France, Germany, and Italy. Ploscowe, "Measures of Constraint in European and Anglo-American Criminal Procedure" (1935) 23 Geo.L.J. 762, 767. In 1929 it was used in England in 77 per cent of all cases; and in France, in 92 per cent. In England, its use is completely in the discretion of the magistrate even as to felonies. See Howard, Criminal Justice in England (1931) 297, 298; Kenny, Outlines of Criminal Law (15th ed.1942) 532; Lawson and Keedy, "Criminal Procedure in England" (1910) 1 J.Crim.L. 565, 602.

[111] The A.L.I. Code of Crim. Proc., Sec. 12, and Federal Rule 4(a) are to the opposite effect. It has been pointed out that a third of American arrests, summonses, and "tickets" are for motor vehicle offenses. Warner, "Modern Trends in the American Law of Arrest" (1943) 21 Can.B.Rev. 192.

14. Duty to Bring Before Magistrate

The law of arrest includes not only apprehension but also detention. The law is clear and definite that the officer making the arrest must bring the arrested party before a magistrate and that he must do this without delay.[112] Hence, where a chief of police found the plaintiff intoxicated, took him to the police station, held him there for a short time, and discharged him sober, without bringing him before a magistrate, judgment for the plaintiff in the sum of three hundred dollars was affirmed by the appellate court.[113] Want of damage to the plaintiff is immaterial, as is actual benefit to him. The duty of the officer is to produce the arrested party in court. When there is detention for investigation, even if the officer's suspicions prove unfounded, the prisoner must still be brought before the court.[114] Likewise in the case of an arrest on behalf of a foreign jurisdiction, the prisoner must be brought before a magistrate.[115] It has been held that when a party has been arrested on a warrant issued by a court which had adjourned when the party was taken into custody and the party was imprisoned for six months in the county jail, the state's attorney might order his release if he thought justice required it.[116]

[112] A.L.I. Code of Crim. Proc. (1931) §§ 6, 35, and 36; Perkins, "The Law of Arrest" (1940) 25 Iowa L.Rev. 201, 255-257; Bohlen and Shulman, "Effect of Subsequent Misconduct Upon a Lawful Arrest" (1928) 28 Col.L.Rev. 841, 852-853. See Rule 5(a) of the Federal Rules of Criminal Procedure.

[113] Brock v. Stimson, 108 Mass. 520 (1871).

[114] Keefe v. Hart, 213 Mass. 476, 100 N.E. 558 (1913); Hall, "The Law of Arrest in Relation to Contemporary Social Problems" (1936) 3 U. of Chi.L.Rev. 345, 356-357.

[115] Cochran v. Toher, 14 Minn. 305 (1869); Davis v. Carroll, 172 App. Div. 729, 159 N.Y. Supp. 568 (1916).

[116] Kent v. Miles, 68 Vt. 49, 33 Atl. 768 (1895).

15. Release of Persons Arrested

The statistics indicate that the police arrest many persons against whom they can make no justifiable charge.[117] One writer indicates that of the 80,000 persons whose arrests are noted in the various surveys of criminal justice, 47.7 per cent were released by the police or by the magistrate without being charged.[118] Of 650,000 arrests compiled from a number of police department reports, 44 per cent were released without being charged. In Europe the percentage of unjustifiable arrests is said to be less.[119]

Despite the duty to bring arrested parties before a magistrate it appears that for many offenses, one of every three persons arrested is released by the police without being brought before any judicial officer.[120] During 1928-1933 all persons arrested in Boston for disorderly conduct were released by the police without appearance in court. In Detroit large numbers of persons charged with drunkenness or "detained for investigation" have been

[117] Conversely, arrests are frequently not made because the criminal has not been apprehended. In New York City in a recent year from the middle of 1937 to the middle of 1938 arrests were made in only 50.2 per cent of the known burglaries. Twelve Months of Crime in New York City; A Report by the Citizen's Committee on the Control of Crime (Dec. 1938) 4-5, reprinted in Michael and Wechsler, Criminal Law and Its Administration (1940) 378: "Data collected in St. Louis and Kansas City demonstrate . . . that an overwhelming majority of persons committing felonies in these cities are never apprehended at all." Missouri Crime Survey (1926) 165-166. In 1921 in Philadelphia, arrests occurred in 40 per cent of the crimes reported. Report of the Crimes Survey Committee, Law Association of Philadelphia (1926) 451. See also Michael and Adler, An Institute of Criminology and of Criminal Justice (1932) 292-294.

[118] Hopkins, Our Lawless Police (1931) 34; Beeley, The Bail System in Chicago (1927) 17; Glueck, Crime and Justice (1936) 82.

[119] Ploscowe, "Measures of Constraint under European and Anglo-American Criminal Procedure" (1935) 23 Geo.L.J. 762, 770-771.

[120] Hall, "The Law of Arrest in Relation to Contemporary Social Problems" (1936) 3 U. of Chi.L.Rev. 345, 359, 362.

thus released. In Los Angeles many persons arrested for robbery, burglary, and larceny have been so released. Possibly the law should be changed so as to authorize the officer in charge of each police station to release arrested persons as soon as their innocence is established.[121] Certainly this should be extended to some classes where guilt is established, such as drunkards.[122]

To correct these defects in the law, Section 10 of the Uniform Act permits any officer in charge of a police department, or any officer delegated by him, to release certain prisoners.[123] Since the number and kind of officers who can release is limited, no indiscriminate release of prisoners, accompanied by bribery and corruption, is likely to result. Persons arrested under a warrant would not be releasable. The officer in charge may release only three classes of persons arrested without a warrant: (1) those who establish their innocence; (2) intoxicated persons whom the department does not wish to prosecute; and (3) misdemeanants who sign an agreement to appear in court, and who the officer is satisfied are residents of the state and will appear at the time designated. The decrease in the number of magistrates and the increase in the number of trained police officers is a strong practical argument for this procedure.[124]

121 Warner, "Investigating the Law of Arrest" (1940) 26 A.B.A.J. 151, 155. See A.L.I. Restatement of Torts (1934) § 136, comments e and f; Perkins, "The Law of Arrest" (1940) 25 Iowa L.Rev. 201, 254.

122 Report of the Crimes Survey Committee, Law Association of Philadelphia (1926) 148. In 1921, out of 25,000 persons arrested for drunkenness in Philadelphia, 23,000 were discharged.

123 Warner, "The Uniform Arrest Act" (1942) 28 Va.L.Rev. 315, 336-339. As to tort liability for release of a prisoner without presentment to a magistrate, see Bohlen and Shulman, "Effect of Subsequent Misconduct Upon a Lawful Arrest" (1928) 28 Col.L.Rev. 841, 853-855.

124 Warner, "Modern Trends in the American Law of Arrest" (1943) 21 Can.B.Rev. 192, 194, 212-213.

16. Delay in Bringing Before Magistrate

Both at common law and under statutes an officer who has made an arrest must bring his prisoner before a magistrate as soon as practicable or without unreasonable delay.[125] This does not mean that the magistrate must work around the clock. If a person is arrested after court hours, the prisoner is to be brought in when the court next convenes.[126] If a person is arrested during court hours for an offense not requiring further investigation, such as speeding, he must be brought before a magistrate at once.[127] The problem is more difficult with respect to arrests for serious felonies or in the exceptional cases in which the prisoner is thought to be wanted in another state for a serious crime. In practice prosecuting attorneys often instruct the police to bring to them all persons arrested for major felonies for examination.[128] This examination may take so long that the prisoner misses court for that day. In some cases even a longer delay may be necessary. For instance, it may be necessary to establish a prisoner's identity by sending his fingerprints to the Federal Bureau of Investigation in Washington.[129]

It appears that there is a public need for a longer period of investigation in the exceptional cases just mentioned. Against this need there must be balanced the inter-

125 A.L.I. Code of Crim. Proc. (1930) § 35; Fed. Rules of Crim. Proc. (1944) Rule 5(a).

126 Wiggins v. Norton, 83 Ga. 148, 9 S.E. 607 (1889); James v. United States, 38 F. (2d) 431, 437 (C.C.A. 9th, 1931).

127 Moses v. State, 6 Ga. App. 251, 64 S.W. 699 (1909); cf. People v. Imamura, 26 Cal. App. 432, 435, 147 § 219, 221 (1915).

128 "It is usual in the United States for the prosecutor or the police to conduct an official examination of the suspect immediately after the arrest." Baker and DeLong, "The Prosecuting Attorney: The Process of Prosecution" (1935) 26 J.Crim.L. 3, 4.

129 Peloquin v. Hibner, 231 Wis. 77, 285 N.W. 380 (1939).

est of the individual in a speedy preliminary hearing, the effective exercise of the right to a writ of habeas corpus, admission to bail, the right to counsel, and freedom from self-incrimination.

Relief as to some cases of unavoidable delay may be afforded by allowing the peace officer to release the prisoner on bail.[130] By special legislation in a few states the peace officer himself may release on bail conditionally, if sufficient bail is offered and the arrest is made at a time when normal proceedings for a hearing would be delayed.

The Uniform Arrest Act, Section 11, reaffirms the existing rule that a person arrested must be brought before a magistrate "without unreasonable delay" and provides that the delay shall not exceed certain periods.[131] Section 2 provides that a suspect may be detained before arrest for a period not exceeding two hours. Section 11 provides that the period between arrest and bringing before a magistrate shall not exceed twenty-four hours except in two cases. The words "if possible" are inserted because in several large western states it is physically impossible during the winter to get a prisoner to a magistrate within twenty-four hours of arrest. The second exception allows a person arrested to be held for a period not to exceed forty-eight hours in excess of the twenty-four hour period, if a judge so orders after good cause shown. The requirement of convincing a judge that good cause exists for postponing should speed up police investigation and reduce long

[130] Perkins, "The Law of Arrest" (1940) 25 Iowa L.Rev. 201, 257. Under the English law the accused may be released upon entering into a recognizance. Howard, "Criminal Justice in England" (1931) 302; Criminal Justice Administration Act of 1914, 485 Geo.V, c.58, § 22; Criminal Justice Act, 1925, 15 & 16 Geo.V, c.86, § 45.

[131] See discussion, Warner, "The Uniform Arrest Act" (1942) 28 Va.L. Rev. 315, 339-342.

periods of detention. The provision would seem constitutional as being reasonable.

17. Evidence Required

A defendant will be discharged by the examining magistrate unless the police have immediately available enough evidence, if uncontradicted, to prove his guilt. The effect of the rule in preliminary examinations is to tighten the rules with respect to arrest, if the police intend to obey the law.[132] A policeman in making an arrest will bear in mind his obligation to take the defendant forthwith before a magistrate and will make sure that he has enough evidence to make out a case against him, before he arrests him. If he brought the defendant before a magistrate without the proper evidence the defendant would immediately be released. If he is arrested and not brought before a magistrate, he may be released on habeas corpus. Because of this dilemma, the police sometimes disregard the law, fail to report his arrest, and hide him in a hotel room. If they then find no evidence, they release him; if they do, they bring him before a magistrate. Thus, while on the whole the requirement of immediate preliminary examination of an arrested person is sound, it does produce some practical difficulties.

18. Identification of Witnesses

In some states the efforts of the police are hindered by the unwillingness of witnesses to give their names. They may be unwilling because they fear gang vengeance or odious publicity or, as in automobile accident cases, because they wish to avoid inconvenience. The Uniform Arrest Act contains an optional section, Section 12, permit-

[132] Waite, Criminal Law in Action (1934) 51-53.

ting a peace officer to stop any person he reasonably believes was present at the commission of any crime, irrespective of its nature and the time it occurred.[133] The officer may demand only the person's name and address. He does not, however, have to accept an unverified answer, but may require the person to identify himself on penalty of being taken forthwith before a magistrate. Since witnesses, like defendants, may be forced to give bail and may be confined pending trial,[134] the requirement of identification should not be regarded as an unreasonable restraint upon this liberty. It is certainly a lesser restraint than the duty to aid in making an arrest.[135]

19. Duty to Assist

There is a duty to assist in arresting a felon when called upon by an officer.[136] This duty goes back to the days of the hue and cry.[137] Thus when a police officer jumps on the running board and orders the driver to chase another car in order to arrest its occupant, it is the duty of the driver to follow the order. In the words of Judge Cardozo: "Still, as in the days of Edward I, the citizenry may be called upon to enforce the justice of the state, not faintly and with lagging steps, but heartily and bravely and with whatever implements and facilities are convenient and at hand." [138] But in the absence of a specific statute so com-

[133] See discussion, Warner, "The Uniform Arrest Act" (1942) 28 Va.L. Rev. 315, 342-343.

[134] In re Grzyeskowiak, 267 Mich. 697, 255 N.W. 359 (1934); United States v. von Bonim, 24 F. Supp. 867 (S.D. N.Y. 1938).

[135] Shawano County v. Industrial Commission, 239 Wis. 513, 263 N.W. 590 (1935).

[136] See A.L.I. Code of Crim. Proc. (1930) § 27.

[137] 2 Pollock and Maitland, History of English Law (1st ed.1895) 580.

[138] Babington et al v. Yellow Taxi Corporation, 250 N.Y. 14, 164 N.E. 726, 61 A.L.R. 1354 (1928), (1929) 29 Col. L.Rev. 637. The case goes very

manding, a private citizen is not under a penal duty to disclose to the police upon his own initiative the commission of a felony by others.[139] The common-law offense of misprision of felony is not recognized in the state courts. An act of congress makes criminal the misprision of a federal felony.[140]

20. Fresh Pursuit

One of the most recent reforms in the law of arrest is embodied in the Uniform Act on Fresh Pursuit.[141] This act gives to officers of another jurisdiction "in fresh pursuit" of one believed to have committed a felony in such other jurisdiction the power to cross the boundary line and come into the state with the same authority to arrest the fugitive and hold him in custody as local officers have in regard to one believed to have committed a local felony. The act places no restriction on the distance the foreign official can travel in the state as long as he continues in fresh pursuit. Fresh pursuit does not necessarily imply instant pursuit, but pursuit without unreasonable delay. If arrested, the fugitive is taken before a magistrate in the county of the arrest. Modern methods of rapid transportation justify the act.

---

far in holding either that property may be taken by peace officers even when the owner is not present, or that a private person may be required to aid with any property that may be in his custody.

139 People v. Lefkowitz, 294 Mich. 263, 293 N.U. 642 (1940); (1941) 54 Harv.L.Rev. 506, (1941) 20 Neb.L.Rev. 66.

140 18 U.S.C.A. § 251; Neal v. United States, 102F. (2d) 643 (1939).

141 Up to 1938, twenty-three states had adopted the Act. The Handbook on Interstate Crime Control (1938). The Act is set out in (1936) 26 J.Crim. L. 773-774. See also Wigmore, "State Cooperation for Crime Repression" (1937) 28 J.Crim.L. 327.

21. Breaking of Doors

If an officer's searches reveal that a breach of the peace or a felony is being committed in a house, the law allows him to break open the door and make an arrest, though only after he has announced his official character and demanded admittance.[142] Suppose, as is often the case, that the officer has no personal knowledge of what has occurred or is occurring in the house, but has responded to a radio call. Under present practice when he gets there and finds the house dark, he may simply pound on the door and inquire of the neighbors. But many police officers feel that the law should allow them to break in, arguing that if no crime is being committed in the house their entry will occasion little inconvenience, while, if one is, it may prevent death or serious harm.[143]

22. Search Incidental to Arrest

One rightfully making an arrest may search the person of the suspected person [144] to discover and seize any articles which appear to have been acquired by means of the crime charged,[145] or which may serve as evidence to prove commission of that crime,[146] or which can be used by the

[142] See A.L.I. Code of Crim. Proc. (1930), commentary to § 28, pp.253-255; Perkins, "The Law of Arrest" (1940) 25 Iowa L.Rev. 201, 244-247.

[143] Warner, "Investigating the Law of Arrest" (1940) 26 A.B.A.J. 151, 153.

[144] People v. Chiagles, 237 N.Y. 153, 142 N.I. 583, 32 A.L.R. 676 (1923); Keigwin, Cases on Criminal Procedure (1939) 16. See A.L.I. Code of Crim. Proc. (1932) § 32. As to search under illegal arrest, see Note (1941) 32 J.Crim.L. 439, 442.

[145] Weeks v. United States, 232 U.S. 383, 34 Sup.Ct. 841, 58 L. Ed. 652 (1914).

[146] United States v. Kirschenblatt, 16 Fed. (C.C.A. 2d, 1926) 202, 51 A.L.R. 416. As to the English law, see Kenny, Outlines of Criminal Law (15th ed.1942) 525-526; Harris and Wilshere, Principles and Practice of

prisoner in effecting an escape or as a means of doing harm to himself or other persons.[147] Such search may be extended also to the immediate surroundings of the person arrested, as a vehicle in which he is found[148] and to articles that are visible in the room in which the arrest was made.[149] Where, however, the officer has no search warrant, he may not go through the house,[150] nor open closets or desks to find things which may prove incriminating.[151] An arrest cannot properly be made for the sole purpose of searching.[152]

23. Right to Counsel

A basic question in connection with the law of arrest is whether or not the accused should have the right to counsel. Obviously he is to have no such right preceding or during the arrest. But it would seem that to protect him fully he should have the right immediately subsequent to the arrest.[153] With respect to persons accused for

---

the Criminal Law (17th ed.1943) 403; Wade, "Police Search" (1934) 50 L.Q.Rev. 354; Radzinowicz and Turner, The Modern Approach to Criminal Law (1945) c.6.

147 People v. Garrett, 232 Mich. 366, 205 N.W. 95 (1925).

148 Carroll v. United States, 267 U.S. 132, 45 Sup.Ct. 250, 60 L.Ed. 543, 39 A.L.R. 790 (1925).

149 Marron v. United States, 275 U.S. 192, 48 Sup.Ct. 74, 72 L.Ed. 285 (1927).

150 State v. Adams, 103 W. Va. 77, 1365 to 703, 51 A.L.R. 407 (1927). See Note (1932) 33 J.Crim.L. 111.

151 United States v. Lefkowitz, 285 U.S. 452, 52 Sup.Ct. 420, 76 L.Ed. 877, 82 A.L.R. 775 (1932).

152 People v. Ford, 356 Ill. 572, 191 N.E. 315 (1934).

153 "In practically every state this right to counsel is interpreted to mean right to counsel during the trial of the case. Although competent counsel is of great value at that time, the time when an accused person really needs the help of a lawyer is when he is first arrested and from then on until trial. The intervening period is so full of hazards for the accused person that he may have lost any legitimate defense long before he is arraigned

the first time, the Danish law so provides. "The accused should therefore always be assisted by a legal advisor and if he cannot afford the fees himself, counsel should be appointed and fully paid for by the Crown—otherwise it is not to be expected that his services would be very effective. And this appointment of counsel for the defense by the Crown is especially necessary immediately a suspect is arrested, since the very fact that a person is detained will usually prevent him from securing the services of anyone himself." [154]

24. Petty Offenses

This book is designed to deal primarily with the procedure with respect to serious offenses. Passing mention should, however, be made of petty offenses. The Wickersham Crime Commission has pointed out: "At common law all prosecutions began with arrest and this is the staple method of beginning petty prosecutions in the United States. The practice of summons in such cases

and put on trial." Miller, J., "Lawyers and the Administration of Criminal Justice" (1934) 20 A.B.A.J. 77, 78. "Those who think of the accused as one at an unfair disadvantage with all the powers of the state arrayed against him . . . if they think intelligently and not merely as emotional romanticists . . . think of that half-concealed, unsupervised procedure which precedes the appearance of the accused in the court of record. Here it is that we find the third degree, the bail bond broker, the stool pigeon, the crooked interpreter, the shyster lawyer, the lame-duck magistrate, and all the rest of the motley of underworld characters and methods. The poor man . . . often is the victim of a grotesque burlesque on the administration of justice." Miller, J., quoted in Moley, Our Criminal Courts (1930) 67-68.

[154] Munch-Petersen, "The Social Aspect of Procedure from a European Point of View" (1927) 11 Minn.L.Rev. 624, 630. Section 37 of the A.L.I. Code of Crim. Proc. (1930) provides that an attorney should, at the request of the arrested person or of one acting on his behalf, be permitted to visit the arrested person.

should be introduced wherever it is not provided for, and its use should be extended everywhere."[155] It also concluded: "There should be a wider use of administration rather than arrest and prosecution with respect to police regulations."[156]

25. Antiquated Character of Law of Arrest

The modern law of arrest is old, having undergone virtually no revision since its formulation in England in the seventeenth and eighteenth centuries.[157] "There has been some legislation in the United States on the subject of arrest during the past fifty years, but surprisingly little."[158]

The common-law rules governing arrest by peace officers seem out of date because of the great changes which have occurred in police organization, prisons, and other phases of criminal procedure.[159] Modern police departments date back little more than a century. Bail for felonies has become easily attainable. Prisoners are not kept

155 Nat. Com. on Law Obs. and Enf., Rep. on Crim. Proc. (1931) 14. See also p.47.

156 *Ibid.* 46-47.

157 Warner, "Investigating the Law of Arrest" (1940) 26 A.B.A.J. 151; Nat. Com. on Law Obs. and Enf., Rep. on Proc. (1931) 18; 1 Stephen, A History of the Criminal Law of England (1883) 194. "The rules as to arrest are the same, although in the nineteenth century the institution of the police, and in the twentieth century automatic pistols and motor vehicles introduced radically new situations of fact." Pound, Criminal Justice in America (1930) 108.

158 Warner, "Modern Trends in the American Law of Arrest" (1943) 21 Can.B.Rev. 192, 195.

159 Warner, "The Uniform Arrest Act" (1942) 28 Va.L.Rev. 315. Social changes occurring have been "the vast increase in the number of misdemeanors, the carrying of pistols by both police and criminals, the great increase in the number of trained police officers and the increase in the number of magistrates, and by no means of least importance, the lack of rapport between the police and the public." Warner, "Modern Trends in the American Law of Arrest" (1943) 21 Can.B.Rev. 162.

in jail for years before trial. Living conditions in jails are not dangerous to life as they once were. Today arrests are usually made by police officers instead of by private persons. Today they are usually made without a warrant by officers in patrol cars in response to requests coming over the police radio. Today an arrested person is usually released after a short detention in a police station, so that neither jail nor bail are probably in store for him. Thus, as one careful student has stated, "today the great majority of arrests by police officers are illegal in their inception, continuance or termination." [160]

26. Increasing Powers of Police

The Wickersham Crime Commission favored making it easier to arrest. The report states: "It is of the first importance that the officers charged with enforcement of the law themselves obey the law. But it is of no less importance to have legal rules governing their action consonant with the practical exigencies of enforcement, so that they will not be driven to exceeding their powers in order to do what is expected of them, or subjected to harassing liabilities in the practical execution of their duties. Not the least cause of non-observance of law is to be found in the screwing up of legal requirements beyond the limits of practical observance. The rules applicable to arrest and its incidents should be restated with reference to the conditions in the cities of the present century." [161] The English experience has been otherwise. A Royal Commission stated [162] ". . . with regard to the powers [of arrest by

[160] Warner, "The Uniform Arrest Act" (1942) 28 Va.L.Rev. 315.

[161] Nat. Com. on Law Obs. and Enf., Rep. on Crim. Proc. (1931) 21.

[162] Report of the Royal Commission on Police Powers and Procedure (1929) 51.

the police] . . . it only remains to add that we have had no evidence leading us to the conclusion that they are either excessive or inadequate."

From the point of view of strict law enforcement, mention should be made of loopholes that may exist in the law or its administration at the stage of arrest. In the words of the Minnesota Crime Commission Report of 1927: "To present the picture in a different light, what must the criminal think of society's effort to deal with him? If he be familiar with the actual operation of the criminal law, he must know that he may escape arrest altogether; that if arrested, he may not be held by the police or sheriff." [163]

27. Basic Considerations

In considering improvement in the law of arrest, two basic questions arise: (1) what methods of making arrests are likely to be most effective; (2) of such effective methods, which should the police be permitted to employ? [164] The first problem is the less serious because it involves only a selection of means to a single end and rather adequate data exist for making the choice. But the second problem raises real difficulty because it is one of ends as well as means; the apprehension of suspected persons is not the sole end of government. That is to say, police practices which constitute efficient methods of apprehension may be incompatible with such other ends as the preservation of the general security.

Present seeming technicalities in the law of arrest appearing unduly to favor the suspected person may be based on the hard facts that policemen may make errors

[163] Minnesota Crime Commission Report (1927) 16.

[164] Wechsler, "A Caveat on Crime Control" (1937) 27 J.Crim.L. 629, 634.

of judgment and moral slips and may even become the tools of persons or groups indifferent or hostile to the public good. More extensive powers of arrest "may make it easier to catch criminals; they may also achieve other results ranging from the industrial black list and the shooting of wrongly suspected persons to the facilitation of a fascist coup d'etat." [165]

A satisfactory law of arrest thus involves a proper balancing between two opposing principles.[166] On the one side there is the demand for security sought to be achieved through protection by professional police. On the other side are certain political sentiments and ideals calling for protection against such professionals. As an English writer has said, "the ideal police force [is] the one which affords a maximum of protection at the cost of a minimum of interference with the lawful liberty of the subject." [167]

[165] Wechsler, "A Caveat on Crime Control" (1937) 27 J.Crim.L. 629, 635.

[166] Ploscowe, "Measures of Constraint in European and Anglo-American Criminal Procedure" (1935) 23 Geo.L.J. 762; Hall, "The Law of Arrest in Relation to Contemporary Social Problems" (1936) 3 U. of Chi.L. Rev. 345; Fraenkel, "From Suspicion to Accusation" (1942) 51 Yale L.J. 748, 754; Warner, "Modern Trends in the American Law of Arrest" (1943) 21 Can.B.Rev. 192, 196-197.

[167] Lee, A History of Police in England (1901) xii.

CHAPTER II

PRELIMINARY EXAMINATION

1. Stage in Proceedings

IN the case of petty offenses, the step following arrest or summons is trial in the inferior court with conviction and sentence or acquittal.[1] In the case of other offenses, there is normally a preliminary examination by the magistrate to determine whether there is probable cause for maintaining a criminal proceeding.[2] At this examination the defendant may be discharged or may be bound over to await the action of the grand jury or of the district attorney.

Accurately speaking this chapter might better be entitled "Proceedings before the Magistrate." [3] The defen-

[1] No preliminary examination is required in cases in which the magistrate is himself competent to try. State v. Solomon, 158 Wis. 146, 147 N.W. 640 (1914).

[2] Nat. Com. on Law Obs. and Enf., Rep. on Crim. Proc. (1931) 16; Kenny, Outlines of Criminal Law (15th ed.1942) 523; Wharton, Criminal Pleading and Practice (9th ed.1889) § 70, p.46. For full discussions of the preliminary examination, see Miller, J., "The Preliminary Hearing" (1929) 15 A.B.A.J. 414; Martin, J., "The Preliminary Hearing: Canadian Practice" (1937) 1 J.Crim.L. (Eng.) 107, 121; Moley, Our Criminal Courts (1930) 3-42; 1 Stephen, A History of the Criminal Law of England (1883) 216-233; Kauper, "Judicial Examination of the Accused—A Remedy for the Third Degree" (1932) 30 Mich.L.Rev. 1224; Report of the Crimes Survey Committee, Law Association of Philadelphia (1926) 167-179; 14 Am. Jur., Criminal Law, §§ 240-248, pp.933-939; 22 C.J.S., Criminal Law, §§ 331-352, pp.483-515.

[3] Rule 5 of the Federal Rules of Criminal Procedure is entitled "Proceedings before the Commissioner," subsection (c) being entitled "Preliminary Examination." Since the modern proceeding is a hearing rather than an examination, it would be more precise to talk of preliminary hearing. Kauper, "Judicial Examination of the Accused—A Remedy for the Third Degree" (1932) 30 Mich.L.Rev. 1224, 1231, n.30.

dant is normally brought before a magistrate following his arrest.[4] He does not, however, invariably undergo a preliminary examination. If he wishes he may waive such examination.

2. Not a Constitutional Right

The right to a preliminary examination, though widely recognized in the United States and all English-speaking countries, is not a constitutional right but rather a right granted by statute.[5] In the opinion of the Wickersham Crime Commission it is one of the essentials of any criminal proceeding.[6] As a federal judge has stated: "One threatened with the charge of the commission of a crime has two rights. One is, of course, the right to a fair and impartial trial upon which the question of his guilt is determined; the other is the no less valuable right, that he shall not be even called upon to answer to a criminal charge until some duly constituted tribunal has passed upon the preliminary question of whether he ought to be brought to trial." [7] In the case of one arrested under a warrant there are thus three preliminary scrutinies of the case against the defendant before his trial. In the first place the magistrate may refuse to issue the warrant on

[4] In some jurisdictions the preliminary examination must be before the magistrate who is issued the warrant if he is available. See Section 6 of the Illinois Code. In other jurisdictions, any magistrate having jurisdiction of the offense may examine. See "Defects in Criminal Justice" (1925) 11 A.B.A.J. 297, 299.

[5] State ex rel. Germain v. Ross, 39 N.D. 630, 170 N.W. 121 (1918). It is true that one type of preliminary examination existed for several centuries in England, but such examination was radically altered by statutes in the middle of the nineteenth century.

[6] Nat. Com. on Law Obs. and Enf., Rep. on Crim. Proc. (1931) 16.

[7] Dickinson, J., in United States v. Fitzgerald, 29 F. (2d) 573, 574 (D.C. Pa.1928).

the facts presented to him under the complaint. In the second place the magistrate may refuse to bind the defendant over at the preliminary examination following the arrest. In the third place, the grand jury may refuse to indict or the prosecuting attorney may conclude not to file an information unless the statute in the jurisdiction compels him to do so.

3. Waiver

Most states allow the defendant to waive his preliminary examination with the result that he is held to answer.[8] Section 40 of the American Law Institute Code of Criminal Procedure permits such waiver, but preserves the right of the prosecution to require such an examination.[9] Under Rule 5 (c) of the Federal Rules of Criminal Procedure, the defendant has an absolute right to waive; no provision is made for examination when he waives. It has been held in a number of cases that it is not essential, as a matter affecting the jurisdiction of the court, that it shall appear affirmatively that the defendant has had or has waived an examination.[10] A failure to accord an ex-

[8] A.L.I. Code of Crim. Proc. (1930) commentaries 276-279. As to waiver by implication, see 14 Am. Jur., Criminal Law, § 242, p.935; 22 C.J.S. Criminal Law, § 333, p.488. A considerable number and variety of acts have been held to constitute waiver by implication. A plea to the merits without demanding a hearing is a waiver. See Waite, Note (1932) 30 Mich.L.Rev. 928, 933.

[9] See in accord: State v. Pigg. 80 Kan. 481, 103 P. 121, 18 Ann. Cas. 521 (1909). In Canada a defendant may waive the preliminary hearing, and have his case sent to trial without it. In England, however, once the case is before the magistrate the depositions must be taken. Martin, J., "The Preliminary Hearing: Canadian Practice" (1937) 1 J.Crim.L. (Eng.) 107, 108, 112.

[10] State v. Pippey, 335 Mo. 121, 71 S.W. (2d) 719 (1934); State v. Shears, 119 Wash. 275, 205 P. 417 (1922). Possibly some of the cases are based on broad doctrines of waiver by implication.

amination goes only to the regularity of the proceedings.[11] It should be taken advantage of by appropriate motion.[12] There is, however, authority holding that, where there is a conviction, the failure amounts to a miscarriage of justice [13] warranting a reversal or setting aside of the judgment of conviction.[14]

4. As a Prerequisite to Accusation

No preliminary examination is necessary prior to the finding of an indictment unless made so by statute.[15] A few states require preliminary examination in certain cases before indictment. Thus in general where prosecution is by indictment, there is no preliminary examination as a matter of right. The American Law Institute Code of Criminal Procedure is silent upon the point. Since today most prosecutions are by information rather than by indict-

[11] State v. Jeffries, 210 Mo. 302, 109 S.W. 614, 14 Ann. Cas. 524 (1908).

[12] Buckley v. Hall, 215 Mo. 93, 114 S.W. 954 (1908).

[13] People v. Bomar, 73 Cal. App. 372, 238 P. 758 (1925).

[14] Davis v. State, 121 Neb. 399, 237 N.W. 297 (1931); State v. Trow, 499 S.D. 485, 207 N.W. 466 (1926); 22 C.J.S., Criminal Law, § 332, p.487.

[15] Keigwin, Cases in Criminal Procedure (1939) 167; 14 Am. Jur., Criminal Law, § 240; Moley, Our Criminal Courts (1930) 23; State v. Mooney, 49 W.Va. 712, 399 E. 657 (1901); Hale v. Henkel, 201 U.S. 43, 26 Sup.Ct. 370, 50 L.Ed. 652 (1906). See also Note (1940) 49 Yale L.J. 1059, 1070; Dession, "From Indictment to Information—Implications of the Shift" (1932) 42 Yale L.J. 163, 168. It has been pointed out that the preliminary examination is, generally speaking, used in connection with indictments as well as informations. Miller, J., "Lawyers and the Administration of Criminal Justice" (1934) 20 A.B.A.J. 77, 79. If the magistrate finds the evidence sufficient and orders the defendant held, the law in twenty odd states requires a second examination of the evidence by a grand jury, who in their turn may find it insufficient and refuse to indict. Waite, Criminal Law in Action (1934) 54. "Even in states not providing for the use of the information, a preliminary examination is often held, though not required in felony cases." Moley, Politics and Criminal Prosecution (1929) 138. See also Dession and Cohen, "The Inquisitorial Functions of Grand Juries" (1932) 41 Yale L.J. 687, 704.

ment, proceedings where there is no preliminary examination will be exceptional.

In general there must have been a preliminary examination or a waiver thereof as a prerequisite to the filing of an information.[16] Some jurisdictions have dispensed with such a requirement.[17] Section 115 of the American Law Institute Code of Criminal Procedure requires such an examination. But Section 60 prohibits the discharge of a defendant on a writ of habeas corpus and the holding invalid of a preliminary examination "because of any informality or error, which does not prejudice the accused in the commitment or the proceedings prior thereto." It would seem that the disregard of technical errors, particularly at a preliminary proceeding, is desirable. Nonprejudicial errors should not prevent the holding of a defendant for trial before a jury upon the merits.

5. History in England

The preliminary hearing is one of the modern developments of criminal procedure. The early law did not contemplate any preliminary inquiry into the guilt or innocence of a defendant.[18] The defendant was tried fol-

[16] Keedy, "The Drafting of a Code of Criminal Procedure" (1929) 15 A.B.A.J. 7, 8.

[17] Connecticut, Florida, Indiana, Iowa, Louisiana, Vermont, and Washington. The Missouri Crime Survey (1926) 129 states: "There is much support of the view that the preliminary hearing now provided for contributes nothing to the cause of justice, but on the contrary increases the costs, is one of the main causes of delay in prosecution, and gives the defendant an undue advantage over the state." The survey suggests that if the preliminary examination be retained, it be conducted by the clerk of court. *Ibid.* 130-131, 381-382. Moley states: "Nearly everyone in the system believes the preliminary hearing to be practically unnecessary. . . . The prosecution views the preliminary hearing as a mere perfunctory detail." Our Criminal Courts (1930) 31.

[18] 1 Holdsworth, History of English Law (3d ed.1923) 295-297; A.L.I.

lowing the action of the grand jury or the finding of a coroner's inquest.[19] If he was taken in the act, he was generally executed immediately.

The inquest of the coroner always had some of the characteristics of a preliminary examination.[20] Moreover the powers of the coroner with respect to taking depositions and binding over witnesses to appear at the trial have been enlarged by statute. During the reign of Philip and Mary there were two statutes conferring similar powers on the justices of the peace. These statutes originated the jurisdiction of the justices of the peace as to preliminary examinations.[21] In 1554 it was enacted that defendants arrested for felony should not be granted bail or mainprize except by two justices in open sessions. These justices "shall take the examination of the said prisoner and information of them that bring him," and shall put into writing the material evidence against the defendant before they release him on bail. In 1555 it was enacted that, whether or not the defendant was actually bailed, such examination should take place, and that the justices could bind over to appear at the trial any witnesses against the defendant whose evidence they regarded as essential. Of the effect of these statutes Stephen states: "I do not

---

Code of Crim. Proc. (1930) § 39, commentaries 266-268; Nat. Com. on Law Obs. and Enf., Rep. on Crim. Proc. (1931) 9-10. Compare Kauper, "Judicial Examination of the Accused—A Remedy for the Third Degree" (1931) 30 Mich.L.Rev. 1224, 1231-1235.

19 Pound, Criminal Justice in America (1930) 87-88.

20 "The earliest instance that occurs of any sort of preliminary inquiry into crime with a view to subsequent proceedings is the case of the coroner's inquest." 1 Stephen, A History of the Criminal Law of England (1883) 217.

21 "It is probable, however, that from the very earliest times magistrates would make a more or less formal inquiry before they took steps towards the arrest or bail of a suspected person." 1 Stephen, A History of the Criminal Law of England (1883) 219.

think any part of the old procedure operated more harshly upon prisoners than the summary and secret way in which justices of the peace, acting frequently the part of detective officers, took their examinations and committed them for trial." [22]

It seems clear that these statutes were aimed to increase the powers of the justices with respect to defendants. They did not appear to contemplate a strictly judicial inquiry into the facts of the case.[23] There can be no question but that in the seventeenth century the examination assumed an inquisitorial character.[24] There was a close examination of the defendant as to all the circumstances of the alleged offense. The witnesses for the prosecution were examined out of his presence, their evidence being viewed as only for the information of the court. As a matter of fact as late as 1823 the grand jury were told that, when a magistrate was conducting the preliminary examination, he was not acting judicially but inquisitorially; that such proceedings should be conducted in secret,[25] and that information thus obtained might be given to the prosecutor but not to the defendant. In 1836, however, the Pris-

[22] 1 Stephen, A History of the Criminal Law of England (1883) 225.

[23] "We have seen that these statutes contemplated an inquisitorial examination of the prisoner, not a judicial enquiry into the facts of the case. They gave, as they were designed to give, the executive some of the advantages against prisoners which were conferred by the inquisitorial procedure of foreign states; and it is not till the reforms of the last century that the examination lost its original character, and became an enquiry of a judicial nature. Such a procedure may seem strange to our modern ideas. But in the sixteenth century, it was necessary in order to secure the observance of the law and to protect the state against its enemies." 4 Holdsworth, History of English Law (3d ed.1923) 529. See also Pound, Criminal Justice in America (1930) 87.

[24] Torture was not, however, resorted to as a regular part of the practice. 1 Stephen, A History of the Criminal Law of England (1883) 221-222.

[25] Prior to 1848 the preliminary examination was generally held in a private residence. Jackson, The Machinery of Justice in England (1940) 81.

oner's Counsel Act permitted defendants to inspect all depositions taken against them. Finally in 1848 Parliament enacted that the witnesses for the prosecution should be examined in the presence of the defendant.[26] Moreover the defendant could make any statement he pleased or call any witnesses he desired, but was not obliged to do either. It was made the duty of the magistrate to inform him of this.[27] Judicial interrogation of the defendant is regarded as improper in England today. Thus less than a century ago the preliminary examination became an entirely judicial proceeding.[28] Previously the magistrate had acted the part of a prosecutor.

The establishment of a modern professional police force in the nineteenth century had a significant effect. It made more clear the differences between the functions of the magistrate and the policeman. The justice of the peace found it easier to act as a judge, now that there was an adequate police force. Arrest under a warrant became less open to suspicion. What Coke had protested against in the seventeenth century was the issuance of a warrant and the examination of the defendant by the detective who was getting up the case. Today the defendant is

[26] Stephen states that "till the year 1849 prisoners certainly had no legal right to know beforehand what evidence was to be given against them." 1 Stephen, A History of the Criminal Law of England (1883) 226. Even today the public cannot insist on admission. Kenny, Outlines of Criminal Law (15th ed.1942) 532.

[27] 1 Stephen, A History of the Criminal Law of England (1883) 441.

[28] "It may indeed admit of a doubt whether it is not too judicial, and whether it does not tend to become a separate trial." 1 Stephen, A History of the Criminal Law of England (1883) 229. For descriptions of the present English system, see Howard, Criminal Justice in England (1931) 330-336; Kenny, Outlines of Criminal Law (15th ed.1942) 532-542; Maitland, Justice and Police (1885) 129-130; Stephen, A Digest of the Law of Criminal Procedure (1883) 69-86; Harris and Wilshere, Principles and Practice of the Criminal Law (17th ed.1943) 404-411.

brought before a magistrate who has no interest in acting otherwise than judicially.

The court may in proper cases assign to the defendant a solicitor and a right to a counsel under the Poor Prisoners' Defense Act, 1930.[29] This Act authorizes justices of the peace, upon committing a defendant for trial, to certify that a solicitor and counsel ought to be assigned to him, and the cost of his defense defrayed out of police funds.[30] This power is to be exercised only where the defendant is too poor to pay for his own defense and it appears, having regard to all the circumstances of the case including the nature of such defense as may have been set up, that it is desirable in the interests of justice that legal aid should be granted.[31] Where the circumstances are exceptional or in cases of extreme gravity, legal aid may be granted by justices so that a prisoner may be defended before them on a preliminary examination or on summary proceedings. Only a solicitor is assigned in such cases except where the charge is for murder. It has been pointed out that the fact that "legal aid is not normally given for the preliminary examination often results in unnecessary expense through the committal of persons subsequently acquitted." [32]

A summary of the differences between the early Eng-

[29] 20 & 21 Geo. V, c. 32. An earlier more limited act had been passed in 1903. Stephen, "Criminal Law Reforms Since 1822" (1922) 57 The Law Journal 419, 421.

[30] The act and rules under it are set out in Archbold, Criminal Pleading, Evidence and Practice (30th ed.1938) 167-170.

[31] It has been thought that the justices are too willing to assign free legal aid for the mere asking without making searching inquiry whether the defendant is really without means, and whether the interest of justice requires it. Butler, "Developments in Criminal Law—1910-1935" (1935) 179 The Law Times 325, 326.

[32] Kenny, Outlines of Criminal Law (15th ed.1942) 542.

lish inquisitorial examination and the present judicial one reveals the following: Under the new law the magistrate sits as a judge with no interest in the case prior to the examination, whereas under the old law he served as a public prosecutor who often was responsible for the arrest. Under the new law there is no compulsory examination of the defendant, although he is invited to make a statement; under the old law he was examined without any significant restrictions. Under the new law the testimony is open, accusatory, and confrontative, whereas under the old it was secret and for the information of the court only. Under the new law there is a right to counsel and to cross-examination; under the old law the defendant had no right to counsel. Under the new law the defendant is entitled to copies of the testimony given in open court and also to inspect all depositions taken against him; under the old law he could not obtain such evidence.[33]

Some weaknesses in the English system have been pointed out.[34] The holding of a preliminary examination amounts to requiring a double hearing with delay and expense. The magistrate very seldom takes the responsibility of deciding that there is not a prima facie case for trial. Since only a very small fraction of prisoners are not committed, no great hardship would result from its abolition. The magistrate would of course have to investigate the statements of the principal witnesses before deciding to commit, but such investigation could be brief and private.

[33] Modern English procedure on preliminary examination is described by Keedy, "Preliminary Examination of Accused Persons in England" (1934) Am. Phil. Soc. Proc. (2) pp.103-116.

[34] Kenny, Outlines of Criminal Law (15th ed.1942) 540.

6. Defects of Inquisitorial System

There are two wholly distinct types of preliminary examinations. The Anglo-American type, which may be described as a judicial inquiry, has as its primary purpose the determination whether there is probable cause for holding the defendant for further proceedings, so that he may be released if no such probable cause appears, and exists secondarily to perpetuate the evidence and to determine the amount of bail if the defendant is not discharged.

The other type of preliminary examination is inquisitorial in character and has for its purpose the obtaining of evidence of guilt by interrogating the defendant.[35] It is the system used in European countries such as France[36] and Italy. The drafters of the American Law Institute Code of Criminal Procedure, after a careful study of that system, concluded that it should not be adopted. They discovered that the tendency in the European countries having this system was to abolish or restrict it.[37] For

[35] Esmein, A History of Continental Criminal Procedure (Simpson's trans. 1913) 8-11.

[36] For a recent description of the French system, see Keedy, "The Preliminary Investigation of Crime in France" (1940) 88 U. of Pa.L.Rev. 385, 692, 915. See also Ploscowe, "Development of Inquisitorial and Accusatorial Elements in French Procedure" (1932) 23 J.Crim.L. 372; Esmein, A History of Continental Criminal Procedure (Simpson's trans. 1913) 539-569; Garner, "Criminal Procedure in France" (1916) 25 Yale L.J. 255, 256-260; Note, "Reform in Criminal Procedure" (1940) 50 Yale L.J. 107, 111; Auld, "The Comparative Jurisprudence of Criminal Process" (1935) 1 U. of Toronto L.J. 82; Moley, Our Criminal Courts (1930) 36-42; Hogg, "French Criminal Procedure" (1945) 23 Can.B. Rev. 846. As to the practice in other European countries, see Esmein, A History of Continental Criminal Procedure (1913) 599-602.

[37] "It is curious to note that at a time when some American scholars look with favor upon the *juge d'instruction* and recommend his introduction here, there is a large body of opinion in Europe which would either materially curtail his powers or eliminate him entirely." Ploscowe, "The De-

instance in France he is permitted to have counsel and is cautioned that he need not answer. The inquisitorial system requires trained officials. In Continental Europe the examining judges are not only lawyers, but they have received special training in the examination and weighing of evidence. In the United States and England magistrates are often laymen. Most American as well as English [38] lawyers are antagonistic on the grounds that it violates fundamental principles of personal liberty and might result in the conviction of innocent persons.[39] While the chief reason advanced in favor of the system is that it would do away with the "third degree," there is no assurance that such result would follow. Resort to the third degree has occurred in France.[40] It would be necessary to amend the constitutions of all but two states to adopt the system. Finally, even if the necessary constitutional changes could be secured and the necessary legislation

---

velopment of Present-Day Criminal Procedures in Europe and America" (1935) 48 Harv.L.Rev. 433, 472.

[38] The English writer, R. C. K. Ensor, states in his book, Courts and Judge in France, Germany and England (1933) 35: "It is he (the *juge d'instruction*) who has the power to order, or to delay ordering, the arrest of a suspect person, and in France where there is no habeas corpus act and where a person once arrested may easily languish in custody for long periods (over a year in extreme instances), this is a very formidable power indeed. He, too, does the orders, searches, and seizures of documents or other property and conducts the interrogation of suspects. He represents one of the points at which anyone concerned to exert improper influence over the judicature is most likely to bring it to bear—the more hopefully because the post is not a very high one and its occupant is apt to be of an age when promotion means a great deal to him."

[39] The views of a few friendly American lawyers are cited by Garner, "Criminal Procedure in France" (1916) 25 Yale L.J. 255, 260, n.19. See also Carman, "A Plea for Withdrawal of Constitutional Privilege from the Criminal" (1938) 22 Minn.L.Rev. 200.

[40] Keedy, "The Third Degree and Legal Interrogation of Suspects" (1937) 85 U. of Pa.L.Rev. 761, 766-777; Warner, "How Can the Third Degree be Eliminated?" (1940) 1 Bill of Rights Review, 24.

adopted, it was thought that the system could not be successfully operated because there are no properly equipped officers and because the bulk of public opinion would be against it. The only methods [41] for introducing something comparable to the well implemented preliminary examination on the Continent are greatly improved judicial personnel and drastic modification of the privilege against self incrimination.[42] In the absence of such reforms reliance must be placed on the grand jury.[43]

7. The Third Degree

What is or should be the significance to the defendant of his preliminary examination before a magistrate? It would be difficult to exaggerate the significance. Resort to the third degree is checked. The constitutional privilege of protection against self incrimination is made effective. Judicial proceedings involve the appearance of counsel for the criminal defendant. Bail may be granted. It becomes definitely known that the defendant is in the custody of the police, hence habeas corpus may be resorted to. Other legal guarantees come into play so that the whole level of official activity is apt to be improved. As one writer has stated, "arrest without a warrant followed by imprisonment and delay or failure to bring the arrestee before a magistrate is the likeliest area for 'official lawlessness.' " [44] The Wickersham Commission found

[41] Note, Reform in Criminal Procedure (1940) 50 Yale L.J. 107, 111-112.

[42] Note, The Privilege Against Self-Incrimination (1940) 49 Yale L.J. 1059.

[43] Dession and Cohen, "The Inquisitorial Functions of Grand Juries" (1932) 41 Yale L.J. 687; Note (1938) 17 N.C.L.Rev. 43.

[44] Hall, "The Law of Arrest in Relation to Contemporary Social Problems" (1936) 3 U. of Chi.L.Rev. 345, 357. See also Nat. Com. on Law Obs.

that, out of 106 cases reported between 1920 and 1930 in appellate courts where the use of the third degree was charged, there were only seven cases in which the prisoner declared that the third degree was used after he had been brought before a committing magistrate.[45]

The last section of the chapter on Arrest of the American Law Institute Code of Criminal Procedure, Section 38, deals with the subject of the third degree. It provides: "No peace officer, or other official engaged in administering the criminal law, shall use oppressive methods of any kind for the purpose of securing a confession or other evidence of guilt from an arrested person." The Wickersham Commission states: "After reviewing the evidence obtainable the authors of this report reach the conclusion that the third degree—that is, the use of physical brutality, or other forms of cruelty, to obtain involuntary confessions or admissions—is widespread." [46] There seems to be no one remedy for eliminating the third degree. Certainly reform in criminal procedure alone is not the solu-

---

and Enf., Report on Lawlessness in Law Enforcement (1931) 6, 173-180, 201-204; American Bar Association Report of the Commission on Lawless Enforcement of Law (1930); Glueck, Crime and Justice (1936) 75; 258 N.Y. 394, 180 N.E. 94 (1932); Chambers v. Florida, 309 U.S. 227, 240, 60 Sup.Ct. 472 (1940); 2 Wigmore, Evidence (3d ed.1940) § 851, pp.319-320; Chafee, "Remedies for the Third Degree" (1931) 148 Atl. Monthly, 621, 622. Compare Miller, J., "Lawyers and the Administration of Criminal Justice" (1934) 20 A.B.A.J. 77, 78, who points out that the third degree is used not to secure a confession, but rather an admission or a plea of guilty.

[45] Nat. Com. on Law Obs. and Enf., Report on Lawlessness in Law Enforcement (1931) 169, 210-211.

[46] Nat. Com. on Laws Obs. and Ent., Report on Lawlessness in Law Enforcement (1931) 4. See Note, "The Third Degree" (1930) 43 Harv.L.Rev. 617. For an opposite view as to the widespread existence of the third degree, see Waite, "Report on Lawlessness in Law Enforcement" (1931) 30 Mich.L.Rev. 54; Waite, Criminal Law in Action (1934) 138-141.

tion. Some of the leading proposals[47] made are: (1) a statute making confessions obtained by police officers inadmissible in evidence;[48] (2) improvement of the efficiency of police officers;[49] (3) employment of scientific methods, such as the "lie detector";[50] (4) extension of the public defender system;[51] (5) allowance of comment on failure of the defendant to testify;[52] (6) legislation authorizing judicial interrogation of persons suspected of crime;[53] and (7) statutes making the third degree a criminal offense.[54]

One of the remedies sometimes suggested for avoiding the third degree is to deprive the police of opportunity for questioning suspects. In criticism it is argued that the remedy is impractical.[55] It is true that such a remedy

[47] These are listed by Keedy, "The Third Degree and Legal Interrogation of Suspects" (1937) 85 U. of Pa.L.Rev. 761, 765-766.

[48] Report of the Crimes Survey Committee, Law Association of Philadelphia (1926) 467. See discussion, Kauper, "Judicial Examination of the Accused—A Remedy for the Third Degree" (1932) 30 Mich.L.Rev. 1224, 1226.

[49] 3 Wigmore, Evidence (3d ed.1940) § 851, pp.319-320; Larson, "Present Police and Legal Methods for the Determination of the Innocence or Guilt of the Suspect" (1925) 16 J.Crim.L. 219, 252. The remedy is to obtain "police and prosecutors who prefer not to use and who are able to protect the public without resorting to it." Warner, "How Can the Third Degree be Eliminated?" (1940) 1 Bill of Rights Review 24.

[50] Chafee, "Remedies for the Third Degree" (1931) 148 Atl. Monthly 621, 627.

[51] Hopkins, Our Lawless Police (1931) 354.

[52] "On the Third Degree" (1932) 23 J.Crim.L. 370.

[53] Knox, J., "Self-Incrimination" (1925) 74 U. of Pa.L.Rev. 139, 153. See criticism by Miller, J., "Lawyers and the Administration of Criminal Justice" (1934) 20 A.B.A.J. 77, 78.

[54] Keedy, "The Third Degree and Legal Interrogation of Suspects" (1937) 85 U. of Pa.L.Rev. 761, 765.

[55] Waite, Criminal Law in Action (1934) 143; Kauper, "Judicial Examination of the Accused—A Remedy for the Third Degree" (1932) 30 Mich.L.Rev. 1224, 1226-1228.

would deprive the police of opportunity to use force in questioning. Unfortunately it would equally prevent questioning of a suspect directly and without force by the police. Since the magistrate does not interrogate, there could be no interrogation by anybody.[56] If the police were required to turn over a defendant to a magistrate without having had the opportunity to question, and if the magistrate cannot question, arrested persons cannot be questioned at all.

In England when the police make an arrest, though the law does not actually require it, in practice they warn the suspect not to say anything that might help the state to prove his guilt.[57] In the United States a policeman's fail-

[56] "In actual practice, from the time a man is arrested until arraignment he is quizzed with a view to inducing him to admit his offense or give some evidence that may convict him." Train, From the District Attorney's Office (1939) 36.

[57] The simplest, clearest, and most effective rule against police interrogation is that of Scotland: "Interrogations of arrested persons by the police are forbidden and confessions and admissions obtained in this way are inadmissible in evidence. . . . 'Police authorities are not permitted to examine him [the prisoner] without the protection of a magistrate.'" Keedy, "Criminal Procedure in Scotland" (1913) 3 J.Crim.L. 728, 743. See also "H. M. Advocate v. Aitken" (1926) J.C. 83; Renton and Brown, Criminal Procedure According to the Law of Scotland (2d ed.1928) 28, 29, 33-35. In England judges have formulated and approved rules regulating the questioning by police of a person in custody. See Rex v. Voisin, L. R. (1918) 1 K. B. 531, 539; (1933) 6 Police Journal 353-356. See also Report of the Royal Commission on Police Powers and Procedure (1929) 61, recommending that questioning by police of persons in custody or on bail should not be permitted. These recommendations have, however, been largely ignored. Radzinowicz and Turner, Penal Reform in England (1940) 80-83. The rules are a handicap to the English police. Jackson, The Machinery of Justice in England (1940) 141. "In the last analysis the only safeguards are to be careful training of the investigating officer in a tradition of fair behavior, and watchful judicial control, in public trials." "Questioning an Accused Person" (1928) 92 Justice of the Peace and Local Government 743, 758, 759. 3 Wigmore, Evidence (3d ed.1940) § 847; Waite, Criminal Law in Action (1934) 144; Baty, "A Revolution in Eng-

ure to caution a suspect against telling the truth does not make the latter's confession unusable against him. But a magistrate's failure to caution the defendant at his preliminary examination that anything he said might be used against him has been held ground for the reversal of a conviction.[58]

Under Rule 5(b) of the First Preliminary Draft of the Federal Rules of Criminal Procedure, there was rendered inadmissible in evidence at the trial any statement made by the defendant in response to interrogation by a government officer, if the interrogation occurred while the defendant was confined in violation of the requirement that he be brought before a magistrate without unnecessary delay.[59] Because of much criticism all later drafts of the Rules omitted it.[60] A like rule is, however, laid down in a recent decision of the Supreme Court.[61] A Committee of the American Bar Association has opposed a bill in Congress to repeal the effect of that decision.[62] They have pointed out that it is the only effective safeguard against arbitrary imprisonment except the denial of mileage fees.[63]

---

lish Criminal Procedure" (1913) 47 Am.L.Rev. 648; Warner, "How Can the Third Degree Be Eliminated?" (1940) 1 Bill of Rights Rev. 24, 27-28.

58 McNish v. State, 45 Fla. 83, 34 So. 219 (1903). Compare 3 Wigmore, Evidence (3d ed.1940) § 852.

59 See also Note to Rule 5(b) in the First Preliminary Draft, 12-16.

60 Comment by Waite (1944) 42 Mich.L.Rev. 679, 688-693; (1943) 29 A.B.A.J. 603-604.

61 McNabb v. United States, 318 U.S. 332, 63 Sup.Ct. 608 (1943), (1943) 56 Harv.L.Rev. 1008, (1943) 28 Minn.L.Rev. 73, (1944) 42 Mich.L.Rev. 909 (Waite). See also Note (1944) 53 Yale L.J. 758; Dession, "The New Federal Rules of Criminal Procedure: I" (1946) 55 Yale L.J. 694, 706-714.

62 A Statement by the Committee on the Bill of Rights of the American Bar Association on H.R. 3690 (1944).

63 In 1943 there were at least a dozen cases in which detention ran from 12 hours to 8 days. See Runnels v. United States, 138 F. (2d) 346 (C.C.A. 9th,1943); Anderson v. United States, U.S. 350 (1943); Haupt v. United States, 136 (2d) 661 (C.C.A. 7th,1943); Gros v. United States,

No penalties had been previously imposed on federal officers who had detained a defendant in custody for a longer time than the federal statutes permit.[64] The jury would favor the police officer in a damage suit, and even if it did not, few police officers could pay any large amount of damages. Police officers need give no bond covering unlawful detentions, hence sureties could not be sued. His superior officers will not discipline him, as he is regarded as having done his duty. If the statutes were to allow some period, such as eight days, the constitutional right of the defendant to habeas corpus, bail, the right to counsel, and freedom from self-incrimination would be violated. A possible solution is to permit investigatory imprisonment, provided consent of the federal courts is obtained. Another solution is for the courts summarily to punish any officer who detains a prisoner beyond the statutory time limit without special judicial authorization.[65] Or the statute might provide that the trial judge shall have discretion to keep the confession out or let it in. That is the English practice. Oral consent to prolonged custody, when given by a prisoner without benefit of counsel should not be treated as excusing a failure to bring the prisoner promptly before a magistrate.[66]

---

136 (2d) 878 (C.C.A. 9th,1943). See also Bullock v. United States, 121 F. (2d) 213 (D.C. App. 1941).

[64] The cases do not authorize a person to be detained for the purposes of facilitating investigation. Leger v. Warren, 62 Ohio. St. 500, 508-509 (1900); People v. Frugoli, 334 Ill. 324, 333 (1929); Nat. Com. on Law Obs. and Enf., Report on Lawlessness in Law Enforcement (1931) 34.

[65] See Note by Waite (1944) 42 Mich.L.Rev. 909, 915; (1943) 56 Harv. L.Rev. 1008; A Statement by the Committee on the Bill of Rights of the American Bar Association on H.R. 3690 (1944) 44.

[66] See reasoning in United States v. Mitchell, 88 L.Ed. 812 (1944).

8. Preliminary Examination in the United States

Suppose that an arrested person has been admitted to bail [67] before a preliminary examination. He is still entitled to another hearing before a magistrate.[68] The purpose of such hearing is to determine whether the known evidence against him is sufficient to justify further proceedings against him. Today this hearing is almost wholly for the benefit of the defendant, whereas historically it was for the benefit of the prosecution.[69] The examining magistrate makes no effort to obtain any evidence. The defendant is permitted to make a statement in his own defense if he desires. The magistrate may not, however, ask him questions for the sake of getting any evidence against him. In the absence of statute no power of interrogation is vested in the magistrate at all.[70] Although the proceeding is called an "examination," it is in no sense an examination of the defendant. Instead, it is an examination by the state to ascertain and evaluate what evidence the state has already acquired. Its basic purpose is to save the defendant the annoyance and costs of having to defend himself against further proceedings, unless there is enough

[67] In comparison with the law as laid down by Blackstone, the "system of commitment and bail is the same, variously modified in its details by statutory tinkering in the several states." Pound, Criminal Justice in America (1930) 108-109.

[68] Examination is before a single magistrate as it is in England. An English writer has stated, however, that "it may well be that the preliminary examination before a single magistrate is the normal procedure, yet the English precedent might well make one hesitate to exclude the possibility of a bench of magistrates." Brunyate, "The American Draft Code of Criminal Procedure, 1930" (1933) 49 L.Q.Rev. 192, 206.

[69] Wood and Waite, Crime and Its Treatment (1941) 410; Waite, Criminal Law in Action (1934) 51-53, 143-146; Puttkammer, "Criminal Law Enforcement" (1941) University of Chicago Magazine; Latimer v. State, 55 Neb. 609, 76 N.W. 207, 70 Am. St. Rep. 403 (1898).

[70] Kelly v. State, 72 Ala. 244 (1882).

evidence to indicate at least a probability that he is guilty.[71] The examining magistrate does not pass on the guilt or innocence of the defendant but only on the probabilities thereof. If he concludes that there is not enough evidence to justify further proceedings, he discharges the defendant from any custody or from any obligation under the bail bond.[72] It will not prevent a discharge that he thinks the police could eventually get enough evidence; they must already have enough at the hearing. On the other hand if he thinks that the evidence is sufficient so that a conviction could reasonably ensue, he orders the defendant held for further proceedings.[73] In the latter event the defendant is normally entitled to release on bail.

9. Interrogation of Defendant

Preliminary hearings as now conducted have occasionally been criticized on the ground that they are not utilized even slightly as a means of obtaining evidence.[74] Such criticisms, of course, concede that any compulsion of a defendant to give evidence against himself would violate the constitutional privilege against self-incrimination. Nevertheless questions might be asked at the hearing even though the defendant could not lawfully be compelled to

[71] "The object or purpose of the preliminary investigation is to prevent hasty, malicious, improvident and oppressive prosecutions, to protect the person charged from open and public accusations of crime, to avoid both for the defendant and the public the expense of a public trial, and to save the defendant from the humiliation and anxiety involved in a public prosecution, and to discover whether or not there are substantial grounds upon which a prosecution may be based." Rosenberry, J., in Thies v. State, 178 Wis. 98, 103, 189 N.W. 539, 541 (1922).

[72] A.L.I. Code of Crim. Proc. (1930) § 54.

[73] *Ibid.* § 55.

[74] Wood and Waite, Crime and Its Treatment (1941) 410; Waite, Criminal Law in Action (1934) 51-53, 143-146, 149-155; Waite, "Report on Lawlessness in Law Enforcement" (1931) 30 Mich.L.Rev. 54, 58.

answer. The questions might concern such matters as where the defendant was at the time of the crime or who was with him. His answers might bring out the truth from a defendant not prepared with a consistent story. On the other hand his failure to answer would look suspicious and when presented to the trial jury might injure him. Suppose the procedure were to tell him that he need not answer if he did not wish, but that his refusal to answer might be pointed out to the jury.[75] It seems likely that most suspects would elect to answer. In this sense a guilty person is under compulsion to incriminate himself. It is argued, however, that the constitutional provision was not intended to forbid this sort of compulsion and that the preliminary hearing could be developed into a search for truth as well as an evaluation of the evidence.[76] The solution is said to be immediate delivery by the police to a magistrate and prompt interrogation by the magistrate. This is a compromise between interrogation by the police with its danger of third-degree methods, and immediate delivery to a magistrate without any interrogation. Simeon E. Baldwin made such a suggestion sixty years ago.[77] Wigmore pro-

[75] This is advocated and its constitutionality defended in Report of the Commission on Administration of Justice in New York State (1939) 43-45, Chapter on Preliminary Examination, 15; Kauper, "Judicial Examination of the Accused—A Remedy for the Third Degree" (1932) 30 Mich. L.Rev. 1224, 1251. The English rule does not allow comment. Kenny, Outlines of Criminal Law (15th ed.1942) 533-534. The Livingston Penal Code of more than a century ago had some interesting provisions: "To avoid tricking the accused, the magistrate's examination was to be limited to specified questions; the answers were to be recorded, corrected, signed by the accused, and transmitted with the record, to the trial court. The accused, being protected from catch-questions, must have his refusal to answer militate against him." Hall, "Edward Livingston and His Code" (1936) 22 A.B.A.J. 191, 193.

[76] Waite, Criminal Law in Action (1934) 151; Waite, Cases on Criminal Law and Procedure (2d ed.1938) 629.

[77] Baldwin, "Preliminary Examinations in Criminal Procedure" (1885),

poses "to provide a means of speedy confession which shall be less susceptible to abuses, while still taking advantage of the inherent psychological situation. . . . Let every accused person be required to be taken before a magistrate, or the district attorney, promptly upon arrest, for private examination; let the magistrate warn him of his right to keep silence; and then let his statement be taken in the presence of an official stenographer, if he is willing to make one." [78] Roscoe Pound states that "there should be express provision for a legal examination of suspected or accused persons before a magistrate; that those to be examined should be allowed to have counsel present to safeguard their rights; that provision should be made for taking down the evidence so as to guarantee accuracy." [79]

Professor John B. Waite has suggested the adoption of the following language as a federal rule of court: "At the time of holding a preliminary hearing the commissioner may interrogate the accused person concerning his possible connection with the alleged crime, his whereabouts at the time, or other matters that may tend to show his guilt or innocence; provided, however, that the commissioner

---

6 A.B.A. Rev. 225, 237-238. See also Knox, J., "Self-Incrimination" (1925) 74 U. of Pa.L.Rev. 139, 153; Untermeyer, The Third Degree (1931) 133 Nation. 600; Note (1940) 49 Yale L.J. 1059, 1070.

[78] 3 Wigmore, Evidence (3d ed.1940) § 851, pp.319-320. Professor Kauper proposes "(1) that the accused be promptly presented before a magistrate for interrogation; and (2) that the interrogation be supported by the threat that refusal to answer questions of the magistrate will be used against the accused at the trial." Kauper, "Judicial Examination of the Accused—A Remedy for the Third Degree" (1932) 30 Mich.L.Rev. 1224, 1239. See also Nat. Com. on Law Obs. and Enf., Report on Lawlessness in Law Enforcement (1931), 5.

[79] Pound, "Legal Interrogation of Persons Accused or Suspected of Crime" (1934) 24 J.Crim.L. 1014, 1017. See also Glueck, Crime and Justice (1936) 237.

shall not so question an accused person until he has first informed him of the right to the advice of counsel, that he is under no obligation to answer any question, that any answer he chooses to give may possibly be used as evidence against him, and that his refusal to answer cannot be used in evidence against him." [80]

All the other members of the United States Supreme Court Advisory Committee rejected this proposal as being contrary to the basic traditions of our criminal procedure and as probably violative of the constitutional guarantee against self incrimination.[81] Such guarantee is understood as including not simply the right to refuse to answer questions, but also the right not to be questioned in a judicial proceeding and before a judicial officer unless the defendant voluntarily takes the stand.[82] From a practical standpoint moreover such examination would have little value. Most commissioners are part-time officers and many of them are not lawyers. They are not skilled in conducting interrogations that would bring out the facts. Even if they had the skill they would previously have to make a detailed study of the case, as by means of examining investigative reports and interviewing witnesses. Commission-

[80] Fed. Rules of Crim. Proc., First Preliminary Draft (1943) 249. He cites as supporting his view: Baldwin, "Preliminary Examinations in Criminal Proceedings" (1883) 6 A.B.A. Rep. 225, 238; 2 Wigmore, Evidence (2d ed.1923) 199; Irvine, "The Third Degree and the Privilege Against Self Crimination" (1928) 13 Corn.L.Q. 211, 216; Pound, Criminal Justice in America (1930) 88; Knox, J., "Self-Incrimination" (1925) 74 U. of Pa.L. Rev. 139, 153; Kauper, "Judicial Examination of the Accused—A Remedy for the Third Degree" (1932) 30 Mich.L.Rev. 1224, 1239; National Crime Commission, "Outline of Code of Criminal Procedure" (1926) 12 A.B.A.J. 690, 692; Nat. Com. on Law Obs. and Enf., Report on Lawlessness in Law Enforcement (1931) 5.

[81] Fed. Rules of Crim. Proc., First Preliminary Draft (1943) 253-254.

[82] Kelly v. State, 72 Ala. 244 (1882).

ers have neither the facility nor the time for pursuing this course.

The chief objection to a system of interrogation by the magistrate is the danger of its abuse.[83] In the words of Wigmore: "In the hands of petty bureaucrats, whether under James the First, or under Philip the Second, or in the Twentieth Century under an American Republic, such a system is always certain to be abused." [84] The magistrate is likely to proceed on the assumption that the defendant is guilty. He may become domineering and overzealous to secure incriminating evidence. He may lose his judicial disinterestedness, and resort to leading, ambiguous, and confusing questions. In cases in which little or no objective evidence has been secured, the interrogation might become a "fishing expedition." A combination of numerous groundless arrests and unscrupulous magistrates might make the system very vicious.

10. Functions of Preliminary Examination

What are the purposes of the preliminary examination from the point of view of the defendant? The nature of the accusation against the defendant is at once revealed.[85] Those who made the accusation are forced to state their case. The defendant is given an opportunity to correct any misconceptions which may have arisen with respect to his conduct.[86] He is offered prompt protection against vicious-

[83] Kauper, "Judicial Examination of the Accused—A Remedy for the Third Degree" (1932) 30 Mich.L.Rev. 1224, 1244.

[84] 8 Wigmore, Evidence (3d ed.1940) § 2251, pp.307, 308.

[85] Miller, J., "The Preliminary Hearing" (1929) 15 A.B.A.J. 414; Moley, Our Criminal Courts (1930) 21; Criminal Law, 22 C.J.S. pp.483-484; Report of the Crimes Survey Committee, Law Association of Philadelphia (1926) 175, 182; Nat. Com. on Law Obs. and Enf., Rep. on Crim. Proc. (1931) 33.

[86] "Furthermore, it provides the defense honestly unable to anticipate

ness, ignorance, or weakness on the part of the police or of the prosecution, who may have acted under the influence of persons having a selfish interest. If he is clearly innocent he may be spared the ignominy resulting from a trial. Subsidiary purposes are said to be the perpetuation of testimony, keeping witnesses within control by requiring recognizances, and the determination of the amount of bail if the defendant is bound over.[87]

Although the preliminary examination may exist primarily or solely for the benefit of the defendant, quite clearly it has some value to the prosecution.[88] It offers a method for testing the complaints of prosecuting witnesses, ascertaining their motives, and eliminating prosecutions based upon misinformation or prejudice.[89] It also affords an opportunity for compelling unwilling or unfriendly witnesses to testify, thus revealing the existence or nonexistence of criminal offenses. Testimony may be

---

the charges against it with an early occasion—perhaps too early if the State's case is not at all prepared—on which to force the prosecutor's hand." Note, "Reform in Criminal Procedure" (1940) 50 Yale L.J. 107, 111. See also 1 Stephen, A History of the Criminal Law of England (1883) 506.

[87] State v. Pigg, 80 Kan. 481, 103 Pac. 121, 18 Ann. Cas. 521 (1909); State ex rel. Germain v. Ross 39 N.D. 630, 170 N.W. 121 (1918); Kauper, "Judicial Examination of the Accused—A Remedy for the Third Degree" (1931) 30 Mich.L.Rev. 1224, 1237.

[88] Miller, J., "The Preliminary Hearing" (1929) 15 A.B.A.J. 414; Maitland, Justice and Police (1885) 132. In Missouri prosecutors who favor the preliminary examination usually assign as their reason that it enables the prosecutor to keep the docket clear of weak cases and to test the strength of the case for the prosecution. Missouri Crime Survey (1926) 130.

[89] "This brief hearing serves some useful purposes, such as providing an opportunity for getting the stories of witnesses on oath and formal record—a particular advantage where the grand jury has fallen into disuse as a regular part of the procedure." Note, "Reform in Criminal Procedure" (1940) 50 Yale L.J. 107, 111. See also Moley, Our Criminal Courts (1930) 21, 24.

perpetuated and witnesses kept within control. Benefit to both the defendant and the prosecution arises from the avoidance of the expense, delay, and consumption of time involved in the trial of the case where the determination is against the necessity for further prosecution.

Although in recent years there has been much agitation for compelling the defendant to reveal his defense before trial, such agitation has not extended to the preliminary examination. The defendant need not reveal his defense either before or at the preliminary examination.[90] As Wharton states, "It is proper, in view of the immense power a government is capable of exercising in the influencing and intimidating of witnesses, as well as of the importance on other grounds to the defendant of keeping his case in reserve until the period of its final disclosure, that he should not be compelled to exhibit it at a preliminary hearing, subject to the mercies of whatever magistrate the prosecution might select." [91] It has, however, been contended that one of the most patent inequalities between the defendant and the prosecution is the "so-called right of the accused to know the prosecution's case," including "the right (if prosecution be commenced by preliminary hearing) to have the state's case presented in prima facie form (and in some jurisdictions in full) with no counter obligation upon the accused to reveal the nature of his defense." [92] In Canada if new evidence comes

[90] He thus has a distinct advantage over a defendant in a civil action. See 1 Stephen, A History of the Criminal Law of England (1883) 507.

[91] Wharton, Criminal Pleading and Practice (9th ed.1889) § 73, p.49. See also Baty, "A Revolution in English Criminal Procedure" (1913) 47 Am.L.Rev. 648, 650-653.

[92] Dean, "Advance Specifications of Defense in Criminal Cases" (1934) 20 A.B.A.J. 435, 436. See also "Defects in Criminal Justice" (1925) 11 A.B.A.J. 297, 298. In Canada the prosecution is expected to bring forward its whole case upon the preliminary hearing. See Martin, J., "The Preliminary Hearing: Canadian Practice" (1937) 1 J.Crim.L. (Eng.) 107, 118.

to light after preliminary hearing and prior to trial, the defendant's attorney will be notified of it before witnesses are called when there was no opportunity to examine on the previous occasion; and the defendant may look upon the hearing much the same way as he would look upon the examination for discovery of the opposite party in a civil action.[93]

The abolition or non-use of the grand jury broadens the scope of the prosecutor's discretion. Many fear that such discretion will be abused. Proponents of procedure by information argue that the desired check on the prosecutor can be supplied by the preliminary hearing.[94] Such argument does not take account of the practical situation. Magistrates and justices of the peace are frequently scattered throughout the county and ignorant of the law as compared with the prosecutor. Hence they are more likely to be dominated and overridden by the prosecutor than they are to exercise an effective checking influence.[95] A better check than a weak preliminary hearing is the grand jury.

11. Complaint

A fundamental prerequisite to a valid preliminary examination is a complaint.[96] If the defendant has been ar-

This is not the American practice. Miller, J., "Informations on Indictments in Felony Cases" (1924) 8 Minn.L.Rev. 379, 394.

[93] Martin, J., "The Preliminary Hearing: Canadian Practice" (1937) 1 J.Crim.L. (Eng.) 107, 118.

[94] "In Missouri the preliminary hearing was provided for by the statute to guard against the abuse of the information." Report of the Minnesota Crime Commission (1934) 139.

[95] Dession, "From Indictment to Information—Implications of the Shift" (1932) 42 Yale L.J. 163, 172; Moley, Our Criminal Courts (1930) 34-36; cf. Seabury, Investigation of New York City Magistrate's Courts (1932); Note, "Reform in Criminal Procedure" (1940) 50 Yale L.J. 107, 109.

[96] Likewise a complaint precedes an arrest unless the arrest is without

rested upon a warrant, the hearing may proceed upon the charge or complaint made in the complaint filed to obtain a warrant.[97] If arrest is without a warrant, a complaint should be subsequently drawn for the examination.[98] It must usually be in writing,[99] and must substantially set out an offense. Although it is commonly stated that it need not be as complete or as technically correct as an indictment, a number of cases hold that it must be as full and precise as an indictment. It is the better practice to draw the complaint precisely like an indictment or information. The magistrate may not conduct a "fishing expedition." [100] The complaint must specify a particular offender.[101]

In some states the complaint is required to be based upon personal knowledge and belief. In most states, however, it is sufficient that it is based on information and belief.[102] The Federal Rules of Criminal Procedure are silent on the matter, thus leaving it to local rules.

It has been said that "the fundamental and outstanding procedural difference between the administration of criminal justice in England and the United States lies in the management of prosecutions." [103] In the United States,

---

a warrant. Baker and De Long, "The Prosecuting Attorney: The Process of Prosecution" (1935) 26 J.Crim.L. 3.

[97] Keigwin, Cases in Criminal Procedure (1939) 2-5, 168-169; A.L.I. Code of Crim. Proc. (1931) § 1. In Canada it is the practice for the same magistrate who passes on the complaint to conduct the preliminary examination; in England it is not. Martin, J., "The Preliminary Hearing: Canadian Practice" (1937) 1 J.Crim.L. (Eng.) 107, 108, 112.

[98] A.L.I. Code of Crim. Proc. (1931) §§ 35 and 36.

[99] At common law it need not be in writing. Robinson, Cases on Criminal Law and Procedure (1941) 309-310.

[100] Dession and Cohen, "The Inquisitorial Functions of Grand Juries" (1932) 41 Yale L.J. 687, 690.

[101] People ex rel. Livingston v. Wyatt, 186 N.Y. 383, 79 N.E. 330 (1906).

[102] Robinson, Cases on Criminal Law and Procedure (1941) 310.

[103] Howard, Criminal Justice in England (1931). On the Continent the

though the original complaint is commonly made by a private person,[104] the prosecuting attorney supersedes the private complainant immediately after a formal complaint has been drawn. In England the theory is that the bulk of criminal proceedings is left to private persons, who are not legally bound to prosecute and who are repaid their costs only on a very inadequate scale. But in actual practice the great majority of English prosecutions are instituted and carried on by the police.[105] Cases of exceptional gravity and importance are conducted by the Director of Public Prosecutions, whose office was created in 1879. The Director may take charge of any prosecution at any stage of the criminal proceedings, and thus prevent the improper abandonment of a prosecution by a private person.

12. Time Interval from Arrest to Preliminary Hearing

Unfortunate delay may be caused by a postponement of the examination. Section 43 of the American Law Institute Code of Criminal Procedure limits the time for which postponements of the examination may be had to six days except for good cause shown.[106] Rule 5 (c) of the Federal

principle of official prosecution prevails. Auld, "The Comparative Jurisprudence of Criminal Process" (1937) 1 U. of Toronto L.J. 82, 92-93.

[104] In Iowa, Michigan, Minnesota, North Dakota, and Oregon, no prosecutions for adultery can be commenced except on the complaint of the husband or wife. See Comment (1921) 5 Minn.L.Rev. 389.

[105] Kenny, Outlines of Criminal Law (15th ed.1942) 555.

[106] Some states already so provide. A.L.I. Code of Crim. Proc. (1930) commentaries 282-283. In England the defendant may be remanded to jail up to eight days, unless a longer term is agreed on, or may be released on his recognizance. Harris and Wilshere, Principles and Practice of the Criminal Law (17th ed.1943) 410. In Russia the case must be either sent to the trial court or dropped within two months. Hazard, "Soviet Criminal Procedure" (1941) 15 Tulane L.Rev. 220, 227.

Rules of Criminal Procedure provides that if the defendant does not waive examination the commissioner shall hear the evidence within a reasonable time. Such rules are designed to prevent arbitrary or oppressive action by the prosecution and also delays by defendants to spirit away witnesses or otherwise interfere with the proper prosecution of the case.[107]

The statistics gathered by the Illinois Crime Survey with respect to the period from the complaint to the disposition at preliminary hearing show little delay at this stage.[108] Oregon statistics show similar results, the intervals ranging from no days to 200 days, with a median interval of three days.[109] In Boston, Massachusetts, in 1933, in 29 per cent of the larceny cases, 95 per cent of the robbery cases, and 98 per cent of the prosecutions for breaking and entering, the preliminary examination occurs on the day the complaint is dated.[110] The time interval between arrest and preliminary examination seldom exceeds twenty-four hours unless a Sunday or a holiday intervenes. This should hold true in all jurisdictions enforcing the common-law rule of a prompt preliminary examination.

[107] A frequent cause of a continuance is the desire of the defendant and the private prosecutor to effect a settlement. Report of the Crimes Survey Committee, Law Association of Philadelphia (1926) 170.

[108] Illinois Crime Survey (1929) 92-100. Cases eliminated in the preliminary hearing for the state of Illinois take about ten and a half days from the date of the complaint. *Ibid.* 93-94.

[109] Survey of the Administration of Criminal Justice in Oregon (1932) 11 Ore. L.Rev. 170-177, 186. For the statistics as to cities in a number of states, see Nat. Com. on Law Obs. and Enf., Report on Prosecution (1931) Table XXIV, p.215.

[110] Warner and Cabot, Judges and Law Reform (1936) 96. In many of the cases, the arrest occurred before the complaint, since the period between arrest and preliminary examination is somewhat longer.

13. Right to Counsel

Before the Act of 1848, the defendant in England was not entitled to counsel at the preliminary examination.[111] There is some doubt whether this statute confers such a right, but in practice the defendant is always permitted counsel.[112] The state and federal constitutions do not expressly provide for counsel at this stage, though some state statutes do. The state decisions are divided as to whether the constitutional guarantee concerning counsel applies.[113] Rule 39 of the American Law Institute Code provides that the magistrate shall inform the defendant of his right to the aid of counsel during the preliminary examination.[114] Rule 5 (b) of the Federal Rules of Criminal Procedure provides that the commissioner shall inform the defendant of his right to counsel and shall allow him reasonable time and opportunity to consult counsel.[115] If the preliminary examination is to serve all its purposes in full, it would seem that the defendant should have the right to procure counsel and to be advised of such right, even though there is no provision for the assignment of counsel as is the usual practice in the trial court. The arguments against the right to counsel have been as follows: The additional time required to procure counsel will de-

111 Cox v. Coleridge (1822) 1 B.&C. 37.

112 A.L.I. Code of Crim. Proc. (1930) commentaries, 268.

113 A.L.I. Code of Crim. Proc. (1930) commentaries, 276. The federal rule is against the right. Ex parte Bollman, 4 Cranch 75 (1807); Goldsby v. United States, 160 U.S. 70 (1895). There has been such a right in France since 1897. Garner, Criminal Procedure in France (1916) 255, 258.

114 Rule 41 provides that the magistrate shall allow the defendant a reasonable time to send for counsel and shall, if necessary, postpone the examination for that purpose. For a proposal to extend this right to non-indictable offenses summarily triable, see Report of New York Law Revision Commission for 1940 (1940) 91-104.

115 See Schwellenbach, J., "Information vs. Intuition in the Imposition of Sentence" (1943) 27 J. Am. Jud. Soc. 52, 54.

prive the examination of its effectiveness since psychologically interrogation is most effective immediately after arrest; and the presence of counsel will discourage spontaneity of responses by the defendant and make him more guarded and evasive.[116] On the other hand as an English writer has said: "It is also a matter of expert advice as to whether the defence should be disclosed at that stage: disclosure may induce the magistrates to refuse to commit for trial, or may strengthen the prosecution's case by warning them of the weak points in their case." [117]

14. Right to Copy of Complaint

On demand counsel for the defendant has a right to examine the complaint.[118] Under some statutes the defendant has a right to have the complaint read and to have a copy thereof.[119] He may waive such right by failing to object and to make a demand for a copy.[120] As will be later seen the right to a copy of the indictment or information is somewhat more extensive. It has been recommended that if the defendant is held to answer, the magistrate or

[116] Kauper, "Judicial Examination of the Accused—A Remedy for the Third Degree" (1932) 30 Mich.L.Rev. 1224, 1247; Baldwin, "Preliminary Examinations in Criminal Proceedings" (1883) 6 A.B.A. Rep. 225, 238; A Statement by the Committee on the Bill of Rights of the American Bar Association (1944) 47-48.

[117] Jackson, The Machinery of Justice in England (1940) 121. The constitutional right to counsel in federal criminal cases "becomes meaningless when the prisoner cannot afford to hire a lawyer to give him the help which he needs before appearing in the commissioner's office." A Statement by the Committee on the Bill of Rights of the American Bar Association (1944) 48.

[118] People ex rel. Steinhardt v. Fuller, 68 N.Y.S. 742, 15 N.Y.Cr.R. 344 (1901).

[119] Haggard v. State, 51 Okla. Cr. 233, 1 P. (2d) 180 (1931); Ex parte Schaeffer, 54 Okla. Cr. 292, 19 P. (2d) 619 (1933).

[120] Ex parte Schaeffer, 54 Okla. Cr. 292, 19 P. (2d) 619 (1933).

his clerk having the custody of the depositions made on the taking of the complaint and the testimony taken on the examination, shall, within two days after demand, furnish to the defendant, or his counsel, a copy of the depositions and testimony or permit either of them to take a copy.[121]

15. Pleas at Preliminary Examination

Under Rule 5 (c) of the Federal Rules of Criminal Procedure, the defendant is not to be called upon to plead in commitment proceedings before the commissioner.[122] The rule is based upon fairness to the defendant who is usually not represented by counsel before the commissioner and also upon the fact that the commitment proceeding, even if a preliminary examination is demanded, is not a trial of an issue of guilt or innocence and is not a court proceeding.[123]

[121] Report of the Commission on Administration of Justice in New York State (1939) 54. Under existing law there is no such right, 23 C.J.S., Criminal Law, § 957, p.268.

[122] Such a rule was laid down in Wood et al v. United States, 128 F. (2d) 265 (App. D.C. 1942), discussed by Morgan, "The Law of Evidence, 1941-1945" (1946) 59 Harv.L.Rev. 481, 523-526. In the absence of any statute or rule, it is not necessary to ask the defendant to plead, or to enter a plea of guilty or not guilty to the complaint. Latimer v. State, 55 Neb. 609, 76 N.W. 207 (1898). Under the Canadian practice, while the complaint is read, the defendant is not asked to plead. Martin, J., "The Preliminary Hearing: Canadian Practice" (1937) 1 J.Crim.L. (Eng.) 107, 117. On the other hand in 1922 the Section of Criminal Law of the American Bar Association recommended that it be possible to dispose of a case finally on a plea of guilty at the preliminary hearing. Note (1922) 8 A.B.A.J. 643.

[123] Moreover it is the general rule that a plea of guilty before a committing magistrate is admissible in subsequent criminal proceedings, even though the defendant pleads not guilty in court when arraigned. Note (1940) 40 Col.L.Rev. 915. A 1934 California constitutional amendment allows a defendant to plead guilty before a committing magistrate, if the

16. Presence of Defendant

At common law there were no requirements that witnesses must be examined in the presence of the defendant and that he might cross-examine them. Section 46 of the American Law Institute Code of Criminal Procedure now lays down such a requirement.[124] Rule 5(c) of the Federal Rules of Criminal Procedure provides that the defendant may cross-examine the witnesses against him. If a secret inquiry were desired it could be obtained by grand jury proceedings. If the preliminary examination is to be a genuine and judicial investigation calling for participation by the defendant, it is to the interest of both parties that there be the fullest revelation of the facts of the case. This is not possible without both confrontation and cross-examination. It is not enough that the defendant has such rights at the trial since one of the objects of the preliminary examination is to determine whether there is a case against the defendant which will stand up at the trial. If the evidence for the prosecution cannot survive the processes of confrontation and cross-examination, the prosecution as well as the defendant is better served by early

---

magistrate and prosecuting attorney assent and counsel for defendant is present. See Note (1935) 25 J.Crim.L. 797. No real good is attained by such speed as to the plea, since the prosecuting attorney must obtain information about prior convictions, charge them in the indictment, and prove them at the trial. Beecher, "The 1934 California Constitutional Amendments in the Field of Criminal Law" (1939) 29 J.Crim.L. 668.

[124] As to present English procedure, see Kenny, Outlines of Criminal Law (15th ed.1942) 533-534; as to Canadian procedure, see Martin, J., "The Preliminary Hearing: Canadian Practice" (1937) 1 J.Crim.L. (Eng.) 107, 117-121. At common law it was in the discretion of the magistrate whether witnesses for the defendant should be heard. Sections 45 and 49 of the American Law Institute Code of Criminal Procedure grant him an absolute right. Opponents contend that this results in actual trial of the case before the inferior court.

determination at the preliminary examination. As to the danger of intimidation of the witnesses for the prosecution, it should be remembered that the names and the testimony of the witnesses are available in the record and that such cases ought to be presented to a grand jury rather than to a magistrate.[125]

As has been seen the defendant today has a right to be present at the preliminary examination. His presence is not, however, jurisdictional and the right may be waived.[126]

17. Unsworn Statement

In England since 1848, the defendant has been given an opportunity publicly to make any statement and may answer any question regarding the charge. Several purposes may be served by the making of such a statement. In the first place, by making such a statement the defendant may be able to convince the magistrate of his innocence and should at least be entitled to such an opportunity. In the second place the defendant is very likely to tell a direct, truthful story at this early stage which will prevent his concocting a perjured defense prior to the trial. The prosecution is given a better opportunity to prepare for trial. Some believe that the police will then have no excuse for conducting secret, unregulated, and oppressive examinations.[127] This third aim is not always attainable, however, since the police are often more interested in finding out from the defendant who were the other per-

[125] Miller, J., "The Preliminary Hearing" (1927) 15 A.B.A.J. 414, 415.

[126] State v. McLain, 13 N.D. 368, 102 N.W. 407 (1905); A.L.I. Code of Crim. Proc. (1930) §§ 287-291.

[127] See statement of the Committee on Criminal Procedure and Judicial Administration of the National Crime Commission, 12 A.B.A.J. 692 (1926); Missouri Crime Survey (1926) 358-359.

sons involved in the crime, or where stolen property has been hidden, or in persuading the defendant to plead guilty.[128] It is a noteworthy fact that from 70 to 90 per cent of all persons against whom judgments are entered plead guilty without trial.[129]

In every state but Georgia provision is made by constitutional or statutory provision that the defendant may testify as a witness in criminal cases. In several states, however, this privilege does not extend to the preliminary examination.[130] The latter states seem to regard the preliminary examination as serving the same purpose as the grand jury hearing at which the defendant is not usually required or permitted to appear. The states of Delaware, Louisiana, New Hampshire, New Jersey, and North Carolina provide that the magistrate may or shall examine the accused. But in practice the defendant is not in fact examined by the magistrate except in North Carolina, in which state, however, he is entitled to counsel, must not be examined in the presence of the other witnesses, the examination shall not be on oath, the defendant before he is examined must be informed of the charge against him, and he is to be informed by the magistrate that he need not answer and that his refusal shall not later be used against him.[131]

Section 47 of the American Law Institute Code provides for the taking of an unsworn statement from the defendant if he wishes to make such a statement.[132] The

[128] Miller, J., "The Preliminary Hearing" (1929) 15 A.B.A.J. 414, 416.

[129] Moley, "The Vanishing Jury" (1928) 2 So.Calif.L.Rev. 97.

[130] A.L.I. Code of Crim. Proc. (1930) commentaries 294-297.

[131] A.L.I. Code of Crim. Proc. (1930) commentaries 291-293. See also Baldwin, "Preliminary Examinations in Criminal Proceedings" (1883) 6 A.B.A. Rep. 225, 230; State v. Parker 132 N.C. 1014, 43 S.E. 830 (1903).

[132] This is to follow the examination of witnesses for the prosecution. Under Section 49 the examination of witnesses for the defendant follows

magistrate is to inform the defendant that he may make such a statement. Section 48 provides for the reduction of such a statement to writing by the magistrate or by a reporter. Section 49 provides that the defendant may, if he desires, be sworn and testify in his own behalf. Sections 47, 48, and 53 make such statements or testimony admissible in evidence against the defendant at the trial. It is, however, provided in Section 47 that his refusal to make any statement may not be used against him. He is also to be warned that he may refuse to make any statement, and that such refusal may not be used against him at the trial.

18. Record of Testimony

Only about eight states provide in all cases for the reduction to writing, or the taking in shorthand and transcribing by a reporter, of the testimony of the witnesses and of the defendant.[133] Section 51 of the American Law Institute Code of Criminal Procedure makes such provision. This seems wise whether or not the defendant is held to answer. If he be held to answer and goes to trial the evidence should be available either for purposes of impeachment or in case the witnesses cannot be found. On

---

the defendant's statement. Much the same order of procedure is followed in England. Kenny, Outlines of Criminal Law (15th ed.1942) 533-534; Howard, Criminal Justice in England (1931) 330-336. As to Scottish procedure, see Mill, "Criminal Law and Procedure in England and Scotland Compared" (1939) 3 J.Crim.L. (Eng.) 605, 616-617.

[133] The Missouri Crime Survey (1926) 381 suggests that in the case of every discharge the magistrate state his reasons therefor in writing and that a transcript of the evidence be made in every preliminary examination. Favoring stenographic reports in felony and certain misdemeanor cases, see Criminal Justice in Cleveland (1922) 203-204, 650. See also Baker and DeLong, "The Prosecuting Attorney: The Process of Prosecution" (1935) 26 J.Crim.L. 185, 187; Moley, Our Criminal Courts (1930) 29; Report of the Crimes Survey Committee, Law Association of Philadelphia (1926) 169-170, 469; Glueck, Crime and Justice (1936) 82.

the other hand if he be not held to answer for his own protection and that of the prosecution a record of the examination should be available. It may be objected that it is too expensive and troublesome to transcribe the reporter's notes in all cases especially if the defendant is discharged. The answer seems to be to eliminate the fee system of paying reporters and to require such transcribing as a part of the regular work of such officers; and to require transcribing only where the defendant is held to answer, but require the filing of the reporter's notes in other cases.[134]

19. Use of Testimony at Trial

Under certain circumstances the testimony of witnesses taken at the preliminary hearing may be admitted in evidence at the trial of the defendant. In seventeen states it may be received if the witness is dead; in three states, when the witness is absent from the trial by the procurement of the defendant; in seven states, when the witness is absent from the state at the time of the trial; and in four states, when the witness is insane or too ill to attend.[135] Section 53 of the American Law Institute Code of Criminal Procedure admits such testimony "if, for any reason the testimony of the witness cannot be obtained at the trial and the court is satisfied that the inability to pro-

[134] On Jan. 12, 1944, Congress passed a bill authorizing the appointment of salaried reporters in the federal district courts. The reporter will be required to record all official proceedings had in open court. "Federal Court Reporter Bill Passed" (Feb. 1944) 30 A.B.A.J. 59. Presumably, however, the reporter will serve only in the district court and not with the commissioners.

[135] In England they may be received if the witness is dead or too ill to travel or to give evidence at the time of the trial. Kenny, Outlines of Criminal Law (15th ed.1942), 538; Roscoe, Law of Evidence (15th ed. 1928) 59.

cure such testimony is not due to the fault of the party offering it." Such a discretionary rule avoids arbitrary results.

20. Public Hearing

The trial in a criminal proceeding is public in this country. It does not necessarily follow that a preliminary examination is. With respect to the practice in Canada, a writer has stated: "A preliminary inquiry is not a 'trial', but is subject to a wider power of exclusion contained in section 679, viz., the justice may order that no person other than the prosecutor and accused, their counsel and solicitors, shall have access to or from any room or building in which the inquiry is held, if it appears to him that the ends of justice will be best answered by so doing." [136] In practice the preliminary examination is open to the public in England and America.[137] The following provision has been recommended: "The magistrate may also exclude from the examination every person except the complainant and his counsel, the prosecuting attorney of the county, the defendant and his counsel and the officer

[136] Auld, "The Comparative Jurisprudence of Criminal Process" (1935) 1 U. of Toronto L.J. 82, 99-100; Martin, "The Preliminary Hearing: Canadian Practice" (1937) 1 J.Crim.L. (Eng.) 107, 108. In England the public cannot insist on admission. Kenny, Outlines of Criminal Law (15th ed.1942), 532; Harris and Wilshere, Principles and Practice of the Criminal Law (17th ed.1943) 405. But use of the power to exclude is infrequent. Maitland, Justice and Police (1885) 129.

[137] Kauper, "Judicial Examination of the Accused—A Remedy for the Third Degree" (1931) 30 Mich.L.Rev. 1224, 1234; 22 C.J.S., Criminal Law, § 338, p.498. "It is public; but it provides none of the conditions which a public hearing is supposed to guarantee. The proceedings take place in a courtroom usually crowded with all sorts and conditions of people. Noise and disorder prevail. Cases are heard with such great speed that no opportunity is permitted for an orderly presentation of evidence." Moley, Our Criminal Courts (1930) 29. See also Glueck, Crime and Justice (1936) 43-46.

having the defendant in custody." [138] In Europe, publicity of proceedings is generally confined to the trial stage.[139] It has been pointed out by an English lawyer that grave prejudice may sometimes be caused by the publicity given in the press to the evidence at a preliminary hearing; possibly reports of such evidence should be completely forbidden.[140]

21. Evidence

The same strict rules of evidence applied in the trial of a criminal case are not applied to the preliminary hearing.[141] The finding of the Illinois Crime Survey is that the "rules of evidence are dispensed with to such an extent that proceedings are marked by hearsay and other incompetent forms of testimony." [142] In practice hearsay evidence is considered, leading questions are permitted, and insufficient opportunity is given for cross-examination.[143]

[138] Report of the Commission on Administration of Justice in New York State (1939) 54.

[139] Ploscowe, "The Development of Present-Day Criminal Procedures in Europe and America" (1935) 48 Harv.L.Rev. 433, 435. The procedure in Scotland is private. Keedy, "Criminal Procedure in Scotland" (1913) 3 J.Crim.L. 728, 744, 747.

[140] Butler, "Developments in Criminal Law—1910-1935" (1935) 179, The Law Times 325, 326-327. See also Jackson, The Machinery of Justice in England (1940) 126-128.

[141] 22 C.J.S., Criminal Law, § 340, p.499; Harmer v. State, 121 Md. 731, 238 N.W. 356 (1931); Ex parte Hollingsworth, 49 Idaho 455, 289 Pac. 607 (1930). See, however, Ex parte Bollman, 4 Cranch (U.S. 1807) 75.

[142] Illinois Crime Survey (1929) 308.

[143] Moley, Our Criminal Courts (1530) 32; Baker and DeLong, "The Prosecuting Attorney: The Process of Prosecution" (1935) 26 J.Crim.L. 185, 186.

22. Committing for Different Offense

In some states defendants can be held to answer only for the crime charged in the original complaint.[144] There seems no good reason why the magistrate, having before him evidence that a crime has been committed and that the defendant has committed it, should not hold him to answer.[145] He should not be bound by a complaint often filed in haste by a person frequently not fully informed as to the laws defining criminal offenses. It is not a satisfactory answer that the defendant may be proceeded against upon a new complaint because that involves the expense and delay of holding another preliminary examination. Nor may it properly be argued that the defendant has not had an opportunity to defend himself upon the new charge, since the proceeding is not a trial on the merits but simply a determination whether or not an offense has been committed and whether there is evidence to indicate the probable guilt of the defendant sufficient to warrant holding him to answer before a jury in the trial court. A bill of particulars may be supplied. Moreover, grand juries may find indictments without even a complaint or an opportunity for the defendant to be heard. It may be that a grand jury hearing will follow the preliminary examination. Section 55 of the American Law Institute Code of Criminal Procedure provides that the magistrate shall

[144] State v. Pay, 45 Utah, 146 Pac. 300 (1915); State v. Anderson, 60 S.D. 187, 244 N.W. 119 (1932), (1933) 31 Mich.L.Rev. 281. See 22 C.J.S., Criminal Law, § 348, pp.509-510.

[145] Miller, J., "The Preliminary Hearing" (1929) 15 A.B.A.J. 414, 416-417. Under a proposed Illinois Code of Criminal Law and Procedure, complaints might be amended or substituted if the magistrate conducting the examination believes that the complaint is insufficient or does not name that offense of which the offender may probably be guilty. Note, "The Draft Code of Criminal Law and Procedure" (1935) 30 Ill.L.Rev. 226, 231-232.

order the defendant to be held to answer for "any public offense" which appears to have been committed by the defendant.[146] Rule 5(c) of the Federal Rules of Criminal Procedure is to the same effect.

23. Test for Committing

One of the most important rules concerning the preliminary examination is that providing for the determination by the magistrate whether or not the defendant should be held to answer and the tests therefor. If it appears that an offense has been committed and that there is probable cause to believe the defendant has committed it, the magistrate is to order him to be held to answer.[147] The Missouri Crime Survey suggests that, in the case of all discharges, the magistrate state his reasons therefor in writing.[148]

146 Under Section 60(2): "The defendant shall not be discharged on a writ of habeas corpus or otherwise nor shall the preliminary examination be held invalid because the offense for which the defendant is held to answer is other than that stated in the complaint or warrant of arrest." The Canadian practice is in accord. Martin, J., "The Preliminary Hearing: Canadian Practice" (1937) 1 J.Crim.L. (Eng.) 107, 115.

147 A.L.I. Code of Crim. Proc. (1930) § 55. See also Rule 5(c) of the Federal Rules of Criminal Procedure, which, however, applies the element of probable cause to both the offense and the defendant's guilt. In the absence of some evidence that an order of commitment is justified habeas corpus will lie. Ex parte Samuel and Slivoo, 82 W.Va. 486, 96 S.E. 95 (1918); State ex rel. Germain v. Ross, 39 N.D. 630, 170 N.W. 121 (1918); Housel and Walser, Defending and Prosecuting Federal Criminal Cases (1938) § 214, p.249.

148 Missouri Crime Survey (1926) 381. The Survey further states: "As an inducement to the magistrate to keep a complete record of each case he should not be deprived of his fee in case a prisoner is discharged." See also Report of the Commission on the Administration of Justice in New York State (1939) 55.

24. Commitment

The term "commitment" is used with respect to the latter part of the proceedings before the magistrate.[149] Where it appears that an offense has been committed and that there is probable cause to believe the defendant guilty thereof, the magistrate is to hold him to answer. If the defendant is not admitted to bail, the magistrate then commits him to custody. The commitment is a formal action of the magistrate and must be regularly ordered and entered upon the record. The defendant is committed to jail to be held there for the higher court. To authorize the detention of the defendant after he is committed, a mittimus or warrant to the jailer is necessary. Errors in the commitment do not generally affect the validity of the examination and subsequent proceedings.[150]

The writ of habeas corpus is available to secure the release of a person improperly held by a committing magistrate. The writ may be used to test the sufficiency of the evidence to warrant his detention.[151]

[149] "The next step to the preliminary inquiry held by the magistrates is the discharge, bail, or committal of the suspected person. Little need be said as to the discharge or committal of the suspected person. It is obvious that, as soon as justices of the peace were erected into intermediate judges, charged to decide the question whether there was or was not ground fcr the detention of a suspected person, they must have acquired, on the one hand, the power of discharge, and, on the other, the power of committal." 1 Stephen, A History of the Criminal Law of England (1883) 233. See also Beale, Criminal Pleading and Practice (1899) § 38, p.33; Clark, Handbook of Criminal Procedure (2d ed. by Mikell, 1918) § 44, pp.118-121; 22 C.J.S., Criminal Law, § 349, pp.510-511; A.L.I. Code of Crim. Proc. (1930) § 55; Rule 5(c), Fed. Rules of Crim. Proc. Kenny labels the stage of a criminal proceeding following arrest "commitment for trial." Outlines of Criminal Law (13th ed.1929) 445, 452-459.

[150] A.L.I. Code of Crim. Proc. (1930) § 60(1) and commentaries, pp.333-334.

[151] People v. Wells, 57 App. Div. 140, 151 (1901); People v. Warden,

A significant question is that concerning the effect of a binding over on subsequent procedure, particularly on procedure by information. Section 117 of the American Law Institute Code of Criminal Procedure provides that it is the duty of the prosecuting attorney to file an information,[152] in the case of every defendant held to answer at a preliminary examination "unless after full consideration of the preliminary examination he shall determine that an information ought not to be filed." In the latter event, the matter is referred to the trial court, which, if it is of the opinion that the case should proceed, directs the prosecuting attorney either to file the proper information or to present the case to the grand jury, as the prosecuting attorney may determine.[153] Though they did not do so in clear language, the drafters also intended to extend the duty to file an information to cases where the defendant had waived preliminary examination. It seems doubtful that the intervention of the grand jury for this particular occasion serves any useful purpose. The case has already been examined by the magistrate, and has then been carefully re-examined in turn by the prosecuting attorney and

---

180 App. Div. 336 (1917); Report of the Special Committee on the Revision of the Code of Criminal Procedure to the Commission on the Administration of Justice, (1935) Chapter on Grand Jury, p.8.

[152] Such information shall charge the commission of an offense according to the evidence presented at the preliminary examination. Thus the information need not be based on the complaint or on the complaint and warrant. As has been seen, a defendant may also be committed for an offense other than that charged in the complaint. For a suggestion that the prosecuting attorney must file within ten days after preliminary examination, see Note (1934) 24 J.Crim.L. 1113. In 1927, California shortened the time from 30 to 15 days. Note (1927) 13 A.B.A.J. 703.

[153] For a discussion of legislative attempts to limit the discretion of the prosecuting attorney, see Baker and DeLong, "The Prosecuting Attorney, Powers and Duties in Criminal Prosecution" (1934) 24 J.Crim.L., 1025, 1060.

by the trial court, and the magistrate and the trial court agree that further proceedings should be taken against the defendant.[154]

25. Rehearing

In general the jurisdiction of the magistrate terminates when he remands the defendant, or when he takes his recognizance or admits him to bail, and he has no authority to grant a rehearing or new examination.[155] An order of committal for trial at once confers jurisdiction on the trial court.[156] If injustice has been done, relief is by way of a writ of habeas corpus.[157]

26. Jeopardy

The pendency or failure of preliminary proceedings on one complaint is not as a matter of double jeopardy a bar to a second complaint for the same offense.[158] Under some statutes there may be a second examination on the same charge before another officer or tribunal.[159] On the other hand, statutes sometimes provide that after discharge on preliminary examination, no further prosecution of the of-

[154] Brunyate, "The American Draft Code of Criminal Procedure (1930)" (1933) 49 L.Q.Rev. 192, 197.

[155] Com. v. Harbeson, 25 Dist. 109 (Pa. 1915); Butler v. State, 36 Tex. Cr. 483, 38 S.W. 46 (1896); 22 C.J.S., Criminal Law, § 346, p.507; Report of the Crimes Survey Committee, Law Association of Philadelphia (1926), 174.

[156] Nelson v. People, 38 Mich. 618 (1878).

[157] Butler v. State, 36 Tex. Cr. 483, 38 S.W. (1896); State v. Randolph, 26 Mo. 213 (1858).

[158] Van Buren v. State, 65 Neb. 223, 91 N.W. 201 (1902); Dreps v. State, 219 Wis. 279, 262 N.W. 700 (1935); Collins v. Loisel, 262 U.S. 426 (1923); Martin, J., "The Preliminary Hearing: Canadian Practice" (1937) 1 J.Crim. L. (Eng.) 107, 119.

[159] Petition of McNair, 324 Pa. 48, 187 Atl. 498, 106 A.L.R. 1373 (1936).

fense shall be had.[160] The American Law Institute Code of Criminal Procedure provides in Section 116 that, if upon the preliminary examination the defendant is discharged, an information may be filed against him only by leave of the court.

27. Bail for Witness

When the defendant is held to answer, it is often the practice to require each material witness to enter into a written undertaking to secure his presence at the trial.[161] Any witness who refuses to enter into such an undertaking or to provide sureties as required may then be committed to jail.[162] Section 58 of the American Law Institute Code of Criminal Procedure, however, provides for a conditional examination and the taking of the deposition of witnesses so held, on application made by either party, after notice to the other. Such deposition may be admitted in evidence. Only seven states have provided for such a conditional examination. It seems inexcusable to hold innocent persons merely because they are material witnesses and unable to provide undertakings or sureties for this release.[163] Rules 15(a) and 46(b) of the Federal

160 Morrissey v. People, 11 Mich. 327, 341, 343 (1863); McCann v. Commonwealth, 14 Gratt. (Va.) 570 (1857).

161 A.L.I. Code of Crim. Proc. (1930) § 56 and commentaries 316-320; Note (1931) 41 Yale L.J. 293, 298. In England, witnesses need only give their own recognizances. Kenny, Outlines of Criminal Law (13th ed.1929) 458.

162 A.L.I. Code of Crim. Proc. (1930) § 58(1) and commentaries 322-327. See Brown, "The Crime of Being a Witness" (Nov. 1937) American Mercury 284-288. In Canada a person may not be arrested and held as a witness while the accused is being sought. Martin, J., "The Preliminary Hearing: Canadian Practice" (1937) 1 J.Crim.L. (Eng.) 107, 113. The history of binding over material witnesses in England goes back to 1554. See 1 & 2 Ph. & Mary, c.13; 1 Stephen, A History of the Criminal Law of England (1883) 219.

163 Warner refers to the "American practices of setting high bail for

Rules of Criminal Procedure contain somewhat similar provisions.[164]

28. Transmission of Papers

About forty states provide that all papers and any bail taken shall be transmitted to the clerk of the court having jurisdiction of the offense.[165] Section 59 of the American Law Institute Code of Criminal Procedure and Rule 5(c) of the Federal Rules of Criminal Procedure so provide.

29. Reform of Procedure

In the view of the Wickersham Crime Commission with respect to the improvement of preliminary examinations "the chief need is competent magistrates, properly organized, and a proper organization of the prosecutor's office. So far as procedural improvements are called for, reference may be made to the model Code of Criminal Procedure of the American Law Institute." [166]

The best possible rules for the conduct of the preliminary examination will not necessarily mean that the administration will be in the public interest. Crime commission reports and surveys have revealed much casualness,

---

witnesses so that they will not skip across a state line and of keeping them in confinement for long periods pending trial." Warner, "Modern Trends in the American Law of Arrest" (1943) 21 Can.B.Rev. 192, 195.

[164] Under the Institute rule, however, the magistrate must release the witness, whereas under the proposed federal rule he may do so. See Waite, "The Proposed Federal Rules of Criminal Procedure" (1943) 27 J.Am.Jud. Soc. 101, 102.

[165] See Report of the Crimes Survey Committee, Law Association of Philadelphia (1926) 176-179.

[166] Nat. Com. on Law Obs. and Enf., Rep. on Crim. Proc. (1931) 21. On p.13 it is stated: "As to procedure in the inferior criminal courts of the states, there is relatively little to be done." See also Glueck, Crime and Justice (1936) 238.

carelessness, and unpreparedness in the conduct of the case for the prosecution by the prosecuting attorney in the municipal or police courts.[167] Witnesses are almost never interviewed before their appearance, and the prosecuting attorney or his assistant regards the preliminary examination as of slight importance. The responsibility for the bringing out of evidence should not be placed upon the sheriff nor upon the magistrate but upon the prosecuting attorney.[168]

30. Importance of Preliminary Examination

The Report on Prosecution of the Wickersham Crime Commission urged the desirability of "an intensive study of the need of and the appropriate function to be performed by the preliminary hearing under contemporary American urban conditions." [169] The Missouri Crime Survey stated: "The courts of preliminary hearing play an unimportant role in the administration of justice." [170] This may be a statement of the present situation. The writer does not concede that it is a correct statement of principle. It is certainly important that there be a thorough sifting of cases at the beginning of prosecution.[171] Innocent per-

[167] Nat. Com. on Law Obs. and Enf., Report on Prosecution (1931) 92-95; Cleveland Crime Survey (1922) 94, 104, 114; Illinois Crime Survey (1929) 305-307 and 406.

[168] Illinois Crime Survey (1929) 258.

[169] Nat. Com. on Law Obs. and Enf., Report on Prosecution (1931) 182. On pp.122-123, it is stated that "the surveys to date do not contain anything like a thorough facing or discussion of the problem of the need for a preliminary examination, what shall be the nature of the tribunal holding same, what shall be the scope of its function, and what shall be the procedure."

[170] Missouri Crime Survey (1926) 164.

[171] "Manifestly the burden of the prosecutor is greatly increased if the examining magistrate commits indiscriminately, while enforcement of the

sons may be saved from humiliation, expense, delay, and inconvenience. From the point of view of the prosecution, dangerous criminals should not escape at this stage and at the same time the state should not be put to the expense and trouble of further prosecution as to certain other defendants.

As the Wickersham Report on Criminal Procedure pointed out: "Moreover, citizens came before these tribunals as complainants and witnesses at preliminary hearings much more frequently than before the superior courts." [172]

The Illinois Crime Survey points out that the large percentage of eliminations in the preliminary hearing especially in large cities "indicates again the vast importance of the preliminary hearing in the conduct of felony cases in our large cities." [173] It is not uncommon that half the cases brought into a municipal court for preliminary examination are eliminated by discharge because there is not probable cause, by dismissal for want of prosecution usually involving the failure of witnesses to appear, and by nolle prosequi filed by the prosecuting attorney.[174] In Missouri, the "preliminary hearing, taking the state as a whole, eliminates slightly over one-fourth of all the cases (26.08 per cent); in the cities it accounts for slightly over four-

law is relaxed if he discharges indiscriminately." Nat. Com. on Law Obs. and Enf., Report on Prosecution (1931) 21.

[172] Nat. Com. on Law Obs. and Enf., Report on Prosecution (1931) 6-7.

[173] Illinois Crime Survey (1929) 36. See also 204-205, 258-260, 296-298, 398-400; Miller, J., "The Compromise of Criminal Cases" (1927) 1 So. Calif.L.Rev. 1; Illinois Crime Survey (1929) 36, 204-205, 297-298, 398-400.

[174] Illinois Crime Survey (1929) 36, 204-205, 297-298, 305-308, 398-400. "A majority of all felony cases which appear in the courts are disposed of on preliminary hearings by magistrates. . . . As a consequence, the police magistrate and the prosecuting attorney loom up as by far the most important officials in our system with reference to the disposition of the greatest number of cases." Hall, Theft, Law and Society (1935) 113.

tenths (41.73 per cent); in the country districts slightly over one-tenth (10.67 per cent)." [175]

Back in the middle of the decade from 1920 to 1930, 58 per cent of all felony arrests in New York City were eliminated at preliminary hearing, 55 per cent in Cincinnati, 49 per cent in Chicago, 41 per cent in Kansas City, 26 per cent in Cleveland, 22 per cent in Baltimore, 17 per cent in Milwaukee and 17 per cent in St. Louis.[176] As Raymond Moley points out: "The two unmistakably important tendencies in present day criminal justice are the vast discretion exercised by the prosecutor and by the committing magistrate and the incredible proportion of felony cases which are terminated through the discretion of these officers. In rural districts the magistrate is largely overshadowed by the prosecutor but in the cities the prosecutor largely through his own indifference permits the magistrate to cut liberally into the cases initiated by the police." [177]

With respect to the reasons for eliminations at the stage of preliminary hearings the surveys indicate that in order of importance they are: (1) dismissal for want of prosecution, usually for failure of witnesses to appear;

[175] Missouri Crime Survey (1926) 275. Eliminated by discharge were 8.16 per cent of all cases, by dismissal for want of prosecution 9.80 per cent, by nolle prosequi 2.59 per cent, by disposition as a misdemeanor 2.77 per cent, and by other dispositions, 2.76 per cent. *Ibid.* p.276.

[176] Moley, Politics and Criminal Prosecution (1929) 28. In England during 1883 the number of persons arrested for crime and not summarily tried was 20,450. Of these 5,192 were discharged by the magistrates. Maitland, Justice and Police (1885) 132.

[177] Moley, Our Criminal Courts (1930) 14. "A majority of all felony cases which appear in the courts are disposed of on preliminary hearings by magistrates." Hall, Theft, Law and Society (1935) 113. In Oregon one half of the felony charges on arrest were eliminated in the preliminary hearing stage. "Survey of Administration of Criminal Justice in Oregon" (1931) 17 A.B.A.J. 212, 213.

(2) discharge for want of a finding of probable cause; and (3) the filing of a nolle prosequi.[178]

It is apparent from the crime surveys that the magistrates have freely exercised their power to discharge defendants or to reduce the charge.[179] Since, however, there was also a large percentage of cases "nolled" or dismissed for want of prosecution, the responsibility is not exclusively that of the magistrate. In Illinois the prosecuting attorney was responsible for the majority of the cases eliminated in preliminary hearings.

In England it is the theory that the burden of deciding whether or not the evidence is sufficient to warrant placing the defendant on trial is the function of the examining magistrate.[180] It is felt that there is no need for any other public official to review the matter. In the United States, on the other hand, it is the practice for prosecuting attorneys to give little weight to the fact that the defendant has been committed by the magistrate or indicted by the grand jury and to recommend the discharge in any proceeding where their own independent investigation of the facts leads them to believe that the case does not justify further prosecution.[181] They defend this practice on the ground that magistrates and grand juries neglect to use fearlessly and intelligently their power to dismiss cases when the evidence is insufficient or untrustworthy. They insist that if they did not do so the number of acquittals by trial juries would be much higher than it now is.

178 Report of the Minnesota Crime Commission (1934) 140.

179 Report of the Minnesota Crime Commission (1934) 140. Of course it should be borne in mind that the elimination of many arrested persons does not necessarily indicate anything wrong with the preliminary examination. It is entirely possible that too many arrests have been made.

180 Howard, Criminal Justice in England (1931) 137.

181 Moley, Politics and Criminal Prosecution (1929) cc. 7 and 8.

The Illinois Crime Survey found the stage of preliminary examination to be of supreme importance particularly in large cities. "The underworld and friends of the underworld know that less difficulty is experienced in getting a case out of the way in the preliminary hearing than in any other stage of prosecution. It is a poor and ineffective 'fixer' who permits his case to get into the more difficult stages of the grand jury proceedings and the trial court stages. The place to get cases out of the way quietly and unobtrusively and painlessly is in the preliminary hearing; consequently, the underworld exercises all sorts of efforts to prevent cases from being prosecuted." [182] The preliminary hearing may result in the release of important defendants who are guilty and who are likely to commit further serious crimes. As Raymond Moley states: "Therefore, while the preliminary hearing is ordinarily neglected and despised by commentators, it is in every respect a most important link in the process of administering justice. It might be concluded with a great deal of justification that so far as the effective enforcement of the criminal law is concerned the preliminary hearing is more important than the trial itself." [183]

[182] Illinois Crime Survey (1929) 307. "If there is to be any 'fixing' of criminal cases, the wise and effective politician does his work here. He is protected by confusion and haste, and he deals with but one person. If his case slips through the preliminary hearing, his task is multiplied manyfold. He must deal with more persons in a more rarefied atmosphere." Moley, Our Criminal Courts (1930) 29-30.

[183] Moley, Our Criminal Courts (1930) 26. See also Glueck, Crime and Justice (1936) 81-83.

CHAPTER III

BAIL

1. Stage in Proceedings

STEPHEN states that the "next step to the preliminary inquiry held by the magistrates is the discharge, bail or committal of the suspected person." [1] Bail may be granted at several stages. As the Wickersham Crime Commission states: "After arrest, or after binding over, or after indictment, or again pending appeal, the accused may be admitted to *bail,* i.e., may be released from custody upon giving security for appearance in court at the required time." [2]

2. History of Bail in England

The right to bail is as old as English law itself.[3] It is expressly referred to by the earliest English writers such as Glanville and Bracton. In the earliest days, arrest involved imprisonment without preliminary inquiry, at least

[1] Stephen, A History of the Criminal Law of England (1883) 233. For general discussions of bail, see Beeley, The Bail System in Chicago (1927); Moley, Our Criminal Courts (1930) 43-61; Ploscowe, "Measures of Constraint in European and Anglo-American Criminal Procedure" (1935) 23 Geo.L.J. 762; Report of the Minnesota Crime Commission (1934) 142-147, 165-166; 6 Am. Jur., Bail and Recognizance, §§ 1-200, pp.48-125; 8 C.J.S., Bail, §§ 29-111, pp.48-219.

[2] Nat. Com. on Law Obs. and Enf., Rep. on Crim. Proc. (1931) 16. Bail is chiefly arranged in the inferior courts and after preliminary examination. *Ibid.* 23. See also Beeley, The Bail System in Chicago (1927) 7-10.

[3] 1 Stephen, A History of the Criminal Law of England (1883) 233-243. With respect to the origin and historical development up to 1275, see De Haas, Antiquities of Bail (1940). See also De Haas, "Concepts of the Nature of Bail in English and American Law" (1946) 6 U. of Toronto L.J. 385.

until the sheriff held his tourn, and in more serious cases until the arrival of the justices. The latter might be delayed for years. Obviously it was a matter of the greatest importance to be able to obtain a provisional release from custody.[4] Moreover, the conditions of incarceration were such that many prisoners died from them.[5]

The sheriff, as the legal representative of the crown and as the head of the executive part of the administration of criminal justice, arrested and imprisoned suspected persons and, if he thought proper, admitted them to bail. His discretionary power was poorly defined. This resulted in great abuses which were corrected by the Statute of Westminster the First, enacted in 1275. For 550 years this statute was the chief basis of the law of bail. Under this statute certain classes of persons could not be bailed; on the other hand, certain classes of persons who had committed less serious offenses were to be bailed. Between 1275 and 1444 the sheriff's powers were to a great extent transferred to the justices of the peace by a series of statutes. Because of overliberality in granting bail to dangerous felons, a statute of 1486 was enacted that the power of granting bail should be exercised only by two

[4] "It was not common to keep men in prison. This apparent leniency of our law was not due to any love of an abstract liberty. Imprisonment was costly and troublesome. Besides, any reader of the eyre rolls will be inclined to define a gaol as a place that is made to be broken, so numerous are the entries that tell of escapes. . . . The sheriff did not want to keep prisoners; his inclination was to discharge himself of all responsibility by handing them over to their friends." 2 Pollock and Maitland, History of English Law (2d ed.1905) 584.

[5] As late as the seventeenth century there was no provision of adequate food for defendants awaiting trial. Hence, 19 Car. II, c.4 recites that "they many times perish before their trial." A malignant form of typhus known as "gaol fever" often swept over the jails. In 1759 an English authority estimated that each year a fourth of the people in prison died there. Warner, "Investigating the Law of Arrest" (1940) 26 A.B.A.J. 151, 15-

justices and that the courts of oyer and terminer were to be notified of the granting of bail.[6]

The procedure established in 1554 by the Statute of Philip and Mary, which also provided for the preliminary examination, was much stricter. This statute was intended to guard against collusion between the justices and the prisoners brought before them. It provided that, whenever a prisoner was bailed, the depositions of the witnesses were to be taken and returned to the court. In 1826, a statute for the first time consolidated the law of bail. The latter statute was superseded in 1848 by a statute still remaining in force. This statute states that the committing justice may, in his discretion, admit to bail any person charged with a felony, or any of certain specified misdemeanors. The net result is that the justice may, in his discretion, either bail or refuse to bail any person accused either of felony or of any common misdemeanor except certain specified ones. As to the latter and as to misdemeanors created by special acts, bail cannot be refused. In case of treason no bail may be taken except by order of a secretary of state or by the High Court.

Of the power of the higher English courts to grant bail, Stephen states: "The power of the superior courts to bail all cases whatever, even high-treason, has no history. I do not know, indeed, that it ever has been disputed or modified. It exists in the present day precisely as it has always existed from the earliest times." [7]

[6] It should be noted, however, that the sheriffs in early times refused to grant bail in cases in which they were legally bound to do so. Certain royal writs, now obsolete, against the sheriffs were developed in order to protect the defendant. 1 Stephen, A History of the Criminal Law of England (1883) 239-243. In addition, from the earliest times the superior courts and the lord chancellor could issue the writ of habeas corpus.

[7] 1 Stephen, A History of the Criminal Law of England (1883) 243.

Briefly speaking, the present system of bail in England is as follows: The judges have discretion as to the granting of bail in felony cases and even in misdemeanor cases.[8] In practice they have been too strict in the allowance of bail.[9] From 1911 to 1921, from 30 to 50 per cent of the persons who were ultimately acquitted had been held without bail. In England there are no professional bondsmen nor corporate sureties, and it is improper for a bondsman to enter into an agreement by which he will be indemnified in case of forfeiture. England requires much less amounts for bail than does this country for offenses of a similar nature and involving a similar risk. In cases of forfeiture the penalty is prompt and severe.

3. Purposes of Bail

The purpose of requiring bail after arrest is to secure the presence of the defendant at the trial.[10] Neither the requirement of bail nor pre-trial detention in default of bail is a punitive device.[11] Forfeiture for nonappearance

[8] Moley, Our Criminal Courts (1930) 59-61; Howard, Criminal Justice in England (1931) 336-342; Kenny, Outlines of Criminal Law (15th ed. 1942) 536-542; Archbold, Criminal Pleading, Evidence and Practice (30th ed.1938) 71-83; Stephen, A Digest of the Law of Criminal Procedure (1883) 88-92; Lawson and Keedy, "Criminal Procedure in England," (1901) 1 J.Crim.L. 595, 601; Harris and Wilshere, Principles and Practice of the Criminal Law (17th ed.1943) 411-415.

[9] Jackson, The Machinery of Justice in England (1940) 126; Kenny, Outlines of Criminal Law (15th ed.1942) 538.

[10] The Forgotten Adolescent (1940) A Publication of the New York Law Society; Wood and Waite, Crime and Its Treatment (1941) 407; A.L.I. Code of Crim. Proc. (1931) § 61; 4 Bl.Comm. *296.

[11] To be distinguished is the practice which has grown up in relation to traffic law violators whereby the defendant can put up a specified amount of money, which is often spoken of as "bail," then forfeit that sum by not appearing for trial, and thereafter be absolved from further liability for the particular offense.

does not bar prosecution for the crime. The problem is to obtain, by a method that is least burdensome or injurious to the defendant, reasonable assurance that he will appear for trial. The need for a system of bail is manifest where arrests are as numerous and indiscriminate and the use of summons is as rare as they are in the United States.[12]

On first thought, one might regard bail as intended solely or primarily for the benefit of the defendant. But that the public interest is also served is easily demonstrable.[13] If the defendant is placed in jail, the government is put to expense to maintain him. Furthermore, the defendant is then likely to lose his job and his family goes on relief. Moreover, in the case of adolescent defendants,[14] and adult defendants who turn out to be innocent, humiliation and injury to morale occur. On the other hand, it may be argued that bail is socially undesirable to the extent that it results in the failure of the defendant to appear at the time set for trial and that it causes delay in bringing cases to trial.[15]

In view of the proper purpose of bail, it would seem sound to develop a policy of keeping as many youthful

[12] Nat. Com. on Law Obs. and Enf., Rep. on Crim. Proc. (1932) 22.

[13] United States v. Barber, 140 U.S. 164, 11 Sup.Ct. 749, 35 L.Ed. 396 (1891); Note, "Criminal Bail Bonds" (1921) 21 Col.L.Rev. 592; Beeley, The Bail System in Chicago (1927) 59.

[14] The extension of juvenile court jurisdiction to include older delinquents is a possible remedy. Beeley, The Bail System in Chicago (1927) 166.

[15] Waite, "Code of Criminal Procedure: The Problem of Bail," (1929) 15 A.B.A.J. 71. "This evidence reveals at once the difficult course which any reform of bail bond procedure must steer. It must be made easier for the poor, casual misdemeanant to avoid wasting in jail, with the resultant loss of earning power and reputation, harmful to society and to the individual. And it must be made harder for the professional criminal to slip out with the aid of the professional bondsman and the professional indemnitor." Note, "Criminal Bail Bonds" (1921) 21 Col.L.Rev. 592.

defendants as possible out of pre-trial jails. Nevertheless in the year ending June 30, 1938, 78 per cent of all defendants between the ages of sixteen and twenty-one, charged with felonies and serious misdemeanors in the boroughs of Manhattan, Brooklyn, and Queens in New York City, were committed to detention prisons because they were unable to post bail required for their release.[16] Yet 1,431 or 64 per cent of these defendants ultimately were discharged, acquitted, given suspended sentences, or placed on probation. Consequently, of these 1,431 boys who were not ultimately sent to prison or otherwise institutionalized, 74 per cent were incarcerated in a city jail at this initial stage of the proceeding. This appears even more regrettable when it is remembered that four out of every five had no record of previous arrests. The paradoxical situation is that the criminal law now takes account of immaturity after conviction by providing special reformatories, but takes no account of immaturity before conviction. The paradox is all the more striking when it is remembered that before conviction the law is dealing with adolescents presumptively innocent, many of whom will be adjudged innocent and most of whom will not be sent to prison.[17] The answer appears to be to set up specialized procedures before the trial for dealing with adolescents.

[16] The Forgotten Adolescent (1940) A Publication of the New York Law Society.

[17] That too many adults are also incarcerated who should have been bailed is pointed out by Morse and Beattie, "Survey of the Administration of Criminal Justice in Oregon" (June 1932) 11 Ore.L.Rev. (Supp. 1, 100, 117.) They point out that only 28 per cent of the cases were released from custody in the bail stage after arrest, 32.6 per cent in the bail stage after bind-over, and 21.6 per cent in the bail stage after indictment.

4. Habeas Corpus

As has been seen in connection with the law of arrest and of preliminary examination, when an arrest has been made, the arrested person must be promptly brought before a magistrate. As a result the opportunity of an arrested person to obtain bail is almost immediate, and he may escape incarceration in the local jail. The magistrate may grant bail before or at the preliminary examination.

If an arrested person is denied release on bail, or if excessive bail is required, his remedy is to apply to the proper judge or court for a writ of habeas corpus.[18] After a hearing, the court will admit him to bail if his offense is bailable, and will fix the amount of bail.[19] But where the judge denying bail could exercise discretion in the granting of bail, the higher court will not interfere, except where that discretion has been exercised in an arbitrary manner.[20]

5. Constitutional Guarantee

Thirty-five states by constitutional provision and one by statute have altered the common law and guarantee that "All persons shall be bailable by sufficient sureties except for capital offenses where the proof is evident or the presumption great." [21] Four states, Indiana, Michigan, Nebraska, and Oregon, except only murder and treason

[18] As to habeas corpus in relation to bail in England, see 1 Stephen, A History of the Criminal Law of England (1883) 243.

[19] Evans v. Foster, 1 N.H. 374 (1819).

[20] Lester v. State, 33 Ga. 192 (1862); Lynch v. People, 38 Ill. 494 (1865).

[21] Note, "The Administration of Bail" (1931) 41 Yale L.J. 293. The situation is thus the reverse of that in England where the courts have practically complete discretionary power as to whether or not they will release a defendant on bail. Waite, "Code of Criminal Procedure: The Problem of Bail" (1929) 15 A.B.A.J. 71, 72.

from the constitutional guarantee. In three states, Georgia, Maryland, and New York, statutes provide that bail is a matter of right in misdemeanor cases. In five states, Massachusetts, New Hampshire, North Carolina, Virginia, and West Virginia, there is enforced the common-law rule allowing almost unlimited discretionary power in granting or refusing bail. The guarantee of bail in most American states has had some unfortunate results. A defendant is entitled to bail even though he has previously absconded and probably will abscond again.[22] A defendant is also entitled to bail even though he is charged with an offense committed while he was on bail previously granted.[23] Amendment of the state constitution is the only available remedy.

Although discretion in granting bail is greatly limited by constitutional provisions, judicial action still has significant consequences. This may be seen in the different results arrived at, in interpreting and applying the clause excepting from the guarantee capital cases where the proof is evident or the presumption great. In three states, the burden is placed on the applicant to show that the proof is not evident nor the presumption great.[24] In four states the burden is placed on the prosecution.[25]

Likewise, in determining what weight shall be given

[22] Kendrick v. State, 180 Ark. 1160, 24 S.W. (2d) 859 (1930).

[23] "A man was arrested in Detroit on the charge of picking pockets; he secured release on bail and while the first case was pending, he was arrested four additional times for picking pockets and secured bail each time." Sutherland, Criminology (1924) 213.

[24] Ex parte Paige, 82 Cal. App. 576, 255 Pac. 887 (1927); Ex parte Tully, 70 Fla. 1 (1914); Ex parte Andrews, 39 Okl. Cr. Rep. 359, 265 Pac. 144 (1928).

[25] In re Haigler, 15 Ariz. 150, 137 Pac. 423 (1913); State v. District Court, 35 Mont. 504 (1907); State v. Kauffman, S.D. 620, 108 N.W. 246 (1906); Ex parte Donohoe, 112 Tex. Cr. App. 124, 14 S.W. (2d) 848 (1929).

an indictment for a capital offense, there has been a great variety of views. In three states the indictment is conclusive proof that proof of guilt is evident.[26] In seven states it creates a rebuttable presumption that proof is evident.[27] In four states it is given no weight.[28] It has been argued by the Kentucky court that, in view of the rule that the presumption of innocence remains until conviction and since bail is generally granted, the burden of proving evidence of guilt so as to warrant a denial of bail should rest on the state after as well as before indictment.[29] Under Section 68(2) of the Institute Code, the burden is on the defendant.

Where the death penalty has been abolished in the state, it has been held that the exception of capital cases from the constitutional guarantee is ineffective and that consequently bail is mandatory in all cases before conviction.[30] At the same time, in states in which the death penalty may be inflicted, a case is capital even though a sentence of life imprisonment has been imposed.[31] This distinction seems sound in the light of general definition of capital cases as those in which the death penalty might be imposed.

[26] State v. Butler, 40 La. Ann. 3, 3 So. 350 (1887); State v. Kuchler, 129 Atl. 632 (N.J. 1925); State v. Diehl, 115 Ohio St. 454, 154 N.E. 726 (1926).

[27] Alabama, Colorado, Florida, Indiana, New Mexico, Oklahoma, and Wyoming. See Ex parte Towndrow, 20 N.M. 631, 151 Pac. 761 (1915); (1916) 16 Col.L.Rev. 65; (1927) 11 Minn.L.Rev. 553.

[28] Jordan v. State, 25 Ariz. 249, 215 Pac. 926 (1923); Ford v. Dilley, 174 Iowa 243, 156 N.W. 513 (1916); Ex parte Verden, 291 N.W. 552, 237 S.W. 734 (1921); Ex parte Howard, 99 Tex. Cr. App. 456, 270 S.W. 550 (1925).

[29] Commonwealth v. Stahl, 237 Ky. 388, 35 S.W. (2d) (1931).

[30] Ex parte Ball, 106 Kan. 536, 188 Pac. 424 (1920); see In re Welisch, 18 Ariz. 517, 163 Pac. 264 (1917).

[31] People v. St. Lucia, 315 Ill. 258, 146 N.E. 183 (1925); State v. Barone, 96 N.J.L. 374, 114 Atl. 809 (1921). *Contra:* Walker v. State, 138 Ark. 517, 209 S.W. 86 (1919).

Certainly one of the most fundamental questions in the law of bail is whether or not the courts should be allowed any discretion in refusing release on bail and, if so, to what extent.[32] The English practice of large discretion seems sound. The American Law Institute Code of Criminal Procedure is so drawn as to permit a reasonable degree of discretion. Section 66 continues the existing satisfactory rule that bail may not be granted to defendants charged with a capital offense, if the proof is evident or the presumption great. Section 67 introduces an innovation, involving constitutional amendment in most states, by providing that the granting of bail shall be a matter of discretion and not of right in capital cases where the proof is not evident or the presumption not great.[33] Section 70 introduces an even greater innovation by providing, with respect to noncapital offenses, that bail shall be discretionary when the defendant is in custody for the commission of murder, treason, arson, robbery, burglary, rape, kidnapping, or any offense against the person likely to result in death under such circumstances that if death would result the offense would be murder.[34]

The general constitutional guarantee of bail is appli-

[32] Waite, "Code of Criminal Procedure: The Problem of Bail" (1929) 15 A.B.A.J. 71, 72.

[33] Under Rule 46(a)(1) of the Federal Rules of Criminal Procedure, a person arrested for an offense punishable by death may be admitted to bail in the exercise of discretion, giving due weight to the evidence and to the nature and circumstances of the offense.

[34] One writer would suspend the bail privilege entirely in such cases "as (1) hardened offenders charged with felony, (2) accused persons obviously mentally disordered, and (3) convicted persons petitioning for or granted an appeal or a new trial." Beeley, The Bail System in Chicago (1927) 166. See also Moley, Our Criminal Courts (1930) 57; Report of the Minnesota Crime Commission (1934) 45; Note (1926) 26 Col.L.Rev. 752.

cable only before conviction.[35] The constitution or statutes of more than twenty states give a right to bail after conviction in various cases less than capital. The constitutions of ten states use the phrase "before conviction" or an equivalent term in defining the right to bail. Thus ordinarily the power to admit a defendant to bail after his conviction is entrusted to the discretion of the trial court.

In cases of interstate rendition [36] and international extradition,[37] there is no constitutional right to bail. In rendition cases bail is generally refused, although it does not appear whether in the exercise of discretion or not.[38] In extradition cases, the power to grant bail after committal is denied by statute.[39] When application is made before committal, it has been refused because no power was expressly given by statute.[40] The sounder view favors the existence of discretionary power, although admittedly it should be exercised with care.

The Eighth Amendment provides that "excessive bail shall not be required." [41] This implies and safeguards the right to bail at least before trial.[42] Its purpose is to prevent the practical denial of bail by fixing the amount so

[35] Orfield, Criminal Appeals in America (1939) 170; Notes (1931) 41 Yale L.J. 293, 295, (1922) 19 A.L.R. 807.

[36] Ex parte Erwin, 7 Tex. App. 288 (1879).

[37] In re Carrier, 57 Fed. 578 (D. Colo. 1893).

[38] State ex rel. Stringer v. Quigg, 91 Fla. 197, 107 So. 409 (1926), 10 Minn.L.Rev. 623.

[39] Wright v. Henkel, 190 U.S. 40 (1903).

[40] In re Wright, 123 Fed. 463 (C.C.S.D.N.Y. 1903). But see In re Mitchell, 171 Fed. 289 (S.D.N.Y. 1909): 9 Col.L.Rev. 727, 4 Am.J.Int.L. 422; In re Gannon, 27 F. (2d) 362 (E.D.Pa. 1928), 42 Harv.L.Rev. 276. See Reuschlein, "Provisional Arrest and Detention in International Extradition" (1934) 23 Geo.L.J. 37, 68-73.

[41] For the history of the adoption of the Eighth Amendment, see Weems v. United States, 217 U.S. 349, 54 L.Ed. 793 (1910).

[42] United States v. Motlow 10 F. (2d) 657, 659 (1926).

unreasonably high that it cannot be given.[43] Mere inability to procure bail does not of itself make the amount excessive.[44]

Bail is excessive only if the amount required is unnecessary to secure the compliance of the defendant with the conditions of the bail bond. The wide discretionary power vested in the magistrate is shown by the fact that he may at any time require additional security or may revise its amount.[45]

If the discretion is to be exercised rightly, there should be a careful consideration of the character, previous record, and economic circumstances of the defendant, nature of the crime charged, the weight of the evidence against the defendant, and the severity of its penalty.[46] Unfortunately bail is often administered in routine fashion,[47] and the amount of bail is endorsed on the indictment without any examination of the defendant.[48] It seems likely that there could safely be a reduction in the amount of bail which would make bail possible for defendants who ought to have it.[49]

[43] Bail in the amount of $50,000 on a charge of vagrancy from a habitual criminal is excessive. People ex rel. Sammons v. Snow, Bailiff, et al. 340 Ill. 469, 173 N.E. 8, 72 Ala. 798 (1930). As to amounts fixed for various crimes, see "Crime and the Georgia Courts—A Statistical Analysis" (1925) 16 J.Crim.L. 169, 205-208; Morse and Beattie, "Survey of the Administration of Criminal Justice in Oregon" (June 1932) 11 Ore.L.Rev. (Supp.) 89-98.

[44] Ex parte Malley, 50 Nev. 248, 256 Pac. 512, 53 A.L.R. 395 (1927).

[45] People v. Eiserman, 69 Col. App. 143, 230 Pac. 669 (1924). See also A.L.I. Code of Crim. Proc. (1930) § 91.

[46] Ex parte Bice, 107 Tex. Cr. 87, 296 S.W. 541 (1927); People v. Searles, 229 App. Div. 603, 243 N.Y. Sup. 15 (3d Dept.1930). See Rule 46(c), Fed. Rules of Crim. Proc.; Beeley, The Bail System in Chicago (1927) 167.

[47] Beeley, The Bail System in Chicago (1927) 31, 33, 159; Nat. Com. on Law Obs. and Enf., Rep. on Crim. Proc. (1931) 22.

[48] Ex parte Reis, 33 S.W. (2d) 435 (Tex. 1930).

[49] Beeley, The Bail System in Chicago (1927) 167.

The power to admit to bail has been viewed as a judicial one. Fixing the amount of bail or determining whether an offense is bailable is regarded as a judicial function and a state statute conferring such power on a clerk of court has been held unconstitutional.[50] While historically the sheriff was the principal bailing officer, he possessed both judicial and ministerial powers; later by statute the authority gradually became vested in the superior court and the justices of the peace.[51] On the other hand, approving and accepting bail after it has been fixed by competent authority is a ministerial act performable by a ministerial officer. At the stage between arrest and preliminary hearing, it appears that in practice the police often exercise the right to accept bail.[52]

6. Fingerprinting

In some jurisdictions, an applicant for bail cannot secure it until his fingerprints have been taken. In New York, no person charged with felony or with any of specified misdemeanors may be admitted to bail in any court un-

[50] Gregory v. The State, ex rel. Gadgel, 94 Ind. 384, 48 Am. Rep. 162 (1883). *Contra:* State v. Sureties of Krohne, 4 Wyo. 347, 34 Pac. 3 (1893). "Admission to bail is the order of an authorized court or official that a person be discharged from custody on his giving bail." A.L.I. Code of Crim. Proc. (1930) § 62.

[51] 1 Stephen, A History of the Criminal Law of England (1883) 233. About the year 1900, there were a number of bills introduced in the Massachusetts legislature to permit police officers to grant bail. Warner and Cabot, Judges and Law Reform (1936) 26.

[52] Moley, Our Criminal Courts (1930) 45; Morse and Beattie, "Survey of the Administration of Criminal Justice in Oregon" (1932) 11 Ore.L.Rev. (Supp.) 1, 87. In England bail may under certain circumstances be accepted by the police at the time of arrest. Howard, Criminal Justice in England (1931) 336; Kenny, Outlines of Criminal Law (15th ed.1942) 532, n.3; Harris and Wilshere, Principles and Practice of the Criminal Law (17th ed.1943) 412.

less his fingerprints have been taken to ascertain whether he is a habitual criminal.[53] Since this condition precedent to bail applies only in localities with proper fingerprint facilities, there seems little likelihood of delay in securing bail for merely technical felons to whom it would otherwise be granted.

7. Shopping for Bail

One of the chief abuses of bail is that a defendant refused bail by one judge applies to other judges until he finds one less strict.[54] To remedy this, Section 72 of the Institute Code provides that, in cases of denial of bail where bail is discretionary, no court of equal or inferior jurisdiction shall admit to bail, unless an affidavit is filed with the application, stating that new evidence material to the defense has been discovered and stating the substance of the new evidence. Possible abuse of discretion by the judge is guarded against by the fact that the section only precludes other applications to judges of equal or inferior jurisdiction. This section is made effective through Section 71, requiring an affidavit for bail to state under oath what previous application has been made. Magistrates should regard previous orders denying bail as presumptively correct.

8. Sickness

Hardship to a defendant who has been refused bail may arise through serious illness. Under Section 73 of

[53] Note (1926) 26 Col.L.Rev. 752, 753. See also Moffatt, "Taking Fingerprints upon Arrest" (1926) 12 A.B.A.J. 175.

[54] Waite, "Code of Criminal Procedure: The Problem of Bail" (1929) 15 A.B.A.J. 71, 75; Note, "The Administration of Bail" (1931) 41 Yale L.J. 293, 296. On the other hand if bail is once granted, no review is open to the prosecution. In re Pantages, 209 Calif. 535, 291 Pac. 831 (1930).

the Institute Code, the court, when satisfied upon investigation that any confinement will endanger his life, may admit the defendant to bail.

9. Delay as Ground for Bail

Delay in the prosecution of a case, through failure either to indict [55] or to try promptly,[56] constitutes a reason to allow bail, as there may be great hardship on the defendant. The American Law Institute Code of Criminal Procedure goes even further in protecting the defendant. Under Section 292 when a person has been committed to custody to answer for an offense, if an indictment is not found or an information filed against him for the offense within approximately three months, the prosecution shall be dismissed in the absence of a showing of good cause.[57] The same rule is applied where a person who has been indicted or informed against for an offense is not brought to trial within the same length of time after the indictment or information. Where good cause is shown, the case may be continued, in which event the defendant shall be released on bail either on his own recognizance or on the undertaking of sureties.

10. Notice to Prosecuting Attorney

The amount of bail must depend largely on the circumstances of each case, except of course that excessive

[55] 39 L.R.A. (N.S.) 767; 1 Ann. Cas. 12.

[56] People v. Tinder, 19 Cal. 539, 81 Am. Dec. 77 (1862).

[57] In England the Habeas Corpus Act provides that if a defendant, who has been committed on a charge of either treason or felony, be not indicted at the next Assizes after his commitment, he must be released on bail unless the witnesses for the Crown cannot appear; and, if at the next subsequent Assizes he is not both indicted and tried, he must be entirely discharged. Kenny, Outlines of Criminal Law (15th ed.1942) 563.

bail may not be required. But there is always the possibility that the amount of bail will be set by some official who is not entirely acquainted with the significant facts of the case.[58] To reduce this danger, Section 74 of the Institute Code provides that, before bail is fixed in serious cases, the official to whom an application for bail is made must notify the prosecuting attorney, and that notice may be given in any case. Under Section 91, if the defendant applies for reduction in the amount of bail, notice is also required.

11. Conditions

The condition of the obligation is that the obligors shall be discharged if the accused shall appear at some specified time or times. The date fixed for such appearance is usually the first day of the next term, but it is usual to stipulate that the principal shall continue in attendance upon the court, shall not depart therefrom without leave of the court, or shall appear from day to day as required. The purpose of such additions is to insure that the accused will be present at such time as the court may call the case for hearing.[59] In some states it regularly is further stipulated that the accused shall abide the judgment and orders of the court, the effect being that he must appear after conviction for imposition of sentence or other direction.[60]

If the bail bond binds the defendant to appear *ad respondendum,* generally, and not to answer for any particular offense, it binds him to appear to answer any offense with which he may be charged.[61] But if the bond is

[58] Warner and Cabot, Judges and Law Reform (1936) 27.

[59] Commonwealth v. Teevens, 143 Mass. 210, 9 N.E. 524, 58 Am. Rep. 131 (1887); Keigwin, Cases in Criminal Procedure (1939) 173-174.

[60] State v. Bryant, 55 Iowa 451, 8 N.W. 303 (1881).

[61] State v. Randolph, 22 Nev. 474 (1856); People v. Gillman, 125 N.Y.

special there should be no obligation beyond its terms.[62] The condition has been held to cover a charge for a different offense, differing merely in degree, and arising out of the same transaction.[63] One case held the obligor where the offense charged did not arise out of the same transaction as the offense declared in the bond.[64]

12. Number of Bail Bonds

The bail bond system may involve an unnecessary number of steps. For example, it was found in Cleveland that in every felony case bound over to the grand jury three was the minimum number of successive bail bonds required, and, if a case was carried to a higher court, the number would go to five or seven.[65] The bond given at the time of arrest to secure appearance at the preliminary examination is one which the defendant wishes to give quickly and for which he has had no opportunity to prepare in advance. It should not be made difficult to obtain this bond, and therefore it should not be required that sureties be found who will stand good for his appearance at all later stages of the case.[66] He will, however, have

---

372, 26 N.E. 469 (1891). Cf. State v. Bryant, 55 Iowa 451, 8 N.W. (1881); Keigwin, Cases in Criminal Procedure (1939) 174.

[62] State v. Young, 20 La.Ann. 397 (1868).

[63] Gresham v. State, 48 Ala. 625 (1872); Commonwealth v. Teevens, 143 Mass. 210, 9 N.E. 524, 58 Am. Rep. 131 (1887). In the latter case the recognizance specified the offense and also provided that the defendant should not depart without leave.

[64] Pernetti v. People, 91 N.Y.Supp. 210 (1905), 5 Col.L.Rev. 329.

[65] Criminal Justice in Cleveland (1922) 184, 213. The number of bonds necessary is reduced in Sections 82 and 83 of the American Law Institute Code of Criminal Procedure.

[66] "There are now altogether too many bonds required at different stages of a felony case, especially in St. Louis. In certain counties this difficulty is eliminated by the more frequent use of recognizances of record. There should be but four bonds, one from arrest to appearance in the court of preliminary hearing, one at the end of the preliminary hearing,

sufficient time to prepare for subsequent proceedings, hence the second bond, given if and when he is bound over, should hold good throughout the case and secure his appearance at all later stages, including his surrender for imprisonment if he finally loses.[67]

13. Kinds of Bail

Any of several types of bail may be required as a condition of release. These types are: a deposit of cash,[68] a pledge of specified property, or a mere promise by sureties, who should be financially responsible, that they will themselves pay a stated sum of money if the person released fails to do what is required of him.[69] The magistrate may, if he chooses, require that these sureties recog-

---

one from that point to conviction and one on appeal." Missouri Crime Survey (1921) 218. In Oregon, bail is fixed at three different points: after arrest, after preliminary examination, and after indictment by the grand jury. Morse and Beattie, "Survey of the Administration of Criminal Justice in Oregon" (June 1932) 11 Ore.L.Rev. (Supp.) 1, 87. In Chicago, the amount of bail required after indictment is usually more than that fixed at the preliminary examination. Baker and DeLong, "The Prosecuting Attorney: The Process of Prosecution" (1935) 26 J.Crim.L. 185, 188.

[67] It has been suggested after a survey of Philadelphia that, in the case of all arrests without warrants for minor offenses, the lieutenants in charge of the police station houses might be given the authority to fix and take bail for appearance at the next magistrate's hearing; in the case of arrest under a warrant, the amount of bail should be set out in the warrant. Report of the Crimes Survey Committee, Law Association of Philadelphia (1926) 463. In England bail may be granted before preliminary hearing, unless the offense appears to be of a serious nature, by a superior police officer where the defendant cannot be brought before a magistrate within twenty-four hours after the arrest. Harris and Wilshere, Principles and Practice of the Criminal Law (17th ed.1943) 412; Kenny, Outlines of Criminal Law (15th ed.1942) 532, n.3.

[68] Such bail must be provided for by statute. It is provided for by Section 87 of the American Law Institute Code of Criminal Procedure (1930) and by Rule 46(d) of the Federal Rules of Criminal Procedure (1944).

[69] Wood and Waite, Crime and Its Treatment (1941) 408.

nize their bond as a lien upon specified real estate. The type and amount of bail are largely matters of discretion. The amount should be large enough so that the defendant will appear rather than forfeit it; and should be of such a character as to make fairly certain the collection of it in case it is forfeited.

14. Collection Procedure

A great evil has been the carelessness in the type of security demanded by judges and the laxity in the collection of forfeitures.[70] For instance, a certain surety was accepted by the magistrates for $100,000 of bail bonds, although his financial worth was represented by a half interest in property valued at $25,000 and covered by a mortgage of $11,500.[71] This evil may be relieved by statutes or rules making certain qualifications essential for sureties on bail bonds and imposing penalties on magistrates who accept sureties not so qualified. The magistrates, if they chose, could correct the evil without legislation.

Certainly one of the most difficult problems in the administration of bail is the assurance of financial responsi-

[70] Waite, "Code of Criminal Procedure: The Problem of Bail" (1929) 15 A.B.A.J. 71, 73; Nat. Com. on Law Obs. and Enf., Report on Prosecution (1931) 22.

[71] (1920) 11 J.Crim.L. 386. "The 'straw' bondsman has the world beaten for high finance. I am familiar with a case where a professional bondsman with an equity of $6,750 in an apartment building went surety on $269,500 worth of bonds scheduling this one piece of property in all cases. But that is not all. He continued in business after his equity was reduced by the entry of a judgment of $3,500 on a forfeited bond to the extent of furnishing $160,000 worth of bail. In another case a professional bondsman went surety on bonds aggregating $304,600 after and while there stood against him an unsatisfied judgment of $3,000 on bonds previously forfeited. In this connection, I am glad to state that the prosecuting attorney and judges in Chicago promptly established procedure under which such occurrences are now impossible." Sims, "Speedy Justice in Criminal Cases" (1921) 46 A.B.A.Rep. 596, 601.

bility without making it unreasonably difficult for defendants to furnish bail. The notion back of bail is that the defendant will appear at the appointed time rather than lose or have someone else lose the amount of his bail. The incentive cannot exist if the bondsman is financially irresponsible. It must be obvious that actual collectibility of the bond is a basic requirement of effective bail.

As has been seen, one remedy suggested has been the setting up of certain simple standards to which acceptable sureties must conform; and then providing that any judge accepting sureties not coming up to the standard be personally liable in case of default and failure of the surety to pay. In other words, the judge would be held responsible for his own dereliction of duty in accepting sureties not permitted by the law, and not as a guarantor of the collectibility of bonds. English statutes of the thirteenth and sixteenth centuries were based on this principle.[72] The American Law Institute Code of Criminal Procedure does not adopt this proposal, but it does provide in Section 112 that any official who takes bail knowing it to be insufficient, or accepts a surety knowing such surety not to possess the legal qualifications or sufficiency, is guilty of a misdemeanor.

Often there is no statutory requirement that the proposed surety give a list of his property. Nor is there any requirement for a record of bonds. Thus often there is no sufficient basis to determine whether the bond proffered represents any real security. The Minnesota Crime Commission in its 1927 report has recommended that all bail bonds, where the surety justifies as the owner of real property, contain a legal description of such property, and that they be filed and indexed in the office of the clerk of

[72] Edw. I, c.15 (1275); 1 & 2 Ph. & Mary, 13 (1554).

the trial court of general jurisdiction, and that similar provisions be made applicable to recognizances.[73]

The collectibility of forfeited bail would of course be assured if release were prohibited, unless the amount of bail was deposited in cash with the court.[74] On the other hand, such a requirement would mean that many persons who ought to be released would be unable to furnish such bail. In the last analysis the bail bond is an inescapable necessity. The problem is to assure its collectibility. To this end it might be proposed that when a release is on bond, the bond must be secured by a lien on specific real estate. The bondsman would have to show that the real estate offered as security had a net value over and above all other liens sufficient to secure the bond. Three arguments might be made in favor of such a proposal. In the first place, it would assure the collectibility of the bond. In the second place, it would expedite the collection of forfeited bonds. There would be an incentive for the owner of the real estate to pay the amount and clear the lien on his own initiative; if he were unwilling, the foreclosure of the lien could be accomplished very speedily. In the third place, the setting of the case for trial would be expedited. The professional bondsman could make a profit only by rapid turnover.

The American Law Institute Code of Criminal Procedure does not adopt proposals to require a deposit or pledge of specific property for every bail bond. Certain sections of the Code do, however, require that sureties have certain qualifications. Thus under Section 78, if there

[73] Minnesota Crime Commission Report (1927) 35, 65-66.

[74] For an indication of the too limited extent to which cash bail is used in practice, see Beeley, The Bail System in Chicago (1927) 155. See also Note, "Criminal Bail Bonds" (1921) 21 Col.L.Rev. 592, 593. In Missouri cash bonds are seldom accepted. Missouri Crime Survey (1926) 193.

is only one surety, he must be worth the amount specified in the undertaking, exclusive of the amount of any other undertaking on which he may be principal or surety and exclusive of property exempt from execution and over and above all liabilities. A similar rule is applied in the case of several sureties. Under Section 79 each surety shall justify by affidavit that he possesses the qualifications and sufficiency just described.[75] Moreover in such affidavit he shall describe the property in respect to which he proposes to justify as to his sufficiency, stating the encumbrances thereon, and stating the number and amount of undertakings, if any, entered into by him and remaining undischarged. If the judges require the observance of those provisions, and if the sureties do not falsify in their affidavits, the evils which have been described should be eliminated.

Section 102 of the Institute Code provides that the undertaking shall be a lien on any real property described in the affidavit required by Section 84 from the time of the recording of the undertaking and affidavit in the county in which the property is situated.[76] Thus, a surety having scheduled real estate as constituting his necessary property could not prevent collection of a forfeiture by hasty sale, because the bond, if recorded, would constitute a lien thereon.

An additional attempt to reduce the evil arising from professional bondsmen, at the same recognizing its bene-

[75] In accord, see Rule 46(e) of the Federal Rules of Criminal Procedure.

[76] Section 102 provides for transmittal of the affidavit and undertaking to certain officials and its proper recording. See Note, "Criminal Bail Bonds" (1921) 21 Col.L.Rev. 592, 594; Criminal Justice in Cleveland (1922) 187.

fits, is to be found in Section 85 of the Institute Code.[77] This section requires every surety to make affidavit as to what consideration or security he has received. A false statement is treated as perjury and the rights of the surety against others are limited to the premises set forth in his affidavit. Under Section 81 all professional bondsmen are to be registered.[78] Those sections should help to avoid existing evils: too many arrests and too few releases on the recognizance of the accused.[79] Historically, a person released on bail was regarded as being delivered into the personal custody of his sureties, who normally were relations or friends.[80] Because of this personal relation, the defendant would be deterred from forfeiting his bail and thus inflicting a loss on his sureties. Furthermore, such sureties might keep close watch over the defendant and might at any time surrender him into court and secure their exoneration. Even today in England bail is still usually required to be furnished by friends or relatives of the defendant.[81] In the United States, however, the large scale

[77] Six objections to the professional bondsman have been voiced: His character is often bad, as shown by police records. Of necessity, he becomes acquainted with and associates with criminals. He charges excessive fees, sometimes as much as twenty per cent of the face of the bond. More of their bonds, though only slightly more, are forfeited. Many of them are permitted to sign bonds far in excess of their property value. There is apt to be an alliance formed between them and public officials, so that the latter serve as runners for the former. Missouri Crime Survey (1926) 207. See also Glueck, Crime and Justice (1936) 160-162.

[78] The value of mere registration has been thought to be illusory. Brunyate "The American Draft Code of Criminal Procedure, 1930" (1933) 49 L.Q.Rev. 192, 206.

[79] Note (1929) 17 Calif.L.Rev. 537, 539.

[80] 4 Bl. Comm. * 297.

[81] Howard, Criminal Justice in England (1931) 339, 340. For an argument that the English approach is the sound one, see Hayes, "Contracts to Indemnify Bail in Criminal Cases" (1937) 6 Fordham L.Rev. 387, 405. Compare, however, Note (1921) 21 Col.L.Rev. 592.

operations of surety companies and professional bondsmen have stripped the relationship between the defendant and his sureties of any personal element, thus reducing the obligation. Then, to make matters worse, worthless sureties are accepted and forfeitures are not enforced.

In England the courts have been unwilling to take the view that bail is a mere contract of suretyship and that an agreement to indemnify bail therefore does not involve any illegality.[82] An opposite view has been taken in this country since state statutes often provide that a personally responsible surety be altogether omitted if the defendant prefers to make a deposit of money.[83] Since a friend may indemnify bail, the defendant should have the same right.

It has been seen that many bonds under the existing system in many states are not collectible. To cap the climax, bail bond investigations have revealed that in many cases no genuine attempts have been made to collect with respect to bonds seemingly collectible.[84] For instance, in Detroit

[82] Rex v. Porter 1 K.B.D. 369 (1910), 23 Harv.L.Rev. 560. Under this view the surety may not accept property from the defendant. The bail may not bring *indebitatus assumpsit* against the principal; and an agreement to indemnify by either the defendant or a third party is invalid.

[83] Moloney v. Nelson, 158 N.Y. 351, 53 N.E. 31 (1899); Carr v. Davis, 64 W.Va. 522 63 S.E. 326 (1908), (1909) 22 Harv.L.Rev. 530. Compare United States v. Ryder, 110 U.S. 729, 4 Sup.Ct. 190, 28 L.Ed. 308 (1884) holding that, in the absence of express contract, there is no implied promise to indemnify a surety. In Leary v. United States, 224 U.S. 567, 32 Sup.Ct. 599 (1912), an express agreement by the defendant to indemnify the bail was enforced. See Hayes, "Contracts to Indemnify Bail in Criminal Cases" (1937) 6 Fordham L.Rev. 387, 396.

[84] Waite, "Code of Criminal Procedure: The Problem of Bail" (1929) 15 A.B.A.J. 71, 75; Note, "Criminal Bail Bonds" (1921) 21 Col.L.Rev. 592, 595; Criminal Justice in Cleveland (1922) 155, 185, 212; Illinois Crime Survey (1929) 216-218; Missouri Crime Survey (1926) 196-197; Hayes, "Contracts to Indemnify Bail in Criminal Cases" (1937) 6 Fordham L.Rev. 387, 396; Nat. Com. on Law Obs. and Enf., Rep. on Crim. Proc. (1931) 22; Nat. Com. on Law Obs. and Enf., Report on Prosecution (1931) 89;

in 1928 the only informed officials stated that, although they were certain that less than twenty per cent of forfeitures were ever collected, they had no records from which could be ascertained just what had been done. That is to say, no systematic attempts at collection had been made. Such a situation is usually excused by the contention that proceedings to collect cost too much in time and effort because of the complication and cumbersomeness of ordinary procedure. The Institute Code therefore attempts to set up a simplified procedure for collection. Under Section 103, if there is a breach of the undertaking, the court before which the case is proceeding shall make a record thereof and shall declare the undertaking forfeited. Under Section 104 if, at any time within ten days after the undertaking has been forfeited, the breach is satisfactorily explained and the defendant has in all other respects complied with the conditions of the undertaking, the court may direct the forfeiture to be discharged upon such terms as are just.[85] Under Section 105, if the forfeiture is not thus discharged, it shall be the duty of the prosecuting attorney, immediately after the lapse of ten days [86] after the forfeiture, to proceed against the defendant or his surety as follows: The prosecuting attorney shall file a certified copy of the order of the court forfeiting the bond in the office of the official whose duty it is to enter judgments of

---

Beeley, The Bail System in Chicago (1927) 47; Moley, Our Criminal Courts (1930) 46.

85 In Chicago in 1926, of bonds forfeited in felony cases 76 per cent were set aside. Illinois Crime Survey (1929) 217, 219, 388. The Survey recommended: "That the judges be urged to discourage the practice of setting aside bond forfeitures except on a clear showing of good faith and a meritorious excuse." *Ibid.* p.220.

86 Sixty days is recommended in Missouri Crime Survey (1926) 217. Such is the rule in Baltimore under rule of court. See Note (1941) 32 J.Crim.L. 211.

the county wherein such order shall have been made; thereupon such official shall docket the same and enter judgment against the person bound for the amount of the penalty, and execution shall be issued to collect the amount of the undertaking.[87] Although a few states have this procedure in force, some of the most inefficient in collecting forfeitures resort to collection as in civil suits,[88] or to procedure by *scire facias*. Under Section 106 there may be a remission of the forfeiture.[89] Here a distinction should be noted. Setting aside or discharge is the release of the liability of the surety before the final adjudication of forfeiture upon the unexcused default by the defendant. Remission is the release of the surety after entry of final judgment of forfeiture and operates either to stay execution or to refund part or all of the collected penalty.

15. Jumping Bail

In most states the only penalty for jumping bail is the forfeiture of the bail bond. It is true that jumping bail is rare where the sureties are friends or relatives of the accused.[90] But different is the case of the professional criminal who posts a bond furnished by a surety company and who would rather lose money than risk being convicted.

[87] See also Rule 46(f)(3) of the Federal Rules of Criminal Procedure.

[88] "The best procedure would be that the forfeiture of the bond itself automatically constitute a judgment on the bond. When, as now, suit on the bond is required, there is no reason why the suit should not be filed immediately after forfeiture and judgment and execution obtained at the earliest moment allowed by law." Criminal Justice in Cleveland (1922) 212.

[89] See also Rule 46(f)(4) of the Federal Rules of Criminal Procedure.

[90] Only from one to two per cent of cases go unpunished because of forfeited bail. Report of the Minnesota Crime Commission (1934) 144-145.

Since bonding companies generally insist on adequate security, the accused has in reality bought his freedom, and, even if he is later arrested, the likelihood of being convicted is reduced by the lapse of time. But if the act of jumping bail were made a crime, the accused would face almost certain conviction when apprehended.[91]

16. Exoneration

Performance of the condition of the bond is excused by an act of God, such as the death of the accused.[92] While sickness of the accused will not discharge the sureties, since they stand bound until he is able to appear,[93] if they later bring him into court, his sickness will be a good defense to an action on the bond,[94] or a ground for vacating a judgment rendered against them.[95] Insanity has been held not to excuse.[96] Where the accused has disappeared and his continued absence is unexplained, death may be inferred from circumstances presenting a strong probability of death.[97] The disappearance of the accused at the time of a tornado has been held not to exonerate his bail.[98]

Incarceration in another state for a second and different offense is generally held not to operate as a discharge of

[91] Report of the Minnesota Crime Commission (1934) 46. Pursuant to recommendations made by the New York Crime Commission in 1927 and 1928, such legislation was enacted in New York in 1928. See § 1694-a, New York Penal Law. Making jumping bail a felony has been recommended in California. Note (1934) 24 J.Crim.L. 1113, 1114.

[92] Conner v. State, 30 Tex. 94 (1867); Pynes v. State, 45 Ala. 52 (1871).

[93] Ringeman v. State, 136 Ala. 131, 34 So. 351 (1903); Piercy v. People, 10 Ill. App. 219 (1881).

[94] People v. Tubbs, 37 N.Y. 586 (1868).

[95] Russell v. State, 45 Ga. 9 (1872).

[96] Adler v. State, 35 Ark. 517, 37 Am. Rep. 48 (1880).

[97] Merritt v. Thompson, 1 Hilt. 550 (N.Y. 1858).

[98] Bryan v. State, 167 S.W. 484 (Ark. 1914), (1915) 15 Col.L.Rev. 270.

the sureties on a bail bond.[99] This is for the reasons that performance in such case has not been prevented by any act of the state in reference to whose laws the contract of bail was made;[100] that the failure to appear was a result of the accused's own voluntary act;[101] and that the sureties, having friendly custody of the accused, are at fault in permitting him to go into another jurisdiction.[102] Where, however, an accused was incarcerated for life in another state, a wife was permitted remission of the forfeiture.[103]

When the condition of the bond has been satisfied or the forfeiture of the bond has been set aside or remitted, the court should exonerate the obligors and release any bail.[104] A surety should be able to exonerate himself by a deposit of cash or by a timely surrender of the defendant into custody.

17. Material Witnesses

Just as it is not desirable that all defendants be incarcerated pending trial, so it is even more undesirable that material witnesses be thus incarcerated.[105] Almost all states have enacted statutes permitting or requiring the committing magistrate to cause material witnesses for the prosecution to enter into a recognizance for their appearance to testify.[106] In some states the statutes limit the

[99] State v. Horn. 70 Nev. 466, 35 Am. Rep. 437 (1879).

[100] Taylor v. Taintor, 83 U.S. 366, 21 L. Fed. 287 (1872).

[101] King v. State, 18 Neb. 375, 25 N.W. 519 (1885).

[102] Withrow v. Commonwealth, 1 Bush (Ky.) 17 (1866).

[103] State v. Williams, 48 N.D. 1259, 189 N.W. 625 (1922), 23 Col.L.Rev. 71, 21 Mich.L.Rev. 94, 7 Minn.L.Rev. 54.

[104] A.L.I. Code of Crim. Proc. (1930) § 108; Rule 46(g), Fed. Rules of Crim. Proc.

[105] Criminal Justice in Cleveland (1922) 313-314.

[106] These statutes, discretionary and mandatory, are listed in Note

amount at which the recognizance can be kept to a figure so low as to make it ineffective where there is a powerful inducement to refrain from testifying.[107] In some states there is no statutory authority to require sureties, in which case the magistrate must accept a personal recognizance.[108] On the other hand, an absolute requirement of sureties may be unfair to a witness who is honestly unable to procure sureties.[109] The conditional examination provided by Section 58(2) of the American Law Institute Code seems a fair solution.[110]

18. Chief Defects in Bail

According to a recent book, in Boston there "are three general lines of criticism of the bail system. It is alleged that the defendant often has difficulty in finding an officer empowered to release him. Secondly, the cost of bail has become oppressive through unscrupulous bondsmen and bail commissioners. Finally, as administered, the system

---

(1931) 41 Yale L.J. 293, 298, n. 41. There is some authority allowing the witness to collect witness fees for the period of confinement. (1912) 21 Yale L.J. 327.

107 Alabama, Idaho, Tennessee, and Utah.

108 Ex parte Shaw, 61 Cal. 58 (1882). In England witnesses need give only their own recognizances. Kenny, Outlines of Criminal Law (15th ed.1942) 540. Under the Criminal Justice Act, 1925, § 13, witnesses whose evidence seems likely to be unnecessary at the trial must attend only if they receive from the prosecutor or the defendant a notice to attend.

109 Medalie, Symposium on National Witnesses (1930) 8 Panel 1.

110 A somewhat more rigid rule is laid down in Rules 46(b) and 15(a) of the Federal Rules of Criminal Procedure. The American Bar Association interested itself in the subject in 1912. It found that 18 states detained and imprisoned innocent witnesses long enough to take depositions, 21 states provided for detention, and 7 states forbade such detention. The Committee on Jurisprudence was asked to condemn the practice of detention, but concluded against the proposal. (1912) 37 A.B.A.Rep. 32, 431-433.

does not insure the presence of the defendant in court for trial."[111]

One of the chief evils in connection with bail is its employ to secure the liberty of the defendant while his lawyer attempts to wear out the case for prosecution by delay.[112] Jail cases are tried first and quite properly so. Thus the defendant on bail starts off with an opening wedge of delay. There is a considerable time interval between arrest and trial. This evil involves an improvement in judicial administration so that judges would be ready to try criminal cases promptly after the accusation is filed.[113] As long as the courts are behind in their calendars, release on bail will be necessary, and long delay between release and trial will continue. This evil, it should be noted, arises not out of the practice of release on bail, but in the slowness of action of the courts.

The outstanding weaknesses in American bail are two: denial of release to many who should be released, and release of many who should not be. Under the first head it appears that release is denied to many defendants without financial means, who are subsequently acquitted or otherwise discharged, and who could be relied on not to jump bail. Under the second head, by virtue of constitutional provisions, bail is granted to many grave offenders, who

[111] Warner and Cabot, Judges and Law Reform (1936) 26.

[112] Bail cases move more slowly. Warner and Cabot, Judges and Law Reform (1936) 98. Fewer bailed persons are convicted than persons without bail. Illinois Crime Survey (1929) 86-90, 101-102; Missouri Crime Survey (1926) 197-200. See also Moley, Our Criminal Courts (1930) 47; Morse and Beattie, "Survey of the Administration of Criminal Justice in Oregon" (1932) 11 Ore.L.Rev. (Supp.) 1, 99-112.

[113] In a number of cities the record shows a median time of as much as four months between arrest and trial. In Baltimore, Maryland, the median time interval has been reduced to one week. Wood and Waite, Crime and Its Treatment (1941) 409, n.8.

will commit other crimes while out on bail and will jump bail. "This American failure to understand the underlying problems involved is the fundamental cause of the widespread bail bond evil, which exists in no other country in the world." [114]

The great number of defendants kept in jail while awaiting trial in nearly all American cities shows quite clearly that bail is in fact beyond the means of many defendants.[115] In 1930, there were some three million commitments to American jails, of which half were of persons awaiting trial.[116] Moreover, even when bail is furnished, its cost will impoverish many families. The delay in arranging for it often costs the defendant his job. It is of course expensive for the state to maintain defendants in jail awaiting trial, especially if as a consequence their families go on relief.

To require the expense and inconvenience of providing bond in all cases seems unjust, as where the defendant is charged with a petty offense, is well established in the locality, and is certain not to attempt to leave the jurisdiction.[117] One remedy has already been considered in connection with the law of arrest, namely, the resort to summons instead of arrest so that the defendant is not incarcerated pending trial.[118] A second remedy is the substitu-

[114] Ploscowe, "Measures of Constraint in European and Anglo-American Criminal Procedure" (1935) 23 Geo.L.J. 762, 779. See also Glueck, Crime and Justice (1936) 160-161.

[115] Warner, "Modern Trends in the American Law of Arrest" (1943) 21 Can.B.Rev. 192, 210; Warner and Cabot, Judges and Law Reform (1936) 26.

[116] Sutherland, Principles of Criminology (1939) 264.

[117] Note, "The Administration of Bail" (1931) 41 Yale L.J. 293, 298.

[118] Beeley, The Bail System in Chicago (1927) 13-22; Champlin, "Reform in Criminal Procedure" (1893) 7 Harv.L.Rev. 189, 198. The courts look with disfavor upon arrests for petty offenses at night or on Sunday

tion of a personal recognizance for a bond with sureties.[119] The latter proposal is possibly not valid in states in which constitutional provisions prescribe that persons shall be bailable only by sufficient sureties, unless the requirement of sureties be interpreted as merely directory. Where an appeal is taken by the prosecution, it may be that no surety or security should be required.

On the other hand, an English writer has stated that the "English observer is apt to be shocked by the apparent ease with which bail is obtainable in America by prisoners who are charged with grave offences and who thus remain at liberty while the numerous stages of a somewhat dilatory procedure are carried through." [120] Unfortunately, constitutional revision is almost impossible to secure.

The Wickersham Crime Commission has suggested as a major subject requiring further research: "Development of recommendations or conclusions upon the organization, methods and principles of the administration of the fixing of bail and enforcement of bail, in the direction of the individualization of bail determinations based on the his-

---

or at other times when bail is hard to obtain. Perkins, "The Law of Arrest" (1940) 25 Iowa L.Rev. 201, 257.

[119] Beeley, The Bail System in Chicago (1927) 166-167; Criminal Justice in Cleveland (1922) 290; Morse and Beattie, "Survey of the Administration of Criminal Justice in Oregon" (1932) 11 Ore.L.Rev. (Supp.) 1, 98, 117. In England the magistrate may dispense with sureties. Archbold, Criminal Pleading, Evidence and Practice (30th ed.1938) 74. Under Rule 46(d) of the Federal Rules of Criminal Procedure, "in proper cases no security need be required." In France and elsewhere on the Continent before the war, bail was demanded only from wealthy defendants. Ploscowe, "Measures of Constraint in European and Anglo-American Criminal Procedure" (1935) 23 Geo.L.J. 762, 777-778. See also Hazard, "Soviet Criminal Procedure" (1941) 15 Tulane L.Rev. 220, 227.

[120] Brunyate, "The American Draft Code of Criminal Procedure, 1930" (1933) 49 L.Q.Rev. 192, 193.

tory, character, standing, personality and record of the accused." [121]

The Wickersham Crime Commission found the weaknesses in bail to be in administration rather than in procedure. "The causes of the unsatisfactory workings of the bail system in so many parts of the country are to be found, in varying degrees in different localities at different times, in (1) the lack of sufficiently strong magistrates or administrative officials to administer the system wisely and discriminately; (2) too much pressure of work to enable it to be done intelligently, due to the excessive number of arrests in comparison with the prosecutions which are carried out to trial for the offense charged; and (3) the influence of politics, particularly active in this connection, and the bane of inferior courts in all connections." [122] As to what may be done by legislation, the Commission refers to the American Law Institute Code of Criminal Procedure.

In large cities a centralized municipal criminal court would seem to be necessary to improve the administration of bail.[123] Centralization makes possible a closer scrutiny

[121] Nat. Com. on Law Obs. and Enf., Report on Prosecution (1931) 184.

[122] Nat. Com. on Law Obs. and Enf., Rep. on Crim. Proc. (1931) 22-23. See also Moley, Our Criminal Courts (1930) 56-59; Pound, Criminal Justice in America (1930) 186. It has been said that the "alliance of professional bondsmen with underworld characters on the one hand and unscrupulous lawyers and officials on the other are on the whole still among the unsolved problems of Justice." Glueck, Crime and Justice (1936) 162. The procedure on bail is about the same as in the days of Blackstone. Pound, Criminal Justice in America (1930) 108-109.

[123] That has been the experience in Detroit. Harley, "Detroit's New Model Criminal Court" (1920) 11 J.Crim.L. 389. See also "Detroit Court Solves Bail Problem" (1933) 16 J.Am.Jud. Soc. 143; Comment (1942) 26 J.Am.Jud.Soc. 40. In 1927 a bail bond branch of the municipal court was established in Chicago. Illinois Crime Survey (1929) 410. See also Mis-

of bondsmen by restricting their activities to one court. It makes more difficult the peddling of applications for bail. It should make easier the observation of bail administration.

---

souri Crime Survey (1926) 215-217; Moley, Our Criminal Courts (1930) 57-59.

CHAPTER IV

GRAND JURY

1. Stage in Proceedings

AFTER preliminary examination and grant or denial of bail, "next follows presentation of the case to a grand jury, which may find there is no probable cause for the prosecution to go on, or may find an *indictment* or formal accusation." [1] A criminal proceeding may be initiated by a grand jury finding an indictment against persons not bound over by magistrates.[2] In that event, arrest or summons follows the indictment.

In most cases considered by the grand jury, arrests already have been made, preliminary hearings held, and the defendant released on bail or committed to jail.[3] It seems likely that the cases originated by the grand jury are those which can be best investigated by the secret procedure of a grand jury hearing prior to arrest.[4] That is to say, cases originate with the grand jury where the local authorities and the prosecutor refuse to act. Or they may originate there as a matter of convenience when the first suspicion

[1] Nat. Com. on Law Obs. and Enf., Rep. on Crim. Proc. (1931) 16-17.

[2] Such indictment has been called an "original" indictment. Illinois Crime Survey (1929) 298.

[3] Nat. Com. on Law Obs. and Enf., Report on Prosecution (1931) 175, 211, 224; Criminal Justice in Cleveland (1922) 232; Illinois Crime Survey (1929) 196, 298; Miller, J., "Informations or Indictments in Felony Cases" (1924) 8 Minn.L.Rev. 379, 389; Dession, "From Indictment to Information—Implications of the Shift" (1932) 42 Yale L.J. 163, 177, 180. This was true in England when the grand jury existed there. Kenny, Outlines of Criminal Law (13th ed.1929) 470.

[4] Survey of the Administration of Criminal Justice in Oregon (1932) 11 Ore.L.Rev. (Supp.) 62, 84.

that certain charges should be brought comes to light in the course of a grand jury investigation. The proper consideration of cases originated elsewhere keeps the grand jury from originating many itself.

In a few states a preliminary examination before a magistrate is a prerequisite to action by the grand jury.[5] But in practically all indictment jurisdictions, including the federal, the holding of a preliminary examination has never been required as a condition precedent to the further progress of a felony prosecution.[6] The prosecuting attorney can thus ignore this first step and initiate a prosecution by securing an indictment. If a preliminary examination is held and the accused discharged, an indictment may still be found and the accused brought in on a bench warrant. If the accused is bound over, the prosecuting attorney may change the bindover charge to one more serious in securing an indictment. The majority rule has not been much criticized, although in 1849 the New York Code Commissioners felt that so unrestricted a form of accusation was dangerous because indictments based on little or no evidence would be found, on charges which the accused might have satisfactorily explained if afforded an opportunity to do so before a committing magistrate; it was also urged that a compulsory preliminary examination

[5] 27 Am. Jur., Indictments and Information, § 13, p.596; Ann. Cas. 1912 D 147.

[6] Dession, "From Indictment to Information—Implications of the Shift" (1932) 42 Yale L.J. 163, 168. This was substantially the situation in England at the date of abolition of the grand jury. "In 1859 the Vexatious Indictments Act made committal by justices one of the necessary conditions to the preferring of an indictment in certain cases which were added to by statute from time to time. Still, in the case of most crimes until 1933, an indictment could be preferred by a private individual on his own initiative, and there has certainly been at least one recent example of the exercise of this right." Burrows, "Criminal Law and Procedure" (1935) 51 L.Q.Rev. 36, 50.

involved a responsible accuser from whom redress might be sought if the accusation was malicious or unfounded.[7]

The grand jury is an Anglo-American institution. France had it for a brief time and then abolished it.[8] There is no grand jury in Alberta, British Columbia, Manitoba, Quebec, and Saskatchewan.[9]

2. History in England

Stephen points out that since the Norman Conquest there have been three modes of accusation in criminal cases; namely, appeal or accusation by a private person, indictment or accusation by a grand jury, and informations which are accusations either by the Attorney General or by the Master of the Crown Office.[10]

The consecutive history of the grand jury goes back to the Assize of Clarendon issued by Henry II in 1166, based not on Anglo-Saxon precedents, but the Frankish inquests as adopted in Normandy.[11] The law required

[7] Fourth Report of the New York Commissioners on Practice and Pleadings (Code of Criminal Procedure) (1849) xxxvii-xxxviii; Dession and Cohen, "The Inquisitorial Functions of Grand Juries" (1932) 41 Yale L.J. 687, 704.

[8] Esmein, A History of Continental Criminal Procedure (Simpson's trans. 1913) 410, 432, 440, 444, 475, 498. It was established in 1791 and abolished in 1808. However, the dossier must be referred to and found sufficient by three judges of a superior court. Note (1921) 21 Col.L.Rev. 376, 378.

[9] Martin, J., "The Preliminary Hearing: Canadian Practice" (1937) 1 J. Crim.L. 109 (Eng.). See Kains, How Say You? A Review of the Movement for Abolishing the Grand Jury System in Canada (1893); Kains, "The Grand Jury" (1902) 1 Can.L.Rev. 219.

[10] 1 Stephen, A History of the Criminal Law of England (1883) 244. The history of appeals as a method of accusation is discussed by Stephen at 245-250. See also Orfield, Criminal Appeals in America (1939) 14-15; 2 Holdsworth, A History of English Law (3d ed.1923) 197-198, 256-257, 320-364; 3 Holdsworth, A History of English Law (3d ed.1923) 608-609.

[11] "Under the Carlovingian monarchy an actual jury of denunciation,

twelve knights or other freemen of every hundred, and four men of every township, to send in accusations of murder, robbery, larceny, and harboring of criminals.[12] Arson and forgery were added in 1176 under the Assize of Northampton. The law as to the number and qualifications of the jurors to be summoned by the sheriff was somewhat indefinite. In practice at the Assizes, the grand jury was composed of the county magistrates whose names were called over until twenty-three at most had appeared. Other good and lawful men of the county might serve, no special qualifications being required. In the time of Blackstone they were usually gentlemen of the best figure in the county.

The earliest recorded juries were employed to discover and present facts in answer to inquiries from the king. The grand jury is directly descended from such juries since its function is to discover, and present to the king, persons suspected of serious crime. Just as in modern times, the grand jury could present from their own knowledge or from the information of others.[13] In the thirteenth

---

'jury de denonciation,' is seen to be in operation. It appears both in the secular courts, where the text shows it first from the beginning of the 800's, and in the ecclesiastical courts." Esmein, A History of Continental Criminal Procedure (Simpson trans. 1913) 83.

[12] 4 Bl. Comm. *301; 1 Stephen, A History of the Criminal Law of England (1883) 185-186, 251-254; 1 Holdsworth, History of English Law (3d ed.1923) 321-323; 1 Pollock and Maitland, History of English Law (2d ed.1905) 137-155, and Vol. 2, pp.647-653; Moley, Politics and Criminal Prosecution (1929) 127-131; McCrimmon, "The Grand Jury" (1901) 1 Can.L.Rev. 127; Langbein, "The Jury of Presentment and the Coroner" (1933) 33 Col.L.Rev. 1329. The history of the grand jury in England during the seventeenth and eighteenth centuries is discussed in Esmein, A History of Continental Criminal Procedure (Simpson's trans. 1913) 332-350.

[13] Historically the grand jury could not summon witnesses in a general investigation to discover crimes. Note (1938) 38 Col.L.Rev. 1943, 1498.

and earlier part of the fourteenth centuries, all or some of the grand jury always formed part of the petit jury; and the judges sometimes took the view that, when the members of a petit jury which had indicted a defendant acquitted him, they had contradicted themselves and could be punished. The separation of the grand jury from the petit jury revealed the true function of the grand jury as being merely to say whether from the evidence for the prosecution there was probable ground for suspicion.[14]

At the date of its abolition in England the grand jury consisted of from twelve to twenty-three, with twelve required to indict.[15] There were no property qualifications for grand jurors at Assizes, and women were eligible. The presiding judge charged them concerning the bills to be laid before them. They heard the witnesses for the prosecution, but did not hear the defendant or his witnesses, nor was counsel for the defendant present. They were not bound by rules of evidence. It was conducted in private, without records except for the names of the witnesses examined. The grand jurors usually acted without

[14] It has, however, been said: "The ancestors of our 'grand jurors' are from the first neither exactly accusers, nor exactly witnesses; they are to give voice to common repute." 2 Pollock and Maitland, History of English Law (2d ed.1905) 642. In the time of Blackstone, a "grand jury, ought to be thoroughly persuaded of the truth of an indictment so far as their evidence goes, and not to rest satisfied merely with remote probabilities; a doctrine that might be applied to very oppressive purposes." 4 Bl. Comm. *301.

[15] 1 Stephen, A History of the Criminal Law (1883) 273-274; Stephen, A Digest of the Law of Criminal Procedure (1883) 119-124; Kenny, Outlines of Criminal Law (13th ed.1929) 462; Howard, Criminal Justice in England (1931) 352-354; Harris, Principles of the Criminal Law (11th ed.1908) 352-355; Roscoe, Criminal Evidence (15th ed.1928) 244-245. For a description of the English grand jury at the beginning of the nineteenth century by a French lawyer, see Cottu, On the Administration of Criminal Justice in England (1822) c.2.

having the depositions before them. Of the bills laid before them they ignored about two per cent. If a bill was not found, a bill might be preferred before a subsequent grand jury. The grand jury had the power to find a bill of indictment without any previous inquiry before a magistrate into the truth of the accusation, although this had been limited by the Vexatious Indictments Act of 1859.[16]

With insignificant exceptions the grand jury was abolished in England in 1933.[17] The abolition was effected on a plea of economy. On the merits the reform in the procedure on preliminary examination and the separation of the functions of the police and the justices of the peace had made the grand jury less essential. The argument for retention that the grand jury might be a protection of accused persons against oppression did not convince the English.[18] If the evidence showed a prima facie case, it was the duty of the grand jury to return a true bill. If on the other hand they found no true bill because the legislation was viewed as oppressive, a government passing such legislation would find other ways. Historically, grand juries have, except on rare occasions, been willing to return true bills in "political" cases.

[16] Kenny, Outlines of Criminal Law (13th ed.1929) 470-471; Harris, Principles of the Criminal Law (11th ed.1908) 354-355.

[17] See Administration of Justice (Miscellaneous Provisions) Act, 1933, 23 & 24 Geo. V, c.36, § 1; Lieck, "Abolition of Grand Jury in England" (1935) 25 J.Crim.L. 623; Heyting, "The Abolition of Grand Juries in England" (1933) 19 A.B.A.J. 648; Elliff, "Notes on the Abolition of the English Grand Jury" (1938) 29 J.Crim.L. 3; Burrows, "Criminal Law and Procedure" (1935) 51 L.Q.Rev. 36, 49-51; Archbold, Criminal Pleading, Evidence and Practice (30th ed.1938) 59; Kenny, Outlines of Criminal Law (15th ed.1942) 545.

[18] Burrows, "Criminal Law and Procedure" (1935) 51 L.Q.Rev. 36, 51n.; Lieck, "Abolition of the Grand Jury in England" (1935) 25 J.Crim. L. 623; Butler, "Developments in Criminal Law—1910-1935" (1935) 129 The Law Times 325, 326.

The last notable defense of the grand jury in England was made by Professor Holdsworth in a letter dated July 13, 1933. He wrote, "Ever since 1681, when the ignoramus of a grand jury saved Lord Shaftesbury from a trial for treason, it is clear that the grand jury is capable of being a real safeguard for the liberties of the subject. These liberties need safeguards even more today than they did in 1681, because bureaucrats of Whitehall who dominate the Cabinet which in turn dominates the House of Commons have established a more effectual and a more oppressive tyranny than the Stuarts ever succeeded in establishing. We cannot in these days afford to lose one of our few remaining securities for freedom of speech and action." [19]

Under the present English procedure any person may prefer a bill of indictment charging an indictable offense, provided that the accused has been committed for trial or that the bill is preferred by the direction or with the consent of a judge of the High Court.[20] The preferment of a bill with such consent offers the prosecutor an opportunity to secure the reversal of a decision of examining magistrates with which he is not satisfied. Some flexibility in drawing the indictment of a defendant committed for trial is permitted. Any counts founded on evidence disclosed in

[19] Quoted by Elliff, "Notes on the Abolition of the English Grand Jury" (1938) 29 J.Crim.L. 3, 20. The Marquess of Hartington stated: "Suppose it came to pass that we had in this country a Fascist Government which created a whole mass of new offenses—such as holding views disrespectful of the Government. . . . [In such case] the grand jury might be a very constitutional safeguard and prove of immense value." *Ibid.* 21.

[20] Lieck, "Abolition of the Grand Jury in England" (1935) 25 J. Crim. L. 623, 624; Administration of Justice (Miscellaneous Provisions) Act, 1933; Harris and Wilshere, Principles and Practice of the Criminal Law (17th ed.1943) 432-436.

the depositions, which might be lawfully joined in the same indictment with the counts charging the offense for which the defendant is committed, may either be substituted or included, and a charge of previous conviction, or of being a habitual criminal or a habitual drunkard, may be added. A bill becomes an indictment when signed by the proper officer of the court, who has been satisfied that there has been a committal or a direction or consent. The judge may, if satisfied that these requirements have been complied with, direct the proper officer to sign.

3. Constitutional Guarantee

With respect to prosecutions in the federal courts, the Fifth Amendment provides: "No person shall be held to answer for a capital, or otherwise infamous crime, unless on a presentment or indictment of a grand jury, except in cases arising in the land or naval forces, or in the militia, when in actual service in time of war or public danger." Many state constitutions have similar provisions.[21] The constitutions of ten states provide that the legislature may modify or abolish the grand jury.[22] The due process clause of the Fourteenth Amendment is not violated by a state statute permitting prosecution without indictment.[23]

There are certain constitutional restrictions on legislative regulation of the grand jury. In cases where a defendant has the right to an indictment, he may insist on his right to one drawn by a grand jury. A statute depriving a certain class of the right would be unconstitutional.[24]

[21] A.L.I. Code of Crim. Proc. (1930) commentaries 414-431.

[22] A.L.I. Code of Crim. Proc. (1930) commentaries 431.

[23] Hurtado v. California, 110 U.S. 516, 4 Sup.Ct. 111, 28 L.Ed. 232 (1884). Nor is the due process clause of the state constitution. State v. Saunders, 66 N.H. 39, 87 (1889). Jones v. Robbins, 8 Gray (Mass.) 329, 342 (1857).

[24] Davis v. Pierse, 7 Minn. 13 (1862).

A change in the common-law number of jurors has been held invalid.[25] At common law the grand jury consisted of from twelve to twenty-three jurors, of whom twelve had to favor an indictment.[26] A provision impairing the secrecy of grand jury hearings has been held invalid; [27] as has one providing that irregularity in the drawing should not prevent qualified jurors from returning a valid indictment.[28] It has been held that the common-law territorial jurisdiction of the grand jury cannot be enlarged.[29] Improper legislative interference might be attacked on the ground that the legislature is trenching upon the judicial domain, the grand jury being an integral part of the court.[30]

Pending the conclusion of an admittedly valid investigation preparatory to impeachment, the legislature may not suspend an equally proper judicial inquiry into the same facts.[31] On principle the legislature may not act prospectively either; that is to say, forbid the courts to order a grand jury investigation until the legislature shall have concluded. Consistently with this reasoning, the courts should not themselves interfere with the legislative proceedings. Both investigatory bodies may legally proceed concurrently, although this may impair the efficiency of both and the confidence of the public. As a matter of public

[25] State v. Barker, 107 N.C. 913, 12 S.E. 115 (1890); State v. Hartley, 22 Nev. 342, 40 Pac. 372 (1895).

[26] 4 Bl. Comm. *302, *306.

[27] Opinion of the Justices, 232 Mass. 601, 123 N.E. 100 (1919).

[28] Commonwealth v. Brown, 121 Mass. 69 (1876). But the legislature may regulate qualifications and methods of impaneling. Thompson and Merriam, Juries (1882) §§ 480-486.

[29] Ex parte Slater, 72 Mo. 109 (1880). *Contra:* Mack v. People, 82 N.Y. 235 (1880).

[30] Imboden v. People, 40 Colo. 142, 90 Pac. 608 (1907); Wilson v. United States, 77 F. (2d) 236 (C.C.A. 8th, 1935).

[31] In re Investigation by the September 1938 Dauphin County Grand Jury, (1938) 52 Harv.L.Rev. 151, 156, (1938) 38 Col.L.Rev. 1493.

policy, except for the completely unsatisfactory record of impeachment proceedings, the legislature should have precedence. Possibly the solution is a grand jury chosen to represent the state as a whole.[32]

4. Present Status in the United States

In many states statutes have been passed giving the prosecutor the option of proceeding by indictment or information, and permitting the defendant to waive indictment. As a result in some counties a grand jury has not been called for many years, while in others its use is confined to conducting investigations.[33] Even in this field its supremacy has been threatened, statutes having been passed allowing investigations to be carried on before a magistrate who thus becomes a one-man grand jury.[34] Connecticut and Michigan now have such statutes.[35]

5. Purpose and Function

It is not the function of the grand jury to pass on guilt or innocence, but only to decide whether or not there is sufficient evidence to justify the standing of trial.[36] The

[32] (1938) 52 Harv.L.Rev. 151, 157.

[33] Moley, "The Initiation of Criminal Prosecutions by Indictment or Information" (1931) 29 Mich.L.Rev. 403; Morse, "A Survey of the Grand Jury System" (1931) 10 Ore.L.Rev. 101.

[34] Marsh, "Michigan's One Man Grand Jury" (1924) 8 J. Am. Jud. Soc. 121; Dession and Cohen, "The Inquisitorial Functions of Grand Juries" (1932) 41 Yale L.J. 687, 689, 692; Moley, Politics and Criminal Prosecution (1929) 146-148; Dession, "From Indictment to Information—Implications of the Shift" (1932) 42 Yale L.J. 163, 191-192; Winters, "The Michigan One-Man Grand Jury" (1945) 28 J. Am. Jud. Soc. 137; Gallagher, "The One-Man Grand Jury—A Reply" (1945) 29 J. Am. Jud. Soc. 20.

[35] Note (1942) 26 J. Am. Jud. Soc. 42, 79.

[36] Wood and Waite, Crime and Its Treatment (1941) 413. But where evidence for the accused is heard, it may almost amount to a trial.

purpose of grand jury proceedings is to secure the citizen "from an open and public accusation of crime and from the trouble, expense and anxiety of a public trial before a probable cause is established by the presentment or indictment of a grand jury." [37] The grand jury "is justly regarded as one of the securities to the innocent against hasty, malicious and oppressive public prosecutions." It is organized for the purpose of discovering and reporting to the court all offenses committed within its jurisdiction.[38] At first that was its sole purpose. The United States Supreme Court has stated that the "most valuable function of the grand jury was not only to examine into the com-

[37] Shaw, C. J., in Jones v. Robbins, 8 Gray (Mass.) 329 (1857); Ex parte Bain, 121 U.S. 7 Sup.Ct. 781, 30 L.Ed. 849 (1887). See also Note (1931) 65 U.S.L.Rev. 528, 532. "It is supposed to serve as an effective 'filter' through which unjustified accusations cannot pass, and is thus a protection of innocence." Wood and Waite, Crime and Its Treatment (1941) 414. Maitland states that it "saves a certain number of innocent persons from the shame and annoyance of a public trial." Justice and Police (1885) 139. Historically this was the second purpose developed. "But with the abuse of power by royal officers, the grand jury developed into the judicial protector of liberty that was so highly prized as a check against royal persecution." Note (1938) 38 Col.L.Rev. 1493, 1496. "The recognized function of the grand jury and the justification for its existence, aside from its inquisitory powers, is the protection it affords suspected persons against the hardship of actual trial upon accusations not warranted by the usable evidence." Waite, Note (1932) 30 Mich.L.Rev. 928, 929.

[38] "Historical evidence seems to indicate that the original purpose of the grand jury was to provide a method of initiating prosecutions by means of a group of the best men of the community." Moley, Politics and Criminal Prosecution (1929) 127. See also Commonwealth v. Woodward, 157 Mass. 516, 32 N.E. 939 (1893). An English writer states it was established "in order to multiply accusations of crime." Kenny, Outlines of Criminal Law (13th ed.1929) 462. "The power to inquire by a grand jury, which dates back to 1166, was originally a power to compel the grand jury to disclose those who were suspected of grave criminal offenses and present the offender by sworn accusation. It was the most important method of enforcing the law in the absence of adequate police or a prosecutor's office." Note (1938) 38 Col.L.Rev. 1493, 1496.

mission of crimes, but to stand between the prosecutor and the accused, and to determine whether the charge was founded upon credible testimony or was dictated by malice or personal ill will."[39] It is not their function, where no crime is found, to criticize individuals,[40] although they may make statements as to general conditions within their jurisdiction. Today it may serve as a citizen agency for the exercise of general inquisitorial powers with respect to social conditions and the conduct of public officers.[41] It should cooperate with the prosecuting attorney, hence it may accurately be said that its "function with respect to accusation is simply to control prosecution in the exceptional case."[42]

6. Manner of Selection

There are two chief methods of selecting grand jurors in the United States.[43] By one method, grand jurors are drawn by lot from some such lists as the tax rolls or registration list. By the second and preferable method, they are chosen by some official or officials who may exercise discretion in the selections. In most states grand jury lists are prepared by jury commissioners or boards of super-

[39] Hale v. Henkel, 201 U.S. 43, 20 Sup.Ct. 370, 50 L.Ed. 652 (1906).

[40] In re Report of Grand Jury Appeal of Perring, 152 Md. 616, 137 Atl. 370 (1927); Bennett v. Kalamazoo Circuit Judge, 183 Mich. 200, Ann. Cas. 1916 E. 233 (1914); 22 A.L.R. 1366; 24 Am. Jur., Grand Jury, § 36, p.859; Dession and Cohen, "The Inquisitorial Functions of Grand Juries" (1932) 41 Yale L.J. 687, 705-711; Nahum and Schatz, "The Grand Jury in Connecticut" (1931) 5 Conn.B.J. 111, 144-145; Konowitz, "The Grand Jury as an Investigating Body of Public Officials" (1936) 10 St. John's L.Rev. 219, 225-227.

[41] Willoughby, Principles of Judicial Administration (1929) 193-194.

[42] Dession, "From Indictment to Information—Implications of the Shift" (1932) 42 Yale L.J. 163, 177.

[43] Morse, "A Survey of the Grand Jury System" (1931) 10 Ore.L.Rev. 217, 226-239.

visors or town officials. In most states also grand jurors and petit jurors are selected from the same jury list. On the whole, the caliber of grand jurors is perhaps higher than that of petit jurors.[44]

7. Additional Grand Juries

In some states constitutional provisions are deemed to prevent the legislature from authorizing the impaneling of a special or additional grand jury to function at the same time and in the same county with a regular grand jury attending on the same court.[45] In other states where there is no such constitutional restraint, the legislature may authorize additional juries.[46] Rule 6(a) of the Federal Rules of Criminal Procedure permits the court to order one or more grand juries to be summoned at such times as the public interest requires. The American Law Institute Code is silent on the subject.

8. Size, Race, and Sex

The size of the grand jury ranges from 23 in 13 states, to 5 to 7 in two states.[47]

[44] Morse, "A Survey of the Grand Jury System", (1931) 10 Ore.L.Rev. 295, 307.

[45] In re Opinion to the Governor, 62 R.I. 200, 4 Atl. (2d) 487, 121 A.L.R. 806 (1939). See 38 C.J.S., Grand Juries, § 3, p.895; 24 Am. Jur., Grand Jury, § 17, p.843.

[46] People v. Grayden, 333 Ill. 429, 164 N.E. 832 (1929). See Henry B. Chamberlin, "Special Grand Juries in Illinois" (1931) 22 J.Crim.L. 163.

[47] Indiana has six. Indiana Ann. Statutes (Burns, 1933) § 9-801. In Virginia and Iowa it may be from 5 to 7. See State v. Cavanaugh, 32 N.M. 404, 258 Pac. 209, 53 A.L.R. 706 (1927); Willoughby, Principles of Judicial Administration (1929) 187. Reduction to 7 jurors is recommended by Deck, "Some Needed Reforms in Criminal Procedure" (1917) 8 J.Crim.L. 325, 328. In Canada there are 13. Riddell, "The Judiciary and the Administration of Justice in the Province of Ontario" (1922) 6 J. Am. Jud. Soc.

Protection against racial discrimination is secured by recent holdings that if, in the selection of grand jurors, the members of a race are intentionally and systematically excluded from grand jury service solely on account of race, the conviction of a member of that race will be reversed as a denial of equal protection of the law as guaranteed by the Fourteenth Amendment.[48]

At common law the "grand jury" was limited to men.[49] The present status of women as jurors is purely statutory.[50] Several decisions have assumed, however, that jury service is a privilege which accompanies that of voting, and that the Nineteenth Amendment qualified them to act as jurors.[51]

9. Irregular Organization

Irregularities in drawing, selecting, summoning, or impaneling a grand jury are not grounds for reversal of a conviction, unless the appellant can show such errors to have been prejudicial.[52] But the presence of a disqualified

---

6, 16. In England at its abolition, the grand jury could consist of any number from 12 to 23. Kenny, Outlines of Criminal Law (13th ed.1929) 462. The federal grand jury consists of from 16 to 23. See Fed. Rules of Crim. Proc., Rule 6(a), retaining the existing rule. See "Defects in Criminal Justice" (1925) 11 A.B.A.J. 297. A grand jury of from 7 to 15 was proposed in an Illinois bill of 1937, which failed of passage.

[48] Pierre v. Louisiana, 306 U.S. 354, 59 Sup.Ct. 536, 83 L.Ed. 757 (1939); Smith v. Texas, 311 U.S. 128, 61 Sup.Ct. 164, 85 L.Ed. 84 (1940).

[49] 3 Bl. Comm. *362; State v. Hartley, 22 Nev. 342, 40 Pac. 372 (1895).

[50] People v. Jensen, 167 Pac. 406 (Cal. App. 1917).

[51] Commonwealth v. Maxwell, 144 Atl. 825 (Pa. 1921), 31 Yale L.J. 108. See also Parus v. District Court, 174 Pac. 706 (Nev. 1918), (1922) 20 Mich.L.Rev. 669. The contrary view has been taken in Massachusetts, New Jersey, and New York. In re Opinion of the Justices, 130 N.E. 685 (Mass. 1921); State v. James, 114 Atl. 553 (N.J. 1921); In re Grilli, 110 Misc. 45, 179 N.Y.Supp. 795 (Sup.Ct. 1920).

[52] Gravitt v. State, 279 Pac. 968 (Okla. Cr. App. 1929); Gaughan v.

juror is held reversible error, although only those expressly excluded by statute from service on the grand jury will be found disqualified.[53] A minority view, in construing the statutes, defines the method of selecting and impaneling the grand jury as mandatory rather than directory, hence any technical departure from the prescribed method is reversible error, even though no bias or prejudice is shown. For instance, reversible error was found when a vacancy on the grand jury was filled by calling a bystander instead of notifying the clerk to draw additional names from the jury box as directed by statute.[54] But all jurisdictions agree that delayed objections to the constitution of the grand jury are unavailing. Furthermore, defects must be pleaded with great particularity, anticipating all such matters as would defeat the plea if alleged by the prosecution.[55] These defects may be attacked by a plea in abatement.[56] Under Sections 215 and 216 of the American Law Institute Code of Criminal Procedure, the plea in abatement would be abolished and objections to irregularities in the constitution of the grand jury would be taken by motion to quash the indictment.[57]

It has been held that an indictment found by a grand jury from which the court had excused certain members of its panel on its own motion should be quashed.[58] But not

---

United States, 19 F. (2d) 897 (C.C.A. 8th, 1927); cf. Canada Criminal Code (1927) § 899.

[53] Crowley v. United States, 194 U.S. 461, 24 Sup.Ct. 731 (1904); cf. Sledge v. State, 208 Ala. 154, 93 So. 875 (1922) (cousin of injured party not disqualified).

[54] Eshelman v. State, 169 N.E. 861 (Ind. 1930), 39 Yale L.J. 1063.

[55] State v. Lowe, 164 N.E. 857 (Ind. 1929).

[56] Hicks v. State, 97 Fla. 199, 120 So. 330 (1929); 2 Bishop, New Criminal Procedure (2d ed.1913) §§ 883, 889.

[57] This is the rule in Delaware. Del. Laws (1925) c.239, § 4847A.

[58] State v. Smith, 145 La. 1091, 83 So. 264 (1919), (1920) 33 Harv.L.Rev.

every departure from prescribed methods of selecting a grand jury should lead to this result. If the court is given some latitude and no prejudice is shown, there should be no reversal. It should not be valid to argue that the court reduced unduly the elements of chance which might have worked in favor of the defendant.

In a recent decision, seemingly the first of its kind, the court denied the application of a citizen to inquire into the right of a grand jury, alleged to have been fraudulently chosen, to hold office.[59] It was held that a grand juror is not an officer, since his office lacks the element of duration and tenure, and therefore may not be subjected to quo warranto proceedings. It would seem, however, that since the grand juror performs a function prescribed by law he is considered a public officer.[60] The grand juror exercises some part of the sovereign power of the state. If, however, it be conceded that a grand juror is not a public officer against whom quo warranto may be brought, mandamus would be the only proper remedy to test his authority.[61] Although mandamus is said to be discretionary, in the absence of quo warranto, the court should grant it, because it is then the only method by which society can control an important public function.[62]

It seems clear that the federal and state constitutional provisions as to the grand jury reflect the importance at-

---

866. The trial judge, after examining the first 12 men drawn from the panel as to their qualifications, of his own motion excused 6 of them. Three of the 6 clearly would have been entitled to the exemption had they claimed it.

59 McDuffie v. Parkerson, 173 S.E. 151 (Ga. 1933), 43 Yale L.J. 1317.

60 Mechem, A Treatise on the Law of Public Offices and Officers (1880) § 1 *et seq.*

61 Johnson v. Superior Court, 102 Cal. App. 178, 283 Pac. 331 (1929); Ferris, The Law of Extraordinary Legal Remedies (1926) §§ 187-191.

62 Note (1934) 43 Yale L.J. 1317, 1319.

tached to the grand jury as a safeguard against governmental oppression. The attainment of that objective requires that the grand jury be fairly drawn and that it be impartial.[63] But the rights of the accused are not violated because the grand jury which indicted him, a Socialist, was composed entirely of persons belonging to other political parties and of property owners.[64]

10. Challenges

Under the historic English practice, the sheriff was directed to summon for service as grand jurors "good and lawful men"; that is to say, residents of his county, over twenty-one years of age, citizens, and not having been convicted of any infamous crime.[65] They must also be freeholders. In this country the qualifications are specified by statute.[66]

The fact that a grand juror has personal knowledge concerning a case does not disqualify him;[67] nor does a prejudice held by the grand juror,[68] nor his having formed

[63] Rottschaefer, Handbook of American Constitutional Law (1939) 779.

[64] Ruthenberg v. United States, 245 U.S. 480, 38 Sup.Ct. 168, 62 L.Ed. 414 (1918).

[65] Keigwin, Cases in Criminal Procedure (1939) 237; Nahum and Schatz, "The Grand Jury in Connecticut" (1931) 5 Conn.B.J. 111, 125.

[66] State v. Easter, 30 Ohio St. 542 (1876). The lack of qualifications required decreases the value of the grand jury. Miller, J., "Informations or Indictments in Felony Cases" (1944) 8 Minn.L.Rev. 379, 402n. In 36 states there are no qualifications as to education or ownership of property. "Defects in Criminal Justice" (1925) 11 A.B.A.J. 297.

[67] People v. Looney, 314 Ill. 150, 145 N.E. 365 (1924). *Contra:* 1 Bishop, New Criminal Procedure (4th ed.1895) § 852.

[68] 24 Am. Jur., Grand Jury, § 10, p.839; 38 C.J.S. § 6(f), p.989; Coblentz v. State, 164 Md. 558, 166 Atl. 45 (1933); Commonwealth v. Brown, 147 Mass. 585, 18 N.E. 587, 1 L.R.A. 620, 9 Am. St. Rep. 736 (1888). See criticism by Nahum and Schatz, "The Grand Jury in Connecticut" (1931) 5 Conn.B.J. 111, 128; 24 Am. Jur., Grand Jury, § 11, p. 840.

or expressed an opinion upon it.[69] Even the aggrieved person or persons closely related to him have been permitted to sit.[70] An early case held that a state employee was not a competent grand juror.[71] It has been held that nothing but what is specified in the statute will disqualify a grand juror.[72] Section 120 of the American Law Institute Code of Criminal Procedure permits a challenge of an individual grand juror for bias, thus altering the common-law rule. Rule 6(b) of the Federal Rules of Criminal Procedure simply permits challenge on the ground that the juror is not legally qualified. In practice challenges are seldom made.[73] There are no peremptory challenges as at the trial itself. The finding of an indictment, though followed by an acquittal, is a serious and a humiliating matter. Hence the right to challenge should not be abolished.[74]

Challenges may be to the panel or array for some ir-

69 Commonwealth v. Woodward, 157 Mass. 516, 32 N.E. 939 (1893); State v. Chairs, 9 Baxt. (Tenn.) 196 (1877). *Contra:* Wharton, Criminal Pleading and Practice (9th ed.1889) § 346, p.239; Bishop, New Criminal Procedure (4th ed.1895) § 852, p.491; § 881, p.509.

70 State v. Russell, 90 Iowa 469, 58 N.W. 915, 28 L.R.A. 195 (1894).

71 Crawford v. United States, 212 U.S. 183, 29 Sup.Ct. 260, 35 L.Ed. 465 (1908). Compare United States v. Wood, 57 Sup.Ct. 177 (1936), (1937) 21 Minn.L.Rev. 608.

72 Territory v. Hart, 7 Mont. 42, 14 Pac. 768 (1887).

73 Report of the Crimes Survey Committee, Law Association of Philadelphia (1926) 185; 5 Longsdorf, Cyclopedia of Federal Procedure (1929) § 2003, p.505.

74 A New York state judge has pointed out that numerous improper and unwarranted indictments are returned. See Note (1922) 8 A.B.A.J. 326. During the First World War, English grand juries were often carried away by war hysteria. Burdick, "Criminal Justice in America, Possibility of Improvement by Statutory Changes and Constitutional Amendments Affecting Procedure" (1925) 11 A.B.A.J. 510, 511. But that serious delay results and that there is little danger of harm to the accused even though he cannot challenge are asserted by Sloss, J., "Reform of Criminal Procedure" (1911) 1 J.Crim.L. 705, 716; Lawler, J., "Needed Reforms in Criminal Law and Procedure" (1911) 1 J.Crim.L. 877, 884.

regularity in the manner of selecting or summoning those presented as members, or to the individual or individuals summoned because of their disqualifications.[75] Some cases hold that such challenges can be interposed only before the jury is sworn.[76] The United States Supreme Court has held valid a state statute requiring that objections to the composition of a grand jury must be made before the indictment, although in the particular case the defendant was indicted for a crime committed after the impaneling of the grand jury.[77] The objection may be raised at this early stage by one who apprehends that he will be indicted or by another person as *amicus curiae*.[78] This rule may be fair enough if the accused is notified that his case is to be brought before the coming grand jury, and he is in position to be present.[79] Otherwise it would operate harshly.

[75] A.L.I., Code of Crim. Proc. (1931) § 118. In this country the cases have usually held that there is a common-law right of challenge. *Ibid.* commentaries 452. Under § 118, the prosecuting attorney or a defendant who has been told to answer may challenge. In some states there is no right to challenge the grand jury. In some states individual jurors may be challenged but not the panel. 38 C.J.S., Grand Jury, §§ 29 and 30. See also Steiner, "Impaneling a Grand Jury in Illinois" (1936) 2 John Marshall L.Q. 63; Report of the Commission on the Administration of Justice in New York State (1939) 67. In a few states the prosecution may not challenge, though the defendant may. "Defects in Criminal Justice" (1925) 11 A.B.A.J. 297, 298. Section 118 of the American Law Institute Code of Criminal Procedure allows both defendant and prosecution the right to challenge.

[76] Section 121 of the A.L.I. Code of Crim. Proc. (1931); Fed. Rules of Crim. Proc. Rule 6(b)(1); State v. Ames, 90 Minn. 183, 96 N.W. 330 (1903); Musick v. People, 40 Ill. 268 (1866); Lascelles v. State, 90 Ga. 347, 16 S.E. 945 (1892); State v. Smith, 192 Iowa 218, 180 N.W. 4 (1920); Crowley v. United States, 194 U.S. 461, 24 Sup.Ct. 73, 48 L.Ed. 1075 (1904). But see United States v. Gale, 109 U.S. 65, 3 Sup.Ct. 1, 27 L.Ed. 857 (1883).

[77] Lang v. New Jersey, 209 U.S. 467, 28 Sup.Ct. 594, 52 L.Ed. 894 (1908).

[78] Tucker's Case, 8 Mass. 286 (1811).

[79] Agnew v. United States, 165 U.S. 36, 17 Sup.Ct. 235, 41 L.Ed. 624

When, however, the accused has had no opportunity to object before the bill was found, the weight of modern authority is that he may take advantage of the objection by motion to quash the indictment or by plea in abatement.[80] The latter is the proper remedy in all cases of contested fact. Under this rule, the accused may allege any defects which he discovers before pleading to the indictment. Since, however, pleading to an indictment admits its genuineness as a record and is a waiver of all irregularities antecedent to its return,[81] the defendant is not free, after a plea of not guilty, to take advantage of any impropriety which may come to his knowledge upon subsequent information.[82] Hence, objections on these accounts cannot be raised by motion or plea during the trial,[83] or after the verdict.[84] If, however, any substantial defect in the organization appears upon the face of the record, a motion in arrest of judgment has been held to lie.[85]

(1897); Wharton, Criminal Pleading and Practice (9th ed.1889) § 350, p.241.

[80] Wharton, Criminal Pleading and Practice (9th ed.1889) § 350, p.242; 38 C.J.S., Grand Jury, § 28 c.; Keigwin, Cases in Criminal Procedure (1939) 239; Pointer v. State, 89 Ind. 255 (1883). Some jurisdictions allow the accused to except on arraignment. State v. Rockafellow, 6 N.J. Law, 332 (1796); Newman v. State, 14 Wis. 393 (1861). It was held too late after pleading in bar. State v. Carver, 49 Me. 588, 77 Am. Dec. 275 (1861); State v. Heffernan, 28 R.I. 477, 68 Atl. 364 (1907). See (1922) 21 Mich.L.Rev. 98.

[81] Frisbie v. United States, 157 U.S. 160, 15 Sup.Ct. 586, 39 L.Ed. 657 (1894); 1 Bishop, New Criminal Procedure (4th ed.1895) § 884.

[82] Agnew v. United States, 165 U.S. 36, 17 Sup.Ct. 235, 41 L.Ed. 624 (1897).

[83] 1 Bishop, New Criminal Procedure (4th ed.1895) § 886.

[84] Gamble v. State, 164 Md. 50, 163 Atl. 859 (1933); People v. Robinson, 2 Parker Cr. Rep. 235 (1855).

[85] People v. Gray, 261, Ill. 140, 103 N.E. 552, 49 L.R.A. (U.S.), 1215 (1913); Rodriguez v. United States, 198 U.S. 156, 25 Sup.Ct. 617, 49 L.Ed. 994 (1905).

Section 210 of the Institute Code provides for a motion to quash an indictment on the grounds; (a) that there was ground for challenge to the panel or to an individual grand juror and that the defendant had not been held to answer at the time the grand jurors were sworn; (b) that a person, other than a grand juror, was present while the grand jurors were deliberating or voting and there is reasonable cause to believe that the defendant was in fact prejudiced thereby; (c) that the requisite member of grand jurors did not concur in finding the indictment; and (d) that the grand jury had no authority to inquire into the offense charged. Rule 6(b)(2) of the Federal Rules of Criminal Procedure allows a motion to dismiss, if not previously determined upon challenge, but such motion must be made before trial. An indictment shall not be dismissed on the ground that one or more members of the grand jury were not legally qualified if it appears from the record kept that twelve or more jurors, after deducting the members not legally qualified, concurred in finding the indictment.[86]

11. Discharge and Excuse

At common law the grand jury usually serves during the entire term of court at which it has been summoned to attend.[87] Under Rule 6(g) of the Federal Rules of Criminal Procedure, a grand jury shall serve until discharged by

[86] See Mitchell, "Reform in Federal Criminal Procedure" (1932) 18 A.B.A.J. 732, 734.

[87] Riley v. State, 209 Ala. 505, 96 So. 599 (1923); 38 C.J.S., Grand Juries, § 32, p.1022; 24 Am. Jur., Grand Jury, § 6, p.836. Under Section 330 of the proposed Illinois Act of 1937, not enacted into law, the judge, by the order convening a grand jury, would fix the duration of its service at not more than sixty days, but could prolong it for the sole purpose of disposing of matters pending at the expiration of the original period.

the court but no grand jury may serve more than eighteen months; tenure and powers are not affected by the beginning or expiration of a term of court. The American Law Institute Code is silent on this matter.

A court may discharge or excuse a grand juror at any time before he is sworn.[88] It has been held that in the absence of statutory authority, a court has no power to excuse grand jurors for any cause after they have once been impaneled and sworn.[89] Under the Federal Rule 6(g), at any time for cause shown, the court may excuse a juror either temporarily or permanently, and in the latter event may impanel another person in place of the juror excused. The American Law Institute Code is silent on this subject.

12. Order of Procedure

When the grand jurors appear in court they are organized by the choice of a foreman, such choice being usually by the court.[90] The jurors are then sworn to make inquiry about crimes, to keep the proceedings secret, and to present none for malice, nor leave any unpresented for fear, favor, or affection.[91] The jurors are then instructed by the judge, who may direct their attention to specific matters requiring their action, and may advise them as to the law and as to their duties.[92] After the charge by the court, the grand jury withdraws to receive and pass on accusations of crime.[93] Ordinarily the prosecuting attorney presents written accusations and supports such accusations

[88] Robinson v. State, 92 Tex. Cr. 527, 244 S.W. 599 (1922).

[89] Ex parte Love, 49 Tex. Cr. 475, 93 S.W. 551 (1906); 38 C.J.S., Grand Juries, § 31, p.1021; 24 Am. Jur., Grand Jury, § 22, p.848.

[90] A.L.I. Code of Crim. Proc. (1930) § 125.

[91] *Ibid.* § 126.

[92] *Ibid.* § 127.

[93] *Ibid.* § 128.

by evidence.[94] The written accusation is called a bill. If a majority of the jurors agree that the allegations of the bill are correct, the bill is indorsed "a true bill," and the foreman signs it.[95] If a bill is found a true bill, it is returned by the foreman in open court.[96]

13. Difference Between Indictment and Presentment

One of the most confusing distinctions in the law is that between indictment and presentment. Both indictment and presentment are "presented" to the court.[97] Both are accusations.[98] The presentment, however, is made by the grand jury. An indictment, on the other hand, is someone else's accusation which has been drawn up into a bill of indictment and preferred to the grand jury, who examine the evidence in support of it and then find it to be a true bill. In finding an indictment the grand jury is acting like a trial jury, except that it hears but one side of the case.[99] In making a presentment the grand jury is playing the role of a prosecutor. For that reason a presentment must be drawn up into a bill of indictment and resubmitted to the grand jury.[100] In a number of states the practice is for the grand jury to examine the witnesses for the prosecutor

[94] *Ibid.* § 135.

[95] *Ibid.* §§ 140-141.

[96] *Ibid.* § 147. Fed. Rules of Crim. Proc. Rule 6(f) of the Federal Rules of Criminal Procedure provides for return by the grand jury to a judge in open court. The Constitution does not require that the grand jury as a body deliver the report. Breese v. United States, 226 U.S. 1, 33 Sup.Ct. 1, 57 L.Ed. 97 (1912).

[97] Respublica v. Honeyman, 2 Dall. 228 (U.S. 1795).

[98] 1 Chitty, Crim. Law, 162. See Keigwin, Cases in Criminal Procedure (1939) 198-200.

[99] Commonwealth ex rel. Jack v. Crans, 3 Pa. L.J. 442, 453 (1844). See Note (1938) 38 Col.L.Rev. 1493, 1497, n.24.

[100] Commonwealth v. Green, 126 Pa. 531, 539 (1889).

without the charge having been drawn up into a formal bill of indictment. If the jury then finds the charge to be true, an indictment is drawn up.[101]

The presentment is not included in the Federal Rules of Criminal Procedure as a third type of accusation. There may be some argument that the Fifth Amendment uses the term "presentment" as an alternative for "indictment." [102] It may be granted that if the term is used in the Fifth Amendment with the meaning it had when the Constitution was adopted, it means a statement of facts by grand jurors upon which an indictment would be subsequently framed by a United States attorney, or it may mean an accusation by the grand jurors upon presentation of facts to them by a special prosecutor acting for a private individual.[103] But it is no longer used in the federal courts because of the constant availability of a United States attorney to assist the grand jury and because of the decline of prosecution by private individuals.[104]

14. Powers

The grand jurors have plenary inquisitorial powers and may upon their own motion originate charges against offenders, even though no preliminary proceedings have been had before a magistrate and though neither the prosecuting attorney nor the court has laid the matter before them.[105] They may investigate any matter appearing to in-

[101] State v. Freeman, 13 N.H. 488 (1843); Field's Charge to the Grand Jury (1872) 2 Sawyer 667, 668 (C.C.D. Cal. 1872).

[102] Compare Ex parte Wilson, 114 U.S. 417 (1885).

[103] See 4 Bl. Comm. *301; Charge to the Grand Jury (Field, J.) 2 Sawyer 667 (C.C.D. Cal., 1872); McKinney v. United States, 199 Fed. 25 (C.C.A. 8th, 1912).

[104] Hughes, Federal Practice, Jurisdiction and Procedure (1932) § 7012.

[105] Blaney v. State, 74 Md. 153, 21 Atl. 547 (1891); People v. Sheridan, 349 Ill. 202, 181 N.E. 617 (1932). It has, however, been held that it can-

volve violation of the criminal law, whether their attention is directed by the court or the prosecuting attorney, or the supposed guilt is brought to their notice by the personal knowledge of some member of the jury or by information communicated to one or more of those members.[106] To justify such an inquiry, it is not necessary that any formal charge or the allegation of any specific wrongdoing be preferred; witnesses may be summoned and questioned with a view to ascertaining the existence of conditions which will justify the drawing up of charges and the accusation of specific crimes.[107]

In some states the authority of the grand jury is limited by long usage or by statute. In Pennsylvania, indictments cannot be brought except for offenses which are of public notoriety, or which are referred to the grand jury by the prosecuting attorney or the court.[108] In certain states there can be no indictment unless there has previously been a preliminary examination.[109] In a few states the summon-

---

not employ detectives and set about trapping criminals. Burns v. Holt, 138 Minn. 165, 164 N.W. 590 (1917), (1922) 7 Minn.L.Rev. 59. See also (1928) 12 Minn.L.Rev. 761, (1935) 35 Col.L.Rev. 613; Note (1923) 26 A.L.R. 605.

106 Hale v. Henkel, 201 U.S. 43, 26 Sup.Ct. 370, 50 L.Ed. 652 (1906), 6 Col.L.Rev. 347; Note (1923) 22 A.L.R. 1351; 2 Wilson's Works (Andrews ed.1876) 213-214; A.L.I. Code of Crim. Proc. (1930) §§ 132 and 136; Wharton, Criminal Pleading and Practice (9th ed.1889) § 334, p.228. In Virginia the grand jury may find an indictment on the unsworn statement of two of its members or on the sworn statement of one member. In Canada the grand jury may not pass upon any matter not submitted to them by Crown counsel. Riddell, "Criminal Law in Canada" (1926) 10 Minn.L.Rev. 557, 561.

107 Blair v. United States, 250 U.S. 273, 39 Sup.Ct. 468, 63 L.Ed. 979 (1919).

108 Commonwealth v. Green, 126 Pa. St. 531, 17 Atl. 878 (1889); Wharton, Criminal Pleading and Practice (9th ed.1889) § 338, p.230. As to the rule in North Carolina, see (1938) 17 N.C.L.Rev. 43.

109 Keigwin, Cases in Criminal Procedure (1939) 167, 241; Wharton, Criminal Pleading and Practice (9th ed.1889) § 339, p.233.

ing of witnesses comes under the complete control of the court.[110] Under New York and California statutes grand juries seeking further information may order the district attorney to issue subpoenas for such other witnesses as they direct.[111]

In most states the inquisitorial powers of the grand jury are very broad. But there are limits. It may not inquire into those matters which are not within the jurisdiction of the court to which it is an appendage.[112] In the absence of civil statutes it may not inquire into civil matters. It may not make a general investigation upon the chance or speculation that commissions of some crimes may be discovered. It may receive only legal evidence, although this limitation is more theoretical than real because the receipt of illegal evidence is usually not sufficient to require that an indictment be quashed. It may not receive evidence in favor of the accused. It may not employ private detectives to aid in the exercise of its inquisitorial powers. It should not violate the constitutional guarantees against unreasonable searches and seizures, nor compel a person to be a witness against himself in a criminal proceeding. Where it is abusing its powers, the court to which it is an appendage may prevent such abuse by denying use of the court's processes,[113] or by discharging the grand jury,[114] or by the issuance of a writ of prohibition.[115]

[110] Lewis v. Commissioners, 74 N.C. 194 (1876).

[111] (1938) 17 N.C.L. Rev. 43, 51.

[112] It has been held, however, that a state statute authorizing an indictment for lynching to be brought by the grand jury of a county adjoining the one where the crime was committed is constitutional. State v. Lewis 55 S.E. 600 (N.C. 1906), (1907) 20 Harv.L.Rev. 404.

[113] In re National Window Glass Workers, 287 Fed. 219 (D.C. Ohio, 1922).

[114] Baker v. State, 183 Ind. 1, 5, 108 N.E. 7, L.R.A. 1915 D., 1061 (1915).

[115] Petition of McNair, 324 Pa. 48, 187 Atl., 498 (1936).

The contumacious and unlawful refusal by a witness to answer truthfully and without evasion proper interrogations before a grand jury has been treated as a contempt of court.[116] The refusal of a witness before a federal grand jury to answer questions, with an allegation of self incrimination for a state crime as his excuse when brought before the court and admonished, is also a contempt of the court of which the grand jury is a part.[117] Contempts must be dealt with by the court and not by the grand jury.[118]

During the whole time of their proceedings grand jurors are protected in the discharge of their duties, and no action lies against them for their findings even when predicated upon malice.[119] One of the arguments frequently advanced by opponents of the grand jury is that it is irresponsible. The evidence does not clearly indicate, however, that grand juries frequently find indictments when the magistrate would not have bound over or the prosecuting attorney would not have filed an information.[120]

116 Finkel v. McCook, 247 App. Div. 57, 286 N.Y.S. 755 (1936), affirmed, 271 N.Y. 636, 3 N.E. (2d) 460 (1936); Schleier v. United States, 72 F. (2d) 414 (C.C.A. 2d, 1934).

117 Camarota v. United States, 111 F. (2d) 243 (C.C.A. 3d, 1940).

118 In re Gannon, 69 Cal. 541, 11 Pac. 240 (1886).

119 Hunter v. Mathis, 40 Ind. 356 (1872); Sidener v. Russell, 34 Ill. App. 446 (1890); 1 Bishop, New Criminal Procedure (4th ed.1895) § 870(b), p.504.

120 It has been stated that grand juries in England during the First World War were abolished, in part because they "were being carried away by war hysteria, and bringing accusations against persons against whom one exercising calm judgment would find no ground for suspicion." Burdick, "Criminal Justice in America" (1925) 11 A.B.A.J. 510, 511.

15. Evidence

The investigation made by the grand jury is an *ex parte* inquiry, in which only the evidence for the prosecution is heard.[121] One whose conduct is being investigated by a grand jury has no right to petition the grand jury or to appear before it. It is improper to send a letter to the grand jury, showing on its face the intention that it shall be considered with respect to a pending case.[122] The accused has no right to have witnesses testify in his favor.[123] In some jurisdictions the court in the exercise of discretionary or statutory authority grants the privilege.[124] The grand jury should not, however, return an indictment unless persuaded that, from the evidence available, the accused is guilty. If the testimony preponderates in favor of innocence or does not show probable cause, no indictment should be found.[125]

Only competent evidence should be heard by the grand

[121] The defendant is not entitled to notice of a grand jury investigation. United States v. Lewis, 192 Ed. 633 (D.C. Mo. 1911); Edwards, The Grand Jury (1906) 103. In New York a defendant may testify. Packer (Nov. 1941) 45 Law Notes 17, 20.

[122] Duke v. United States, 90 F. (2d) 840, 112 A.L.R. 316 (C.C.A. 4th, 1937). Furthermore no individual may, acting as a volunteer, approach the grand jury as to matters before them or which may come before them. United States v. Kilpatrick, 16 Fed. 765 (N.C. 1883), (1938) 17 N.C.L. Rev. 43, 46.

[123] Commonwealth v. McNary, 246 Mass. 46, 140 N.E. 255, 29 A.L.R. 483 (1923); Charlton v. Kelly, 229 U.S. 447, 57 L.Ed. 1374, 46 L.R.A. (N.S.) 397 (1913).

[124] State v. Hamlin, 47 Conn. 95 (1879); Note (1938) 38 Col.L.Rev., 1493, 1498; A.L.I. Code of Crim. Proc. (1931) § 139; Nahum and Schatz, "The Grand Jury in Connecticut" (1931) 5 Conn.B.J. 111, 131, 133.

[125] Field's Charge to Grand Jury (1872) 2 Sawyer 667, Fed. Cas. No. 18, 255. A century ago, however, it was urged that grand jurors were never agreed as to whether they were trying the case or ascertaining if it was fit to be tried. Elliff, "Notes on the Abolition of the English Grand Jury System" (1938) 29 J.Crim.L. 3, 9.

jury, that is to say, testimony or documentary proof presented under oath and by witnesses qualified to testify before a petit jury.[126] If some improper evidence is heard by the grand jury, the indictment is valid unless it is shown that there was no other and competent proof upon which the indictment was found.[127] It is a controversial question as to what extent, if any, the courts may inquire into the evidence upon which a grand jury acted. In several states it has been held that in no case will an inquiry be made into the evidence with a view to setting aside an indictment.[128] This is a minority view.[129] Other courts hold that only in extreme cases will the court consider such an allegation,[130] as where there is no legal evidence at all,[131] or there was no competent testimony going to prove some fact essential to the guilt of the accused.[132] In a third group of states, an indictment will be quashed if the testimony of one or more incompetent witnesses was heard by the grand jury.[133] Under the generally accepted rule, the indictment is not vitiated by illegal evidence if there was some competent proof taken by the grand jury of a kind

[126] Nanfito v. United States, 20 Fed. (24) 376 (C.C.A. 8th, 1927).

[127] People v. Lauder, 82 Mich. 109, 46 N.W. 956 (1890); Tinkhoff v. United States, 86 Fed. (2d) 868 (C.C.A. 9th, 1937). See 5 Longsdorf, Cyclopedia of Federal Procedure (1929) § 1988, pp.498-499; (1929) 38 Yale L.J. 680.

[128] Pick v. State, 143 Md. 192, 121, 918 (1923); State v. Dayton, 23 N. J.L 49 (1850); Noll v. Dailey, 72 W.Va. 520, 79 S.E. 668, 48 L.R.A. (N.S.) 1207 (1913).

[129] *Contra:* Beale, Criminal Pleading and Practice (1899) 45.

[130] McKinney v. United States, 199 Fed. 25 (C.C.A. 8th, 1912).

[131] State v. Cole, 145 Mo. 672, 47 S.W. 895 (1898); Sparrenberger v. State, 53 Ala. 581 (1875).

[132] Brady v. United States, 24 Fed. (2d) 406 (C.C.A. 8th, 1918).

[133] Nanfito v. United States, 20 Fed. (2d) 376 (C.C.A. 8th, 1927). See People v. Burleson, 195 N.Y.S. 284, 119 Misc. 107 (1921), (1929) 27 Mich. L.Rev. 955.

to establish every substantial element of the case.[134] It has been argued that the minority rule against reviewing the evidence before the grand jury is preferable, since the indictment is merely an accusation and because such review results in delay and another loophole for the defendant.[135] Inquiry has sometimes been refused with respect to evidence obtained by illegal search and seizure,[136] and in the case of a violation of the accused's privilege against self incrimination.[137]

In some cases the view is taken that an inquiry into the evidence before the grand jury is objectionable because in many states the proceedings of the grand jury can be proved only by the testimony of grand jurors themselves, who are not competent to disclose what occurred in the jury room. But in several states, under statute or by established usage, the testimony is preserved by a stenographic or other written report. This transcript, known as the minutes of the grand jury, should give a satisfactory indication of the proof. The prevalent view is that it is in

[134] Keigwin, Cases in Criminal Procedure (1939) 242-243; Friscia v. United States, 63 F. (2d) 977 (C.C.A. 5th, 1933); Clark, Handbook of Criminal Procedure (2d ed. by Mikell, 1918) 132, 135; McKinney v. United States, 199 Fed. 25 (C.C.A. 8th, 1912), (1913) 13 Col.L.Rev. 168.

[135] (1929) 27 Mich.L.Rev. 955, 956, (1921) 30 Yale L.J. 421, (1929) 38 Yale L.J. 680. In Canada the proceedings before the grand jury may not be re-examined. Riddell, "The Judiciary and the Administration of Justice in the Province of Ontario" (1922) 6 J. Am. Jud. Soc. 6, 16. See also A.L.I. Code of Crim. Proc. (1931) § 138; Report of the Special Committee on the Revision of the Code of Criminal Procedure to the Commission on the Administration of Justice (N.Y. 1935) chapter on Grand Jury, pp.11-12, 19-20.

[136] United States v. Harbin, 27 F. (2d) 892 (N.D. Miss. 1928), (1929) 38 Yale L.J. 680; State v. Foell, 37 Idaho 722, 217 Pac. 608 (1923).

[137] Mencheca v. State, 28 S.W. 203 (Tex. Cr. App. 1894); State v. Lloyd, 152 Wis. 24, 139 N.W. 514 (1913).

the discretion of the court to determine when access may be had to such records.[138]

Suppose the extreme case of one ultimately to be indicted is recognized as such from the start. If the proceeding were by way of preliminary examination by a magistrate, the accused would not have to answer.[139] But in a grand jury proceeding no charge need be laid against him, and he is not yet as a matter of form a party. Some courts refuse to recognize the actual facts of the situation, and the accused must therefore testify.[140] The feeling is sometimes expressed that the witness's privilege of refusing to answer specific incriminating questions should be enough.[141]

Many cases are less clear in their holdings. While the court will talk about a proceeding "in fact aimed against one," yet it will avoid its application in the particular case.[142] For instance, it may be concluded that the objection was not raised in the correct manner; [143] or that the error was not prejudicial; [144] or that reversal of a conviction would only mean the circuity of a proper re-indictment.[145] But the privilege lurks in the background, avail-

[138] State v. Rhoads, 81 Ohio St. 397, 91 N.E. 186, 27 L.R.A. (N.S.) 558, 18 Ann. Cas. 415 (1910); People v. Sweeney, 213 N. Y. 37, 106 N.E. 913 (1914); Havenor v. State, 125 Wis. 444, 104 N.W. 116 (1905).

[139] 8 Wigmore, Evidence (3d ed.1940) § 2360.

[140] United States v. Kimball, 117 Fed. 156 (C.C.S.D.N.Y. 1902); Pick v. State, 143 Md. 192, 121 Atl. 918 (1923); People v. Lauder, 82 Mich. 109, 46 N.W. 956 (1890), two judges dissenting. See Comment (1940) 49 Yale L.J. 1059, 1070.

[141] State v. Comer, 157 Ind. 611, 62 N.E. 45 2 (1902). See Note (1937) 27 J.Crim.L. 746.

[142] Radinsky v. People, 66 Colo. 179, 180 Pac. 88 (1919); People v. Page, 116 Colo. 386, 48 Pac. 326 (1897).

[143] State v. Andersen, 10 Ore. 448 (1882).

[144] State v. Donelson, 45 La. Ann. 745 (1893).

[145] Lindsey v. State, 69 Ohio St. 215, 224, 69 N.E. 126, 129 (1903).

able where abuse is strongly felt. It has even been held that it is enough that the accused has been required to appear and testify and that it is not essential that the indictment be based upon the statements made by the accused before the grand jury or that the statements injured him in any way.[146]

A number of cases[147] have held that where the investigation before the grand jury is in fact a proceeding against the defendant, the defendant's constitutional right to freedom from self incrimination is violated if he is subpoenaed before the grand jury, sworn, and questioned though he makes no claim of privilege.[148] If, on the other hand, the person testifying is a mere witness, he must claim his privilege. A defendant is protected even though he is not under arrest, or openly charged with the crime or proceeded against in name. The indictment should be quashed apparently without inquiry as to whether there was other and unobjectionable evidence to support the charge.[149]

[146] Dession and Cohen, "The Inquisitorial Functions of Grand Juries" (1932) 41 Yale L.J. 687, 703. See also Nahum and Schatz, "The Grand Jury in Connecticut" (1931) 5 Conn.B.J. 111, 136-137.

[147] State v. Gardner, 82 Minn. 130, 139, 92 N.W. 529 (1902); see United States v. Edgerton, 80 Fed. 374, 376 (D.C. Mont. 1897).

[148] (1909) 9 Col.L.Rev. 80, (1931) 15 Minn.L.Rev. 344; 68 A.L.R. 1501; People v. Bermal, 71 Misc. 356, 128 N.Y.S. 524 (1911); Boone v. People, 148 Ill. 440, 36 N.E. 99 (1894); Ex parte Gauss, 223 Mo. 277, 122 S.W. 741 (1909); State v. Froiseth, 16 Minn. 296, Gilf 260 (1871). *Contra:* People v. Lauder, 82 Mich. 109, 46 N.W. 956 (1890), two judges dissenting; Gamble v. State, 164 Md. 50, 163 Atl. 859 (1933); United States v. Pleva, 66 F. (2d) 529 (C.C.A. 2d, 1933).

[149] Boone v. People, 148 Ill. 440, 36 N.E. 99 (1894). *Contra:* People v. Lauder, 82 Mich. 109, 46 N.W. 956 (1890); United States v. Brown, 1 Sawy. 531, Fed. Cas. No. 14, 671 (D.C. Ore. 1871).

16. Secrecy

Grand jurors take an oath of secrecy.[150] This oath is in accordance with a concept of public policy which prescribes that the inquiry made by a grand jury shall be conducted in privacy and that the proceedings prior to indictment shall not be revealed to the general public. At common law, members of a grand jury are not competent witnesses to prove facts going to invalidate their indictment.[151] As a general rule a juror cannot be required or even permitted to testify to any things which occurred in the jury room. No grand juror can be required to disclose how any juror voted, or what opinions were expressed in the deliberations of that body, or to state in detail the evidence upon which the action was had, or even to state whether or not an indictment was under consideration.[152] A grand juror may not testify that an indictment did not receive twelve votes,[153] or that there was no evidence supporting the charge made by an indictment.[154] Some cases

[150] 8 Wigmore, Evidence (3d ed.1940) §§ 2360-2362; 1 Bishop, New Criminal Procedure (4th ed.1895) § 856; In re Atwell, 140 Fed. 368 (D.N.C. 1905), (1906) 6 Col.L.Rev. 366; State v. Hamlin, 47 Conn. 95, 36 Am. Rep. 54 (1879). In actual fact, grand jury proceedings are often far from secret. Miller, J., "Informations or Indictments in Felony Cases" (1924) 8 Minn.L.Rev. 379, 389.

[151] McDonald v. Pless, 238 U.S. 264, 35 Sup.Ct. 783, 59 L.Ed. 1300 (1915); Lewis v. State, 132 Miss. 200, 96 So. 169 (1923); Vaise v. Delaval, 1 T. R. 11 (1785). See 8 Wigmore, Evidence (3d ed.1940) §§ 2361-2362; Wharton, Criminal Pleading and Practice (9th ed.1889) §§ 378-379, pp. 264-266.

[152] Keigwin, Cases in Criminal Procedure (1939) 244; A.L.I. Code of Crim. Proc. (1930) §§ 143-144.

[153] State v. Baker, 20 Mo. 338 (1855); Gitchell v. People, 146 Ill. 175, 33 N.E. 757 (1893). *Contra:* Sparrenberger v. State, 53 Ala. 481 (1875).

[154] State v. Beebe, 17 Minn. 241 (1871); State v. Davis, 41 Iowa, 311 (1875).

base secrecy on the grand juror's oath to keep counsel,[155] or on considerations of public policy; [156] in some there is a statutory requirement.[157]

The rule as to secrecy is subject to limitations. After an indictment has been made public, the need for secrecy is largely gone, and justice may require disclosure of some phases of the investigation.[158] It has been held that a grand juror may testify whether or not a certain person was examined by that body; [159] or that a witness before the grand jury swore to facts different from those which he stated upon the trial of the case.[160] Likewise a juror may be a witness to prove facts extrinsic to the evidence considered by the panel, such as the misconduct of a grand juror or of another person, the presence of one not a member, and similar matters.[161] Some cases go so far as to permit disclosure, whenever in the court's discretion justice demands it.[162] This is the position recommended in the American Law Institute Code of Criminal Procedure.[163]

[155] Cf. Gordon v. Commonwealth, 92 Pa. 216, 37 Am. Rep. 672 (1879).

[156] Cf. Sands v. Robison, 12 Sm. and M. 704 (Miss. 1849).

[157] Cf. Tindle v. Nichols, 20 Mo. 326 (1855).

[158] United States v. Reid, 12 How. (U.S.) 361, 13 L.Ed. 1023 (1851); State v. Wood, 53 N.H. 484 (1873). A witness may testify what he stated to the grand jury. R. v. Gibson, Car. & M. 672 (1842).

[159] Commonwealth v. Hill, 11 Cush (Mass.) 137 (1853); Ex parte Schmidt, 17 Cal. 212, 12 Pac. 55 (1886).

[160] Commonwealth v. Mead, 12 Gray (Mass.) 167, 71 Am. Dec. 741 (1858); State v. Wood, 53 N.H. 484 (1873); Gordon v. Commonwealth, 92 Pa. 216, 37 Am. Rep. 672 (1879). As to perjury prosecution, see Izer v. State, 77 Md. 110, 26 Atl. 282 (1893). See also A.L.I. Code of Crim. Proc. (1930) § 145.

[161] Mattox v. United States, 146 U.S. 140, 13 Sup.Ct. 50, 36 L.Ed. 917 (1892); State v. Kifer, 186 La. 674, 173 So. 169, 110 A.L.R. 1017 (1937).

[162] State v. Campbell, 73 Kan. 688, 85 Pac. 784 (1906); Attorney General v. Pelletier, 240 Mass. 264, 134 N.E. 407 (1920). See (1937) 37 Col. L.Rev. 315, 316; United States v. Socony-Vacuum Oil Co., 310 U.S. 658, 60 Sup.Ct. 1091, 84 L.Ed. 1129 (1940).

[163] Section 145. *Contra:* Tindle v. Nichols, 21 Mo. 326 (1855); Fother-

It has been stated: "Where the situation calls for public exposure of whole systems of corruption rather than merely prosecution of particular individuals there would appear to be no necessity for the prohibition against any disclosure of what takes place in the grand jury room." [164]

17. Minutes

At common law it was not necessary to keep full records of the testimony before the grand jury. It has been recommended that . . . "a stenographic report and transcript should be made of all testimony before the grand jury. This will have the effect of spurring the assistant prosecutor to his best efforts; will have the effect of reducing careless or perjured testimony; will have the effect of placing in the hands of the trial prosecutor information which will assist him in the adequate presentation of the case to the trial judge and jury." [165]

Where a written record of the grand jury proceedings is kept, there arise not only questions of admissibility but also of access to the record. Although it is a matter of discretion, the tendency of the courts has been not to allow the defendant to examine notes taken for their own pur-

---

ingham v. Adams Exp. Co., 34 Fed. 646 (C.C.E.D. Mo. 1888). Compare Fed. Rules of Crim. Proc., Rule 6(e); Nahum and Schatz, "The Grand Jury in Connecticut" (1931) 5 Conn.B.J. 111, 138-140; Edwards, The Grand Jury (1906) 118; Bishop, New Criminal Procedure (4th ed.1895) § 857, p.494; 24 Am. Jur., Grand Jury, § 50, p.867; 38 C.J.S., Grand Juries, § 43, 1062.

164 Dession and Cohen, "The Inquisitorial Functions of Grand Juries" (1932) 41 Yale L.J. 687.

165 Criminal Justice in Cleveland (1922) 211. Under § 130 of the American Law Institute Code of Criminal Procedure (1930), the foreman on the demand of the prosecuting attorney or of the grand jurors shall appoint a stenographer to take in shorthand the testimony received. See also Morse, "A Survey of the Grand Jury System" (1931) 10 Ore.L.Rev. 295, 330-332.

poses by the grand jurors or by the prosecutor.[166] The Federal Rules of Criminal Procedure do not provide for inspection of the minutes of the grand jury. In a number of states there are statutes which require or permit minutes to be kept.[167] Under some of these statutes the minutes are always available to the defense.[168] In New York there may be disclosure upon the written order of the court; a motion to inspect is addressed to the discretion of the court.[169] Lack of a preliminary examination before a magistrate may make a difference.[170] A bona fide attempt to quash the indictment on the ground that there was no competent evidence before the grand jury [171] or that defendant was unconstitutionally compelled to be a witness [172] will merit disclosure. The New York courts are divided as to whether mere insufficiency of evidence is enough,[173] and on inspection as an aid to defendant's preparation for trial.[174]

[166] State v. Rhoads, 81 Ohio St. 397, 91 N.E. 186 (1910); Franklin v. Commonwealth, 105 Ky. 237, 48 S.W. 986 (1898). See Nahum and Schatz, "The Grand Jury in Connecticut" (1931) 5 Conn.B.J. 111, 145; 3 C.J.S., Criminal Law, § 956, p.265; 38 C.J.S., Grand Juries, § 43, p. 1063.

[167] N. Y. Code Crim. Proc., § 952 I (Laws 1885, c.348, § 5).

[168] Iowa Code (1935) § 13730; Ky. Code Ann. (Carroll, 1932) Crim. Prac. § 110. See 23 C.J.S., Criminal Law, §§ 956, 1036; (1910) 1 J.Crim.L. 118; Perkins, "The Short Indictment Act" (1929) 14 Iowa L.Rev. 385, 395.

[169] People v. Strauss, 165 App. Des. 58, 150 N.Y.Supp. 991 (2d Dept. 1914). See *contra* report of a committee of the Bar Association of New York City (1934) 20 A.B.A.J. 89, 91. But compare Packer (Nov. 1941) 45 Law Notes 17.

[170] People v. Molineux, 27 Misc. 60, 57 N.Y.Supp. 936 (Gen. Sess. 1899). *Contra:* People v. Steinhardt, 47 Misc. 252, 93 N.Y.Supp. 1026 (1905).

[171] People v. Steinhardt, 47 Misc. 252, 93 N.Y.Supp. 1026 (1905).

[172] People v. Steinhardt, 47 Misc. 252, 93 N.Y.Supp. 1026 (1905).

[173] People v. Molineux, 27 Misc. 60, 57 N.Y.Supp. 936 (Gen. Sess. 1899) (granted); People v. Steinhardt, 47 Misc. 252, 93 N.Y.Supp. 1026 (Sup.Ct. 1905) (not granted).

[174] People v. Kressel, 142 Misc. 88, 254 N.Y.Supp. 193 (Sup.Ct. 1931)

There is not much authority concerning the minutes of a previous grand jury. It has been held that the court has no jurisdiction.[175] But inspection has been granted to a commissioner appointed by the governor to investigate accusations against a district attorney,[176] and to a police commissioner seeking to reopen a case in which the grand jury had failed to indict.[177] The Attorney General of the United States, prosecuting an indictment returned by a federal grand jury, applied to a state court for inspection of the minutes of the earlier state grand jury and was granted it.[178] Those decisions seem justifiable. The rule of secrecy is based on the following considerations of policy: (1) the avoidance of subornation of perjury;[179] (2) or of flight by the accused; (3) freedom of action in the grand jury room; and (4) protection of the reputation of an innocent accused from public knowledge that charges are being preferred against him.[180] The first two considerations have no application to a proceeding subsequent to that of the grand jury involved. The third appears to be for the benefit of the prosecution and may therefore be ignored when outweighed by other interests of the prosecution. The fourth loses its force when it once becomes known that the accused is being examined or tried. Since

(granted); People v. Coney Island Jockey Club, 68 Misc. 302, 123 N.Y. Supp. 669 (Sup.Ct. 1910) (not granted).

175 Man v. Delaware, L. & W. R. R., 99 Misc. 358, 163 N.Y.Supp. 1050 (Sup.Ct. 1917).

176 Matter of Crain, 139 Misc. 799, 250 N.Y.Supp. 249 (Gen. Sess. 1931). Cf. People v. Ewald, 144 Misc. 657, 259 N.Y.Supp. 314 (Sup.Ct. 1932).

177 People v. Luckman (County Court, N.Y. 1935), cited in (1937) 37 Col.L.Rev. 315, 317.

178 Matter of Attorney General of United States (1936), (1937) 37 Col. L.Rev. 315.

179 Commonwealth v. Mead, 12 Gray 167, 170 (Mass. 1858); People v. Ewald, 144 Misc. 657, 660, 259 N.Y.Supp. 314, 316 (Sup.Ct. 1932).

180 Sands v. Robison, 12 Sm. and M. 704, 711 (Miss. 1849).

the secrecy doctrine has been subjected to limitations for the defense, it is arguable that it should be similarly limited with respect to the prosecution.[181] There appears to be a continuing tendency to make exceptions to the rule of secrecy whenever warranted by the particular facts.

18. Witnesses

It has been held that witnesses called before the grand jury cannot testify to what took place before that body, as secrecy would not otherwise be possible.[182] At common law no oath of secrecy was required of witnesses before grand juries.[183] Thus in the absence of a statute providing for such oath, there should be no such oath required. It has been held, however, that a witness before a federal grand jury may be required to take an oath of secrecy, even though no federal statute imposes such an oath.[184] On the merits the rule seems sound, since considerations of public policy require that secrecy surround the activities of the grand jury. The witness should have no more freedom of disclosure than the grand juror.

It would appear that a witness who has taken the oath of secrecy may be released from his pledge when the

[181] See Fed. Rules of Crim. Proc., Rule 6(e).

[182] State v. Fasset, 16 Conn. 457 (1844). A witness has been held guilty of contempt of court even for a breach of the rule after discharge of the grand jury. In re Atwell, 140 Fd. 368 (D.N.C. 1905). *Contra:* People v. James Naughton, 38 How. Prac. 430 (N.Y. 1870); State v. Fish, 90 N.J.L. 17, 100 Atl. 181 (1917), affd., 91 N.J.L. 228, 102 Atl. 378, L.R.A. 1918 E. (1917); Edwards, The Grand Jury (1906) 120.

[183] Regina v. Hughes, 1 Car. & K. 519, 174 Eng. Rep. 919 (N.P. 1844). Witnesses take an oath that they will tell the truth. A.L.I. Code of Crim. Proc. (1930) § 137 and commentaries 499-503.

[184] Goodman v. United States, 108 Fed. (2d) 516 (C.C.A. 9th, 1939), (1940) 14 So. Calif.L.Rev. 80. An oath of secrecy is required in 37 districts. Rule 6(e) of the Federal Rules of Criminal Procedure does not apply to witnesses.

furtherance of justice so requires.[185] When the subject of the grand jury proceedings has been indicted or is in custody, he should be entitled to all information pertinent to his defense, even though such information must be got from one who appeared before the grand jury as a witness and who testified to the same facts before the grand jury.[186]

Often witnesses upon leaving the grand jury room immediately disclose to the suspected person the testimony against him, with the result that the defendant either prepares his defense or leaves the jurisdiction before he can be arrested. To remedy this, it has been proposed that it be made a misdemeanor for such a witness to disclose any part of his testimony until after the defendant shall have been arrested, and that such disclosure shall also be a contempt of court.[187]

19. Presence of Non-Jurors

It is a principle of public policy that the inquiry made by a grand jury shall be conducted in privacy and that the proceedings prior to an indictment be kept secret.[188] Accordingly no person who is not a member of the grand jury may be present when it is deliberating whether an indictment should be returned. The presence of such a per-

[185] As to when there may be a disclosure, see: United States v. Farrington, 5 Fed. 343 (N.D.N.Y. 1881); Atwell v. United States, 162 Fed. 97, 15 Ann. Cas. 253, 17 L.R.A. (N.S.) 1049 (C.C.A. 4th, 1908); Commonwealth v. Mead, 12 Gray, 167 (Mass. 1858).

[186] State v. Kemp, 124 Conn. 639, 1 Atl. (2d) 761 (1938).

[187] Campbell, "Some Needed Reforms in the Criminal Law" (1903) 6 Rep. Proc. Bar Assoc. of Ark. 53, 67. See also Deck, "Some Needed Reforms in Criminal Procedure" (1917) 8 J.Crim.L. 325, 331-332.

[188] Nahum and Schatz, "The Grand Jury in Connecticut" (1931) 5 Conn.B.J. 111, 140; Note (1920) 30 Yale L.J. 196.

son during the deliberations is ground to quash an indictment or for a plea in abatement.[189]

When testimony is taken, there must of course be present the grand jurors and the witness under examination. There may also be a prosecuting attorney or one of his assistants, to conduct the questioning and to advise the panel upon the import of the evidence and upon points of law.[190]

In some states it has been held that a stenographer must not be present at this stage.[191] But by the weight of authority, sometimes based on statute, it is permissible for a stenographer to be present.[192] In the federal courts, attorneys not regularly appointed assistants to the district attorney, but specially authorized by the attorney general to prosecute particular cases, are authorized to attend the

[189] State v. Coulter, 104 Miss. 764, 61 S. 706, 44 L.R.A. (N.S.) 1142 (1913); 1 Bishop, New Criminal Procedure (4th ed.1895) § 861, p.497; (1926) 24 Mich.L.Rev. 856; 24 Am. Jur., Grand Jury, § 42, p. 862; L.R.A. 1916D, 1123; (1911) 1 J.Crim.L. 783. One witness may not be present while another is testifying: Commonwealth v. Harris, 121 N.E. 409 (Mass. 1919) 28 Yale L.J. 712.

[190] McCullough v. Com., 27 Pa. St. 30 (1870); Shattuck v. State, 11 Ind. 473 (1858); Hale v. Henkel, 201 U.S. 43, 26 Sup.Ct. 370, 50 L.Ed. 652 (1906). As to assistant prosecutors, see United States v. Reed, 2 Blatchford, 435, Fed. Cas. No. 16134 (1852). For an interesting case in which the grand jury excluded a special prosecuting attorney, see Bruce, "The Judge and the Grand Jury" (1932) 23 J.Crim.L. 10, 13. See also Baker and DeLong, "The Prosecuting Attorney, Powers and Duties in Criminal Prosecutions" (1934) 24 J.Crim.L. 1025, 1058; First Report of Judicial Council of Connecticut (1928) 28-29.

[191] State v. Bowman, 90 Me. 363, 38 Atl. 331 (1898); United States v. Goldman, 28 Fed. (2d) 424 (D. Conn. 1928).

[192] State v. Bates, 148 Ind. 610, 48 N.E. 2 (1897); State v. Rhoads, 81 Ohio St. 397, 91 N.E. 186 (1910); (1916) 16 Col.L.Rev. 158; (1898) 11 Harv.L.Rev. 411; Re Montgomery, 126 App. Div. 309, 110 N.Y.S. 793 (1908); Act of Congress, May 18, 1933. See A.L.I. Code of Crim. Proc. (1930) § 133; Rule 6(d), Fed. Rules of Crim. Proc.

grand jury when it investigates their cases.[193] No one else, such as an unofficial attorney, employed by persons interested in obtaining an indictment, may be present.[194] No one other than the grand jurors should be present while the grand jury is voting or deliberating.

Under Rule 6(d) of the Federal Rules of Criminal Procedure, the following may be present while the grand jury is in session, though not while it is deliberating or voting: attorneys for the government, the witness under examination, interpreters when needed, and, for the purpose of taking the evidence, a stenographer. Section 133 of the American Law Institute Code of Criminal Procedure is similar in character. Under Section 210 of the Institute Code, a motion to quash an indictment lies on the ground that a person, other than a grand juror, was present while the grand jurors were deliberating or voting and there is reasonable cause to believe that the defendant was in fact prejudiced thereby.

20. Resubmission After Failure to Indict

It is an interesting question whether or not a grand jury may indict after an earlier failure to do so. The rules governing reconsideration after an ignoramus seem to allow resubmission, although the decisions and the statutes are not in complete agreement concerning the conditions under which this action is proper.[195] Blackstone recognized re-

[193] United States v. Fall, 56 App. D.C. 83, 10 Fed. (2d) 648 (1925). But see United States v. Goldman, 28 Fed. (2d) 424 (D. Conn. 1928). See People v. Hartonblower, 208 Ill. App. 465 (1917); Wharton, Criminal Pleading and Practice (9th ed.1889) § 366, p.257.

[194] Coblentz v. State, 164 Md. 558, 166 Atl. 45, 88 A.L.R. 886 (1933); Wilson v. State, 70 Miss. 595, 13 So. 225 (1893).

[195] 2 Bishop, New Criminal Procedure (2d ed.1913) 668; Joyce, Indictments (1908) 137; (1920) 69 U. of Pa. L.Rev. 80; (1933) 31 Mich.L.Rev. 1160.

submission to a new grand jury.[196] The federal courts allow complete freedom in resubmission.[197] A court may order resubmission, although the first indictment is dismissed on motion of the prosecution.[198] According to one view the resubmission must be in the form of a new bill.[199] In line with this view it has been held that new evidence is required; [200] and that a court should not grant permission to resubmit unless there is new evidence or the first grand jury hearing has been defective or incomplete because of fraud, mistake, ignorance, or negligence.[201] Where a court order is necessary, there must be a new order each time the jury reconsiders a rejected bill.[202] Of course there is nothing in the doctrine of double jeopardy, or in the nature of grand jury proceedings, to prevent reconsideration. Limitations on the right to reconsider are rather to be justified on the basis of policy. In fairness to the accused, he should not be subject to repeated harassment by means of resubmission if charges are found groundless.[203] Section 146 of the American Law Institute Code of Criminal Procedure takes account of this by requiring an order of the trial court as a prerequisite to resubmission.[204]

[196] 4 Blackstone (Wendell's ed.1854) 305. See also Beale, Criminal Pleading and Practice (1899) 44.

[197] United States v. Thompson, 251 U.S. 407, 40 Sup.Ct. 289, 64 L.Ed. 333 (1920); United States v. Bonavia, 41 F. (2d), 366 (D.N.Y. 1930).

[198] State v. Wright, 122 Ore. 377, 257 Pac. 699 (1927).

[199] State v. Brown, 81 N.C. 568 (1879).

[200] Richards v. State, 22 Neb. 145, 34 N.W. 346 (1887).

[201] People v. Dziegiel, 140 Misc. 145, 250 N.Y.S. 743 (1931).

[202] People v. Clements, 5 N.Y.Crim. 288 (1887).

[203] State v. Ledford, 203 N.C. 724, 166 S.E. 917 (1932), (1933) 31 Mich. L.Rev. 1160.

[204] This rule, however, covers only persons who have been held to answer. The cases of the original submission to the grand jury of a case against a person who has been held to answer are rare. Brunyate, "The American Draft Code of Criminal Procedure, 1930" (1933) 49 L.Q.Rev. 192, 198.

21. Dismissal for Failure to Indict

When a defendant has been committed for an offense and the grand jury fails to act within reasonable time, the defendant should be discharged.[205] Section 292 of the American Law Institute Code of Criminal Procedure provides for such a dismissal unless good cause to the contrary is shown, in which event there may be a continuance. In the event of such dismissal, under Section 294 there may not be another prosecution for the same offense without the order of the court in which the cause is pending.

22. Eliminations by Grand Jury

In the middle of the decade from 1920 to 1930, 12 per cent of all felony arrests in New York City, Cincinnati, and Cleveland were eliminated by the grand jury, 11 per cent in Chicago, 5 per cent in Baltimore, 3 per cent in St. Louis, and 2 per cent in Kansas City.[206] In the proportion of cases disposed of, the grand jury plays a much smaller part than do the magistrates at the preliminary examination.[207] Thus in Illinois, only 12 per cent of the cases were eliminated at the grand jury stage, compared to 44 per cent at the preliminary examination. In New York in

[205] 1 Bishop, New Criminal Procedure (4th ed.1895) § 870(a), p.504. See Rule 48(b), Fed. Rules of Crim. Proc.

[206] Moley, Politics and Criminal Prosecution (1929) 28. "In Illinois the grand jury is more important, being responsible for the elimination of 12% of all cases in which warrants were issued, and representing 21% of all cases presented to the grand jury. In other words, only about 80% of all cases entering the grand jury result in indictments. In Cleveland the grand jury eliminates 16% of all cases in which warrants were issued and 21% of all cases entering the grand jury. In New York (1925), 25% of all cases bound over were eliminated by this body." Report of the Minnesota Crime Commission (1934) 141.

[207] Glueck, Crime and Justice (1936) 84.

1933, 12 per cent were eliminated by the grand jury and 55 per cent at preliminary examination.

In 1925, 29.77 per cent of all cases submitted to the grand jury in New York City were eliminated and in 1926, 30.53 per cent of all cases so submitted in Chicago.[208] In 1919, 21.54 per cent of all cases submitted to the grand jury in Cleveland were eliminated by a no-bill.[209] In Missouri the grand jury "plays a negligible role in elimination." [210] In 1927 and 1928, 17.6 per cent of all cases submitted to the grand jury in Oregon were eliminated by it.[211] The proportion of eliminations throughout the country ranges from 2 to 30 per cent with a median proportion of 18.5 per cent.[212] Responsibility for improper eliminations rests largely on the prosecuting attorney [213] and the investigating officers, who have not been sufficiently diligent in procuring the necessary evidence.

23. Criticisms of Grand Jury

The grand jury system has been criticized as inflexible and overly formal. It has been contended that the use of indictments should be optional, instead of mandatory as under the present system. Grand jury proceedings should

208 Moley, Politics and Criminal Prosecution (1929) 41; Illinois Crime Survey (1929) 298-299.

209 Criminal Justice in Cleveland (1922) 179.

210 Missouri Crime Survey (1926) 275, 284. From 1922 to 1924, only .17 per cent of all the cases were eliminated by "no true bills."

211 "Survey of the Administration of Criminal Justice in Oregon" (1932) 11 Ore.L.Rev. (Supp.) 31, 63.

212 Nat. Com. on Law Obs. and Enf., Report on Prosecution (1931) 207. As to eliminations in Philadelphia from 1910 to 1923, see Report of the Crimes Survey Committee, Law Association of Philadelphia (1926) 401.

213 Criminal Justice in Cleveland (1922) 176; Illinois Crime Survey (1929) 299.

not be required for all types of felony cases, some of which may be solved better administratively. The amendment of indictments is almost impossible.[214] The indictment is often verbose, artificial, antiquated, and contains errors of a kind resulting in reversal of the conviction.

The historical situation making a grand jury indispensable has been substantially altered. In the days of royal and baronial despotism, the grand jury came to be viewed as an institution which would protect the people against the deprivation of their freedom. Today trial courts are not responsible to the executive, and other institutions give adequate protection against executive tyranny.[215] Moreover, the grand jury sits in secret and hears only the evidence for the prosecution, and the accused is given no opportunity to defend himself.[216] A preliminary hearing, on the other hand, is conducted in public with the defendant present.

It has even been claimed that the grand jury simply

[214] "Under the grand jury system an indictment is in theory, although not in fact, the statement of the grand jury, and therefore no amendment in it can be made except by the grand jury, and as the grand jury is ordinarily dismissed as soon as it has reported its indictments, a defect discovered after that time is fatal." Chaplin, "Reform in Criminal Procedure" (1893) 7 Harv.L.Rev. 189, 192.

[215] Criminal Justice in Cleveland (1922) 211-212. Moreover, in the early days, there were some two hundred capital crimes, while today there are very few.

[216] Stevenson, "Our Grand Jury System" (1886) 8 Crim.L.Mag. 711, 719; Chaplin, "Reform in Criminal Procedure" (1893) 7 Harv.L.Rev. 189, 190; Willoughby, Principles of Judicial Administration (1929) 184; Elliff, "Notes on the Abolition of the English Grand Jury" (1938) 29 J.Crim.L. 3, 16. See, in defense of secrecy, Edwards, The Grand Jury (1906), 42; Note (1921) 21 Col.L.Rev. 676. "The purpose of the constitutional preservation of indictment—protecting the accused—is to a large extent incompatible with the purpose of a grand jury investigation—obtaining evidence by which he may be convicted." (1938) 38 Col.L.Rev. 1493, 1495.

rubber-stamps the opinion of the prosecuting attorney.[217] It depends upon him for its knowledge of the law and for its information on the facts. On the other hand, when the grand jury was first developed there was no public prosecutor [218] nor official police force nor magistrates. The grand jury may provide a means by which the prosecuting attorney, while exercising his own discretion and expressing his own will, escapes responsibility. Since the grand jury is so largely subject to the influence of the prosecutor, it is asserted that it no longer fulfills its historic function of protection against hasty and unfounded prosecutions. The considerable percentage of cases in which the grand jury finds a "no true bill" tends to show it is no mere rubber stamp.[219]

Indeed it may be argued that normally the grand jury and the prosecuting attorney should agree, and that the fact of agreement shows a proper spirit of cooperation. Finally, it should be pointed out that the grand jury, while

[217] Chaplin, "Reform in Criminal Procedure" (1893) 7 Harv.L.Rev. 189, 190; Criminal Justice in Cleveland (1922) 176, 211-212; Moley, Politics and Criminal Prosecution (1929) 127, 143; Miller, J., "Informations or Indictments in Felony Cases" (1924) 8 Minn.L.Rev. 379, 397; Nat. Com. on Law Obs. and Enf., Report on Prosecution (1931) 34; Morse, "A Survey of the Grand Jury System" (1931) 10 Ore.L.Rev. 295, 304; Illinois Crime Survey (1929) 206, 218, 299. The grand jury "has in fact become a secret tribunal wherein the state's attorney is practically judge, prosecutor, and administrator." Illinois Crime Survey (1929) 299.

[218] Nat. Com. on Law Obs. and Enf., Report on Prosecution (1931) 34. The grand jury served as a check on private prosecutions, insuring that such proceedings would not go forward unless a representative body of men in the neighborhood found there was probable cause therefor. See also Pound, Criminal Justice in America (1930) 109, 187.

[219] Hall, "Analysis of Criticism of the Grand Jury" (1932) 22 J.Crim.L. 692, 697-698. It should be noted, however, that of the cases heard by grand juries only about five per cent are initiated by them. Moley, "The Initiation of Criminal Prosecutions by Indictment or Information" (1931) 29 Mich.L.Rev. 403; Morse, "A Survey of the Grand Jury System" (1931) 10 Ore.L.Rev. 295, 306.

concurring in most cases, would differ "in any case where public opinion felt that executive power was undertaking to crush opposition to it by baseless prosecution of its opponents." [220]

When a preliminary hearing has preceded a grand jury proceeding, some have thought that there is nothing useful left for the grand jury.[221] One preliminary examination is enough. If the preliminary examination shows probable cause, the prosecuting attorney should file an information promptly thereafter. If there be both a preliminary hearing and grand jury proceedings, the accused has two chances to escape before he can be put on trial, either by discharge by the examining magistrate, or by refusal of the grand jury to return a true bill.[222] It is unfair to witnesses to be dragged before the magistrate, the grand jury, and the trial court. The grand jury may indulge in "fishing expeditions" and impertinent and unnecessary questions.[223]

[220] McClintock, "Indictment by a Grand Jury" (1942) 26 Minn.L.Rev. 153, 161.

[221] Criminal Justice in Cleveland (1922) 211-212; "Grand Jury Reform" (1920) 4 J. Am. Jud. Soc. 77, 79; Moley, Politics and Criminal Prosecution (1929) 137; Report of the Crimes Survey Committee, Law Association of Philadelphia (1926) 168, 175, 182; Lieck, "Abolition of the Grand Jury in England" (1935) 25 J.Crim.L. 623; Elliff, "Notes on the Abolition of the English Grand Jury" (1938) 29 J.Crim.L. 3, 16; Burrows, "Criminal Law and Procedure" (1935) 51 L.Q.Rev. 36, 51; Kenny, Outlines of Criminal Law (13th ed.1929) 462; Nat. Com. on Law Obs. and Enf., Report on Prosecution (1931) 34. However, repetition of proceedings may insure a full presentation at the trial. Hall, "Analysis of Criticism of the Grand Jury" (1932) 22 J.Crim.L. 672, 703.

[222] "If the magistrate finds the evidence sufficient and orders him held, the law in twenty odd states requires a second examination of the evidence by a grand jury, who in their turn may find it insufficient and refuse to indict." Waite, Criminal Law in Action (1934) 54. The grand jury may find an indictment even though the magistrate discharges.

[223] Keeble, "The Grand Inquest of the County" (1925) The American Mercury, 146.

It has frequently been pointed out that grand juries are expensive.[224] They involve more than the expenditure of money, such as for jurors' and witnesses' fees, mileage fees, and bailiff's fees. In large cities there may be an excessive drain on busy men who may have to sit for months. There is economic waste with respect to witnesses who may have to go before the magistrate, the grand jury, and the trial court. There seem to be an ample number of citizens who can be voluntarily enlisted in grand jurors associations.[225] Monte Lemann of the Wickersham Crime Commission thought that grand jury service does not "call for more than the citizen may reasonably be expected to do." [226] The cost of the grand jury is a very small part of the total cost of crime, and perhaps is a cost that society ought to pay.[227]

The intervention of the grand jury often involves delay.[228] It can be called in only when a court is in session. Months may elapse without the court being in session. If the accused cannot furnish bail he remains in prison. It

224 Nat. Com. on Law Obs. and Enf., Report on Prosecution (1931) 35; Morse, "A Survey of the Grand Jury System" (1931) 10 Ore.L.Rev. 295, 338-344.

225 Dession, "From Indictment to Information—Implications of the Shift" (1932) 42 Yale L.J. 163, 184.

226 Nat. Com. on Law Obs. and Enf., Rep. on Crim. Proc. (1931) 50.

227 Hall, "Analysis of Criticism of the Grand Jury" (1932) 22 J.Crim.L. 692, 698-699; Pollock, "The King's Peace in the Middle Ages" (1900) 13 Harv.L.Rev. 177, 188.

228 Barnes, J., "Causes of Delay in Criminal Cases" (1916) 7 J.Crim.L. 330, 331; Chaplin, "Reforms in Criminal Procedure" (1893) 7 Harv.L. Rev. 189, 197; Warner and Cabot, Judges and Law Reform (1936) 104; Moley, Politics and Criminal Prosecution (1929) 136; Miller, J., "Informations or Indictments in Felony Cases" (1924) 8 Minn.L.Rev. 379, 382; Morse, "A Survey of the Grand Jury System" (1931) 10 Ore.L.Rev. 250, 296; Nat. Com. on Law Obs. and Enf., Report on Prosecution (1931) 36-37; Illinois Crime Survey (1929) 218. See, however, Hall, "Analysis of Criticism of the Grand Jury" (1932) 22 J.Crim.L. 692, 699-700.

would be less oppressive to be examined at a preliminary hearing by a magistrate, particularly in cases where the defendant wishes to plead guilty. Witnesses may scatter and leave the jurisdiction.[229] Delay may thus be equally injurious to the prosecution. Statutory requirements as to the drawing and composition of grand juries give rise to dilatory objections to the indictment, as do rules of procedure, such as those dealing with who may be present during their inquiries and deliberations.[230] Legislation and rules of court may, however, eliminate these technicalities.[231]

In Oregon the time interval between binding over by the magistrate and disposition by the grand jury ranges from 0 to 194 days, with a median interval of 21 days.[232] In Oregon the delay at this stage appears to be the longest delay at any stage of the proceedings.[233] In Illinois the time interval appears to be slightly shorter than in Oregon.[234] The period between binding over and the filing of

[229] It is estimated that 20 per cent of the cases have to be dropped at this stage for lack of witnesses. Moley, Politics and Criminal Prosecution (1929) 137.

[230] Mitchell, "Reform in Federal Criminal Procedure" (1932) 18 A.B.A.J. 732, 734.

[231] Dession, "From Indictment to Information—Implications of the Shift" (1932) 42 Yale L.J. 163, 187-189.

[232] Morse and Beattie, "Survey of the Administration of Criminal Justice in Oregon" (1932) 11 Ore.L.Rev. 177-182. As to other states, see Moley, "The Initiation of Criminal Prosecutions by Indictment or Information" (1931) 29 Mich.L.Rev. 403, 426-430; Nat. Com. on Law Obs. and Enf., Report on Prosecution (1931), Table XXV, p.216.

[233] "Survey of the Administration of Criminal Justice in Oregon" (1932) 11 Ore.L.Rev. 170-191. Moley states: "Data collected in the various surveys show forcefully that the most important cause for delay is in the stage of procedure in which action by the grand jury is being awaited." Moley, "The Initiation of Criminal Prosecutions by Indictment or Information" (1931) 29 Mich.L.Rev. 403, 427.

[234] Illinois Crime Survey (1929) 95, 97. For somewhat similar figures

an information appears to be substantially equivalent, and in any case the period in grand jury cases is reasonably brief.[235] This should not cause surprise since grand juries are frequently impaneled in the larger cities. The delays are admittedly greater in smaller cities and urban counties. Even in their case the statutes appear to indicate that a shortening of the interval from binding over to information is compensated by a lengthening of the interval between information and arraignment. In other words, while the wait for a grand jury is eliminated, there may still be a long wait for a term of court.[236] Delay may be avoided at this stage by waiver of indictment. A second remedy is that found in a North Dakota statute providing that a defendant bound over and prepared to plead guilty may be brought before a district judge sitting anywhere within the judicial district of which the county is part, and that the defendant may thereupon be arraigned before the district judge in chambers, may plead, and be sentenced without waiting for a term of court.[237]

24. Advantages of Retention of Grand Jury

Some modifications of the grand jury have been recommended by almost all writers and crime surveys. They have favored the necessary statutory or even constitu-

---

in Cleveland, see Criminal Justice in Cleveland (1922) 304, Table 17. See also Morse, "A Survey of the Grand Jury System" (1931) 10 Ore.L.Rev. 217, 250-257.

235 Dession, "From Indictment to Information—Implications of the Shift" (1932) 42 Yale L.J. 163, 180.

236 Dession, "From Indictment to Information—Implications of the Shift" (1932) 42 Yale L.J. 163, 182-183.

237 N. D. Comp. Laws Ann. (1913) § 10628(6). See also Section 231 of the A.L.I. Code of Crim. Proc.; Second and Final Report of the Royal Commission on Delay in the King's Bench Division (1913) 16 *et. seq.*

tional changes necessary to permit waiver of indictment by the defendant, the use of the information as an alternative to the indictment, liberal rules of amendment, and shorter, simpler indictments.[238] Abler jurors should be chosen; there should be fewer exemptions and excuses from service; persons should not be called on to serve at too frequent intervals nor for too long periods of time. In some jurisdictions they may be reduced in size.

In accordance with the tendency to dispense with the intervention of the grand jury, Section 113 of the American Law Institute Code of Criminal Procedure provides that "All offenses heretofore required to be prosecuted by indictment may be prosecuted either by indictment or information." Moreover under Section 114 "No grand jury shall be summoned to attend at any court except upon the order of a judge thereof when in his opinion public interest so demands, except that a grand jury shall be summoned at least once a year in each county." [239]

[238] Nat. Com. on Law Obs. and Enf., Rep. on Crim. Proc. (1931) 33; Nat. Com. on Law Obs. and Enf., Rep. on Prosecution (1931) 34, 47, 124-126. See also the reports of the crime surveys of Cleveland (1922) 176, 210-212; Minnesota (1927) 29; Minnesota (1934) 47-48; New York (1928) 167; and Illinois (1929) 218. In accord, are the A.L.I. Code of Crim. Proc. (1930) 49, 70, 80; "Grand Jury Reform" (1920) 4 J. Am. Jud. Soc. 77; Miller, J., "Informations or Indictments in Felony Cases" (1924) 8 Minn.L.Rev. 379; Burdick, "Criminal Justice in America" (1925) 11 A.B.A.J. 510, 511; Morse, "A Survey of the Grand Jury" (1931) 10 Ore.L.Rev. 101; Roberts, J., "Trial Procedure—Past, Present and Future" (1929) 15 A.B.A.J. 667, 669; Moley, "The Use of the Information in Criminal Cases" (1931) 17 A.B.A.J. 292; Kenny, Outlines of Criminal Law (13th ed.1929) 462-463; Stevenson, "Our Grand Jury System" (1886) 8 Crim.L.Mag. 711, 727; Glueck, Crime and Justice (1936) 84; "Light on Grand Jury Procedure" (1931) 15 Am. Jur. Soc. 121.

[239] In criticisms of Section 114 it has been stated that the requirement that a grand jury be summoned at least once a year in each county subjects a county to needless expense since grand juries are not always needed that often. It has also been stated that the grand jury should be convened

The most conspicuous procedural provision of a proposed Illinois Code of Criminal Law and Procedure which failed of adoption was the abolition of the grand jury. However, a board of inquiry was proposed to take its place.[240] Unlike the grand jury the board of inquiry was not to be called into existence at stated intervals, but only at the request of the prosecuting attorney or attorney general or on the court's own motion to deal with matters requiring exceptional handling. The board was to consist of seven regular nominees and fourteen alternate nominees drawn from the regular jury rolls. In more serious crimes a preliminary examination or its waiver was a prerequisite to the filing of an information, except when it was presented by the board. The board, while normally presenting cases called to its attention by the prosecuting attorney, might also act on its own initiative. The board would never act where there had been a preliminary examination.

Although modifications have frequently been suggested, very few advocate the outright abolition of the grand jury in this country.[241] The English example is not necessarily properly applicable to this country.[242] England has been more successful in developing a highly efficient system of police and of minor courts, thus making action by the grand jury an unnecessary duplication. In this country the assistance of the grand jury seems necessary or useful on

---

whenever the prosecuting attorney asks the judge for the assistance of a grand jury, and not simply when the judge orders it. Morse, "A Survey of the Grand Jury System" (1931) 10 Ore.L.Rev. 295, 364-365.

240 Freeman, "The Draft Code of Criminal Law and Procedure" (1935) 30 Ill.L.Rev. 226, 233; Notes (1935) 26 J.Crim.L. 136, 139, (1935) 21 A.B.A.J. 269.

241 Robinson, Cases on Criminal Law and Procedure (1941) 298-299.

242 The A.L.I. Code of Crim. Proc., c.4, provides for its retention. Keedy, "The Drafting of a Code of Criminal Procedure" (1929) 15 A.B.A.J. 7, 10.

various occasions. It is well suited to investigate riots [243] and public disorders of a like nature, corruption in office,[244] certain extensive conspiracies, and cases with religious and racial [245] aspects which ought to be conducted in a manner beyond suspicion of prejudice. Occasionally the proper protection of the complaining party is best achieved by basing the prosecution on a grand jury indictment rather than on his personal complaint. He will thus be better protected from reprisals and from suits for malicious prosecution. The prosecuting attorney is enabled to obtain the statements of witnesses on record. Unwilling witnesses may finally testify to avoid repeated subpoenas and appearances before the grand jury. He is enabled to

[243] Hale v. Henkel, 201 U.S. 43, 20 Sup.Ct. 370, 50 L.Ed. 652 (1906).

[244] Criminal Justice in Cleveland (1922) 211-212; Willoughby, Principles of Judicial Administration (1929) 193; Lawyer, "Should the Grand Jury be Abolished?" (1906) 15 Yale L.J. 178; "Grand Jury Reform" (Oct. 1920) 4 J. Am. Jud. Soc. 77; "Light on Grand Jury Procedure" (1931) 15 J. Am. Jud. Soc. 120; Note (1934) 20 A.B.A.J. 200; Miller, J., "Informations or Indictments in Felony Cases" (1924) 8 Minn.L.Rev. 379, 405-408; Morse, "A Survey of the Grand Jury System" (1931) 10 Ore.L.Rev. 295, 333-338. Hinton states: "The grand jury is so necessary in some cases, where the state's attorney is unwilling to take responsibility or when the facts are impossible to discover without a secret investigation that its total abolition would be a mistake." Illinois Crime Survey (1929) 196. "In Nebraska, in Lancaster County during the past twenty-five years only six grand juries were summoned, and for the purpose of investigating the corruption of county officials, corrupt practices of members of the bar, and illegal banking and sales of stock." Moley, Politics and Criminal Prosecution (1929) 145-146. It has been pointed out that noncriminal investigating agencies may be better suited than grand juries to situations calling for the public exposure of whole systems of corruption; since no requirement of secrecy is imposed, there is the privilege for fair comment, and full scope for publicizing the findings is consequently afforded. Dession and Cohen, "The Inquisitorial Functions of Grand Juries" (1942) 41 Yale L.J. 687, 707-711.

[245] Hurtado v. California, 110 U.S. 516, 554, 4 Sup.Ct. 111, 28 L.Ed. 232 (1884).

obtain possession of documents by bringing them before the grand jury under a *subpoena duces tecum.* Finally, in cases of unusual difficulty, he is enabled to obtain the views of a representative group of substantial citizens before filing an accusation.[246]

In recent decades there has been considerable agitation for the replacement of indictment by information. This involves the elimination of the grand jury and a consequent broadening of the discretion of the prosecuting attorney. At the same time many have feared that the increased powers of the prosecuting attorney would be attended with abuse of discretion.[247] The proponents of procedure by information argue in reply that the preliminary examination can supply the desired check.[248] But, as was seen in the chapter on preliminary examination, magistrates who are frequently scattered throughout the county and untrained in law are more likely to be dominated by the prosecuting attorney than they are to restrain him.[249]

246 The late Federal District Attorney George Z. Medalie states with respect to federal grand juries that "in many sections of the country Washington is regarded more or less as a distant agency. Unless the people through their own representatives are able to voice the local sentiment concerning the law, and the local sense of justice, they will feel decidedly insecure, and the grand jury is the particular body that breathes the spirit of the community." Quoted by Dession, "From Indictment to Information—Implications of the Shift" (1932) 42 Yale L.J. 163, 164 from (1931) The Panel, No. 2, at 16. See also Elliff, "Notes on the Abolition of the English Grand Jury" (1938) 29 J.Crim.L. 3, 17-18; Note, Dewey (1941) 32 J.Crim.L. 217.

247 Nat. Com. on Law Obs. and Enf., Report on Prosecution (1931) 18-20. See the views of state judges cited by Morse, "A Survey of the Grand Jury System" (1931) 10 Ore.L.Rev. 295, 351-356.

248 Chaplin, "Reform in Criminal Procedure" (1893) 7 Harv.L.Rev. 189, 190-191.

249 Kains, How Say You? A Review of the Movement for Abolishing the Grand Jury System in Canada (1893) 50-51, 95, 100; Edwards, The Grand Jury (1906) 37-38; Notes (1921) 21 Col.L.Rev. 376, 378, "Reform

Roscoe Pound has pointed out that opportunities for abuse of the prosecutor's discretion are found particularly in the larger cities of today.[250] This is true since the check of an informed local opinion may be absent. In such areas clearly some check is desirable. But the best equivalent of an informed local opinion is not a weak preliminary hearing or court supervision of nolle prosequis, but the grand jury,[251] for which even the American Law Institute Code of Criminal Procedure makes some rather ambiguous provisions.[252] "Unlike a committing magistrate under one of the prevailing types of information system, a grand jury is amply endowed with legal powers for the exercise of its function as a lay leaven of bureaucracy, a check on corruption, and in general a citizen's agency for overseeing and controlling the initiatory activities of the prosecution." [253]

A prosecuting attorney may inquire generally, but in most states has no subpoena power.[254] Calling in the witnesses is not the same thing, as they may be hostile or unwilling. The magistrate may issue a subpoena after a com-

---

in Criminal Procedure" (1940) 50 Yale L.J. 107, 109. *Contra:* Miller, J., "Informations or Indictments in Felony Cases" (1924) 8 Minn.L.Rev. 379, 399.

[250] Pound, Criminal Justice in America (1930) 149-151.

[251] Dession, "From Indictment to Information—Implications of the Shift" (1932) 42 Yale L.J. 163.

[252] Although the Code contains long detailed sections (118-147) on grand jury procedure, yet Section 114 provides that the grand jury shall be summoned when in the judge's opinion "public interest so demands," except that it must be summoned "at least once a year in each county." This does not assure that it will be used very often.

[253] Dession, "From Indictment to Information—Implications of the Shift" (1932) 42 Yale L.J. 163, 176.

[254] It has been argued, however, that the power and duty to investigate violation of the law is executive. See Notes (1938) 38 Col.L.Rev. 1493, 1499, (1923) 33 Yale L.J. 96.

plaint but is bound in his investigations by the confines of a specific charge.[255] "The proceedings before a grand jury constitute the only general criminal investigation known to the law." [256] Prior to the stage where specific accusations are supportable, investigation must be free from any restraint comparable to the specific charge and showing of probable cause required to confer jurisdiction on the magistrate. Since the establishing of the occurrence of a suspected criminal act is likely to depend on the production of evidence by unwilling witnesses, there must be the power to issue subpoenas and to punish for contempt.[257] Detectives and the prosecuting attorney have no such power. Historically only the grand jury has had it. The absence of such power is likely to result in holding suspects incommunicado for questioning of a third-degree character. Questioning in the office of the prosecuting attorney is likely to develop in the same direction. Or the prosecuting attorney may throw up his hands and confine himself to cases prepared by the police.

[255] Dession and Cohen, "The Inquisitorial Functions of Grand Juries" (1932) 41 Yale L.J. 687, 689; A.L.I. Code of Crim. Proc. (1930) § 1. As to the limits on inquisitorial powers, see (1937) 21 Minn.L.Rev. 605.

[256] Ward Baking Co. v. Western Union Tel. Co., 205 App. Div. 723, 728, 200 N.Y. Supp. 865, 869 (3d Dept. 1923). See also (1937) 35 Mich.L. Rev. 1018; Konowitz, "The Grand Jury as an Investigating Body of Public Officials" (1936) 10 St. John's L.Rev. 219; Elliff, "Notes on the Abolition of the English Grand Jury" (1938) 29 J.Crim.L. 3, 17; Nahum and Schatz, "The Grand Jury in Connecticut" (1931) 5 Conn.B.J. 111, 120.

[257] "In a few of the information states, notably Missouri, Indiana and Iowa, the prosecution has kept such grand juries in frequent session to avail of the power to subpoena and examine witnesses in secret and get their testimony on record at an early stage. But more generally the adoption of an information system has meant the disappearance of grand juries and with them the facilities embodied in grand jury powers." Dession, "From Indictment to Information—Implications of the Shift," (1932) 42 Yale L.J. 163, 190.

The Wickersham Crime Commission states: "Today the grand jury is useful only as a general investigating body for inquiring into the conduct of public affairs and in cases of large conspiracies. It should be retained as an occasional instrument for such purposes." [258] In the same vein, Section 114 of the American Law Institute Code of Criminal Procedure retains the possibility of impaneling occasional grand juries for purposes of investigation by providing that a grand jury shall be summoned at least once a year in each county.

The abolition of the grand jury would deprive the prosecuting attorney, in investigating probable cause, of those aids which are or can be made available through the device of grand jury.[259] It has been seen that the Anglo-American preliminary examination, in comparison with constitutional procedure, is utterly inadequate as an energetic investigatory device. The grand jury, much more than the preliminary examination, seems to have the potential effectiveness of the Continental procedure. It presents a fertile field for development along those lines. Even now, chiefly through its *ex parte* character and its subpoena power, it can supply valuable aids to the prosecutor's investigation.[260]

Back as far as 1825, Jeremy Bentham is said to have stated that the grand jury had outlived its usefulness for over a century.[261] Doubtless, however, because of some

[258] Nat. Com. on Law Obs. and Enf., Report on Prosecution (1931) 37.

[259] Criminal Justice in Cleveland (1922), 212. "There will always be instances in which the inquisitorial powers of the grand jury are necessary for the initial discovery or proof of a violation of law, and in which, just as at present, the prosecution will be begun before the grand jury."

[260] Dession and Cohen, "The Inquisitorial Functions of Grand Juries" (1932) 41 Yale L.J. 687; Note (1938) 17 N.C.L.Rev. 43; Lindsey, "Functions of the Grand Jury" (1913) 4 J.Crim.L. 169.

[261] 3 Bentham, Rationale of Judicial Evidence, c.15, § II.

positive merits, the grand jury has survived the campaigns waged against it. It is used extensively in federal anti-trust prosecutions,[262] as well as in such large and important metropolitan areas as New York City.[263] The American Law Institute Code of Criminal Procedure appears to recognize merit in the grand jury without clearly stating or implying what its advantages are.[264]

The grand jury may be of no use in England and still serve a purpose in this country. An English authority has said about its use in England: "Judging by one's own experience upon English grand juries, one would be tempted to anticipate that independent enquiry by the grand jury with a view to direct presentment would be clumsy and ineffective in working and would add nothing of value to the measure of protection against crime already enjoyed by the citizens as a body." [265] Yet he seems to recognize its possible value in this country when he goes on to say: "It must, however, be recognized that when magistrates and prosecuting attorneys are elective officers, with definite political affiliations, there may from time to time be cases in which some alternative procedure for bringing offenders to trial, however clumsy and ineffective in its working, may prove a valuable safeguard." As Professor McClintock states, "at this time, when rights of individuals have been completely subordinated to the will of the executive in many countries, and when fears are expressed in our

[262] Lewin, "The Conduct of Grand Jury Proceedings in Antitrust Cases" (1940) 7 Law & Contemp. Prob. 112.

[263] See The Panel, publication of the New York Grand Jurors Association; Warner and Cabot, "Changes in the Administration of Criminal Justice During the Past Fifty Years" (1937) 50 Harv.L.Rev. 583, 597.

[264] Brunyate, "The American Draft Code of Criminal Procedure, 1930" (1933) 49 L.Q.Rev. 192, 197-198.

[265] Brunyate, "The American Draft Code of Criminal Procedure, 1930" (1933) 49 L.Q.Rev. 192, 197.

own country that the expansion of the executive power is endangering the rights of the individual, it would be the height of folly to make an attempt to eliminate it so long as any substantial part of the people continue to regard it as a bulwark against executive tyranny. Our concern now is to investigate what reforms in the system are constitutionally possible and desirable." [266]

[266] McClintock, "Indictment by a Grand Jury" (1942) 26 Minn.L.Rev. 153, 156-157. For writings on the grand jury, see: Stevenson, "Our Grand Jury System" (1886) 8 Crim.L.Mag. 711-729; Edwards, The Grand Jury (1906) 1-219; Lawyer, "Should the Grand Jury System be Abolished?" (1906) 15 Yale L.J. 178; Adkins, "The Grand Jury" (1924) 2 Geo.L.J. 6-15; Thompson, "Shall the Grand Jury in Ordinary Criminal Cases be Dispensed with in Minnesota?" (1922) 6 Minn.L.Rev. 615-616; "Grand Jury Reform" (1920) 4 J. Am. Jud. Soc. 77-82; Note (1921) 21 Col.L.Rev. 376-379; Miller, J., "Informations or Indictments in Felony Cases" (1924) 8 Minn.L.Rev. 379-408; Morse, "A Survey of the Grand Jury System" (1931) 10 Ore.L.Rev. 101, 217, 295; Nahum and Schatz, "The Grand Jury in Connecticut" (1931) 5 Conn.B.J. 111-147; Chamberlin, "Special Grand Juries in Illinois" (1936) 22 J.Crim.L. 163-170; Dession and Cohen, "Inquisitorial Functions of Grand Juries" (1932) 41 Yale L.J. 687-712; Dession, "From Indictment to Information—Implications of the Shift" (1932) 42 Yale L.J. 163-193; Konowitz, "The Grand Jury as an Investigating Body of Public Officials" (1936) 10 St. John's L.Rev. 219-235; 24 Am. Jur., Grand Jury, §§ 1-50; 38 C.J.S., Grand Juries, §§ 1-47.

CHAPTER V

INDICTMENT AND INFORMATION

1. History of Information

FROM a very early period in the common law the two most important methods of beginning criminal prosecution have been by indictment and by information.[1] The information is almost as old as the indictment.[2] This is not surprising, but came very naturally to the centralized royal justice of the thirteenth century. What could be more normal than for the king by his counsel to inform his courts of some facts which had legal consequences? The procedure was also in accord with the existing notion that all men, including the king, were subject to law.

A considerable number of types of information were developed by the various courts in civil as well as in criminal cases. The criminal information in the developed common law fell under two heads: those brought by a subject on a penal statute on behalf of himself and the crown, which "are a sort of *qui tam* actions, only carried on by the criminal instead of the civil process"; and those brought solely at the suit of the king.[3] The latter in turn was of two types: "first, those which are truly and properly his own suits, and filed *ex officio* by his own immediate officer, the Attorney General: Secondly, those in which, though the king is the nominal prosecutor, yet it is at the relation of

[1] Holdsworth, "The History of the Criminal Information" (1923) 1 Can. B.Rev. 300. This article also appears in 9 Holdsworth, History of English Law (3d ed.1923) 236-245.

[2] Bl. Comm. *309. See also 1 Stephen, A History of the Criminal Law of England (1883) 294-297; 2 Pollock and Maitland, History of English Law (2d ed.1905) 662.

[3] Bl. Comm. *303.

some private person or common informer; and they are filed by the King's coroner and attorney in the court of the King's Bench, usually called the Master of the Crown Office, who is for this purpose the standing officer of the public." [4]

During the reign of Edward I, the king could, by information to his court, bring a man to trial for treason or felony.[5] Very likely, however, before the end of the medieval period, the right to use informations had been restricted to misdemeanors.[6] This restriction arose out of the extensive and abusive use made by the Council of the process of information, and the medieval statutes passed to restrict the jurisdiction of the Council in criminal cases. Common-law lawyers had long been jealous of such jurisdiction. This restriction on cases coming before the Council very likely reacted on the proceedings at the suit of the Crown by way of information in the common-law courts, though there seems to be no express authority for restriction on the Crown. The king could, however, proceed by information for offenses under the degree of felony.[7]

In the seventeenth century we get the first hint of the theory that an information is not a legitimate mode of proceeding in criminal cases. During that century the procedure by ex officio information was used for purely political purposes. The nature of the cases in which it was

[4] Bl. Comm. *304.

[5] 2 Pollock and Maitland, History of English Law (2d ed.1905) 662.

[6] Holdsworth, "The History of the Criminal Information" (1923) 1 Can. B.Rev. 300, 303; 9 Holdsworth, History of English Law (3d ed.1923) 238.

[7] 2 Hawkins, Pleas of the Crown, c.26, §§ 1 and 3. An act of Parliament in 1495 gave power to the judges of Assize and the justices of the peace to bring to trial persons accused of misdemeanors upon an information instead of an indictment. 4 Holdsworth, History of English Law (3d ed.1923) 524.

used meant inevitably that its legality would be attacked. The hardship on defendants was often pointed out. Thus even if the accused were acquitted he could get no costs against the king. He must plead instantly, a hardship, however, also experienced in the case of an indictment. The Master of the Crown Office failed to take care that the complainant had a probable cause of complaint before he allowed him to exhibit an information. This want of care enabled "all private persons to prosecute criminally any person who had offended them by any act which could be treated as a misdemeanor without the sanction of a grand jury." [8] Many persons abused the power to prosecute; an information would be exhibited, the defendant would plead to the issue, and then the prosecution would be abandoned.

The procedure by information was attacked in the House of Commons. In several cases attempts were made to prove that all criminal informations were illegal.[9] But while the legality of criminal informations was established, Parliament took steps to mitigate the hardships which resulted from those exhibited by the Master of the Crown Office at the suit of private persons.[10] It was provided that no such informations were to be exhibited without an express order of the court and without taking a recognizance for effectual prosecution. If the information was not effectually prosecuted within a year, or the verdict was for the defendant, the court could award costs to the defendant. Baseless or frivolous informations were

[8] 1 Stephen, A History of the Criminal Law of England (1883) 296.

[9] The argument was considered and overruled by Holt, C. J. See Prynn's Case (1690) 5 Mod. 459, 463-464, 87 Eng. Reprint 764.

[10] 4 & 5 Wm. & Mary, c.18 (1692). The statute did not limit, in fact expressly excepted from its operation, the ex officio information. See Note (1922) 36 Harv.L.Rev. 204.

thereby checked, since a motion for an information made to the court operates, just as a preliminary examination before the magistrate, to stop at the outset merely frivolous prosecutions.[11] The courts have varied with respect to the manner of exercising their discretion. They appear to have been lax at the end of the eighteenth and the beginning of the nineteenth centuries, but returned to a stricter practice in the latter half of the nineteenth century.

Throughout its history, the difference between the procedure by way of indictment and by way of information was only a difference as to the method by which the proceedings were initiated. As Blackstone states: "The same notice was given, the same process was issued, the same pleas were allowed, the same trial by jury was had, the same judgment was given by the same judges, as if the prosecution had originally been by indictment." [12] It has, of course, always been easier to amend an information than an indictment.

2. History of Indictment

The history of indictment in England has already been partially covered in the prior chapter on "Grand Jury." As Stephen has pointed out: "The indictment is the foundation of the record in criminal cases and is indeed the only document connected with the trial which in all

[11] 1 Stephen, A History of the Criminal Law of England (1883) 296. The present information in England is described in Kenny, Outlines of Criminal Law (15th ed.1942) 543-544; Archbold, Criminal Pleading, Evidence and Practice (30th ed.1938) 113-125; Harris and Wilshere, Principles and Practice of the Criminal Law (17th ed.1943) 440-441.

[12] 4 Bl. Comm. *305; 9 Holdsworth, History of English Law (3d ed.1923) 245.

cases is in writing."[13] The extreme strictness as to the form of the indictment seems to have been derived very largely from the rules relating to the other historic method of prosecution, namely, appeal. Stephen states that the "history of indictments is a branch of the history of the law of special pleading."[14] In the normal case the pleadings in a criminal case have always consisted of an indictment "engrossed in parchment," and a plea given by the defendant orally in open court of guilty or not guilty. The requisites of an indictment have remained the same from early times up to 1915.[15]

The common law gave what appear to us as irrational advantages to both the accused and the Crown. A technical flaw might in effect result in the complete discharge of the accused. The likelihood of his being re-indicted and of the prosecution's being able to show that the defect in the first indictment was such that he had never been legally in peril, and so could not plead former jeopardy, was not very great. On the other hand, the accused was not entitled to a copy of the indictment in felony cases, but only

[13] 1 Stephen, A History of the Criminal Law of England (1883) 274. Holdsworth states that the "indictment was always a written document." 3 History of English Law (3d ed.1923) 618. According to Beale it has been in writing since the reign of Edward I. Beale, Criminal Pleading and Practice (1899) 80.

[14] 1 Stephen, A History of the Criminal Law of England (1883) 275. According to Holdsworth, "the formality, certainty, and verbal precision required in an indictment has always been one of the most salient characteristics of English criminal procedure." 3 History of English Law (3d ed.1923) 616. Moreover, the verbal exactness required in civil cases was carried over into criminal procedure. *Ibid.* 618-619.

[15] The Statute of Additions (1 Hen. V, c.5) provided that the names of the defendants should be followed by a statement of "their estate or degree or mystery, and of the towns, hamlets, or place, and counties, in which they were." The statute of 4 Geo. II, c.26, enacted that all indictments should be in English.

to have it read over to him when called upon to plead.[16] Thus he scarcely had an opportunity to discover and take advantage of any defect. Any person could, however, point out such a flaw and it was the duty of the judge as counsel for the accused to do so.[17]

If the indicted person was not in custody and could not be apprehended, he could be outlawed.[18] In cases of treason and felony, outlawry had the effect of a conviction and involved forfeiture. From the earliest time, it was the duty of the sheriff and other officials entrusted with the preservation of the peace to arrest persons who had been indicted.[19] As early as the reign of Edward III it was held that the killing of a person indicted, who was forcibly resisting arrest by one who had a sheriff's warrant for his arrest, was a case of justifiable homicide and needed no pardon.

16 For several centuries indictments were in French. In 1362 it was provided that they be in Latin. It was not until 1751 that a statute provided that indictments and other pleadings should be "in the English tongue and language only." (1925) 3 Proc. Am. L. Inst. 499-500.

17 However, some flaws were not waived by pleading to the indictment. See 1 Stephen, A History of the Criminal Law of England (1883) 284, 398, 399; compare 9 Holdsworth, History of English Law (3d ed.1923) 233.

18 1 Stephen, A History of the Criminal Law of England (1883) 292; 3 Holdsworth, History of English Law (3d ed.1923) 604-607. The last judgment of outlawry was in 1859. Kenny, Outlines of Criminal Law (15th ed.1942) 584, n.3. See Richards, "Is Outlawry Obsolete?" (1902) 18 L.Q.Rev. 297. Outlawry was abolished in 1938. Harris and Wilshere, Principles and Practice of the Criminal Law (17th ed.1943) 437-438.

19 2 Pollock and Maitland, History of English Law (2d ed.1905) 581. As to modern procedure after indictment to secure the appearance of the defendant, see Archbold, Criminal Pleading, Evidence and Practice (30th ed.1938) 63-71.

3. Modern English Procedure

In the past thirty years the form of indictment has been materially changed in England.[20] In 1885 the indictment, though much more simplified than it had been, was in substance set forth in one long sentence affirming the guilt of the defendant.[21] Each felony was required to be set forth in a separate indictment. Any number of misdemeanors could be joined in the same indictment, but a felony and a misdemeanor, whether closely connected or not, could never be made counts in the same indictment. The indictment was unnecessarily long and defendants often found it difficult to understand what they were asked to plead to. It was not necessary to cite the statute upon which the charge was based. This might be a hardship to the defendant when the prosecution might have been based on more than one statute.

The Indictments Act of 1915 remedied these defects.[22]

20 As to reforms proposed in 1898, see Stephen, "Indictments and the Rule Committee" (1898) 14 L.Q.Rev. 260. For the liberal Canadian rules, see Crouse, "A Critique of Canadian Criminal Legislation" (1934) 12 Can.B.Rev. 545, 574, 575.

21 The procedure is described in Harris, Principles of the Criminal Law (11th ed.1908) 328-345; Archbold, Criminal Pleading, Evidence and Practice (23d ed.1905) 51-94; Stephen, A Digest of the Law of Criminal Procedure (1883) 151-168; Lawson and Keedy, "Criminal Procedure in England" (1910) 1 J.Crim.L. 595, 604. It has been said that "by the end of the fifteenth century, at least, the indictment had acquired the rigid form it has today." Beale, Criminal Pleading and Practice (1899) 81.

22 5 & 6 Geo. V, c.90. "In England a complete change has been brought about by providing for short indictments, stating the offense charged and specifying in brief phrase the acts constituting it in the particular case." Nat. Com. on Law Obs. and Enf., Rep. on Crim. Proc. (1931) 33. See also Howard, Criminal Justice in England (1931) 355-358; Kenny, Outlines of Criminal Law (15th ed.1942) 548-557; Archbold, Criminal Pleading, Evidence and Practice (30th ed.1938) 23-25, 41-55; Harris and Wilshere, Principles and Practice of the Criminal Law (17th ed.1943) 417-431.

The new form states the necessary particulars with respect to the court, the defendant, the charge, and if a statute is involved, the act and the section of the act, and a short nontechnical statement of the particulars. Each charge must be placed in a separate count. Any number of felonies and misdemeanors may be joined in the same indictment, provided they arise out of the same transaction or series of transactions.[23] If in the opinion of the court the interests of justice require it, the counts may be separated or tried one or more at a time. It is easier to prepare and to understand this form than the old forms, although even today the defendant may be somewhat puzzled after the reading of the indictment.[24]

The English indictment now consists of three parts: (1) the commencement, (2) the statement of the offense, and (3) the particulars of the offense.[25] The commencement states the place of the court's jurisdiction, usually a

[23] It is preferable in England to multiply counts rather than indictments. Two indictments cannot, even by consent, be tried together. Kenny, Outlines of Criminal Law (15th ed.1942) 552, n.2. For a full discussion of joinder of offenses in England, see Archbold, Criminal Pleading, Evidence and Practice (30th ed.1938) 50-54; Harris and Wilshere, Principles and Practice of the Criminal Law (17th ed.1943) 427-431.

[24] Burrows, "Criminal Law and Procedure" (1935) 51 L.Q.Rev. 36, 51. "By the Indictment Act, 1915, and the rules made thereunder, indictments have been entirely remodeled. Instead of being a pleading governed by strict rules of art occasionally involving immense quantities of detail and repetition, and susceptible of very little amendment, an indictment is now written in almost popular language, and made as nearly intelligible as possible to the unlearned and ignorant. All the longer indictments, especially those for fraud, conspiracy, and perjury, have consequently been very much shortened and simplified and the court has an exceedingly wide power, and indeed duty, of amendment." Stephen, "Criminal Law Reforms Since 1822" (1922) 57 L.J. 419, 421.

[25] Kenny, Outlines of Criminal Law (15th ed.1942) 548. For typical forms, see Kenny, 623-625; Harris and Wilshere, Principles and Practice of the Criminal Law (17th ed.1943) 666-674.

county or a borough. Then come one or more paragraphs, each called a "count," and describing an offense with which the accused is charged. If there is more than a single paragraph, each is to be consecutively numbered. The statement of offense, with which every count must begin, names the crime charged, for example, "murder." It must be in ordinary language, and need not set out all the essential elements of the crime. If the offense is statutory, the statute and particular section involved must be specified in the statement.[26]

Next follow the particulars of the offense, the purpose of which is to inform the defendant as to the circumstances of the crime alleged with respect to time, place, conduct, and subject matter. The particulars may be very brief, but must be sufficient to indicate to the accused "with reasonable clearness" the accusation and circumstances of his offense.[27] The purpose of this requirement is to enable the defendant to know what defense to offer and to protect himself against double jeopardy. If the count is too general, it may be quashed. A count may be in the alternative in the case of any statutory offense defined by alternatives.[28] If the count charges the defendant with two different offenses, it may still be held bad for duplicity.[29]

[26] The following model form is proper: "Arson, contrary to section 2 of the Malicious Damage Act, 1861." See Archbold, Criminal Pleading, Evidence and Practice (30th ed.1938) 41.

[27] The following model form is proper: "AB on the 9th day of March A.D. 1916 in the county of London maliciously set fire to a dwelling house, one CD being therein." Archbold, Criminal Pleading, Evidence and Practice (30th ed.1938) 41.

[28] Compare A.L.I. Code of Crim. Proc. (1930) § 176, which is even broader.

[29] *Contra:* A.L.I. Code of Crim. Proc. (1930) § 185(1)(c). See Comments (1903) 17 Harv.L.Rev. 204, (1928) 37 Yale L.J. 522, (1933) 11

To be valid a count should state in the particulars of the offense the party indicted, the party injured, and the facts and intent that are necessary ingredients of the offense.[30] The party indicted should be described but only in such a manner "as is reasonably sufficient to identify him," without necessarily stating his residence, occupation, or even his correct name. Likewise the party injured should be described but only with similar reasonable sufficiency. The acts, circumstances, and state of mind constituting the offense should be set forth in ordinary language without any need of using such technical expressions as "feloniously."[31]

Under Section 5 of the Act of 1915, where before trial, or at any stage of the trial, it appears to the court that the indictment is defective, the court shall make such order amending the indictment as it deems necessary to meet the circumstances of the case unless upon the merits of the case the required amendments cannot be made without injustice.[32] There are of course no constitutional restrictions on amendments of indictments such as exist in the United States.

Neb.L.Bull. 458; Levitt, "Duplicity in Indictments brought under section 37, Criminal Code of the United States" (1924) 6 Ill.L.Q. 135.

[30] Kenny, Outlines of Criminal Law (15th ed.1942) 550-551. Although most of the older technical rules have been abolished, it is clear that even yet "the nature and circumstances of the offense must be stated with reasonable clarity." Howard, Criminal Justice in England (1931) 357.

[31] A similar rule is set out in the A.L.I. Code of Crim. Proc. (1930) § 164.

[32] But an amendment may not add a new false pretense, Rex v. Errington 16 Cr. App. 148 (1922); nor substitute a representation of an existing fact where the false pretense charged was consistent with mere futurity. Rex v. Hughes 20 Cr. App. 4 (1927). See Archbold, Criminal Pleading, Evidence and Practice (30th ed.1938) 48-50; Harris and Wilshere, Principles and Practice of the Criminal Law (17th ed.1943) 426.

4. Necessity of Formal Accusation

"The basic and indispensable document in a criminal prosecution is the written accusation." [33] It is a fundamental tenet of Anglo-American law that no person can be subjected to trial until he has been informed formally and in writing [34] what the charge is against which he must be prepared to defend himself.[35] The Illinois court has

[33] Robinson, Cases on Criminal Law and Procedure (1941) 265. "A formal accusation is essential to every trial for crime." Clark, Handbook of Criminal Procedure (2d ed. by Mikell, 1918) 122.

[34] "The indictment is the foundation of the record in criminal cases, and is indeed the only document connected with the trial which in all cases is in writing." 1 Stephen, A History of the Criminal Law of England (1883) 274. "Like all judicial proceedings everywhere, a criminal prosecution must be founded upon a statement of the charge against the defendant." Beale, Criminal Pleading and Practice (1899) 80. "The indictment is the foundation for the judgment of the court in a criminal proceeding, the same as a declaration or bill in equity in a civil action." Ricks, J., in Klawanski v. People, 218 Ill. 481, 75 N.E. 1028 (1905). One of the seven "essentials of a criminal proceeding" is "notice to the accused of the offense charged." Nat. Com. on Law Obs. and Enf., Rep. on Crim. Proc. (1931) 16. "Justice can be done to the man who is tried without any formal charge against him, as is the case now when petty offenses are summarily tried; and it is possible to do justice where the formal charge is written after all the evidence on both sides is in, and the proper legal authority has found the facts. Practically there are serious limitations upon both methods. Although justice can be done, injustice is too likely to result. It is elemental that an accused person should have an opportunity to prepare a defense and the best way of insuring to him this opportunity is to present a formal charge against him." Scott, "Reform of Criminal Procedure, With Reference Particularly to the Defendant" (1913) 61 U. of Pa. L.Rev. 458, 468-469.

[35] Wood and Waite, Crime and Its Treatment (1941) 411. Waite points out that the courts have been even stricter than that. "The courts have held, and some still do hold, that a valid indictment is 'jurisdictional' and that a trial, however fairly conducted, is a nullity if it eventually appears that the accusation is formally insufficient." Waite, Criminal Law in Action (1934) 56. Under Section 369 of the American Law Institute Code of Criminal Procedure (1930), it is ground for motion in arrest of judgment that "the indictment or information does not charge an offense." The Federal

stated: "To give a court jurisdiction of the subject matter in a criminal case it is essential that the accused be charged with a crime. If that is not done, a plea of guilty in manner and form as charged does not authorize the court to render a judgment of conviction for some criminal offense, and if a judgment is so rendered, it is void and may be attacked collaterally." [36] The defendant may not waive the absence of an accusation.[37] As later appears, he may waive indictment and be prosecuted by information, but that is not equivalent to waiving any and all written accusations. Since waiver of trial by jury is admissible upon consent of the defendant despite the constitutional right to a jury trial, the question has been asked why trial without *formal* accusation is not valid if the defendant has consented thereto.[38] In Virginia where the constitution is

---

Rules of Criminal Procedure, Rule 34, is to the same effect. See Ex parte Hopkins, 17 Cox C.C. 444 (1891), in which a release on a writ of habeas corpus was permitted. Habeas corpus was permitted after sentence under a void indictment in Aderhold v. Schiltz, 73 Fed. (2d) 381 (C.C.A. 5th, 1934).

[36] People v. Buffo, 318 Ill. 380, 149 N.E. 271 (1925). See also People v. Campbell, 4 Parker Cr. R. 386 (N.Y. 1859); Gibbons v. Territory, 5 Okla. Cr. App. 212, 115 Pac. 129 (1911); Keigwin, Cases in Criminal Procedure (1939) 190; Note (1932) 18 Va.L.Rev. 460, 463.

[37] People v. Minto, 318 Ill. 293, 149 N.E. 241 (1925); People v. Pilawski, 295 Ill. 58, 60 (1920); Clark, Handbook of Criminal Procedure (2d ed. by Mikell, 1918) 122. Brandeis, J., states in Albrecht v. United States, 273 U.S. 1, 47 Sup.Ct. 250, 71 L.Ed. 505 (1927): "The invalidity of the warrant is not comparable to the invalidity of an indictment. A person may not be punished for a crime without a formal and sufficient accusation even if he voluntarily submits to the jurisdiction of the court."

[38] Waite, Cases on Criminal Law and Procedure (2d ed.1938) 667, n.2. Compare the argument quoted by Waite, pp.718-720. "Just why a statute would not be constitutional which would provide that the court should have jurisdiction where the accused was as a matter of fact informed of the nature and cause of the accusation without a formal written charge is not clear, but that such a statute would not be constitutional seems firmly established by the cases." Scott, "Simplified Criminal Accusations

silent with regard to the method of prosecuting criminal cases, the court has stated: "While the constitution guarantees to every man the right to demand the cause and nature of his accusation, it does not prescribe the manner in which this demand shall be complied with. It does not require that it shall be by way of indictment or in any other prescribed manner. It may be by presentment or information, or in any other manner the legislature may provide. Furthermore, the right guaranteed by the constitution is the right to demand 'the cause and nature of his accusation'. If he does not choose to demand it, he is under no obligation to do so. It is a right that he may waive if he chooses, and which he will be held to have waived unless he asserts it." [39] It is probable that most courts today would insist on there being a written accusation and not permit waiver.[40] The real problem, then, is rather what is the proper source of the accusation, grand jury or prosecuting attorney?

It has been held that an indictment which does not allege facts constituting a crime will be good after verdict

---

and the Supplementing and Amending Thereof" (1913) 61 U. of Pa. L.Rev. 540, 550.

[39] Pine v. Commonwealth, 121 Va. 812, 939 S.E. 652, syll. 17 (1917). In Sullivan v. Commonwealth 161 S.E. 297 (Va. 1931), the defendant was in effect held to have waived the right to be tried under the section of the statute under which he was indicted. See Comments (1932) 45 Harv.L. Rev. 934, 23 J.Crim.L. 486, 18 Va.L.Rev. 460. See also Note (1911) 25 Harv.L.Rev. 179.

[40] 1 Bishop, New Criminal Procedure (4th ed.1895) §§ 79, 95; Clark, Handbook of Criminal Procedure (2d ed. by Mikell, 1918) 122; 27 Am. Jur., Indictments and Informations, § 3, p.585. Likewise they could insist that the defendant be tried only for the crime for which he was indicted. Under Section 369(d) of the American Law Institute Code of Criminal Procedure, it is a ground for motion in arrest of judgment that the "defendant was convicted of an offense of which he could not be convicted under the indictment or information."

and judgment, if the defendant fails to object in the manner prescribed by the statutes and provided the facts necessary to constitute the crime intended to be charged appeared upon the trial.[41] This raises the question of whether aider by verdict is applicable to criminal as well as civil cases. While it has been suggested that the doctrine does not apply to criminal cases in England,[42] a modern case has held that an indictment which does not charge a crime could be aided by a verdict rendered upon proof of all the necessary facts.[43]

It does not follow that American courts will apply a similar doctrine, since constitutional provisions possibly make the right to an indictment more than a personal privilege, and make it mandatory. The constitutional restriction may go to the jurisdiction of the court, and jurisdiction may not be broadened by acts of the parties.[44]

The same considerations should apply where the defendant pleads guilty when arraigned upon an indictment which does not state facts sufficient to constitute an offense. A plea of guilty confesses only the facts charged, and does not constitute a waiver of other than formal defects. A majority of decisions support this view.[45]

It has been held that, where an indictment omits one essential averment but there is proof of every element at the trial, the defendant cannot on appeal first raise the de-

41 People v. Wiechers, 179 N.Y. 459 (1904), (1905) 5 Col.L.Rev. 237. Accord: State v. Malish, 15 Mont. 506 (1895); State v. Hinckley, 4 Idaho, 490 (1895).

42 King v. Mason, 2 D. & E. 581 (1788).

43 Heyman v. Queen, 12 Cox C.C. 383 (1873).

44 Note (1905) 5 Col.L.Rev. 237; Newcomb v. State, 37 Miss. 383 (1859); Clark, Handbook of Criminal Procedure (2d ed. by Mikell, 1918) 369; Keigwin, Cases in Criminal Procedure (1939) 511.

45 Fletcher v. State, 12 Ark. 170 (1851); Boody v. People, 48 Ill. 481, 75 N.E. 1028 (1905), (1906) 6 Col.L.Rev. 273, (1906) 15 Yale L.J. 374.

fect in the indictment.[46] It has been said that the general view is *contra*.[47]

The imperative necessity of having an indictment which states an offense as well as the hardship from the point of view of the defendant where it is thus deficient is shown by the prevalent view that, where the defendant has been convicted in such a case, he can be tried again and cannot plead former jeopardy.[48] Trial under a void accusation is regarded as no trial at all.

In common practice the accusation takes the form of an indictment, an information, or a complaint.[49] Those forms are exactly the same in that part of each form, called the body, which sets forth the facts alleged as the charge or accusation. Each of the three has a different signer. The indictment is signed by the foreman of the grand jury and by the prosecuting attorney; the information is signed by the prosecuting attorney; and the complaint is signed by the peace officer or by a private individual.[50]

[46] Serra v. Mortiga, 204 U.S. 470 (1907), 20 Harv.L.Rev. 573. Accord: Eaves v. State, 113 Ga. 749 (1901).

[47] (1907) 20 Harv.L.Rev. 573; Commonwealth v. Doyle, 110 Mass. 103 (1872). See Orfield, Criminal Appeals in America (1939) 96; Note (1941) 54 Harv.L.Rev. 1204, 1208.

[48] State v. Collins, 112 Wash. 201, 21 Pac. 831 (1920), 20 Col.L.Rev. 915; A.L.I., Administration of the Criminal Law, Double Jeopardy (1935) § 10. Section 9 of the Institute provision on Double Jeopardy, however, allows the defendant to plead jeopardy if he has been acquitted on the merits. See also Note (1940) 24 Minn.L.Rev. 522, 526.

[49] In England today the "accusation may be made either (1) by a crown official's information, or (2) by an indictment or (3) in the case of murder, manslaughter or infanticide by a coroner's inquisition." Kenny, Outlines of Criminal Law (15th ed.1942) 542.

[50] Under Rule 7(c) of the Federal Rules of Criminal Procedure (1944), both an indictment and an information require the signature of the prosecuting attorney. The A.L.I. Code of Crim. Proc. (1930) § 151 requires the signature of the prosecuting attorney on the information only.

5. Methods of Prosecution

There are constitutional provisions in all states except Georgia, Kansas, Maryland, Massachusetts, Michigan, Minnesota, New Hampshire, Vermont, Virginia, and Wisconsin prescribing the methods for prosecuting criminal cases.[51] Prosecution by indictment in all but a few exceptional cases, such as cases of impeachment, cases arising in the land and naval forces or in the militia when in actual service in time of war or public danger, and cases cognizable by justices of the peace, is expressly required in Alabama, Delaware, Kentucky, Mississippi, New Jersey, North Carolina, Oregon, Pennsylvania, South Carolina, Tennessee, and West Virginia. Prosecution by indictment for serious offenses with similar exceptions are required by express constitutional provisions in Illinois, Maine, New York, Ohio, Rhode Island, and Texas. The constitutions expressly provide that indictable offenses may also be prosecuted by information in Arkansas,[52] Arizona, California, Connecticut (except for offenses punishable by death or imprisonment for life), Idaho, Louisiana (except in capital cases), Missouri, Montana, Nevada,

[51] Keedy, "The Drafting of a Code of Criminal Procedure" (1929) 15 A.B.A.J. 7. In Kansas, Vermont, and Wisconsin, statutes providing in effect that information and indictment shall be concurrent remedies have been held constitutional. The validity of an 1859 Michigan statute to the same effect has never been questioned. There are intimations in Maryland and Massachusetts that the bill of rights guarantees prosecution by indictment for all crimes involving capital or infamous punishment, but New Hampshire has taken an opposite view. The use of the information does not seem to be barred in Georgia and Virginia. In Minnesota it may be used where the punishment is less than imprisonment for ten years. See Comment (1923) 7 Minn.L.Rev. 166.

[52] Arkansas is the latest state to so provide, having adopted a constitutional amendment in November 1936. See Proc. Bar. Assoc. of Arkansas (1937-1939) 115, 116.

New Mexico, Oklahoma, South Dakota, Utah, and Washington.

The Indiana legislature, which is empowered by the constitution to modify or abolish the grand jury system, has passed statutes permitting all public offenses except treason and murder to be prosecuted by affidavit.[53] In Florida the constitution provides for prosecution by indictment, but also authorizes except in capital cases prosecutions by information in Escambia County and in any counties for which the legislature may so provide. The constitutions of Colorado, Nebraska, North Dakota, and Wyoming provide for the use of the indictment in felony cases but empower the legislature to provide otherwise. The Iowa constitution requires prosecution by indictment for all offenses where the punishment exceeds a fine of one hundred dollars or imprisonment for thirty days, but likewise authorizes the legislature to provide otherwise. In these five states legislation has been passed authorizing prosecution by information in all cases where an information may be used. Section 113 of the American Law Institute Code of Criminal Procedure provides: "All offences heretofore required to be prosecuted by indictment may be prosecuted either by indictment or information." [54] In

[53] The procedure is described in Robinson, Cases on Criminal Law and Procedure (1941) 315-316. The approval of the prosecuting attorney, though not of the court, is required. The affidavit may be made by the injured party or any other person. It must allege the statutory elements of the offense. No preliminary examination is required. The statute has been in effect since 1905, and has been held constitutional.

[54] "In twenty-four states it is now possible . . . to initiate prosecutions for major offenses by an information." Moley, "The Use of the Information in Criminal Cases" (1931) 17 A.B.A.J. 292. See also Morse, "A Survey of the Grand Jury" (1931) 10 Ore.L.Rev. 101, 122. This reform has long been urged. See "Criminal Procedure, Draft Report" (1910) 1 J.Crim. L. 584. More than a hundred years ago, Connecticut began to prosecute

states where its use is permitted, information is used to a very large extent in prosecuting both felonies and misdemeanors.[55] The following leading advantages have been claimed for the use of the information in preference to the indictment by a grand jury. In the first place, it is said that the time interval required to conduct a criminal prosecution is materially reduced.[56] It is less expensive, not only in the saving of the cost of grand juries but also in the lessened burden which is imposed upon the other agencies of law enforcement. In the third place, it is asserted that cases are disposed of more efficiently in that not so many unsuccessful prosecutions are initiated. Finally, it is said that it properly centers responsibility upon the prosecutor for actions which are seemingly largely within his control, even when indictments only are used.

The Minnesota Crime Commission Report of 1927 recommended that the power of the county attorney to file informations be extended to include all offenses the maximum punishment for which does not exceed twenty years.[57] Under existing law, informations could be filed only where the maximum sentence is not more than ten

---

without indictment in cases of felonies where the punishment did not extend to death or life imprisonment. Nat. Com. on Law Obs. and Enf., Report on Prosecution (1931) 35. California early made such provision. The use of the information in federal criminal procedure for prosecuting lesser crimes has been common since 1870. Albrecht v. United States, 273 U.S. 1, 47 Sup.Ct. 250, 71 L.Ed. 505 (1927). In 1934 it was one of four major reforms in criminal procedure approved by the American Bar Association. (1934) 20 A.B.A.J. 647, 651.

[55] Missouri Crime Survey (1926) 119; Report of the Minnesota Crime Commission (1934) 47, 97-98.

[56] Moley, "The Initiation of Criminal Prosecution by Indictment or Information" (1931) 29 Mich.L.Rev. 403, 404, 430. These alleged advantages have been discussed in the prior chapter on "Grand Jury."

[57] Minnesota Crime Commission Report (1927) 29. The reason assigned was avoidance of delay.

years. The Minnesota Crime Commission of 1934 recommended that the power of the county attorney to file informations be extended to include all felonies except those punishable by life imprisonment.[58]

In the federal courts, in the absence of waiver, prosecution for infamous crimes must be by indictment. An infamous crime is one which may be punished by death, or by imprisonment for a term exceeding one year, or by imprisonment for any term with hard labor.[59] This includes all felonies, but only those misdemeanors which provide penalties of imprisonment for a term exceeding one year or of imprisonment at hard labor. Under the Federal Rules of Criminal Procedure, Rule 7(a), it is required that offenses punishable by death shall be prosecuted by indictment, there being no possibility of a waiver.

6. Waiver of Indictment

Even if it should be concluded that informations are preferable to indictments, the right of the defendant to an indictment in various criminal cases is fixed by the Fifth Amendment for the federal courts and by similar provisions in several state constitutions. An intermediate solution, however, suggests itself, that of waiver of indictment.[60] For example, Rule 7(b) of the Federal Rules of

[58] Report of the Minnesota Crime Commission (1934) 47-48. If the defendant pleads guilty, he must be represented by counsel under this proposal. That indictment be required only in homicide cases is proposed in the Fifth Report of the Judicial Council of Ohio (1941) 7-8.

[59] Ex parte Wilson, 114 U.S. 417, 427, 5 Sup.Ct. 935, 29 L.Ed. 89 (1885); United States v. Moreland, 258 U.S. 433, 24 A.L.R. 992, 1002 (1922). See Keigwin, Cases in Criminal Procedure (1939) 200-201.

[60] It was rejected in the Report of the Minnesota Crime Commission (1934) 47, although a subcommittee of the Commission reported in its favor. But waiver was recommended by the Judicial Conference of Senior

Criminal Procedure provides: "An offense which may be punished by imprisonment for a term exceeding one year may be prosecuted by information if the defendant, after he has been advised of the nature of the charge and of his rights waives in open court prosecution by indictment." It will be noted that the case for waiver is clearer if there is a statute or rule of court providing for it. In the absence of such provisions for waiver, the courts are likely to take the view that such procedure is unknown to the common law and cannot be availed of.[61]

Assuming there is a statute, there may still be difficulties with respect to constitutionality. The New York court has held a statute providing for waiver unconstitutional.[62] There are, however, a number of state decisions,[63] as well as a lower federal court ruling [64] upholding the validity of waiver. Since the United States Supreme Court has up-

---

Circuit Judges in 1941 and 1942 and by the attorney general of the United States in 1931, 1932, 1933, 1936, 1937, 1938, and 1939. In 1934 it was one of four major proposals for criminal procedural reform approved by the American Bar Association. (1934) 20 A.B.A.J. 647, 651. See also Ninth Report of Judicial Council of Massachusetts (1933) 38-40.

[61] Wright v. State. 16 Ga.App. 216 (1915); United States v. Gill, 55 Fed. (2d) 399 (D.N.M. 1931); (1929) 14 Corn.L.Q. 206, 208. There are statutes permitting waiver in Arkansas, Georgia, Maryland, Massachusetts, North Carolina, Pennsylvania, and Rhode Island.

[62] People ex rel. Battista v. Christian, 249 N.Y. 314, 164 N.E. 111, 61 A.L.R. 797 (1928), 28 Col.L.Rev. 976, (1929) 14 Corn.L.Q. 206, 24 Ill.L. Rev. 319, (1932) 30 Mich.L.Rev. 928. See also (1942) 21 Neb.L.Rev. 178; See also Kyser v. State, 22 Ala. App. 431, 117 So. 157 (1928). Compare Garnsey v. State, 4 Okla. Cr. 547, 112 Pac. 24, 38 L.R.A.N.S. 600 (1910).

[63] Cook v. Wier, 185 Ga. 418 (1938); Edwards v. State, 45 N.J.L. 419 (1883); Lavery v. Commonwealth, 101 Pa. 560 (1882); Commonwealth ex rel. Stanton v. Francies, 250 Pa. 496, 95 Atl. 527 (1915), (1916) 29 Harv.L.Rev. 326; State v. Faile, 43 S.C. 52. 20 S.E. 827 (1894).

[64] United States v. Gill, 55 Fed. (2d) 399 (D.N.M., 1931); Comment (1938) 38 Col.L.Rev. 1318. See, however, Joyce on Indictments, §§ 31 and 32; Zoline, Federal Criminal Law and Procedure, § 138; Ex parte McClusky, 40 Fed. 71 (C.C. Ark. 1889).

held the waiver of jury trial[65] there should be no serious doubts about the waiver of grand jury proceedings. The contrary argument of the New York court was that a question of jurisdiction was involved and that public injury would result; thus the right to waive was not treated as a personal privilege. It should be noted that the federal rule does not require the prosecuting attorney to resort to information even when the defendant wishes that mode of prosecution. Just as in the case of waiver of jury trial, the consent of the prosecution is necessary. The federal rule provides for waiver whether the defendant pleads guilty or not.[66]

7. Necessity of Preliminary Examination

In most of the states where a substantial use of the information is permitted, there is either a constitutional or a statutory requirement that a preliminary examination before a magistrate be had or waived whereupon information may be filed.[67] Section 115 of the American Law Institute Code provides that no information may be filed against any person, except a fugitive from justice, for any

[65] Patton v. United States, 381 U.S. 276, 50 Sup.Ct. 253 (1930). It should be noted that there was no federal statute expressly providing for waiver of trial by jury. The United States Supreme Court has also held that the Fourteenth Amendment does not guarantee a grand jury indictment in the state courts. Hurtado v. California, 110 U.S. 516, 4 Sup.Ct. 111, 28 L.Ed. 232 (1884).

[66] A proposal by President Hoover in 1932 seemed to include only the case of a plea of guilty. See Note (1932) 30 Mich.L.Rev. 928, 930. In many New York counties, over half of those indicted by the grand jury plead guilty upon arraignment. Report of the New York Crime Commission (1928) 157.

[67] Keedy, "The Drafting of a Code of Criminal Procedure" (1929) 15 A.B.A.J. 7, 8. Substitution of examination before a law judge instead of before a magistrate is discussed by Lindsey, "Suggested Improvements in Criminal Procedure" (1917) 8 J.Crim.L. 2.

offense which may be punished by death or imprisonment in the penitentiary until there has been a preliminary examination or a waiver of such examination.[68] It also provides, however, that the fact that a preliminary examination was neither had nor waived shall in no case invalidate any information, unless the defendant objects before pleading to the merits.

About half the states limit the requirement of preliminary examination to felony cases. In the other states it applies to all cases where prosecution may be by information. In Arkansas,[69] Connecticut, Florida, Iowa, Louisiana, Vermont, and Washington, it is not necessary that there be a preliminary examination of the accused before an information is filed; or in Indiana before an affidavit is filed. In Iowa, Louisiana, and Pennsylvania it is necessary, however, that the consent of the trial judge be obtained.[70] There is no unanimity of opinion as to whether it is essential to the right to file an information that the accused be held to answer. Section 116 of the Institute Code provides

68 The American Law Institute Code of Criminal Procedure rule seems desirable. It does not cover misdemeanors. As Waite states: "Thus innocence is protected by the magisterial examination, under the information system, just as it is protected by the grand jury examination of the evidence under the indictment system." Wood and Waite, Crime and Its Treatment (1941) 414. In England procedure by information is regarded as disadvantageous to the defendant, since there is no preliminary examination. Jackson, The Machinery of Justice in England (1940) 94. The Federal Rules of Criminal Procedure do not make a preliminary examination a prerequisite to an information.

69 The Arkansas Supreme Court ruled that the omission of this requirement from the 1936 Arkansas Constitutional Amendment did not deprive the defendant of due process under the Fourteenth Amendment to the Federal Constitution, Penton v. State, 109 S.W. (2d) 131, 136 (Ark. 1937). A preliminary examination is not required in federal criminal procedure. Housel and Walser, Defending and Prosecuting Federal Criminal Cases (1938) § 34, pp.50-51.

70 See 120 A.L.R. 363.

that, if upon the preliminary examination the defendant is discharged, an information may be filed against him only by leave of court.

8. Leave of Court

The filing of an information, though it involves in most states the requirement of a prior preliminary examination, does not [71] require leave of the court except in Iowa, Louisiana,[72] and Pennsylvania [73] where statutes expressly require it. At common law, informations were brought, either ex officio by the attorney general in the king's own suit, or were filed by the Master of the Crown Office in the Court of King's Bench in cases where the king was the nominal prosecutor on the relation of some informer.[74] At common law, informations were merely the accusation of these officers, who were perfectly free in bringing them.[75] But the law was modified by an early statute [76] which in effect required the Master of the Crown Office to

[71] Code of Iowa, 1935, § 13650. That this results in a more dependable safeguard against persecution than the requirement of a grand jury is asserted by Perkins, "The Trial Information in Iowa" (1928) 13 Iowa L.Rev. 264, 287.

[72] The statute has been construed as giving the court very little discretion. State v. Judge of Tenth Judicial Circuit, 33 La. Ann. 1222 (1881). Cf. State v. Cole, 38 La. Ann. 843 (1886).

[73] Reports of the Crimes Survey Committee, Law Association of Philadelphia (1926) 120, 180. See also Walker v. People, 22 Colo. 415, 45 Pac. 388 (1896) where no preliminary examination was had. See also State v. Bratt (Mont. 1895) 40 Pac. 873 to same effect. See also 120 A.L.R. 359 annotating State ex rel. Juhl v. District Court, 107 Mont. 309, 84 Pac. (2d) 979, 120 A.L.R. 353 (1938).

[74] Bl. Comm. *308. This procedure became exceedingly rare and was abolished in 1938. Jackson, The Machinery of Justice in England (1940) 94.

[75] Note (1922) 36 Harv.L.Rev. 204, 205.

[76] See 4 & 5 Wm. & Mary, c.18 (1692). See 1 Stephen, A History of the Criminal Law of England (1883) 296.

procure leave of court to file an information.[77] The power of the court to deny leave, even though there was a prima facie case for the prosecution, was quite broad.[78] This statute expressly excepted the ex officio information. It followed that the attorney general had a right to file informations merely on his oath of office and without court leave as well after the passage of this statute as before.[79] The weight of authority in the state courts is that it is the ex officio information which obtains in our law.[80] The United States Supreme Court resolved prior doubts as to federal procedure by holding it to be necessary to obtain leave of court as recently as 1927.[81] The First Preliminary Draft of the Federal Rules of Criminal Procedure, Rule 8 (c), expressly retained this rule, but Rule

[77] The practice under this act was to grant leave only after certain preliminary steps had been taken, a motion supported by affidavit made in open court, a rule to show cause, and the filing of a recognizance by the prosecutor. See 2 Hawkins, Pleas of the Crown (8th ed.1824) c.26, § 8.

[78] The King v. Morgan, 1 Doug. 314 (1780); The King v. Compton, Cold. 246 (1783). For other examples of the exercise of the discretion, see Archbold, Criminal Pleading, Evidence and Practice (30th ed.1938) 120-121.

[79] The King v. Philipps, 3 Burr. 1564 (1764). But such practice has become practically obsolete. Kenny, Outlines of Criminal Law (15th ed.1942) 543. The latest case was Rex v. Mylius (London Times, Feb. 2, 1911) for a libel on the king.

[80] State v. Dover, 9 N.H. 468 (1838). Cf. State v. Kelm, 79 Mo. 515 (1883). See Note (1922) 36 Harv.L.Rev. 204, 205; Report of the Crimes Survey Committee, Law Association of Philadelphia (1926) 119; Clark, Handbook of Criminal Procedure (2d ed. by Mikell, 1918) 146; 31 C.J., Indictments and Informations, § 133, p.626.

[81] Albrecht v. United States, 273 U.S. 1, 47 Sup.Ct. 250, 71 L.Ed. 505 (1927). See also In re Informations under Migratory Bird Treaty Act, 281 Fed. 546, 548 (D. Mont. 1922), 36 Harv.L.Rev. 204. The practice has been formal and an assumed rather than an actual leave. United States v. Simon, 248 Fed. 980 (D.Pa. 1918). See also 5 Longsdorf, Cyclopedia of Federal Procedure (1929) § 2057, pp.542-544. In Russia the trial court makes a preliminary review of the indictment. Hazard, "Soviet Criminal Procedure" (1941) 15 Tulane L.Rev. 220, 228.

7(a) of the present Rules expressly abolishes it. The American Law Institute Code does not require it.

While the historical development does not support the requirement of leave of court, practical considerations may support the rule. If the courts are flooded with prosecutions for petty offenses, the court rather than some executive should say whether the court's time should be used for the trial of petty cases. This was particularly true in the days of prohibition. Even more important, accused persons are given some protection against persecution, in addition to the preliminary examination and corresponding to the protection afforded by a grand jury.

9. Alleged Strict Construction of Indictments

A generation ago and occasionally even today critics of criminal procedure point to the strictness with which the technical rules as to the sufficiency of indictments and informations have been enforced. They often quote or paraphrase the statement of Sir Matthew Hale made in the seventeenth century: "That in favor of life great strictnesses have been in all times required in points of indictments, and the truth is, that it is grown to be a blemish and inconvenience in the law, and the administration thereof; more offenders escape by the over easy ear given to exceptions in indictments, than by their own innocence, and many times gross murders, burglaries, robberies, and other heinous and crying offenses, escape by these unseemly niceties to the reproach of the law, to the shame of the government, and to the encouragement of villainy, and to the dishonor of God."[82] Doubtless many guilty

[82] Hale, History of the Pleas of the Crown (1st Am. ed.1847) 193. See also 1 Stephen, A History of the Criminal Law of England (1883) 284;

persons escaped in the days of Blackstone who lamented that one hundred and seventy offenses were punishable by death.[83] But it does not follow that the same situation prevails today. The meager statistics that are available indicate that the number of guilty persons escaping because of technical rulings with respect to the sufficiency of indictments is much smaller than many have supposed.[84]

In the American Law Institute's Study of the Business of the Federal Courts,[85] of the 34,420 cases studied,

---

Beale, Criminal Pleading and Practice (1899) 82; Clark, Handbook of Criminal Procedure (2d ed. by Mikell, 1918) 180; Pound, Criminal Justice in America (1930) 161-162; "Defects in Criminal Justice" (1925) 11 A.B.A.J. 297, 299; Waite, Criminal Law in Action (1934) 55; "How Long Must We Endure It?" (1918) 1 J. Am. Jud. Soc. 187; Ballantine, "Technicalities in Criminal Procedure" (1917) 1 Ill.L.Bull. 92; Caruso, "The Short Indictment" (1935) 23 Ky.L.J. 362; Wigmore, "Comment" (1910) 4 Ill.L.Rev. 580; Perkins, "Short Indictments and Informations" (1929) 15 A.B.A.J. 292; Perkins, "Absurdities in Criminal Procedure" (1926) 11 Iowa L.Rev. 297, 300, 330; Fessenden, "Improvement in Criminal Pleading" (1896) 10 Harv.L.Rev. 98.

[83] 4 Bl. Comm. *18. "This practice of extreme strictness in dealing with criminal indictments has been the cause of much ridicule in modern times, but its origin was humane and was one of the methods by which the courts 'administered' practical justice at a time when the inertia of the community was such that it still allowed excessive penalties to remain upon the statute books." Grinnell, "Probation as an Orthodox Common Law Practice in Massachusetts Prior to the Statutory System" (1917) 2 Mass. L.Q. 591, 600.

[84] It has been pointed out "that a rule which with the design of preventing escape for defect in pleading brings criminals to trial on an indictment that states conclusions instead of facts, will facilitate their escape for defect of proof, if it leads prosecutors to forego a careful consideration of the facts necessary to be established, and a preliminary examination of witnesses, searchingly and in detail, such as they would be likely to make if they were obliged to draw an accusation which explicitly sets forth the elements and circumstances of the crime." Green, "Is an Indictment Merely a Pleading?" (1911) 1 J.Crim.L. 925, 926; Book Review (1870) 5 Am.L.Rev. 732, 734; Ballantine, "Technicalities in Criminal Procedure" (1917) 1 Ill.L.Bull. 92, 94-95.

[85] A.L.I., A Study of the Business of the Federal Courts (1934) Pt. I,

"pleadings"[86] were filed by defendants in only 1,857. Of the pleadings filed, only 13.2 per cent were motions to quash the indictment or information, and 4.4 per cent were motions in arrest of judgments, which were often based on some claimed defect in the indictment or information. In 51.6 per cent of these pleadings, the ruling was in favor of the United States. In only 28 per cent of the pleadings was the ruling in favor of the defendant. The other pleadings were accounted for under the headings "No entry" or "Other rulings." In only a fraction of one per cent of the criminal cases in the federal courts is the indictment held to be defective,[87] and this small fraction doubtless includes many cases where the defect was one of substance and not merely of form.

The state crime surveys have shown similar results. In Missouri, out of 4,969 cases lodged in the circuit court, only 251 were disposed of by action of the court, and of these only 16 were discharged on motion to quash.[88] In the highest appellate court of Missouri, of 329 reversals in 745 cases studied, only 28 were for defective indictment.[89] This is all the more striking when it is recalled that some of the most technical decisions on indictment have come from Missouri.[90] In Illinois the cases elimi-

---

Criminal Case P. 72, and Detailed Tables 15, p.127, and 17, p.129. See also Comment (1937) 35 Mich.L.Rev. 456.

[86] The term is employed to include any motion or paper filed in the case except a guilty or not guilty plea.

[87] Comment (1937) 35 Mich.L.Rev. 456.

[88] Missouri Crime Survey (1926) 167.

[89] Missouri Crime Survey (1926) 223, 234, 253, 264. The New York decisions have not been overly technical. Nutting, "The Indictment in New York" (1934) 19 Corn.L.Q. 580, 584.

[90] For instance, in State v. Campbell, 210 Mo. 202, 109 S.W. 807 (1908) a conviction for rape was reversed on the ground that the indictment concluded "Against the peace and dignity of state," instead of "Against the peace and dignity of *the* state" as required by a clause in the constitution.

nated by discharges by the court for defective indictments were negligible.[91] In the supreme court 39 per cent of the cases appealed were affirmed. Of the reversals, only 4.6 per cent were for defective indictment or information. As a matter of fact, reversals on appeal are usually for errors in instructions to the jury or in admission or exclusion of evidence, and seldom for defects in the accusation.[92] Thus the elimination of all the cases where accusations are held defective would have only a slight effect on the percentage of convictions of criminal defendants. This does not mean that improvement would not be worth while, inasmuch as there is widespread criticism of these decisions both by lawyers and laymen.[93]

10. Constitutionality of Reform of Indictments

When the Fifth Amendment to the Federal Constitution guaranteeing indictment by a grand jury was adopted, it seems likely that it was understood to refer to the strict technical indictment of the common law.[94] The drafters of the amendment were more concerned with the protection of the individual than with the efficient operation of the government. At an early date, however, the legislatures

[91] Illinois Crime Survey (1929) 123-131, 211.

[92] Orfield, Criminal Appeals in America (1939) 206-207. "As far as indictments are concerned, the metamorphosis is now complete, for supreme court reports contain little reference to faulty indictments. Drafting indictments has degenerated from a fine art to the filling in of blanks, work which is well within the competence of a stenographer." Warner and Cabot, "Changes in the Administration of Criminal Justice During the Past Fifty Years" (1937) 50 Harv.L.Rev. 583, 588.

[93] Such decisions occupy a prominent position in the "show window of the bar." Stassen, "The Show Window of the Bar" (1936) 20 Minn.L.Rev. 577. See the view of Hadley in Missouri Crime Survey (1926) 359-360; and of Harno in Illinois Crime Survey (1929) 123-131.

[94] McClintock, "Indictment by a Grand Jury" (1942) 26 Minn.L.Rev. 153, 157.

and Congress began to pass legislation correcting the worst abuses of the common-law rules respecting the validity of an indictment.[95] Where these statutes have been limited to merely formal parts of the indictment, they have been held valid. In the small number of cases in which laws prescribing the sufficiency of indictments have been held invalid, the courts have thought that they permitted the omission of allegations substantially necessary to charge the offense.[96] It appears that the constitutional guarantee permits modifications in the form, but not in the substance, of the indictment as it was known at common law. There thus became necessary an examination of the functions performed by the indictment to ascertain what are the essential elements that must be retained.

11. Functions of Accusation

Today the basic function of the accusation is to give notice.[97] Such notice would seem to be required by due

[95] While legislation may bring about immediately needed improvements, in the long run it is preferable to improve criminal pleading by rules of court. Nat. Com. on Law Obs. and Enf., Rep. on Crim. Proc. (1931) 31-32, 46.

[96] State v. Learned, 47 Me. 426 (1859); State v. Mace, 76 Me. 64 (1884); Murphy v. State, 24 Miss. 590 (1852); Williams v. State, 12 Tex. App. 396 (1882). See Note (1907) 20 Harv.L.Rev. 573.

[97] Robinson, Cases on Criminal Law and Procedure (1941) 277. On the other hand it has been stated: "But if there has been a preliminary examination, accused knows well enough the nature of the charge and the evidence by which it is to be maintained, and if he has waived such examination he is not likely to be ignorant of these things." Nat. Com. on Law Obs. and Enf., Rep. on Crim. Proc. (1931) 33. "To our mind, in the average case, the person who is being prosecuted as the person who, whether guilty or innocent of the crime, does as a matter of fact know at least as much about it as the prosecution. He has had some connection therewith, or suspicion would have been directed to him. It is possible to presume a man innocent of the offense, and still to presume that he knows

process of law. The accusation must notify the defendant of the criminal act and intent which are charged against him so that he may prepare his defense. It ought to indicate the criminal statute which he is accused of having violated. It operates to limit the subsequent proceedings to the exact scope of its main allegations. The jurors, the lawyers, and the court are also given notice by its terms for their assistance in the discharge of their functions. The specifications of the charge shape and control the pleadings, the trial, and the judgment. It serves to protect the accused against further prosecutions for the same crime.

A leading student of the pleading problem in criminal procedure has said: "In the United States the scope and content of the indictment have been determined by two general factors: first, the rule to be found in all our constitutions to the effect that the accused shall be fully informed of the accusation against him and, secondly, the rule of judicial law that the accusation shall express all the constituent elements of the offense charged." [98] Where an indictment accomplishes both of these objectives, there can be no contention that it is not valid. Difficulty arises where it accomplishes the former objective but not the latter. One group of reformers of criminal pleading would treat the indictment as still valid. Another group has serious doubts as to constitutionality.

Historically, the indictment performed only the function of informing the king's officers of the crimes which had been committed in the jurisdiction from which the

---

a great deal about it." Scott, "Reform of Criminal Procedure, With Reference Particularly to the Indictment" (1913) 61 U. of Pa.L.Rev. 458, 469.

[98] Millar, "The Function of Criminal Pleading" (1922) 12 J.Crim.L. 500.

grand jury was called.[99] This narrow and relatively unimportant function doubtless explains in part why, until comparatively recently, the accused was not given a copy of the indictment or permitted to examine it, but had to get his knowledge of its contents from hearing it read to him at his arraignment. Such a rule was logical with respect to an accusation for the benefit of the king, but scarcely consistent with the subsequently announced purpose of the indictment to inform the defendant of the exact accusation against him.

Prior to the settlement of America, the indictment had come to perform a second function. It served as the pleading of the prosecution, and was accordingly subjected to the strict construction that then applied to all pleadings.[100] The statutes of jeofails alleviated the most obnoxious features of the strict rules when applied to civil proceedings. But these statutes did not apply to criminal proceedings.[101] Hence we adopted with the indictment the old rules of strict construction.[102]

[99] 3 Holdsworth, History of English Law (3d ed.1923) 615; Note (1929) 24 Ill.L.Rev. 319, 322. "But here, my Lords, I would first observe the reason and use of a presentment or indictment, it is to apprise the king of such an offense committed, as it is of an office, to inform him of a title in civil matters." R. v. Berchet (1691) 1 Shower at p.120, argument by Shower.

[100] Two common-law doctrines have been generally followed in American jurisdictions: "First, that the indictment shall set forth all the juristic elements of the offense, shall allege with completeness the State's cause of action; and, secondly, that its allegations shall answer the test of certainty as fixed by the common law." Millar, "The Reform of Criminal Pleading in Illinois" (1917) 8 J.Crim.L. 336, 338. See also Scott, "Reform of Criminal Procedure, With Reference Particularly to the Indictment" (1913) 61 U. of Pa.L.Rev. 458, 471-474; 1 Stephen, A History of the Criminal Law of England (1883) 275, 280-282. A high degree of certainty was required. See the opinion of Lumpkin, J., in Wingard v. State, 13 Ga. 391 (1853).

[101] 2 Hale, History of the Pleas of the Crown (1st Am. ed.1847) 193;

The third and final function of an indictment was protection of the citizen against arbitrary action by the sovereign. Although this was not the original purpose of the indictment, eventually it became so important in popular opinion that it was guaranteed in the bill of rights during the struggle between Parliament and the Stuarts. At a time when officials and even judges were under the influence of the king, the subject had some protection against arbitrary prosecution, so long as no prosecution could be begun without an indictment by the grand jury. It seems reasonable to conclude that the guarantee of indictment

---

3 Holdsworth, History of English Law (3d ed.1923) 618. It followed that the defendant could raise the objection on motion in arrest of judgment as well as earlier. It has been pointed out that "the requirement as to indictments grew up at a time when the only review of a criminal proceeding was by writ of error for errors apparent on the face of the record, that is, of the indictment, recital of trial and verdict, and the sentence. Hence the indictment at common law had to do much more than apprise the accused as to what was charged against him. It had to set forth a complete case against him sufficient on its face and without more to sustain the judgment of conviction and sentence." Nat. Com. on Law Obs. and Enf., Rep. on Crim. Proc. (1931) 21. See also p.33 of the Report. The indictment must state the offense with sufficient certainty so as to "make it appear on the record of what particular offense the defendant was charged, for the purpose of review in case of conviction." Clark, Handbook of Criminal Procedure (2d ed. by Mikell, 1918) 177.

[102] 4 Holdsworth, History of English Law (3d ed.1923) 531. The American Law Institute Code of Criminal Procedure "changes the function of the indictment by limiting it to a bare statement of the offense." Perkins, "Short Indictments and Informations" (1929) 15 A.B.A.J. 292, 293. On the other hand it has been asserted: "An indictment is not in substance or form a mere accusation. It is a finding of guilt." Green, "Is an Indictment Merely a Pleading?" (1911) 1 J.Crim.L. 925, 926. He adds: "The same thing is substantially true of an information. The degree of particularity with which the circumstances of the alleged offense must be set out has hitherto been determined, it would seem, not alone by what is sufficient to apprise the prisoner of the charge, but quite as much by what was regarded as sufficient to enable the court to see that the question of his guilt has been investigated with proper care."

by a grand jury was intended to preserve the functions of the indictment, first as a pleading and second as an accusation by an unofficial body of laymen, based on a determination by that body that the accused was guilty of the specified crime for which he was to be placed on trial, and that the latter function was regarded as far more important.[103] The substantial impairment of either function would violate the bill of rights.

12. Pleading Aspect of Indictment

At common law, the opening pleading[104] by one who initiates a civil or criminal proceeding must satisfy three requirements.[105] In the first place, it must set forth sufficient facts to show that the court in which the proceeding is brought has jurisdiction of the subject matter, and to

[103] McClintock, "Indictment by a Grand Jury" (1942) 26 Minn.L.Rev. 153, 159; Comment (1936) 35 Mich.L.Rev. 456, 461. It has been contended that formalities in the written document were required to show that the grand jury had considered all essential elements of a case. (1929) 24 Ill. L.Rev. 319. On the other hand, under present practice the indictment is prepared by the prosecuting attorney and may have little relation to what takes place in the grand jury room. See Note (1939) 53 Harv.L.Rev. 122, 129.

[104] The indictment constitutes the first pleading in a criminal action. Housel and Walser, Defending and Prosecuting Federal Criminal Cases (1938) 284.

[105] McClintock, "Indictment by a Grand Jury" (1942) 26 Minn.L.Rev. 153, 159. See United States v. Cruikshank, 92 U.S. 542 (1875); Miller v. United States, 133 Fed. 337, 341 (C.C.A. 8th, 1904). "The objects of the indictment, then, are these: (1) to enable the accused to prepare his defense, (2) to enable him in case he is again prosecuted for the same crime to plead as a defense his former conviction or acquittal, and (3) to give the court an opportunity to decide the case on the indictment without hearing the evidence, and the accused an opportunity to elect as to how he shall present his defense." Willard, "The Seventeenth Century Indictment in the Light of Modern Conditions" (1911) 24 Harv.L.Rev. 290. See also (1930) 30 Col.L.Rev. 1051, 1053; Wingard v. State, 13 Ga. 396, 400 (1853).

enable it to render the proper judgment; in a criminal proceeding it must show that the acts which defendant is charged with committing amounted to a specified crime which the court could punish, and that it was committed within the territorial jurisdiction of the court.[106] In the second place, the pleading must inform the defendant of the nature of the charge against him. In the third place, it must form a record from which it can be determined whether a subsequent proceeding is barred by the former adjudication.

The first of these requirements was satisfied by the common-law indictment, often with great prolixity.[107] The judge could easily recognize the nature of the crime charged, and the indictment was required specifically to allege the county in which the act had been committed. In the seventeenth century and before, the second requirement was met very inadequately. No copy of the indictment was furnished to the defendant and he was not guaranteed the right to counsel. The reading of the in-

106 "The indictment must state the offense, and must state it with sufficient certainty (a) to enable the court to say that, if the facts stated are true, an offense has been committed by the defendant. (b) To enable the court to know what punishment to impose in case of conviction. (c) To enable the court to confine the proof to the offense charged, so that the defendant may not be accused of one offense and convicted of another." Clark, Handbook of Criminal Procedure (2d ed. by Mikell, 1918) 177.

107 It has been asserted that this function could easily be eliminated, that it involves trying the case on the papers and not on the proof, and that it is not important to the court to know whether or not the facts alleged constitute an offense when after the evidence has been presented it will have an opportunity to determine whether or not the facts proved constitute an offense. Willard, "The Seventeenth Century Indictment in the Light of Modern Conditions" (1911) 24 Harv.L.Rev. 290, 291. See also Millar, "The Reform of Criminal Pleading in Illinois" (1917) 8 J.Crim.L. 337, 339; Criminal Procedure, Draft Report of Committee E (1910) 1 J.Crim.L. 584, 587.

dictment to him would not help, since it was lengthy, replete with technical legal terms, and in Latin. That it might even be misleading was shown by the fact that, although it was required to state the date on which the alleged crime was committed, a conviction would be valid if the proof showed another day, so long as the prosecution was not barred by the statute of limitations. Even at the present time, when the defendant is furnished with a copy of the indictment, he may be unable to understand it unless aided by counsel.[108] Moreover, convictions are held valid even where there is a variance between allegations which must be included in the indictment so as to inform the defendant of the charge against him, and the proof adduced by the prosecution. The third requirement of protection against a second prosecution[109] is doubtless

[108] Yet it has been stated: "Of the three objects of the indictment there remains for consideration the first—to enable the accused to prepare his defense. It is confidently submitted that in any country where the object of its laws is the punishment of the guilty only, this should be the sole and exclusive object of an indictment, complaint, or criminal charge." Willard, "The Seventeenth Century Indictment in the Light of Modern Conditions" (1911) 24 Harv.L.Rev. 290, 293. "The primary function of the indictment is manifestly that of complying with the just command of the constitution that it informs the accused of the nature and cause of the accusation against him." Millar, "The Function of Criminal Pleading" (1922) 12 J.Crim.L. 500, 501-502.

[109] It has been claimed that this theory "has led to more absurd decisions than almost any other. It is chiefly responsible for the rule that the indictment must state all the ingredients of the offense." Willard, "The Seventeenth Century Indictment in the Light of Modern Conditions" (1911) 24 Harv.L.Rev. 290, 292. Mr. Willard states that this function can be eliminated without prejudice to the essential rights of the defendant. This could be done by a provision that in case of a second indictment the entire proceedings of the first trial may be examined to find out just what was decided. See also, Case v. United States, 6 F. (2d) 530 (C.C.A. 9th, 1925). Under Section 186 of the American Law Institute Code of Criminal Procedure (1930), there may be an amendment of the accusation after verdict to avoid another prosecution for the same offense. It has been

met in most cases, but it should be noted that in most cases there is little likelihood of a second prosecution for the same offense. In those cases where there is such a likelihood, the record is usually not sufficient to determine the question, and the defendant must allege facts outside of the record to support his plea of former conviction or acquittal.

With respect to the pleading aspect, it may well be argued that a short form of indictment or information is inadequate. As one writer states: "It may seem sufficient for all purposes of fairness to the prisoner that the formal accusation whether by indictment or information, should name the offense, and that it should be described in the charge by its specific name only, supplemented by a bill of particulars when this is demanded. But it is one of the functions of pleading to formulate the issues which are to be tried."[110] He adds that "good results in the trial are

---

stated: "Moreover when the forms of indictment became settled there were no such means of establishing what was tried as are now available everywhere. . . . There is no longer reason for requiring more than such notice of the offense charged as will assure a fair trial." Nat. Com. on Law Obs. and Enf., Rep. on Crim. Proc. (1931) 22. See also Millar, "The Reform of Criminal Pleading in Illinois" (1917) 8 J.Crim.L. 337, 339-340; Millar, "The Function of Criminal Pleading" (1922) 12 J.Crim.L. 500, 501; Scott, "Reform of Criminal Procedure, With Reference Particularly to the Indictment" (1913) 61 U. of Pa.L.Rev. 458, 472.

[110] Ballantine, "Technicalities in Criminal Procedure" (1917) 1 Ill.L. Bull. 92, 95. "Notwithstanding all the pedantry and technicalities, by which the law relating to indictments was disfigured, it ought to be said they had at least one valuable feature. The rule that the indictment must set out all the elements of the offences charged, was some sort of security against the arbitrary multiplication of offences and extension of the criminal law by judicial legislation in times when there were no definitions of crimes established by statute, or indeed by any generally recognized authority. . . . The fact is that looseness in the legal definitions of crimes can be met only by strictness and technicality in indictments." 1 Stephen, A History of the Criminal Law of England (1883) 292-293. According to

not likely to follow from loose and slip-shod methods of pleading. If the charge contains the essential propositions which have to be proved by the prosecution, there is less likely to be a mis-trial by failure of proof."

13. Proposed Reforms

On the basis of the functions of the indictment, one may attempt to evaluate proposals for reform. Proposed reforms have been of two types. One type involves general provisions relaxing the strictness of the common-law requirements, permitting amendments to eliminate the freeing of defendants for errors in the indictments, or broadening the common-law rules as to the defects which are waived by failure to plead them expressly or cured by the verdict. A second type undertakes to provide simplified forms which have been declared to be sufficient.

Reforms of the first type have been quite successful. For the most part their validity has not been questioned.[111] When the question has been raised, they have

---

Holdsworth the common-law rules had three advantages: (1) looseness in legal definitions is counteracted by the strictness in the indictment; (2) compelling the Crown to state its case with particularity and formality was security against arbitrary power of the Crown; and (3) since the Crown must prove its case, any defenses which could disprove that case were open to the defendant. Moreover, it fostered and kept alive the idea of the presumption of innocence. 3 History of English Law (3d ed.1923) 620.

[111] With respect to a federal criminal proceeding, however, it has been held that surplusage cannot be stricken from an indictment, at least not without the consent of the defendant. Ex parte Bain, 121 U.S. 1, 7 Sup. Ct. 781, 30 L.Ed. 849 (1887). Rule 7(d) of the Federal Rules of Criminal Procedure provides that the court may on motion strike surplusage from the indictment or information. Section 183 of the American Law Institute Code of Criminal Procedure (1930) allows the disregarding of surplusage without limitation. With respect to the Canadian procedure, see

usually been upheld. The reason they have not attained complete success is because the courts have often construed them so narrowly as to nullify much of the good which their advocates intended they should accomplish.

Since 1881 in New York, the statutes have required only a "plain and concise statement of the act constituting the crime, without unnecessary repetition." [112] Similar provisions are found in most other states.[113] Other statutes make unnecessary technical allegations, the omission of which would not prejudice the defendant. Still other statutes deal with crimes which were particularly difficult to charge. Thus homicide may be charged without setting out the manner and means of killing,[114] perjury by setting out only the substance of the false testimony,[115] and libel by a general allegation of the defamation of the complaining witness.[116]

With respect to the old indictment, minimum standards of sufficiency required a statement of the acts of the defendant and of the elements of the crime.[117] Some examples of the problems of alleging the acts are reckless driving, conspiracy, and violations of the narcotic laws. Usually a charge in the language of the statute is proper but, where that language is too general, its use may be condemned as a conclusion of law which does not succeed in apprizing the defendant of the particular acts of which

---

Crouse, "A Critique of Canadian Criminal Legislation" (1934) 12 Can.B. Rev. 545, 574.

112 New York Code of Criminal Procedure, § 275. See (1929) 53 Harv. L.Rev. 122.

113 E.g., Ill. Ann. Stat. (Smith-Hurd, 1935) c.38, § 716; A.L.I. Code of Crim. Proc. (1930) 538 *et seq*. See Supplemental Report of Rhode Island Judicial Council (1932) 3-9.

114 Wis. Stat. (1937) § 355, 24.

115 Mass. Ann. Laws (1933) 277, § 43.

116 Cal. Pen. Code (Deering, 1937) § 964.

117 People v. Dumar, 106 N.Y. 502, 13 N.E. 325 (1887).

he is accused.[118] In fact, sometimes the language of the statute, when read apart from its definitive sections, embraces noncriminal acts.[119] Another bar to conciseness is the line of cases holding that the defendant is prejudiced unless all the elements of the offense are set out. For example, the particular intent necessary to make an act unlawful must be alleged.[120] To charge larceny it must be stated that the property was taken from the possession and without the consent of the owner,[121] and statutory exceptions must be negatived.[122]

The second type of reform, legislative enactment of specific forms, has not been so successful.[123] The form has been held invalid where it fails to allege some particular fact essential to the completion of the crime. The reasons assigned have been either that it fails to inform the defendant of the nature of the accusation against him, or because it does not conform to the requirements of an indictment as that term was used in the constitutional guarantee of indictment by a grand jury.[124] In a leading New

[118] People v. Green, 368 Ill. 242, 13 N.E. (2d) 278 (1938); State v. Verdin, 192 La. 275, 187 So. 666 (1939). Reasons of public policy require a different rule with respect to indictment for the publication of obscene literature. Bartell v. United States, 227 U.S. 427 (1913).

[119] Mastoras v. State, 180 So. 113 (Ala. App. 1938). But courts are inclined to feel that a perusal of the statute will give the defendant the information to which he is entitled. (1939) 37 Mich.L.Rev. 1325.

[120] People v. Santro, 229 N.Y. 277, 128 N.E. 234 (1920).

[121] Slusher v. Commonwealth, 267 Ky. 140, 101 S.W. (2d) 663 (1937).

[122] People v. Stachler, 175 N.Y. 57, 67 N.E. 132 (1903).

[123] For the American Law Institute Code of Criminal Procedure forms, see Section 188. The Code does not require the use of such forms but permits them. The old forms can still be used if desired. See Section 187.

[124] State v. Mace, 76 Me. 64 (1884); Murphy v. State, 24 Miss. 590 (1852); Brinster v. State, 12 Tex. App. 612 (1882). See Note, 13 Tex.L. Rev. 101 (1935) on the constitutionality of the short form of indictment in Texas. See also Wharton, Criminal Pleading and Practice (9th ed. 1889) § 90, p.66.

York case[125] the highest New York appellate court with three judges dissenting upheld an indictment which, as permitted by statute, merely charged that defendants on a day stated committed murder in the first degree contrary to a specified section of the penal statutes. The court pointed out that the statutes required the prosecuting attorney, on demand of the defendant, to furnish a bill of particulars which became part of the record, and that such a bill was furnished in this case. The court stated that its decision should not be regarded as a judicial approval of the form of indictment used. While sufficient in the particular case, it would not be in any case where doubt as to its meaning could exist. Probably, because of the strict limitations placed upon its decision by the court, the statutory forms are not in common use in New York.[126]

14. The Institute Code

The American Law Institute Code of Criminal Procedure contains forty-seven sections in Chapter 6 thereof dealing with the regulation of indictments and informations.[127] To the extent that they provide for the elimination of useless technicalities of the common-law rules regarding criminal pleading, they are to be commended.[128]

[125] People v. Bogdanoff, 245 N.Y. 16, 171 N.E. 890 (1930); Note (1930) 30 Col.L.Rev. 1051. For the history of New York legislation with respect to indictments, see Nutting, "The Indictment in New York" (1934) 19 Corn.L.Q. 580.

[126] Note (1939) 53 Harv.L.Rev. 122.

[127] Many of these provisions are suggested in Mikell, "A Proposed Draft of a Code of Criminal Procedure" (1913) 5 J.Crim.L. 827. See also Millar, "The Reform of Criminal Pleading in Illinois" (1917) 8 J.Crim.L. 337.

[128] The purpose of the Code is to "get away entirely from the needless formalism and verbosity in criminal pleading—a need urgently felt for a long time both within and without the legal profession." Perkins, "Short Indictments and Informations" (1929) 15 A.B.A.J. 292, 293. He adds that

There is a very complete and detailed specification of needless requirements which may be eliminated from the accusation. Section 184 is a very broad general section dealing with defects, variances, and amendments. If this section is afforded a reasonable scope, it will prevent the freeing of defendants in all cases where it does not appear affirmatively that the defendant was in fact prejudiced thereby in his defense on the merits.

15. Amendment

At common law there can be no amendment, either as to form or substance, without the consent of the grand jury finding the indictment.[129] Quite clearly any amendment changing the nature of the offense would appear to amount to a change of substance, violating the constitu-

---

the heart of the Institute plan is to be found in Sections 152, 153, 154, 155, 184, and 188. Section 152 covers form of indictment, 153 form of information, 154 charging the offense, 155 bill of particulars, 184 defects, variances, and amendments, and 188 forms for specific offenses. Several states have adopted the Code provisions on indictment. Iowa Code (1935) § 13732 *et seq.;* R.I. Gen. Laws (1938) c.625, § 3; Utah Rev. Stat. Ann. (supp. 1939) §§ 105-121 *et seq.* In New Mexico the short form has been adopted by rule of court. State v. Roy, 40 N.M. 397, 60 P. (2d) 646 (1936). The same has been true in Arizona. Waite, "Arizona's Code of Criminal Procedure" (1940) 23 J. Am. Jud. Soc. 175. Proposed reforms in Illinois failed of adoption. See Freeman, "The Draft Code of Criminal Law and Procedure" (1935) 30 Ill.L.Rev. 226, 234. "We recommend the provisions as to indictment and information in the model code of criminal procedure of the American Law Institute for general consideration." Nat. Com. on Law Obs. and Enf., Rep. on Crim. Proc. (1931) 33. See also p.47 of the Report.

129 Ex parte Bain, 121 U.S. 1, 7 Sup.Ct. 781 (1887); Clark, Handbook of Criminal Procedure (2d ed. by Mikell, 1918) 363; Keigwin, Cases in Criminal Procedure (1939) 201; Joyce, Indictments (2d ed.1924) § 13; 2 Bishop, New Criminal Procedure (4th ed.1895) § 708; Comments (1918) 27 Yale L.J. 969; (1930) 10 B.U.L.Rev. 388; (1928) 37 Yale L.J. 383. In many states statutes have been passed permitting amendments in form. Some cases allow amendments in form even in the absence of statute.

tional right to presentment by a grand jury.[130] Occasionally there will be difficulties in determining what is a change in the nature of the offense.[131] It is immaterial that the amendment charges a lesser crime.[132] The consent of the defendant to the change should make no difference as no waivable right appears to be involved,[133] nor should the court find an amendment which the parties themselves did not expressly contemplate.

Amendment of the information or indictment should be allowed as to all formal matters. It should be allowed before or during trial to prevent variance, on such terms as will give the defendant reasonable notice and an opportunity to make his defense. It should be allowed after trial in order to make the indictment or information conform to the proof, where no objection to the variance was made upon the trial.[134]

The Minnesota Crime Commission Report of 1927 recommended that the court have the power to amend indictments and informations at any time, provided that such

130 State v. Goodrich, 46 N.H. 186 (1865); Wilbur v. State, 101 Miss. 392, 58 So. 7 (1912); Joyce, Indictments (2d ed.1924) § 137; Millar, "The Reform of Criminal Pleading in Illinois" (1917) 8 J.Crim.L. 337, 358-359.

131 Sullivan v. Commonwealth, 161 S.E. 297 (Va. 1931), (1932) 45 Harv.L.Rev. 934; 23 J.Crim.L. 486; 18 Va.L.Rev. 460. Separate sections and separate penalties were involved.

132 Commonwealth v. Adams, 92 Ky., 134, 17 S.W. 276 (1891); People v. Motello, 157 App. Div. 510, 142 N.Y.Supp. 622 (1919).

133 But compare the view of Beale: "By consent of the defendant, however, an indictment may be amended, except, perhaps, an indictment for a capital offense." Beale, Criminal Pleading and Practice (1899) 116.

134 Burdick, "Criminal Justice in America: Possibility of Improvement by Statutory Changes and Constitutional Amendments Affecting Procedure" (1925) 11 A.B.A.J. 510, 512; Report of Committee on Law Enforcement (1923) 48 A.B.A. Rep. 415, 423, 434; Lawson and Keedy, "Criminal Procedure in England" (1910) 1 J.Crim.L. 595, 604; "Report of Committee on Criminal Procedure" (1910) 1 J.Crim.L. 584, 586-590; Campbell, "Some Needed Reforms in the Criminal Law" (1903) 6 Rep. Proc. Bar Assoc. of Ark. 53, 64.

amendments should not prejudice substantial rights of the defendant, and provided further that the defendant be afforded reasonable notice and opportunity to make his defense.[135]

Largely because of constitutional doubts,[136] the Federal Rules of Criminal Procedure make no provision for amendment of indictments. Rule 7(e) of the Federal Rules of Criminal Procedure provides: "The court may permit an information to be amended at any time before verdict or finding if no additional or different offense is charged and if substantial rights of the defendant are not prejudiced."

An information may, on leave of the court, be amended by a successor in office of the prosecuting attorney who filed the information.[137] In the absence of the prosecuting attorney the assistant prosecutor has the power.[138]

It has been held that an unauthorized amendment of an information, made by the county solicitor after it had been filed, rendered it void.[139]

16. Variance

Even if an indictment is sufficient, there may be a variance between the crime charged and the proof. An illustra-

[135] Report of the Minnesota Crime Commission (1927) 30, 73. The reasons assigned were the avoidance of delay and the prevention of the failure of prosecutions because of mere irregularities. See also MacChesney, "A Progressive Program for Procedural Reform" (1912) 3 J.Crim.L. 528, 531.

[136] It has been held that an amendment authorized by the court, by which five words were stricken out of the indictment as surplusage, was a fatal interference with the functions of the grand jury. Ex parte Bain, 121 U.S. 1, 7 Sup.Ct. 781, 30 L.Ed. 849 (1887).

[137] State v. Barrell, 54 Atl. 183 (Vt. 1903), 12 Yale L.J. 510; State v. Meacham, 67 Vt. 707 (1895).

[138] People v. Henssler, 48 Mich. 49 (1882).

[139] State ex rel. Wentworth v. Coleman, 121 Fla. 13, 163 So. 316, 101 A.L.R. 1252 (1935).

tion may be found in the attempt to distinguish larceny by trick from obtaining property by false pretenses or embezzlement. An indictment for one of these crimes is not supported by proof of the other.[140] It is true that the short-form indictment need not set out the theory of the accusation. But such theory must be set out in the bill of particulars and, if the bill is to be read with the indictment,[141] a variance between bill and proof would be fatal.[142] Recent simplified forms for New York indictments diminish the possibility of variance by charging the crime in several counts drawn upon different theories. This avoids the necessity of electing before proof is in, upon what theory the case is to be submitted to the jury. Even this cannot entirely avoid the danger that the jury will be instructed on the wrong theory. It is possible to solve the problem as to larceny by legislation modeled after Massachusetts and California statutes providing that one form of charge shall be sufficient to support a conviction on any of the three theories.[143]

The best legislative solution of the problem of variance is provision for liberal amendment. Statutes in New York and eighteen other states have long allowed the amendment of allegations as to time and names and descriptions of places and things to conform to the proof.[144] But under such statutes no change can be made in the crime charged, since this would bring about an indictment not found by the grand jury.[145]

140 People v. Noblett, 244 N.Y. 355, 155 N.E. 670 (1927).

141 Cf. People v. Bogdanoff, 254 N.Y. 16, 171 N.E. 890 (1930).

142 State v. Schuling, 216 Iowa 1425, 250 N.W. 588 (1933), (1934) 19 Iowa L. Rev. 628.

143 Mass. Ann. Laws (1933) c.277, § 41; Cal. Pen. Code (Deering, 1937) § 952; Note (1938) 22 Minn.L.Rev. 211.

144 N.Y. Code Crim. Proc. § 293.

145 People v. Bromwich, 200 N.Y. 385, 93 N.E. 933 (1911).

Section 184(2) of the American Law Institute Code of Criminal Procedure provides that no variance between the allegations of the indictment and the evidence in support thereof shall be ground for acquittal, but that the indictment may be amended to conform to the evidence. This would appear to violate the constitutional guarantee in all of those cases where there is nothing to show that the grand jury had in mind, in finding the indictment, the facts as they appeared by the evidence at the trial rather than those they stated in the indictment.[146]

17. Bill of Particulars

The Institute Code provisions just mentioned are negative in character.[147] In the affirmative provisions as to what the indictment shall contain [148] and in the forms suggested,[149] the Code follows the technique of reducing the indictment to the smallest possible compass, and then providing that its function as a pleading shall to a large degree be performed by a bill of particulars,[150] which must

146 McClintock, "Indictment by a Grand Jury" (1942) 26 Minn.L.Rev. 153, 175. The provision is defended by Perkins, "Short Indictments and Informations" (1929) 15 A.B.A.J. 292, 296. See also Perkins, "Absurdities in Criminal Procedure" (1926) 11 Iowa L.Rev. 297, 304.

147 It has been suggested that the American Law Institute Code of Criminal Procedure should have set out the minimum requirements in affirmative terms. Brunyate, "The American Draft Code of Criminal Procedure, 1930" (1933) 49 L.Q.Rev. 192, 209. Rule 7(c) of the Federal Rules of Criminal Procedure (1944) provides: "The indictment or the information shall be a plain, concise and definite written statement of the essential facts constituting the offense charged."

148 Sections 152, 153, and 154. See Perkins, "The Short Indictment Act" (1929) 14 Iowa L.Rev. 385; Perkins, "Short Indictments and Informations" (1929) 15 A.B.A.J. 292.

149 Section 187.

150 Section 155. It should be noted that the bill of particulars is made

be filed in all cases where demanded by the defendant and which the court may require the prosecuting attorney to file in any case.[151] The Code quite clearly assumes that the defendant has the constitutional right to have the nature of the accusation against him stated, but seems to overlook the additional constitutional guarantee of the right to an indictment by the grand jury.[152] The commentaries to the code with respect to the bill of particulars are meager,[153] and deal only with the Massachusetts statute, which has been held valid.[154]

It would thus appear that the use of a bill of particulars to eliminate the need for a setting forth of all of the elements of the crime charged was adopted by the American Law Institute on the basis of very little previous experience. It is true that the common law recognized the use of

---

compulsory when the defendant demands it. At common law the grant of such a bill was discretionary.

[151] The gist of the method is "by differentiating between the offense proper and the particulars of the offense, and asking the grand jury to make a finding upon defendant's commission of the offense only, leaving the particulars to be furnished by the prosecuting attorney in the form of a bill of particulars." Perkins, "Short Indictments and Informations" (1929) 15 A.B.A.J. 292, 293. See also Mikell, "A Proposed Draft of a Code of Criminal Procedure" (1915) 5 J.Crim.L. 827, 828.

[152] This is pointed out by McClintock, "Indictment by a Grand Jury" (1942) 26 Minn.L.Rev. 153, 164. For a similar omission, see Note (1930) 30 Col.L.Rev. 1051, 1053; Millar, "The Reform of Criminal Pleading in Illinois" (1917) 8 J.Crim.L. 337, 358; Millar, "The Function of Criminal Pleading" (1922) 12 J.Crim.L. 500. It is, however, conceded by Scott that the right to indictment by a grand jury does not require that the indictment identify the transaction as well as its offense. Scott, "Simplified Criminal Accusations and the Supplementing and Amending Thereof" (1913) 61 U. of Pa.L.Rev. 540, 551, 577-578.

[153] *Ibid.* 542, 543.

[154] Commonwealth v. Bennett, 118 Mass. 443 (1875); Commonwealth v. Farmer, 218 Mass. 507 (1914). See Scott, "Simplified Criminal Accusations and the Supplementing and Amending Thereof" (1913) 61 U. of Pa. L.Rev. 540, 554.

a bill of particulars, granted in the discretion of the judge, but it recognized it when the indictment, prolix and verbose as it was, might fail to give the defendant enough information as to the nature of the crime to enable him properly to prepare his defense.[155] Such a bill, however, could only supplement the accusation in the indictment; it could not furnish the allegations which the law treated as essential to a complete accusation of the crime charged. The Institute proposed this very significant change in procedure without any considerable prior agitation therefor.[156] Moreover, there seems never to have been any clear statement of any benefits that would result from stating the matter essential to the accusation of an offense in two documents instead of one. Thus the reform may turn out to be neither constitutional nor desirable on the merits.

The principal advantages of stating the details of a crime in a bill of particulars, rather than in the indictment itself, would be a saving of effort if the defendant did not insist on a bill of particulars, as he probably would not in a great many cases; facility of amendment; and greater scope for the application of the doctrine of waiver and aider by verdict.[157] Where the prosecution is begun by in-

[155] Commonwealth v. Snelling, 15 Pick. (Mass.) 321, 329 (1834); 3 Encyc. Pl. & Pr. 554; McClintock, "Indictment by Information" (1942) 26 Minn.L.Rev. 153, 164.

[156] The chief writings in favor of the proposed change are: Mikell, "A Proposed Draft of a Code of Criminal Procedure" (1915) 5 J.Crim.L. 827; Scott, "Reform of Criminal Procedure, With Reference Particularly to the Indictment" (1913) 61 U. of Pa.L.Rev. 458; Scott, "Simplified Criminal Accusations and the Supplementing and Amending Thereof" (1913) 61 U. of Pa.L.Rev. 540; Millar, "The Reform of Criminal Pleading in Illinois" (1917) 8 J.Crim.L. 337.

[157] McClintock, "Indictment by a Grand Jury" (1942) 26 Minn.L.Rev. 153, 165.

formation, only the first of these advantages would be present.

The first advantage is not very significant. The time necessary to draft an indictment is a small fraction of the time required in the entire proceeding. In the case of statutory crimes, where much care and labor may be involved, it is not unlikely that a bill of particulars would be demanded so that no saving of labor would occur. Since the bill of particulars is furnished by the prosecuting attorney, there would be no need of reference to the grand jury for an amendment, and therefore much time might be saved. The amendment must fall within the limits of the particular acts which the grand jury had found to constitute the crime charged, hence there could not be much freedom of amendment. It would seem unconstitutional to permit an amendment at the trial to conform to the proof there adduced, if the proof differed from that heard by the grand jury so that there was no finding by the grand jury that the defendant should be prosecuted for those particular acts. In the third place, it is doubtful whether there would be substantially greater scope for the application of the doctrine of waiver and aider by verdict. It is doubtful whether the courts will permit waiving any substantial element of the indictment, particularly if the court refuses waiver of indictment.[158] Courts have liberally applied statutes providing for waiver of formal defects, but any failure to allege the existence of some essential element of the crime could not be waived.[159]

[158] Waiver of indictment was held unconstitutional in People ex rel. Battista v. Christian, 249 N.Y. 314, 164 N.E. 111, 61 A.L.R. 793 (1929).

[159] Compare State v. Ostby, 203 Iowa 333, 210 N.W. 934, 212 N.W. 550 (1927), with State v. Delerno, 11 La. Ann. 648 (1856); Newcomb v. State, 37 Miss. 383 (1859).

The advantages just enumerated would seem to be outweighed by the disadvantages. In the first place, the procedure is of doubtful constitutionality.[160] It is true that Massachusetts has had the procedure for quite some time and that there is a fairly extensive line of cases construing such procedure. The first Massachusetts statutes dealt with a few designated crimes.[161] After such statutes had been upheld, the legislature applied the procedure to all of the usual crimes. These statutes have been attacked always on the basis of the guarantee of a written accusation stating the nature of the crime charged, and never on the basis of the guarantee of indictment by a grand jury. The Massachusetts courts have never considered a case in which there was a claim that the particulars set forth in the bill of particulars were not the same as those on which the grand jury based its charge. In the decision upholding the New York short-form indictment, no claim was made that the acts set forth in the bill of particulars differed from those on which the grand jury found its indictment.[162] The Iowa statute has also been sustained, but in the first case the objection to the validity was based solely on the guarantee of the right to know the nature and cause of the accusation.[163] In the second case the statute was attacked as violating the guarantee of indictment by a grand jury, and the court relied on the New York hold-

[160] "Unhappily some States have rigid constitutional provisions as to the form and contents of indictments." Nat. Com. on Law Obs. and Enf., Rep. on Crim. Proc. (1931) 33.

[161] Fessenden, "Improvements in Criminal Pleading" (1896) 10 Harv.L. Rev. 98, 107-110.

[162] People v. Bogdanoff, 254 N.Y. 16, 171 N.E. 890 (1930), 30 Col.L.Rev. 1051, 8 N.Y.U.L.Q.Rev. 328. See also (1931) 29 Mich.L.Rev. 636. Compare State v. Ray, 7 S.E. (2d) 654 (W.Va. 1940), (1941) 47 W.Va.L.Q. 336.

[163] State v. Henderson, 215 Iowa 275, 243 N.W. 289 (1932).

ing.[164] But in neither case was there any suggestion or contention that the bill of particulars did specify acts which were not made the basis of the action of the grand jury in voting the indictment. In fact, it has been vigorously contended that the Code provisions, if applied to federal procedure, would conflict with the guarantee of indictment by a grand jury in the Fifth Amendment to the Federal Constitution, as that guarantee has been construed by the courts of the United States.[165] Thus it is not at all clear that the function of the indictment of expressing the finding of the grand jury as to the particular acts of the defendant which amounted to the crime charged can be so transformed.

In some jurisdictions, minutes of the grand jury are kept and such minutes are accessible to the defendant. In such jurisdictions the defendant could determine whether the bill of particulars set out the facts on which the grand jury acted. Possibly the view might be taken, especially in other jurisdictions, that the bill of particulars prima facie sets out the facts on which the grand jury acted. This would seem to deprive the defendant of the substance of the guarantee. On the other hand, it would impose an impossible task on the prosecution, if it were held that the guarantee required the prosecution to be ready to prove in every case that the particulars set out in the bill are the same as those on which the grand jury acted.

Even if the use of the bill of particulars to perform the function of the grand jury indictment be held valid, it does

[164] State v. Engler, 217 Iowa 138, 251 N.W. 88 (1933).

[165] Comments (1937) 35 Mich.L.Rev. 456, (1941) 47 W.Va.L.Q. 336; Willard, "The Seventeenth Century Indictment in the Light of Modern Conditions" (1911) 24 Harv.L.Rev. 290, 297.

not follow that its use is wise or desirable.[166] It seems paradoxical to simplify procedure by providing that allegations which are essential to a record which will sustain a conviction shall be contained in two pleadings instead of one as previously. To justify such separation, it ought to be clearly shown that the resulting benefits will outweigh the manifest disadvantages. The general use of the practice is likely to lead to a great many questions as to the identity of the charges in the two instruments, particularly where the crime is a continuing one, or one that has been repeated on different occasions.[167] In jurisdictions such as Massachusetts and New York, permitting the liberalized procedure, it is not a uniform practice to use such procedure. It was not used in the prosecution of Sacco and Vanzetti. It was not followed by the district attorney for New York County in the drafting of model forms of indictments for use in that office.[168] On the whole it seems best not to follow the American Law Institute Code provisions for the use of the extreme short form of indictment. The real purpose of the short indictment is to

[166] "While brevity is a cardinal element in the indictment, practically it should not be sought at the expense of prudence or, as said Pollock, C. B., by 'making experiments to see with how small amount of legal averment an indictment can be sustained.' " 1 Bishop, New Criminal Procedure (4th ed.1895) § 336, p.215. "The idea expressed holds human life too cheaply. The best way for a man to get right on this point is to put himself into the place of the man who is brought into court to defend his life. It will require no argument to convince that man, whether he be guilty or not guilty, that he should be permitted to know specifically the acts with which he is charged. I do not mean the *legal name* of the law's conclusions from the acts, but the acts themselves, so far as that can be done." Brooks, "Procedure in Criminal Law" (1912) 21 Yale L.J. 267, 271.

[167] Comment (1935) 35 Mich.L.Rev. 456, 465. See Hall, "Objectives of Federal Criminal Procedural Revision" (1942) 51 Yale L.J. 723, 736.

[168] Note, "Streamlining the Indictment" (1939) 53 Harv.L.Rev. 122.

change the underlying functions of the indictment,[169] and to make available some of the advantages of the information as a method of prosecution. But this is unconstitutional and strives to do what should be done by waiver of indictment or by constitutional amendment validating use of the information.

The modern English rule seems preferable to the Code rule.[170] It provides: "Every indictment shall contain, and shall be sufficient if it contains, a statement of the specific offense or offenses with which the accused person is charged, together with such particulars as may be necessary for giving reasonable information as to the nature of the charge."[171] Along the same line, Rule 7(c) of the Federal Rules of Criminal Procedure provides: "The indictment or information shall be a plain, concise and definite written statement of the essential facts constituting the offense charged." Mr. Justice Sutherland has stated the problem as follows: "The rigor of common-law rules

[169] As a writer has said: "Statutory changes have reduced an indictment from a series of finding of fact to a statement of a conclusion." Green, Note (1930) 24 Ill.L.Rev. 319, 324.

[170] See the argument quoted in Waite, Cases on Criminal Law and Procedure (2d ed.1938) 718-720. See also "The Indictments Act, 1915" (1916) 16 J. Comp. Leg. (N.S.) 236.

[171] The Indictments Act, 5 & 6 Geo. V, c.90, § 3 (1915). The Act also sets up a rules committee with power, subject to the approval of the Lord Chancellor to alter the rules with respect to the form of the indictment. For the earlier law, see 1 Stephen, A History of the Criminal Law of England (1883) 280-282, 286-288. The Canadian Code provides that every count of an indictment shall be sufficient if it contains in substance a statement that the accused has committed some offense therein specified; the statement may be made in any words sufficient to give the accused notice of the offense with which he is charged. Crouse, "A Critique of Canadian Criminal Legislation" (1934) 12 Can.B.Rev. 545, 574; see Note (1937) 1 U. of Toronto L.J. 127. But see Riddell, "The Sacco-Vanzetti Case from a Canadian Viewpoint" (1927) 13 A.B.A.J. 683, 684; "Jargon in Pleadings" (1919) 2 J. Am. Jud. Soc. 184.

of criminal pleading has yielded in modern practice, to the general principle that formal defects, not prejudicial, will be disregarded. The true test of the sufficiency of an indictment is not whether it could have been made more definite and certain, but whether it contains the elements of the offense intended to be charged, 'and sufficiently apprised the defendant of what he must be prepared to meet and, in case any other proceedings are taken against him for a similar offense, whether the record shows with accuracy to what extent he may plead a former acquittal or conviction.' "[172]

Section 155 of the American Law Institute Code grants to the defendant an absolute right to a bill of particulars when an indictment "fails to inform the defendant of the particulars of the offense sufficiently to enable him to prepare his defense." The Federal Rules of Criminal Procedure contemplate that the necessary particulars be set out in the original accusation, as is also the English rule.[173] They contemplate a bill of particulars in the discretion of the court as at common law.[174] Rule 7(f) provides: "The court for cause may direct the filing of a bill of particulars."

[172] Hagner v. United States, 285 U.S. 427, 52 Sup.Ct. 417, 76 L. Fed. 861 (1932). See also State v. Cornellison, 166 Tenn. 106, 59 S.W. (2d) 514 (1933).

[173] This has been labeled merely a difference in form, but it would appear to be a difference in substance. See Millar, "The Reform of Criminal Pleading in Illinois" (1917) 8 J.Crim.L. 337, 344. The Canadian and Indian Codes require that the indictment contain a complete statement of the offense. See Scott, "Simplified Criminal Accusations and the Supplementing and Amending Thereof" (1913) 61 U. of Pa.L.Rev. 540, 547-548.

[174] Likewise the English Act proceeds on the theory that, when the indictment has been drawn in accordance with its provisions, the accused has a right to no more. See Millar, "The Reform of Criminal Pleading in Illinois" (1917) 8 J.Crim.L. 337, 344-345.

A motion for such a bill may be made only within ten days after arraignment or within a shorter time as prescribed by rule or order.

18. Commencement and Conclusion

Under Section 149 of the Institute Code, the technical common-law requirements with respect to caption and commencement [175] are declared obsolete by permitting a caption or commencement to be supplied or amended as of course at any stage of the proceedings. Along similar lines, Section 150 provides that the accusation need contain no formal conclusion.[176] It should be noted, however, that the constitutions of half the states require that an accusation should conclude "against the peace and dignity of the State." [177] Rule 7(c) of the Federal Rules of Criminal Procedure provides: "It need not contain a formal commencement, a formal conclusion or any other matter not necessary to such statement."

19. Name

Section 157 of the Code makes adequate provision with respect to the name of the defendant, whether the accused

[175] As to the history of the rule in England, see 1 Stephen, A History of the Criminal Law of England (1883) 275-280.

[176] Section 148, the special definition clause of the American Law Institute Code of Criminal Procedure, which is contained in Chapter 6 on "Indictment and Information," should have been transferred to a general definition clause governing the entire code, and contains no definition of "caption," "commencement," or "conclusion." Brunyate, "The American Draft Code of Criminal Procedure, 1930" (1933) 49 L.Q.Rev. 192, 209.

[177] While historically a conclusion was one of the three essential parts of an indictment in England, for quite some time no formal conclusion has been required. 1 Stephen, A History of the Criminal Law of England (1883) 275, 282-283.

is an individual or a corporation.[178] In part the provision as to the former reads that "it is sufficient to state a surname and one or more given names, or a surname and one or more abbreviations or initials of a given name or names." If the accusation as originally drawn gives the wrong name and the true name is discovered in the course of the proceedings, the court shall cause the true name to be inserted and the proceedings shall be continued against him in his true name.

20. Time and Place

It was a peculiarity of the common law that, although an indictment was held invalid if it did not contain a precise averment of the time of the offense, nevertheless, if a time was duly stated, some other time would serve just as well when it came to the introduction of evidence at the trial. In many states statutes have endeavored to correct this anomalous rule. Section 158 of the Code provides: "An indictment or information need contain no allegation of the time of the commission of the offense unless such allegation is necessary to charge the offense under section 154." This section does not contemplate withholding from the defendant information relative to the time of the offense. This is one of the particulars which may be stated in the indictment or furnished in a bill of particulars. The Code at the same time safeguards the defendant more adequately than existing law, for, if there is a variance between the time stated and that shown at the trial, Section 184 permits the court to postpone the trial "to be had before the same or another jury" if the court "is of the

[178] Compare Rule 7 of the rules made under the English Indictments Act, 1915, set forth in Archbold, Criminal Pleading, Evidence and Practice (30th ed.1938) 44.

opinion that the defendant has been prejudiced in his defense upon the merits." The mere allegation that the defendant committed the offense is considered under Section 158(2) an allegation that it was committed after the act became an offense, before the finding of the accusation [179] and within the period of limitations. Under Section 156, however, the court is authorized to quash the indictment if it appears from the bill of particulars that the prosecution is barred by the statute of limitations.[180]

Section 159 of the Code provides that no allegation of place is required, "unless such allegation is necessary to charge the offense under section 154." It also provides that all allegations unless stated otherwise shall be deemed to refer to the same place. Section 158 contains a similar provision as to time. The two provisions when taken together eliminate the need for the "then and there" clause with which common-law indictments were burdened. Another novel provision in Section 159 is that the allegation that the defendant committed the offense "shall in all cases be considered an allegation that the offense was committed within the territorial jurisdiction of the court." This eliminates the need for encumbering the accusation with the phrase "in the county aforesaid," but does not affect the necessity of proving the venue at the trial.[181]

[179] The general rule is that an indictment charging the commission of a felony at a date subsequent to the finding thereof is fatally defective. State v. Runyon, 131 S.E. 466 (W.Va. 1926), 10 Minn.L.Rev. 622.

[180] See Comment (1932) 10 Neb.L.Bull. 475.

[181] Comment (1933) 31 Mich.L.Rev. 728. As to allegations of time and place, compare Rule 9 of the rules made under the English Indictments Act, 1915, set forth in Archbold, Criminal Pleading, Evidence and Practice (30th ed.1938) 45.

21. Means, Value, Price, and Ownership

Under Section 160 of the Code the accusation need not allege the means by which the offense was committed, unless this is necessary to state the offense itself as distinguished from the particulars.[182] Value and price are sometimes used to distinguish between offenses that are indictable and those which must be dealt with in a summary proceeding before the magistrate. In a case of that kind the indictment cannot ignore the value or price, but under Section 161 "it is sufficient to aver that the value or price of the property exceeds the certain value or price which determined the offense." In other cases value or price need not be alleged. Under Section 162, ownership of property involved in an offense need not be stated in the accusation. Whenever it appears, an allegation of ownership is satisfied by proof of possession or the right of possession, and any statement which implies possession or the right of possession is a sufficient allegation of ownership.

22. Intent

Under Section 163, the accusation need contain no allegation of the intent with which an act was done, except in certain cases in which this is necessary to the charge itself, as for example charging an assault with intent to inflict great bodily harm. Furthermore, where allegations of intent to defraud are used, it is not necessary to specify the particular person who was to be injured or defrauded.

[182] See 1 Stephen, A History of the Criminal Law of England (1883) 287n., cf. 290n.; 2 Bishop, New Criminal Procedure (4th ed.1895) § 553. Rule 7(c) of the Federal Rules of Criminal Procedure (1944) provides: "It may be alleged in a single count that the means by which the defendant committed the offense are unknown or that he committed it in one or more specified ways."

Under Section 164, characterization of the act by such words as "feloniously,"[183] "traitorously," "unlawfully," "with force and arms," "burglariously," "wilfully," "knowingly," "maliciously," or "negligently" is not required, "unless such characterization is necessary to charge the offense under section 154." Under Section 165 no accusation need state any matter not necessary to be proved.

23. Other Matters

The same general plan has been followed in other sections dealing with such matters as descriptive allegations, name of person other than defendant, property described as money, description of written instruments, description of spoken or written words or pictures, naming of words and phrases, previous convictions, private statutes, judgments, libel, and perjury.

24. Habitual Offender Statutes

Prior convictions must be alleged in the indictment for the defendant's information, but neither the allegation of prior conviction, nor the issue of the defendant's identity should be submitted to the jury until they return a verdict of guilty on the principal issue of the specific crime charged.[184] Section 172 of the Institute Code provides:

[183] See Comments (1922) 17 Ill.L.Rev. 322 by Millar. For a recent reversal on appeal because of an omission of the word "feloniously," see State v. Pryor, 119 S.W. (2d) 253 (Mo. 1938), (1939) 23 Minn.L.Rev. 226.

[184] State v. Ferrone, 96 Conn. 160, 113 Atl. 452 (1921), (1922) 31 Yale L.J. 440. See also Comments (1927) 11 Minn.L.Rev. 261, (1927) 36 Yale L.J. 1019, (1934) 9 Ind.L.J. 534, 537. The courts are almost unanimous in holding that in order to validate the sentence of increased punishment the defendant must be told in the indictment of the entire charge against him; that is to say, of the subsequent offense and the prior convictions. State v. Campagno, 125 La. 659, 51 S.W. 681 (1910); Commonwealth v. O'Reilly,

"No indictment or information shall contain an allegation of a prior conviction of the defendant unless such allegation is necessary to charge the offense under section 154."

25. Negativing Exceptions

A section which will eliminate much confusion is Section 175, under which no accusation shall be invalid merely for failure "to negative any exception, excuse or proviso contained in the statute creating or defining the offense." There has been no hardship to defendants from statutes which, while creating certain specific crimes, have included an express provision that exceptions contained therein need not be negatived, nor from rules requiring the exception to be insisted upon affirmatively by the defendant if it is not contained in the enacting clause,[185] or if it is not part of the description of the offense, regardless of its location in the statute.[186] The Code rule represents a real step in advance.

---

94 Conn. 698, 110 Atl. 550 (1920). A statute permitting an increased sentence without allegation of prior convictions has been held unconstitutional. Commonwealth v. Harrington, 130 Mass. 35 (1880). Three jurisdictions allow omission of the allegation of prior conviction. MacWhorter v. State, 118 Ga. 55, 44 S.E. 873 (1903); State v. Parris, 89 S.C. 140, 71 S.E 808 (1911); Okla. Gen. Sts. 1903, c.5574.

185 At common law an indictment had to negative an exception contained in the enacting clause of the statute defining the offense. Davis v. State, 39 Ala. 521 (1865); People v. Priestly, 17 Cal. app. 171 (1911). See Comments (1914) 62 U. of Pa.L.Rev. 741, (1929) 13 Minn.L.Rev. 512, (1932) 10 Neb.L.Bull. 331; Illinois Crime Survey (1929) 127-130; Beale, Criminal Pleading and Practice (1899) 222-225; Keigwin, Cases in Criminal Procedure (1939) 403-407.

186 Recent cases have held that the indictment must negative the exception if it is part of the description of the offense, irrespective of its location in the statute. State v. Moore, 166 N.Y. 284, 81 S.E. 294 (1914). Wehunt v. State. 136 Tenn. 223, 188 S.W. 939 (1916). It is often difficult to determine when an exception or provision is part of the description of an offense. Comment (1929) 13 Minn.L.Rev. 512.

26. Indirect Allegations

The common law insisted that every essential element of a crime must be alleged positively and directly, without being aided in any way by inference or intendment. For example, an allegation of receiving a deposit "after the bank was insolvent" was held not to allege that the bank was insolvent at the time of the receipt of the deposit.[187] Section 177 of the Code provides that no accusation shall be held invalid "for the reason that it alleges indirectly and by inference or by way of recital any matters, facts or circumstances connected with or constituting the offense."

27. Degrees of Crime

Section 180 of the American Law Institute Code of Criminal Procedure provides that, where the offense is one which is divided into degrees, the indictment need only charge that defendant committed the offense, without specifying the degree. This is another provision which does not appear to be in conformity with the spirit of the guarantee of the right to an indictment by a grand jury.[188] To be sure the cases support such a provision even where there is no statute.[189] They do so on the theory that the indictment is sufficient at common law to charge that of-

187 Fleming v. State, 62 Tex. Cr. App. 653, 139 S.W. 598 (1911).

188 McClintock, "Indictment by a Grand Jury," (1942) 26 Minn.L.Rev. 153, 169. See also Notes (1916) 16 Col.L.Rev. 241, (1936) 11 Wis.L.Rev. 413; Scott, "Simplified Criminal Accusations and the Supplementing and Amending Thereof" (1913) 61 U. of Pa.L.Rev. 540, 571-573.

189 Graves v. State, 45 N.J.L. 203 (1883), affirmed 45 N.J.L 347, 46 Am. Rep. 778 (1883); State v. Cole, 132 N.C. 1069, 44 S.E. 391 (1893). It has been stated that the present practice "is to charge the highest degree that might by any possibility be supported by the evidence," and that Section 180 would make this dodge unnecessary. Perkins, "Short Indictments and Informations" (1929) 15 A.B.A.J. 292, 295.

fense and that the statute dividing the offense into separate degrees merely affects the punishment, not the nature of the offense. In numerous instances, however, it is largely a matter of accident whether the legislature chooses to modify the common-law definition of a crime and create a new crime which will include the acts eliminated from the common-law definition or whether it will call the different forms of the former crime different degrees of the same crime. The determination of whether the different acts constitute different offenses or different degrees of the same offense depends usually on historical considerations. In most states there is much less difference in both legal consequences and moral condemnation between the highest degree of manslaughter and the lowest degrees of murder than there is between the different degrees of murder. If the right to release on bail depends on whether the indictment is for first or second degree murder, a rule that the grand jury may use one form of indictment for either permits the refusal of bail even in cases where the grand jury concluded that an accusation for first degree murder would not be proper under the evidence. A rule thus unfair to the defendant should not be perpetuated.[190]

28. Accessory Before the Fact

It has been provided by statutes in many states that an accessory before the fact may be prosecuted and punished

[190] Preferable is the rule earlier prepared by Mikell, "A Proposed Draft of a Code of Criminal Procedure" (1915) 5 J.Crim.L. 827, 838: "In an indictment for murder it is sufficient to charge that the accused murdered the deceased, adding a statement of the degree of murder, if murder in the first degree is not intended to be charged, and in an indictment for manslaughter, it is sufficient to charge that the accused killed the deceased, adding a statement of the degree or form of manslaughter if the highest degree or form of manslaughter is not intended to be charged."

as if he were the principal offender. The effect of such a statute is that it is sufficient for the indictment to charge that an accessory before the fact committed the crime.[191] Section 180 of the American Law Institute Code provides: "Every person concerned in the commission of an offense, whether he directly commits the offense, or procures, counsels, aids, or abets its commission, may be indicted or informed against as principal."

29. Surplusage and Repugnance

At common law the mere inclusion of allegations which were immaterial and superfluous was never held to render an indictment defective. Such statements could be rejected as surplusage and the pleading supported without them if otherwise sufficient. Unfortunately, however, the common law had a rule that no allegation was to be regarded as superfluous if it was descriptive of the identity of the subject matter. It followed that, however unnecessary such an allegation may have been, any variance or failure of proof was held to be fatal. For example, although there was no necessity of mentioning the material of which a stolen sheet was composed, an indictment for stealing "one white woolen flannel sheet" was held not to be sustained by proof of stealing one made partly of cotton and partly of wool.[192] Moreover, differences of opinion as to just what allegations are descriptive of the identity of material matters have introduced a large element of uncertainty. This confusion has been eliminated by Section 183 providing that "any allegation unnecessary under existing law or under the provisions of this chapter may, if con-

[191] Comment by Orfield (1931) 10 Neb.L.Bull. 170, 172; Comment by Sears (1931) 25 Ill.L.Rev. 854.

[192] Alkenbreck v. People, 1 Denio 80 (N.Y. 1845).

tained in an indictment or information or bill of particulars, be disregarded, as superfluous."[193] The evils flowing out of common-law rules as to repugnancy are eliminated by Section 182 of the Code.

30. Indorsing Names of Witnesses

In order to apprise the accused of the evidence which he may have to meet at the trial, some states provide, as does Section 194 of the American Law Institute Code of Criminal Procedure, that the names of the witnesses examined by the grand jury shall be indorsed on the indictment.[194] This provision is generally regarded as being directory rather than mandatory, so that an omission to comply with it does not invalidate the indictment.[195] Other witnesses may be called. In New York the provision is said to be a prolific source of motions to dismiss the indictment.[196] Often the defendant relies solely upon the

[193] For discussions of surplusage, see Notes (1918) 12 Ill.L.Rev. 555, 13 Ill.L.Rev. 124, (1919) 89 Cent.L.J. 203. In the federal courts it appears that surplusage cannot be stricken from an indictment unless the defendant consents. Ex parte Bain, 121 U.S. 1 (1887). For criticism of the case, see Scott, "Simplified Criminal Accusations and the Supplementing and Amending Thereof" (1913) 61 U. of Pa.L.Rev. 540, 559-560, 579. Compare Ford v. United States, 273 U.S. 593 (1927). If a defendant may waive an indictment, *a fortiori,* he should have power to consent to the striking out of surplusage. Rule 7(d) of the Federal Rules of Criminal Procedure provides: "The court on motion of the defendant may strike surplusage from the indictment or information."

[194] See discussion of the Code Section in (1930) 8 Proc. Am. L. Inst. 132-140. This was the practice in England. 1 Stephen, A History of the Criminal Law of England (1883) 273-274. The common law does not require it except in capital crimes. Abbott, Criminal Trial Practice (4th ed. 1939) § 253, p.470.

[195] State v. Shores, 31 W. Va. 491, 7 S.E. 413, 13 Am. St. Rep. 875 (1888). See Edwards, The Grand Jury (1906) 135; Wharton, Criminal Pleading and Practice (9th ed.1889) § 358, p.247; Bishop, New Criminal Procedure (4th ed.1895) § 869(a), p.503.

[196] Report of the Special Committee on the Revision of the Code of

enumeration of the witnesses to substantiate a motion to dismiss. Moreover the defendant is under no reciprocal duty to acquaint the prosecuting attorney with the names of his witnesses.[197] It has been contended that there is possibility of intimidation of witnesses. On the other hand, it has been argued that the rule forces the prosecution to put all its cards on the table and that it has worked well in most states having the rule.[198] A report to the Wickersham Commission favored a requirement "that the state shall seasonably furnish a list of its witnesses to the accused." [199] Wigmore considers its omission a great injustice.[200]

31. Citation of Statutes

The American Law Institute Code of Criminal Procedure contains no provision requiring the citation of the statute alleged to have been violated by the defendant.[201] Under Rule 4 carrying out the English Indictments, Act

---

Criminal Procedure to the Commission on the Administration of Justice (1935) c. "Grand Jury," p.24. See also report of the Special Committee of the New York City Bar Association (1934) 20 A.B.A.J. 89, 91.

197 Such a reciprocal duty is advocated by Millar, "The Function of Criminal Pleading" (1922) 12 J.Crim.L. 500, 504; Note (1924) 38 Yale L.J. 650, 652, 656. So providing, see Wash. Laws 1925, 420. § 2; 50 & 51 Vict. 29, § 36 (1887).

198 See (1930) 16 A.B.A.J. 351, 398, 399. "The furnishing of such a list should be an essential feature of any system of criminal procedure." Millar, "The Function of Criminal Pleading" (1922) 12 J.Crim.L. 500, 503.

199 Nat. Com. on Law Obs. and Enf., Report on Lawlessness in Law Enforcement (1931) 284, 341.

200 6 Wigmore, Evidence (3d ed.1940) § 1850, p.391. The subject is fully discussed in Sections 1850-1855.

201 Under Section 154(2) the statute may be cited. At common law the statute need not be cited. Biskind v. United States, 281 Fed. 47 (C.C.A. 6th, 1922); People v. Mason, 186 N.Y.Supp. 215 (1921). Reference to an inapplicable statute is not reversible error. Pruett v. United States, 3 Fed. (2d) 353 (C.C.A. 9th, 1925), 25 Col.L.Rev. 839; Clemens v. State, 185 N.W. 209 (Wis. 1921), (1922) 31 Yale L.J. 676.

of 1915, the statement of the offense, if the offense charged is one created by statute, shall contain a reference to the section of the statute creating the offense.[202] Under Rule 7(c) of the Federal Rules of Criminal Procedure: "The indictment or information shall state for each count the official or customary citation of the statute, rule, regulation or other provision of law which the defendant is alleged therein to have violated. Error in the citation or its omission shall not be ground for dismissal of the indictment or information or for reversal of a conviction if the error or omission did not mislead the defendant to his prejudice." The ever increasing number and complexity of both federal and state criminal statutes and general rules and regulations makes such provision desirable. To know the statute may be as important as to know the facts intended to be proved.[203] German and Italian law have long so provided. Jeremy Bentham had proposed it for civil procedure.[204]

32. Joinder of Offenses

Section 185 deals with misjoinder of defendants and of offenses charged.[205] It provides that no accusation shall be

[202] Archbold, Criminal Pleading, Evidence and Practice (30th ed.1938) 40.

[203] Millar, "The Function of Criminal Pleading" (1922) 12 J.Crim.L. 500, 502; Scott, "Simplified Criminal Accusation and the Supplementing and Amending Thereof" (1913) 61 U. of Pa.L.Rev. 540, 543-544.

[204] Plaintiff's demand should contain "reference to the article or articles . . . of the body of the law upon which the demand is grounded." 7 Bentham, Rationale of Judicial Evidence, 271.

[205] It has been pointed out that this section is the only section dealing with joinder of charges, while the British Indian chapter on "Charges," containing but twenty sections, has eight dealing with joinder. Brunyate, "The American Draft Code of Criminal Procedure, 1930" (1933) 49 L.Q. Rev. 192, 210.

invalid because of misjoinder of the parties defendant, or of the offenses charged; and the court is empowered to require the severance of the accusation into separate accusations or counts, as shall be proper. Logically, misjoinder presupposes positive rules as to the circumstances under which joinder is permissible. But no such rules are found in the Code.[206] Thus the courts must apply the pre-existing law of the several states, with varying results. In about thirteen states any joinder of more offenses than one would constitute misjoinder.

Many states by decision or statute adhere strictly to the rule that the indictment must allege but one offense, distinguishing cases in which the prosecution seeks only one conviction and employs several counts to avoid a variance.[207] A more liberal rule allows joinder of offenses of the same nature.[208] A recent Kansas case went even further in allowing joinder of rape and robbery occurring at the same time and place.[209] A similar result should be reached in states having code provisions which allow joinder of offenses connected together in their commission.[210] The federal and English cases stress the view that joinder is

[206] Rule 8 of the Federal Rules of Criminal Procedure, sets out affirmative rules with respect to both joinder of offenses and joinder of defendants.

[207] Kotter v. People, 150 Ill. 441, 37 N.E. 932 (1894); State v. Link 314 Wis. 192, 286 S.W. 12 (1926); see Notes (1926) 26 Mich.L.Rev. 192, (1899) 9 Yale L.J. 67.

[208] Simmons v. State, 165 Md. 155, 167 Atl. 60 (1933) (9 larcenies); Forney v. State, 123 Neb. 179, 242 N.W. 441 (1932) (selling mortgaged property on three different occasions). See Note (1933) 11 Neb.L.Bull. 415; Beale, Criminal Pleading and Practice (1899) c.21.

[209] State v. Thompson, 139 Kans. 59, 29 P. (2d) 1101 (1934), (1935) 48 Harv.L.Rev. 510.

[210] Wash. Rev. Stat. Ann. (Remington, 1932) § 2059; State v. McMahon, 145 Wash. 672, 261 Pac. 639 (1927) (robbery and murder). Cf. People v. Covington, 28 P. (2d) 687 (Calif. 1934).

ultimately a matter of discretion.[211] The proper basis for objecting to joinder is that juries are likely to use evidence addressed in support of one charge to convict the accused of another charge not independently nor adequately proved.[212] Whether or not such improper use of evidence is likely would appear to depend on the nature of the offenses and the effect of their consolidation in each case rather than on a rigid general rule or classification of offenses. The new statutes do not violate the constitutional right to trial by jury,[213] to be informed of the nature and cause of the accusation,[214] or to indictment by a grand jury.[215]

The Federal Rules of Criminal Procedure provide a model rule with respect to joinder of offenses, based substantially on existing federal statutes and decisions. Under Rule 8(a) "Two or more offences may be charged in the same indictment or information in a separate count for each offense if the offenses charged, whether felonies or misdemeanors or both, are of the same or similar character or are based on the same act or transaction or on two or more acts or transactions connected together or constituting parts of a common scheme or plan." Rule 3 laid down under the English Indictments Act, 1915, provides: "Charges for any offenses, whether felonies or misdemeanors, may be joined in the same indictment if those charges are founded on the same facts or form or are a

[211] Pointer v. United States, 151 U.S. 396 (1894); Rex. v. Lockett (1914) 2 K.B. 720.

[212] Comment (1937) 22 Minn.L.Rev 112. See Note (1915) 5 J.Crim.L. 923.

[213] People v. Kelly, 203 Cal. 128, 263 Pac. 226 (1928).

[214] State v. Fox, 56 S.D. 294, 228 N.W. 382 (1929).

[215] People ex rel. Pincus v. Adams, 274 N.Y. 447, 9 N.E. (2d) 46 (1937), 22 Minn.L.Rev. 112.

part of a series of offenses of the same or a similar character."

Such joinder will permit joinder in a considerable group of cases. There may be joinder in separate counts for distinct offenses if they are based on the same act or transaction.[216] There may be joinder if they are based on two or more acts or transactions connected together.[217] There may be joinder if they are of the same class or character.[218] The words "constituting parts of a common scheme or plan" are taken from the New York Code.[219] The rule continues the present federal rule permitting joinder of felonies and misdemeanors.[220] It also continues the present rule that there be a separate count for each offense.[221]

[216] Rooney v. United States, 203 Fed. 928 (C.C.A. 9th, 1913).

[217] Dillard v. United States, 141 Fed. 303 (C.C.A. 9th, 1905).

[218] Pointer v. United States, 151 U.S. 396, 403 (1894). The word "character" is used in the English Indictments Act, 1915, 5 & 6 Geo. V, c.90, § 1, Rule 3, and in the New York Code of Criminal Procedure, § 279.

[219] New York Laws, 1936, c.328, § 1, New York Code of Criminal Procedure, § 279, (1937) 37 Col.L.Rev. 1027, (1937) 22 Minn.L.Rev. 112, (1937) 14 N.Y.U.L.Q.Rev. 250. For a classification of states according to rules of joinder, see A.L.I. Code of Crim. Proc. (1930) Commentary to § 185 at 588.

[220] The rule in England is similar. See the Indictments Act, 5 & 6 Geo. V, c.90, § 1, Rule 3 and § 4. On joinder of offenses in England, see Archbold, Criminal Pleading, Evidence and Practice (30th ed.1938) 51-54; Harris and Wilshere, Principles and Practice of the Criminal Law (17th ed.1943) 427-431.

[221] At common law the joinder of two or more offenses in the same count was known as duplicity, and rendered the indictment bad. Wharton, Criminal Procedure (10th ed.1896) § 335, p.385; (1940) 31 J.Crim.L. 314; (1933) 11 Neb.L.Bull. 458. But the joinder in one indictment of distinct counts, each charging a different offense, was permissible if the offenses were of the same general character and the mode of trial was the same. In England duplicity is demurable and appealable. Archbold, Criminal Pleading, Evidence and Practice (30th ed.1938) 48.

33. Joinder of Defendants

There is of course a distinction between joinder of offenses and joinder of defendants.[222] The Federal Rules of Criminal Procedure provide a model rule with respect to the latter as well as the former. Rule 8(b) provides: "Two or more defendants may be charged in the same indictment or information if they are alleged to have participated in the same act or transaction or in the same series of acts or transactions constituting an offense or offenses. Such defendants may be charged in one or more counts together or separately and all of the defendants need not be charged in each count."

The federal rule lays down a new rule for the federal courts as there is no federal statute and the decisions do not go so far. At common law defendants who commit an offense by joint participation may be indicted jointly on the same count or counts of an indictment or separately in different indictments in the discretion of the prosecuting attorney.[223] The rule which has generally existed in federal procedure permits two or more defendants to be named as joint defendants in a count or counts of an indictment if they have cooperated in the offense, or if they have been under a joint legal duty.[224] If the indictment charges conspiracy or a scheme to defraud, the cooperation required to support joinder of defendants need not

[222] See Keigwin, Cases in Criminal Procedure (1939) 445 (Joinder of Defendants) and (441) (Joinder of Counts); Robinson, Cases on Criminal Law and Procedure (1941) 394 (Joinder of Defendants) and 456 (Joinder of Offenses).

[223] 2 Bishop, New Criminal Procedure (4th ed.1895) § 463; Clark, Handbook of Criminal Procedure (2d ed. by Mikell, 1918) 347. For the present English rule, see Archbold, Criminal Pleading, Evidence and Practice (30th ed. 1938) 50-51; Harris and Wilshere, Principles and Practice of the Criminal Law (17th ed.1943) 426-427.

[224] Dillon v. United States, 113 F. (2d) 334 (C.C.A. 8th, 1940).

be as close as the cooperation required for joinder in other offenses.[225] Likewise under the rule which has existed in the past, defendants not acting jointly cannot be charged in the same indictment, either jointly in the same count or in separate counts.[226]

Under the federal rule, defendants who have participated in the same transaction or transactions can be joined in the same indictment as separate defendants in separate counts as well as joint defendants in one or more counts in the indictment.[227] Moreover, defendants charged jointly need not be named in each count of the indictment.[228] Even without the federal rule, joinder of this type is widely practiced when indictments are consolidated for trial under the federal statutes. Defendants named in indictments consolidated for trial frequently are not all named in all the counts of the consolidated indictments, and the charges of the indictments are often not the same against all defendants.[229]

Traditionally it was held that there could be no joint indictment for a crime which from its nature cannot be jointly committed.[230] Thus there could be no joint indictment for exercising a trade without apprenticeship,[231] nor

[225] Sasser v. United States, 29 F. (2d) 76 (C.C.A. 5th, 1928).

[226] United States v. Dietrich, 126 F. 664 (C.C.Neb., 1904).

[227] This principle was applied in Morris v. United States, 128 F. (2d) 912 (C.C.A. 5th, 1942).

[228] See United States v. Tuffanelli, 131 Fed. (2d) 890, 894 (C.C.A. 7th, 1942). Compare Culjak v. United States, 53 F. (2d) 554 (C.C.A. 9th, 1931).

[229] Davis v. United States, 12 F. (2d) 253 (C.C.A. 5th, 1926), cert. denied, Laud v. United States, 271 U.S. 688 (1926). See Bucklin v. United States, 159 U.S. 682 (1895). Compare McElroy v. United States, 164 U.S. 76, 77 (1896); State v. Blackley, 191 Wash. 23 70 P. (2d) 799 (1937).

[230] Wharton, Criminal Pleading and Practice (9th ed.1889) § 302; (1916) 29 Harv.L.Rev. 334.

[231] Rex v. Weston, 1 Strange 623, 93 Eng. Rep. 740 (1726).

for perjury.[232] This was the early American view.[233] It is still the law in some states.[234] It has even been held that two persons cannot be jointly drunk.[235] The rule was seemingly formal, since the insertion of the word "separaliter" made a joint indictment for a crime of this kind valid.[236] It is not shocking to hold that the word "several" can be implied where from the nature of the act the crime is several.[237] It has been held that there may be a joint indictment for practicing medicine without a license.[238] The test should be practical, rather than logical, turning on substantial fairness to the parties rather than the nature of the crime.[239]

34. Arrest After Indictment

An arrest may come at a considerably later stage than just after the committing of the criminal act or even after the filing of the complaint.[240] After an indictment has been found, the court is bound to issue a warrant of arrest, even though the prosecuting attorney has presented no facts to the court indicating probable cause.[241] The grand jury de-

232 Rex v. Philips, 2 Strange 921, 93 Eng. Rep. 943 (1733).

233 United States v. Kazinski, 26 Fed. Cas. 682 (1855); Vaughn v. State, 4 Mo. 530 (1837).

234 State v. Wilson, 115 Tenn. 725, 91 S.D. 195 (1906); Walker v. Commonwealth, 172 S.W. 109 (Ky. 1915).

235 State v. Deaton, 92 N.C. 788 (1885).

236 1 Starkie, A Treatise on Criminal Pleading (1814) 43.

237 See State v. Mills, 39 N.J.L. 587 (1877).

238 State v. McAninch, 154 N.W. 399 (Iowa 1915), (1916) 29 Harv.L. Rev. 334.

239 State v. Winstandley, 151 Ind. 316, 51 Me. 92 (1898).

240 "In early times the formal accusation was often, perhaps usually, the first step in the procedure, and the prisoner was not arrested until after he had been indicted." 1 Stephen, A History of the Criminal Law of England (1883) 217.

241 Ex parte United States, 287 U.S. 241 (1932), reversing United States v. Wingert, 55 F. (2d) 960 (E.D. Pa., 1932); Fraenkel, "From

termination of probable cause is conclusive. It is immaterial that the prosecutor uses secret proceedings to obtain an indictment and that no preliminary hearing before a magistrate is afforded. Under Rule 9 of the Second Preliminary Draft of the Federal Rules of Criminal Procedure, the clerk instead of the court might issue the warrant upon the request of the prosecuting attorney. This is in accord with the general state practice.[242] Prior to the proposed rule it was necessary to obtain an order of the court for the issuance of a warrant.[243] Rule 9 of the Federal Rules of Criminal Procedure adheres, however, to the earlier rule.

BIBLIOGRAPHY

Chaplin, "Reform in Criminal Prŏcedure" (1893) 7 Harv.L.Rev. 189, 193-195; Fessenden, "Improvement in Criminal Pleading" (1896) 10 Harv. L.Rev. 98; Willard, "The Seventeenth Century Indictment in the Light of Modern Conditions" (1911) 24 Harv.L.Rev. 290; "The Indictments Acts, 1915" (1916) 16 J. Comp. Leg. 236; Kenny, "Abbreviation of Indictments in India" (1899) 1 J. Comp. Leg. 390; Marshall, "The Indictment and Its Preparation in Illinois" (1911) 6 Ill.L.Rev. 162-169; Scott, "Reforming Criminal Procedure, With Reference Particularly to the Indictment" (1913) 61 U. of Pa.L.Rev. 458; Scott, "Simplified Criminal Accusations and the Supplementing and Amending Thereof" (1913) 61 U. of Pa.L. Rev. 540; Mikell, "A Proposed Draft of a Code of Criminal Procedure" (1915) 5 J.Crim.L. 827; Sprague, "Criminal Pleadings and Procedure" (1936) 15 Mich. S.B.A.J. 350-356; Perkins, "Short Indictments and Informations" (1929) 15 A.B.A.J. 292; Perkins, "Abridged Indictments and Informations" (1927) 12 Iowa L.Rev. 209, 355; Millar, "The Function of Criminal Pleading" (1922) 12 J.Crim.L. 500; Lawson, "Technicalities in Procedure, Civil and Criminal" (1909) 1 J.Crim.L. 63; "Criminal Procedure, Draft Report of Committee E" (1910) 1 J. of Crim.L. 584; Caruso, "The Short Indictment" (1935) 23 Ky.L.J. 362; Millar, "The Reform of Criminal Pleading in Illinois" (1917) 8 J.Crim.L. 337; McClintock, "Indictment by a Grand Jury" (1942) 26 Minn.L.Rev. 153; 27 Am. Jur., Indictments and Informations; 30 C.J., Indictments and Informations.

Suspicion to Accusation" (1942) 51 Yale L.J. 748, 756; A.L.I. Code of Crim. Proc. (1930) §§ 195-198.

242 Clark, Handbook of Criminal Procedure (2d ed. by Mikell, 1918) 28.

243 Ex parte United States, 287 U.S. 241 (1932).

CHAPTER VI

ARRAIGNMENT AND PREPARATION FOR TRIAL

1. Stage in Proceedings

NEXT in order[1] following indictment or information "come *arraignment,* or a formal reading of the charge to the accused in open court, and the *plea* or pleas of the accused. At common law he may demur to the indictment or information i.e., challenge its sufficiency in point of law, or plead to the jurisdiction (by a written pleading) or plead in abatement (also by a written pleading) that the grand jury was irregularly constituted or that its proceedings were fatally irregular. Today the latter objections are usually raised by a motion to quash. If the indictment is found to be insufficient in point of law or fatal irregularities are

[1] "It is the first step in the prosecution after the return of an indictment or the filing of the information; and formerly took place with great formality [4 Bl. Comm. *322], and was a *sine qua non* to a successful criminal prosecution." Housel and Walser, Defending and Prosecuting Federal Criminal Cases (1938) 346. "The arraignment takes place as soon after the return of the indictment or the filing of the information as the presence of the defendant can be secured." *Ibid.* 348. See also 2 Bishop, New Criminal Procedure (4th ed.1895) § 728, p.574. In Oregon the median time interval between indictment and arraignment in 1927 to 1928 was 7 days. Morse and Beattie, Survey of the Administration of Criminal Justice in Oregon (1932) 182. In New York in 1926 such interval was 1 day in New York City and in large upstate cities, 5 days in small cities, and 2 in rural areas. In Chicago in the same year the median time interval was 25 days. Moley, "The Initiation of Criminal Prosecutions by Indictment or Information" (1931) 29 Mich.L.Rev. 403, 427-428. As to cities in a number of states, see Nat. Com. on Law Obs. and Enf., Report on Prosecution (1931) Table XXVI, p.217. For discussions of the topics in this chapter see 22 C.J.S., Criminal Law, §§ 406-465; 23 C.J.S. Criminal Law, §§ 927-960; 14 Am. Jur., Criminal Law, §§ 249-303.

shown, the prosecution is brought to an end and a new one must be instituted. Or, instead, the accused may plead in bar (again by a written pleading) that he has been previously acquitted or convicted or put in jeopardy for the same offense or he may plead orally to the merits, pleading guilty or not guilty." [2]

2. History in England

In the period before Edward I, the only plea which a defendant could make seems to have been a flat denial.[3] But the growing elaboration of the law thereafter made it possible for the defendant to plead many other pleas. The pleas of benefit of clergy [4] and sanctuary,[5] taken over from the ecclesiastical law in the thirteenth century and known as declinatory pleas, could be used to question the jurisdiction of the court. The former plea could be made after conviction, and this became the usual practice. There were also pleas in abatement. Such pleas were very com-

[2] Nat. Com. on Law Obs. and Enf., Rep. on Crim. Proc. (1931) 17. See also 1 Stephen, A History of the Criminal Law of England (1883) 297; 4 Bl. Comm. (5th ed.1773) cc.25-26, pp.322-341. "Upon being called upon to plead, there are several courses which he may take. He may move to quash the indictment. He may plead to the jurisdiction in abatement, or a special plea in bar, such as former conviction or acquittal. He may demur, or he may plead not guilty. All these present questions for some court to decide." Willoughby, J., in Whitehead v. The Commonwealth, 19 Gratt. (Va.) 640, 644 (1870).

[3] 2 Holdsworth, History of English Law (3d ed.1923) 106, 109; 2 Pollock and Maitland, (2d ed.1905) 607-620; 3 Holdsworth, History of English Law (3d ed.1923) 614.

[4] 3 Holdsworth, History of English Law (3d ed.1923) 293-302; Hall, Theft, Law and Society (1935) 68-86. It was abolished in 1827. See 4 Bl. Comm., c.26; Starkie, Criminal Pleading (1st American ed.1824) 343.

[5] 3 Holdsworth, History of English Law (3d ed.1923) 303-307. It was abolished in 1623-1624. See also 4 Bl. Comm., c.26; Starkie, Criminal Pleading (1st American ed.1824) 343; 1 Stephen, A History of the Criminal Law of England (1883) 491-492.

mon because of the strictness required in the wording of indictments. They were also usually urged after conviction, and counsel might be assigned for the defendant to make them.[6] There were also pleas in bar: pardon, former acquittal, and former conviction.[7] Even during the medieval period a mass of learning grew up concerning those pleas, both with respect to the manner in which they could be proved and the circumstances under which they were available. Upon indictments for treason or felony the defendant could, if the finding on such pleas was against him, plead over the general issue not guilty.

Pleading in criminal cases was always oral. The indictment was in writing because it was in form and in fact a presentment to the king on which the king took action. The pleas advanced by the defendant were not only oral but simple. That is to say, the form of the plea was simple, although there was much technical learning with respect to the circumstances under which it could be pleaded. The form was necessarily simple in contrast to the form of pleading in civil cases partly because criminal cases usually involve less elaborate facts, but chiefly from the fact that in civil cases the parties could employ attorneys who spoke or later on drew their pleadings. But in treason and felony cases the defendant could not be represented by counsel. For this same reason the defendant was allowed to plead over though his special pleas had failed. For the same reason the courts were willing to let the defendant

[6] Counsel was assigned to prepare a plea to the jurisdiction in a treason case. Fitzharris' Case (1681) Vent. 354. See also Note (1929) 24 Ill.L. Rev. 319, 322-323; 3 Holdsworth, History of English Law (3d ed.1923) 614.

[7] The plea of autrefois attaint was early abolished. See Note (1913) 13 Col.L.Rev. 76. Only a single decision recognized it in the United States. Crenshaw v. State, 1 Mart. & Y. 122 (Tenn. 1827).

on a plea of not guilty urge anything he could in his defense.

At common law the order of pleading was as follows: (1) pleas to the jurisdiction, (2) demurrers, (3) dilatory pleas including pleas in abatement, (4) pleas in bar, such as former conviction, former acquittal, former attainder, and pardon, and (5) pleas to the matter of the indictment; that is to say, not guilty and special pleas.[8]

3. Modern English Procedure

Today in England a defendant who has been indicted must appear in person at the bar of the court to be arraigned by hearing the indictment read; and to plead to it.[9] The defendant must remain in court during all the proceedings including the imposition of sentence. In cases of misdemeanor, however, the court may permit him to be absent after he has pleaded. Under the Indictments Act of 1915, it is the duty of the clerk of the court to supply to the defendant on request a copy of the indictment free of charge.[10] Formerly one charged with a felony could not even buy one for fear of his bringing an action for malicious prosecution on it.

[8] 1 Chitty, Criminal Law (2d ed.1826) 434. But this order was not rigidly adhered to. 2 Bishop, New Criminal Procedure (4th ed.1895) §§ 746-747, pp.586-587. While Chitty states that double pleading was not permissible, Bishop cites Hawkins to the contrary. Bishop, *ibid.* §§ 748-752, pp.587-591.

[9] Kenny, Outlines of Criminal Law (15th ed.1942) 557. "The arraignment of prisoners, against whom bills of indictment have been preferred and signed, consists of three parts, first, calling the prisoner to the bar by name; secondly, reading the indictment to him; thirdly, asking him whether he is guilty or not." Archbold, Criminal Pleading, Evidence and Practice (30th ed.1938) 159.

[10] Rule 13(1). At common law he was not entitled to a copy because it was in its written form a presentment to the king. 3 Holdsworth, History of English Law (1923) 615; 2 Hale, Pleas of the Crown (1st American ed.1847) 236.

After the indictment has been read to him the defendant may pursue several courses. He may plead guilty, or stand mute, or take some legal objection to the indictment, or plead to it.[11]

If he pleads guilty, as do nearly half of the defendants indicted at Assizes or Quarter Sessions,[12] he may be sentenced immediately. In serious cases, however, because he may have pleaded guilty through some mistake as to the law or even as to the facts of his case, the court frequently advises him to withdraw his plea of guilty and permit the matter to be fully investigated. If the defendant stands mute, a jury must be impaneled to try whether he is mute "of malice" or by "visitation of God." In the latter event, the question will come up whether or not he can be made to understand by signs. But in the former event, a plea of guilty will be entered at once. At common law in cases of treason and misdemeanor, standing mute was treated as a plea of guilty. But in felony cases trial was regarded as necessary. He could not, however, be tried without his consent. To obtain that consent he was until 1772 subjected to the *peine forte et dure,* by being laid under a heavy mass of iron and deprived of food.[13] Many defendants chose to die under this torture, because by dying without having been convicted they saved their families from forfeiture

[11] Kenny, Outlines of Criminal Law (15th ed.1942) 558-563. See also Howard, Criminal Justice in England (1931) 358-360; Archbold, Criminal Pleading, Evidence and Practice (30th ed.1938) 140-158, 160-165; Roscoe, Criminal Evidence (15th ed.1928) 260-267; 2 Hale, Pleas of the Crown (1st American ed.1847) 216, 236; Stephen, A Digest of the Law of Criminal Procedure (1883) 169-176, 182-186; Harris and Wilshere, Principles and Practice of the Criminal Law (17th ed.1943) 447-456.

[12] Kenny, Outlines of Criminal Law (15th ed.1942) 558, 572.

[13] 1 Stephen, A History of the Criminal Law of England (1883) 297-301; 2 Pollock and Maitland, History of English Law (2d ed.1905) 650-652.

of property. Since 1827 a plea of not guilty is entered in such cases.

In the third place, he may show that the indictment, on the face of it, is open to some legal objection. Legal objections may be raised by a demurrer [14] or more commonly by a motion to quash. The motion to quash may be made at any time before the verdict. The court in its discretion may refuse to quash; hence if the defendant presses his objection, he must demur.

In the fourth place, he may put in a plea to the indictment. The more important pleas are: (1) pleas to the jurisdiction, (2) plea in abatement, (3) general plea in bar, and (4) special plea in bar. A plea to the jurisdiction is rarely made, since the same result may often be achieved by a demurrer or by a general plea in bar.[15] A plea in abatement lies for an error of form, but the plea has been rendered obsolete by the powers given to amend indictments.[16] A plea in bar means a defense on the merits. A general plea in bar raises the general issue and denies the whole indictment by alleging that the defendant is not guilty.[17] This is the most common and advantageous plea

[14] It has been stated that "demurrers may in practice be regarded as obsolete." Archbold, Criminal Pleading, Evidence and Practice (30th ed. 1938) 143; see also Kenny, Outlines of Criminal Law (15th ed.1942) 586. In misdemeanor cases, where the ruling is against the defendant, the court in its discretion may allow him to plead over, although it is not clear that there is such discretion in felony cases. Archbold, p.145; Regina v. Faderman (1850) 3 Car. 353. While Blackstone treats demurrers as pleas, they are in fact objections that there is not sufficient case in point of law to oblige the accused to plead. Harris, Principles of the Criminal Law (11th ed.1908) 368.

[15] Pleas to the jurisdiction and pleas in abatement are termed "dilatory pleas." Harris, Principles of the Criminal Law (11th ed.1908) 368.

[16] According to Blackstone, a "plea in abatement is principally for a misnomer, a wrong name, or false addition to the prisoner." 4 Bl. Comm. *328.

[17] "The general issue is pleaded by the prisoner *ore tenus* at the bar,

for the defendant to make. A special plea in bar is very unusual, as almost any defense can be raised under a general plea in bar, that is to say, under a plea of not guilty.[18] Such a plea, if successful, results in no trial for the crime charged. The principal special pleas in bar are: (1) justification, in cases of libel, (2) a pardon, (3) former acquittal, and (4) former conviction. The two latter pleas are available only if the defendant was in jeopardy under a valid indictment, if a final verdict was rendered, and if the two charges are substantially identical. In misdemeanors, a judgment on those two pleas is final, and sentence follows if the pleas fail.[19] But in felony or treason cases the defendant may plead over, and put in a further plea of not guilty.

All in all it would appear that the pleadings of the defendant in response to the indictment continue much as at common law in England.[20]

---

in these words, '*not guilty*'; by which plea, without further form, every person not having privilege or peerage, upon being arraigned upon any indictment for treason, felony, or piracy, is deemed to have put himself upon the country for trial." Archbold, Criminal Pleading, Evidence and Practice (30th ed.1938) 157.

[18] The only instance in which a special plea in bar seems requisite, with the exception of former acquittal, former conviction, and pardon is where a party or county is indicted for not repairing a road or bridge, and wishes to throw the burden of repairing upon some person not bound of common right to repair it. Archbold, Criminal Pleading, Evidence and Practice (30th ed.1938) 145.

[19] This seems unsound and is not followed in this country. 14 Am. Jur., Criminal Law, § 285, p.960; 22 C.J.S., Criminal Law, § 447, p.697.

[20] Archbold, Criminal Pleading, Evidence and Practice (30th ed.1938) 140. The "method of pleading in criminal cases, unlike that in civil cases, has always adhered more closely to the old forms." 3 Holdsworth, History of English Law (3d ed.1923) 615. No notice of alibi is required. Kenny, Outlines of Criminal Law (15th ed.1942) 534, 539.

4. Arraignment

According to Blackstone: "To arraign is nothing else but to call the prisoner to the bar of the court to answer the matter charged upon him in the indictment." [21] The arraignment precedes the plea of the defendant and is distinct from them. "When a criminal is arraigned, he either stands mute or confesses the fact, which circumstances we may call incidents to the arraignment, or else he pleads to the indictment, which is to be considered as the next stage of the proceedings." [22] The arraignment is the act of the court, while the plea is the act of the defendant. "It is true that in the form of proceeding, what is called an arraignment, generally includes the pleading of the accused; but I think the more strict meaning of the word is confined to the action of the court." [23] The purpose of arraignment is to inform the defendant of the charge against him and to obtain an answer from him.[24]

Under Section 201 of the American Law Institute Code of Criminal Procedure, the defendant is "arraigned by having the charge stated to him by the clerk in open court and by being called upon to plead thereto. If the defendant so demands before he pleads, the indictment or information shall be read to him by the clerk." This provi-

[21] 4 Bl. Comm. *322.

[22] 4 Bl. Comm. *324. See also 5 Longsdorf, Cyclopedia of Federal Procedure (1929) § 2171, p.604.

[23] Willoughby, J., in Whitehead v. The Commonwealth, 19 Gratt. (Va.) 640, 643-644 Sup.Ct. (1870). See Crain v. United States, 162 U.S. 625, 16 Sup.Ct. 952, 40 L.Ed. 1097 (1896); Johnson v. United States, 225 U.S. 405, 32 Sup.Ct. 748, 749, 56 L.Ed. 1142 (1912).

[24] Garland v. State of Washington, 232 U.S. 642, 644, 34 Sup.Ct. 456, 58 L.Ed. 772 (1914); 5 Longsdorf, Cyclopedia of Federal Procedure (1929) § 2171, p.604; 2 Bishop, New Criminal Procedure (4th ed.1895) § 728, p.574. And to identify the defendant, 14 Am. Jur., Criminal Law, § 249, p.939; 22 C.J.S., Criminal Law, § 406, p.625.

sion makes it possible to dispense with the reading of a lengthy and more or less technical accusation unless the defendant demands otherwise. Rule 10 of the Federal Rules of Criminal Procedure provides that the arraignment "shall consist of reading the indictment or information to the defendant or stating to him the substance of the charge and calling on him to plead thereto." Thus the option whether to read the indictment or not is not left with the defendant as it is in the Institute Code. The Code rule provides that it will be the clerk who states the charge or who reads the indictment. The federal rule is silent on that subject.

Arraignment except in capital cases is one of the rights which may be waived.[25] Due process does not require that there be a formal arraignment and plea in order to sustain a conviction.[26] The older cases are to the effect that ordinary criminal procedure requires this, on the ground that until arraignment and plea there is no issue to try.[27] It has also been said that any change is for the legislature.[28] A more liberal rule has been laid down as to misdemeanors.[29] It is scarcely sensible to try to assert that

[25] Notes (1911) 25 Harv.L.Rev. 179, (1907) 6 Mich.L.Rev. 82, (1929) 27 Mich.L.Rev. 703.

[26] Garland v. Washington, 232 U.S. 642, 34 Sup.Ct. 456, 58 L.Ed. 772 (1914), 27 Harv.L.Rev. 760. The court pointed out that in former times defendant had no right to counsel, could not testify, and punishment for slight offenses was severe and shocking.

[27] People v. Corbett, 28 Cal. 328 (1865); State v. Fontenette, 45 La. Ann. 902, 12 So. 937 (1893); Burroughs v. State, 94 Neb. 519, 143 N.W. 450, Ann. Cas. 1915 C. 1070 (1913). Jeopardy does not attach where there is no arraignment and plea. Note (1940) 24 Minn.L.Rev. 522, 527.

[28] State v. Vanderhook, 88 Mo. 105 (1885). *Contra:* Hack v. State, 141 Wis. 340, 124 N.W. 492, 45 L.R.A. (N.S.) 664 (1910), 10 Col.L.Rev. 361, (1911) 1 J.Crim.L. 688; Ray v. State, 40 Okla. Crim. 413, 269 Pac. 509 (1928).

[29] Allyn v. State, 21 Neb. 593, 33 N.W. 212 (1887); State v. Moore, 30 S.C. 69, 8 S.E. 437 (1888).

the defendant does not know with what he is charged until he has been arraigned. Section 206 of the American Law Institute Code of Criminal Procedure provides: "Neither a failure to arraign nor an irregularity in the arraignment shall affect the validity of any proceeding in the cause if the defendant pleads to the indictment or information or proceeds to trial without objecting to such failure or irregularity."

The defendant must be present at his arraignment in all felony cases, but there is authority not requiring his presence in misdemeanor cases.[30] Section 287 of the Institute Code requires his presence in felony cases, and Section 288 in misdemeanor cases. Rule 43 of the Federal Rules of Criminal Procedure does not require presence in misdemeanor cases, although the defendant has a right to be present if he wishes. It provides that in prosecutions "for offenses punishable by fine or by imprisonment for not more than one year or both, the court, with the written consent of the defendant, may permit arraignment, plea, trial and imposition of sentence in the defendant's absence."

In carefully avoiding any confusion between arraignment and preliminary examination, it should be remembered that arraignment is usually before the trial court, whereas the preliminary examination is before the justice. Arraignment follows indictment while preliminary examination follows arrest. Section 204 of the Institute Code provides that arraignment shall normally be in the court in which the indictment or information is filed.

[30] Housel and Walser, Defending and Prosecuting Federal Criminal Cases (1938) 349; A.L.I. Code of Crim. Proc. (1930) commentaries 878; Wharton, Criminal Pleading and Practice (9th ed.1889) § 545, p.392; Frank v. Mangum, 237 U.S. 309, 35 Sup.Ct. 582, 592, 59 L.Ed. 969 (1914); Davis v. State 51 Neb. 301, 360, 70 N.W. 984 (1897).

Counsel may be very necessary or helpful to a defendant at arraignment.[31] Section 203 of the Institute Code provides that before the defendant is arraigned on a charge of felony "if he is without counsel the court shall, unless the defendant objects, assign him counsel to represent him in the cause." [32] Rule 44 of the Federal Rules of Criminal Procedure does not specifically refer to arraignment but provides: "If the defendant appears in court without counsel, the court shall advise him of his right to counsel and assign counsel to represent him at every stage of the preceeding unless he elects to be present without counsel or is able to obtain counsel." [33]

[31] The right to counsel "should be afforded a defendant at a time he is in a position to make a complete defense beginning, in the case of a felony, with the arraignment and plea." 2 Moore, Illinois Criminal Law and Procedure (3d ed.1932) 838-839. See also People v. Kurant, 331 Ill. 470, 480 (1928); Note (1942) 42 Col.L.Rev. 271, 275, 276. In Chicago cases of indigent defendants are turned over to the public defender by assignment at arraignment. Baker, "The Public Defender's Work in Cook County" (1934) 25 J.Crim.L. 5, 8, n.6.

[32] Compare the earlier proposal: "The Defendant shall have the right to be represented by counsel of his own selection, but if he is unable to secure counsel, he shall be represented by the Public Defender (in case the laws provide for such an official) or by counsel appointed by the Court, to whom a reasonable fee may be allowed by the Court and taxed as costs in the case. The Judge in every criminal court shall maintain a list of reputable attorneys who are willing to act for defendants unable to pay and shall secure the assistance of the local or state bar association in this matter." Hadley, "Outlines of a Code of Criminal Procedure" (1926) 12 A.B.A.J 690, 692. It will be noted that the American Law Institute Code of Criminal Procedure provision fails to include misdemeanors.

[33] The past federal practice has been that the court always inquired of the defendant upon his arraignment whether or not he had counsel, and then assigned him counsel if he had none and lacked funds to engage one. Housel and Walser, Defending and Prosecuting Federal Criminal Cases (1938) 349.

5. Copy of Indictment

Under Rule 10 of the Federal Rules of Criminal Procedure, at the time of arraignment the defendant is to be given a copy of the accusation before he is called upon to plead. Section 193 of the Institute Code provides for the furnishing of a copy, whether requested or not, at least twenty-four hours before the defendant is required to plead.[34] It would seem that if the defendant does not desire a copy "there is no propriety in forcing a copy upon him and charging the government with the expense." [35]

6. List of Jurors

In the absence of statute, a defendant is not entitled to a list of the jury panel.[36] In England he has had the right since 1708 to such a list only in cases of high treason.[37] In a number of jurisdictions, statutes provide for the furnishing of such lists. Federal statutes provide that a list of trial jurors and witnesses be delivered to the defendant in

[34] But if he pleads he waives such right. The English rule is like the federal rule. The defendant is furnished a copy upon request without charge. Rule 13(1) under Indictments Act, 1915. The defendant was always entitled to a copy of the indictment in misdemeanor cases. Kenny, Outlines of Criminal Law (15th ed.1942) 568. He got the right in treason cases in 1695. 1 Stephen, A History of the Criminal Law of England (1883) 416. In Russia a copy of the indictment must be delivered to the defendant three days before trial. Hazard, "Soviet Criminal Procedure" (1941) 15 Tulane L.Rev. 220, 228.

[35] United States v. Van Duzee, 140 U.S. 169, 11 Sup.Ct. 758, 35 L.Ed. 399 (1891).

[36] Cooley v. State, 174 Tenn. 168, 124 S.W. (2d) 250, 253 (1939); 23 C.J.S., Criminal Law, § 960, p.270. Nor is he entitled to interview witnesses for the prosecution or to a disclosure of what their testimony will be. 23 C.J.S., Criminal Law, § 1025, p.395.

[37] Archbold, Criminal Pleading, Evidence and Practice (30th ed.1938) 187. The value of a list of jurors has been doubted. 1 Stephen, A History of the Criminal Law of England (1883) 399.

treason cases at least three days before trial and in other capital cases at least two days before trial.[38] In the exercise of discretion, federal courts have ordered that such lists be furnished defendants in other than capital cases.[39] The right to a list may be waived, as when the defendant declares himself ready for trial and goes to trial without objection.[40] The Institute Code and the Federal Rules of Criminal Procedure contain no provisions on the subject.

7. List of Witnesses

In most jurisdictions, the prosecution is required to furnish the defendant with a list of witnesses to be called on behalf of the state. According to Bishop, this list is "differently regarded according to the terms of the varying statutes. Under same the prosecuting attorney must either examine all or have all in court to be called by the defendant if he wishes. Widely he is not required to produce all on the witness stand. On this question, opinions as well as statutes are not quite uniform. A witness not named in the list may, in most localities, testify, as of favor or of right, either by having his name first added to the list or without; but there are exceptional states in which this is not allowed." [41] It has been argued that the defendant

[38] 18 U.S.C., § 562. See Logan v. United States, 144 U.S. 263 (1892). This statute does not require that lists of witnesses before the grand jury be furnished. Moore v. Aderhold, 108 F. (2d) 729 (C.C.A. 10th, 1939).

[39] Spivey v. United States, 109 F. (2d) 181 (C.C.A. 5th, 1940), cert. denied 310 U.S. 631 (1940); United States v. Aviles, 222 Fed. 474 (D. Col. 1915).

[40] Mackie v. State, 138 Miss. 740, 103 So. 379 (1925).

[41] 1 Bishop, New Criminal Procedure (4th ed.1895) 966c. In France a list of the witnesses for the prosecution must be furnished the defendant 24 hours before trial. Wright, "French Criminal Procedure" (1929) 45 L.Q.Rev. 92, 94.

should be under a reciprocal duty to furnish a list of his witnesses.[42]

It is of course true that when an unscrupulous defendant is furnished with the names of witnesses and a description of the evidence to be used against him, an opportunity is afforded him to tamper with or to intimidate the witnesses, manufacture false evidence in opposition, or otherwise practice chicanery. But an innocent defendant needs protection from false charges and, in order that he may prepare to meet them, advance notice must be given him. This is in accord not only with a policy of fairness, but also protects the prosecution from convicting an innocent defendant. Moreover, the general policy of securing the just and expeditious settlement of controversies, whether civil or criminal, is hampered by the lack of such information.[43] It has finally been recognized in England and in many states that merely to furnish the defendant a copy of the indictment or information does not give him enough information so that he may adequately prepare his defense. As the government has grown more powerful, the risks of tampering have decreased. It can safely furnish the defendant the evidence and the witnesses on which it relies. The preliminary examination is no substitute for two reasons. There need be none where prosecution is by indictment. Even if there is one, since the hearing is limited only to the finding of probable cause, the prosecution need not usually put on a full-dress proceeding.

[42] Millar, "The Function of Criminal Pleading" (1922) 12 J.Crim.L. 500, 503-504. See also "Defects in Criminal Justice," (1925) 11 A.B.A.J. 297, 298; Hadley, "Criminal Justice in America: Present Conditions Historically Considered" (1925) 11 A.B.A.J. 674, 676; Report of Judicial Council of Idaho (1930) 26.

[43] 6 Wigmore, Evidence (3d ed.1940) ¶ 1845, 1850-1855b.

8. Procedure in Cases of Present Insanity

A defendant should not be tried while so insane as not to be able to conduct a rational defense.[44] At common law the mode of deciding this issue lay within the discretion of the trial court.[45] The customary procedure is to try the matter before a special jury.[46] If the question is raised only after the trial has begun, it may in some states be left to the trial jury.[47] The purpose of the rule against trying insane persons is to avoid the conviction of defendants whose disabilities have prevented them from raising valid defenses or disclosing exculpating facts. Hence, even after verdict, a defendant should be allowed to show that he was insane despite his failure to object earlier.[48]

A person presently insane cannot plead to an arraignment.[49] Under Section 307 of the Institute Code, if before

[44] Freeman v. People, 4 Denio 9 (N.Y. 1847); see 3 Bishop, New Criminal Procedure (4th ed.1895) § 667(2); 23 C.J.S., Criminal Law, § 940, p.236.

[45] Youtsey v. United States, 97 Fed. 937 (C.C.A. 6th, 1899).

[46] People v. Ah Ying, 42 Cal. 18 (1871). In some states this is expressly required by statute. Ill. Rev. Stat. (Cahill, 1927) c.38, § 622.

[47] State v. Khoury, 149 N.C. 454, 62 S.E. 638 (1908).

[48] United States v. Lancaster, Fed. Cases, No. 15, 555 at 552 (C.C. Ill. 1877). *Contra:* People v. Hart, 333 Ill. 169, 164 N.E. 156 (1928), (1929) 42 Harv.L.Rev. 830. See also (1918) 27 Yale L.J. 698.

[49] Youtsey v. United States, 97 F. 937, 940 (C.C.A. 6th, 1899); Housel and Walser, Defending and Prosecuting Federal Criminal Cases (1938) 441; Dession, "The Mentally Ill Offender in Federal Criminal Law and Administration" (1944) 53 Yale L.J. 684. For the common-law view to the same effect, see 1 Hale, History of the Pleas of the Crown (1st American ed.1847) 34, 35; 4 Bl. Comm. *24, 25; 2 Bishop, New Criminal Procedure (4th ed.1895) § 666. For a comparison of common-law and present procedure, see Glueck, Mental Disorder and the Criminal Law (1925) 53-72; Weihofen, Insanity as a Defense in Criminal Law (1933) 255, 346, 372. Questions of both present insanity and insanity at the time of the act are usually raised for the first time upon arraignment. Weihofen, Insanity as a Defense in Criminal Law (1933) 255, 346. As to modern English procedure, see Archbold, Criminal Pleading, Evidence and Practice (30th ed.1938) 162-164.

or during the trial the court has reasonable ground to believe that a defendant, against whom an indictment has been found or an information filed, is insane to the extent that he cannot understand the proceedings against him or assist in his defense, the court shall immediately fix a time for a hearing to determine the defendant's mental condition. The court may appoint two disinterested qualified experts to examine the defendant. In case the defendant is found insane, steps are taken to have him committed to a proper institution. If not, the court proceeds with the trial. A more far-reaching reform is the Massachusetts law providing for routine examination before trial.[50]

The Massachusetts law, known as the Briggs Law, has been thought to have the following virtues: By providing in advance of trial an impartial and competent mental examination, it avoids the expense and ordeal of numerous trials. It almost entirely eliminates the battle of experts. There can be a more scientific examination out of court than in court. It protects the right of the psychotic or otherwise mentally incompetent defendant who might otherwise go unrecognized. It educates judges and the bar to a realization of the value of psychiatry. "It is no exaggeration to say that the Briggs Law represents the most significant step yet found towards a harmonious union of psychiatry with the criminal law." [51]

[50] Glueck, Mental Disorder and the Criminal Law (1925) 55-56, 58-72, 474-476; Weihofen, Insanity as a Defense in Criminal Law (1933) 401-407; Overholser, "The Massachusetts Procedure Relative to the Sanity of Defendants in Criminal Cases" (1935) 19 Minn.L.Rev. 308; Glueck, "Psychiatric Examination of Persons Accused of Crime" (1927) 36 Yale L.J. 632; Tulin, "The Problem of Mental Disorder in Crime: A Survey" (1932) 32 Col.L.Rev. 933, 958.

[51] Overholser, "The Massachusetts Procedure Relative to the Sanity of Defendants in Criminal Cases" (1935) 19 Minn.L.Rev. 308, 317. It is "easily the most far-sighted piece of legislation yet passed on this subject."

9. Pleadings and Motions Before Trial

Counsel for the defendant is likely to proceed as follows with respect to the defendant's pleadings.[52] After he has examined the indictment or information, he may request postponement of arraignment or may arrange with the prosecuting attorney for arraignment. He may seek to provide bail if the defendant has not appeared before in the case. If he discovers that the indictment is defective for some reason not shown on its face, as for example the failure to draw grand jurors in the manner provided for by statute, he may file a plea in abatement.[53] A statutory motion to quash the accusation, or in some states a demurrer,[54] may be filed to raise an objection to a defect which is apparent on the face of the accusation. If the motion to quash or a demurrer is not filed, or if it is overruled, counsel may enter a plea of guilty or not guilty, depending upon the results of conferences with the defendant and investigation of the law and facts.

Glueck, "Psychiatric Examination of Persons Accused of Crime" (1927) 36 Yale L.J. 632, 635. "The Briggs Law, in theory and in practice, is far ahead of any other device dealing with the problem of mental disorder and the criminal law." Tulin, "The Problem of Mental Disorder in Crime: A Survey" (1932) 32 Col.L.Rev. 933, 961.

[52] Robinson, Cases on Criminal Law and Procedure (1941) 218.

[53] A plea in abatement should precede a plea of not guilty, because the latter waives all preceding irregularities. People v. Beak, 291 Ill. 449, 126 N.E. 201 (1920). Likewise a demurrer must be filed before pleading to the indictment; People v. Kinsley, 118 Cal. App. 593, 5 Pac. (2d) 938 (1931); and a motion to quash is subject to the same rule, State v. Riffe, 10 W.Va. 794 (1877); Keigwin, Cases in Criminal Procedure (1939) 498, n.4; and a plea to the jurisdiction. Ford v. United States, 273 U.S. 593, 606, 71 L.Ed. 793, 799 (1927).

[54] For a case permitting a demurrer to the evidence where there is a fatal variance between the indictment and the proof, see State v. Franklin, 204 N.C. 157, 167 S.E. 569 (1933). See also Wharton, Criminal Pleading and Practice (9th ed.1889) § 407, p.284.

The filing of pleadings by a criminal defendant, other than pleas of guilty or not guilty, is not as common as might be supposed. In a study of 34,240 federal criminal cases, pleadings were filed by defendants in only 1,857 cases. Of the 2,965 pleadings filed, only 403 or 13.2 per cent were motions to quash.[55] On 1,530 or 51.6 per cent of these pleadings, the ruling was in favor of the United States, and on only 827, or 28 per cent of the pleadings, was the ruling in favor of the defendant. In Missouri, out of 4,969 cases entering the trial court, only 251 were terminated by action of the court, of which six were dismissed on pleas in abatement and eighteen on motions to quash.[56] In 1926 in Philadelphia, it was found that there is "practically no delay in the trial of cases caused by the making of technical objections to the indictment. Cases in which indictments are quashed or demurrers sustained because of inadequacy as to form are exceedingly infrequent." [57]

Statutes in several states provide that if, on the arraignment the defendant requires it, he must be allowed a reasonable time not less than one day to answer the indictment or information.[58] Section 207 of the Institute Code provides that upon being arraigned "the defendant shall immediately, unless the court grants him further time,

[55] A.L.I., A Study of the Business of the Federal Courts (1934) pt. I, Criminal Cases, p.72, and Detailed Tables 15, p.127, and 17, p.129. See McClintock, "Indictment by a Grand Jury" (1942) 26 Minn.L.Rev. 153, 154.

[56] Missouri Crime Survey (1926) 166-167.

[57] Report of the Crimes Survey Committee, Law Association of Philadelphia (1926) 472.

[58] One of the seven essentials of a criminal proceeding is "opportunity to prepare for trial, procure witnesses, and make needed investigations." Nat. Com. on Law Obs. and Enf., Rep. on Crim. Proc. (1931) 16. In Virginia in 1917 and 1927, the average time between indictment and plea was one month. Fuller, Criminal Justice in Virginia (1931) 159.

either move to quash the indictment or information or plead thereto or do both." Rule 12(b)(3) of the Federal Rules of Criminal Procedure gives the defendant more time in providing: "The motion shall be made before the plea is entered, but the court may permit it to be made within a reasonable time thereafter."

At common law if the defendant's demurrer was overruled he had no absolute right to plead over. This was also true as to a number of other pleadings. Statutes in many states, however, now permit him to do so. Section 207 of the Institute Code provides with respect to the broadened motion to quash: "If he moves to quash, without also pleading, and the motion is withdrawn or overruled he shall immediately plead." [59]

Rule 12(b)(3) of the Federal Rules of Criminal Procedure permits the motion raising defenses and objections to be made after the plea of not guilty. This alters the older federal practice, which, like the common law, took the view that the defendant acknowledged the legal sufficiency of the indictment by entering a plea of not guilty.[60]

It is true that a defendant might be permitted to withdraw his plea of not guilty and then move to quash. But the defendant had no absolute right to withdraw his plea of not guilty, it being a matter of discretion for the trial court. Modern criminal pleading is designed to get away from older rules as to a fixed chronological order of pleading, as to the prohibition of more than one plea at a time, and limiting the right to plead over.

[59] Rule 12(b)(5) of the Federal Rules of Criminal Procedure provides: "If a motion is determined adversely to the defendant he shall be permitted to plead if he had not previously pleaded."

[60] In Canada demurrers and motions to quash must be made before plea except by leave of court. Bayley, "Canadian Criminal Law and Procedure as Administered in the Province of Ontario" (1926) 4 Can. B.Rev. 552, 557.

It is now generally provided by statute that, on failure to plead, a plea of not guilty shall be entered.[61] Section 208 of the Institute Code provides: "If the defendant is a corporation and fails to appear or if any defendant stands mute or pleads evasively a plea of not guilty shall be entered of record." [62]

In most states there are statutes to some extent simplifying the common-law pleas.[63] Section 209 of the American Law Institute Code carries this still further by substituting a motion to quash the indictment for demurrers and all pleas except the pleas of guilty and not guilty.[64] The Wickersham Commission states: "The matter is not of great importance but we think the change a distinct step forward in the development of procedure and recommend it." [65] Rule 12(a) of the Federal Rules of Criminal Procedure provides for a motion to dismiss corresponding to the Code motion to quash. The common-law pro-

[61] Reg. v. Bernard, 1 Fost L.F. 240 (1858); Commonwealth v. Place, 153 Pa. 314, 26 Atl. 620 (1893).

[62] See also Rule 11 of the Federal Rules of Criminal Procedure; Criminal Justice Act, 1925, 15 & 16 Geo. V, c.86, § 33, subsec. 3.

[63] But it has been stated that the "various motions, demurrers and pleas which may be made upon arraignment remain virtually the same today as when Hale, Hawkins, and Blackstone expounded upon them." Dean, "Advance Specifications of Defense in Criminal Cases" (1934) 20 A.B.A.J. 435, 436. "Arraignment, plea and issue, trial, judgment, review, reprieve, and pardon stand fundamentally as in the fourth book of Blackstone." Pound, Criminal Justice in America (1930) 109. See also note to Rule 12(a), Fed. Rules of Crim. Proc. (1944) Second Preliminary Draft.

[64] This was embodied in the proposed Illinois Code. See Freeman, "The Draft Code of Criminal Law and Procedure" (1935) 30 Ill.L.Rev. 226, 232. There appear to be no constitutional objections to such reforms. Willard, "The Seventeenth Century Indictment in the Light of Modern Conditions" (1911) 24 Harv.L.Rev. 290, 291-292.

[65] Nat. Com. on Law Obs. and Enf., Rep. on Crim. Proc. (1931) 33. See also Report of the Commission on the Administration of Justice in New York State (1939) § 282, 283; Missouri Crime Survey (1926) 166; Stephen, "Indictments and the Rule Committee" (1898) 14 L.Q.Rev. 260, 264.

cedure made for delay[66] and for confusion as to the proper motion or plea[67] by the defendant.

A critic of existing criminal procedure has said: "There needs no argument to show that demurrers and motions to quash delay the progress of the case."[68] To correct this, Section 215 of the Institute Code provides that its broadened motion to quash shall be heard "immediately on its being made unless, for good cause, the court postpones the hearing." Rule 12 b(4) of the Federal Rules of Criminal Procedure introduces more flexibility by providing: "A motion before trial raising defenses or objections shall be determined before trial unless the court orders that it be deferred for determination at the trial of the general issue."

Some objections raisable by a defendant may be raised during the trial as well as before trial. Rule 12 (b) (1) of the Federal Rules of Criminal Procedure provides: "Any defense or objection which is capable of determination without the trial of the general issue may be raised before trial by motion." In federal practice this would include the defense and objections of lack of jurisdiction, former

[66] Willard, "The Seventeenth Century Indictment in the Light of Modern Conditions" (1911) 24 Harv.L.Rev. 290, 291. It would not be fair to the defendant, however, to abolish all pleas and motions other than guilty or not guilty. If the defendant's motion is sustained, he is often saved the expense and humiliation of having to go to trial.

[67] For example, in federal practice pleas in abatement and motions to quash have overlapped in an uncertain fashion. United States v. Goldman, 28 F. (2d) 424, 426 (D. Conn. 1928). In United States v. Oppenheimer, 242 U.S. 85, 86 (1916), the same defense "was presented in four forms entitled respectively, demurrer, motion to quash, plea in abatement, and plea in bar."

[68] Willard, "The Seventeenth Century Indictment in the Light of Modern Conditions" (1911) 24 Harv.L.Rev. 290, 291. See also Barnes, J., "Cause of Delay in Criminal Cases" (1916) 7 J.Crim.L. 330, 332; Fuller, Criminal Justice in Virginia (1931) 127.

acquittal, former conviction, former jeopardy, pardon, statute of limitations, and insanity at the time of the trial of the general issue.[69]

Other defenses raisable by a defendant can be raised only before trial. Failure to raise them then waives the defense. Rule 12(b)(2) of the Federal Rules of Criminal Procedure provides: "Defenses and objections based on defects in the institution of the prosecution or in the indictment or information other than that it fails to show jurisdiction in the court or to charge an offense may be raised only by motion before trial. The motion shall include all such defenses and objections then available to the defendant. Failure to present any such defenses or objection as herein provided constitutes a waiver thereof, but the court for cause shown may grant relief from the waiver." Defenses based on "defects in the institution of the prosecution," include objections that the grand jury was not legally selected or organized, that members of the grand jury were not legally qualified, and that proceedings of the grand jury were not legally conducted. Defenses based on defects in the indictment include duplicity, misjoinder of offenses, misjoinder of defendants, and misnomer. All these must now be raised before trial under the proposed rule. The rule changes the older practice of presenting various defenses in successive demurrers, motions to quash and also in abatement, thus avoiding unnecessary delay.

In general under liberalized criminal pleading, the defendant must move to quash or dismiss the indictment at an early stage in the criminal proceedings or waive his right to raise the objection. This avoids delay and resort to strategy. Section 220 of the Institute Code provides as

[69] Note to Rule 12(b) of the Fed. Rules of Crim. Proc.

to the broadened motion to quash: "If the defendant does not move to quash the indictment or information before or at the time he pleads thereto he shall be taken to have waived all objections which are grounds for a motion to quash except those which are also grounds for a motion in arrest of judgment."

Where does the defendant stand if the courts grant a motion to quash or dismiss an indictment? His release does not necessarily follow. Under Rule 12 (b) (5) of the Federal Rules of Criminal Procedure, "If the court grants a motion based on a defect in the institution of the prosecution or in the indictment or information, it may also order that the defendant be held in custody or that his bail be continued for a specified time pending the filing of a new indictment or information." Section 218 of the Institute Code, while longer and more elaborate, is to the same general effect.

10. Trial of Issues of Fact

It is not usual to leave to the court, rather than the jury, the determination of the existence of a fact occurring during the commission of a crime, when that fact extends the amount of punishment which may be imposed.[70] To be sure, where the court has a discretion in imposing sentence, it may consider the character of the defendant, his previous offenses, and the circumstances of the particular crime.[71] A statute requiring the court after a plea of guilty to determine the degree is valid.[72] The

[70] People v. Caruso, 249 N.Y. 302, 164 N.E. 106 (1928). *Contra:* People v. Krennen, 264 N.Y. 108, 190 N.E. 167 (1934), 48 Harv.L.Rev. 334.

[71] Foster v. United States, 47 F. (2d) 892 (C.C.A. 7th, 1931); (1933) 86 A.L.R. 832. *Contra:* People v. Corry, 349 Ill. 122, 181 N.E. 603 (1932), 46 Harv.L.Rev. 334.

[72] People v. Chew Lan Ong, 141 Cal. 550, 75 Pac. 186 (1904).

plea includes all the elements of any degree. On a plea of benefit of clergy where available, if the prosecution alleged that the defendant had availed himself of the plea on a former conviction, the defendant was entitled to jury trial on his identity with the person previously convicted.[73] In statutes providing increased punishment for habitual offenders, there is usually some provision giving a right to jury trial as to identity.[74] But it has been held valid for a statute to leave the question of identity in these prior offender cases to the judge.[75] Where the amount of punishment depends on the defendant's age, the court and not the jury determines the age.[76]

Most courts hold that entrapment is a question of fact which the jury may consider under the general issue.[77] There has also been authority that the court itself should decide the question, and that the defense may be asserted at any stage in the proceedings.[78]

Issues of fact raised by the plea of not guilty are at common law triable by a jury. But there was more complexity at common law as to the trial of issues of fact or law raised by other pleas or motions.[79] Doubtless as a

[73] State v. Carroll, 24 N.C. 257 (1842) semble.

[74] Cf. Graham v. West Virginia, 224 U.S. 616 (1912); People v. Gowasky, 244 N.Y. 451, 155 N.E. 737 (1927).

[75] State v. Guidry, 169 La. 215, 124 So. 832 (1929); cf. A.L.I. Code of Crim.Proc. (1930) § 403.

[76] State v. Lavner, 30 Mo. 44 (1860); People ex rel. Ziegler v. Justice of Special Sessions, 10 Hun. 224 (N.Y. Sup.Ct. 1877).

[77] Sorrells v. United States, 287 U.S. 435, 53 Sup.Ct. 210 (1932), (1933) 46 Harv.L.Rev. 848, three judges dissenting. See Mikell, "The Doctrine of Entrapment in the Federal Courts" (1942) 90 U. of Pa.L.Rev. 245.

[78] United States v. Healy, 202 Fed. 349 (D. Mont. 1913); United States v. Mathues, 22 F. (2d) 979 (D. Pa. 1927).

[79] See A.L.I. Code of Crim. Proc. (1930) commentaries 655-658; 14 Am. Jur., Criminal Law, § 284, p.959; 22 C.J.S., Criminal Law, §§ 426, 434, 446. See also the note to Rule 12(b)(4), Fed. Rules of Crim. Proc. (1944) Second Preliminary Draft.

matter of efficiency the court ought to try such issues. Section 216 of the Institute Code provides: "All issues, whether of law or fact, which arise on a motion to quash shall be tried by the court." In some states this provision would be unconstitutional as to issues of fact arising under pleas of former jeopardy, pardon, or grant of immunity by law from prosecution.[80] Rule 12(b)(4) of the Federal Rules of Criminal Procedure provides: "An issue of fact shall be tried by a jury if a jury trial is required under the Constitution or an Act of Congress. All other issues of fact shall be determined by the court with or without a jury or on affidavits or in such other manner as the court may direct."

11. Meaning of Pleading

Where a criminal statute uses the words "pleading of a party" it has reference to an allegation made by the parties to a criminal case "for the purpose of definitely presenting the issue to be tried and determined between them."[81] The Institute Code uses the term "plead" quite narrowly in connection with the defendant. Under Section 221: "The defendant shall plead to the indictment either by a plea of guilty or of not guilty." No provision is made for the plea of *nolo contendere*. On the other hand, Rule 11 of the Federal Rules of Criminal Procedure provides: "A defendant may plead not guilty, guilty, or, with the consent of the court, *nolo contendere*." Under Rule 12 of the Federal Rules: "Pleadings in criminal proceedings

[80] The American Law Code of Criminal Procedure in a note to Section 216 proposes that in such states such issues of fact shall be decided by a jury before the defendant is tried for the offense for which he is indicted or informed against.

[81] Tucker v. United States, 151 U.S. 164, 168, 14 Sup.Ct. 299, 38 L.Ed. 112, 114 (1894).

shall be the indictment and the information, and the pleas of not guilty, guilty and *nolo contendere*." [82]

Under Section 222 of the Institute Code, every plea must be pleaded orally and in open court and must be immediately entered of record. But a failure to enter it shall not affect the validity of any proceeding in the case.

It has been held that, in a felony case where the record showed arraignment, demurrer, and overruling of demurrer, trial, and conviction, it is not sufficient if it does not also show affirmatively that a plea had been entered by or for the defendant.[83] The theory was that the record in criminal cases must show affirmatively that every step essential to a valid trial has been properly taken, and that unless a plea is entered there is no issue for the jury to try.[84] This was formerly the weight of authority.[85] Under Section 236 of the Institute Code, the "fact that the defendant does not plead shall not affect the validity of any

[82] As to the origin of the term "pleading," see Millar, "The Lineage of Some Procedural Words" (1939) 25 A.B.A.J. 1023, 1025, 1026. According to Hand, J., "An indictment is not a pleading of the United States, but the charge of a grand jury." Falter v. United States, 23 F. (2d) 420, 425 (C.C.A. 2d, 1928).

[83] State v. Walter, 50 Ore. 142, 91 Pac. 490 (1907), 21 Harv.L.Rev. 217. "Without plea, there can be no valid trial. It is so even though the defendant went voluntarily and without objection to trial, knowing there was no plea. It must be before the jury is sworn; afterward, the plea is too late." 2 Bishop, New Criminal Procedure (4th ed.1895) § 733, subdiv. 4.

[84] Crain v. United States, 162 U.S. 625, 16 Sup.Ct. 952, 40 L.Ed. 1097 (1896) overruled in Garland v. United States, 232 U.S. 642, 32 Sup.Ct. 456, 58 L.Ed. 772 (1914).

[85] (1907) 21 Harv.L.Rev. 217. But, in a misdemeanor case, when the record of a trial is silent as to an arraignment or plea of the defendant, and the matter was never presented to the trial court, and not assigned as error, and not called to the attention of the appellate court, except by the brief of counsel, there will be no reversal. Williams v. State, 92 Fla. 648, 109 So. 805 (1926).

proceeding in the cause if the defendant proceeds to trial without a plea." There is some authority that, while arraignment may be waived, the entry of a plea is essential.[86]

12. Plea of Nolo Contendere

Modern conceptions about the pleas of *non vult* or *nolo contendere* have arisen out of descriptions in early treatises.[87] Such descriptions were based on a colloquy between the court and counsel in a Year Book of 1430.[88] Not all the incidents of the plea were clearly defined.[89] Although it is not a direct admission of guilt, it has been treated as a plea of guilty for the purpose of the particular case.[90] But one limitation is said to be that it may not be used in subsequent proceedings as an admission to prove the facts alleged in the indictment.[91] In New Hampshire a conviction under such a plea may be shown in criminal prosecutions against the same defendant, but not in civil suits.[92] There may be a prison sentence after such plea.[93] The plea cannot be entered without the consent of the court, which

[86] People v. Evenow, 355 Ill. 451, 189 N.E. 368 (1934); Note (1910) 10 Col.L.Rev. 361. The record must affirmatively show the entry of a plea of not guilty. No such distinction is taken in Garland v. United States, 232 U.S. 642, 34 Sup.Ct. 456, 58 L.Ed. 772 (1914).

[87] 2 Hawkins, Pleas of the Crown (1716) c.31, § 3; Viner, Abridgment (1799) Estoppel F 35, 36.

[88] Y.B. 9 Hen. VI, 60 (1430). See (1934) 48 Harv.L.Rev. 128.

[89] Lambard, Eirenarcha (1607) 500; Hudson v. United States, 272 U.S. 451, 454 (1926), (1927) 36 Yale L.J. 421.

[90] People ex rel. Peacock v. Judges, 46 N.J.L. 112 (1884); United States v. Norris, 281 U.S. 619 (1930).

[91] Chester v. State, 107 Miss. 459, 65 So. 510 (1914); Lafferty v. Houlihan, 81 N.H. 67, 121 Atl. 92 (1923); Note (1941) 50 Yale L.J. 499, 505.

[92] State v. Fagan, 64 N.H. 431, 14 Atl. 727 (1888); Collins v. Bensen, 81 N.H. 10, 120 Atl. 724 (1923); Teslovich v. Fireman's Fuel Ins. Co. of San Francisco, 110 Pa. Super. 245, 168 Atl. 354 (1923).

[93] Hudson v. United States, 272 U.S. 451 (1926). *Contra:* Roach v. Commonwealth, 157 Va. 954, 162 S.E. 50 (1932).

the court in its discretion may refuse. If granted, it cannot be withdrawn without the consent of the court. The plea is an anomaly, of doubtful value in the state courts.[94] It has been extensively used in the federal courts, particularly in anti-trust prosecutions.[95] Lengthy and expensive trials are thus avoided. Rule 11 of the Federal Rules of Criminal Procedure provides for its continuance. It has not been used in English practice since 1702.[96] It is not provided for in the Canadian Criminal Code, nor in the American Law Institute Code of Criminal Procedure. The plea may have disturbing consequences to a defendant, such as is found in holding that a *nolo contendere* plea is a conviction, and makes a person after a second conviction a second offender;[97] and that a *nolo contendere* plea may be introduced to impeach a witness's credibility in a subsequent action.[98] It would also appear that a previous plea of *nolo contendere* amounts to a conviction under the numerous forms of questionnaires, such as in civil service applications inquiring whether a person has ever been convicted of a crime.[99]

13. Plea of Guilty

Under Section 224 of the Institute Code, where the defendant is not represented by counsel the court shall not

[94] (1934) 48 Harv.L.Rev. 128.

[95] Lenvin and Meyers, "Nolo Contendere: Its Nature and Implications" (1942) 51 Yale L.J. 1255; (1940) 7 Law and Contemporary Problems 1.

[96] Hudson v. United States, 272 U.S. 451 (1926). The last reported English case is Queen v. Templeman, 1 Salk. 55 (Q.B. 1702).

[97] State v. Suick, 195 Wis. 175, 177, 217 N.W. 743, 744 (1928); People v. Daibock, 265 N.Y. 125, 129, 191 N.E. 859, 860 (1934); United States ex rel. Bruno v. Reimes, Commissioner of Immigration, 98 F. (2d) 92 (C.C.A. 3d, 1938).

[98] State v. Herlihy, 102 Me. 310, 66 Atl. 643 (1906).

[99] Lenvin and Meyers, "Nolo Contendere: Its Nature and Implications" (1942) 51 Yale L.J. 1255, 1267.

accept a plea of guilty until it shall have explained to the defendant the consequences of such a plea.[100] Rule 11 of the Federal Rules of Criminal Procedure goes considerably further in protecting a defendant by providing: "The court may refuse to accept a plea of guilty, and shall not accept the plea without first determining that the plea is made voluntarily with understanding of the nature of the charge." The First Preliminary Draft also required that, prior to acceptance of the plea, the court must determine that the indictment charges an offense. This was criticized as resulting in undue delay in the case of long and complicated indictments.

Under Sections 223 and 287 of the Institute Code the defendant, except in the case of a corporation, must be present when a plea of guilty is made or accepted.[101] No similar rule is laid down with respect to a plea of not guilty.

At common law an attorney for the defendant could not plead guilty for the defendant, even when the defendant stood by in apparent acquiescence.[102] This rule was relaxed only in the case of misdemeanors.[103] In the latter

[100] Section 225 provides that the court may refuse to accept a plea of not guilty and may order a plea of not guilty to be entered of record. At common law in capital cases it was the duty of the judge to make certain that the defendant understood the nature and consequences of his act. Commonwealth v. Battis, 1 Mass. 95 (1804). In some states the duty extended to other cases. People v. Cooper, 366 Ill. 113, 7 N.E. (2d) 882 (1937); Caruth v. State, 77 Tex. Cr. 150, 177 S.W. 973 (1915). An insane person should not be allowed to plead guilty. See Note (1933) 24 J.CrimL. 604.

[101] For a discussion of the common-law rule to that effect, see Comment (1940) 40 Col.L.Rev. 722, 723.

[102] Orbell v. Ward, Carth. 54, 90 Eng. Rep. 636 (K.B. 1689); see State v. Meekins, 41 La. Ann. 543, 544, 6 So. 822 (1889); 1 Bishop, New Criminal Procedure (4th ed.1895) § 268; 14 Am. Jur., Criminal Law, § 259, p. 944.

[103] See Jacobs v. Commonwealth, 5 S. & R. 315, 317 (Pa. 1819).

case the attorney could plead in the defendant's absence after showing of authorization.[104] The necessity of personal action by the defendant logically results from the general rule that the defendant must be present during the criminal proceedings.[105] Moreover, in former days a plea of guilty to any serious offense involved the possibility of a death sentence. There are a few modern cases holding that the defendant's attorney may plead guilty for him in his presence.[106] But the courts are reluctant to deviate from the rule.[107] It is possible that a defendant may be too confused or too ignorant to follow the proceedings in court and might not know that a plea of guilty is being entered for him. It is the duty of the judge to see that the defendant is fairly tried.

It may be desirable that a defendant consult counsel before he makes a plea of guilty. A defendant may, however, make a plea of guilty without the advice of counsel if he has competently and intelligently waived his right to counsel.[108]

In New Jersey, the statutes forbid the acceptance of a plea of guilty of first degree murder.[109] On the other hand,

104 There can be no plea of guilty in the absence of authorization from an absent defendant. Note (1940) 4, J.Crim.L. (Eng.) 1.

105 See Comment (1940) 40 Col.L.Rev. 722, 723.

106 Bearden v. State, 13 Ga. App. 264, 79 S.E. 79 (1913); Conway v. State, 5 Wyo. 107, 38 Pac. 354 (1894); United States v. Moe Liss, 105 F. (2d) 144 (C.C.A. 2d, 1939), (1940) 40 Col.L.Rev. 722; United States v. Denniston, 89 F. (2d) 696, 110 A.L.R. 1296 (C.C.A. 2d, 1937).

107 People v. McCrory, 41 Colo. 458 (1871); Bowley v. MacFadden, 146 Atl. 788 (N.J. 1929), 28 Mich.L.Rev. 204.

108 Buckner v. Hudspeth, 105 F. (2d) 396, (C.C.A. 10th, 1939) cert. denied 308 U.S. 553, 60 Sup.Ct. 99, 84 L.Ed. 465 (1939); Notes (1943) 27 Minn.L.Rev. 533, 534, (1942) 42 Col.L.Rev. 271, 279.

109 State v. Barth, 114 N.J.L 112, 176 Atl. 183 (1935); Wood and Waite, Crime and Its Treatment (1941) 421. In Louisiana and New York, pleas of guilty will not be received in capital cases. See annotations: 6 A.L.R. 696; 35 L.R.A. (N.S.) 1149.

Section 225 of the Institute Code provides that the "defendant may plead guilty to an indictment or information for any offense." It adds, however, that the court may refuse to accept the plea.

It has often been held that the defendant may plead guilty to a lesser offense than that charged in the indictment.[110] Section 226 of the Institute Code permits such plea with the consent of the court and of the prosecuting attorney. An English statute permits the making of such a plea.[111]

The Minnesota Crime Commission Report of 1927 recommended that, whenever a plea of guilty is accepted for an offense less than that charged, a written record should be made of the reasons therefor.[112] A statute passed in 1927 so provided.[113]

In some states, when a defendant makes a plea of guilty the criminal proceeding is substantially completed.[114] In Oregon from 1927 to 1928 in those cases in which the defendant pleaded guilty upon arraignment, sentence was usually imposed on the same day without any pre-sentence investigation.[115] In cases where his plea of guilty came after the time of arraignment, the time interval was thirty-two days when he pleaded guilty to the crime charged and

[110] People v. Smith, 78 Hun. 179 (N.Y. 1894); State v. McDonald, 10 Okla. Cr. 413 (1914).

[111] 4 & 5 Geo. V, c.58, § 39.

[112] Minnesota Crime Commission Report (1927) 31. The Commission assigned as a reason the abuse of a power it conceded to be a necessary one. For a recommendation by Governor Lehman of New York that the prosecuting attorney be required to submit a written statement of reasons, see Note (1936) 26 J.Crim.L. 948, 950.

[113] Mason's Minnesota Stat., 1927, § 10696-1.

[114] In this country and in England a plea of guilty takes a case out of the hands of the jury. On the Continent this is not true because of the fear that improper pressure may have been used to obtain the plea.

[115] Morse and Beattie, "Survey of the Administration of Criminal Justice in Oregon" (1932) 11 Ore.L.Rev. Supp. 183.

twenty-seven days when he pleaded guilty to a lesser offense.[116]

An appeal will lie with respect to an indictment which does not charge an offense even though the defendant has pleaded guilty.[117] Fatal defects may be raised for the first time on appeal.[118] But where the defect is merely formal and curable by amendment it cannot be raised for the first time on appeal.[119] It has been said that there is no right of appeal from a plea of guilty in the absence of collateral questions, such as the fact that the court does not satisfy itself concerning the voluntary character of the plea or where the question raised on appeal is the validity of the indictment.[120]

Many pleas of guilty are obtained through the out-of-court action of the prosecuting attorney. "The first and most favored way of securing a plea is to permit the defendant to plead guilty to a charge less serious than the one originally made in the indictment or information. The second is to induce a plea of guilty by the promise of a suspended sentence." [121]

The extreme importance of the plea of guilty may be seen from the fact that in some districts 95 per cent of all convictions are on plea of guilty.[122] The average through-

[116] *Ibid.* 184.

[117] Klawanski v. People, 218 Ill. 481, 75 N.E. 1028 (1905), (1906) 15 Yale L.J. 374; Fletcher v. State, 7 Eng. (Ark.) 69 (1851).

[118] Pattee v. State, 109 Ind. 545 (1886); Cancemi v. People, 18 N.Y. 128 (1858).

[119] People v. Kelley, 99 Mich. 82 (1894).

[120] (1923) 7 Minn.L.Rev. 588.

[121] Moley, "The Use of the Information in Criminal Cases" (1931) 17 A.B.A.J. 292, 293. See also Baker, "The Prosecutor-Initiation of Prosecution" (1933) 23 J.Crim.L. 770, 786.

[122] Hall, Theft, Law and Society (1935) 113; Moley, Politics and Criminal Prosecution (1929) 160. Even in England almost half of those indicted plead guilty. Kenny, Outlines of Criminal Law (15th ed.1942) 558, 572.

out the country is around 85 per cent.[123] "The vast majority of all persons who are punished for serious criminal offenses have filed pleas of guilty." [124] It follows that the prosecuting attorney is, together with the magistrate, who eliminates more than half of the cases at preliminary examination, the most important official as practically judged by the disposition of the greater number of cases. A practice has grown up that is so common that it forms the chief technique employed; namely, waiver of the major felony charge and acceptance of a plea of guilty of a lesser offense.[125] It is not improbable that, in the majority of cases in which defendants charged with felonies have pleaded guilty of misdemeanors, they have in fact committed more serious crimes.[126] In Chicago in 1926, 78.81 per cent of all pleas of guilty in felony cases were entered

[123] Wood and Waite, Crime and Its Treatment (1941) 421; Missouri Crime Survey (1926) 149; Report of the Crimes Survey Committee, Law Association of Philadelphia (1926) 228. In 1933 in the federal courts, out of 73,207 convictions, 67,904 were on pleas of guilty. "Address of Chief Justice Hughes at the American Law Institute Meeting" (1934) 20 A.B.A.J. 341, 342.

[124] Hall, Theft, Law and Society (1935) 113; Clark, "Law Enforcement and Public Administration" (1935) 30 Ill.L.Rev. 273, 282-283; Fuller, Criminal Justice in Virginia (1931) 151. There is a greater percentage of guilty pleas in states using the information than in states using the indictment. Moley, "The Use of the Information in Criminal Cases" (1931) 12 A.B.A.J. 292, 293.

[125] Nat. Com. on Law Obs. and Enf., Report on Prosecution (1931) 95-97; "Survey of Administration of Criminal Justice in Oregon" (1932) 17 A.B.A.J. 212; Criminal Justice in Cleveland (1922) 322. "It seems to be generally true that conviction by a jury brings a severer sentence than a plea of guilty, especially one made on arraignment." Hall, Theft, Law and Society (1935) 113. See Missouri Crime Survey (1926) 149, 314; Report of the Minnesota Crime Commission (1934) 160; Illinois Crime Survey (1929) 101; Weintraub and Tough, "Lesser Pleas Considered" (1942) 32 J.Crim.L. 506.

[126] Hall, Theft, Law and Society (1935) 114-115. Cf. Wallace, "Nullification: A Process of Government" (1930) 45 Pol.Sci.Q. 347.

to minor offenses.[127] Reduction was most frequent in property crimes such as robbery, burglary, and larceny, and not so frequent in cases of homicide, rape, and other sex crimes.

While there has been much criticism of waiver of felonies there has been "no attempt to go deeply into the causes, or to discuss the effective remedies, or to present principles and procedures which should govern acceptance of pleas." [128] The common criticism has ascribed the waivers to political and corrupt influences.[129] On the other hand, it has been pointed out (1) that crimes have greatly increased in numbers, (2) that the courts are unable to care for the increased volume of cases, (3) that there is a heavy burden upon the public by way of jury and witness duties, and (4) that persons are reluctant to admit criminal liability since it carries the stigma of moral delinquency.[130] There are other even more deep-seated

[127] Hall, Theft, Law and Society (1935) 115. With respect to burglaries in New York City from the middle of 1937 to the middle of 1938, of the 1,499 defendants brought to pleading or to trial, 1,289 entered pleas of guilty—201, or 13.4 per cent, to the offense charged, and 1,088, or 72.5 per cent, to lesser offenses. Michael and Wechsler, Criminal Law and Its Administration (1940) 378, 380.

[128] Nat. Com. on Law Obs. and Enf., Report on Prosecution (1931) 96-97.

[129] But questionnaires sent to 225 Bar Association committees in all states showed that, "The policy of bargaining with the offender for a plea of guilty of a lesser offense is abused in scarcely more than one community out of ten." Shafroth, "The Bar Reports on Several Phases of Criminal Law" (1934) 20 A.B.A.J. 463. Cf. (1934) 20 A.B.A.J. 533. "It is not so often the corrupt politician, as interested members of the public who intercede with officials on behalf of known offenders." Hall, Theft, Law and Society (1935) 118-119; Pope, J. (1928) 1 So. Calif.L.Rev. 151. The guilty plea technique would of course be eliminated if all sentences were indeterminate. Gausewitz, "Considerations Basic to a New Penal Code" (1936) 11 Wis.L.Rev. 480, 495.

[130] Miller, J., "The Compromise of Criminal Cases" (1927) 1 So. Calif. L.Rev. 1; Warner and Cabot, "Changes in the Administration of Crimi-

causes.[131] Officials may regard the law as too severe in any case. More frequently, mitigating circumstances provided by the facts or the reputation of the defendant lead officials to conclude that it is preferable to inflict a lesser penalty than that fixed by the statute for the crime actually committed. In the third place, the case for the state may be weak for reasons beyond the control of the prosecuting attorney, such as want of thorough investigation by the police and lack of necessary witnesses. Finally, the ambition to establish a record for numerous convictions for use in future election compaigns plays a significant part. Discretion there must be, and possibly it can be exercised more deliberately by the prosecuting attorney than by the jury which was formerly the chief repository of such powers.[132]

14. Withdrawal of Plea of Guilty

Since a plea of guilty is a confession in open court and a waiver of trial, it has always been received with great caution. It is the duty of the court to see that the defendant thoroughly understands the situation and acts voluntarily before receiving it.[133] The defendant should be

nal Justice During the Past Fifty Years" (1937) 50 Harv.L.Rev. 583, 597; Moley, Politics and Criminal Prosecution (1929) 166-192.

[131] Hall, Theft, Law and Society (1935) 117-118. See also Arnold, "Law Enforcement—An Attempt at Social Dissection" (1932) 42 Yale L.J. 1, 8-11.

[132] "It follows that the task of legal reform lies not in the direction of eliminating discretion, but rather in the direction of securing a wiser use of it by intelligent delegation of authority, a more competent, honorable personnel and careful checks." Hall, Theft, Law and Society (1935) 121. Possibly a written statement of reasons for acceptance of a plea of guilty to lesser offenses should be required. Criminal Justice in Cleveland (1922) 650; Minnesota Crime Commission Report (1927) 31.

[133] Gardner v. People, 106 Ill. 76 (1883); State v. Stephens, 71 Mo. 535 (1880).

permitted to withdraw the plea when induced to make it through ignorance, fraud, or intimidation.[134] Withdrawal may be before sentence.[135] It has been permitted after sentence quite frequently.[136] Where the trial court clearly abuses its discretion, it should be subject to reversal upon appeal.[137]

Under Rule II(4) of the Criminal Appeals Rules of the United States Supreme Court laid down in 1934: "A motion to withdraw a plea of guilty shall be made within ten (10) days after entry of such plea and before sentence imposed." Section 230 of the Institute Code goes much further when it provides: "The court may in its discretion at any time before sentence permit a plea of guilty to be withdrawn and, if judgment of conviction has been entered thereon, set aside such judgment, and allow a plea of not guilty, or, with the consent of the prosecuting attorney, allow a plea of guilty of a lesser included offense,

[134] Myers v. State, 115 Ind. 554, 18 N.E. 42 (1888); Swang v. State, 2 Cold (Tenn.) 212 (1865); Comments (1912) 12 Col.L.Rev. 373, (1941) 20 Neb.L.Rev. 173, (1931) 30 Mich.L.Rev. 307, (1931) 79 U. of Pa.L.Rev. 484, (1935) 26 J.Crim.L. 457, (1941) 32 J.Crim.L. 199.

[135] Rex v. Plummer (1902) 2 K. B. 339, 20 Cox. C.C. 269. See also 20 A.L.R. 1445; 66 A.L.R. 828. In England the plea may be withdrawn after verdict, but not after judgment.

[136] 22 C.J.S., Criminal Law, § 421, p.645; 14 Am. Jur., Criminal Law, § 288, p.363; City of Salena v. Cooper, 45 Kan. 12, 25 Pac. 233 (1890); People v. Aseltine, 139 Cal. App. 768, 341P (2d) 830 (1934); Little v. Commonwealth, 142 Ky. 92, 133 S.W. 1149 (1911); (1901) 14 Harv.L.Rev. 609; (1913) 27 Harv.L.Rev. 86; (1936) 20 Minn.L.Rev. 223; (1941) 32 J.Crim.L. 199; (1923) 23 Col.L.Rev. 195; (1931) 79 U. of Pa.L.Rev. 484, 488; (1943) 146 A.L.R. 1430, 1437. *Contra:* Clark, Handbook of Criminal Procedure (2d ed. by Mikell, 1918) 429-430. Howington v. State, 235 Pac. 931 (Okla. Crim. App. 1925), 74 U. of Pa.L.Rev. 94.

[137] Deloach v. State, 77 Miss. 691, 27 So. 618; Hardzog v. State, 49 Okla. Cr. Rep. 244, 293 Pac. 1107 (1930); (1901) 14 Harv.L.Rev. 609; (1936) 20 Minn.L.Rev. 223; (1928) 27 Mich.L.Rev. 926; Hopkins, "Withdrawal of Plea of Guilty" (1889) 11 Crim.L.Mag. 479. As to habeas corpus, see (1912) 12 Col.L.Rev. 373.

or of a lesser degree of the offense charged, to be substituted for the plea of guilty."

Rule 32(d) of the Federal Rules of Criminal Procedure goes along with the Institute Code provision by providing: "A motion to withdraw a plea of guilty or of *nolo contendere* may be made only before sentence is imposed or imposition of sentence is suspended; but to correct manifest injustice the court after sentence may set aside the judgment of conviction and permit the defendant to withdraw his plea."

A defendant who contemplates making a plea of guilty runs the risk in some jurisdictions that if he withdraws such plea and pleads not guilty, it may be admitted in evidence as a confession.[138] The weight of authority is, however, that the withdrawn plea is a nullity and cannot be used in evidence.[139] The Supreme Court of the United States has followed the majority view.[140] The majority rule is based on the view that the jury are likely to attach undue weight to the plea,[141] and that the plea is in fact often relied on as a tactical move. The contrary argument is that a judicial confession should be conceded at least as much probative value as an extrajudicial confession, since the withdrawn plea shows conduct on the part of the defendant inconsistent with his claim of innocence before

[138] People v. Steinmetz, 240 N.Y. 411, 148 N.E. 597 (1925), 35 Yale L.J. 231. See also Notes (1940) 40 Col.L.Rev. 915, (1916) 16 Col.L.Rev. 421, (1937) 15 Tex.L.Rev. 379, (1916) 25 Yale L.J. 587, (1916) 14 Mich.L.Rev. 586, (1918) 28 Yale L.J. 168.

[139] Comments (1927) 37 Yale L.J. 119, (1916) 3 Va.L.Rev. 622, (1941) 27 Va.L.Rev. 703.

[140] Kercheval v. United States, 274 U.S. 20, 47 Sup.Ct. 582, 71 L.Ed. 1009 (1927), 37 Yale L.J. 119.

[141] Comments (1918) 28 Yale L.J. 168, 171, (1931) 79 U. of Pa.L.Rev. 484, 490.

the jury.[142] Moreover in many cases withdrawal of the plea is permitted though no mistake is clearly shown.[143]

15. Plea of Not Guilty: Affirmative Defenses

The Wickersham Commission has recommended that the defendant shall give notice of affirmative defenses along with a plea of not guilty.[144] It points out that one of the great advantages of the defendant is that he may prove any defense except former jeopardy under a general oral plea of not guilty. In civil procedure, on the other hand, a defendant must plead specially all affirmative defenses.[145] In a criminal case the defendant learns from the preliminary examination substantially what will be shown against him, while the prosecuting attorney is often in ignorance until the defendant's evidence is presented at the trial. Occasionally the prosecuting attorney is forced to prepare on rebuttal what proves to be the real case. As a result of grave abuses of the insanity defense, some jurisdictions more than a generation ago provided by statute that insanity be pleaded specially. Under Section 235 of the American Law Institute Code, a written notice of pur-

142 Comments (1916) 25 Yale L.J. 587, (1916) 16 Col.L.Rev. 421, (1916) 29 Harv.L.Rev. 782, (1922) 37 Yale L.J. 119.

143 Comment (1925) 35 Yale L.J. 231.

144 Nat. Com. on Law Obs. and Enf., Rep. on Crim. Proc. (1931) 34, 47. See "Defects in Criminal Justice" (1925) 11 A.B.A.J. 297, 298.

145 "Civil pleading at common law labored in almost metaphysical detail to narrow issues of both law and fact." Note (1928) 38 Yale L.J. 650. "Criminal pleading thus abandons one of the great functions of pleading in civil cases, that of reducing the matter in controversy to the specific proportions or issues in dispute, and gives no indication as to the grounds upon which the defendant bases his defense." Ballantine, "Technicalities in Criminal Procedure" (1917) 1 Ill.L.Bull. 92, 102. Until the Hilary Rules of 1834, civil pleading did not narrow the issues and defendant's plea of the general issue was broad in its effect. Holdsworth, "The New Rules of Pleading of the Hilary Term, 1834" (1923) 1 Camb. L.J. 261.

pose to show insanity must be filed by the defendant at the time of the plea of not guilty or not later than four days before the trial. The Wickersham Commission would extend this requirement of written notice to all affirmative defenses, for example, justifications and excuses, such as self-defense, thus leaving as the scope of the plea of not guilty, the questions of whether or not the acts charged took place and whether the accused committed them.[146] Thus, as Judge Charles E. Clark states, recent reforms tend toward "simpler pleading statements on the part of the prosecution and more detailed on the part of the defense." [147]

Doubtless to a large extent because of the severity of criminal penalties and because of the absence of substantial procedural rights,[148] such as the right to counsel, the pleadings of a defendant in a criminal proceeding were

[146] Millar seems to go almost equally far. See "The Modernization of Criminal Procedure" (1920) 11 J.Crim.L. 344, 351; as does Dean, "Advance Specifications of Defense in Criminal Cases" (1934) 20 A.B.A.J. 435, 438, and Ballantine, "Technicalities in Criminal Procedure" (1917) 1 Ill. L.Bull. 92, 102. See also (1925) 3 Proc. Am. L. Inst. 503; Comment (1942) 26 J. Am. Jud. Soc. 106, 107; Moley, Our Criminal Courts (1930) 95.

[147] Clark, "Law Enforcement and Public Administration" (1935) 30 Ill. L.Rev. 273, 283.

[148] Prior to the eighteenth century "an accused was secretly confined before trial without opportunity to prepare a defense; he was given no intimation of the evidence or witnesses to be used against him; he was not permitted counsel, either prior to or at trial; there was no guarantee of confrontation of witnesses; confessions of accomplices were regarded as specially cogent evidence; and the trial was an unequal battle between a battery of prosecution counsel (each one of which would devote himself to a particular segment of the case) on the one side, and the privilege shorn suspect on the other." Dean, "Advance Specifications of Defense in Criminal Cases" (1934) 20 A.B.A.J. 435. Moreover, "criminal pleadings, unlike those in civil actions have always been required to be made orally and by the defendant in person, a practice which obviously precludes accurate affirmative pleading." Note (1904) 17 Harv.L.Rev. 208, 209.

so developed as to give him wide latitude in defense, through the means of a single simple plea. Under the plea of not guilty he could at common law, and in most states still can, and even must,[149] raise such issues as insanity,[150] alibi,[151] self-defense,[152] intoxication,[153] and the statute of limitations.[154]

At common law he was, however, compelled to plead former acquittal and former conviction, especially in bar.[155] Ten states and Alaska have expressly incorporated the common-law rule into their statutes. It was held in one case that such a statute permits the defense of former jeopardy under a plea of not guilty.[156] But the holding is likely to be different in the seven states which have an ad-

[149] Special pleas of matter which might be raised under a plea of not guilty are properly disallowed. State v. Karagavoorian, 32 R.I. 477, 79 Atl. 1111 (1911); Stacks v. State, 20 Ala. App. 462, 103 So. 70 (1925).

[150] Johnson v. State, 57 Fla. 18, 49 S. 40 (1909); State v. Potts, 100 N.C. 457, 6 S.E. 657 (1888). "At common law, the defense that the accused at the time of the act (if he committed it) was too insane to be criminally responsible was admissible under a plea of not guilty, and this is the law today in forty American states. No special plea of 'not guilty by reason of insanity' is required, and it has even been held in some of these states that such a special plea is not permitted." Weihofen, Insanity as a Defense in Criminal Law (1933) 257-258. See also Glueck, Mental Disorder and the Criminal Law (1925) 21-22.

[151] Albritton v. State, 94 Ala. 76, 77, 10 So. 426 (1892).

[152] State v. Linden, 154 La. 65, 97 So. 299 (1923).

[153] People v. Collins, 30 Cal. App. 656, 159 Pac. 229 (1916).

[154] James v. State, 110 Ark. 170, 160 S.W. 1090 (1913); People v. Bailey, 103 Misc. 366, 171 N.Y.Supp. 394 (Sup.Ct. 1918). Compare United States v. Cook, 17 Wall (U.S.) 168, 21 L.Ed. 538 (1872). Comments (1908) 8 Col.L.Rev. 52, (1910) 10 Col.L.Rev. 159. See (1935) 33 Mich.L.Rev. 805.

[155] 2 Bishop, New Criminal Procedure (4th ed.1895) § 806. In Illinois, all special pleas, including former jeopardy, have been abolished and the plea of not guilty raises every possible defense. See criticism by Ballantine, "Technicalities in Criminal Procedure" (1917) 1 Ill.L.Bull. 92, 102.

[156] People v. Cage, 48 Cal. 323, 17 Am. Rep. 436 (1874). Former jeopardy, not amounting to conviction or acquittal, may be so pleaded.

ditional and inclusive plea of former jeopardy. In the states in which there are no statutes it has usually been held that the common-law practice is the proper procedure,[157] although an exception has been made when all the facts are of record and may be judicially noticed.[158] The special plea is tried separately, ahead of the issue of not guilty.[159] The defense of former jeopardy under a plea of not guilty is allowed in only four states.[160] The special plea is abolished by Section 209 of the Institute Code, and under Section 210 it is to be raised by a broadened motion to quash, although under Section 212 the motion is to set out the facts constituting the jeopardy.[161]

The other common-law special plea, that of pardon, has been continued in force by statutes [162] and by decisions.[163] It is abolished by the Institute Code.[164] A special plea has been held necessary to set up an immunity from prosecu-

157 State v. Johnson, 11 Neb. 273, 276 (1876); State v. Reilly, 94 Conn. 698, 703, 110 Atl. 550, 552 (1920). The purpose is notice to the prosecution.

158 State v. White, 71 Kan. 356, 80 Pac. 589 (1905); People v. Taylor, 117 Mich. 583, 76 N.W. 158 (1898). See George v. State, 59 Neb. 163, 168, 80 N.W. 486, 487 (1899).

159 Parsons v. State, 179 Ala. 23, 24, 60 So. 864, 865 (1913); United States v. Hopkins & Co., 228 Fed. 173, 175 (S.D. N.Y. 1912).

160 People v. Hawkinson, 324 Ill. 285, 155 N.E. 318 (1927); Barker v. State, 188 Ind. 263, 120 N.E. 593 (1918); State v. Salter, 256 S.W. 1070 (Mo. App. 1923); State v. Conlin, 27 Vt. 318 (1885). See also Morrissey v. People, 11 Mich. 327 (1863).

161 To the same effect see A.L.I., Administration of the Criminal Law, Double Jeopardy (1935) §§ 28 and 29.

162 Neb. Rev. Stat. (1943) § 29-1817; Crim. Code (Patterson 1924) § 13630; Wyo. Comp. Stat. Ann. (1920, § 7492).

163 Michael v. State, 40 Ala. 361, 370 (1867); State v. Blalock, 61 N.C. 242, 247 (1867). *Contra:* Powers v. Commonwealth, 110 Ky. 386, 61 S.W. 735 (1901). Perhaps it may be raised on motion. United States v. Wilson, 32 U.S. 150, 163 (1833).

164 Section 209. It may be raised under Section 210, although under Section 213 it is to set out the material facts concerning the pardon.

tion.[165] The pleas just discussed were the compulsory special pleas.[166] According to many decisions the defendant could plead the statute of limitations specially, but he was not required to.[167] Canada has not departed from the common-law procedure. Its statute provides: "The following special pleas and no others may be pleaded according to the provisions hereinafter contained, that is to say, a plea of *autrefois acquit,* a plea of *autrefois convict,* a plea of pardon, and such pleas in cases of defamatory libel as are hereinafter mentioned. All other grounds of defense may be relied on under the plea of not guilty." [168].

The proponents of compulsory special pleading of affirmative defenses contend that it will serve several functions.[169] In the first place, it will narrow the issues by excluding all except those which are pleaded. In the second place, it will give notice to the prosecution of the defense which will be relied on and may save the state unnecessary expense. In the third place, it will possibly separate the issues for the consideration of the jury. On the theory of notice, special pleas amounting in reality to an outline of the defense have been advocated as a method of placing

[165] Scribner v. State, 90 Okla. Cr. 465, 132 Pac. 933 (1913); State v. Sine, 91 W. Va. 608, 114 S.E. 150 (1922). Section 209 of the American Law Institute Code of Criminal Procedure abolishes this plea. It may be raised under Section 210, although under Section 214 it is to set out the material facts upon which immunity is claimed.

[166] Note (1929) 38 Yale L.J. 650, 652. See Keigwin, Cases in Criminal Procedure (1939) 535.

[167] 2 Bishop, New Criminal Procedure (4th ed.1895) § 799(5). Some cases appear to require a special plea. People v. Murphy, 296 Ill. 532, 129 N.E. 868 (1921). Others refuse to permit it at all. See United States v. Barber, 219 U.S. 72, 31 Sup.Ct. 209 (1911). The special plea does not require a separate preliminary trial of the issue. State v. Snyder, 182 Mo. 462, 82 S.W. 12 (1904).

[168] Crankshaw's Criminal Code of Canada (5th ed.1924) § 905.

[169] Note (1929) 38 Yale L.J. 650, 652.

the prosecution in as effective a position as the defendant.[170]

If the almost all-inclusive plea of not guilty is to be broken up, this must come about by statute or rule of court. The state and federal courts have not gone through any such process; only Scotland has. In Scotland it is not "competent for the person accused to state any special defense unless a plea of special defense shall be tendered and recorded."[171] Under a Scottish statute there must be pleas for alibi, insanity, and self-defense.[172] Under this same statute the defendant must furnish the prosecution a list of his witnesses, and in certain cases what they are to prove. Full notice is thus given to the prosecution, and the issues are narrowed. The Scottish statute is silent as to separation of issues for the jury. In this country, no provisions for special pleas of self-defense or the statute of limitations have been found, and until quite recently there were none as to alibi.[173] In eight states there is a requirement of a special plea of the defense of insanity.[174]

[170] Millar, "The Function of Criminal Pleading" (1922) 12 J.Crim.L. 500, 503; Freeman, "Should the Defendant in a Criminal Case File a Written Pleading Outlining His Defense?" (1924) 8 Minn.L.Rev. 357; Dean, "Advance Specifications of Defense in Criminal Cases" (1934) 20 A.B.A.J. 435, 436.

[171] 50 & 51 Vict., c.29, § 36 (1887).

[172] Renton and Brown, Criminal Procedure According to the Law of Scotland (2d ed.1928) 68. See Millar, "The Reform of Criminal Pleading in Illinois" (1917) 8 J.Crim.L. 337, 359-360.

[173] At present 14 states require, either by statute or by rule of court, that a defendant who intends to present evidence of alibi shall give notice before trial. See the full note to Rule 16 of the Federal Rules of Criminal Procedure (1944) Second Preliminary Draft.

[174] Weihofen, Insanity as a Defense in Criminal Law (1933) 258. Such a plea has been recommended in the Missouri Crime Survey (1926) 371, 399; Report of the Minnesota Crime Commission (1934) 42. But it has been thought that such a view is too harsh. Tulin, "The Problem of Mental Disorder in Crime: A Survey" (1932) 32 Col.L.Rev. 933, 943.

In the eight states having compulsory special pleas of insanity, certain common characteristics of such pleas are to be found.[175] In the absence of such a plea, no evidence of insanity can be introduced, no argument made, and instructions on the crime need not be given. A written plea is usually required. It is to be presented at the time of arraignment, but may be allowed later in the discretion of the court. It is in the form of a separate plea rather than a specification under the plea of not guilty. It is not exclusive, and may be interposed with other pleas. Until recently it was not usual to provide for a separate trial of the special issue in advance of the trial on the merits.[176]

A leading student of criminal pleading would require the defendant to give notice of alibi by written specification "under the plea of guilty or otherwise." [177] He further proposes that "any defense which involves an admission of the fact charged, such as former jeopardy or the statute of limitations should be made the subject of a special plea." [178] The special plea should be required to

[175] Weihofen, Insanity as a Defense in Criminal Law (1933) 258-259; Note (1929) 38 Yale L.J. 650, 654. See also Glueck, Mental Disorder and the Criminal Law (1925) 21-26. It should be noted that the insanity defense is raised in comparatively few cases. Dean, "Advance Specifications of Defense in Criminal Cases" (1934) 20 A.B.A.J. 435, 475; Illinois Crime Survey (1929) 213, 757; Nat. Com. on Law Obs. and Enf., Report on Prosecution (1931) 129.

[176] Such a trial is discretionary in Colorado. In California alone, the trial on the merits is to come first. There is also a separate trial in Louisiana and Maryland. See Weihofen, Insanity as a Defense in Criminal Law (1933) 259-262, 291-292.

[177] Millar, "The Function of Criminal Pleading" (1922) 12 J.Crim.L. 500, 503. "If the defense is one by way of confession and avoidance, a special plea would be proper; if essentially a denial, then the vehicle of notice should be a written specification under not guilty." Millar, "The Modernization of Criminal Procedure" (1920) 11 J.Crim.L. 344, 351.

[178] He would provide for written specifications as to self-defense and insanity. Millar, "The Reform of Criminal Pleading in Illinois" (1917) 8

state the elements of a defense only so far as coincident with the giving of necessary information to the opposite party.[179] The prosecution should be given the right to demand further particulars of the defense, just as the defendant may obtain a bill of particulars with regard to an indictment.

"The defendant has, under all systems of criminal justice a great advantage in the matter of pleading. The prosecutor must formulate his charges with precision and accuracy; but the plea of not guilty leaves him utterly ignorant of the defense by which he is to be met. It may be an alibi, a justification, a claim of temporary insanity. Whatever it be, he learns it for the first time when the trial is begun, and must be ready to meet and disprove it on the instant, with no possibility of a postponement on the ground of surprise. . . . We have relieved the prisoner from the necessity, ordinarily imposed in civil cases, of pleading the nature of his defense." [180]

A possible objection to requiring the defendant to give advance notice of all his defenses is that counsel might make a practice of enumerating all defenses in their specifications.[181] To this it has been replied that statutes might provide against the enumeration of inconsistent defenses; or the prosecuting attorney might be given the right to comment upon the fact that defenses specified were not established at the trial, or that the defenses were incon-

---

J.Crim.L. 337, 359-360; Millar, "The Modernization of Criminal Procedure" (1920) 11 J.Crim.L. 344, 350-351.

[179] Full notice seems most necessary in the case of the defense of alibi. Millar, "The Reform of Criminal Pleading in Illinois" (1917) 8 J.Crim.L. 337, 360; Note (1929) 38 Yale L.J. 650, 656.

[180] Baldwin, "Preliminary Examination in Criminal Proceedings" (1883) 6 A.B.A.Rep. 225, 235-236.

[181] Note (1929) 38 Yale L.J. 650, 656.

sistent.[182] But such a procedure would revive all the evils apparent in any system which must place stress on particularity and nicety of pleading. The introduction of such a source of legal hairsplitting would perhaps defeat the purpose of establishing a simple and clear code of criminal procedure.

16. Alibi

In recent years, the chief defense of the defendant to receive attention is that of alibi.[183] It is true that there is no rule or statute on the subject in England.[184] Nor does the American Law Institute Code contain any provision on the subject. But in recent years [185] fourteen American

[182] Dean, "Advance Specifications of Defense in Criminal Cases" (1934) 20 A.B.A.J. 435, 438. It has been pointed out, however, that the defendant may have acted in good faith and should not be penalized. Millar, "The Statutory Notice of Alibi" (1934) 24 J.Crim.L. 849, 854.

[183] It was suggested by Millar in a number of articles: "The Reform of Criminal Pleading in Illinois" (1917) 8 J.Crim.L. 337, 359-360, "The Modernization of Criminal Procedure" (1920) 11 J.Crim.L. 344, 350-351, "The Function of Criminal Pleading" (1922) 12 J.Crim.L. 500, 503. See also Burdick, "Criminal Justice in America" (1925) 11 A.B.A.J. 512; Willoughby, Principles of Judicial Administration (1929) 450-451; Report of the Minnesota Crime Commission (1934) 42. Questionnaires sent out in 1938 to prosecuting attorneys in all states, however, revealed a "more or less general air of indifference to the whole question, which may or may not cast some doubt on the real or ultimate value of statutory change." Stayton and Watkins, "Is Specific Notice of the Defense of Alibi Desirable?" (1940) 18 Texas L.Rev. 151, 158.

[184] The English procedure is adversely criticized by Kenny. Outlines of Criminal Law (15th ed.1942) 534, 539. The court may, however, comment freely on the evidence. Note (1935) 21 Va.L.Rev. 940, 941. In Scotland for more than half a century, notice of alibi has been required. Renton and Brown, Criminal Procedure According to the Laws of Scotland (2d ed. 1928) 68, 187.

[185] Before 1934 only 2 states had adopted statutes, Michigan in 1927 and Ohio in 1929; New Jersey acted in 1934; 9 states in 1935, Arizona in 1940, and Iowa in 1941. The 10 states acting in 1934 and 1935 were doubtless stimulated to do so by the American Bar Association program

states have laid down, by statute or rule of court, that a defendant who intends to present evidence of alibi shall give notice to the prosecuting attorney before trial of such intention. Moreover, Rule 16 of the Federal Rules of Criminal Procedure as proposed by the Advisory Committee provided for notice of alibi. The Rules as finally adopted were silent as to alibi. It has been thought that the practice at common law wrongly permitted evidence of an alibi to come in as a surprise after the state had rested its case and after there was little or no opportunity for the state to investigate the truth of the alibi.[186]

Eleven of the fourteen state statutes require the defendant to take the first step in commencing the notice procedure. The proposed federal rule (eliminated by the Supreme Court) likewise provided that the defendant shall take the initiative. It is important to note, however, that the initiative required by the proposed federal rule, differing from that required by the state statutes, was a disclosure not of a specific objective fact but of a personal intention. The first disclosure of a specific fact required by the rule was from the government.

Six of the state statutes require that the defendant give the names of the witnesses by whom he proposes to prove his alibi. The federal rule was more favorable to the defendant and made no such requirement.

---

of 1934, making alibi one of its six chief proposals. (1934) 20 A.B.A.J. 647, 651; (1934) 59 A.B.A.Rep. 112. The Michigan and Ohio statutes are discussed by Millar, "The Statutory Notice of Alibi" (1934) 24 J.Crim.L. 849; Esch, "Ohio's New Alibi Defense Laws" (1931) 9 Panel 42; Toy, "Michigan Law on Alibi and Insanity Reduces Perjury" (1931) 9 Panel 52.

[186] On the other hand, many prosecuting attorneys have concluded that the defense of alibi is seldom raised, that it rarely if ever comes as a surprise to the state, and that the state should be able, if its case has been properly prepared, to rebut any false alibi that may be offered. See opinions cited by Stayton and Watkins, "Is Specific Notice of the Defense of Alibi Desirable?" (1940) 18 Texas L.Rev. 151, 154.

Ten of the state statutes provide that, if the defendant fails to give the notice, the court may exclude his evidence of alibi. The federal rule was in accord. Several state statutes provide that, if the defendant fails to give the notice but the court nevertheless in its discretion admits the evidence, the government may request a recess or permission to reopen its case or other appropriate relief. The federal rule likewise so provided.

There may be controversy as to whether or not the defendant should have to take the first step in commencing the notice procedure.[187] It may be contended that, under such a rule, a defendant may be surprised and handicapped because of a lack of knowledge of the requirement and because his counsel, if any, may not protect his rights. On the other hand, the government should not be required to anticipate a possible alibi defense, since the matter is one peculiarly within the knowledge of the defendant. To require the government to make the first move would tend to make the rule ineffective, since the government would thereby be placed in the position of practically inviting an alibi defense. With respect to the element of surprise to the defendant, it should be noted that the federal rule expressly provided that the court may relieve a defendant of the consequences of a failure to serve a notice of alibi.

An alibi statute is not in violation of the self incrimination provision of a constitution. In a New York case the defendant moved to set aside a demand served in pursuance of a statute, which provided that a defendant who intends to deny his presence at the scene of the crime must,

[187] The Second Preliminary Draft of the Federal Rules of Criminal Procedure required the defendant to take the first step, while the First Preliminary Draft placed the burden on the prosecution. For the differing views of the Advisory Committees on Rules of Criminal Procedure, see the Second Preliminary Draft, 239-243.

on demand of the prosecutor within eight days of the trial, designate the place where he will claim to have been and the names and addresses of the witnesses who will testify to that effect; that otherwise such evidence may be excluded at the trial or, if it is allowed, the court must grant an adjournment at the request of the prosecutor.[188] It was held in a lower New York decision that since the defendant must first voluntarily choose to offer the evidence, he would not be compelled to testify against himself.[189] An alibi statute was upheld by the highest Ohio court.[190]

The argument made against constitutionality rests on improper deduction from cases holding that a witness may not be compelled to give testimony which, though inadmissible in a future prosecution, might lead to the discovery of other evidence which could be used against him.[191] By an extension of these cases, the information which the defendant must produce in advance of trial is in a sense incriminating for the reason that it might lead to denying evidence which rebuts the alibi. Moreover, forbidding the admission of alibi testimony as the penalty for noncompliance is sufficient compulsion.[192] But before any compulsion to produce the evidence for the trial arises, the defendant must of his own free will choose to offer it at trial. Thus the compulsion from the statute con-

188 New York Code of Criminal Procedure, § 295l.

189 People v. Slade, N.Y. Sup.Ct. (1936), (1937) 50 Harv.L.Rev. 523.

190 State v. Thayer, 124 Ohio St. 1, 176 N.E. 656 (1931); Millar, "The Statutory Notice of Alibi" (1934) 24 J.Crim.L. 849, 852; Legis. (1935) 21 Va.L.Rev. 940, 944.

191 Counselman v. Hitchcock, 142 U.S. 547 (1892); Matter of Doyle, 257 N.Y. 244, 177 N.E. 489 (1931). See Dean, "Advance Specifications of Defense in Criminal Cases" (1934) 20 A.B.A.J. 435, 440; Robinson, "Proposed Federal Rules of Criminal Procedure" (1943) 27 J. Am. Jud. Soc. 38, 46; Millar, "The Statutory Notice of Alibi" (1934) 24 J.Crim.L. 849, 852.

192 See 4 Wigmore, Evidence (3d ed.1940) § 2273.

cerns only the time when the evidence becomes available to the prosecution. This amounts to arguing that it would be unconstitutional to deprive the defendant of the accidental advantage obtained from the physical incapacity of the prosecution to make timely investigation of evidence first given at trial. The same deprivation would result from the granting of an adjournment after such testimony had been offered, with opportunity for the prosecution to give evidence in rebuttal. Such a regulation of trial would unquestionably be valid.[193] But proposed Rule 16 was rejected by the Supreme Court.

17. Time to Prepare for Trial

After a defendant has pleaded not guilty, he will usually need some time to prepare for trial. Statutes in some states give him one day, in others two days, in others three days, in one four days, in one five days, and in some a reasonable time.[194] Section 237 of the Institute Code provides: "After a plea of not guilty the defendant is entitled to at least two days to prepare for trial unless the court for good cause shown should allow further time." [195] A report to the Wickersham Commission recommended the

[193] Leighton v. People, 88 N.Y. 117 (1882) (rebuttal evidence); Walker v. State, 116 Ga. 537, 42 S.E. 787 (1902) (adjournment to enable prosecution to procure witness).

[194] A.L.I. Code of Crim. Proc. (1930) commentaries 687. Until the seventeenth century the "prisoner was kept in confinement more or less secret till his trial, and could not prepare for his defence." 1 Stephen, A History of the Criminal Law of England (1883) 350. Theoretically, even in the days of Stephen, the grand jury might indict without notice to the accused, he might be arrested on proof of his identity, need not undergo a preliminary examination, and might be tried without knowing who the witnesses were or having a copy of the indictment. *Ibid.* 399.

[195] The Reporter had proposed five days, but the Council overruled him. (1929) 8 Proc. Am. L. Inst. 143. See Note (1932) 10 Neb.L.Bull. 478.

"establishment of a statutory minimum time for the preparation of the defense." [196]

18. Relief from Prejudicial Joinder

It has been seen in connection with indictments and informations that there may be a joinder of offenses or of defendants under certain circumstances. It does not follow that there will necessarily be a joint trial in such cases. In other words, joinder in connection with indictments and informations is to be distinguished from joinder in connection with trial. The joinder, though otherwise right or appropriate, may be such as to prejudice the defendant or the prosecution. In such cases the court in its discretion ought to be able to order an election [197] or separate trials of counts and to grant a severance [198] of defendants.

Section 185 of the Institute Code deals with misjoinder of offenses, though it would seem that it does not necessarily cover prejudicial joinder, the latter term being more inclusive. Under this section, in case of misjoinder of offenses the court may order the prosecuting attorney to sever the indictment into separate indictments or into separate counts.[199] Rule 14 of the Federal Rules of Criminal Procedure provides that, if it appears that a defendant or the government [200] is prejudiced by a joinder of

[196] Nat. Com. on Law Obs. and Enf., Rep. on Lawlessness in Law Enforcement (1931) 340. See also pp.273-278 of the Report.

[197] Clark, Handbook of Criminal Procedure (2d ed. by Mikell, 1918) 342-343; Beale, Criminal Pleading and Practice (1899) §§ 301-303, pp. 341-344.

[198] Clark, Handbook of Criminal Procedure (2d ed. by Mikrell, 1918) 355, 503; Beale, Criminal Pleading and Practice (1899) § 13, p.15.

[199] See Comments (1933) 11 Neb.L.Bull. 415, (1935) 48 Harv.L.Rev. 510.

[200] The American Law Institute Code of Criminal Procedure provision does not clearly seem to contemplate the case of prejudice to the government.

offenses in an indictment or in a trial, the court may order an election or separate trials of counts or give whatever other relief justice requires.

The English Indictments Act provides: "Where, before trial, or at any stage of the trial, the Court is of opinion that a person accused may be prejudiced or embarrassed in his defense by reason of being charged with more than one offense in the same indictment, or that for any other reason it is desirable to direct that the person should be tried separately for any one or more offenses charged in an indictment, the court may order a separate trial of any count or counts of such indictment." [201]

The problem of severance involves the balancing of the conflicting demands of securing fair trials for defendants with administrative expediency. The common law left the solution of the problem to the discretion of the court,[202] whether the motion for severance was made by the defendants [203] or the prosecution.[204] Possibly the problem of severance at common law arose from the difficulty in obtaining jurors at a time when the number of permissible peremptory challenges was very high.[205] By reducing the number of challenges, statutes have removed this difficulty. In the statutes today there are three approaches

[201] 5 & 6 Geo. V, c.90, § 5(3). See Note (1941) 5 J.Crim.L. (Eng.) 75.

[202] United States v. Marchant & Colson, 25 U.S. 480 (1827); State v. Soper, 16 Me. 293 (1839).

[203] Cockran v. United States, 41 F. (2d) 193 (C.C.A. 8th, 1930).

[204] State v. Claypoole, 5 N.J. Misc. 627, 137 Atl. 893 (N.J. Sup. 1927). There is authority that the court may order separate trials on its own motion. 2 Hale, Pleas of the Crown (1st Am. ed.1847) 296; see Woodsmall v. State, 181 Ind. 613, 618, 105 N.E. 155, 157 (1914).

[205] Comment (1936) 36 Col.L.Rev. 1359. By 9 Edw. IV, § 27 b (1470), even if 20 men were jointly indicted, each was allowed 35 peremptory challenges. By 25 Hen. VIII, c.3 (1534) the number of challenges was reduced to 20, except in cases of treason. See the opinion of Story, J., in United States v. Marchant & Colson, 25 U.S. 480, 481 (1827).

taken as to severance. The group departing the most from the common law grants severance as of right in all cases. An intermediate group allows severance as of right only in felony cases. A third group adheres to the common-law view that severance is in the discretion of the court. The trend is to adopt the common-law doctrine.[206] The considerations favoring the common-law rule are discouragement and intimidation of witnesses, the cost to the state, the necessity of numerous panels of jurors, hardship in preparation of the cases by the prosecuting attorney, and a slower judicial administration.[207] These will often outweigh a personal injustice to defendants from a joint trial.[208] But in certain cases real injustice may result unless a severance is permitted: The weight of evidence against one defendant may adversely affect another;[209] evidence admissible as to one may be inadmissible against the other;[210] the witnesses competent for one may be incompetent on behalf of the other;[211] defenses may be extremely antagonistic and mutually recriminatory;[212] there may be variance in pleading, one defendant pleading guilty and another not guilty;[213] or the law applicable to

[206] "A Summary of Laws Relating to Proposed Changes in Criminal Procedure" (1925) 9 Minn.L.Rev. 301, Pt. I.; Comment (1934) 13 Neb.L. Bull. 151.

[207] Comment (1936) 36 Col.L.Rev. 1359, 1360; 23 C.J.S. § 935, p.224.

[208] Hiscock, "Criminal Law and Procedure in New York" (1926) 26 Col.L.Rev. 257, 258; Note (1926) 26 Col.L.Rev. 752, 755.

[209] Note (1926) 26 Col.L.Rev. 752, 756; 2 Wharton, Criminal Evidence (1935) § 730.

[210] White v. People, 81 Ill. 333 (1876); United States v. Rockefeller, 222 Fed. 534, 536 (S.D. N.Y. 1915).

[211] Watson v. State, 84 Tenn. 604 (1886); O'Brien v. United States, 299 Fed. 568, 570 (C.C.A. 8th, 1924).

[212] United States v. Noble, 294 Fed. 689 (D. Mont. 1923); see People v. Minnecci, 200 N.E. 853, 855 (Ill. 1935).

[213] Marler v. State, 67 Ala. 55 (1880); Woodley v. State, 103 Ala. 23, 15 So. 820 (1894).

one defendant may not apply to another.[214] Possibly there should be a severance where a habitual criminal is jointly indicted with a first offender, not only where statutes provide that habitual criminality may be one count in an indictment but also where the hostile feeling of the jury toward the habitual offender may operate against the first offender.[215]

Section 185 of the Institute Code provides that, in case of a misjoinder of the parties defendant, the court may order the prosecuting attorney to sever the indictment into separate indictments or counts. Section 312 more clearly covers the case of prejudicial joinder of defendants. It provides: "When two or more defendants are jointly charged with any offense, whether felony or misdemeanor, they shall be tried jointly, unless the court in its discretion on the motion of the prosecuting attorney or any defendant orders separate trials." [216] Furthermore, the court may split the defendants into groups of one or more for separate trials. Rule 13 of the Federal Rules of Criminal Procedure, Second Preliminary Draft, provided that, in case of prejudicial joinder of defendants, the court may grant a severance of defendants or provide whatever other relief justice requires; but such severance may be granted only before trial.[217] This is now Rule 14 in the

[214] United States v. Rockefeller, 222 Fed. 534 (S.D.N.Y. 1915) (on indictment for violation of the Clayton Anti-Trust Act, some defendants were elected directors before and some after its passage).

[215] Rex v. Lonsdale (1931) 1 K.B. 191.

[216] Leaving the matter to the discretion of the judge is also approved by the Missouri Crime Survey (1926) 356; Minnesota Crime Commission Report (1927) 32; Report of the Minnesota Crime Commission (1934) 43; and by Report of the Commission on the Administration of Justice in New York State (1930) 126. See also Notes (1931) 70 A.L.R. 1171; (1936) 104 A.L.R. 1519; (1941) 131 A.L.R. 917; (1934) 13 Neb.L.Bull. 151.

[217] Under the federal rule, the court may sever of its own motion; the

final draft, and the provision as to granting only before trial is omitted. It may be noted that Rule 14 states substantially existing federal law concerning relief from prejudicial joinder.

The Minnesota Crime Commission Report of 1927 recommends that, in the discretion of the court, those jointly indicted or informed against may be tried jointly, as is the rule in the federal courts.[218] The Minnesota Crime Commission of 1934 renewed the recommendation.[219]

19. Consolidation of Indictments

It may happen that separate indictments may have been drawn up with respect to offenses or defendants where under the rules of joinder single indictments could properly have been found. In such cases consolidation should be permitted.[220] The Institute Code has no provision on the subject. Rule 13 of the Federal Rules of Criminal Procedure provides: "The court may order two or more indictments or informations or both to be tried together if the offenses, and the defendants if there is more than one, could have been joined in a single indictment or information. The procedure shall be the same as if the prosecution were under such single indictment or information."

American Law Institute Code of Criminal Procedure rule does not specifically so provide. See Comment (1934) 13 Neb.L.Bull. 151, 160.

218 Minnesota Crime Commission Report (1927) 32. Avoidance of the necessity of several trials was assigned as a reason.

219 Report of the Minnesota Crime Commission (1934) 43.

220 Approving consolidation of offenses, see Beale, Criminal Pleading and Practice (1899) § 200, pp.227-228; Clark, Handbook of Criminal Procedure (2d ed. by Mikell, 1918) § 155, p.504. See also 23 C.J.S., Criminal Law, § 931, p. 209. In England there may be no consolidation either as to offenses or defendants. Archbold, Criminal Pleading, Evidence and Practice (30th ed.1938) 198-199; Harris and Wilshere, Principles and Practice of Criminal Law (17th ed.1943) 427.

20. Elimination of Surprise

The most far-reaching reformers of the criminal law have prepared a series of rules, the purpose of which is to reduce the element of surprise and maneuvering at the trial to an irreducible minimum. They would make provision for a much fuller disclosure by both the prosecution and the defense in advance of trial. They assume that equality of position at the trial must be maintained for both sides.[221] The prosecution must be accorded the same advantage within constitutional limits as is the defendant, with respect to antecedent notice. The right of the defendant involves such steps as securing a copy of the indictment or information, together with names of the witnesses upon whose testimony it was found, the jury panel, bills of particulars, a copy of the grand jury minutes when necessary, a list of the witnesses to be called against him, and inspection and copy of the documents and objects in the prosecution's hands on a showing that such inspection seems reasonably necessary for the preparation of the defense. The complementary right of the government involves notice of the names of the witnesses upon whom the defendant will rely, and through them advance notice of his defenses; and inspection of the evidence which he will introduce, so far as the Constitution permits. For both sides there should also be further provision for the taking of depositions, and their use upon trial, and more extensive use of the pre-trial conference.

The contrast between criminal and civil procedure is most striking. In civil cases the sporting theory has been abandoned. The equity courts, influenced by ecclesiastical

[221] Millar, "The Function of Criminal Pleading" (1922) 12 J.Crim.L. 500.

and continental procedures, early required a limited pretrial disclosure through the bill of discovery in aid of an action at law.[222] A systematic and continuous development of fuller disclosure through such efforts as the Field Code, have culminated in the Federal Rules of Civil Procedure.[223] "Discovery, deposition, interrogatories, inspection, and other devices have made enormous inroads on this theory so that it may be said with some approximation to the truth that in the trial of a civil action one plays the game with the cards face up. In criminal cases, however, the old theory still prevails."[224]

The pleadings in civil actions apprise the parties of the issues. Each party has an opportunity to learn the strength of his own and his opponent's case. Little room is left for surprise, dramatic climax, or resulting miscarriage of justice. The administration of criminal justice is quite different. "The old theory was that a prosecution for crime was a contest between the injured person, or his relatives, and the accused. That theory has gradually yielded to the milder view that the contest is between the public and the accused. We ought now to be ready for the theory that a criminal prosecution is not a contest at all, but an investigation, conducted by the state, before a tribunal of its own appointment, with as great a desire to clear the defendant, if not guilty, as to convict him, if guilty."[225] A criminal trial is more of a contest between able lawyers

[222] 6 Wigmore, Evidence (3d ed.1940) § 1846; Millar, "The Mechanism of Fact Discovery: A Study in Comparative Civil Procedure" (1937) 32 Ill.L.Rev. 261, 424.

[223] Pike and Willis, "The New Federal Deposition—Discovery Procedure" (1938) 38 Col.L.Rev. 1179, 1436.

[224] Kidd, "Secrecy v. Inspection of Grand Jury Minutes" (1928) 6 The Panel, No. 1, 4.

[225] Chaplin, "Reform in Criminal Procedure" (1893) 7 Harv.L.Rev. 189, 199.

confusing real issues than an investigation to ascertain truth. It may well be asserted that the outcome of the contest may depend more on the skill of the hired champions than on the guilt or innocence of the defendant, just as was true in the old wager of battle.[226]

21. Pre-trial Procedure

One of the new and important innovations in federal practice introduced by the Federal Rules of Civil Procedure is found in Rule 16 providing for pre-trial procedure. This rule establishes a procedure under which the court, as well as the parties, may participate in the pretrial investigation and sifting of the issues and evidence in actions proceeding before it.[227] The purpose of the rule is to simplify, shorten, and perhaps make unnecessary a trial. Passing a statute or adopting a rule on pre-trial procedure does not enlarge the fundamental powers of a court, but simply specifies them for use.

Pre-trial procedure has been occasionally employed in the state courts,[228] and in the federal courts.[229] It has proved helpful in conspiracy cases involving a number of

[226] Stevens, "Archaic Constitutional Provisions Protecting the Accused" (1914) 5 J.Crim.L. 18.

[227] 1 Moore, Federal Practice (1938) 816.

[228] It has been used in the North Dakota state courts. "Experience with pre-trial in criminal cases has not been common, but where tried, it has yielded results of great value. A plea of guilty or an order of acquittal and release not only benefits both state and respondent, but goes far in protecting security. Further it builds confidence in the courts and in the legal profession." "Pre-trial is Readily Adapted to Rural Counties" (1942) 26 J. Am. Jud. Soc. 106, 107. It has also been used in the Wisconsin state courts. Comment (1941) 25 J. Am. Jud. Soc. 121, 122.

[229] Way, "New Technique Facilitates Criminal Trials" (1941) 25 J. Am. Jud. Soc. 120; Annual Report of the Director of the Administrative Office of the United States Courts (1941) 77; Shafroth, "Pre-Trial Techniques of Federal Judges" (1944) 28 J. Am. Jud. Soc. 39, 42.

defendants and the taking of a mass of evidence. In a particular case defendants might be induced to agree that a conspiracy existed, leaving as the only issue for trial whether particular defendants were connected with the conspiracy. In some cases a waiver of trial by jury may be agreed upon.

Rule 15 of the Federal Rules of Criminal Procedure, as proposed by the Advisory Committee, provided for pre-trial procedure in federal criminal procedure. It was modeled very largely on Rule 16 of the Federal Rules of Civil Procedure. The pre-trial conference may be held at any time after the filing of the indictment or information. The court is not required to hold any such conference, but may invite the attorneys to appear before it for a conference. The defendant is given the right to be present at such conference. The rules as finally adopted are silent as to pre-trial procedure.

The pre-trial conference may deal with four subjects: the simplification of the issues; the possibility of obtaining admissions of fact and of documents which will avoid unnecessary proof; the number of expert witnesses or character witnesses or other witnesses who are to give testimony of a cumulative nature; and such other matters as may be related to the disposition of the proceeding. Following the conference the court is to make an order, reciting the agreement made by the parties as to any of the matters considered. The order is to control the subsequent course of the proceeding unless modified at the trial to prevent manifest injustice. If a defendant is not represented by counsel, this rule is not to be invoked. This should serve to allay any fear that defendants not represented by counsel might be induced to make improvident concessions. But Rule 15 was stricken out by the Supreme Court.

22. Depositions

In civil cases, evidence which is not likely to be available at the trial may be preserved by taking the depositions of witnesses.[230] This cannot readily be done in criminal cases because of the constitutional guarantee that the accused shall be confronted with the witnesses against him. This guarantee serves a real purpose. Witnesses are more disposed to talk freely and untruthfully in the absence of the defendant. But much material evidence becomes unavailable because of this rule. There are many formal or noncontroversial matters where depositions are safe. Advantage is often taken of the existing rule by persuading or intimidating material witnesses for the prosecution to go into another state. Witnesses may be old and infirm, and unable to attend court. It has therefore been strongly urged that statutes be enacted providing for the taking of the testimony of witnesses, either for the prosecution or the defense, in the presence of the defendant, to be used if the witness cannot be produced at the trial.[231] In the opinion of the Wickersham Commission "testimony by deposition is at best unsatisfactory. Also, unless

230 The relation between criminal and civil cases and between a deposition and former testimony is clarifyingly discussed in 5 Wigmore, Evidence (3d ed.1940) §§ 1401-1418.

231 Report of the Minnesota Crime Commission (1934) 44; Missouri Crime Survey (1926) 360. See Comment (1908) 8 Col.L.Rev. 663; Chaplin, "Reform in Criminal Procedure" (1893) 7 Harv.L.Rev. 195; Note (1934) 24 J.Crim.L. 1113, 1114; (1936) 10 Kansas Judicial Council Bulletin 24-26; Campbell, "Some Needed Reforms in the Criminal Law" (1903) 6 Rep. Proc. Bar. Assoc. of Ark. 53, 67; Burdick, "Criminal Justice in America, Possibility of Improvement by Statutory Changes and Constitutional Amendments Affecting Procedure" (1925) 11 A.B.A.J. 510, 513; Hiscock, "Criminal Law and Procedure in New York" (1926) 26 Col.L. Rev. 253, 258; "Defects in Criminal Justice" (1925) 11 A.B.A.J. 297, 298; Moley, Our Criminal Courts (1930) 95; Evans, J., "Recommendations for Reforms in Criminal Procedure" (1929) 24 Ill.L.Rev. 111, 116.

constitutional provisions are changed, the depositions would have to be taken in the presence of the accused and so would not be feasible in the cases of chief concern, namely, those in which the witnesses are run out of the state. Conceding that the situation is far from satisfactory, we are not able to make any specific recommendation." [232] Seventeen states have, however, passed statutes permitting the prosecuting attorney to take depositions.[233] Chief Justice Taft once stated: "Another principle of the law of evidence embodied in the constitutional limitations is that the defendant must be confronted with the witnesses who testify against him. This seems to impose unnecessary hardships upon the government, because it certainly would not injure the defendant if depositions were taken and the defendant or his counsel were permitted to cross-examine. It is not a case of undue tenderness toward the defendant. There is no such restriction upon the defendant when he is seeking to prove his innocence for he may use depositions without number." [234]

There is no infringement of the constitutional guarantee of confrontation when the defendant is given means and an opportunity to be present with counsel at each examination desired by the prosecution, and when it is required that the defendant be brought to such examination if he is in custody.[235]

[232] Nat. Com. on Law Obs. and Enf., Rep. on Crim. Proc. (1931) 36. The use of depositions is opposed by Smith, "Criminal Justice in America" (1925) 11 A.B.A.J. 797.

[233] Alabama, California, Colorado, Idaho, Indiana, Louisiana, Maine, Massachusetts, Montana, Nevada, New York, Ohio, South Carolina, Vermont, Washington, Wisconsin, and Wyoming.

[234] Taft, C. J., "The Administration of the Criminal Law" (1905) 15 Yale L.J. 1, 10.

[235] 5 Wigmore, Evidence (3d ed.1940) § 1398, p.136; § 1401, p.147. There are a few jurisdictions which regard the constitutional provision requir-

Rule 17 of the Federal Rules of Criminal Procedure, as proposed by the Advisory Committee, provided for the taking of depositions at the instance of both the defendant and the government. The court may order the taking of a deposition if it appears "that a prospective witness may be unable to attend or prevented from attending a trial or hearing." [236] The deposition of a witness committed for failure to give bail may be taken.[237] The rule expressly confers the right to counsel at the taking of the deposition. If he "cannot bear the expense thereof, the court may direct that the reasonable expenses of the defendant and his attorney in taking the deposition be paid by the government." Depositions may be taken only when the court is convinced that they are necessary. The rules do not go as far as the Federal Rules of Civil Procedure which encourage depositions and permit them to be used as examinations before trial for the purpose of discovery, as well as for the purpose of securing testimony.

Resembling Rule 26(d) of the Federal Rules of Civil Procedure, Criminal Rule 15(e) allows a deposition to be used in five groups of situations: (1) if it appears that the

---

ing the confrontation of witnesses as preventing any use by the prosecution of depositions and former testimony. But a century ago there was a real doubt as revealed in the omission of the legislature, when providing authority for taking depositions generally, to include provisions authorizing the taking of depositions on behalf of the prosecution.

[236] Most of the cases involving depositions in criminal cases appear to involve the use of former testimony. According to Wigmore: "There is on principle no distinction between a *deposition* and *former testimony* as to the conditions upon which either may be used at the trial." 5 Wigmore, Evidence (3d ed.1940) § 1401, p.146. He also states: "There is on principle no distinction, as to the conditions of necessity for using depositions and former testimony, between civil and *criminal cases.*" *Ibid.* § 1401, p. 147.

[237] This is also provided for in Section 58 of the A.L.I. Code of Crim. Proc. (1930).

witness is dead; (2) if the witness is out of the United States; (3) if the witness is unable to testify because of sickness or infirmity; (4) if the party offering the deposition has been unable to procure the attendance of the witness by a subpoena; and (5) to contradict or impeach the testimony of the defendant as a witness.[238]

The Second Preliminary Draft laid down additional requirements if the deposition was at the instance of the government. If the defendant is in custody, the officer having custody is to be notified of the time and place of the examination, is to produce him at the examination, and to keep him in the presence of the witness during the examination. If the defendant is not in custody, he shall be given notice and shall have the right to be present. The government must pay in advance to the defendant's attorney and to a defendant not in custody the expense of travel and subsistence. These provisions afford to the defendant his right secured by the Sixth Amendment to confront the witnesses against him. The Rules as adopted make no provision as to depositions by the government.

23. Discovery and Inspection

In civil cases the power of the courts to compel production of documents for inspection by the opposite party is fairly well defined. But, in criminal cases, courts differ as to the existence and limitations of such a power.[239] In contrast to the situation in civil cases, up to 1928 only one state has recognized such jurisdiction by statute.[240] Per-

[238] Compare 5 Wigmore, Evidence (3d ed.1940) §§ 1403-1410, pp.149-165.

[239] Notes (1928) 41 Harv.L.Rev. 519, (1942) 51 Yale L.J. 687, (1945) 45 Col.L.Rev. 461; 23 C.J.S., Criminal Law, § 955, p.262.

[240] Iowa Code (1924) § 9326, 9339. But the statutes are directory and

haps the privilege of the defendant against self incrimination would prevent inspection by the prosecution.[241] A number of courts have denied inspection by the defendant.[242] Such right is doubtless not so badly needed by the defendant as it was at a time when he had no right of counsel, could not testify in his own behalf, and had no right to be informed of the nature of the charge against him.

It is argued against the right of the defendant to inspect that there is no precedent at common law suggesting it. It is true that an early English case denied the power.[243] Subsequent English cases established the contrary a century ago.[244] A reasonable basis for upholding the power is the supervisory control that courts exercise over public officers.[245] A bill of particulars does not serve the function of discovery of the evidence, since it merely gives addi-

---

not mandatory. State v. Howard, 191 Iowa 728, 183 N.W. 482 (1921); State v. Burris, 198 Iowa 1156, 198 N.W. 82 (1924).

241 Rex v. Purnell, 1 Wm. Bl. 37 (1748); State v. Wallahan, Tappan 48 (Ohio 1816); 8 Wigmore, Evidence (3d ed.1940) § 2224. Compare the cases where the documents or chattels are found on the defendant when he is arrested, or are brought into court by proper warrant. People v. Adams, 176 N.W. 351, 68 N.W. 636 (1903). "The state should have the right under proper restrictions, to compel accused persons to produce any paper or thing of importance in connection with the trial." MacChesney, "A Progressive Program for Procedural Reform" (1912) 3 J.Crim.L. 528.

242 Rex v. Holland, 4 D. & E. 691 (1792); State ex rel. Robertson v. State, 117 Wis. 385, 135 N.W. 1128 (1912); State v. Jeffries, 117 Kan. 742, 232 Pac. 873 (1925); State v. Yeoman, 112 Ohio St. 214, 147 N.E. 3 (1925).

243 Rex. v. Holland, 4 D. & E. 691 (1792).

244 Rex v. Harrie, 6 C. & P. 105 (1833); Regina v. Colucci, 3 Fost. & F. 103 (1861).

245 People ex rel. Lemon v. Supreme Court, 245 N.Y. 24, 30, 156 N.E. 84, 85 (1927).

tional information regarding the crime charged.[246] Inspection at the trial is not adequate since sometimes the evidence, inspection of which is sought, can be met only by extensive expert examination;[247] and in other ways time may be essential in preparing the defense.[248] It has also been contended that to allow inspection before trial will induce false testimony. But that contention has been long ago discredited in analogous fields;[249] and it would apply to some extent to inspection at the trial. With the assistance of cross-examination, the knowledge previously obtained by the defendant will not seriously reduce the probative force of the evidence, if the theory of the prosecution is correct. It will give the defendant an opportunity to demonstrate that the theory of the government is incorrect.[250] In fact the defendant might argue that to deny the right to inspect would be out of harmony with the policy of the state to give every defendant a fair and impartial trial, and an opportunity to meet every charge preferred against him.[251]

Of course, too sweeping a right of inspection would be socially undesirable. One case suggests a rule that the defendant is entitled to the disclosure of any material in the hands of the government, whether it be admissible as evidence or not, so long as it is reasonably calculated to aid the defense.[252] Such a rule, according to one view, would

246 Commonwealth v. Jordan, 207 Mass. 259, 265, 93 N.E. 809, 810 (1911).

247 United States v. Riera, 10 Porto Rico 186, 188 (1917).

248 People v. Gerrold, 265 Ill. 448, 107 N.E. 165 (1914).

249 2 & 6 Wigmore, Evidence (3d ed.1940) §§ 576, 1859, 1863.

250 See United States v. Rich, 6 Alaska 670, 671 (1922).

251 See Fitzpatrick v. Commonwealth, 135 Va. 504, 506, 115 S.E. 522, 523 (1923).

252 People v. Tippett, 317 Mo. 319, 296 S.W. 132 (1927), (1928) 41 Harv. L.Rev. 519, overruled in State ex rel. Page v. Terte, 324 Mo. 925, 25 S.W.

allow "fishing expeditions" into the state's evidence which would not be allowed even in civil cases.[253] The defendant, it is asserted, does not need so wide a scope adequately to protect his interests. Prosecuting attorneys would be embarrassed and impeded and convictions rendered very difficult.[254] Another view is that the accused be allowed to inspect if he can show that the paper is a material item in the preparation of his defense.[255]

Should the defendant ever be permitted to inspect statements of witnesses before trial? Should he be permitted to inspect the statement or confession of a codefendant? Should he be permitted to inspect the grand jury minutes, or the transcript of an administrative investigatory hearing? May he require the physical examination of a witness?[256]

The solution seems to be a rule between the extremes of no inspection and unrestricted inspection. Whenever the defendant in good faith seeks the inspection of documents or chattels which will be admissible or substantial evi-

---

(2d) 459 (1930). Defendant was charged with violating the statutory crime of leaving the scene of an automobile accident in which he was implicated. A witness gave a statement of the accident to the district attorney. The court held it was error to deny the motion of the defendant for inspection.

[253] Padgett v. State, 64 Fla. 389, 59 So. 946 (1942).

[254] State ex rel. Robertson v. Steele, 117 Minn. 384, 135 N.W. 1128 (1912).

[255] In United States v. Burr, 25 Fed. Cas. 30, 187 (C.C.D. Va. 1807), pre-trial inspection of a letter in the hands of the prosecution was permitted in a showing that "it may be material" to the defense.

[256] It was held not in State v. Allen 222 Pac. 502 (Wash. 1924) 22 Mich.L.Rev. 740. Defendant on trial for rape moved for an order requiring the prosecuting witness to submit to a physical examination by a physician. It seems a hardship not to permit such examination and some cases permit it. Walker v. State, 12 Okla. Cr. 179 (1915); State v. Pucca, 4 Pennewill (Del.) 71 (1902); People v. Preston, 19 Calif. App. 675 (1912).

dence whether for or against him, and which are necessary for the proper preparation and prosecution of his defense, it should be discretionary with the court to grant an inspection.[257] Defendant should be entitled to a new trial only if he can show material prejudice. If the document is a public one,[258] or is the subject of the indictment,[259] or is such a document or chattel as would require an investigation by experts in order to bring the facts before the jury,[260] or in any case where the exigencies of the situation would entail the denial of a fair opportunity to prepare an adequate defense,[261] the refusal of a motion for inspection would be an abuse of discretion. Where the document sought is inadmissible or may be admissible solely for impeachment purposes, the court should not be precluded from ordering inspection if the circumstances of the particular case warrant it.

In federal criminal cases the defendant is said to be entitled to production and inspection of documents and chattels when they constitute evidence, and when suppression may result in a failure of justice.[262] But the decisions reveal that even within this restricted framework this right is infrequently granted. Inspection is usually denied

[257] Such a rule is broader than the old equity practice which allowed discovery where the material sought by the applicant was admissible for him but did not allow it when it was admissible against him. But in several cases, inspection of documents which were admissible in evidence against the accused was refused. Morrison v. State, 40 Tex. Cr. 473, 51 S.W. 388 (1899) (admission by the defendant); Goode v. State, 57 Tex. Cr. 220, 123 S.W. 597 (confession).

[258] Daly v. Dimock, 55 Conn. 579, 12 Atl. 405 (1887). Cf. In re Greenbaum, 249 Fed. 468 (C.C.A. 6th, 1918).

[259] State v. Bramhall, 134 La. 1, 63 So. 603 (1903).

[260] Gray v. State, 55 Tex. Cr. 90, 114 S.W. 635 (1908).

[261] People v. Gerrold, 265 Ill. 448, 107 N.E. 165 (1914).

[262] 2 Wharton, Criminal Evidence (11th ed.1935) § 785. See Edwards v. United States, 312 U.S. 473 (1944).

on two related grounds: the fear of "fishing expeditions" and reluctance to force the government to disclose the evidence constituting its case.[263] There would seem to be less danger of harm resulting than may result from the granting of a list of jurors and witnesses. Tampering and subornation are far more feasible when living witnesses rather than unimpeachable papers and documents are involved. If examination and copying are properly supervised, the integrity of the document or object can hardly be endangered.[264]

Rule 16 of the Federal Rules of Criminal Procedure grants the defendant a considerable right of discovery and inspection.[265] Upon motion of a defendant at any time after the filing of the indictment or information, the court may order the attorney for the government to permit the defendant to inspect and copy or photograph designated books, papers, documents, or tangible objects obtained from or belonging to the defendant or obtained from others by seizure or by process, upon a showing that the

263 United States v. Rosenfeld, 57 F. (2d) 74 (C.C.A. 2d, 1932), cert. denied, sub nom. Nachman v. United States, 286 U.S. 556 (1932); United States v. Oley, 21 F. Supp. 281 (E.D. N.Y. 1937).

264 6 Wigmore, Evidence (3d ed.1940) § 1859 g.

265 The defendant is liberally protected in England. "Modern practice concedes to every accused person the right to know, before his trial, what evidence will be given against him. Hence, if any one who was not produced before the committing justice is to be called as a witness, full information should be furnished to the accused, both as to his name and as to the evidence he will give. If this has not been done, his evidence should not be pressed at the trial if the accused objects (per Hawkins, J., in Reg. v. Harris (1882), C.C.C. Sess. Pap. XCV, 525). The same principle applies to letters or other documents. And every witness whose depositions have been taken before examining justices must be made to attend at the trial, in order that if the Crown does not call him, the prisoner may be able to do so." Kenny, Outlines of Criminal Law (15th ed.1942) 563, n.3. See also Lawson and Keedy, "Criminal Procedure in England" (1911) 1 J.Crim.L. 748, 749.

items sought may be material to the preparation of his defense and that the request is reasonable. No corresponding right is granted to the government, since this might violate the privilege of freedom from self incrimination. Some equality might be obtained by requiring the defendant to reveal his defenses and the names of his witnesses.

24. Subpoena

In England where there has been a preliminary examination and commitment for trial, the witnesses are generally bound over by recognizance to appear at the trial and give evidence.[266] Where the witnesses have not been bound over and it is not certain that they will attend voluntarily, their appearance at trial may be compelled by subpoena. It may be obtained at the Crown Office of the High Court, or from the clerk of the peace or clerk of assize of the court in which the defendant is to be tried. Personal service is required if enforcement is to be sought by contempt procedure. It may be served in any part of the United Kingdom. No tender of expenses is necessary either by the Crown or by the defendant.[267]

Many American books and writings on criminal procedure neglect or omit the subject of subpoena. The Institute Code has no provision on the subject.[268] The Sixth

[266] Archbold, Criminal Pleading, Evidence and Practice (30th ed.1938) 492.

[267] As to payment out of local funds in the case of indigent prisoners, see Archbold, Criminal Pleading, Evidence and Practice (30th ed.1938) 272 *et. seq.*

[268] See, however, "Summoning Witnesses in One State to Testify in Another" (1931) 17 A.B.A.J. 392; (1931) 9 Proc. Am. L. Inst. 173-178, containing the draft approved by the American Law Institute; Note (1911) 25 Harv.L.Rev. 188. Section 45 of the American Law Institute Code of Criminal Procedure provides for process to summon witnesses for the preliminary examination. See also Hadley, "Outline of Criminal Procedure"

Amendment provides with respect to federal criminal cases: "In all criminal prosecutions the accused shall enjoy the right . . . to have compulsory process for obtaining witnesses in his favor." [269] Rule 45 of the Federal Rules of Civil Procedure lays down a rule as to subpoena in federal civil cases. Rule 17 of the Federal Rules of Criminal Procedure is patterned after the civil rule and offers almost a lone model for the states on the subject of subpoena in criminal cases. A subpoena shall be issued by the clerk under the seal of the court.[270] It shall command each person to whom it is issued to attend and testify at the time and place therein specified.

Under the federal rule, the court may order that a subpoena be issued upon the motion or request of an indigent defendant. The motion or request must be supported by an affidavit in which the defendant shall state the name and address of each witness and the testimony which he is expected to give, and it shall show that such evidence is material to the defense, that the defendant cannot safely go to trial without the witness, and that the defendant is unable to pay the witness fees. If the court orders the issuance of the subpoena, the costs incurred and the witness fees shall be paid in the same manner as in case of witnesses for the government. In the discretion of the court,

(1926) 12 A.B.A.J. 690, 293. The Report of the Minnesota Crime Commission of 1934, p.43, proposed that the state enter into reciprocal agreement with other states for the extradition of witnesses in criminal cases.

[269] There have been only a few cases interpreting this provision. Rottschaefer, Handbook of American Constitutional Law (1939) 797. In England it was not until 1702 that witnesses could be called expressly on behalf of a felon. Kenny, Outlines of Criminal Law (15th ed.1942) 107, 565. The right has often been violated in the state courts. Nat. Com. on Law Obs. and Enf., Report on Lawlessness in Law Enforcement (1931) 284.

[270] In some states it may be issued by attorneys. Cf. New York Code of Criminal Procedure (1938) §§ 194, 611.

witnesses may be required to attend in behalf of indigent defendants from any place in the United States. There may also be a subpoena for the production of documentary evidence and of objects.[271] Service may be by the marshal or by any other person who is not a party and who is not less than eighteen years of age.

A federal statute [272] provides that anyone who is a citizen of the United States or domiciled therein may, though outside the country, be subpoenaed as a witness at the trial of a criminal action when desired by the attorney general or attorney acting under him. There is a provision for personal service by a United States consul, with tender of traveling expenses. On failure to appear, an order to show cause why the recalcitrant should not be punished for contempt may be issued and his property in the United States seized to satisfy the fine assessed. This statute has been held not to violate the Fifth Amendment to the Federal Constitution.[273] It has been held that the right of a defendant to compulsory process under a state constitution does not extend to witnesses beyond the state line.[274] Possibly, a state statute like the federal one might be valid. A state should have the right to demand that its citizens, or persons domiciled in it, return on pain of execution on their property located within the state.[275]

[271] See Note, "Subpoenaed Documents in Federal Criminal Cases" (1942) 51 Yale L.J. 687.

[272] 44 Stat. 835 (1926); 28 U.S.C.A. §§ 711-718 (1927).

[273] Blackmer v. United States, 284 U.S. 421, 52 Sup.Ct. 252, 76 L.Ed. 375 (1932).

[274] Redmond v. State, 4 Ala. App. 190, 59 So. 181 (1912); State v. Yetzer, 97 Iowa 423, 66 N.W. 737 (1896).

[275] Comment (1932) 32 Col.L.Rev. 747.

25. Nolle Prosequi

In England, since the latter part of the seventeenth century, the attorney general has had the power to enter a nolle prosequi after the filing of an indictment and before judgment.[276] Such entry terminates all proceedings under the indictment. A new indictment may be filed, but this seldom happens. The wishes of the private prosecutor need not be consulted. The power is ordinarily exercised in cases in which the indictment cannot be sustained by legal evidence or where it appears that the interests of justice do not require that the defendant be brought to trial. It is sparingly used,[277] full confidence being reposed in the committing magistrate and the trial court.

There are other methods of ending the prosecution in England. In cases handled by the Director of Public Prosecutions, if the Director's investigation establishes either the innocence of the defendant or the legal insufficiency of the case against him, the usual practice of Crown counsel is to wait until the case is reached on the calendar, summarize briefly the facts in open court, explaining that the Director has decided to offer no evidence in view of the facts. The judge must be convinced that this is in the interest of justice. A jury is then sworn, no witnesses are called by the Crown, and the defendant is then acquitted by direction of the court.[278] An entry is made on the papers by the court clerk indicating that the defendant

276 Howard, Criminal Justice in England (1931) 35; Archbold, Criminal Pleading, Evidence and Practice (30th ed.1938) 110-112; Regina v. Allen (1862) 1 Best & S. 850; Note (1919) 13 Ill.L.Rev. 706. Informations could be nol-prossed at an earlier date. Roscoe, Criminal Evidence (15th ed.1918) 274.

277 It is used only six or seven times a year. Howard, Criminal Justice in England (1931) 137.

278 Howard, Criminal Justice in England (1931) 135-136, 360.

was acquitted by direction of the court, no evidence having been offered by the prosecution. No official recommendation is made by the Director other than the statement of Crown counsel in open court. The English theory seems to be that explanations for doing what seems to be necessary or desirable at the time are more likely to create difficulty than to avoid it.

A third method of terminating a case in England is the discharge of recognizances.[279] This is used where the evidence seems insufficient to warrant conviction. The prosecuting attorney states the facts in open court and the presiding judge, if he thinks proper, directs that the defendant be released from custody and the prosecutor and other witnesses who have been bound over to give evidence be excused from further attendance at the court. These two methods of ending prosecutions are not abused, not more than twelve or fifteen cases a year being disposed of at the Central Criminal Court by failure of the prosecution to offer evidence or by the discharge of recognizances.

The prosecuting attorney at common law clearly has the power to enter a nolle prosequi from the return of the indictment,[280] up to the beginning of the trial.[281] But once

[279] Howard, Criminal Justice In England (1931) 136, 360.

[280] He cannot enter it before the filing of the indictment as at preliminary examination or during grand jury proceedings. United States v. Schumann, 2 Abb. (U.S. 1866, C.C. Calif.) 523. The court also stated; "He can do this before the arraignment of the accused; or he may do it after issue joined; he can do it at any time until the jury is impaneled; and after the trial is commenced he can do it with consent of the defendant." Possibly the prosecution should be given the power to nolle prosequi after the defendant has been held to answer, especially in jurisdictions where the grand jury is seldom in session, and the defendant may be unable to obtain bail. See Rule 48(a), Fed. Rules Crim. Proc.

[281] Attorney General v. Tufts, 239 Mass. 458, 537, 131 N.E. 573 (1921).

the trial has begun and a jury has been impaneled, the entry of a nolle prosequi without the consent of the defendant has the effect of an acquittal.[282] Another prosecution is barred.[283] It has been held that, after the return of a verdict of guilty but before sentence, the prosecuting attorney can enter a nolle prosequi on his own authority.[284] But he may not do so after the pronouncement of sentence.[285] In a number of states a nolle prosequi requires the consent of the court.[286] When a nolle prosequi is entered before trial, there may be another prosecution on the basis of a new indictment.[287] The court cannot of its

---

See Comments (1918) 17 Mich.L.Rev. 186, (1923) 23 Col.L.Rev. 683; Bishop, "Nolle Prosequi" (1876) 2 So.L.Rev. (N.S.) 346, 350; Winfield, "Nolle Prosequi" (1884) 5 Crim.L.Mag. 1, 4.

282 Commonwealth v. Hart, 149 Mass. 7, 8, 20 N.E. 310 (1889); Confiscation Cases, 7 Wall. 454, 457 (1868). Rule 48(a) of the Federal Rules of Criminal Procedure is in accord. For the acquittal to be binding, the indictment must be valid. Bishop, "Nolle Prosequi" (1876) 2 So.L.Rev. (N.S.) 346, 354. Compare Winfield, "Nolle Prosequi" (1884) 5 Crim.L. Mag. 1, 4, 5.

283 Note (1940) 24 Minn.L.Rev. 522, 528. A minority of states require an actual acquittal or conviction.

284 Commonwealth v. Tuck, 37 Mass. 356 (1833); Winfield, "Nolle Prosequi" (1884) 5 Crim.L.Mag. 66.

285 Bishop, "Nolle Prosequi" (1876) 2 So.L.Rev. (N.S.) 346, 357; Commonwealth v. Dascalakis 140 N.E. 470 (Mass. 1923), 23 Col.L.Rev. 683. See Commonwealth v. Mead, 10 Allen 396, 397 (Mass. 1865).

286 See A.L.I. Code of Crim. Proc. (1930) commentaries 895-897; Abbott, Criminal Trial Practice (4th ed.1939) § 631, p.1192; see People ex rel. Hoyne, 284 Ill. 315, 120 N.E. 244 (1918), 17 Mich.L.Rev. 186, (1919) 13 Ill.L.Rev. 706; Winfield, "Nolle Prosequi" (1884) 5 Crim.L.Mag. 1, 11; Baker, "The Prosecuting Attorney: Legal Aspects of the Office" (1936) 26 J.Crim.L. 647, 667; Emery, J., "The Nolle Prosequi in Criminal Cases" (1913) 6 Me.L.Rev. 199.

287 In most states there may be no prosecution on the same indictment. Bishop, "Nolle Prosequi" (1876) 2 So.L.Rev. (N.S.) 346, 355; State v. Veterans of Foreign Wars, Post 1856, 223 Iowa, 1146, 274 N.W. 916, 112 A.L.R. 383 (1937). See, however, Winfield, "Nolle Prosequi" (1884) 5 Crim.L.Mag. 1, 3. Allowing no prosecution under the same indictment is

own motion without action by the prosecuting attorney enter a nolle prosequi.[288]

In America the use of the nolle prosequi is of far greater importance than it is in England. "The decline in the use of the grand jury plus the greater increase in criminal prosecutions attendant upon continued urbanization have added materially to the power of the district attorney during the last fifty years. In many places the determination of what felony prosecutions should be brought lies in his hands. In all our large cities more prosecutions are initiated than it is possible to try. Thus the prosecutor must determine not only whether there is sufficient evidence to justify a trial, but whether as a matter of policy he will not nolle prosequi particular cases or classes of cases." [289] Judges exercise their authority in public on the basis of established precedents. The prosecuting attorney acts in private without any rules or standards except his own conscience.

In Cleveland in 1925 more than eleven per cent of all prosecutions initiated by indictment were terminated by nolle prosequi.[290] In St. Louis in 1923-1924, 10.2 per cent were thus eliminated.[291] In Minneapolis in 1923, 28.6 per cent of all indictments were nol-prossed,[292] and in Atlanta,

---

said to be the better view. Beale, Criminal Pleading and Practice (1899) § 304, p.345.

288 Report of the Crimes Survey Committee, Law Association of Philadelphia (1926) 198-199. See Abbott, Criminal Trial Practice (4th ed. 1939) § 631, p.1192; 69 A.L.R. 240.

289 Warner and Cabot, "Changes in the Administration of Criminal Justice During the Past Fifty Years" (1937) 50 Harv.L.Rev. 583, 597.

290 Moley, Politics and Criminal Prosecution (1929) 152; Moley, "The Vanishing Jury" (1928) 2 So.Calif.L.Rev. 97, 99.

291 Missouri Crime Survey (1926) 285, Table IV.

292 Minnesota, Biennial Report of the Attorney General (1926).

Georgia, in 1921, 13 per cent.[293] In 1933, of 131,000 criminal cases entering the trial courts in twenty-four states, about a quarter of them (36,832) were disposed of without prosecution, the greater number being dismissed by the prosecutor.[294]

A true picture of terminations of prosecutions is not obtainable by looking simply at the statistics on nolle prosequi. For instance, in Chicago in 1926, of cases entering the trial court on indictment, while less than 6 per cent were nol-prossed, 4.12 per cent were dismissed for want of prosecution usually because of the absence of witnesses.[295]

The replacement of indictment by information with its broadening of the scope of the prosecutor's discretion has resulted in a fear that his discretion may be abused.[296] A leading proposal for checking the prosecutor is Section 295 of the American Law Institute Code of Criminal Procedure, providing that a prosecution shall not be dismissed except by court order and for good cause amplified in a written statement to be entered on record. The court might act on its own motion. This has been advocated in the Missouri Crime Survey.[297] There are, however, a

293 "Crime and the Georgia Courts" (1925) 16 J.Crim.L. 169.

294 Clark, "Law Enforcement and Public Administration" (1935) 30 Ill. L.Rev. 273, 282-283. Statistics for California, Michigan, Montana, Maine, Minnesota, and Texas are cited in Miller, J., "Information or Indictments in Felony Cases" (1924) 8 Minn.L.Rev. 379, 403, n.91.

295 Illinois Crime Survey (1929) 300, 303-304.

296 Nat. Com. on Law Obs. and Enf., Report on Prosecution (1931) 18-20; Roscoe Pound, Criminal Justice in America (1930) 149-151; Warner and Cabot, "Changes in the Administration of Criminal Practice During the Past Fifty Years" (1937) 50 Harv.L.Rev. 583, 597.

297 Missouri Crime Survey (1926) 146-147, 370-371; Baker, "The Prosecutor-Initiation of Prosecution" (1933) 23 J.Crim.L. 720, 791; Cf. Nat. Com. on Law Obs. and Enf., Report on Prosecution (1931) 97-100. See also, Willoughby, Principles of Judicial Administration (1929) 140-141;

number of rather convincing arguments for not interfering with the prosecutor's discretion.[298] In the first place, he is not in position to prosecute all offenses, as he operates on a budget which is too limited.[299] If he undertakes a prosecution and later discovers that it is not so deserving of the available resources as originally supposed, he should be able to drop it without the need of an open inquiry in court. In the second place, there are a number of cases which he will not want to prosecute because only a personal grudge would be served. In the third place, it is only in the privacy of his office that he can carry on the plea bargaining, which is a practical necessity in criminal administration.[300] The tentative drafts of Federal Rules of Criminal Procedure did not take away the powers of the prosecuting attorney but required him to furnish a statement of reasons. Rule 50 provided: "The Attorney General or the United States Attorney may file a dismissal of the indictment or information with a statement of the reasons therefor and the prosecution shall thereupon

Gemmill, "What Is Wrong with the Administration of Our Criminal Laws?" (1914) 4 J.Crim.L. 698, 703-704, 711; Goodwin, "Community v. Criminal" (May 1926) 11 Mass.L.Q.; Baker and DeLong, "The Prosecuting Attorney, Powers and Duties in Criminal Prosecution" (1934) 24 J.Crim.L. 1025, 1060; Hadley, "Outline of Code of Criminal Procedure" (1926) 12 A.B.A.J. 690, 694.

298 See Note (1940) 50 Yale L.J. 107, 110.

299 Nat. Com. on Law Obs. and Enf., Report on Prosecution (1931) 104.

300 "The ideal that all laws should be enforced without a discretionary selection is impossible to carry out. . . . The prosecutor . . . will be confronted with a long line of offenders caught in the act who are important, but who must be disposed of. His choice will be either to make reasonable compromises with them, or else to clog the machinery with relentless prosecution of comparatively harmless persons." Arnold, "Law Enforcement—An Attempt at Social Dissection" (1932) 42 Yale L.J. 1, 9. See also A.L.I., A Study of the Business of the Federal Courts (1934) Pt. I: Criminal Cases (1934) 57; Miller, J., "The Compromise of Criminal Cases" (1927) 1 So. Calif.L.Rev. 1; Pound, Criminal Justice in America (1930) 187.

terminate. Such a dismissal may not be filed during the trial without the consent of the defendant." The administrative practice has been that the United States attorney secures the approval of the Department of Justice before dismissing a proceeding.[301] Rule 48 of the Federal Rules now provides: "The Attorney General or the United States Attorney may by leave of court file a dismissal of an indictment, information or complaint and the prosecution shall thereupon terminate."

The Minnesota Crime Commission in its Report of 1927 recommended that whenever an indictment or information is dismissed, or a nolle prosequi entered, a written record should be made of the reasons therefor.[302] Rule 50 of the Federal Rules of Criminal Procedure, Second Preliminary Draft, was to the same effect.

301 As to the development of the attorney general's power to supervise prosecutions, see Cummings and McFarland, Federal Justice (1937) 486-520. See also Harker, "The Control of Criminal Prosecutions in Federal Courts" (1914) 8 Ill.L.Rev. 373. As to the powers of a state attorney general to nolle prosequi, see DeLong, "Powers and Duties of the State Attorney General in Criminal Prosecutions" (1934) 25 J.Crim.L. 358, 370, 386.

302 Minnesota Crime Commission Report (1927) 31. A 1922 Massachusetts statute required a statement of reasons. Warner and Cabot, Judges and Law Reform (1936) 29. See also Criminal Justice in Cleveland (1922) 207, 329, 368; Illinois Crime Survey (1929) 270, 278. There is, however, the possibility that the prosecutor will make purely perfunctory statements, such as "insufficient evidence" or "witnesses missing." Illinois Crime Survey (1929) 302; Moley, Politics and Criminal Prosecution (1929) 154; Moley, "The Vanishing Jury," (1928) 1 So. Calif.L.Rev. 97, 101; Bettman, "Criminal Justice in America" (1925) 11 A.B.A.J. 455, 459. For an excellent specimen of a statement setting forth the reasons for the action of the prosecuting attorney, see Cummings, "The State v. Harold Israel" (1924) 15 J.Crim.L. 406, 407-434.

CHAPTER VII

TRIAL

1. Stage in Proceedings

AFTER a plea of not guilty, the next step is trial.[1] "Trial in our system involves the impaneling of a jury, the presentation of evidence, argument by counsel, and the charge of the court. Then follows the *verdict*, which may find the accused guilty or not guilty. If the latter, there is judgment of acquittal and the accused goes free. No further proceedings against him are permitted after that verdict." [2]

Of seven chief essentials of a criminal proceeding suggested by the Wickersham Commission, two of them are a "speedy trial" and a "fair trial before an impartial tribunal." [3]

The cases are not in accord as to the exact stage in a criminal proceeding at which the trial begins. One view is that it does not begin until the jury is impaneled and sworn.[4] A second view is that it begins when the case is called and the jury summoned, even though the jury has

[1] As to the origin of the word "trial," see Millar, "The Lineage of Some Procedural Words" (1939) 25 A.B.A.J. 1023, 1028. It came from the old French word "trier" meaning "to sift."

[2] Nat. Com. on Law Obs. and Enf., Rep. on Crim. Proc. (1931) 17. For full discussion of the law of trial practice, see 23 C.J.S., Criminal Law, §§ 961-1417, pp.274-1114; 2 Bishop, Criminal Procedure (4th ed.1895) §§ 890-1045, pp.682-902; Wharton, Criminal Pleading and Practice (9th ed.1889) §§ 540-758, pp.388-526. For a recent volume devoted chiefly to trial practice, see Abbott, Criminal Trial Practice (4th ed.1939).

[3] A.L.I. Rep. on Crim. Proc. (1931) 16.

[4] Bush v. State, 128 N.E. 443 (Ind. 1920), (1921) 5 Minn.L.Rev. 152. Accord: State v. Kent, 5 N.D. 516, 67 N.W. 1052, 35 L.R.A. 518 (1896); State v. Jackman, 31 Nev. 511, 104 Pac. 13 (1909). This is the minority view, according to Note (1906) 6 Col.L.Rev. 357.

not been sworn.[5] The rule that jeopardy does not attach until the jury is impaneled and sworn does not therefore necessarily determine the time at which the trial commences.[6]

2. Early English Procedure

According to Thayer, there were four chief forms of trial in the beginnings of English legal history: (1) by witnesses, (2) the party's oath, with or without fellow swearers, (3) ordeal, and (4) battle.[7] Trial by witness was the oldest kind of "one-sided" proof. There was no testing by cross-examination and the operative thing was the oath, and not the probative quality of what was said. The second method in its judicial form was compurgation, in which the party swore with the auxiliary oath of others. In criminal cases it is thought to have disappeared by an implied prohibition of the Assize of Clarendon in 1166, although it remained long in the local and ecclesiastical courts. The third method, that of ordeal, is one of the oldest and still exists in various parts of the world. Trial by battle, often classified as an ordeal, survived the ordeal proper by centuries, being abolished in 1819. It was brought into England by the Normans. In actual practice it was not much resorted to.

In the earliest days of the grand jury, indictments found by it were tried by ordeal.[8] Ordeals were abolished

[5] Palmer v. State, 42 Ohio St. 596 (1885); State v. Johnson, 24 S.D. 590, 124 N.W. 847 (1910); Hopt v. Utah, 110 U.S. 574, 4 Sup.Ct. 202, 28 L.Ed. 262 (1884).

[6] Capler v. State, 3 Okla. Cr. Rep. 72, 104 Pac. 493 (1909).

[7] Thayer, "The Older Modes of Trial" (1891) 5 Harv.L.Rev. 45, 47; Thayer, A Preliminary Treatise on Evidence at the Common Law (1898) 16.

[8] Trial by battle was possible only where prosecution was by an appeal.

in 1215 with the result that every indictment had to be referred back to the grand jury, to which other colleagues were sometimes added.[9] Finally after the lapse of a century the practice developed of these new jurors alone undertaking the duty of revision without the presence of the original accusers.[10] A statute of 1352 specifically excluded the original accusers. This history explains the existence of two juries. Both juries, however, proceeded upon common repute or upon the basis of their own knowledge; and men who were acquainted with the circumstances of the crime were often placed on the jury as additional jurors.[11] Finally about the year 1500 such persons were no longer added to the jury itself, but were sent to give evidence before it.[12] Two centuries later witnesses

---

1 Stephen, A History of the Criminal Law of England (1883) 254. See 2 Pollock and Maitland, History of English Law (2d ed.1905) 632-634; 1 Holdsworth, History of English Law (3d ed.1923) 308-310.

9 2 Pollock and Maitland, History of English Law (2d ed.1905) 598, 619, 648, 650; 1 Holdsworth, History of English Law (3d ed.1923) 323, 334. See Thayer, A Preliminary Treatise on Evidence at the Common Law (1898) 47-84; Thayer, "The Older Modes of Trial" (1891) 5 Harv.L.Rev. 45; 1 Stephen, A History of the Criminal Law of England (1883) 251-272, 301-307, 425-426, as to the early history of the jury. For the history from 1554 to 1760, see 1 Stephen, 319-427.

10 See Wells, "Early Opposition to the Petty Jury in Criminal Cases" (1914) 30 L.Q.Rev. 97.

11 It follows that the "impanelling of the jury was in very ancient times equivalent to the choice of the witnesses by whom matters of fact were to be determined." 1 Stephen, A History of the Criminal Law of England (1883) 301. In the thirteenth century, the English law had no word equivalent to trial. Proof is a better term. 2 Pollock and Maitland, History of English Law (2d ed.1905) 588. In that century an indictment in a misdemeanor case was treated not as an accusation but as conclusive testimony, and there was no trial. The penalty was, however, only a fine. 2 Pollock and Maitland, History of English Law (2d ed.1905) 652-653.

12 By the "middle of the fifteenth century the fundamental principles of trial by jury in criminal cases had been established to a great measure, though not entirely." 1 Stephen, A History of the Criminal Law of Eng-

were allowed to be called expressly on behalf of the defendant.[13] Documentary evidence preceded testimony of witnesses in point of historical development. It is not unlikely that the evidence of witnesses was at first received in writing; and the witnesses were not present at the trial. Political cases were at first treated in a different fashion from non-political cases, though the trial was at least public and oral. During the reigns of James I and Charles I, the evidence presented to the jury consisted in most cases of reports of what had been said by witnesses when questioned by royal commissioners in the absence of the defendant and in private. Such interrogation was often made of the defendant himself. The privilege against self incrimination was as yet unknown. Since the middle of the seventeenth century, however, political cases have been tried like non-political cases.[14]

Trial by jury does not seem originally to have involved the right of confrontation or subpoena of witnesses, although these may have developed early in non-political

---

land (1883) 264-265. The right to peremptory challenge is mentioned by Bracton and Britton in the thirteenth century. The right to challenge a fixed number, 35, in felony cases probably arose at the period when the separation between the duties of the jury and the witnesses was coming to be recognized. *Ibid.* 301-302.

[13] 1 Stephen, A History of the Criminal Law of England (1883) 350. Defendants were first allowed to call witnesses during the reign of Queen Mary. Sibley, Criminal Appeal and Evidence (1908) 255. Such witnesses were not at first examined on oath. An Act of Parliament of 1702 provided that defendants' witnesses in case of treason and felony be sworn. 1 Stephen, A History of the Criminal Law of England (1883) 416.

[14] For the history of English trial procedure from 1554 to 1760, see 1 Stephen, A History of the Criminal Law of England (1883) 319-428. See also 9 Holdsworth, History of English Law (3d ed.1923) 222-236. The first fully reported trial occurred in 1664. 1 Stephen, 376. Trial before the thirteenth century is described in 2 Pollock and Maitland, History of English Law (2d ed.1905) 653-656.

cases. Stephen knew of "no precise, clear authority for the proposition that a prisoner is entitled to have the witnesses against him examined in his presence or that he is entitled to call witnesses or examine them upon oath till long after the Revolution" of the seventeenth century.[15]

At common law after the jury had been sworn and charged with the inquiry concerning the prisoner, they could not depart from the custody of the court in cases of treason or felony until they had completed the inquiry.[16] No such requirement was laid down as to misdemeanors. They were required to be unanimous because historically they were witnesses, and the rule was that twelve witnesses must swear to the prisoner's guilt before he could be convicted.[17]

As late as 1554 jurors were imprisoned and heavily fined for acquitting a defendant. The right of the jury to return any verdict they thought right without being punished at the will of the court was finally established in 1670 in Bushel's Case.[18] The earliest method of reviewing the action of the jury seems to have been the attaint, which lay only at the suit of the king and never the defendant. This procedure, originating about the year 1202, involved review by a second jury, double the number of

[15] 1 Stephen, A History of the Criminal Law of England (1883) 358.

[16] Originally they were debarred from "food, drink, and fire." Possibly this was the law until the latter half of the nineteenth century. 1 Stephen, A History of the Criminal Law of England (1883) 305-306. See Winsor v. Regina (1866) L.R. 1 Q.B. 289.

[17] 1 Stephen, A History of the Criminal Law of England (1883) 304; 2 Pollock and Maitland, History of English Law (2d ed.1905) 625. In the thirteenth century a majority verdict seems to have been possible. Britton (Nichols trans.) lib. 1, 12 b.

[18] Vaughan, 135, 6 St. Tr. 999. See 1 Stephen, A History of the Criminal Law of England (1883) 373-375; 1 Holdsworth, History of English Law (3d ed.1923) 342-347.

the original jury. Later on, judges sought unsuccessfully to compel the jury to return special verdicts.[19]

Until 1898 the defendant was not a competent witness.[20] But down to 1688 interrogation of the defendant on his arraignment constituted a most important part of the trial.[21] After the Revolution of 1688 questioning of the prisoner ceased. The civil rule that a party was incompetent as a witness, which prevailed until 1853, was held to apply to criminal cases. But there were two important qualifications. Defendants charged with felonies could not be defended by counsel and therefore had to speak for themselves. They usually spoke, for if they did not they were likely to be convicted. When the law permitted counsel, counsel were likely to contend that their client's mouth was closed, but that if he could speak he would say so and so.[22] In the second place, until 1848 the statutes of Philip and Mary authorized committing magistrates to hold the examination of the person suspected. Under the new system the prisoner was asked whether he wished to say anything and warned that if he did what he said would be taken down and might be used at the trial. Thus before 1898 the defendant was protected against judicial questioning before or at the trial, but he could not give evidence on his own behalf. The theory of exclusion was

[19] On the history of attaint, special verdicts, and punishment of juries for erroneous verdicts, see Orfield, Criminal Appeals in America (1939) 15-17. It will be noted that the early restrictions of the jury protected the Crown against erroneous acquittals, but did not protect the defendant against erroneous convictions.

[20] See Note (1899) 18 L.Q.Rev. 120.

[21] 1 Stephen, A History of the Criminal Law of England (1883) 325, 439-440. See McCormick, "Tomorrow's Law of Evidence" (1935) 24 A.B.A.J. 507, 511; 8 Wigmore, Evidence (3d ed.1940) § 2250.

[22] For many years prior to the Act of 1898, it was the practice of the judges to allow a defendant as well as his counsel to address the jury. Archbold, Criminal Pleading, Evidence and Practice (30th ed.1938) 202.

that a witness is to be believed because he is sworn to tell the truth and is reluctant to lie. It would, however, be very hard for a defendant to lie minutely and circumstantially without being found out.[23]

In trials for misdemeanors the defendant has always been entitled to be defended by counsel.[24] He acquired no such right in felony trials until 1836.[25] Moreover, even in misdemeanor cases (those important on public grounds were usually tried before the Star Chamber) the discretion of the court was so wide and its decisions were so little susceptible of checks except by Parliament that the position of the bar was rather futile.[26]

Early trials were short and did not usually last more than a day.[27] The right of the court to adjourn in cases of treason or of felony was not fully established until the treason trials of 1794.

The turbulent seventeenth century brought few direct

[23] 1 Stephen, A History of the Criminal Law of England (1883) 341, 445.

[24] By the practice of the Star Chamber, defendants were not only allowed counsel but were required to get their answers signed by them. Counsel was often reluctant to sign with the result that the defendant admitted the case against him. 1 Stephen, A History of the Criminal Law of England (1883) 341.

[25] 6 & 7 Wm. IV, c.114, § 1. Previously the rule against counsel in felony cases had been gradually relaxed. A practice, the origin of which cannot be traced, grew up, by which counsel in the eighteenth century could do everything for the prisoner except address the jury for him. 1 Stephen, A History of the Criminal Law of England (1883) 424.

[26] 1 Stephen, A History of the Criminal Law of England (1883) 451-454.

[27] In the seventeenth century, it was still the rule that trials must be finished at a single sitting. 1 Stephen, A History of the Criminal Law of England (1883) 403, 422; Allen, Legal Duties and Other Essays in Jurisprudence (1931) 169. The reason seems to have been the rule, on a treason or felony trial, forbidding the jury to separate before verdict or to eat or drink during their deliberations. 11 Holdsworth, History of English Law (3d ed.1923) 553-554.

legislative changes in criminal procedure. "The most important was the enactment that the judges should hold office, not at the pleasure of the Crown, but during good behavior. This deeply affected the whole administration of justice." [28] When, "in the eighteenth century, further privileges were given to accused persons and the judges conducted the trials with scrupulous fairness to them, the English criminal trial became a model to the nations of Western Europe." [29] However, as recently as a century ago, criminal trials were often conducted with such speed as scarcely to do justice in serious criminal cases.[30]

To summarize the history of English trial procedure: "For many centuries the chief development in criminal procedure was securing the defendant an adequate opportunity to present his defense. Notable landmarks in this direction were supplying him with a copy of the indictment, permitting him to have counsel and witnesses sworn and summoned to appear, and finally allowing him to take the stand as a witness in his own defense." [31]

3. Modern English Procedure

A defendant in English criminal proceedings is assured an early trial.[32] The Habeas Corpus Act provides that, if

[28] 1 Stephen, A History of the Criminal Law of England (1883) 416. Holt, Chief Justice from 1689 to 1710, is said to have been the first judge to conduct a trial in the modern spirit. 6 Holdsworth, History of English Law (3d ed.1923) 518-519. See also Pound, Criminal Justice in America (1930) 100.

[29] 11 Holdsworth, History of English Law (3d ed.1923) 581.

[30] Jackson, The Machinery of Justice in England (1940) 120.

[31] Warner and Cabot, "Changes in the Administration of Criminal Justice during the Past Fifty Years" (1937) 50 Harv.L.Rev. 583, 587.

[32] On modern trial procedure in England, see Kenny, Outlines of Criminal Law (15th ed.1942) 563-573; Archbold, Criminal Pleading, Evidence and Practice (30th ed.1938) 165-223; 1 Stephen, A History of the Crimi-

any man who has been committed on a charge of either treason or felony is not indicted at the next Assizes after his commitment, he must be released on bail, and further that, if at the next subsequent Assizes he is not both indicted and tried, he must be discharged altogether. There is, however, no statutory provision governing misdemeanants committed to Assizes. The Assizes Relief Act enacted in 1889 insures the speedy trial of all persons committed to Quarter Sessions in both felony and misdemeanor cases.

Conversely the defendant is rarely allowed to secure a postponement of the trial. By interposing a plea of not guilty the defendant puts himself upon his trial, which ordinarily takes place as soon as the case is reached on the trial calendar. At this time either the Crown or the defendant may request an adjournment. The court may require that the application be supported by affidavit with a full statement of grounds. Few adjournments are granted; they are short; and only upon proof of exceptional circumstances such as the illness of the defendant or of a material witness.[33]

In felony cases the defendant must be present at his trial and must stand in the dock.[34] A misdemeanant may

---

nal Law of England (1883) 301-307, 428-456; Stephen, A Digest of the Law of Criminal Procedure (1883) 184-194; Howard, Criminal Justice in England (1931) 359-380. Trial procedure in 1880 strongly resembled that in 1760. 1 Stephen, A History of the Criminal Law of England (1883) 428; and even that of 1660. See 1 Stephen, 369. Trial procedure in 1822 is described by an observer for the French Government in Cottu, On the Administration of Criminal Justice in England (1822) 74-102. "The alterations in the conduct of the trial of indictable offenses since 1822 have been remarkably few." Stephen, "Criminal Law Reforms Since 1822" (1922) 57 Law J. 419, 422.

[33] Howard, Criminal Justice in England (1931) 359.

[34] Archbold, Criminal Pleading, Evidence and Practice (30th ed.1938)

be tried in his absence if he has previously pleaded. Trial must be in a public court with open doors, although the general public may be excluded when young persons are called as witnesses in cases involving conduct contrary to decency or morality.[35]

Venue is the common-law term for the neighborhood from which the jurors are to come.[36] At common law only a jury of the district in which the offense was committed could try the case. By the Criminal Justice Act, 1925, a defendant charged with an indictable offense may be proceeded against, indicted, tried, and punished in any county or place in which he was apprehended as if the offense had been committed in that county or place.[37] Exception is made in cases of hardship to the defendant. Prosecution of vagrant criminals is thus made more feasible. Under Section 14 of this act it is provided that, instead of being committed to the court of the locality of the commission

---

165-166, 209. He must be present at the delivery of the verdict in open court. Presence at trial was important historically because defendant had no right to counsel until 1836.

[35] Archbold, Criminal Pleading, Evidence and Practice (30th ed.1938) 198, 209. He need not be present at the return of the verdict.

[36] Archbold, Criminal Pleading, Evidence and Practice (30th ed.1938) 24. For the history of venue, see 1 Stephen, A History of the Criminal Law of England (1883) 276-280; 4 Holdsworth, History of English Law (3d ed.1923) 530.

[37] 15 & 16 Geo. V, c.86, § 11(1). See Kenny, Outlines of Criminal Law (15th ed.1942) 535-536; Burrows, "Criminal Law and Procedure" (1935) 51 L.Q.Rev. 36, 52; Butler, "Developments in Criminal Law—1910-1935" (1935) 179 Law T. 325, 326. In Canada every court of criminal jurisdiction "is competent to try all offenses wherever committed, if the accused is found, or apprehended or is in custody within the jurisdiction of such court, or if he has been committed to trial before such court. The only limitation is that no court in one province can try any person for any offense committed entirely in another province except in the case of defamatory libel." Crouse, "A Critique of Canadian Criminal Legislation" (1934) 12 Can.B.Rev. 545, 575.

of the crime or that of apprehension, a defendant may be committed to the court of some other place if it appears, having regard to the date and place of such other sessions more convenient to commit to it, either to expedite trial or to save expense. This power is not to be exercised if the regular court is normally to be held within one month, or if there would be hardship to the defendant. The King's Bench Division of the High Court may change the place of trial of any felony or misdemeanor, whenever it is necessary for the purpose of securing a fair and impartial trial.[38] Before 1939 cases were removable by certiorari into the King's Bench Division in order to remove to some other court a case which, owing to local prejudice, for example, may not receive a fair trial. They are now removable by a simple direction of the court.[39] The English Business of Courts Committee has concluded that removal to secure fair trial should in the future be direct from one venue to another.[40]

Jurors in criminal trials and in civil cases must have the same qualifications in England. They must be over twenty-one years of age and must be the owner, in fee or for life, of lands or tenements worth £10 a year or by long leaseholds worth £20 a year, or else the occupier of a house rated at £20 a year.[41] They serve without reward of even

[38] Archbold, Criminal Pleading, Evidence and Practice (30th ed.1938) 95, 107; Kenny, Outlines of Criminal Law (15th ed.1942) 498. This power has been seldom, if ever, exercised. 1 Stephen, A History of the Criminal Law of England (1883) 280.

[39] Jackson, The Machinery of Justice in England (1940) 92.

[40] Kenny, Outlines of Criminal Law (15th ed.1942) 498-499.

[41] Kenny, Outlines of Criminal Law (15th ed.1942) 566. For a discussion of the modern English jury by a French judge, see Gorphe, J., "Reform of the Jury System in European Countries: England" (1936) 27 J. Crim.L. 17. For a realistic criticism, see Jackson, The Machinery of Justice in England (1940) 218-232. He points out that jury service is con-

pocket expenses. They may be of either sex, but the trial judge may, on the application of either side or at his own instance, make an order that the jury shall be composed of men only or of women only. A panel or list is returned by the sheriff in each county at every Assize of persons who are thus qualified whom he has summoned. While there is no fixed number, forty-eight is usual at Assizes and thirty-six at Sessions. The clerk calls twelve names from this panel, and the defendant then may challenge any of the jurors.

Although in the United States two or more days may be spent in challenges to the jury, challenges are now rare in England.[42] Challenges may be made to the whole panel, that is to say to the "array," where the sheriff has constituted it in an unfair manner as by choosing jurors on the ground of their religion. Such challenge must be in writing. They may also be made to the polls, that is to say, to individual jurors. An individual may be challenged either for cause shown or peremptorily, that is to say, without showing cause. A challenge for cause may be made *propter affectum,* that is to say, for being closely related to the defendant; *propter defectum,* that is to say, for infancy or alienage; and *propter delictum,* that is to say, for having been convicted of an infamous crime. Challenge for cause may be made by both the Crown and the defendant. Peremptory challenges, on the other hand, can be made only by the defendant.[43] The defendant can so

---

fined to the middle and upper classes. See also Radzinowicz and Turner, The Modern Approach to Criminal Law (1945) c.7.

[42] Moore, "Voir Dire Examination of Jurors: The English Practice" (1928) 16 Geo.L.J. 438; Note (1922) 31 Yale L.J. 514, 770; Lawson and Keedy, "Criminal Procedure in England" (1910) 1 J.Crim.L. 595, 609. Likewise in Canada it seldom takes more than half an hour to obtain a jury. Riddell, "Criminal Law in Canada" (1926) 10 Minn.L.Rev. 557, 561.

[43] Under the Defense (Administration of Justice) Regulations, 1940,

challenge only in cases of treason and felony, being allowed thirty-five challenges in cases of treason and twenty in cases of felony.[44] In misdemeanor cases, however, the defendant is usually allowed to exercise the privilege possessed by the Crown in all criminal cases of requiring any jurors to "stand by," that is to say, not to serve unless a full jury cannot be made up without them.[45]

After challenge the jury is then sworn. In cases of felony or treason the indictment is read over to them. This process is called "charging" them with the inquiry concerning the prisoner. The counsel for the prosecution then addresses the jury for the purpose of directing their minds to the chief issues in dispute, telling them what evidence he plans to introduce, and explaining its bearings upon the case.[46] This process is called "opening" the indictment.[47] His function is said to be "to assist the jury in arriving at the truth," whereas the attorney for the de-

---

R. 13, the right of peremptory challenge was suspended. Harris and Wilshere, Principles and Practice of the Criminal Law (17th ed.1943) 459.

[44] The jurors are sworn separately to give the defendant a full opportunity to challenge each of them. In misdemeanor cases, the jurors are usually sworn in groups of four. Originally the defendant could challenge 35 jurors peremptorily in all felony cases. This was reduced to 20, except in treason cases, in 1533. 1 Stephen, A History of the Criminal Law of England (1883) 302.

[45] Reg. v. Blakeman (1850) 3 C. and K. 97.

[46] There is no such address in Scottish procedure. Keedy, "Criminal Procedure in Scotland" (1913) 3 J.Crim.L. 834, 836. The Scottish rule is intended to protect the defendant.

[47] Kenny, Outlines of Criminal Law (15th ed.1942) 568-569; Howard, Criminal Justice in England (1931) 370-371. See Hewart, C. J. (1933) 25 Cr. App. R., 115. While counsel for the defendant is generally allowed more latitude in examination and cross-examination and in speeches to the jury, nevertheless in practice "there is considerably less tendency on the part of the defense counsel to impede the course of the trial, get error on the record which may serve as the possible basis for an appeal, and otherwise obscure the issues, than in the United States." Howard, Criminal Justice in England (1931) 372.

fendant should do everything he honorably can to protect the interests of the defendant.[48] He must not present arguments that do not carry weight in his own mind, nor endeavor to bar any legal evidence that would be of importance to the defendant.

After he has concluded his address, the prosecuting counsel then calls his witnesses, one after another. Each is or may be examined in chief, cross-examined and re-examined.[49] On the completion of the evidence for the Crown, counsel for the defendant may submit that it is not such as could reasonably satisfy the jury that the accusation has been made out; and he therefore asks the judge to withdraw the case from the jury.

If the request is refused or if none is made, next comes the presentation of the defense. If the defendant has no witnesses to call, other than character witnesses, he may, if he wishes, give evidence under oath and be cross-examined. Beginning in 1872, there were a series of statutes enabling defendants to give evidence in the case of a few specified crimes; ultimately a general enactment was passed, the Criminal Evidence Act, 1898.[50] A defendant may make an unsworn statement instead of giving testimony. After the defendant testifies or declines to do so, he may call character witnesses if any. Then if he has no counsel, he may address the jury in his own defense. If he has counsel, the prosecuting attorney may, if there is adequate cause, make a second speech, summing up the

[48] Until defendants were permitted to have counsel, cross-examination of the witnesses for the prosecution was trifling and of little importance. 1 Stephen, A History of the Criminal Law of England (1883) 431.

[49] Kenny, Outlines of Criminal Law (15th ed.1942) 412-415, 569.

[50] 61 & 62 Vict., c.36. See Kenny, Outlines of Criminal Law (15th ed. 1942) 474; Archbold, Criminal Pleading, Evidence and Practice (30th ed. 1938) 202.

Crown's evidence and commenting on the prisoner's own evidence if any.[51] Then the counsel for the defendant addresses the jury, thus having the last word.[52]

If, however, the defendant has witnesses, as soon as the witnesses for the Crown have finished, his counsel or he "opens" his case. Then his witnesses are examined, cross-examined, and re-examined. His counsel or he then makes a second speech, summing up his defense.[53] The prosecuting counsel then makes the final speech in reply.

The judge takes a very active part during the entire trial.[54] If he is of the opinion at any time during the trial that the evidence for the Crown does not justify conviction, he may direct the jury to return a verdict of not guilty at once and thereby terminate the case. He may call witnesses who have not been called by either the defendant or the Crown.[55] He usually takes longhand notes of the testimony as it is being given, which he uses in his summing up and as an official record of the proceedings.[56] Under a directory provision of the Criminal Appeal Act, 1907, shorthand notes are to be taken of the proceedings

[51] This was provided for in 1865 by 28 & 29 Vict., c.18, § 2. The theory was that facts might come out in evidence which ought to be explained and commented upon by the counsel for the Crown before the defense was made. 1 Stephen, A History of the Criminal Law of England (1883) 450; Archbold, Criminal Pleading, Evidence and Practice (30th ed.1938) 200.

[52] This is not the American rule. 23 C.J.S., § 983, p.328; Beale, Criminal Pleading and Practice (1899) 289.

[53] This right was first given in 1865 by 28 & 29 Vict., c.18, § 2.

[54] The jurors are by no means subservient, however. Howard "American Criminal Justice and the 'Rules of the Game'" (1938) 24 A.B.A.J. 347, 351.

[55] Rex v. Harris (1927) 2 K.B. 587. This is said to be a survival of the former "inquisitorial" character of English criminal trials. Kenny, Outlines of Criminal Law (15th ed.1942) 570, n.1.

[56] Howard, Criminal Justice in England (1931) 376. This practice was of slow growth. 1 Stephen, A History of the Criminal Law of England (1883) 377.

at the trial of any person on indictment, coroner's inquisition, or criminal information, who if convicted is entitled or may be authorized to appeal under that act.[57] Speeches by counsel are not included unless the judge so orders to make clear what issues were raised.

Following these full statements of the cases for each side comes the summing up by the trial judge.[58] He directs the jury as to any points of law that are involved in the case. He also addresses them as to the relevancy and value of the evidence. The creation of the Court of Criminal Appeal has meant the development of improved standards that the summing up be not only accurate but also adequate. The judge may request the jury to answer specific questions of fact, but they may refuse and render a general verdict if they wish. He may comment on the failure of the defendant to give evidence under oath, though counsel for the prosecution is not permitted to do so.[59] While it has been asserted that English juries do as they are told,[60] the court does not order the jury to find a verdict conforming to his wishes, but summarizes and analyzes the evidence in such a fashion as usually to command their respect.

[57] Archbold, Criminal Pleading, Evidence and Practice (30th ed.1938) 198; Kenny, Outlines of Criminal Law (15th ed.1942) 588. The reports of trials by good shorthand writers dates back to the decade from 1678 to 1688. 1 Stephen, A History of the Criminal Law of England (1883) 383.

[58] Lawson and Keedy, "Criminal Procedure in England" (1911) 1 J. Crim.L. 748, 756-757. It dates back as far as 1348. 3 Holdsworth, History of English Law (1923) 614. In the seventeenth century the prisoner was not entitled to instructions to the jury. 1 Stephen, A History of the Criminal Law of England (1883) 403.

[59] In Canada neither judge nor prosecuting attorney may comment on the defendant's failure to testify. Riddell, "Administration of Criminal Law in Canada" (1934) 17 J. Am. Jud. Soc. 141, 144.

[60] Elder, "Trial by Jury: Is It Passing?" Harper's Magazine (April 1928) 578.

After the summing up, the jury then considers its verdict.[61] The verdict must be unanimous.[62] The jury may in their discretion return a general verdict of guilty or not guilty, or a special verdict pronouncing on the facts alone.[63] The verdict may find the defendant guilty or not guilty on all counts, or guilty on some but not guilty on others. The jurors may attach a recommendation of mercy or any other recommendation they think fitting. Modern statutes permit the jury in a few exceptional cases to convict of the crime which has in fact been proved, though it is not the crime charged in the indictment, or to convict of an offense other than that which the evidence has established.[64] The court may direct the jury to reconsider its verdict or may discharge them if they are unable to agree. In the event of disagreement after a second trial there is usually no further prosecution. In practice the jury con-

[61] After the jury has been sworn they may not leave the box without the court's consent. By Section 1 of the Juries Detention Act, 1897, they may, in all cases except treason and murder, be permitted to separate at any time before they begin to consider their verdict. During the Second World War the court might, if it thought fit, allow them to separate even in those excepted cases. Harris and Wilshere, Principles and Practice of the Criminal Law (17th ed.1943) 459-460, 464. After they begin to consider their verdict, they may not separate without leave of the court.

[62] Unanimity was not established until the latter half of the fourteenth century. 2 Pollock and Maitland, History of English Law (2d ed.1905) 625-627. Stephen regards a unanimous verdict as essential and would possibly relax the requirement only to the extent of allowing a large majority to acquit after a certain time. 1 Stephen, A History of the Criminal Law of England (1883) 304-305. The Criminal Justice Act, 1925, Section 15, provides against the death or illness of a juror, or of two jurors, during a trial. The remainder may act, if the prosecutor and the defendant consent in writing.

[63] Special verdicts are rare. For a modern instance, see Reg. v. Dudley (1884) 14 Q.B.D. 273.

[64] Kenny, Outlines of Criminal Law (15th ed.1942) 553-555, 572. Of course one cannot be indicted for murder and found guilty of theft.

victs about two thirds of those tried and acquits one third.[65]

There are four classes of criminal offenses in England today: (1) indictable crimes that must be tried on indictment before a jury; (2) indictable offenses that can be tried either on indictment or in summary courts; (3) summary offenses in which the accused can demand trial on indictment; and (4) petty offenses triable only in the summary courts.[66] All the most serious crimes are in the first group. Cases in the second group are very numerous, the most important being stealing and related offenses. All offenses other than homicide by persons under seventeen are triable in summary courts. The third class includes offenses punishable with more than three months' imprisonment.

Possibly the most important development in the administration of criminal justice in England during the last half century has been the obsolescence of the petit jury through the enlargement of the powers of the courts of summary jurisdiction to hear and determine indictable offenses.[67] This has doubtless resulted in speedier, cheaper, and more efficient trials and the elimination of unwholesome publicity in certain classes of cases. But English writers and High Court judges have pointed out that the practice of dealing summarily with serious offenses is be-

65 Kenny, Outlines of Criminal Law (15th ed.1942) 572-573.

66 Jackson, The Machinery of Justice in England (1940) 85.

67 Howard, Criminal Justice in England (1931) 319. In England in 1926, 69,695 defendants charged with indictable offenses were dealt with in courts of summary jurisdiction and only 7,924 were committed for jury trial at the higher courts. Howard, Criminal Justice in England (1931) 407. The history of jury trial with special reference to summary cases is set forth by Frankfurter and Corcoran, "Petty Federal Offenses and the Constitutional Guaranty of Trial by Jury" (1926) 39 Harv.L.Rev. 917, 922-934.

coming far too common.[68] Many cases are dealt with summarily which, because of their importance or difficulty, should be tried before a jury. In order to bring cases within summary jurisdiction, there is a tendency to prosecute for lesser degrees of a crime; for example, to prosecute for larceny instead of burglary. "Trial by jury probably leads to many guilty persons being acquitted, but undoubtedly provides a greater safeguard for an innocent defendant than trial before a bench of lay magistrates."[69] The penalties are lighter in summary trials, and there is no delay.[70] In cases of trial by jury, the defendant must wait often in jail until the next Assizes or Quarter Sessions.

Indigent defendants are granted legal aid under the Poor Prisoners' Defense Act, 1930.[71] This act removes the onerous condition in the 1903 Act making it necessary for a defendant to have disclosed his defense to the justices who committed him; and the defendant must have pleaded not guilty.[72] Justices are required to grant a legal

[68] Kenny, Outlines of Criminal Law (15th ed.1942) 518-519; Rex v. Bennett (1928) 20 Cr. App. R. 188.

[69] Kenny, Outlines of Criminal Law (15th ed.1942) 519. As to the obsolescence of the jury in Canada, see Crouse, "Trial Juries in Canadian Criminal Practice" (1935) 23 Geo.L.J. 433; Woods, "Criminal Law Administration in Canada" (1936) 14 Tex.L.Rev. 337; Beaumont, "Summary Trials of Indictable Offenses in the Province of Alberta, Canada" (1938) 28 J.Crim.L. 684. Since about 1910 under the Canadian practice "it is possible in most indictable offenses for a defendant to 'elect' to be tried by the judge alone." Moley, Our Criminal Courts (1930) 127. As to proposed changes in Canadian procedure, see Cameron, "The Criminal Code" (1927) 5 Can.B.Rev. 54.

[70] Jackson, The Machinery of Justice in England (1940) 91.

[71] 20 & 21 Geo. V, c.32. The act is set forth in Archbold, Criminal Pleading, Evidence and Practice (30th ed.1928) 167-173.

[72] Howard, Criminal Justice in England (1931) 346, 364. The 1903 Act was rarely made use of except in the case of very serious crimes, such as murder. In the average case a poor defendant was not assured legal aid.

aid certificate to any poor person where it appears to be in the interests of justice that he should have free legal aid, either by reason of the seriousness of the charge or of exceptional circumstances. This applies to all cases, whether they are to be finally dealt with by the justices or are to be committed to trial by jury. When a legal aid certificate is granted, the defendant is entitled to have a solicitor assigned to him. A defense certificate must be granted to a poor person committed upon a charge of murder and may be granted to poor persons committed on other charges if the interests of justice require it. The defense certificate entitles the defendant to have solicitor and counsel assigned to him.

The Poor Prisoners' Defense Act seems broad enough to provide free legal aid in all proper cases. But it has not worked well in practice.[73] There is a very high proportion of refusals of applications, although offers of assistance are rarely declined. For trials on indictments in 1937, 1,693 certificates were given, and 161 defenses without certificates, while the total number of persons tried on indictment was 9,083. But only 499 of the prisoners received free legal aid at the preliminary examination which led to their commitment. The record is even worse as to cases tried summarily. There were 315 free defenses in 840,948 cases tried; 19,000 persons were sent to prison without the option of a fine. Many defendants do not

The harsh situation of the defendant prior to the twentieth century has been pointed out. "It must be remembered that most persons accused of crime are poor, stupid, and helpless." 1 Stephen, A History of the Criminal Law of England (1883) 442. "The safeguards which the experience of centuries has provided in our own days are, I think, sufficient to afford considerable protection to a man who has sense, spirit, and above all, plenty of money; but I do not think it possible to prevent a good deal of injustice where these conditions fail." *Ibid.* 383.

[73] Jackson, The Machinery of Justice in England (1940) 123-125, 253.

know of the facilities for free legal aid. Conspicuous notices ought to be posted in thc courts.

Dignity and decorum in the courtroom is assured in an English trial by the Criminal Justice Act, 1925, which makes it an offense, punishable by a fine of £50, to sketch for publication, or to photograph, in any court whether criminal or civil, any of the persons concerned in a judicial proceeding.[74] Moreover, the courts exercise authority to prevent the newspapers from prejudging a case. "From the day the prosecution is begun until the jury renders its verdict a newspaper is not permitted to comment upon the evidence or express opinions upon the guilt or innocence of the prisoner. Anything beyond a fair report of the evidence, as it is given in the magistrate's or the trial court, is forbidden. For a newspaper to publish a comment upon pending judicial proceedings, either criminal or civil, which comment would be likely to influence the minds of persons who might become jurors, is a contempt of court and is severely punished." [75]

4. Importance of Trial

It has been seen that a very large proportion of cases are eliminated before reaching the trial court.[76] Even in

[74] Kenny, Outlines of Criminal Law (15th ed.1942) 565, n.4.

[75] Lawson and Keedy, "Criminal Procedure in England" (1914) 1 J. Crim.L. 595, 611. See also Robbins, "The Hauptmann Trial in the Light of English Criminal Procedure" (1935) 21 A.B.A.J. 300.

[76] "It is said that, in New York City, only 47 per cent of prosecutions reach jury trial; in St. Louis, 13 per cent; Chicago, 3.8 per cent; Cleveland, 13.6 per cent; and Cincinnati, 11.8 per cent." Wickersham, "The Program of the Commission on Law Observance and Enforcement" (1930) 16 A.B.A.J. 654, 658. "Surveys of the administration of criminal justice, which have been made since 1920, have revealed that about eighty-five per cent of the cases of arrests for crime are disposed of before trial." Miller, J., "Lawyers and the Administration of Criminal Justice" (1934)

the trial court the elimination through jury acquittals is generally less than through other modes. "The percentages of all eliminations in the trial court or trial-court stage represented by jury acquittals are: New York City (1925) 36.7 per cent; Chicago, 11.5 per cent; Cleveland, 24.8 per cent; Cincinnati, 38 per cent; and St. Louis, 27.3 per cent." [77] As Mr. Alfred Bettman states: "The statistics point to the conclusion that, in the attention given to the jury trial and to questions of trial procedure, there has been and still is a mistaken emphasis." [78]

In view of the many eliminations prior to the stage of trial and in view of the many pleas of guilty followed by sentence without any trial, one might be tempted to discount the importance of the trial. But, though trials may be few, it is the stage of trial which receives the most pub-

---

20 A.B.A.J. 77, 78. "Of all felony cases originating in arrest in New York City, about two per cent are eliminated by the police, 57 per cent in the preliminary hearing, 12 per cent in the grand jury, 8 per cent in the trial court, and 5 per cent after guilt is established." Report of the New York Crime Commission (1928). "Eliminations. As a matter of fact in the state as a whole in only 4.45 per cent of the arrests for felonies do the cases ever come before the juries for trial and the remaining 95.55 per cent are disposed of on pleas of guilty or disappear on account of the failure of the state's attorney to prosecute before the magistrate on the preliminary hearing, the failure of proof before that magistrate sufficient to induce him to hold the defendant to the grand jury, a dismissal of the complaint by the state's attorney before the committing magistrate, the failure of the Grand Jury to indict even if the defendant is held over, and, even if an indictment is returned, the dismissal or *nolle prosequi* by the state's attorney." Bruce, "The Administration of Criminal Justice in Illinois" (1929) 19 J.Crim.L. No. 4 (A Summary of the Crime Survey of the Illinois Association for Criminal Justice) 27. During 1938 and 1939 there were no felony trials in Rhode Island. Note (1940) 31 J.Crim.L. 475. As to the percentage of defendants tried who are convicted, see Warner and Cabot, Judges and Law Reform (1936) 69. The percentage runs from 90 in Wisconsin to 42.5 in Chicago.

[77] Nat. Com. on Law Obs. and Enf., Report on Prosecution (1931) 64.

[78] *Ibid.* 65.

licity. Cases coming to trial are often of a very serious character. "The trial process is important both for the results it accomplishes in sorting the innocent from the guity and also for its effect upon other factors in the criminal administration. Where trials are prompt, fair, and accurate, police are encouraged in their work of apprehension, whereas a system which lets many guilty men pass through its net discourages effort. The effect is similar all along the line." [79] On the whole the trial court does a good job. "The real complaint of the public is not with trial procedure, but with what happens before and after trial." [80]

Many reformers of the criminal law feel that modern trial procedure is unduly favorable to the defendant, hence they propose to lighten the burden of the prosecutor during the trial. "Today the chief remedies advocated are to require notice of an alibi defense to prevent surprise, to permit the judge or prosecutor to comment on the defendant's failure to testify, and to permit less than unanimous verdicts and waiver of trial by jury." [81] It is easy to overstate the value of such reforms. Possibly of much greater value would be more thorough preparation on the part of the prosecuting attorney and of the police.[82]

5. Change of Venue

In the ordinary situation a crime must be tried in the county in which it is committed. Historically, this was

[79] Warner and Cabot, "Changes in the Administration of Criminal Justice During the Past Fifty Years" (1937) 50 Harv.L.Rev. 583, 592-593.

[80] *Ibid.* 593.

[81] Warner and Cabot, "Changes in the Administration of Criminal Justice During the Past Fifty Years" (1937) 50 Harv.L.Rev. 583, 589.

[82] Warner and Cabot, Judges and Law Reform (1936) 76-91.

based on the concept that a jury of the vicinage was the source rather than the arbiter of the evidence. Today the basis is the fact that venue must be laid somewhere and the further fact that witnesses are usually most available at the place of commission.[83] In certain cases, however, it may be undesirable that trial be held in a particular county or district because there is a likelihood that prejudice will render the trial unfair to either the defendant or the prosecution. The race of the defendant, the publicity given to the crime, political, economic, and personal factors, or the previous history of the case may induce the community to form preconceptions which impair its ability to decide impartially. The remedies are change of venue to another county within the same state, or in some cases removal to the federal courts, or habeas corpus proceedings in the federal courts.

Where it is the prosecution which seeks a change of venue, the right to such change is not so clear as where it is at the request of the defendant.[84] Statutes expressly giving the right to the defendant without mentioning the prosecution may by implication deny it to the prosecution.[85] In most states, however, there are statutes expressly conferring the right on the prosecution. If the state constitution gives the defendant the right of "trial by jury of the county" of commission of the crime, there can be no trial

[83] In some cases convenience will call for trial elsewhere. United States v. Parker, 19 F. Supp. 450, 459, (D.N.J. 1937), aff'd., 103 F. (2d) 857 (C.C.A. 3d, 1939), cert. denied, 307 U.S. 642 (1939). Cf. Rev. Stat., § 789 (1875), 28 U.S.C. § 101 (1934).

[84] (1921) 69 U. of Pa.L.Rev. 361, (1932) 17 Iowa L.Rev. 399, (1937) 25 Geo.L.J. 1036, (1932) 76 A.L.R. 1034. The prosecution had a right of removal at common law. See Rex v. Harris, 3 Burr. 1330, 1334 (K.B. 1762).

[85] (1939) 52 Harv.L.Rev. 1023. See "Defects in Criminal Justice" (1925) 11 A.B.A.J. 297, 298.

elsewhere unless the defendant consents.[86] But if the constitution simply requires a jury of the "vicinage" or "county" or "trial by jury" without more, the result is different.[87] As a matter of logic and abstract fairness the prosecution should have the right. The right should be conditional on protection of indigent defendants by payment of additional costs for the transportation of defendant's witnesses by the prosecution.[88] Before granting a change to the prosecution, the court should ascertain that the new county is not prejudiced against the defendant.[89]

Where it is the defendant who seeks the change, he must follow certain procedures varying from state to state.[90] He must apply to the trial judge and notify the prosecution within a certain time before trial or after indictment. The time limitation may result in hardship since often the defendant, possibly because of the prejudice warranting a change of venue, has not had the assistance of an attorney until shortly before trial.[91] In some states he must accompany his application with affidavits by a number of "credible persons." This will result in hardship in states holding that this necessitates a person whose

[86] Wheeler v. State, 24 Wis. 52 (1869); State v. Greer, 22 W.Va. 800 (1883). *Contra:* Hewitt v. State, 43 Fla. 194, 30 So. 795 (1901); State v. Holloway, 19 N.M. 528, 146 Pac. 1066 (1914).

[87] People v. Peterson, 93 Mich. 27, 52 N.W. 1039 (1892); Commonwealth v. Hargis, 237 Ky. 591, 36 S.W. (2d) 8 (1931). *Contra:* People v. Powell, 87 Cal. 348, 25 Pac. 481 (1891).

[88] People v. Baker, 3 Abb. Pr. 42 (N.Y. 1856).

[89] Smith v. Commonwealth, 108 Ky. 53, 55 S.W. 718 (1900).

[90] (1941) 54 Harv.L.Rev. 679, 681. See also Blume, "The Place of Trial of Criminal Cases: Constitutional Vicinage and Venue" (1944) 43 Mich. L.Rev. 59.

[91] In Donner v. Dunaway, 53 F. (2d) 586 (C.C.A. 5th, 1931), counsel was appointed one hour before trial; and in Avery v. Alabama, 308 U.S. 444 (1940), three days before trial.

knowledge of the tenor of feeling throughout the county enables him broadly to affirm that the defendant cannot get a fair trial.[92] The prejudice may be so great that there will not be a sufficient number of persons who will swear to it.[93] Moreover, the prosecution is generally allowed to interpose counter-affidavits. .These should be by disinterested parties, although opposing affidavits by the district attorney and the sheriff have been allowed.[94] The court should not be too readily influenced by the mere number of counter-affidavits.[95]

If the prosecution does not counteract the affidavits of the defendant, he will probably be granted a change of venue.[96] But if the prosecution insists, a hearing will be necessary at which oral testimony will be taken. The burden of proof is on the defendant.[97] The most liberal test laid down is that it is sufficient to show "a strong probability that bias exists in the community."[98] The judge usually acts on his own knowledge.[99] Such knowledge should be a factor in granting but not in denying a change since he can often sense the existence of prejudice, yet not be sure of its absence.

The right of appeal in case of denial of a change is not very helpful to the defendant since no appeal lies until after trial and conviction. The appellate court will be

92 Tillman v. State, 121 Ark. 322, 181, S.W. 890 (1915). The more common holding is that "credible" means merely competent to be a witness. Freleigh v. State, 8 Mo. 606 (1844).

93 Fitzgerald v. Commonwealth, 30 Ky. L 349, 98 S.W. 319 (1909).

94 People v. Hall, 330 Cal. 166, 30 P. (2d) 23 (1934).

95 In Jamison v. People, 145 Ill. 357, 34 N.E. 486 (1893) there were 337. So large a number may itself indicate prejudice.

96 Miller v. Commonwealth, 248 Ky. 717, 59 S.W. (2d) 969 (1933).

97 Maxwell v. Commonwealth, 169 Va. 886, 193 S.E. 507 (1937).

98 People v. Nathan, 139 Misc. 345, 346, 249 N.Y. Supp. 395, 397 (Sup.Ct. 1931).

99 People v. Swift, 178 Mich. 473, 138 N.W. 662 (1912).

slow to act since the granting of a change is a matter of discretion.[100] If the appellate court reverses and remands, such remand, though in practice made to the same court, should be to another court.

If change of venue is granted, the case is sent to another county, usually within the discretion of the trial judge.[101] Some states, however, require the nearest county without prejudice, and others a county within a limited contiguous area. The latter may be unfair to the defendant as the prejudice may be widespread. Most states permit only one change of venue,[102] a rule which seems too rigid. The original prosecuting attorney continues the prosecution in the second county.[103]

The existing machinery for change of venue in the state courts may be improved by various state remedies. A few states provide that a requested change be granted automatically in capital cases. Perhaps such rule should be extended to felonies punishable by long imprisonment. Another safeguard is to vest the trial judge with power to order a change on his own motion without the concurrence of either counsel.[104]

Federal remedies also perhaps exist. The defendant may appeal from the highest state court to the United States Supreme Court on the ground of a violation of due process.[105] Or the defendant may seek a writ of habeas corpus in the federal district court.[106] If the case has not

[100] Note (1930) 21 J.Crim.L. 449.

[101] Commonwealth v. Kelly, 266 Ky. 662, 99 S.W. (2d) 774 (1936).

[102] Lee v. State, 164 Md. 550, 165 Atl. 614 (1933) cert. denied, 290 U.S. 639 (1933).

[103] Baker and DeLong, "The Prosecuting Attorney, Powers and Duties in Criminal Procedure" (1934) 24 J.Crim.L. 1025, 1027.

[104] Parrish v. State, 134 Tex. Cr. 545, 116 S.W. (2d) 1706 (1938).

[105] 28 U.S.C., §§ 451, 453 (1934).

[106] 28 U.S.C., § 74 (1934).

gone to trial, the defendant may ask for removal to a federal court.[107] However, isolated judicial action does not warrant removal.

In general in the United States, criminal cases are tried in the county in which the offense was committed. State constitutional provisions guarantee such right to the defendant,[108] hence there is not the same possibility of altering the place of trial that there is in England unless the defendant consents.[109] With respect to federal court trials, Article III, Section 2, Clause 3 of the United States Constitution provides that "Trial shall be held in the state where the said crime shall have been committed," and the Sixth Amendment provides that "In all criminal prosecutions, the accused shall enjoy the right to a speedy and public trial by an impartial jury of the state and district wherein the crime shall have been committed." [110]

Section 240 of the Institute Code is simply carrying out the constitutional mandate when it provides that in "all criminal prosecutions the trial shall be in the county where the offense was committed unless otherwise provided in this Code." The Institute Code and constitutional provisions make reference only to trial and do not refer specifically to proceedings before trial, although in practice the proceedings before trial are also conducted in the county in which the crime was committed.[111] Rule 18 of

[107] Virginia v. Rives, 100 U.S. 313 (1879). A state statute must stand in the way to warrant removal.

[108] See A.L.I. Code of Crim. Proc. (1930) commentaries 688-694.

[109] As has been seen in England, the defendant may be proceeded against, indicted, and tried in the county or place in which he was apprehended. Archbold, Criminal Pleading, Evidence and Practice (30th ed. 1938) 24.

[110] See Dobie, "Venue in Criminal Cases in the United States District Court" (1926) 12 Va.L.Rev. 287.

[111] In some states there are statutes covering not only trial but other

the Federal Rules of Criminal Prócedure is more specific. It provides "Except as otherwise permitted by statute or by these rules, the prosecution shall be had in a district in which the offense was committed, but if the district consists of two or more divisions, the trial shall be had in a division in which the offence was committed." Rule 19 provides with respect to a federal district having more than one division that the "arraignment may be had, a plea entered, the trial conducted or sentence imposed, if the defendant consents, in any division and at any time." Rule 20 goes a step further by providing for criminal proceedings in a federal district other than that of the commission of the crime. A defendant arrested in a district other than that of indictment may state in writing, after receiving a copy of the indictment, that he wishes to plead guilty or *nolo contendere* and to have his case disposed of in the district of arrest. The written approval of the United States attorney for both districts involved is also necessary. But if the defendant pleads not guilty, the proceeding must be completed in the district of indictment.

Section 255 of the Institute Code provides for a change of venue upon the application of either the defendant or the prosecution "on the ground that a fair and impartial trial cannot be had for any reason other than the interest or prejudice of the trial judge." Rule 21(a) of the Federal Rules of Criminal Procedure allows a change of venue to another district or division upon motion of the defendant "if the court is satisfied that there exists in the district or division where the prosecution is pending so great a prejudice against the defendant that he cannot obtain a fair and impartial trial in that district or division."

---

stages in criminal proceedings. A.L.I. Code of Crim. Proc. (1930) commentaries 695-696.

Application for change of venue is usually required to be made at some time before trial. Section 259 of the Institute Code provides that it may be made "only before the jury is sworn, or, where trial by jury is waived, before any evidence is received." Rule 22 of the Federal Rules of Criminal Procedure provides that it may be made "at or before arraignment or at such other time as the court or these rules may prescribe."

6. Change of Judge Before Trial

At common law, a trial before a disqualified judge was not void but voidable.[112] The defect was waived unless timely objection was made.[113] Likewise under most statutes, if the objection is not taken at the earliest opportunity, the proceedings are treated as valid.[114] The defect may be so serious as to violate due process. It was so held in a case tried before a justice of the peace who was given the costs as part of his salary, and such costs were paid by the defendant only in case of conviction.[115]

Many states have provided by statute for recusation or disqualifying of judges for bias.[116] In some the judge may

[112] Fowler v. Brooks, 64 N.H. 423, 13 Atl. 417 (1887); (1863) 84 Am. Dec. 114, 126.

[113] 1 Freeman, Judgments (4th ed.1892) §§ 144-146.

[114] (1928) 41 Harv.L.Rev. 915; Rottschaefer, Handbook of American Constitutional Law (1939) 808-809.

[115] Tumey v. Ohio, 273 U.S. 510, 47 Sup.Ct. 437, 71 L.Ed. 749, 50 A.L.R. 1243 (1927), 40 Harv.L.Rev. 1149, 35 Yale L.J. 1171. As to criminal cases in which the existence of the court or the title to office of a judge is challenged, see Field, "The Effect of an Unconstitutional Statute in the Law of Public Officers: Effect on Official Status" (1939) 13 Minn.L.Rev. 439, 465-470.

[116] Putnam, J., "Recusation" (1923) 9 Corn.L.Q. 1. Under Section 299 of a bill introduced though not passed in Illinois in 1937, provision for change of magistrate for preliminary examination because of prejudice upon application under oath was made.

himself decide, subject to appeal, the existence of bias on his part.[117] In others, as in the federal courts, the judge may pass on the legal sufficiency of the affidavit, but, if on its face it is sufficient, it disqualifies him even though the statements therein are wholly false.[118] But to be legally sufficient they must be such that a reasonable mind may fairly infer bias.[119] The courts should not be only impartial but above suspicion of partiality.[120] Belief in prejudice, like prejudice itself, is a state of mind which often cannot be attributed to any specific set of facts. Hence, in a third group of jurisdictions, an unsupported assertion of bias is sufficient.[121] The federal rule appears to be a reasonable compromise as between two extremes.[122] Possibly an even better solution would be the submission of the affidavits directly to a superior court on an application for a writ of prohibition.[123]

There are two possible tests for bias or prejudice of the court. Under the "real prejudice" rule, no person should be brought to trial in the presence of actual bias.[124]

[117] Notes (1916) 16 Col.L.Rev. 162, (1920) 20 Col.L.Rev. 594, (1941) 51 Yale L.J. 169. At common law the only ground for disqualification was a pecuniary or personal interest in the subject matter of the cause. People v. Williams, 24 Cal. 31 (1864); Notes (1916) 29 Harv.L.Rev. 430, (1920) 20 Col.L.Rev. 594.

[118] Berger v. United States, 255 U.S. 22, 41 Sup.Ct. 230 (1921), 21 Col.L.Rev. 387.

[119] Keown v. Hughes, 265 Fed. 572, 577 (C.C.A. 1st, 1920). While usually prejudice must be personal, prejudice against a class may be so keen as to attach to persons and disqualify. People v. District Court, 60 Colo. 1, 152 Pac. 149 (1915), (1920) 20 Col.L.Rev. 594, 29 Harv.L.Rev. 430.

[120] Garrett v. State, 15 Okla. Crim. 332, 336, 176 Pac. 769 (1918).

[121] Howell v. State, 81 So. 287 (Fla. 1919); Note (1941) 51 Yale L.J. 169, 171-172.

[122] Notes (1921) 21 Col.L.Rev. 387, (1916) 29 Harv.L.Rev. 430. The present trend is toward easier disqualification. Note (1938) 47 Yale L.J. 1403, 1405.

[123] Note (1916) 29 Harv.L.Rev. 430.

[124] Note (1941) 51 Yale L.J. 169, 171.

The reasoning is that there is little likelihood of harm to the interests of a party, unless the judge is in fact prejudiced either against him or in favor of the other party. But it may be unreasonably difficult to show actual prejudice.[125] The test is likely to result in appeals and therefore delay. Moreover, it will not always convince the parties of the fairness of the trial, thus resulting in loss of public confidence. A second test considers whether the circumstances surrounding the trial would create in the mind of the party a reasonable apprehension that he would not receive a fair trial.[126] The advantage of this subjective test is that it increases public confidence in the impartiality of the courts. This test, too, unlike an automatic disqualification, involves the possibility of many appeals.

What about disqualification of judges by peremptory challenges? A California statute permitted any litigant one peremptory challenge of the judge slated to hear any proceeding pending in a municipal or superior court. Even without further action or evidence of disqualification by the challenger, the presiding county judge was required to assign another judge to the case. The statute was found unconstitutional as an excessive delegation of legislative power, on the ground that it permitted an individual litigant to interfere unlawfully with the constitutional prerogatives of the court.[127] This statute carried the trend

[125] In People v. Emmett, 123 Cal. App. 678, 12 P. (2d) 92 (1932), there was an altercation between judge and counsel during the impaneling of a jury, in the course of which the judge stated to counsel that his standing before the courts was not such as to entitle him to any great consideration. The appellate court found no bias demonstrated.

[126] Note (1941) 51 Yale L.J. 169, 172.

[127] Austin v. Lambert, 77 P. (2d) 849 (Cal. Sup.Ct. 1938), 47 Yale L.J. 1403. An automatic disqualification rule exists in England and the British dominions. Notes (1941) 51 Yale L.J. 169, 172, n.66, (1927) 41 Harv.L. Rev. 78. In Russia there may be a challenge of any of the judges upon

toward easier disqualification one step beyond the process of disqualification by simple affidavit. There can be little real difference between an affidavit without proof and a peremptory challenge. In both the operative fact is the demand for removal rather than the actual disqualifying circumstances. The simple affidavit amounts to no more assurance against abuse of the privilege than the peremptory challenge. Limiting the time of filing and the number of challenges would solve the problem.[128]

To be distinguished from change of venue is change of judge. In the latter case the trial will be conducted in the same county but before a different judge. In the former case the trial will be conducted in another county. The Federal Rules of Criminal Procedure contain no provisions on the subject, but the Institute Code does. Under Section 253 of the Code "application for change of judge may be made only before or at the time the case is called for trial."[129] Under Section 250, the defendant or the prosecution "may apply for a change of judge on the ground that a fair and impartial trial cannot be had by reason of the interest or prejudice of the trial judge."[130] Under Section 252, only one such application may be made by any party. Under Section 254, when an application is made, the judge "shall proceed no further in the cause, but a judge who is competent to act shall be substituted for him."

---

the bench, to be passed on by the two colleagues of the challenged judge. Hazard, "Soviet Criminal Procedure" (1941) 15 Tulane L.Rev. 220, 230.

128 Note (1938) 47 Yale L.J. 1403, 1407.

129 The American Law Institute Code of Criminal Procedure provisions are discussed in (1930) 8 Proc. Am. L. Inst. 144-150; (1929) 7 Proc. Am. L. Inst. 155-160.

130 In most courts the prosecution has no right to a change of judges because of prejudice. "Defects in Criminal Justice" (1925) 11 A.B.A.J 297, 298.

7. Absence of Judge

At common law the essential elements of trial by jury were: (1) a jury of twelve men, (2) the presence of a supervising judge with powers to instruct and advise the jury on the law and facts, and (3) a unanimous verdict.[131] The second element is as important as the other two, though there are not so many decisions.[132] The presence of a judge is necessary not only to assemble the jury, administer oaths, enter judgment, and sentence the defendants, but also to instruct the jury on the law, advise them on the facts, and set aside the verdict of guilty if against the law or evidence. Since there can be a waiver of the first and third elements, possibly a waiver should be permitted as to presence of the judge at least as to a part of the proceedings.[133]

It has been said to be the weight of authority that there can be no court without a judge, and that it is his duty to be present during all stages of the trial.[134] Unless the parties consent to his absence there will be ground for re-

[131] Patton v. United States, 281 U.S. 276, 50 Sup.Ct. 253, 74 L.Ed. 854, 70 A.L.R. 263 (1929).

[132] It is discussed in Capital Traction Co. v. Hof, 174 U.S. 1, 19 Sup.Ct. 580 (1899). See also Comments (1905) 5 Col.L.Rev. 476, (1912) 12 Col.L. Rev. 163, (1912) 22 Yale L.J. 165. Where a view is regarded as evidence the judge must be present, and perhaps he should in other cases. Note (1907) 7 Col.L.Rev. 607.

[133] Note (1941) 40 Mich.L.Rev. 113, 114. Absence of the judge for two or three minutes during the argument of defendant's counsel to the jury, when not objected to until after verdict, was not reversible error. Heflin v. United States, 125 Fed. (2d) 700 (C.C.A. 5th, 1942), 21 Neb.L.Rev. 171. See also Note (1912) 12 Col.L.Rev. 163.

[134] People v. Blackburn, 127 Calif. 248 (1899); Turbeville v. State, 56 Miss. 793 (1879); (1912) 22 Yale L.J. 165. See Lehman, "A Critical Survey of Certain Phases of Trial Procedure in Criminal Cases" (1915) 63 U. of Pa.L.Rev. 609, 628-632.

versal.[135] The judge should perhaps even be visibly present at all times.[136] There is some authority, however, that a judge may be out of sight but within hearing and so able to pass on any question that may arise.[137] It has been held that the judge should be present during the summing up of counsel.[138] A number of cases hold that prejudice must be shown to have arisen from the absence of the judge.[139] It has sometimes been held that, if absence is not objected to at the time, there is no error.[140]

8. Substitution of Judge During Trial

In England at common law, judgment could be entered or execution ordered only by the judge who tried the case.[141] In a leading federal decision, the court said that trial by jury in a criminal case means trial before a tribunal "consisting of at least one judge and twelve jurors, all of whom must remain identical from the beginning to the end, and that neither the defendant nor the government can consent to the substitution of judge or jurors." [142] The Patton Case would seem to justify a decision that a

[135] State v. Smith, 49 Conn. 376 (1881).

[136] State v. Beuerman, 59 Kan. 586 (1898); People v. Tupper, 122 Calif. 424 (1898).

[137] Rowe v. People, 26 Colo. 542 (1899); State v. Porter, 105 Iowa 677 (1898).

[138] Hayes v. State, 58 Ga. 35 (1877); Brownlee v. Hewitt, 1 Mo. App. 360 (1876).

[139] Hughes v. State, 149 S.W. 173 (Tex. 1912), 22 Yale L.J. 165.

[140] Pritchett v. State, 92 Ga. 65 (1893).

[141] Commonwealth v. Thompson, 328 Pa. 27, 30, 195 Atl. 115 (1937). See, however, Note (1915) 29 Harv.L.Rev. 83. A substitute judge who had not heard the testimony may not instruct the jury. Commonwealth v. Claney, 113 Pa. Super. 439, 173 Atl. 840 (1934), 83 U. of Pa.L.Rev. 94.

[142] Freeman v. United States, 227 F. 732, 759 (C.C.A. 2d, 1915), 29 Harv.L.Rev. 83.

substituted judge may receive the verdict of the jury, at least if the defendant consents.[143]

On the whole the practice of substituting judges is not to be recommended except in cases of necessity. It may be appropriate at certain stages in the proceedings, as before trial has actually begun or after the jury has retired.[144] In a leading Iowa case[145] after the jury was instructed and had retired, the judge announced that he was going to another town to sit for a judge who was in poor health, but that a second judge would be available to receive the verdict. Defendant's counsel did not object. After this judge had left, the jury desired further instructions, but the defendant objected and they were denied. The second judge received the unqualified verdict of the jury convicting the defendant. It was held on appeal that the defendant had waived his right to have the same judge preside over the trial, and that there was no reversible error unless the defendant made an affirmative showing of prejudice.

Rule 25 of the Federal Rules of Criminal Procedure

143 Note (1941) 40 Mich.L.Rev. 113, 114.

144 Commonwealth v. Thompson, 328 Pa. 27, 195 Atl. 115 (1937); State v. Sereg, 296 N.W. 231 (Iowa, 1941), 41 Mich.L.Rev. 113. In State v. McCray, 189 Iowa 1239, 179 N.W. 627 (1920), (1921) 21 Col.L.Rev. 199, (1921) 30 Yale L.J. 533, (1921) 6 Iowa L.Bull. 118, it was held that defendant might consent to a change of judges in the middle of the trial, where the second judge had familiarized himself with the record. *Contra:* Bland v. People, 41 N.Y. 604 (1870); Commonwealth v. Claney, 113 Pa. Super. 439, 173 Atl. 840 (1934). See 114 A.L.R. 432 (1938).

145 State v. Sereg, 296 N.W. 231 (Iowa, 1941), 40 Mich.L.Rev. 113. Substitution at the time of argument to the jury by stipulation of the parties was upheld in Simons v. United States, 119 F. (2d) 539 (C.C.A. 9th, 1941), (1942) 21 Neb.L.Rev. 171. Substitution to hear a motion for new trial is proper. People v. McConnell, 155 Ill. 192, 40 N.E. 608 (1895); as it is to impose sentence. Lamphere v. State, 114 Wis. 193, 89 N.W. 128 (1902).

deals with the disability of the judge. The rule does not depart from the principle that the judge must be present at all stages of the trial but provides rather for a substitution of judges after a verdict or finding of guilt. Substitution at an earlier stage is not permitted. Based to a considerable extent on Rule 63 of the Federal Rules of Civil Procedure, it provides: "If by reason of absence from the district, death, sickness or other disability the judge before whom the defendant has been tried is unable to perform the duties to be performed by a court after a verdict or finding of guilt, any other judge regularly sitting in or assigned to the court may perform those duties; but if such other judge is satisfied that he cannot perform those duties because he did not preside at the trial or for any other reason, he may in his discretion grant a new trial."

9. Right to a Speedy Trial

The provisions of state constitutions granting a speedy trial are usually supplemented by directory statutes stating the time after indictment within which criminal prosecutions must be tried.[146] In a few jurisdictions, these have been construed as being almost statutes of limitations, under which no demand for trial is necessary.[147] But statutes of this sort are usually regarded as requiring a demand and refusal as a condition precedent to the granting of a notice for discharge or writ of habeas corpus. This is on the theory that the claim to the personal right will be

[146] Cal. Pen. Code (Deering, 1931) § 1382; Commentaries on Code of Criminal Procedure (Am. L. Inst. 1930) § 292, p.890. See Notes (1915) 15 Col.L.Rev. 625, (1923) 7 Minn.L.Rev. 575, (1936) 26 J.Crim.L. 937.

[147] State v. Rosenberg, 71 Ore. 389, 142 Pac. 624 (1914); Ex parte Chalfant, 81 W.Va. 93, 93 S.E. 1032 (1917).

considered waived by non-action.[148] Where there is no such supplementary statute, the Michigan court relies in part on the rule of the federal courts where a demand is required before prejudice under the Sixth Amendment may be claimed.[149] It should be noted, however, that in the federal courts the only remedy seemingly available is mandamus to compel a trial, and this procedure necessarily requires prior demand and refusal.[150] In state courts, on the other hand, the defendant is protected by a dismissal of the prosecution.[151] Yet state courts have held, without a limiting statute, that a demand is essential.[152] There is no real hardship on the defendant who may readily protect himself by formally demanding trial.[153] It has been suggested that it be mandatory to bring the defendant to trial within thirty days after the indictment is filed against him.[154]

In this country as in England the defendant is entitled to a speedy trial.[155] Federal and state constitutions ex-

148 Fox v. State, 102 Ark. 393, 144 S.W. 516 (1912); Harris v. Ogden, 44 Okla.Cr. 418, 281 Pac. 316 (1929).

149 Phillip v. United States, 201 Fed. 259 (C.C.A. 8th, 1912); Worthington v. United States, 1 F. (2d) 154 (C.C.A. 7th, 1920), cert. denied, 266 U.S. 626 (1924).

150 Daniel v. United States, 17 F. (2d) 339 (C.C.A. 9th, 1927), cert. denied 274 U.S. 744 (1927). The various remedies available in the various courts are: mandamus, habeas corpus, motion in trial court to dismiss, appeal after conviction. See Note (1936) 26 J.Crim.L. 937. As to Canadian practice, see (1925) 3 Can.B.Rev. 579.

151 Wash. Rev. Stat. (Remington, 1932) § 2312.

152 State v. Banks, 111 La. 22, 35 So. 370 (1903); People v. Foster et al., 246 N.W. 60 (Mich., 1933), 46 Harv.L.Rev. 1027.

153 See State v. McTague, 173 Minn. 153, 216 N.W. 787 (1927).

154 Note (1934) 24 J.Crim.L. 1113.

155 This is designed to protect from capricious and unreasonable delays while imprisoned before trial. Commonwealth v. Carter, (1831) 11 Pick. (Mass.) 277; Note (1907) 7 Col.L.Rev. 285. It requires that the defendant be tried within a reasonable time after he has been indicted. United

pressly guarantee the right, and statutes have been passed to implement it. Section 292 of the Institute Code provides that, if the defendant is not brought to trial within about three months after the indictment has been found, the prosecution shall be dismissed upon the motion of the defendant, prosecuting attorney, or court itself "unless good cause to the contrary is shown, by affidavit, or unless the cause has not proceeded to trial because of the defendant's consent or by his action."[156] Under Section 294 there may be no further prosecution except by order of the court. Under Section 298 the prosecution as well as the defendant is entitled to a speedy trial.[157] Often delay results from continuances sought sometimes by the defendant and sometimes by the prosecution.[158] To avoid

States v. Fox, 3 Mont. 512 (1880); Note (1915) 15 Col.L.Rev. 625. The defendant was held entitled to be released where he was convicted and sentenced under one of several indictments, the other indictments were withdrawn without his consent until the expiration of his sentence, and he was then put on trial under the latter indictments and convicted. Arrowsmith v. State, 175 S.W. 545 (Tenn. 1915), 15 Col.L.Rev. 625. See also Nat. Com. on Law Obs. and Enf., Report on Lawlessness in Law Enforcement (1931) 272.

156 Good cause for delay is usually of two kinds: (1) unforeseen events over which the prosecution has no control, such as destruction of courthouse by fire; (2) delay caused by law as where the jury disagrees or cannot be obtained. See Note (1931) 29 Mich.L.Rev. 373. See also Rule 48(b), Fed. Rules of Crim. Proc.

157 See Warner and Cabot, Judges and Law Reform (1936) 152-153. Under existing law in many states, the prosecution has no redress if the courts grant a delay to the defendant. "Defects in Criminal Justice" (1925) 11 A.B.A.J. 297, 298.

158 Missouri Crime Survey (1926) 167-172. The prosecutor usually obtains a continuance because the court fears that he will dismiss the case if he does not obtain it. Absence of witnesses is the usual ground. Failure of indigent defendants to obtain effective legal aid sometimes results in the discharge of the defendant because of the lapse of a prescribed statutory period. Baker, "The Public Defender's Work in Cook County" (1934) 25 J.Crim.L. 5, 6. Continuances are granted in the discretion of the trial

such delays Section 299 of the Institute Code provides: "An application for continuance may be made only before or at the time the cause is called for trial, unless good cause for failure so to apply is shown or unless the ground for application arose after the cause was called for trial." Under Section 304, "No continuance shall be granted for a longer time than the ends of justice require."

Delay in bringing a case to trial, if too prolonged, is likely to result in disposition without trial. "As an average proposition in Cleveland, unless the state can bring a criminal to trial within one hundred and fifteen days his case will be nol-prossed or discharged on motion or dismissed for want of prosecution." [159] In Baltimore the average time intervening between indictment and trial has been cut to about six days.[160] In Boston, delays before trial arise out of four causes: (1) the granting of bail or the presence of an attorney for the defendant; (2) spacing of cases so as to keep the same number of judges and prosecutors busy throughout the month; (3) postponement of arraignment and trial secured by parties or counsel in particular cases; and (4) defaults occasioned by the failure of defendants on bail to appear.[161]

Although the preparation of trial calendars appears to be a court function, in state criminal cases and apparently

---

court. See Note (1927) 75 U. of Pa. L.Rev. 377; Lehman, "A Critical Survey of Certain Phases of Trial Procedure in Criminal Cases" (1915) 63 U. of Pa.L.Rev. 609-616.

159 Smith, "Cleveland's Crime Survey" (1921) 5 J. Am. Jud. Soc. 68, 72. In Virginia if a case is disposed of within three months of the filing of the indictment, the chances of establishing guilt are about twice as great as if the case is delayed beyond that time. Fuller, Criminal Justice in Virginia (1931) 122.

160 Ulman, A Judge Takes the Stand (1933) 251. In Cleveland the average time is five days. Cockrell, J., Successful Justice (1939) 319.

161 Warner and Cabot, Judges and Law Reform (1936) 105.

federal as well, this function is actually exercised by the prosecuting attorney, with practically no supervision by the court in which the action is pending. The prosecuting attorney is not only allowed to fix the time of arraignment and trial, but in some cities actually distributes the various cases to be tried among the different judges as he desires. This may prevent a defendant from obtaining an early trial. His remedy of moving to dismiss is seldom used because of fear of incurring the displeasures of the prosecuting attorney. On the other hand, as to defendants not wanting an early trial, the case may be pigeonholed against the interests of the public. The New York Judicial Council has therefore proposed a statute requiring each court with jurisdiction over trials under indictments to provide for the preparation and periodical calling of its pleading and trial calendars and, if it has more than one judge, for the distribution of cases among its various parts independently of the district attorney.[162] With the same objective Rule 50 of the Federal Rules of Criminal Procedure provides: "The district courts may provide for placing criminal proceedings upon appropriate calendars. Preference shall as far as practicable be given to criminal proceedings."[163]

To be distinguished from delay before trial is slowness in the trial process itself. It has been contended that trials

[162] Fourth Report of the New York Judicial Council (1938) 59.

[163] Rule 46(b) of the First Preliminary Draft provided further: "The senior district judge may request of the United States Attorney a report of the status of any criminal case in which an indictment or an information has been filed, or in which the defendant has been held to answer in the district court. After such notice, if any, to the United States Attorney and to the defendants concerned as he considers reasonable, the senior district judge may make such orders for the advancement, conduct, trial, or hearing of the proceedings as will expedite the calendars and promote prompt and just disposition of all pending cases."

are conducted much too slowly.[164] This slowness arises from several sources. The sporting theory of justice still prevails and respectable counsel consider it not only their right but their duty to take the maximum advantage of every possible legal means of obtaining an acquittal. The wide leeway given the defendant in the admission of evidence aggravates this tendency.

10. Right to Public Trial

It is the immemorial usage of the common law to try all prisoners in open court, to which all spectators are admitted.[165] Perhaps owing to the prevalence of this usage there are but few discussions on the subject. It has been said that the court has the power in proper cases to put a reasonable limit to the number of persons who may be admitted to the courtroom and to exclude persons whose presence and conduct tend to interfere with the orderly progress of the trial.[166] The right of a court to try a case

[164] Warner and Cabot, "Changes in the Administration of Criminal Justice During the Past Fifty Years" (1937) 50 Harv.L.Rev. 583, 589. Federal cases are tried speedily, however. Arnold, J., "Progress Report in Study of the Federal Courts, No. 7" (1931) 17 A.B.A.J. 799, 801. Moreover, as to Ohio cases in the year 1930 it has been concluded: "Once the date for trial has been set, there is relatively little delay in finishing the case. . . . It is obvious that the great delays take place in the early stages of procedure and in those cases which result in the failure of the state to make its case." Gehlke, Criminal Actions in the Common Pleas Court in Ohio (1936) 275.

[165] 1 Bishop, Criminal Procedure (4th ed.1895) § 957; (1917) 30 Harv. L.Rev. 771. The Continental law is somewhat stricter. Auld, "The Comparative Jurisprudence of Criminal Process" (1937) 1 U. of Toronto L.J. 82, 99. A different rule is followed in juvenile delinquency cases. Waite, "How Far Can Court Procedure Be Socialized Without Impairing Individual Rights?" (1921) 12 J.Crim.L. 339, 341.

[166] People v. Swafford, 65 Cal. 223, 3 Pac. 809 (1884); State v. Brooks, 92 Mo. 542, 5 S.W. 257 (1887).

with closed doors has been recognized in certain classes of cases; lunacy, wards of the court, and secret processes.[167] It has been held that a court martial might try an Irish rebel *in camera*.[168] The power has been strictly limited to cases where it would not be possible to administer justice in open court.[169] In the United States the constitutional provision for a public trial has been very strictly enforced.[170]

The courts are about evenly divided where the trial involves the permanent exclusion of adults. Some cases hold that under such circumstances the general public cannot be excluded without violating the defendant's rights.[171] Other cases hold that, where, from the character of the charge and the nature of the evidence, public morality would be injuriously affected, the general public may be excluded.[172] Where the evidence relates to indecent and immoral

[167] Mellor v. Thompson, 31 Ch. D. 55 (1885).

[168] King v. Governor of Lewes Prison, 61 Sol. J. 294 (1917), 30 Harv. L.Rev. 771.

[169] Scott v. Scott, A.C. 417, 445 (1913); (1913) 27 Harv.L.Rev. 88.

[170] People v. Murray, 89 Mich. 276, 50 N.W. 995 (1891); People v. Hartman, 103 Cal. 242, 37 Pac. 153 (1894). The Canadian rule permits some restrictions. Auld, "The Comparative Jurisprudence of Criminal Process" (1937) 1 U. of Toronto L.J. 82, 99.

[171] State v. Hensley, 75 Ohio St. 225, 79 N.E. 462, 9 L.R.A. (N.S.) 277, 116 A.S.R. 734, 9 Ann. Cas. 108 (1906), (1907) 7 Col.L.Rev. 212, (1907) 20 Harv.L.Rev. 489, (1907) 5 Mich.L.Rev. 471, (1907) 16 Yale L.J. 341; Davis v. United States, 247 Fed. 394, L.R.A. 1918 C 1164 (C.C.A. 8th, 1917), (1918) 6 Mich.L.Rev. 641. See State v. Beckstead, 96 Utah 528, 88 Pac. (2d) 461 (1939), (1940) 30 J.Crim.L. 983. See also (1921) 5 Minn. L.Rev. 554, (1937) 35 Mich.L.Rev. 474. See Radin, "The Right to a Public Trial" (1931) 6 Temp.L.Q. 381.

[172] Keddington v. State, 19 Ariz. 457, 172 Pac. 273, L.R.A. 1918 D 1093 (1918); State v. Johnson, 26 Idaho 609, 144 Pac. 784 (1914); People v. Hall, 64 N.Y.S. 433 (1900); Reagan v. United States, 202 Fed. 488, 44 L.R.A. (N.S.) 583 (C.C.A. 9th, 1913); Rottschaefer, Handbook of American Constitutional Law (1939) 793.

matters, persons of immature years may be excluded.[173] Likewise, a temporary exclusion of all spectators to alleviate the embarrassment of a particular witness as to an indecent matter is valid.[174] It has been said that the defendant may waive his right to a public trial altogether.[175]

The considerations favoring publicity of trial are the opportunities for discovering new testimony, the wholesome effect on witnesses, jurors, and officers of the court, and the confidence of the community that it knows or can know what the courts are doing.[176] An opposing consideration is that spectators may be subjected to the influences of obscene and vicious testimony. Exclusion may be defended on the ground that it is necessary to sustain order,[177] to prevent the embarrassment of the witness,[178] or to maintain the dignity of the court.[179] These considerations should not be lightly used to circumvent the constitutional provision. Attendance should be limited to the seating capacity of the room. The doors ought not to be locked during the examination of witnesses.[180] The plan of admission by tickets good for limited periods is possibly invalid and offers an opportunity for improper exclusion.[181]

173 State v. Adams, 100 S.C. 43, 84 St. 368 (1914).

174 State v. Callahan, 100 Minn. 63, 110 N.W. 342 (1907).

175 Keddington v. State, 19 Ariz. 457, 172 Pac. 273, L.R.A. 1918 D 1093 (1918); Note (1921) 5 Minn.L.Rev. 554, 555.

176 6 Wigmore, Evidence (3d ed.1940) § 1834; Notes (1907) 20 Harv. L.Rev. 489, (1921) 5 Minn.L.Rev. 554. As to trial at other places than the courthouse, see Note (1912) 10 Mich.L.Rev. 324.

177 Lide v. State, 133 Ala. 43, 63 (1901).

178 Grimmett v. State, 22 Tex. App. 36 (1886).

179 People v. Kerrigan, 73 Cal. 222 (1887).

180 But see Stone v. People, 3 Ill. 326 (1840).

181 But see Jackson v. Commonwealth, 100 Ky. 239 (1896). The use of tickets at French criminal trials has been criticized. Wright, "French Criminal Procedure" (1919) 45 L.Q.Rev. 92, 95.

11. Right to Trial Free from Mob Domination

It is not enough to constitute due process that the court and jury be fair and impartial. The conditions under which the trial is had must be such as to insure a fair and impartial trial.[182] A trial does not meet this standard where a trial is so dominated by a mob that the jury is intimidated and the judge yields to its threats. If a state furnishes no adequate remedies, but executes the judgment on a verdict thus arrived at, there is a failure of due process and the federal courts will interfere by the grant of writs of habeas corpus.[183]

12. Scope of Right to Trial by Jury

A defendant does not have the right to trial by jury in all criminal cases. It has always been held with respect to federal crimes that a jury trial was not guaranteed in the trial of petty offenses which, according to the common law, were summarily triable without a jury by justices of the peace in England or by corresponding judicial officers in the colonies, and which were punishable by commitment to jail, workhouse, or house of correction.[184] Misdemeanors which are punishable by short imprisonment or

[182] Rottschaefer, Handbook of American Constitutional Law (1939) 809.

[183] Moore v. Dempsey, 261 U.S. 86, 43 Sup.Ct. 265, 67 L.Ed. 543 (1923); Notes (1923) 37 Harv.L.Rev. 247, (1931) 44 Harv.L.Rev. 447, (1923) 33 Yale L.J. 82, (1925) 73 U. of Pa.L.Rev. 430, (1923) 7 Minn.L.Rev. 513; Waterman and Overton, "Federal Habeas Corpus Statutes and Moore v. Dempsey" (1933) 1 U. of Chi.L.Rev. 307; Schofield, "Federal Courts and Mob Domination of State Courts: Leo Frank's Case" (1916) 10 Ill.L.Rev. 479.

[184] Callan v. Wilson, 127 U.S. 540, 8 Sup.Ct. 1301, 32 L.Ed. 223 (1888); Rottschaefer, Handbook of American Constitutional Law (1939) 788; Frankfurter and Corcoran, "Petty Federal Offenses and the Constitutional Guaranty of Trial by Jury" (1926) 39 Harv.L.Rev. 917.

a small fine are not crimes requiring jury trial.[185] The criterion usually employed for ascertaining whether an offense is a mere petty offense or a crime requiring jury trial is its nature, and, if it is *malum in se* or involves such obvious depravity as would shock the general moral sense, it is not a petty offense, regardless of the amount of its punishment.[186] Conspiracy[187] and reckless driving of a motor vehicle[188] are offenses in which the defendant may demand a jury. On the other hand, engaging in the business of a dealer in secondhand articles without a license is a petty offense.[189] Severity of punishment may be so great as to require jury trial although the offense appears otherwise petty in its nature.[190] State constitutional provisions are also construed as not requiring the trial by jury of petty offenses, but there are considerable differences in opinion as to what offenses are petty.[191] Determination of the mode of trial of statutory offenses unknown to the common law is said to be discretionary with the legis-

185 Schick v. United States, 195 U.S. 65, 24 Sup.Ct. 826, 49 L.Ed. 99, 1 Ann. Cas. 585 (1904), (1905) 5 Col.L.Rev. 48. Defendant was prosecuted for receiving for sale oleomargarine not stamped according to law, and fined $50.00.

186 District of Columbia v. Colts, 282 U.S. 63, 51 Sup.Ct. 52, 75 L.Ed. 177 (1930), (1931) 31 Col.L.Rev. 325, (1931) 79 U. of Pa.L.Rev. 640, (1931) 40 Yale L.J. 1303.

187 Callan v. Wilson, 127 U.S. 540, 8 Sup.Ct. 1401, 32 L.Ed. 223 (1888).

188 District of Columbia v. Colts, 282 U.S. 63, 51 Sup.Ct. 52, 75 L.Ed. 177 (1930).

189 District of Columbia v. Clawans, 300 U.S. 617, 57 Sup.Ct. 660, 81 L.Ed. 843 (1937); Notes (1922) 70 U. of Pa.L.Rev. 318, (1937) 35 Mich.L. Rev. 1377.

190 District of Columbia v. Clawans, 300 U.S. 617, 57 Sup.Ct. 660, 81 L.Ed. 843 (1937).

191 (1935) 13 Neb.L.Bull. 452. As to petty offenses in seven of the thirteen colonies, see Frankfurter and Corcoran, "Petty Federal Offenses and the Constitutional Guaranty of Trial by Jury" (1926) 39 Harv.L.Rev. 917, 934-965, 983-1019.

lature,[192] unless the offense is treated as analogous to a crime triable by jury before the constitution.[193] Violations of municipal ordinances are usually tried summarily.[194] In some states a jury may be dispensed with only as long as a fine without imprisonment is fixed as the maximum punishment;[195] in others, summary trial is precluded where the maximum fine exceeds a stated amount.[196]

The federal constitution guarantees the right of trial by jury only in the federal courts.[197] The states are not precluded by the Fourteenth Amendment from abolishing trial by jury or from reducing the number of jurors or from abolishing the requirements of unanimity.

13. Waiver of Jury Trial

Trial by jury has been criticized as involving delay, expense, and uncertainty. In England this has led to limitations on the right of trial by jury.[198] This has not occurred in American criminal cases, but there has been an increas-

[192] Caruso v. Porter, 102 N.J.L. 71, 130 Atl. 803 (1925) (driving while intoxicated). See Note (1931) 40 Yale L.J. 1303, 1305.

[193] Bowden v. Nugent, 26 Ariz. 485, 226 Pac. 549 (1924); Note (1922) 70 U. of Pa.L.Rev. 318.

[194] Natal v. Louisiana, 139 U.S. 621, 11 Sup.Ct. 636 (1891). In some states the violation of a city ordinance is not a crime unless the act is also forbidden by state law. See Notes (1922) 35 Harv.L.Rev. 462, (1939) 18 Neb.L.Bull. 67.

[195] Weisner v. State, 168 Ohio 129, 160 N.E. 623 (1928). See Note (1929) 3 U. of Cin.L.Rev. 215.

[196] Ward v. City of Tulsa, 24 Okla. Cr. 77, 216 Pac. 173 (1923).

[197] Dennis, "Jury Trial and the Federal Constitution" (1906) 6 Col.L. Rev. 423. See State v. Osborne, 153 Ore. 484, 57 P. (2d) 1083 (1936), 35 Mich.L.Rev. 146; Maxwell v. Dow, 176 U.S. 581, 604, 20 Sup.Ct. 448, 44 L.Ed. 597 (1900).

[198] See Administration of Justice (Miscellaneous Provisions) Act, 1933, 23 & 24 Geo. V, c.36, § 6. "There has been no trace of any demand that indictable offenses shall be triable without a jury." Burrows, "Criminal Law and Procedure" (1935) 51 L.Q.Rev. 36, 53.

ing extension of the privilege of waiving trial by jury. Half a century ago waiver was common in Maryland,[199] and perhaps in West Virginia.[200] At present it is permitted by constitution, statute, or judicial decision in the federal courts and in more than half of the states.[201] In some states waiver is used more frequently than in others. For instance, in 1934 in the courts of general jurisdiction in Connecticut, New Jersey, and Wisconsin, there were more trials to the court than before a jury; in Wisconsin, seven times as many. But in Ohio jury trials were more numerous, and in California and Michigan they were twice, and in Pennsylvania four times as common as trials to the court.[202]

Waiver has been more frequently and more strongly recommended than almost any other reform in criminal

[199] Frank, "Trying Criminal Cases without Juries in Maryland" (1931) 17 Va.L.Rev. 253; Bond, "The Maryland Practice of Trying Criminal Cases by Judges Alone, Without Juries" (1925) 11 A.B.A.J. 699.

[200] See State v. Cottrill, 31 W.Va. 162, 165, 6 S.E. 428, 429 (1888).

[201] Grant, "Waiver of Jury Trial in Felony Cases" (1932) 20 Calif. L.Rev. 132. Waiver is permitted in all cases in Connecticut, Illinois, Indiana, Maryland, Michigan, Ohio, and Wisconsin. The English reports reveal no attempt to waive a jury in the trial of serious offenses. Cf. Rex. v. Perkins, 90 Eng. Rep. 1122 (1698) (privilege of withdrawing a juror denied); Lord Audley's Case, 3 How. St. Tr. 401 (1631) (findings of waiver of trial by nobleman's peers denied); see Aldrich, J., dissenting in Dickinson v. United States, 159 Fed. 801, 814-818 (1908). Waiver existed to some extent in the Colonial period. See Griswold, "The Historical Development of Waiver of Jury Trial in Criminal Cases" (1934) 20 Va. L.Rev. 655; Note (1930) 30 Col.L.Rev. 1063.

[202] See statistics of the United States Bureau of the Census; Maltbie, "Criminal Trials without a Jury in Connecticut" (1926) 17 J.Crim.L. 335; Goldberg, "Waiver of Jury in Felony Trials" (1929) 28 Mich.L.Rev. 163; Grant, "Felony Trials without a Jury" (1931) 25 Am. Pol. Sci. Rev. 980; First Report of Judicial Council of Massachusetts (1925) 21-28; Report of Oregon Judicial Council for 1929 (1930) 9 Ore.L.Rev. 340-342; Second Report of Rhode Island Judicial Council (1928) 13-20; Second Report of California Judicial Council (1926) 44-45.

procedure.[203] It was one of the four chief points in the criminal law program of the American Bar Association in 1934.[204]

Waiver has been objected to as unconstitutional, particularly as to serious crimes. It has been asserted that public policy prevents an accused giving up jury trial.[205] More frequently it has been objected that the legislature has made no provision for the trying of a case without a jury.[206] In some cases a peculiarly mandatory provision in the state constitution has stood in the way.[207] The trend of recent cases is to allow the power whenever statutory authority can be found.[208] A few cases have permitted it even in the absence of express constitutional or statutory authority.[209]

The United States Supreme Court has held that a waiver of trial by jury requires the consent of both the prosecution and the court.[210] The same view has been

203 Missouri Crime Survey (1926) 366; Illinois Crime Survey (1929) 219; Report of the California Crime Commission (1929) 30 and (1931) 49; Proceedings of the Attorney General's Conference on Crime (1934) 453; Nat. Com. on Law Obs. and Enf., Rep. on Crim. Proc. (1931) 47; Second Report of the Judicial Council of New York (1936) 95-101; Fifth Report of the Judicial Council of New York (1939) 153-178.

204 Harno, "Program on Criminal Law and Its Enforcement" (1934) 20 A.B.A.J. 465, 466.

205 Cancemi v. People, 18 N.Y. 128 (1858); State v. Talken, 316 Mo. 596, 292 S.W. 32 (1927). See Note (1934) 13 Neb.L.Bull. 139.

206 Commonwealth v. Hall, 291 Pa. 341, 140 Atl. 626 (1928).

207 Jackson v. Commonwealth, 221 Ky. 823, 299 S.W. 983 (1927); State v. Cottrill, 31 W.Va. 162, 6 S.E. 428 (1888).

208 Ex parte King, 274 Pac. 682 (Okla. 1929); People v. Henderson, 246 Mich. 481, 224 N.W. 628 (1929). See Note (1927) 36 Yale L.J. 710.

209 State v. Baer, 103 Ohio St. 585, 134 N.E. 786 (1931); State v. Tiedeman, 49 S.D. 356, 207 N.W. 153 (1926); Patton v. United States, 281 U.S. 276, 50 Sup.Ct. 253, 74 L.Ed. 854, 70 A.L.R. 263 (1930).

210 Patton v. United States, 281 U.S. 276, 299, 312, 50 Sup.Ct. 253, 74

taken by a number of state courts.[211] This seems hard to reconcile with the theory that the right to jury trial merely provides a privilege for the defendant.[212] While theoretically the court and prosecutor might serve to protect the defendant against an unwise waiver, such power might be employed to relieve the court of responsibility or to obtain practical advantages for the prosecution. If the defendant waives in open court upon the advice of his attorney, he should be adequately protected.[213] Advantages to the public in reducing the expense and delay of jury trial make desirable the removal of impediments to waiver.[214] If waiver in capital cases is denied altogether, consent of the court and prosecution seems even less desirable.

Section 266 of the Institute Code provides: "In all cases except where a sentence of death may be imposed trial by a jury may be waived by the defendant. Such waiver shall be made in open court and entered of record." It will be noted that there is no provision requiring

---

L.Ed. 854 (1930), 30 Col.L.Rev. 1063, (1930) 44 Harv.L.Rev. 124, (1930) 28 Mich.L.Rev. 1053, (1931) 40 YaleL.J. 1303. A leading English writer believes the consent of the prosecuting attorney desirable. Brunyate, "The American Draft Code of Criminal Procedure, 1930" (1933) 49 L.Q.Rev. 192, 198.

211 State v. Mead, 4 Blackf., 309 (Ind. 1837) (consent of prosecutor); Ickes v. State, 63 Ohio St. 549, 59 N.E. 233 (1900) (consent of court); Braeder v. State, 201 Ala. 76, 77 N. 370 (1917); People v. Scornavache, 347 Ill. 403, 179 N.E. 909 (1931), (1932) 45 Harv.L.Rev. 932, (1932) 27 Ill.L.Rev. 447, (1932) 6 Tulane L.Rev. 660; People v. Eubanks, 7 Calif. App. (2d) 588, 46 Pac. (2d) 789 (1935), (1936) 26 J.Crim.L. 939.

212 Oppenheim, "Waiver of Trial by Jury in Criminal Cases" (1927) 25 Mich.L.Rev. 695, 701; Hall, "Has the State a Right to Trial by Jury in Criminal Cases?" (1932) 18 A.B.A.J. 216; Note (1931) 22 J.Crim.L. 113.

213 Note (1942) 55 Harv.L.Rev. 1209.

214 See Perkins, "Proposed Jury Changes in Criminal Cases" (1931) 16 Iowa L.Rev. 20, 225.

the consent of the prosecuting attorney or of the court, as is required in the Patton Case.[215] Rule 23(a) of the Federal Rules of Criminal Procedure provides: "Cases required to be tried by jury shall be so tried unless the defendant waives a jury trial in writing with the approval of the court and the consent of the government." The federal rule thus includes capital cases and requires a written waiver.[216] It does not alter the rule laid down in a recent decision that a defendant acting freely and intelligently may waive his right to trial by jury after having waived the assistance of counsel.[217] Possibly in case of waiver three judges might be used in capital cases.[218] In Minnesota and Ohio the statutes provide that the waiver may be revoked at any time before the trial. In Connecticut [219] and New Jersey [220] it has been held that the right to withdraw a waiver lies in the discretion of the court. It seems sound to leave the matter in the discretion of the

[215] Patton v. United States, 281 U.S. 276, 50 Sup.Ct. 253, 74 L.Ed. 854, 70 A.L.R. 263 (1930). Five states and the federal courts require consent of both the court and the prosecutor; three, of the court; and four, of the prosecutor. Eight states require only the consent of the defendant. Fifth Report of the Judicial Council of New York (1939) 153, 161.

[216] Seven states require a written waiver while in five states it is oral. Fifth Report of the Judicial Council of New York (1939) 153, 168.

[217] Adams v. United States ex rel. McCann, 317 U.S. 269, 63 Sup.Ct. 236 (1942).

[218] See A.L.I. Code of Crim. Proc. (1930) § 266, n.1. In New York the Court of Special Sessions has long tried serious misdemeanor cases without a jury. See Bayes, J., "Criminal Cases Tried to a Bench of Three Judges" (1941) 24 J. Am. Jud. Soc. 182. The use of three judges in all jury waived cases has been recommended. "The Trial Bench of Three Judges" (1929) 12 J. Am. Jud. Soc. 185. The element of expense is a strong opposing consideration. Jackson, The Machinery of Justice in England (1940) 128. There is also the possibility of congestion of cases not permitting the use of several judges. Third Report of the Judicial Council of Massachusetts (1927), reported in (1927) 13 Mass.L.Q.

[219] State v. Rankin, 102 Conn. 49 (1925).

[220] Edwards v. State, 45 N.L.J. 419 (1883).

courts, subject to such rules for applying that discretion as the courts may develop.[221]

After it had been held that a defendant in a federal court might waive trial by jury, the question arose whether he could do so without the advice of counsel. With three judges dissenting, the United States Supreme Court held that he could.[222] The court had previously held that a defendant in a criminal prosecution may waive his constitutional right to assistance of counsel if, in so doing, he acts competently and intelligently.[223] The dissenting judges adopted the argument of the lower court [224] that, without the aid of counsel, a defendant who is not himself a lawyer is not competent to waive a jury trial understandingly in a felony prosecution. That is to say, the combination of waiver of jury trial and waiver of counsel resulted in inadequate protection of the constitutional rights of the defendant.

The question arises after waiver, what form shall the decision take? The New York Judicial Council proposes that the decision by the court shall have the force and effect of a verdict in a case tried by a jury.[225] In Connecticut the judge must make findings of subordinate facts and conclusions of fact and law from these subordinate facts.[226] In the federal courts, a memorandum decision is

[221] Fifth Report of the Judicial Council of New York (1939) 153, 169.

[222] Adams v. United States, 317 U.S. 269, 63 Sup.Ct. 236 (1942), (1943) 27 Minn.L.Rev. 533.

[223] Johnson v. Zerbst, 304 U.S. 458, 58 Sup.Ct. 1019, 82 L.Ed. 1461 (1938).

[224] United States v. Adams, 126 F. (2d) 774 (C.C.A. 2d, 1942), 55 Harv. L.Rev. 1209, (1942) 41 Mich.L.Rev. 495, (1942) 91 U. of Pa.L.Rev. 76. A leading English writer adopts the same view. Jackson, The Machinery of Justice in England (1940) 121.

[225] Fifth Report of the Judicial Council of New York (1939) 153, 170-171.

[226] State v. Frost, 105 Conn. 326 (1926); Connecticut Practice Book (1934) §§ 336-341.

required in which the court need not set forth special findings of ultimate facts.[227] Rule 23(c) of the Federal Rules of Criminal Procedure provides: "In a case tried without a jury the court shall make a general finding and shall in addition on request find the facts specially." Such a strict requirement on the judges may result in their not consenting to waiver.

14. Trial by Less Than Twelve Jurors

Not so serious a departure from trial by jury is trial by less than twelve persons, as by eleven or ten.[228] Courts which have objected to waiver of a jury have sometimes approved of trial by eleven jurors.[229] Rule 23(b) of the Federal Rules of Criminal Procedure provides: "Juries shall be of 12 but at any time before verdict the parties may stipulate in writing with the approval of the court that the jury shall consist of any number less than 12." Thus they could stipulate before the trial as well as dur-

[227] Mulloney v. United States, 79 F. (2d) 566 (C.C.A. 1st, 1935).

[228] Reduction of the size of the jury is recommended in: Fifth Report of the Rhode Island Judicial Council (1932) 17 Mass.L.Q. 12; Note (1931) 17 Va.L.Rev. 497, 499; Willoughby, Principles of Judicial Administration (1929) 503. See discussion in Report of the Judicial Council of Kansas (1927) 17-18. In Greece, the jury number has been reduced to 10; in Vaud and Berne to 8; in Germany to 6; in Tessin to 5; in Denmark to 4 (only capital cases here go to a jury); and in Bulgaria to 3. Gorphe, J., "Reform of the Jury System in Europe: Results and Conclusions," (1936) 27 J.Crim.L. 473, 477. Six jurors for misdemeanor is recommended by Roberts, J., "Trial Procedure, Past, Present and Future" (1929) 15 A.B.A.J. 667, 669. See also Galston, J., "Civil Jury Trials and Tribulations" (1943) 29 A.B.A.J. 195, 197.

[229] State v. Kaufman, 51 Iowa 578, 2 N.W. 275 (1879); Commonwealth v. Egan, 281 Pa. 251, 126 Atl. 488 (1924), 73 U. of Pa.L.Rev. 106; Commonwealth v. Hall, 291 Pa. 341, 140 Atl. 626, 58 A.L.R. 1023 (1928), 76 U. of Pa.L.Rev. 727; Commonwealth v. Lawless, 258 Mass. 262, 154 N.E. 753 (1927); see Notes (1930) 44 Harv.L.Rev. 124, (1908) 8 Col.L Rev. 577, (1928) 37 Yale L.J. 521.

ing trial.[230] It may be noted that the rule does not state that this smaller number may act by less than a unanimous verdict. In England in case of death or illness, the remainder of the jury, so long as they are not reduced below ten, may, on the written consent of the defendant and the prosecution, bring in a verdict.[231]

By Section 7 of the Administration of Justice (Emergency Provisions) Act, 1939, it is provided that for the purpose of any trial with a jury in any proceedings in England, whether civil or criminal, it shall not be necessary for the jury to consist of more than seven persons.[232] This does not apply to cases of murder or treason, nor to such serious cases as the court directs that it not be applied.

15. Special Jury

At common law in England, a special or struck jury exists to try issues too complex for the ordinary freeholder.[233] Special juries are available today in England in cases other than treason and felony.[234] Statutes in several states in this country provide for special juries.[235] It is permitted as a matter of right upon compliance with the statute.[236]

230 Compare Note (1908) 8 Col.L.Rev. 577, 578. See also Note (1937) 35 Mich.L.Rev. 662.

231 Criminal Justice Act, 1925, § 15; Archbold, Criminal Pleading, Evidence and Practice (30th ed.1938) 220.

232 Harris and Wilshere, Principles and Practice of Criminal Law (17th ed.1943) 457.

233 3 Bl. Comm. *357.

234 Archbold, Criminal Pleading, Evidence and Practice (30th ed.1938) 185; Jackson, The Machinery of Justice in England (1940) 221-222.

235 Note (1922) 31 Yale L.J. 388. There is no violation of the Federal Constitution in the use of struck juries. Brown v. State of New Jersey, 175 U.S. 1712, 20 Sup.Ct. 77, 44 L.Ed. 119 (1899).

236 But it is sometimes allowed only in the discretion of the trial court.

16. Alternate Jurors

In trials of any importance or difficulty jurors may become disabled, with the result that a second trial is necessary at common law. To remedy this situation a number of statutes, as well as the federal government, have provided for the impaneling of alternate jurors.[237] One of the chief proposals of the American Bar Association program on criminal law in 1934 was the adoption of Section 285 of the Institute Code providing for the use of one or two alternate jurors.[238] An act of Congress of 1932 was closely modeled on the Code provision.[239] Rule 47(b) of the Federal Rules of Civil Procedure provides in more concise language for its use in federal civil cases. Rule 24(c) of the Federal Rules of Criminal Procedure follows the Civil Rule closely, except that it allows up to four alternate jurors.

Since 1933 California has provided for the retention of the alternate jurors for possible need after the case is submitted to the jury.[240] The California courts have sustained the constitutionality of such a statute.[241] They

---

State v. Withrow, 133 Mo. 500, 34 S.W. 245 (1896). The abolition of foreign, struck, and special juries is recommended in the Third Report of the New York Judicial Council (1937) 121-128.

[237] Notes (1936) 24 Calif.L.Rev. 735, (1937) 15 Chi. Kent L.Rev. 218, (1935) 26 J.Crim.L. 21, (1942) 21 Neb.L.Rev. 26, (1931) 4 So.Calif.L.Rev. 303, (1935) 9 U. of Cin.L.Rev. 307, (1937) 85 U. of Pa. L.Rev. 539, (1936) 11 Wash.L.Rev. 109; Perkins, "Proposed Jury Changes in Criminal Cases" (1931) 16 Iowa L.Rev. 232; 70 A.L.R. 182; 71 A.L.R. 1385; 96 A.L.R. 793; 102 A.L.R. 1055; 109 A.L.R. 1488.

[238] Harno, "Program on Criminal Law and Its Enforcement" (1934) 20 A.B.A.J. 465, 466.

[239] 28 U.S.C., see 417a.

[240] Cal. Pen. Code (Deering, 1937) § 1089.

[241] People v. Peete, 54 Calif. App. 333 (1921); People v. Davidson, 20 Calif. App. (2d) 720 (1937). See (1936) 11 Wash.L.Rev. 109. The First Preliminary Draft of the Federal Rules of Criminal Procedure contained a similar provision.

pointed out that there is a total of twelve persons participating in hearing witnesses, in deliberating on a verdict, in returning a verdict, and in every other jury function during a trial. The essentials of trial by jury remained; namely, twelve jurors, a unanimous verdict, and impartial deliberations. Alternates may not, however, retire with the regular jurors to the jury room for deliberation, even though instructed not to participate therein.[242]

17. Jury Exemptions

It has often been pointed out that jurors are lacking in experience and intelligence.[243] There are three chief means by which good jury material is often depleted: exemptions, excuses, and challenges.[244] It has been estimated that seventy-five per cent of the people of New York City are excluded by exemptions. A possible solution suggested is the abolition of all exemptions except court officers.[245] An absolute exemption might be replaced by

242 People v. Bruneman, 4 Cal. App. (2d) 75 (1935), 26 J.Crim.L. 121, (1936) 24 Calif.L.Rev. 735; Woods v. Commonwealth, 287 Ky. 312 (1941). See also State v. Dalton, 206 N.C. 507 (1934).

243 Illinois Crime Survey (1929) 231. In 36 states there are no qualifications as to education or ownership of property. "Defects in Criminal Justice" (1925) 11 A.B.A.J. 297.

244 Note, "Proposed Legislation for Jury Reform in New York" (1930) 30 Col.L.Rev. 721.

245 Note (1930) 30 Col.L.Rev. 721, 723. Only clergymen, physicians, druggists, and lawyers should be exempted according to Lawler, J., "Needed Reforms in Criminal Law and Procedure" (1911) 1 J.Crim.L. 877, 891. A recent United States Senate bill would exempt only three classes of persons: (1) persons who have served as jurors within a certain period of time; (2) certain public officers; and (3) persons on active duty with the armed forces. Blume, "Jury Selection Analyzed" (1944) 42 Mich.L.Rev. 831, 858. In 1936 the New York Judicial Council proposed that mandatory exemptions be allowed to only six classes: clergymen, lawyers, doctors and dentists, firemen and policemen, sailors and marines,

discretionary power in the court to postpone the time of service, where the exigencies of his business require his temporary excuse.

But the abolition of exemptions is not enough. In need of curtailing is the large number of excuses granted to individual jurors who are not from the exempted classes.[246] Politicians and court officials have connived at such evasions. As many as fifty per cent of jurors summoned are excused. A suggested remedy is the requirement that excuses be presented to the judge in open court and that a note of the excuse and the reason therefor be made by the judge and transmitted to the commissioners of jurors by the clerk.[247] The result of the existing systems has been that juries are made up of middle-class merchants, manufacturers, salesmen, brokers, clerks, and the like. Not many laborers are used, and men of wealth and prominence are even more rare.

In 1935 Congress passed an act making governmental employees eligible for jury service in the federal courts. This act was sustained by the United States Supreme Court,[248] which reversed an earlier decision holding that a federal employee is disqualified for implied bias to serve as a juror in a criminal case in which the United States is a party, because at common law a servant of either litigant was disqualified.[249] The Sixth Amendment guarantees

---

and merchant sailors. Second Report of the New York Judicial Council (1936) 87-94.

246 Note (1930) 30 Col.L.Rev. 721, 724.

247 A California Bar committee recommends "that it be made a misdemeanor for any attorney (except in a court proceeding) or other person to intercede with the court on behalf of a prospective trial juror." Note (1940) 30 J.Crim.L. 791, 792.

248 United States v. Wood, 299 U.S. 123, 57 Sup.Ct. 177, 81 L.Ed. 78 (1936), 21 Minn.L.Rev. 608, (1937) 27 J.Crim.L. 914.

249 Crawford v. United States, 212 U.S. 183, 29 Sup.Ct. 260, 53 L.Ed. 465, 15 Ann. Cas. 392 (1908).

the right to an impartial jury, but governmental employees are not necessarily biased. The state courts have often held that governmental employees may serve on state juries.[250] Exemption by statute from jury service is not a disqualification but is merely a personal privilege.[251] In a few states governmental employees are disqualified by statute.[252]

18. Challenges for Cause

One of the chief evils of American trial procedure has been the lengthy and costly *voir dire* examination.[253] Such examinations have been known to fill an entire corpulent volume in the printed record on appeal.[254] The remedy seems to be to give the court full authority to conduct the examination as it wishes without domination by counsel.[255]

[250] State v. Galbraith, 150 Wash. 664, 274 Pac. 797 (1929) (member of state senate); State v. McDonald, 59 Kan. 241, 52 Pac. 453 (1898) (school district officer).

[251] Jackson v. State, 74 Ala. 26 (1883) (coroner); State v. Backer, 68 N.J.L. 19, 52 Atl. 284 (1902) (national guardsman).

[252] State v. Johnson, 123 S.C. 50, 115 S.E. 748 (1923) (deputy sheriff).

[253] Illinois Crime Survey (1929) 198, 218, 243; Grant, "Notes on Judicial Organization and Procedure" (1930) 24 Am. Pol. Sci. Rev. 117, 127.

[254] Pound, J., Address (1933) 56 Rep. of N.Y. Bar Assn. 437, 444; Orfield, Criminal Appeals in America (1939) 148. "In the Snyder-Gray trial, the whole of the first five days was consumed in the examination and selection of prospective jurors. Four hundred persons were compelled to leave their businesses and come into court for interrogation. One 63 year old man lost his job as a result, the others lost thousands of dollars in time." Waite, Criminal Law in Action (1934) 298.

[255] "Examination of the panel as to their qualifications, conducted by the court instead of by counsel, a practice obtaining with the best results in some of our older jurisdictions, has proved entirely sufficient to insure impartial juries, has insured a higher level of jurors, and has obviated much delay and expense. It should supersede the practice of examination by counsel" Nat. Com. on Law Obs. and Enf., Rep. on Crim. Proc. (1931) 25. See Notes (1926) 26 Col.L.Rev. 494, (1933) 17 Minn.L.Rev. 299; Moore, "Voir Dire Examination of Jurors: The English Practice" (1928)

Section 275 of the Institute Code provides: "The court shall then examine each juror individually, except that, with the consent of both parties, it may examine the jurors collectively. The court in its discretion may permit either party to question a jury and each party may also submit questions to the court which in its discretion it may ask a juror." The cases seem to justify the control of the interrogation by the court.[256] The wisdom of examination by somebody, court or counsel, before challenge seems established.[257]

Rule 24(a) of the Federal Rules of Criminal Procedure is similar, and closely modeled on Rule 47(a) of the Federal Rules of Civil Procedure in order that there be uniformity of criminal and civil procedure. It provides: "The court may permit the defendant or his attorney and the attorney for the government to conduct the examination of prospective jurors or may itself conduct the examination. In the latter event, the court shall permit the defendant or his attorney and the attorney for the government to supplement the examination by such further inquiry as it deems proper or shall itself submit to the prospective jurors such additional questions by the parties or their attorneys as it deems proper."

The importance of questioning the jurors for disqualification is seen by the fact that the defendant cannot after

---

16 Geo.L.J. 438; Perkins, "Some Needed Reforms in the Methods of Selecting Juries" (1915) 13 Mich.L.Rev. 391, 395; Notes (1924) 8 J. Am. Jud. Soc. 92, 10 A.B.A.J. 875; McCormick, "Function of Judges and Counsel in the Examination of Jurors" (1932) 22 J.Crim.L. 734; Evans, J., "Recommendations for Reforms in Criminal Procedure" (1929) 24 Ill.L. Rev. 112, 114. In England and Canada, there can be no examination of jurors prior to challenge. (1922) 31 Yale L.J. 514, 770.

256 Jones v. State, 35 Fla. 289, 17 So. 284 (1895); Murphy v. United States, 7 Fed. (2d) 85 (C.C.A. 1st, 1925), (1926) 26 Col.L.Rev. 494.

257 Note (1922) 31 Yale L.J. 514.

verdict of guilty move to set aside the verdict or for a new trial because of such disqualification.[258] The defendant is not entitled to a new trial unless he can show that the disqualification was unknown to him at the time of the trial, and that he exercised due diligence to ascertain it.[259] A failure to question the juror upon the matters of alleged disqualification is usually regarded as a lack of diligence.[260] The action of the defendant may be such as to waive the disqualification. Where a person disqualified to act as a juror answers to the name of another and sits in his place, a verdict of guilty has been set aside.[261] In a capital case the defendant, upon learning that one of the jurors was an alien, may move for a new trial.[262]

The proper method of attacking the panel is by a challenge to the array.[263] It is well settled that a prior challenge to the polls is a waiver of any absolute right to challenge the array.[264] The courts adhere strictly to this rule where the challenge to the array was based on a deviation from the statutory regulations for selecting or summoning the panel.[265] But the trial court may in its discre-

[258] Notes (1912) 12 Col.L.Rev. 561, (1912) 22 Yale L.J. 154, (1898) 11 Harv.L.Rev. 545.

[259] Chase v. People, 40 Ill. 352 (1866); Note (1933) 17 Minn.L.Rev. 299, 303.

[260] Gillooley v. State, 58 Ind. 182 (1877).

[261] Rex v. Wakefield, 13 Crim. App. Cas. 56 (1918), 18 Col.L.Rev. 488. *Contra:* Tolbert v. State, 71 Miss. 179, 14 So. 462 (1893).

[262] People v. Bott, 201 N.Y.Supp. 47 (1923), 33 Yale L.J. 215. The weight of authority is against objection after verdict at least in non-capital cases. Okershauser v. State, 136 Wis. 111, 116 N.W. 769 (1908); Fulcher v. State, 82 Miss. 630, 35 So. 170 (1903).

[263] Borrelli v. People, 164 Ill. 549, 45 N.E. 1024 (1897). Abolition of the right to challenge the panel is recommended by Lawler, J., "Needed Reforms in Criminal Law and Procedure" (1911) 1 J.Crim.L. 877, 885.

[264] Forsythe v. State, 6 Ohio 19 (1833); State v. Taylor, 134 Mo. 109, 35 S.W. 92 (1896).

[265] State v. Clark, 121 Mo. 500, 26 S.W. 562 (1894).

tion allow a challenge to the array after a challenge to the polls.[266] The intervention of a party in interest in the selection of the panel furnishes good reason for relaxing the rule.[267]

19. Peremptory Challenges

The United States Constitution does not require Congress to grant peremptory challenges in criminal cases, hence a statute requiring the several defendants in a single trial to be treated as a single party for purposes of determining the number of allowable peremptory challenges does not violate the right to trial by jury.[268] The parties do not have a proprietary interest in the jury panel. This does not mean that it may not be desirable to grant rights not conferred by the Constitution.

In the absence of statutory regulation, the order in which peremptory challenge shall be exercised is in the discretion of the court.[269] The order prescribed by the trial judge is subject to review,[270] although the conviction will not be reversed unless prejudice is shown.[271] It seems settled that requiring the state and the defendant to alternate in the exercise of their challenges and to consider as

[266] Cox v. People, 80 N.Y. 500 (1880). See Note (1918) 27 Yale L.J. 565.

[267] People v. Felber, 61 Mich. 114, 28 N.W. 83 (1886).

[268] Stilson v. United States, 250 U.S. 583, 40 Sup.Ct. 28, 63 L.Ed. 1154 (1919), (1920) 29 Yale L.J. 363. Cf. language in Lewis v. United States, 146 U.S. 370, 13 Sup.Ct. 136, 36 L.Ed. 1011 (1892). At common law, persons tried jointly could exercise the full number of challenges. Smith v. State, 57 Miss. 822 (1880); Note (1913) 11 Mich.L.Rev. 404.

[269] Commonwealth v. Piper, 120 Mass. 185 (1876); State v. Pierce, 8 Iowa, 231 (1859); Note (1942) 21 Neb.L.Rev. 174; (1936) 10 So.Calif.L. Rev. 89.

[270] Kock v. State, 32 Ohio St. 352 (1877); Schumaker v. State, 5 Wis. 324 (1856).

[271] Pointer v. United States, 151 U.S. 396, 411, 14 Sup.Ct. 410, 416 (1894).

waived those challenges not exercised is not in derogation of the defendant's rights.[272] But the cases are in conflict as to whether it is an abuse of the court's discretion to give the state the last peremptory challenge. In an Ohio case, the defendant was denied a challenge after the state had exercised its last peremptory challenge, even though he had exercised only four of his sixteen challenges.[273] It would seem that proper protection of the defendant requires the court to allow the defendant to reserve at least some of his peremptory challenges until after the state has exercised all of its peremptory challenges. This is the practice in the states where statutes regulating the order of exercising peremptory challenges have been enacted.[274] In some jurisdictions the defendant has an absolute right to have a full panel presented every time he is called on to exercise any of his peremptory challenges.[275] Some jurisdictions hold that the right to challenge continues until the jury is sworn.[276] Others hold that the defendant can be required to exercise his peremptory challenges as each juror or set of jurors appear, before more are called.[277]

[272] State v. Shelledy, 8 Iowa, 477 (1859); Johnson v. State, 88 Neb. 565, 130 N.W. 282 (1911). *Contra:* Schumaker v. State, 5 Wis. 324 (1856).

[273] Lyon v. State, 155 N.E. 800 (Ohio, 1927), 27 Col.L.Rev. 1008, 76 U. of Pa.L.Rev. 105.

[274] People v. McQuade, 110 N.Y.S. 284, 18 N.E. 156 (1888); Wyo. Comp. Stat. (1920) § 7502, c.470; cf. State v. Jones, 27 Wyo. 46, 191 Pac. 1075 (1920).

[275] Avila v. United States, 76 F. (2d) 39 (C.C.A. 9th, 1935), (1936) 10 So.Calif.L.Rev. 89; Cal. Pen. Code (1935) § 1088. *Contra:* State v. Shelledy, 8 Iowa, 477 (1859); Funderbark v. State, 75 Miss. 20, 21 So. 658 (1897).

[276] People v. Ah You, 47 Colo. 121 (1873); State v. Spaulding, 60 Vt. 228, 14 Atl. 769 (1888); United States v. Davis, 103 Fed. 457 (C.C.Tenn. 1900).

[277] State v. Potter, 18 Conn. 166 (1846); Nicholson v. People, 31 Colo. 53, 71 Pac. 377 (1903); McDonald v. State, 172 Ind. 393, 88 N.E. 673, 139 Am. St. Rep. 383, 19 Ann. Cas. 763 (1909).

At common law jurors were called one at a time, examined, subjected to challenge—both for cause and peremptory—and sworn. In other words, the defendant's right is to reject and not to select particular jurors.

It has been pointed out that the personnel of juries is reduced in size not only by numerous exceptions and excuses but also by the allowance of many peremptory challenges.[278] New York affords a defendant on trial for murder or other serious felony more peremptory challenges than any other state in the Union.[279] In capital cases there are thirty challenges, in cases punishable by life imprisonment or imprisonment for a term of ten or more years there are twenty; and in other criminal cases there are five. As to the first group, it has been suggested there be a reduction from thirty to twenty, and as to the second, from twenty to ten. In Canada a defendent in a capital case has twenty peremptory challenges; if the offense is punishable by imprisonment for more than five years he has twelve, and for any other offense he has four.[280]

In Arkansas in impaneling the jury to try a felony case, the defendant has twenty peremptory challenges, while the prosecution has only ten. This is true, although the

[278] Note, "Proposed Legislation for Jury Reform in New York" (1930) 30 Col.L.Rev. 721, 726. The number of peremptory challenges allowed varies from 5 to 45. Evans, J., "Recommendations for Reforms in Criminal Procedure" (1929) 24 Ill.L.Rev. 112, 114.

[279] Note (1930) 30 Col.L.Rev. 721, 726. That there are too many challenges in Nebraska is asserted by Letton, J., "Challenges and the Power of Judges" (1911) 23 Green Bag, 684, 685.

[280] Bayley, "Canadian Criminal Law and Procedure as Administered in the Province of Ontario" (1926) 4 Can.B.Rev. 552, 556. Continental Europe allows many peremptory challenges, but many Continental jurists have severely attacked the practice as based only on historical considerations. Mannheim, "Trial by Jury in Modern Continental Criminal Law" (1937) 53 L.Q.Rev. 388, 400.

attorney for the defendant is usually a resident of the county while the prosecuting attorney is not. It has been contended that the state should have an equal number of challenges.[281]

The Institute Code reduces the number of peremptory challenges, and allows the prosecution to have as many as the defendant, and reduces the number of challenges where several defendants are jointly tried.[282] Under Section 282 of the Code ten challenges are allowable when the penalty is death or life imprisonment, six for other felonies, and three for misdemeanors.[283] Under Section 283 there may be a collective challenge for joint defendants in the above number, together with individual chal-

[281] Campbell, "Some Needed Reforms in the Criminal Law" (1903) 6 Rep. Proc. Bar Assoc. of Ark. 53, 66. See also Comment (1926) 10 J. Am. Jud. Soc. 68. On the other hand, it has been argued that the prosecution does not need as many challenges, as it has ample resources to investigate the jury panel and every juror sworn. Smith, "Criminal Justice in America: A Reply" (1925) 11 A.B.A.J. 797, 798.

[282] "As to peremptory challenges, with respect to which the law in too many states gives a grossly unreasonable advantage to the accused, we may refer to the Model Criminal Code of the American Law Institute." Nat. Com. on Law Obs. and Enf., Rep. on Crim. Proc. (1931) 26. See also "Defects in Criminal Justice" (1925) 11 A.B.A.J. 297, 298; Taft, C. J., quoted in Willoughby, Principles of Judicial Administration (1929) 511; Fourth Report of Judicial Council of Kentucky (1936) 9; Report of Illinois Judicial Advisory Council (1931) 17-18; (1925) 3 Proc. Am. L. Inst. 501; Allen, "Needed Reforms in Criminal Procedure" (1906) Ky.S.B.A. 38, 52.

[283] The Missouri Survey would equalize the number of challenges for both sides, and allow six challenges as to offenses punishable by death or life imprisonment, four as to cases punishable by imprisonment in the penitentiary, and three as to all other cases. Missouri Crime Survey (1926) 356-357; see also Moley, Our Criminal Courts (1930) 95. Abolition of peremptory challenges is recommended in Report of the Crimes Survey Committee, Law Association of Philadelphia (1926) 473. In Alabama no peremptory challenges are allowed. Herndon v. State, 2 Ala. App. 118, 56 So. 85 (1911).

lenges of two when the penalty is death or life imprisonment and one as to other felonies, and the prosecution may have as many challenges as are allowed to all the defendants.[284]

Rule 24(b) of the Federal Rules of Criminal Procedure is somewhat more generous to the defendant.[285] If the offense is punishable by death, each side is entitled to twenty peremptory challenges. If the offense is punishable by imprisonment for more than one year, the government is entitled to six peremptory challenges and the defendant to ten; the earlier proposed federal rule gave each side six challenges. If the offense is punishable by imprisonment for not more than one year or by fine or both, each side is entitled to three peremptory challenges. If there is more than one defendant, the court may allow the defendants additional peremptory challenges and permit them to be exercised separately or jointly.

20. Improvement of Jury Trial

The weaknesses of the jury have been well described by the Wickersham Commission.[286] The jury has not been

[284] For a comparable proposal in Illinois, see Miller, "Trial Practice and Review Under the Proposed Criminal Code" (1936) 24 Ill. Bar J. 338.

[285] As to the history of peremptory challenges in the federal courts, see (1942) 21 Neb.L.Rev. 174.

[286] Nat. Com. on Law Obs. and Enf., Rep. on Crim. Proc. (1931) 23-28. See also Waite, Criminal Law in Action (1934) 63-79; Warner and Cabot, Judges and Law Reform (1936) c.6; Nott, "The Juror's Part in Crime" (1926) 79 Scribner's Magazine 94; Sutliffe, Impressions of an Average Juryman (1922); Perkins, "The Great American Game" (1927) 155 Harper's Magazine 750; Garner, "Crime and Judicial Inefficiency" (1907) 29 Annals 601; Train, "The Jury System" (1910) 36 Annals 175; Hall, "Present Day Jury" (1924) 10 A.B.A.J. 111; Note, "Proposed Legislation for Jury Reform in New York" (1930) 30 Col.L.Rev. 74; Robinson, "Revolt of the Jury" (1927) 18 J.Crim.L. 100; Green, Judge and Jury (1930)

prized as an effective tribunal for the ascertainment of the facts, but has been thought of in terms of the seventeenth century contests between the courts and the Crown and of eighteenth century contests between the Colonies and royal authority. The jury was more suitable in a homogeneous pioneer or rural community, where people knew each other and the affairs of the community, than in an urban industrial community where no such knowledge was possible. It demands too much time and energy from urban inhabitants best qualified to serve.[287] Statutes grant exemptions from jury service to too many well-qualified citizens. The selection of trial juries from the panel takes

---

375; Stalmaster, What Price Jury Trials (1931); Criminal Justice in Cleveland (1922) 340-353; Missouri Crime Survey (1926) 178 *et. seq.*, Illinois Crime Survey (1929) 230 *et seq.;* Wigmore, "A Program for the Trial of Jury Trial" (1929) 12 J. Am. Jud. Soc. 166; Note (1931) 41 Yale L.J. 1303, 1307; McWhorter, "Abolish the Jury" (1923) 57 Am.L.Rev. 42; Sebille, "Trial by Jury an Ineffective Survival" (1925) 59 Am.L.Rev. 65; Coxe, "The Trial of Jury Trials" (1901) 1 Col.L.Rev. 286; "Cincinnati Conference Trial by Jury" (1937) 11 U. of Cin.L.Rev. 119-259. On the jury in Italy see Ploscowe, "The Jury System in Italy" (1934) 25 J. Crim.L. 576; and in other countries see Gorphe, J., "The Jury System in Europe" (1934) 27 J.Crim.L. 17, 155. "The jury has by no means been a satisfactory feature in Continental criminal procedure." Pound, Criminal Justice in America (1930) 63-64. See also Mannheim, "Trial by Jury in Modern Continental Criminal Law" (1937) 53 L.Q.Rev. 99, 388; Auld, "The Comparative Jurisprudence of Criminal Process" (1935) 1 U. of Toronto L.J. 82. In Russia decisions are by a majority of a bench of three judges, but the minority judge may prepare a dissenting opinion to aid the higher court. Hazard, "Soviet Criminal Procedure" (1941) 15 Tulane L.Rev. 220-232. The bench consists of one professional and two lay judges. See also Henry, "Story of the Criminal Jury in the Civil Law and in the Common Law" published in Murray, Legal Essays (1935) 135-164; Riesenfeld, "Structure and Phases of a Criminal Trial in Europe" (1936) 11 Calif. State Bar J. 168, 172-175.

[287] Yet jury duty may be far less onerous than witness duty or military duty. See the statement of Lemann, Nat. Com. on Law Obs. and Enf., Rep. on Crim. Proc. (1931) 49, 50.

too long in all hotly contested cases.[288] Impartial jurors are hard to get because of what often amounts to trial of the case in advance in the press. Judges in most states cannot assist the jury by commenting on the facts as they can in England and in the federal courts. In some states, jurors are made judges of the law as well as the facts with the result that the law is ignored or misapplied. In some states the jury assesses the punishment as well as finding the guilt or innocence, thus confusing the jury as to its function. The jury in civil cases is constantly losing ground. Trial by jury is expensive in time and money.[289] Mistrials may result.[290] While it is a guarantee to the accused, he should not be compelled to be tried by jury if he does not wish it.

The case in favor of the jury has been well stated by Wigmore: "We are good friends of jury trial. We believe in it as the best system of trial ever invented for a free people in the world's history. In spite of all suggestions to substitute the trained judge of fact, we believe that a system of trying facts by a regular judicial official, known beforehand and therefore accessible to all the arts of corruption and chicanery, would be fatal to justice. The grand solid merit of jury trial is that the jurors of fact are selected at the last moment from the multitude of citizens. They cannot be warned beforehand, and they melt back into the multitude after each trial." [291]

As Wigmore has pointed out, the jury system has four

[288] But, as has been seen, this is not true in England.

[289] But in countries not using the jury, there is a bench consisting of one senior and two assistant judges. These three judges require assistants, rooms, etc.

[290] But there is no reliable evidence showing that many mistrials occur.

[291] Wigmore, "To Ruin Jury Trial in the Federal Courts" (1925) 9 J. Am. Jud. Soc. 61.

outstanding merits not possessed by trial by judges.[292] In the first place, it prevents or diminishes popular distrust of official justice. Bureaucratic justice cannot secure the same confidence as justice participated in by the citizenry.[293] In the second place, it provides the necessary flexibility in legal rules. The jury in the secrecy of the jury room may dispense popular justice. In the third place, it educates the citizenry in the administration of law. Mere publicity of trials is not sufficient to accomplish this. In the fourth place, there is the improved quality of a verdict based on the reconciliation of varied temperaments and minds. An average judgment is secured. A single judge may easily err in his judgments. If the court consisted of three judges, the junior judges might too readily take their cue from the senior judge.

While there are weaknesses in trial by jury, few thoughtful students would recommend its abolition in criminal cases.[294] The Wickersham Commission stated in

292 Wigmore, "A Program for the Trial of Jury Trial" (1929) 12 J. Am. Jud. Soc. 166, 169-171.

293 "No stronger bulwark, in my judgment, can be devised for protecting the innocent from oppression at the hands of the powerful." Parker, J., "Improving the Administration of Justice" (1941) 27 A.B.A.J. 71, 73.

294 It is well to remember the words of Blackstone as to possible alternatives to jury trial: "And, however convenient these may appear at first, (as doubtless all arbitrary powers, well executed, are the most convenient), yet let it be again remembered that delays and little inconveniences in the form of justice are the price that all free nations must pay for their liberty in more substantial matters." 4 Bl. Comm. *349. "Ever since the 17th century, when juries began to express sentiment against the government, there has been a tendency for the jury to become, at least in popular thought, a safeguard of political liberty." Plucknett, A Concise History of the Common Law (1929) 96. "The great bulwark and protection of the individual against the power of the government and the King, extended through the judges removable at will in criminal prosecutions for political offenses, was trial by jury." Taft, C. J., "The Administration of Criminal Law" (1905) 15 Yale L.J. 1, 4.

spite of its finding of present flaws that it felt "strongly that the jury is on the whole an eminently suitable tribunal for criminal cases." [295] If it is given its common-law characteristics it would function effectively. It should not be made judge of the law. It should not fix the sentence. The judge should assist it by commenting on the evidence and by vigorous direction of the trial; and should play the leading role in selecting it on the *voir dire* examination.

Among the chief reforms of the jury which have been proposed and adopted in some jurisdictions are: waiver of jury trial, alternate jurors, abolition of the requirement of unanimity, reduction of the size of the jury, more careful selection of jurors,[296] and jury pooling and other methods of economizing the time and use of jurors.[297] Jurors should be made more comfortable.[298] The terms of service should be shortened, with an option to serve

295 Nat. Com. on Law Obs. and Enf., Rep. on Crim. Proc. (1931) 28. "These manifestations of distrust, and our fairly justified dissatisfaction with the functioning of the American Jury System, do not necessarily mean that the system ought to be abolished. I believe that it should be retained, despite its occasional injustices to society, for the sake of its obstructive value in preventing possible injustice to individuals." Waite, Criminal Law in Action (1934) 75.

296 Ninth Report of the Judicial Council of Massachusetts (1933) 9; Note, "Proposed Legislation for Jury Reform in New York" (1930) 30 Col.L.Rev. 721; Otis, J., "Qualifications of Jurors" (1942) 25 J. Am. Jud. Soc. 178; Report to the Judicial Conference of Senior Circuit Judges of the Commission on Selection of Jurors (Sept., 1942); Otis, J., "Selecting Federal Court Jurors" (1943) 29 A.B.A.J. 19; Grant, "Methods of Jury Selection" (1930) 24 Am. Pol. Sci. Rev. 117; Blume, "Jury Selection Analyzed" (1944) 42 Mich.L.Rev. 831. Possibly they should undergo a physical examination. Note (1940) 30 J.Crim.L. 791. As to jury selection in Europe, see Mannheim, "Trial by Jury in Modern Continental Criminal Law" (1937) 53 L.Q.Rev. 388, 398.

297 MacChesney, "A Progressive Program for Procedural Reform" (1912) 3 J.Crim.L. 528, 534; McLaughlin, "Jury 'Pooling' Saves Huge Sums and Expedites Justice" (Jan. Feb. 1934) 12 Panel, p.10.

298 Warner and Cabot, Judges and Law Reform (1936) c.6.

longer.[299] They should not be "locked up" unnecessarily. If they must be "locked up," the daily sittings should be lengthened, sessions held on Saturdays and holidays, and publicity severely limited. Their pay should be increased.[300]

21. Presence of Defendant

The United States Supreme Court has held that a state court does not deny due process of law when it permits a defendant indicted for murder to waive by his counsel his presence during the examination of a juror who was after examination discharged.[301] The defendant should be present at the questioning of witnesses.[302] The right based on the Sixth Amendment extends, in the case of capital offenses and felonies, to every stage of the trial from the impaneling of the jury to the reception of the verdict.[303]

[299] A Committee of the California Bar Association recommended in 1940: "The Committee feels that the time of actual trial service should be reduced to fifteen days actual service unless said period must be extended by an actual trial and in no event more than twenty days, whether the juror be used or not, and further that no one should be called for jury service more than once in five years." Note (1940) 30 J.Crim.L. 791, 792.

[300] Note (1930) 30 J.Crim.L. 791, 792.

[301] Howard v. Kentucky, 200 U.S. 164, 26 Sup.Ct. 189 (1905), (1906) 6 Col.L.Rev. 357. The note suggests due process requires presence at the trial, and that the right is therefore not waivable; also that under the Kentucky though not the majority view, trial does not begin until the jury is sworn. For full discussion, see Lehman, "A Critical Survey of Certain Phases of Trial Procedure in Criminal Cases," (1915) 68 U. of Pa.L.Rev. 609, 619-628.

[302] State v. Sheppard, 39 S.E. 676 (W.Va. 1901), (1902) 15 Harv.L.Rev. 412. In this case, before the entrance of the defendant into court, a witness was asked her name and that of her husband; the absence of the defendant was then noted, the questions were then asked again, but reversible error was found.

[303] Diaz v. United States, 223 U.S. 442, 32 Sup.Ct. 250, 56 L.Ed. 500, Ann. Cas. 1913 C, 1138 (1912); Rottschaefer, Handbook of American

Question may arise as to the proper course to follow where a defendant creates commotion during a trial, as where he endeavors to assault the judge or is very noisy. In an English case the court finally proceeded without the presence of the defendant, where he persisted in vociferous and offensive conduct even after being placed in fetters. Possibly the better course, even in such a case, is to put the defendant under whatever restraint is necessary in order to allow the trial to continue.[304] This may not be so essential in the case of a misdemeanor.[305]

Presence at a view is not necessarily on the same basis as presence at other stages of a criminal proceeding. Most jurisdictions recognizing the probative use of a view treat it as evidence.[306] Accordingly they have conceded the defendant's right to accompany the jury either as an element of presence at the trial,[307] or more questionably [308] as an element of the right to confront witnesses.[309] Some courts have found a waiver by a failure to request presence.[310] Absence of prejudice has been found even when the request was expressly denied.[311] The United States Supreme

---

Constitutional Law (1939) 794; (1935) 33 Mich.L.Rev. 1104. He need not be present at the hearing on his appeal. Vowell v. State, 178 S.W. 768 (Tenn. 1915), 64 U. of Pa.L.Rev. 98.

304 Note (1898) 11 Harv.L.Rev. 409.

305 Note (1907) 20 Harv.L.Rev. 235; "Power of Court to Pass Sentence in Absence of Prisoner" (1933) 98 Justice of the Peace and Local Government Review 621.

306 4 Wigmore, Evidence (3d ed.1940) § 1168; (1944) 28 Minn.L.Rev. 201.

307 Noell v. Commonwealth, 135 Va. 600, 115 S.E. 679 (1923).

308 6 Wigmore, Evidence (3d ed.1940) § 1803.

309 Watson v. State, 61 S.W. (2d) (Tenn. 1933); People v. Hartnett, 124 Miss. 418, 208 N.Y.Supp. 247 (County Ct. 1925).

310 State v. Stratton, 103 Kan. 226, 173 Pac. 300 (1918); State v. Much, 156 Wash. 403, 287 Pac. 57 (1930).

311 Haynes v. State, 71 Fla. 585, 72 So. 180 (1916); People v. Raider, 256 Mich. 131, 239 N.W. 386 (1931).

Court has taken the unique view that a view is evidence and yet no part of the trial.[312] The more usual contention is that a view is not a proceeding to which an absolute guarantee of presence attaches.[313] The United States Supreme Court held that due process under the Fourteenth Amendment required personal presence of the defendant only when it bore a reasonably substantial relation to his opportunity to defend.

It has recently been held that it was reversible error for the court, without notice to the defendant and in the absence of the defendant and his counsel, to instruct the jury orally while the jury was deliberating upon its verdict.[314] The instruction consisted chiefly of a sharp reprimand for failure to agree upon a verdict, a reminder that there should be no outside influence, and a request for an early unanimous verdict.

Where a defendant indicted for murder and on bond voluntarily absented himself during the rendition of the verdict, it was held that he could not waive his right to be present in a capital felony case, either expressly or constructively.[315] On the other hand, a court has held in a

[312] Snyder v. Massachusetts, 291 U.S. 97, 54 Sup.Ct. 330, 78 L.Ed. 674, 90 A.L.R. 575 (1933), (1934) 34 Col.L.Rev. 767, 19 Corn.L.Q. 477, 33 Mich.L.Rev. 304.

[313] 6 Wigmore, Evidence (3d ed.1940) § 1803.

[314] Strasheim v. State, 138 Neb. 651, 294 N.W. 433 (1940), (1941) 20 Neb.L.Rev. 47.

[315] Sherrod v. State, 93 Miss. 774, 47 So. 554, 20 L.R.A. (N.S.) 509 (1908), (1909) 9 Col.L.Rev. 178, (1909) 22 Harv.L.Rev. 380. At common law the defendant's presence was imperative in all cases of treason and felony and such right was not waivable. Several states no longer apply this to non-capital felonies, since the defendant should not be allowed to render ineffectual a trial otherwise proper. For full discussion see Goldin, "Presence of the Defendant at Rendition of the Verdict in Felony Cases" (1916) 16 Col.L.Rev. 18-36. See also Notes (1907) 17 Yale L.J. 110, (1928) 13 Minn.L.Rev. 65.

felony case that where counsel, without the defendant's knowledge or consent, waived his presence at the reception of the verdict, and later moved for a new trial not alleging such fact, the defendant had acquiesced in the waiver and could not attack the verdict.[316] The rule requiring presence of the defendant at verdict, unless there be waiver, is based upon the idea that the defendant may personally poll the jury and that he may be in the power of the court for sentencing.[317] If, however, the defendant waives his presence, he should be regarded as properly waiving his personal right to poll the jury, and sentence may be pronounced at some later time.

Section 287 of the Institute Code provides that the defendant shall be present in felony prosecutions at arraignment, where plea of guilty is made, at the calling, examination, challenging, impaneling and swearing of the jury, at all proceedings before the court when the jury is present, when evidence is addressed to the court out of the presence of the jury for the purpose of laying the foundation for the introduction of evidence before the jury, at a view by the jury, and at the rendition of the verdict. It is further provided, however, that, if the defendant is voluntarily absent, all proceedings just mentioned may be had except arraignment and plea if the court so orders. In other words, the entire trial could be conducted in the voluntary absence of the defendant.

Under Section 288 in a misdemeanor case any proceeding except the arraignment and plea of guilty and sentence of imprisonment may be had in the voluntary absence of

[316] Frank v. State, 142 Ga. 741, 83 S.E. 645 (1914), (1915) 15 Col.L.Rev. 166, 189. Waiver by counsel is not binding unless ratified by the defendant. State v. Jenkins, 84 N.C. 812 (1881). See also (1929) 13 Minn.L. Rev. 65.

[317] Note (1915) 15 Col.L.Rev. 166.

the defendant. Under Section 365 the court must grant a new trial, provided substantial rights of the defendant have been thereby prejudiced, if the defendant was not present at any proceeding where his presence is required under the Code.

Rule 43 of the Federal Rules of Criminal Procedure provides: "The defendant shall be present at the arraignment, at every stage of the trial including the impaneling of the jury and the return of the verdict, and at the imposition of sentence, except as otherwise provided by these rules. In prosecutions for offenses not punishable by death, the defendant's voluntary absence after the trial has been commenced in his presence shall not prevent continuing the trial to and including the return of the verdict. A corporation may appear by counsel for all purposes. In prosecutions for offenses punishable by fine or by imprisonment for not more than one year or both, the court, with the written consent of the defendant, may permit arraignment, plea, trial and imposition of sentence in the defendant's absence. The defendant's presence is not required at a reduction of sentence under Rule 35."

22. Right to Counsel

The Scottsboro Cases,[318] decided by the United States Supreme Court in 1932, raised the question of the right to counsel in the state courts under the due process clause of the Fourteenth Amendment. The common-law rule, which did not allow the defendant in England to defense by counsel in the case of treason until 1688 and in case of felony until 1836, was generally rejected in this country.

318 Powell v. State of Alabama, 287 U.S. 45, 53 Sup.Ct. 55, 77 L.Ed. 158, 84 A.L.R. 527 (1932), (1933) 17 Minn.L.Rev. 415, (1932) 32 Col.L.Rev. 1430.

The Sixth Amendment guaranteed the right to counsel in the federal courts and the state constitutions contained similar provisions. The Scottsboro Cases added to defendants in state courts the protection of the due process clause of the Fourteenth Amendment. The due process clause is invoked not only to assure the absolute right to counsel where the accused is unable to employ counsel and is incapable of making his defense adequately because of illiteracy, ignorance, feeble-mindedness, or the like, but also for the purpose of requiring the court, whether there is a request or not, to appoint such counsel at such time and under such circumstances as to give the defendant the full benefit of his rights. The decision was limited expressly to capital cases, but was of such a nature that logically it might have been extended to all criminal cases or at least to felonies.[319]

It was therefore somewhat surprising when a decade later in 1942, the Supreme Court held, three justices dissenting, that where the issue is simple, the accused of ordinary intelligence, the crime less than capital, and the appointment of counsel is not required by state law, the guarantee of the Sixth Amendment of counsel in all criminal prosecutions is not included in the due process clause of the Fourteenth Amendment.[320]

A defendant in a state court is thus not as well protected as one in a federal criminal case. In the federal courts, counsel must be appointed in all criminal cases where the defendant is unable to procure the services of

[319] Notes (1932) 31 Mich.L.Rev. 245, 252, (1933) 17 Minn.L.Rev. 415, 418, (1942) 42 Col.L.Rev. 271, 272; Boyd v. O'Grady, 121 F. (2d) 146 (C.C.A. 8th, 1941).

[320] Betts v. Brady, 316 U.S. 455, 62 Sup.Ct. 1252, 86 L.Ed. 1595 (1942), 42 Col.L.Rev. 1205. See also Notes (1942) 33 J.Crim.L. 49, (1943) 29 A.B. A.J. 61, (1942) 91 U. of Pa.L.Rev. 78, (1942) 31 Ill. Bar J. 139.

an attorney if the right has not been intentionally and competently waived.[321] In the state courts, on the other hand, counsel must be appointed only in capital cases where the defendant is impoverished and ignorant.[322] A majority of the Supreme Court viewed the fact that state laws providing counsel to a defendant have received restrictive applications as a popular judgment that the right to counsel is not fundamental and essential in all cases to a fair trial. Prior Supreme Court decisions arising from state trials are explained on the ground that there were state statutes requiring the appointment of counsel. In the past, however, state law has been said not to be a criterion of conformity with the due process clause of the Fourteenth Amendment. It is true that some practical difficulties may arise, such as whether the right should extend to petty cases where there is no right of trial by jury;[323] possibly numerous habeas corpus actions might burden the courts; and the financial drain might be great if the states reimburse counsel.[324] The right to counsel seems to be so basic a right as to require its uniform availability. It is perfectly clear that the ordinary layman does not under-

321 Johnston v. Zerbst, 304 U.S. 458, 58 Sup.Ct. 1019, 82 L.Ed. 1461 (1938); Walker v. Johnston, 312 U.S. 275 (1941); Holtzoff, "The Right of Counsel under the Sixth Amendment" (1944) 20 N.Y.U.L.Q.Rev. 1.

322 Powell v. Alabama, 287 U.S. 45, 53 Sup.Ct. 55, 77 L.Ed. 158, 84 A.L.R. 527 (1932); Avery v. Albama, 308 U.S. 444, 445 (1940); cf. Smith v. O'Grady, 312 U.S. 329 (1941). Only Maryland and Texas affirmatively sustain a refusal to appoint counsel in serious criminal cases.

323 For a proposal that a defendant charged with a non-indictable offense be advised of his right to counsel, see Report of the New York Law Revision Commission (1940) 91-104.

324 Most defendants, however, wish counsel of their own choice if they can possibly pay for it. "Everyone will admit that defense at the hand of a highly qualified and specialized private attorney is, in general, more effective than the defense of an employed attorney within the framework of a public defender's office." Schweinburg, "What State Defense in Criminal Procedure Presupposes" (1944) 11 U. of Chi.L.Rev. 444, 447.

stand technical questions of practice, pleading, and evidence. The Supreme Court laid down a very uncertain test when it held that the intelligence of the accused and the complexity of the issue must be examined. Such a test overemphasizes the facts of the individual cases.

In general, the right to counsel has been given a broad interpretation, not only in the Scottsboro Cases, but in the state decisions.[325] It has been held to confer every privilege which will make the presence and aid of counsel a valuable right. It has been said to contemplate not only the right to counsel at the trial, but also at every stage of the proceedings.[326] After ample notice of the charge against him, of its consequences, and of his rights,[327] the defendant should be allowed reasonable time to procure counsel[328] who should be allowed every reasonable opportunity for full and confidential consultation with the defendant,[329] and reasonable time for preparation of the defense.[330] Where the defendant is unable to procure counsel,[331] it is the duty of many courts by statute, and the

325 Note (1933) 17 Minn.L.Rev. 415. But for a decision holding no duty by the court to advise a minor defendant of his right to counsel in a first degree murder case where the defendant pleaded guilty, see People v. Crandell, 258 N.W. 224 (Mich. 1935), 83 U. of Pa.L.Rev. 797. See also Note (1946) 46 Col.L.Rev. 647.

326 People v. Naphtaly, 105 Cal. 641, 39 Pac. 29 (1895); Powell v. Alabama, 287 U.S. 45, 53 Sup.Ct. 55 (1932); Sutton v. State, 35 Okla. Cr. 263, 250 Pac. 930 (1926); Note (1942) 42 Col.L.Rev. 271, 275.

327 State v. McDonnell, 165 Minn. 423, 206 N.W. 952 (1926); Commonwealth v. O'Keefe, 298 Pa. St. 169, 148 Atl. 73 (1929).

328 Commonwealth v. O'Keefe, 298 Pa. St. 169, 148 Atl. 73 (1929).

329 State v. Davis, 9 Okla. Cr. R. 94, 130 Pac. 962, 44 L.R.A. (N.S.) 1083 (1913); Note, 23 A.L.R. 1382 (1923).

330 People v. Blumenfeld, 330 Ill. 474, 161 N.E. 857 (1928); Notes (1927) 36 Yale L.J. 574, (1942) 42 Col.L.Rev. 271, 274.

331 Many cases place upon the defendant the burden of showing that he is unable to procure counsel and of requesting that counsel be appointed in his behalf. If he fails to act, he is then deemed to waive his

practice in others by custom, to inform him of his rights to have counsel appointed.

The present status of the right to counsel in the state courts has been thus summarized: "While [as of 1936] all states had provided for assignments in capital cases, nearly one-fourth had not done so in felony cases, and nearly one-half had not done so in misdemeanor cases. Only eight states had provided for assignments in the magistrates' or other lower courts, as distinguished from the regular criminal trial courts; and only two had covered proceedings in appellate courts. Nineteen states had made no provision for compensating the assigned counsel; in most of the remaining states the compensation was meagre or nominal (e.g.: North Carolina, $25 in capital cases; Oklahoma, $25 maximum; Washington, $10 per day; Iowa, life or over, $20 per day, others $10 maximum total; Idaho, capital, $50, felony, $25, misdemeanor, $10; and so on). Finally, only eight states had provided reimbursement for the necessary expenses and disbursements of trial (expert testimony, witness fees, travel, etc.)—and two of these limited the reimbursement to capital cases; so that, with these exceptions, 'either the attorney must pay the incidental expenses out of his own pocket, which, of course, he cannot afford to do, and therefore, does not do, or the defendant must go to trial and do the best he can in spite of an inadequate preparation of his case.' "[332]

---

right to counsel. Holland v. Commonwealth, 241 Ky. 831, 45 S.W. (2d) 476 (1932); but cf. Batchelor v. State, 189 Ind. 69, 125 N.E. 773 (1920).

[332] Garrison, "Legal Service for Low Income Groups in Sweden" (1940) 26 A.B.A.J. 215, 217. New state statutes are also fully discussed in Betts v. Brady, 316 U.S. 455, 62 Sup. 1252, 86 L.Ed. 1595 (1942). The matter of compensation for court appointed counsel is discussed in a Note (1941) 31 J.Crim.L. 731. The United States Judicial Conference of Senior Circuit Judges favors compensation to attorneys appointed by the court to repre-

A state statute providing for the compensation of counsel assigned to a defendant in a criminal proceeding does not violate a constitutional provision which forbids payment of public money for private purposes.[333] Some states even hold it unconstitutional to refuse to pay for such services of counsel on the ground that it would be taking private property for public purposes without compensation.[334]

A defendant if competent may if he chooses conduct his entire defense unaided.[335] But when he elects to retain counsel for the initial stages of the trial, the trial court may, in its discretion, treat such election as final.[336]

In assigning counsel, the court must appoint counsel who are able and willing.[337] Such counsel must have no prejudice toward the defendant.[338] They must have no interest antagonistic to the defendant.[339]

The circumstance that an attorney is young or inexperienced does not show incompetence.[340] Mistakes in

---

sent indigent persons in criminal cases and in habeas corpus proceedings where no provision is made for a public defender, Congress to prescribe maximum amounts and the court to fix the compensation within that amount. Report of the Judicial Conference of Senior Circuit Judges (1941) 11.

333 People ex rel. Acritelli v. Grout, 84 N.Y.Supp. 97 (1903), (1904) 13 Yale L.J. 202.

334 Hall v. Washington County, 2 G. Greene (Iowa) 473 (1850).

335 Dietz v. State, 149 Wis. 462, 136 N.W. 166 (1912); People v. Rose, 42 Cal. App. 540, 183 Pac. 874 (1919); Note (1922) 17 A.L.R. 266.

336 State v. Townley, 149 Minn. 5, 182 N.W. 773 (1921), 5 Minn. L.Rev. 553, (1921) 35 Harv.L.Rev. 86. But cf. Rehfeld v. State, 102 Ohio St. 431, 131 N.E. 712 (1921).

337 People v. Blevins, 251 Ill. 381, 388, 96 N.E. 214, Ann. Cas. 1912 C 451 (1911).

338 State v. Jones, 174 La. 1074, 142 So. 693 (1932), 46 Harv.L.Rev. 335.

339 People v. Bopp, 279 Ill. 184, 116 N.E. 679 (1917).

340 Achtien v. Dowd, 117 F. (2d) 989, 992 (C.C.A. 7th, 1941); cf. Jones v. State, 57 Ga. App. 195 S.E. 316 (1938).

judgment may, though not always, show incompetence.[341] The incompetence of counsel, resulting in failure to introduce evidence favorable to the defendant, especially where the evidence actually introduced is inconclusive, may be sufficient ground for a new trial.[342] Where a defendant is represented by a party representing himself as an attorney, but who has not been admitted to the bar, he should be entitled to a new trial if convicted.[343]

It has been held that an attorney need not be required to defend a person with whom he has had unpleasant relations and with whom he is not in sympathy.[344] It does not clearly follow that the appointment of such an attorney constitutes ground for reversal.[345] On the other hand, where the defendant urges neglect or incompetence of appointed counsel, a patent miscarriage of justice must appear.[346] But the appointment of counsel having adverse interests on behalf of another client has been held reversible without proof of actual harm.[347] Prejudice, like adverse interest, may have consequences impossible to ascertain from the record, such as failure to run down evidence of which no one but the attorney is aware. Reversal will be justified in some cases.

341 Aldredge v. Williams, 188 Ga. 607, 4 S.E. (2d) 469 (1939); Note (1942) 42 Col.L.Rev. 271, 273; (1935) 33 Mich.L.Rev. 445.

342 People v. Schulman, 299 Ill. 490, 132 N.E. 530 (1921), (1922) 22 Col. L.Rev. 276, (1922) 31 Yale L.J. 450. See also Notes (1912) 21 Yale L.J. 505, (1923) 71 U. of Pa.L.Rev. 379, (1912) 6 Ill.L.Rev. 409, (1922) 15 Ill.L.Rev. 40, (1947) 47 Col.L.Rev. 115.

343 Note (1929) 29 Col.L.Rev. 665. If the defense is well conducted and if his guilt clearly appears, perhaps the error should be regarded as harmless.

344 People v. Thompson, 205 App. Div. 581, 199 N.Y.Supp. 868 (1923).

345 But see State v. Jones, 142 So. 693 (La. 1932), 46 Harv.L.Rev. 335.

346 Castro v. State, 196 Ind. 385, 147 N.E. 321 (1925); People v. Andrews, 327 Ill. 162, 158 N.E. 462 (1927); but cf. People v. Blevins, 251 Ill. 381, 96 N.E. 214 (1911).

347 People v. Bopp, 279 Ill. 184, 116 N.E. 679 (1917).

The assistance of counsel guaranteed to federal defendants under the Sixth Amendment contemplates that such assistance be untrammeled and unimpaired by a court order requesting that one lawyer shall simultaneously represent conflicting interests of joint defendants.[348] A defendant might expressly waive his objection, but it is not clear that mere silence would be a waiver.[349] Even without a conflict of interest, an appointment to represent several defendants may be improper because the additional burden of representing so many may conceivably impair counsel's effectiveness.[350]

It is fundamental that counsel should have adequate opportunity to prepare and present his case. Many cases have been appealed because of the trial judge's denial of a continuance which would have given counsel more time to prepare. There is no set rule as to what is adequate time. The court should take into account the familiarity of the attorney with the case,[351] the difficulty of reaching witnesses to interview them,[352] and the inability of defense counsel to give all his time to the case.[353] The possibility of lack of sufficient time to prepare seems greatest in

348 Glasser v. United States, 315 U.S. 60, 62 Sup.Ct. 457 (1942), 26 Minn.L.Rev. 657, 41 Mich.L.Rev. 321, 9 U. of Chi.L.Rev. 733. For a state court decision arriving at the same result, see People v. Rose, 348 Ill. 214, 180 N.E. 791 (1932).

349 Cf. United States v. Rollnick, 91 F. (2d) 911 (C.C.A. 2d, 1937).

350 Glasser v. United States, 315 U.S. 60, 62 Sup.Ct. 457 (1942). For reasons of practicality and economy, possibly the right of the defendant would not be as broad where the counsel was appointed by the court rather than privately retained.

351 Shores v. United States, 80 F. (2d) 942, 947 (C.C.A. 9th, 1935), cert. denied 297 U.S. 705 (1936).

352 Avery v. Alabama, 308 U.S. 444 (1940).

353 People v. Gordon, 30 N.Y.S. (2d) 625 (App. Div. 2d Dept. 1941).

cases where the court appoints counsel for the defendant at the time of arraignment.[354]

In an ideal system, counsel should be present at all stages of a criminal proceeding.[355] The cases, however, are in some conflict as to whether the defendant has been deprived of his constitutional rights if he was unadvised at the time of arraignment.[356] The entering of a plea is one of the most critical stages in the proceedings. In general, a defendant should have counsel before anything is done to prejudice him.[357] It has been held that it was error for a trial judge, in the absence of defense counsel, to communicate with a jury [358] or to have evidence read to a jury at its request.[359]

A violation of the defendant's right would appear to occur where counsel for defendant has not been present at the trial or has withdrawn from the case before the jury rendered the verdict and sentence was imposed.[360] It does

[354] Powell v. Alabama, 287 U.S. 451, 53 Sup.Ct. 55, 77 L.Ed. 158 (1932), 31 Mich.L.Rev. 245.

[355] In Powell v. Alabama, 287 U.S. 45, 69 (1932), the court stated that a defendant "requires the guiding hand of counsel at every step in the proceedings against him." A leading English writer states: "The need for competent legal assistance exists at all stages of a criminal charge." Jackson, The Machinery of Justice in England (1940) 121.

[356] Lack of assistance before arraignment was held unconstitutional in United States ex rel. Mertner v. Hiatt, 33 F. Supp. 545 (M.D.Pa. 1940); People ex rel. Moore v. Hart, 258 App. Div. 24, 16 N.Y.Supp. (2d) 19 (4th Dept. 1939); Ex parte Stinnett, 110 P. (2d) 310 (Okla. 1941). The contrary was held in People v. Crandell, 270 Mich. 124, 258 N.W. 224 (1935).

[357] People v. Terry, 366 Ill. 520, 523, 9 N.E. (2d) 322, 324 (1937).

[358] Shields v. United States, 273 U.S. 583 (1927).

[359] Lett v. Commonwealth, 284 Ky. 267, 144 S.W. (2d) 505 (1940).

[360] Note (1942) 42 Col.L.Rev. 271, 276. Compare majority and dissenting opinions in Kent v. Sanford, 121 F. (2d) 216 (C.C.A. 5th, 1941), cert. denied 312 U.S. 697 (1941); see also Norton v. Henderson, 123 F. (2d) 48 (C.C.A. 5th, 1941).

not seem realistic to argue in criminal cases that an attorney cannot withdraw from the case without the consent of the court and that the relation does not terminate finally until there is a withdrawal of record. At the close of the trial the three chief duties of defendant's counsel are a motion for a new trial, the perfecting of an appeal, and a request for leniency in the sentence where the judge has discretion.[361] It is true that due process does not include the right to appeal.[362] But if the legislature has provided an appellate organization, it may be an unconstitutional discrimination not to provide a means of appeal for indigent defendants.[363] There is authority that the appeal is part of the proceedings in which an accused is entitled to counsel.[364] Even if the statement that an accused is entitled to counsel in every stage of the proceedings merely referred to the proceedings at trial, it could be said that a motion for a new trial is a part of the trial proceedings.

The following elements thus appear to be essential to effective benefit of counsel: (1) that counsel be appointed in cases in which the defendant is indigent; (2) that counsel be competent; (3) that counsel have adequate opportunity to prepare and present the case; and (4) that counsel be present during all stages of the proceeding.[365]

Although a defendant may have the right to counsel, he may under certain circumstances waive such right. In federal criminal cases, unless there be a waiver, the ab-

[361] Kent v. Sanford, 121 F. (2d) 216, 218 (C.C.A. 5th, 1941) (dissenting opinion), cert. denied 312 U.S. 697 (1941).

[362] McKane v. Durston, 153 U.S. 684 (1894).

[363] Boykin v. Hoff, 121 F. (2d) 856, 870 (App. D.C. 1941).

[364] State ex rel. White v. Hilgemann, 34 N.E. (2d) 129 (Ind. 1941); cf. State v. Hudson, 55 R.I. 141, 179 Atl. 130 (1935).

[365] Note (1942) 42 Col.L.Rev. 271.

sence of assistance of counsel voids the conviction because of lack of jurisdiction.[366] It follows that the defendant may collaterally attack the judgment by habeas corpus. The defendant may waive his right only intelligently and competently. Whether a waiver is intelligent and competent will depend upon the particular facts in each case, including the background and conduct of the defendant. But since a judgment of a court of general jurisdiction carries with it a presumption of regularity, it will be up to the petitioner to prove by a preponderance of the evidence that he did not waive competently and intelligently. There ought to be a record of the waiver, though this has been held not absolutely essential to bind the defendant. A mere failure to request counsel ought not to be treated as a waiver.[367]

Of great practical importance to the defendant are the procedural means he may employ to enforce the right to counsel. The increasingly common method for federal defendants is a habeas corpus attack on the jurisdiction of the court which convicted the undefended accused.[368] A state defendant can, except in unusual circumstances, obtain the federal writ only when he has exhausted his state remedies.[369] If he has not appealed to the high court of his state because of his failure to have assistance of counsel, this would be no bar.[370]

[366] Johnson v. Zerbst, 304 U.S. 458, 58 Sup.Ct. 1019, 82 L.Ed. 1461 (1938). See Note (1936) 27 J.Crim.L. 603.

[367] But the cases treat it as a waiver. Note (1942) 42 Col.L.Rev. 271, 279.

[368] Notes (1939) 24 Corn.L.Q. 270, (1938) 24 Iowa L.Rev. 170, (1942) 42 Col.L.Rev. 271, 281. For a Canadian case in accord, see Note (1928) 6 Can.B.Rev. 407, involving merely a summary conviction.

[369] Mooney v. Holohan, 294 U.S. 103, 59 Sup.Ct. 340, 79 L.Ed. 791, 98 A.L.R. 406 (1935); Achtien v. Dowd, 117 F. (2d) 989 (C.C.A. 7th, 1941).

[370] Smith v. O'Grady, 312 U.S. 329 (1941).

Counsel may do various acts which when ratified by the defendant are binding upon him. It has been held even in a capital case that counsel might waive defendant's presence at the rendition of the verdict.[371] There are a few modern cases holding that the defendant's attorney may plead guilty for him in his presence.[372] In the absence of the defendant, his counsel may not plead guilty for him where he has not been authorized to do so or has been instructed to plead not guilty.[373]

Just as it is held that defendant must be present at the trial, there are holdings that the presence of his counsel is necessary. It has been held, for instance, that he must be present when the official stenographer's notes are read to the jury.[374]

23. Order of Trial

It appears to be common practice for the prosecuting attorney to open the case and then offer evidence in support of the indictment, the defendant then opening the defense, and then offering evidence in support of his defense. In New York a statute has changed the order of trial, so that the opening address of the defense follows, as in

[371] Frank v. State, 83 S.E. 645 (Ga. 1914), (1915) 15 Col.L.Rev. 166. Failure of defendant to make any objection in a later motion for new trial was held to constitute acquiescence in the waiver.

[372] United States v. Moe Liss, 105 F. (2d) 144 (C.C.A. 2d, 1939), (1940) 40 Col.L.Rev. 722. The common law did not permit an attorney to make a plea of guilty even where the defendant stood by in apparent acquiescence. 1 Bishop, New Criminal Procedure (4th ed.1895) § 268. A waiver of jury trial by defendant's counsel and the prosecutor in open court in the presence of the defendant has been held insufficient. People v. Spinato, 280 Pac. 691 (Calif. App. 1929), (1930) 28 Mich.L.Rev. 770.

[373] Note (1940) 4 J.Crim.L. (Eng.) 1.

[374] Bartell v. State, 40 Neb. 232, 58 N.W. 716 (1894).

civil cases, that of the prosecuting attorney before any evidence is taken.[375]

The Commission on the Administration of Justice in New York State has recommended the following order of trial:[376]

The jury having been impanelled and sworn, the trial shall proceed in the following order:

1. The prosecuting attorney shall open the case.
2. The defendant or his counsel may then open the defense.
3. The prosecuting attorney shall then offer evidence in support of the indictment.
4. The defendant or his counsel may then offer evidence in support of his defense.
5. The parties may then offer rebutting testimony.
6. The court for good reason shown may permit the prosecuting attorney or the defendant or the defendant's counsel to reopen the case at any time before the verdict is rendered for the purpose of offering additional evidence on his original case.
7. When the evidence is concluded, unless the case is submitted to the jury on either side or on both sides without argument, the defendant or his counsel shall commence and the prosecuting attorney conclude the argument to the jury.
8. The court shall then charge the jury.

[375] Note (1926) 12 A.B.A.J. 386, 387.

[376] Report of the Commission on the Administration of Justice in New York State (1939) § 345, p.125. The American Law Institute Code of Criminal Procedure has been criticized for the brevity of its treatment of this stage. "In view of the detail in which such special cases are dealt with, it comes as somewhat of a surprise to find how small is the number of sections dealing with the actual procedure at the hearing, from the empanelment of the jury down to their retirement, in a case which proceeds normally." Brunyate, "The American Draft Code of Criminal Procedure, 1930" (1933) 49 L.Q.Rev. 192, 199.

24. Evidence

Assuredly one of the most important topics in connection with trial is that of evidence. The importance of the topic may be shown by the fact that most reversals on appeal in criminal cases are on the grounds of error in the instructions and errors in rulings on matters of evidence.[377] It has been asserted that "the practice of reversals for technical errors in the admission or exclusion of evidence has also become less common in the past fifty years." [378] Yet even today counsel for the defendant is on the alert to get error into the record. It follows that there is much wrangling over the admissibility of evidence, and too much time and energy of judges and counsel is spent in this fashion. The judge is likely to rule in favor of the defendant for fear that he will appeal.

25. Expert Witnesses

The National Conference of Commissioners on Uniform State Laws has pointed out: "The use of expert evidence has increased until it has become an important and often controlling factor in an estimated sixty per cent of our more important litigated business. . . . There can be no doubt of the need for expert testimony. The problem is how to eliminate the evils of bias and partisanship." [379] One remedy is to authorize the court to call an

[377] Orfield, Criminal Appeals in America (1939) 206. The present volume does not consider problems of evidence, except on a few topics. Lack of space unfortunately forbids. The American Law Institute Code of Criminal Procedure and the Federal Rules of Criminal Procedure do not deal with the subject at full length.

[378] Warner and Cabot, "Changes in the Administration of Criminal Justice During the Past Eighty Years" (1937) 50 Harv.L.Rev. 583, 588.

[379] Handbook of the National Conference of Commissioners on Uniform State Laws (1937) 337.

expert selected by the judge himself.[380] Wigmore says of such a remedy that, "Modest as it seems, this expedient would remove most of the present abuses."[381] It would appear that the courts have inherent power to appoint, at least in the absence of legislation to the contrary.[382]

An expert witness can be called by the court in "any action or proceeding,—civil or criminal" in California.[383] Expert witnesses may be appointed by the court to testify "in any criminal case" in Wisconsin.[384] The court is required to appoint expert witnesses to testify on the issue of insanity in criminal cases in Indiana,[385] and California.[386] The constitutionality of these statutes has been upheld.[387] Section 308 of the Institute Code permits the court to appoint expert witnesses. Rule 28 of the Federal Rules of Criminal Procedure provides: "The court may

[380] A.L.I., Model Code of Evidence (1942) Rule 403; Second Report of the Judicial Council of New Jersey (1931) 79; Missouri Crime Survey (1926) 371; Uniform Expert Testimony Act, § 1; New York Law Revision Commission (1936) 799; Nat. Com. on Law Obs. and Enf., Rep. on Crim. Proc. (1931) 37, 47.

[381] 2 Wigmore, Evidence (3d ed.1940) § 563, p.648.

[382] Brandeis, J., in Ex parte Petersen, 253 U.S. 300, 312 (1919). The appointment of expert alienists by a trial judge in the absence of any statute conferring such authority was upheld in State v. Horne, 171 N.C. 787, 88 S.E. 433 (1916).

[383] Cal. Code Civ. Proc. (Deering 1941) § 1871 (enacted 1925). See also Rhode Island, Gen. Laws, 1923, c.342, § 5002.

[384] Wis. Stat. (1941) § 357.12 (enacted 1921).

[385] Ind Stat. Ann. (Burns 1933) § 9—1702 (enacted in 1927).

[386] Cal. Pen. Code (Deering 1941) § 1027 (enacted 1929).

[387] Jessner v. State, 302 Wis. 184, 231 N.W. 634 (1930), (1931) 26 Ill. L.Rev. 82, (1931) 6 Wis.L.Rev. 184; Noelke v. State, 214 Ind. 427 (1938); People v. Strong, 114 Calif. App. 522 (1931). The Michigan statute was held unconstitutional. People v. Dickerson, 164 Mich. 148, 129 N.W. 199, 33 L.R.A. (N.S.) 917, Ann. Cas. 1912 B 688 (1910), (1911) 24 Harv. L.Rev. 483, (1911) 9 Mich.L.Rev. 603. The Illinois Court held appointment by the court invalid where no statute permitted. People v. Scott, 326 Ill. 327, 157 N.E. 347 (1927).

order the defendant or the government or both to show cause why expert witnesses should not be appointed, and may request the parties to submit nominations. The court may appoint any expert witnesses agreed upon by the parties, and may appoint witnesses of its own selection. . . . The parties also may call expert witnesses of their own selection."[388]

In some states, by statutory provision, the trial court determines the reasonable compensation of an expert witness appointed by the court and orders payment out of the county funds. Rule 28 of the Federal Rules of Criminal Procedure provides: "The court may determine the reasonable compensation of such a witness and direct its payment out of such funds as may be provided by law." In the absence of available funds the witness could decline appointment. In fact Rule 28 provides: "An expert witness shall not be appointed by the court unless he consents to act."

The defendant should be guarded against surprise and should be informed as to who will testify against him. Section 2 of the Uniform Expert Testimony Act provides: "The appointment of expert witnesses by the court shall be made only after reasonable notice to the parties to the proceedings of the names and addresses of the experts proposed for appointment." Rule 28 of the federal rules provides: "A witness so appointed shall be informed of his duties by the court at a conference in which the parties shall have opportunity to participate. A witness so

[388] The Federal Criminal Rule and the American Law Institute Model Code of Evidence, Rule 403, differ from the Uniform Expert Testimony Act in providing for a hearing. It seems fair to give the parties an opportunity to be heard on the question whether expert evidence is needed or desired as well as to present arguments for or against the selection of specified experts.

appointed shall advise the parties of his findings, if any, and may thereafter be called to testify by the court or by any party. He shall be subject to cross examination by each party."

26. Demurrer to the Evidence

The demurrer to the evidence has today been generally superseded by the motion to enter a nonsuit, to direct a verdict, or to exclude the evidence from the jury. These motions are less technical in character and accomplish the same result of transferring from the jury to the judge the application of the law to the facts. But demurrer to the evidence is still recognized in almost half the states in civil cases. In criminal cases, on the other hand, the use of the demurrer is less common and in fact the propriety of its use is doubted. The West Virginia court has ruled that it does not exist in West Virginia.[389]

Against the use of the demurrer it is argued that, if the defendant has the right to demur to the evidence, the state would have a corresponding right without the consent of the defendant who would thus lose his right to trial by jury. But in criminal cases a joinder in demurrer is optional, not compulsory as in civil suits.[390] It is also contended that it deprives the defendant of the right to be proved guilty beyond every reasonable doubt because, it is said, all doubt must be resolved against the demurrant. But inferences from the evidence need not be taken as strongly against the demurrant in criminal as in civil cases. The effect of a demurrer is that the defendant contends that, upon the evidence presented, the court acting as a

389 State v. Alderton, 50 W.Va. 101, 40 S.E. 350 (1901), (1902) 13 Harv. L.Rev. 738.

390 Duncan v. State, 29 Fla. 439, 10 So. 815 (1892).

jury would not be justified in finding an adverse verdict.[391] The court, therefore, no more than a jury should deprive the defendant of reasonable doubts in his favor. But even if it does, the defendant should have the right to waive at least in jurisdictions where he can waive trial by jury.[392] Admittedly, however, it is an unusual and an antiquated practice. It is in no way more desirable than the modern motions. In fact it has several disadvantages: the demurrant waives the benefit of any exceptions taken to prior rulings of the court and is debarred from introducing more evidence if his demurrer is overruled.

27. Directed Verdict

It is the prevailing doctrine today that the court may instruct the jury as to the law and that the jury should follow and apply the law as laid down by the court.[393] On the other hand, it is clear that the jury may disregard their oath, ignore their moral duty, and return a verdict of not guilty.[394] Suppose, however, the facts of guilt are undisputed. The modern tendency is toward holding that an instruction correctly stating the law and warning the jury against a finding contrary to it is not a direction of a verdict of guilty, although in effect it directs the jury to find the defendant guilty.[395] On the other hand, it is argu-

[391] Trout v. Virginia, etc., R.R.C., 23 Gratt. (Va.) 619, 639 (1873).

[392] Martin v. State, 62 Ala. 240 (1878).

[393] Duffy v. The People, 26 N.Y. 588 (1863).

[394] Comment (1921) 19 Mich.L.Rev. 325.

[395] Nicholson v. Commonwealth, 91 Pa. 390 (1879); Horning v. District of Columbia, 254 U.S. 135, 41 Sup.Ct. 53, 65 L.Ed. 185 (1920); (1921) 5 Minn.L.Rev. 231, (1921) 21 Col.L.Rev. 190; (1921) 19 Mich.L.Rev. 325; (1921) 30 Yale L.J. 42. See Notes (1939) 6 U. of Chi.L.Rev. 494, (1916) 16 Col.L.Rev. 594, (1927) 11 Minn.L.Rev. 663, (1929) 27 Mich.L.Rev. 582; State v. Corey, 182 Minn. 48 233 N.W. 590 (1930), (1931) 15 Minn.L.Rev. 343; (1931) 10 Ore.L.Rev. 269; (1931) 79 U. of Pa.L.Rev. 812.

able that the error is more than formal, for the right to be tried by jury is a constitutional right.[396]

If, when the evidence for the prosecution has been presented, it appears that there has been a failure to make out a prima facie case against the defendant, he may be saved further harassment, expense, and delay by moving for a directed verdict.[397] Such motions are seldom granted, however. In Missouri, "out of the total number of 4,969 felony cases in the circuit courts, during the period of the survey, only 18 were dismissed owing to the failure of the state to make out a prima facie case."[398]

Section 321 of the Institute Code provides for a directed verdict of acquittal on motion of the defendant or on the court's own motion. Rule 50(a) of the Federal Rules of Civil Procedure lays down a rule for federal civil cases. Rule 29(a) of the Federal Rules of Criminal Procedure provides for the abolition of motions for directed verdict and the substitution of motions for judgment of acquittal. The court on its own motion or that of the defendant shall order the entry of judgment of acquittal after the evidence on either side is closed, if the evidence is insufficient to sustain a conviction. A defendant whose motion at the close of the evidence offered by the government is not granted may, even though he did not reserve the right to do so, offer evidence as if the motion had not been made.

396 Brandeis, J., dissenting in Horning v. District of Columbia, 254 U.S. 135, 41 Sup.Ct. 53, 65 L.Ed. 185 (1920). Three other justices also dissented.

397 A failure to raise the question of the sufficiency of the evidence by a motion for a directed verdict precludes a motion for new trial on that ground. Housel and Walser, Defending and Prosecuting Federal Criminal Cases (1938) § 602, p.664.

398 Missouri Crime Survey (1926) 175.

28. Judgment Notwithstanding the Verdict

Criminal judgments *non obstante veredicto,* whereby the court enters a judgment contrary to the jury verdict, were virtually unknown at common law.[399] But they were almost equally unfamiliar in civil cases, a factor causing the United States Supreme Court to hold such judgment violative of the Seventh Amendment, which prohibits re-examination of any fact tried by a jury otherwise than according to the rules of the common law.[400] The court in a subsequent case pointed out that in the earlier case there had been no motion for directed verdict with ruling reserved; and that there were common-law prototypes of judgments notwithstanding the verdict after reserved rulings.[401] Similar criminal prototypes existed at common law. Both civilly and criminally, these devices required the consent of the parties and probably of the jury as well.[402] But several states permit such procedure.[403] The United

[399] Cf. 2 Hale, History of the Pleas of the Crown (1st American ed. 1847) 309-310; Stephen, A History of the Criminal Law of England (1883) 311; Note (1940) 49 Yale L.J. 733, 735. But see Archbold, Criminal Pleading, Evidence and Practice (23d ed.1905) 292-293; Roscoe, Criminal Evidence and Practice (15th ed.1938) 317.

[400] Slocum v. New York Life Ins. Co., 228 U.S. 364 (1913). The Seventh Amendment does not apply to equity cases, and probably not to criminal cases. Shapiro, "Criminal Appeal on the Facts and the Federal Judicial System" (1939) 34 Ill.L.Rev. 332; (1939) 52 Harv.L.Rev. 1358.

[401] Baltimore & Carolina Line, Inc., v. Redman, 295 U.S. 654 (1935).

[402] Morgan, "A Brief History of Special Verdicts and Special Interrogatories" (1923) 32 Yale L.J. 575, 591; cf. Rex v. Huggins, 2 Ld. Raym. 1574 (K.B. 1730).

[403] Sutherland v. Commonwealth, 171 Va. 485, 198 S.E. 452 (1938) (criminal judgment n.o.v. by appellate court); State v. Meen, 171 Wis. 36, 176 N.W. 70 (1920). Cf. Ill. Rev. Stat. (1937) c.110, § 192 (31)(b); Iowa Code (1935) § 14013. In Commonwealth v. Pennsylvania R.R., 72 Pa. Super. Ct. 353 (1919), a statute permitting judgments n.o.v. was construed as inapplicable to criminal cases. In State v. Bossio, 136 Wash.

States Supreme court in an evenly divided opinion upheld such practice in the federal courts.[404]

The chief consideration in favor of the use of such judgments is their utility in protracted trials, sparing the jury prolonged sequestration and avoiding needless new trials.[405] Such judgments should be permitted at least in complex cases. Since a court might direct a verdict of acquittal, it should be able to overrule the jury after it has deliberated.[406]

The chief counter considerations are possible abuse by the courts, and the unfairness to the prosecution of an unappealable acquittal after a jury conviction.[407] A civil judgment on the other hand is appealable. It permits a judge to review a cold record after impressions of the credibility of witnesses have been forgotten. It upsets the allocation of power between trial and appellate courts in permitting the trial judge to review his own decision. It

---

232, 234, 239 P. 553, 555 (1925), mention was made of much the same procedure, though as the case arose the court did not pass on the point.

404 United States v. Stone, 308 U.S. 519, 60 Sup.Ct. 177, 84 L.Ed. 441 (1939). For the lower court decisions, see Ex parte United States, 101 F. (2d) 870 (C.C.A. 7th, 1939), 52 Harv.L.Rev. 1358; (1939) 17 Chi.-Kent Rev. 283; (1939) 25 Va.L.Rev. 987; (1940) 49 Yale L.J. 733; United States v. Standard Oil Co., 23 F. Supp. 937 (W.D. Wis. 1938); (1939) 87 U. of Pa.L.Rev. 351. See also Note, (1942) 21 Neb.L.Rev. 181. In Collenger v. State, 50 F. (2d) 345 (C.C.A. 7th, 1931), it was held that a new trial must be ordered, although the evidence clearly is insufficient, if the trial court makes no reservation of ruling.

405 Notes (1939) 52 Harv.L.Rev. 1358, (1942) 21 Neb.L.Rev. 181, (1939) 25 Va.L.Rev. 987. See Minutes of the Fifth Pennsylvania Judicial Conference (1936) 7-8.

406 Note (1939) 87 U. of Pa.L.Rev. 351.

407 Note (1940) 49 Yale L.J. 733. However, the prosecution cannot appeal from a directed verdict either. Moreover, legislation might properly allow the prosecution the right to appeal. The appellate court need not allow a new trial, but could reinstate the verdict of guilty.

may cause the trial judge to be less attentive during trial since he can review the case later.

The Institute Code has no provision dealing with judgment notwithstanding the verdict. Rule 50(b) of the Federal Rules of Civil Procedure provides for it in federal civil cases. Rule 29(b) of the Federal Rules of Criminal Procedure introduces it definitely into federal criminal procedure and is modeled very largely on the federal civil rule. In effect a defendant against whom a verdict has been returned is permitted to renew a motion which he might have made previously for a directed verdict. Whenever a motion for directed verdict, or as the proposed federal rule calls it, a motion for judgment of acquittal, is made at the close of all the evidence, the court may reserve decision, submit the case to the jury, and decide the motion either before or after the jury has returned a verdict of guilty or has been discharged. If the motion is denied and the case submitted to the jury, the motion may be renewed within five days [408] after the jury is discharged. In case of a verdict of guilty, the court may set aside the verdict and order a new trial or enter judgment of acquittal. If no verdict is returned, the court may order a new trial or enter judgment of acquittal. The result of this rule is that the court no longer loses its power to direct a verdict as soon as the jury retires. Furthermore it is not confined to granting a new trial but may enter judgment of acquittal, thus obviating unnecessary new trials.

29. Separation of the Jury

Historically, except in misdemeanor cases, the jury was bound to remain together from the time of impaneling

[408] The First Preliminary Draft, Rule 27(b), fixed a period of ten days.

and swearing to the rendition of its verdict in open court.[409] In England the Juries Detention Act, 1897, gave the court discretion to allow the jury to separate in all cases but treason and murder at any time before the jury have retired to deliberate on their verdict. In 1940 the rule permitting separation was extended to murder and treason.[410]

Separation of the jury before its deliberations on its verdict has often been sustained.[411] It has been held valid after the impaneling and swearing of the jury,[412] and just before the giving of instructions.[413] In the case of a sealed verdict, it may separate after the finding of its verdict but before rendition.[414] The important stage at which separation should not occur seems to be that at which the jury has retired to consider its verdict.[415] The Massachusetts Judicial Council has suggested and secured the adoption of a rule under which the practice of locking up juries at night while deliberating on a case was given up and the jurors were furnished with sleeping quarters.[416]

[409] Note (1898) 12 Harv.L.Rev. 345; (1906) 6 Col.L.Rev. 466.

[410] Note (1941) 5 J.Crim.L. (Eng.) 29.

[411] Notes (1912) 22 Yale L.J. 59, (1916) 25 Yale L.J. 22. It is approved in the discretion of the trial judge, if the defendant and prosecuting attorney consent, in the Fourth Report of the Judicial Council of Kentucky (1936) 8. For full discussion, see Lehman, "A Critical Survey of Certain Phases of Trial Procedure in Criminal Cases" (1915) 63 U. of Pa.L.Rev. 754, 773-780.

[412] Langford v. State, 32 Neb. 782, 49 N.W. 766 (1891).

[413] Smith v. State, 111 Neb. 432, 196 N.W. 633 (1923).

[414] Griess v. State, 121 Neb. 467, 237 N.W. 405 (1931), (1932) 10 Neb.L. Bull. 341; Note, 34 A.L.R. 1231.

[415] See 23 C.J.S., Criminal Law, § 1449, pp.1189-1194; 39 Am. Jur., New Trial, §§ 90-92; pp.104-107; Abbott, Criminal Trial Practice (4th ed. 1939) § 688, p.1307; (1932) 12 B.U.L.Rev. 518.

[416] Warner and Cabot, Judges and Law Reform (1936) 217; Fifth Report of the Judicial Council of Massachusetts (1929) 34.

After the jury has rendered its verdict and separated, its reassembly to amend or correct a verdict in a matter of form, in a matter as to which there is no dispute, or in a matter which the court could correct without the aid of a jury, has been held valid in any number of civil cases.[417] But because of the possibility of abuse, it cannot be reassembled as to a matter of substance.[418] The jury cannot be reassembled where the failure of the verdict to express the true agreement of the jury is due to the jury's misconception of the effect of the language used in the verdict.[419] Reassembly has been permitted to correct an inadvertent misuse of the word "punishment" for "penitentiary"[420] to complete and verify the verdict.[421] They may be reassembled to correct a formally defective sealed verdict.[422] On the other hand, a jury cannot be reassembled to fix the degree of the crime,[423] to change the punishment,[424] to recommend clemency,[425] to change a verdict from a recommendation of suspension of sentence to the contrary effect,[426] to change a verdict of guilty on one count to guilty on both counts, even though the jury thought that the finding of guilty on one count involved the same find-

[417] Note (1937) 21 Minn.L.Rev. 868.

[418] State v. Dawkins, 32 Sup.Ct. 17, 10 S.E. 772 (1889); Clark v. State, 97 S.W. (2d) 644 (Tenn. 1936), (1937) 21 Minn.L.Rev. 868. There are any number of contrary civil cases.

[419] Sargent v. State, 11 Ohio 472 (1842). There are several civil cases opposed to this view.

[420] Taggart v. Commonwealth, 104 Ky. 301, 20 Ky.L.Rep. 493, 46 S.W. 674 (1898).

[421] Cunningham v. State, 14 Ala. App. 1, 69 So. 982 (1915).

[422] State v. Waltermath, 162 Wis. 602, 156 N.W. 946 (1916).

[423] Allen v. State, 85 Wis. 22, 54 N.W. 999 (1893).

[424] Ellis v. State, 27 Tex. Cr. App. 190, 11 S.W. 111 (1889).

[425] State v. Dawkins, 32 S.C. 17, 10 S.E. 772 (1889). See Note 66 A.L.R. 538 (1930).

[426] Perryman v. State, 102 Tex. Cr. App. 531, 278 S.W. 439 (1925).

ing on the other count,[427] or to correct a mistake in the name of the defendant.[428]

The Institute Code contains a number of provisions dealing with separation of the jury. Under Section 319 the court may direct that the jurors, when they leave the jury box at any time before the case is finally submitted to them, be permitted to separate or be kept in charge of a proper officer. In either event the court shall admonish them not to converse among themselves, or with any one else, about the trial. If the court permits them to separate, it shall admonish them not to view the place of the alleged crime. Under Section 328, unless the jurors had been kept together during the trial, the court may after the final submission of the case order that the jurors may separate for a definite time to be fixed by the court and then reconvene in the courtroom before retiring for consideration of their verdict. Statutes in a number of states provide for the separation of the jury after they have retired to consider their verdict.[429] Section 365 of the Code provides for the granting of a new trial, provided prejudice to the constitutional rights of the defendant is shown, if the jurors after retiring to deliberate upon the verdict have separated without leave of court.

30. Taking of Notes by Jury

In the absence of statutes which provide that jurors may take notes, some courts regard the practice as allowable or even commendable, while others regard it as an

[427] Sargent v. State, 11 Ohio 472 (1842).

[428] State v. McBride, 19 Mo. 239, 240 (1853). But see Commonwealth v. Breyesse, 160 Pa. St. 451, 457, 28 Atl. 824, 40 A.S.R. 729 (1894).

[429] A.L.I. Code of Crim. Proc. (1930) commentaries 983-985.

improper practice.[430] If the defendant having knowledge fails to object, he is presumed to consent.[431] Even if there is no knowledge, note taking is not illegal, and should not be ground for a new trial.[432]

31. Argument to the Jury

The right to fair argument by counsel is a fundamental element of a jury trial.[433] In criminal cases the right to proper argument has been said to be guaranteed as to the federal courts by the Sixth Amendment and by similar provisions in most state constitutions.[434] The right to argument was fostered by the worship of eloquence characteristic of the American pioneer community.[435] Unfortunately the limits of fairness are often transgressed and true trial by jury thus denied.[436] Forensic misconduct has appeared

[430] (1906) 19 Harv.L.Rev. 303. See United States v. Davis, 103 Fed. 457 (C.C. Tenn. 1900); Thomas v. State, 90 Ga. 437 (1892).

[431] State v. Robinson, 117 Mo. 649 (1893).

[432] Packer, "Suggestions with Reference to the New Proposed Federal Rules of Criminal Procedure" (1941) 45 Law Notes 17, 21; Lehman, "A Critical Survey of Certain Phases of Trial Procedure in Criminal Cases" (1915) 63 U. of Pa.L.Rev. 754, 765-767.

[433] The case will be reversed on appeal where the trial court instructs the jury to disregard the arguments of counsel entirely. People v. Ambach, 247 Ill. 451, 93 N.E. 310 (1910). See Note (1936) 36 Col.L.Rev. 931; (1927) 11 Minn.L.Rev. 664.

[434] Meredith v. People, 84 Ill. 479, 482 (1877); Gibbs v. State, 22 Ala. App. 345, 346, 115 So. 693, 694 (1928). Improper argument to the jury is the most common type of misconduct in the prosecution of criminal cases. Baker, "The Prosecuting Attorney: Legal Aspects of the Office" (1936) 26 J.Crim.L. 647, 658.

[435] Pound, The Spirit of the Common Law (1921) 124. "The eloquence of the criminal bar . . . has received the popular applause for many ages." People v. Mull, 167 N.Y. 247, 254, 60 N.E. 629, 631 (1901). But cf. Ulman, A Judge Takes the Stand (1933) 86-88.

[436] Nat. Com. on Law Obs. and Enf., Report on Lawlessness in Law Enforcement (1931) 268; Note (1920) 33 Harv.L.Rev. 956.

in some of the *causes célèbres* of our times.[437] Improper summation has perhaps engendered resentment against the courts and the legal profession, as well as necessitating the delay and the expense of new trials.

An essential principle of proper summation forbids the statement in argument of any elementary proposition of fact which is not already in the record unless it can be judicially noticed.[438] Where reference is made to the race or nationality,[439] the religious views, or to the sectional allegiances of the parties or the witness, the courts will reverse on the theory that an appeal to a pre-existing prejudice has been made. Unless the subject matter is such that it is likely to arouse prejudice, the attorney's histrionic technique is largely a matter of his own judgment.[440] In some situations abusive language may be ground for reversal,[441] as may be certain types of emotional pressure, such as appeals to sympathy[442] and fear.[443] Flattery of the jury seems an accepted custom.[444] The prosecuting attorney, as a high public officer, must, it is said, seek justice, rather than simply to win his case.[445]

437 Hauptmann v. State, 115 N. J. 412, 180 Atl. 809 (1935); State v. Beal, 199 N.C. 278, 154 S.E. 604 (1930), 44 Harv.L.Rev. 1118.

438 6 Wigmore, Evidence (3d ed.1940) § 1806; Note (1936) 36 Col.L. Rev. 932, 933.

439 Miller v. People, 70 Colo. 313, 201 Pac. 41 (1921); Morehead v. State, 12 Okla. Cr. 62, 151 Pac. 1153 (1915) ("coal-black murderer"); Note (1936) 36 Col.L.Rev. 932, 935.

440 State v. Burns, 119 Iowa 663, 670, 94 N.W. 238, 241 (1903). In a civil case it has been said to be not only the privilege but also the duty of counsel to shed tears during his argument. Ferguson v. Moore, 98 Tenn. 342, 352, 39 S.W. 341, 343 (1897).

441 Garrison v. Commonwealth, 169 Ky. 188, 193, 183 S.W. 473, 475 (1916); (1933) 13 B.U.L.Rev. 549.

442 Fall v. United States, 49 F. (2d) 506, 515 (App. D.C. 1931).

443 People v. Mull, 167 N.Y. 247, 60 N.E. 629 (1901).

444 Ulman, A Judge Takes the Stand (1933) 88.

445 Berger v. United States, 295 U.S. 78, 88, 55 Sup.Ct. 629 (1935), 26

In actual practice, however, the public clamor for convictions, the strong and resourceful opposition of organized crime, and the inability of the state to appeal may to some extent justify on the part of the prosecuting attorney an attitude as partisan as that of counsel for the defendant.[446] Although in civil cases, counsel is generally not permitted to argue or read law to the jury, some courts permit it in criminal cases.[447] The jury may, however, be confused by the instructions on the law by the trial judge, and even more confused after argument of counsel.

The trial court has broad discretion in determining whether any statement of counsel is misconduct.[448] Harmless legal error does not require reversal. The statement must have been prejudicial. Improper argument is presumed to be prejudicial.[449] The presumption may be rebutted where the evidence of guilt is free from doubt.[450] If, on the other hand, it is closely contested, it will be considered prejudicial.[451] It is likely to be treated as prejudi-

---

J.Crim.L. 276, (1936) 34 Mich.L.Rev. 1044; State v. Ferrone, 96 Conn. 160, 168-169, 113 Atl. 452, 455 (1921). It follows that a statement of personal opinion by the prosecuting attorney would be more effective with juries than those of ordinary attorneys, and would therefore be more readily excluded. See (1926) 25 Mich.L.Rev. 203. As to expression of opinion as to guilt of defendant, see Note (1932) 22 J.Crim.L. 905.

[446] Illinois Crime Survey (1929) 163; (1926) 24 Mich.L.Rev. 834; (1933) 13 B.U.L.Rev. 549; (1924) 8 Minn.L.Rev. 443.

[447] State v. Whitmore, 53 Kan. 343, 36 Pac. 748 (1894). In some states the trial court has discretion. Commonwealth v. Anderson, 245 Mass. 177, 139 N.E. 436 (1923); see Note (1936) 36 Col.L.Rev. 931, 938.

[448] State v. Bryan, 89 N.C. 531, 534 (1883); (1923) 21 Mich.L.Rev. 947; (1935) 26 J.Crim.L. 276.

[449] See Amsinger v. Najim, 335 Mo. 528, 532, 73 S.W. (2d) 214, 216 (1934).

[450] Hauptmann v. State, 115 N.J.L. 412, 418, 180 Atl. 809, 815 (1935); Spencer v. Commonwealth, 143 Va. 531, 536, 129 S.E. 351, 353 (1925).

[451] Berger v. United States, 295 U.S. 78, 88, 55 Sup.Ct. 629 (1935).

cial if the jury awards severe punishment;[452] or if it is too remote from the ultimate probanda.[453] Some cases give weight to whether or not the improper statement was intentional. This seems improper since a fair trial is the end sought rather than discipline of the attorney.[454] Some cases apply a doctrine of retaliation, offsetting improper summation on the one side by improper summation on the other.[455] This seems undesirable as it is almost impossible to determine accurately the effect of the comparative misconduct of the parties. Some cases point out the cumulative effect of several errors in argument.[456] This is sound so long as it does not tend to persuade the court that single improprieties may not be prejudicial.

In some cases misconduct in summation may be cured by action of the court or of the offending attorney.[457] A voluntary retraction, if not too grudging or casual, may cure the defect.[458] The judge may rebuke and reprimand erring counsel and, even better, may instruct the jury to disregard the improper statements.[459] The prejudice may be so great that the court should declare a new trial.[460] The courts have often held exceptional misconduct of a highly prejudicial nature to be incurable.[461] The mere reci-

452 People v. Milewski, 316 Ill. 288, 291, 147 N.E. 246, 247 (1925).

453 Latham v. United States, 226 Fed. 420, 424 (C.C.A. 5th, 1915).

454 People v. Teiper, 186 App. Div. 830, 844, 175 N.Y.Supp. 197, 207 (4th dept. 1919).

455 State v. Shawen, 40 W.Va. 1, 8, 20 S.E. 873, 875, 876 (1894).

456 Berger v. United States, 295 U.S. 78, 89, 55 Sup.Ct. 629 (1935).

457 Latham v. United States, 226 Fed. 420, 424 (C.C.A. 5th, 1915).

458 Luterman v. United States, 281 Fed. 374 (C.C.A. 3d, 1922).

459 See L.R.A. 1918 D, 4, 7, *et seq.* If the court waits until its charge to the jury, that may be too late. Lauback v. State, 12 Tex. Cr. App. 583 (1882).

460 Spencer v. Commonwealth, 143 Va. 531, 129 S.E. 351 (1925); Lincoln v. State, 191 Ind. 426, 133 N.E. 351 (1921).

461 Miller v. People, 70 Colo. 313, 201 Pac. 41 (1921); Latham v. United States, 226 Fed. 420 (C.C.A. 5th, 1915); Note (1936) 11 Ind.L.J. 298.

tation of a formula may be no cure at all. The error should be objected to at the trial, as otherwise the appellate court is unwilling to review. In certain cases, however, the appellate court should review even though objection was not taken, since often it is difficult to preserve the objectionable language verbatim for purpose of appeal,[462] and since interruption by counsel of his opponent's summation may in the eyes of the jury be made to reflect upon the objector.[463] What are the preventives of improper summation? Disapprobation of the profession and citations for contempt[464] are no great help. The true answer seems to be to allow the trial court to comment on the evidence.

A reasonable time must be allowed for arguing the law and the facts, taking into account the circumstances of the case, the gravity of the charge, the complexity, amount, and character of the evidence, the number of witnesses, and the number and character of the legal questions involved.[465] There is no agreement as to what is an unreasonable limitation on time for argument. In one state it has been held that in a trial for a felony the court should not set a limit on the time before the arguments begin.[466] Limiting the time to one hour for each side in a murder case over the objection of counsel has been held reversible error.[467] In capital cases, the time for argument

462 To have any part of the summation in the record, counsel must generally ask the court to have the stenographer record it.

463 Note (1936) 36 Col.L.Rev. 931, 941-943.

464 Epps v. State, 102 Ind. 540, 552, 1 N.E. 491, 499 (1885); Spencer v. Commonwealth, 143 Va. 531, 537, 129 S.E. 351, 353 (1925).

465 Lucas v. Commonwealth, 149 Ky. 495, 149 S.W. 861, 42 L.R.A. (N.S.) 209 (1912); Rossi v. United States, 9 F. (2d) 362 (C.C.A. 8th, 1925). See Dittenhoefer, J. (1913) 4 J.Crim.L. 565, 567, suggesting an hour and a half per side if the trial lasts over two days.

466 Williams v. State, 60 Ga. 367, 27 Am. Rep. 412 (1878).

467 State v. Cash, 136 S.E. 222 (S.C. 1927), 11 Minn.L.Rev. 664.

should be limited only in very extraordinary and peculiar circumstances.[468]

In every state but Minnesota the final word of counsel to the jury is given to the prosecution.[469] This rule is based on the logic of the situation. The party having the burden of proof is granted the final argument. Particularly should this be true in criminal cases in which the state must prove its case beyond a reasonable doubt. The Minnesota Crime Commission report of 1927 recommended that the state have the right to reply to the argument of the defense to the jury.[470]

It has been held that a defendant who, after the evidence was all in, discharged his attorneys and requested permission to make the closing argument was not entitled thereto.[471] No technical rules should determine the right of the defendant to discharge his counsel and continue the case in person. It is a matter of discretion. Perhaps a greater scope should be allowed to persons accused of political offenses. The original English view was that where a defendant was allowed counsel as to matters of fact, the defendant had no right to make the closing argument.[472] But the English courts have been increasingly

[468] State v. Tighe, 27 Mont. 327, 71 Pac. 3 (1903). In capital cases the court should exercise its discretionary power only to prevent counsel from introducing irrelevant argument or making excursions which delay the trial. People v. Keenan, 13 Cal. 581 (1859).

[469] In Scotland, counsel for the defense has the last speech. Keedy, "Criminal Procedure in Scotland" (1913) 3 J.Crim.L. 824, 839, 852. The same is true in France. Crabites, "Why American Criminal Justice Is a Failure" (1937) 23 A.B.A.J. 697, 700. See Note (1904) 14 Yale L.J. 54.

[470] Minnesota Crime Commission Report (1927) 34. This recommendation is renewed in Report of the Minnesota Crime Commission (1934) 47.

[471] State v. Townley, 149 Minn. 5, 182 N.W. 773, 17 A.L.R. 253 (1921), 35 Harv.L.Rev. 86.

[472] Rex. v. Parkins, 1 C. & P. 548, 171 Eng. Rep. 1311 (1824).

lenient, and have even permitted both defendant and counsel to address the jury.[473]

32. Instructions

The use of instructions by the court to the jury goes far back in English history.[474] Beginning in 1673 the defendant gained the right to new trial in misdemeanor cases tried by the Court of King's Bench.[475] In 1700 the writ of error issued as of right in misdemeanor cases.[476] These two remedies made possible more control of the jury by the trial court and of the trial court by the appellate courts. New trials soon came to be granted because the jury failed to follow the instructions of the trial judges as well as because of misdirection by the judge.[477] In this country, the problem arose of accurately recording what the judge had stated to be the law so that the appellate courts might know whether the juries had followed it.[478] At common law, instructions were oral, hence it was necessary for the person excepting to get them reduced to writing, since recordation was discretionary with the trial judge.[479] Numerous statutes have been passed requiring that instructions be written.[480]

[473] Reg. v. Doherty, 16 Cox C.C. 306 (1887); Reg. v. Walkling, 8 C. & P. 243 (1838).

[474] "It is, however, self-evident that the jurors are in need of some legal assistance if they are obliged to decide the whole question of guilt. The summing up of the judge, therefore, seems to be an essential feature of every trial by jury." Mannheim, "Trial by Jury in Modern Continental Criminal Law" (1937) 53 L.Q.Rev. 99, 110.

[475] 1 Holdsworth, History of English Law (3d ed.1923) 216; Sokolov, "The Judge's Charge to the Jury in Criminal Cases" (1932) 10 Can.B.Rev. 228.

[476] Orfield, Criminal Appeals in America (1939) 23.

[477] Orfield, Criminal Appeals in America (1939) 17-18.

[478] People v. Hersey, 53 Cal. 574 (1879).

[479] Smith v. Crichton, 33 Md. 103 (1870).

[480] They are listed by Farley, "Instructions to Juries—Their Role in the Judicial Process" (1932) 42 Yale L.J. 194, 204, n.59.

Theoretically, at least, the function of instructions is to enlighten the jury on the law.[481] The substantive rules of criminal law governing the particular case are brought to the attention of the jury. Instructions are also a method by which appellate courts control juries and trial courts.[482] More cases are reversed on appeal for errors in instructions than on any other ground.[483] While the appellate court cannot review the findings of fact of the jury, it can pass on whether they might have been misled by an error in the statement of law or whether they might have found differently if requested instructions had been given. Or if the instructions are perfect, an exceptional case, the court may discover that the jury manifestly failed to observe the instructions of the trial judge, thus making it a matter of law rather than of fact. Errors of misdirection, non-direction, and failure to observe directions assure appellate control. Appellate courts have reduced instructions to formalisms by allowing the trial courts to use instructions which have generally been approved by the courts.[484]

481 Farley, "Instructions to Juries—Their Role in the Judicial Process" (1932) 42 Yale L.J. 194, 205-210. But French and other Continental judges do not instruct because it is thought to encroach on the functions of the jury. Sokolov, "The Judge's Charge to the Jury in Criminal Cases" (1932) 10 Can.B.Rev. 228, 230.

482 Sokolov, "The Judge's Charge to the Jury in Criminal Cases" (1932) 10 Can.B.Rev. 210, 214.

483 Orfield, Criminal Appeals in America (1939) 206; Green, Judge and Jury (1930) 351. The same situation seems to be true in England. Butler, "Developments in Criminal Law, 1910-1935" (1935) 179 L.T. 325. "It must be admitted that two causes have tended to render jury trials less efficient than they otherwise would be; one is a poor method of selection of jurors, and the other is inadequate instructions by the judge." Chesnut, "Instructions to the Jury," The Judicial Administration Monographs (1942) 35.

484 State v. Allen, 34 Mont. 403, 87 Pac. 177 (1906); Minich v. People, 8 Colo. 440, 9 Pac. 4 (1885); McAlpine v. State, 47 Ala. 78, 82 (1872).

The appellate courts warn against invading the province of the jury rather than stressing the enlightenment of the jury.

A third actual function of instructions is the setting by lawyers of traps for the courts.[485] At common law, the court has a right to instruct the jury of its own motion. In some states it is under a duty to do so. In all jurisdictions exceptions can be taken to instructions whether they are prepared by court or counsel. Counsel may suggest instructions so that the language, form, and substance of the instruction is guided by the ingenuity of counsel. In states where instructions are in writing, they are usually wholly drafted by counsel, subject to modification by the court. Counsel will seek not to give a correct dissertation on the law for the jury, but to prepare a case for the appellate court based on the grant or refusal of a great number of instructions. He will hope that the busy trial judge will refuse at least some of the instructions proposed. Erroneous instructions will be of no help to the prosecuting attorney, who cannot appeal after acquittal, but will assist the counsel for the defense. The court is likely to give its instructions with its whole attention fixed on the reactions of the appellate court rather than those of the jury. Thus the three persons who should acquaint the jury with the law are thinking of the appellate court and not the jury.

In the fourth place, instructions are a method by which

[485] Farley, "Instructions to Juries—Their Role in the Judicial Process" (1932) 42 Yale L.J. 194, 214-216. "As it has been put, the requests of counsel for instructions to be given the jury became in effect an examination of the judge upon the law applicable to the case, in which he must make no mistake on penalty of vitiating the result of the trial." Pound, Criminal Justice in America (1930) 162.

the trial court maintains its integrity.[486] Such instructions are cautionary and peremptory instructions. Cautionary instructions are in reality not instructions of law, but suggestive, psychological guides to bring into the open the possibility of improperly influential emotional ferment. Their tendency is to put the jury in the correct attitude, so far as their consciences are concerned, and to guard against sympathy and prejudice.[487] When questionable evidence has been admitted, the court may in the light of subsequent developments exclude such evidence by instructions to the jury to disregard it.[488] A judge with a fair amount of sense can by cautionary instructions leave the record cured of many possible objections. Moreover, they are generally held to be within the discretion of the trial court.[489] This makes them an even better weapon to ward off appeals.

The other weapon for maintaining the integrity of the court is overt direction of the verdict, the peremptory instruction. The court may direct a verdict of acquittal, though not of guilty. The peremptory instruction is so unrelated to other types of instructions that it is now seldom treated under the head of instructions. There can be no doubt but that in fact it invades the province of the jury. It differs from setting aside a verdict since a directed verdict is *res judicata,* whereas setting aside the verdict involves new trial.

The trial courts are at the mercy of the appellate courts when it comes to the reform of instructions. The appellate

[486] Farley, "Instructions to Juries—Their Role in the Judicial Process" (1932) 42 Yale L.J. 194, 216-221.

[487] Sheurmann v. Mathison, 67 Ore. 419, 136 Pac. 330 (1913).

[488] State v. McKowen, 126 La. 1075, 53 So. 353 (140) (1910).

[489] Dinsmore v. State, 61 Neb. 418, 85 N.W. 445 (1901). See (1931) 22 J.Crim.L. 596.

courts developed the rules as to misdirection for their own benefit. They can develop them for the benefit of the trial courts by finding non-prejudicial error where the jury clearly was not misled. Memorandum decisions and discretionary appeals are other possible devices.

In approximately half the states only written instructions may be given. It appears that in states requiring written instructions reversals for erroneous instructions are much more frequent.[490] Section 325(2) of the Institute Code provides that the "charge of the court may be either oral or written." "Too often instructions are read hurriedly and in a mumbling manner. Instructions should be read slowly, clearly, audibly, and in consonance with the thought contained in the instructions." [491]

The Institute Code does not go very far with respect to the giving of instructions to the jury. Section 324 provides: "Either party may request the giving of particular instructions. Such request may be oral, unless the court directs it to be in writing." Rule 30 of the Federal Rules of Criminal Procedure is far more explicit and follows Federal Civil Rule 51 in substance. It provides that, at the close of the evidence or at such earlier time as the court directs, any party may file written requests that the court instruct the jury on the law as set forth in the requests, copies to be furnished simultaneously to the adverse parties. The court shall inform counsel of its proposed action prior to their arguments to the jury, but shall instruct the jury after the completion of arguments. No party may assign as error any portion of the charge or omission therefrom unless he objects before the jury re-

[490] Gemmill, J., "Criminal Procedure" (1912) 3 J.Crim.L. 566, 568; Ralston, J., "The President's Address" (1915) 6 J.Crim.L. 490, 503.

[491] Note (1940) 30 J.Crim.L. 791, 793.

tires to consider its verdict, stating distinctly the matter to which he objects and the grounds of his objections.[492]

Some lawyers object to any requirement that objections to the charge must be made before the jury retires. On the other hand, this requirement offers the judge an opportunity to make such corrections as he thinks are proper. Some lawyers urge that the charge should precede argument so that they may discuss the case in the light of the instructions.[493] It seems preferable, however, that the last words heard by the jury should come from a neutral court rather than from interested and impassioned counsel.

In most states it is reversible error to fail to charge, irrespective of any request, that the defendant is presumed to be innocent.[494] Many states also hold that the court must charge that this presumption accompanies the accused throughout the trial and must be considered in

[492] Defendant's counsel should be required "to point out any errors in the form or substance of the instructions immediately after the court has read them to the jury." Missouri Crime Survey (1926) 264. See also MacChesney, "A Progressive Program for Procedural Reforms" (1912) 3 J. Crim.L. 528, 531-532; Gemmill, J., "Criminal Procedure" (1912) 3 J.Crim. L. 566, 572; Kennedy, J., "Instructions to Juries" (1934) Proc. Wyo. State Bar Assn. 73, 74.

[493] In 22 states the charge must be given before the arguments of counsel. Otis, J., "'Governor of the Trial' or 'Referee at the Game'" (1937) 21 J. Am. Jud. Soc. 105. See also Fuller, Criminal Justice in Virginia (1931) 129. "If the power to comment is to be restored to state trial judges, should it not be accompanied by a return to the common law practice of an *oral* summing up on the facts and instructions on the law *before* the arguments of counsel?" McCormick, "Comment on Kolkman v. People" (1933) 16 J. Am. Jud. Soc. 151, 154.

[494] Commonwealth v. Andrews, 245 Mass. 177, 139 N.E. 436 (1923); State v. Tyree, 143 Wash. 313, 255 Pac. 382 (1927). See Notes (1926) 10 Minn.L.Rev. 539, (1929) 8 Neb.L.Bull. 186. *Contra:* State v. Boswell, 139 S.E. 374 (N.C. 1927), (1928) 37 Yale L.J. 523.

reaching the verdict.[495] Some even require a charge that the presumption can be overcome only by evidence which in the jury's mind is sufficient.[496] Others treat the presumption as a corollary of "reasonable doubt" and usually require that it be mentioned.[497] The majority view is said to be that the presumption is not evidence.[498] Logically, those jurisdictions which regard the presumption as evidence and those which hold that it continues with the defendant throughout the trial would always instruct as to the presumption of innocence; while others would not necessarily do so.

This last group of jurisdictions would seem to follow the view of Wigmore that the presumption affects the duty of going forward with the evidence and serves as a warning to the jury not to treat certain facts, such as the fact of defendant's indictment, improperly as evidence.[499] If the presumption is not evidence and does not run with the defendant throughout the trial, there is little value in instructing as to the presumption, especially if there is an instruction as to reasonable doubt.

When it is once decided what propositions of fact the prosecution has the burden of establishing, the jury may be instructed that they must acquit unless they are convinced beyond a reasonable doubt that each of such propositions is true. Most attempts to define reasonable doubt by paraphrase or circumlocution result in obfuscation rather than clarification of the concept.[500] Even today, however,

[495] Sims v. State, 197 Ind. 311, 147 N.E. 520 (1925); State v. Sonnenschein, 37 S.D. 585, 159 N.W. 101 (1916).

[496] People v. McClintic, 193 Mich. 589, 160 N.W. 461 (1916).

[497] Emery v. State, 101 Wis. 627, 660, 78 N.W. 145, 155 (1899).

[498] Note (1926) 10 Minn.L.Rev. 539.

[499] 9 Wigmore, Evidence (3rd ed.1940) § 2511.

[500] State v. Sykes, 248 Mo. 708, 154 S.W. 1130 (1913); People v. Ahrling,

convictions are occasionally set aside for a refusal to define reasonable doubt.[501]

The most widely approved definition of a reasonable doubt is that by Chief Justice Shaw, that it is such a doubt as would cause a prudent and reasonable man to act or to pause or to hesitate to act in the determination of any of the affairs of life of the highest importance to himself.[502] But it is error to charge that a reasonable doubt is one for which a reason could be given, based on the evidence or want of evidence in the case.[503] A juror may feel a reasonable doubt which he may be unable to give a reason for in words. The burden of proof should not be shifted to the defendant.

The fact that erroneous instructions given were asked for by the defendant does not necessarily preclude a new trial. In one case a defendant on trial for murder was convicted of manslaughter under an instruction requested by himself. The instruction was not justified by any evidence. He was held entitled to a new trial.[504] The opposing consideration is that the defendant has "invited error."

In general the court should instruct as to the lesser and included crimes where a conviction for them is authorized under an indictment.[505] Juries are prone, when the evi-

---

279 Ill. 70, 116 N.E. 764 (1917); Morgan, "Instructing the Jury Upon Presumptions and Burden of Proof" (1933) 47 Harv.L.Rev. 59, 63.

[501] Nanfito v. United States, 20 F. (2d) 376 (C.C.A. 8th, 1927); Davis v. State, 46 Fla. 137, 35 So. 76 (1903).

[502] Commonwealth v. Webster, 5 Cush. (Mass.) 295 (1850); (1913) 22 Yale L.J. 622; (1936) 27 J.Crim.L. 130.

[503] Ayer v. Territory, 201 Fed. 497 (C.C.A. 8th, 1912), (1913) 22 Yale L.J. 622. *Contra:* State v. Jefferson, 43 La. Ann. 995 (1891).

[504] Griggs v. State, 17 Ga. App. 301, 86 S.E. 726 (1915), (1916) 29 Harv.L.Rev. 448.

[505] State v. Kline (N.C. 1925) 129 S.E. 417, (1926) 26 Col.L.Rev. 102; see (1920) 33 Harv.L.Rev. 980.

dence shows that the defendant has committed a crime, though perhaps of a lower degree than that charged, to return a verdict of guilty on the latter rather than to acquit absolutely. When the facts show that the defendant is either guilty of the crime charged or not guilty of any crime, instructions as to lesser crimes need not be given.[506] The same is true where the evidence clearly shows that the major crime was committed, the only question being whether the defendant committed it.[507] If no evidence is offered on which conviction of a lower offense could be sustained, the court need not instruct as to such lower offense.[508] But if any evidence is offered warranting a verdict as to a lesser offense, the court must then instruct.[509]

In the few jurisdictions where statutes allow the jury to assess the penalty as well as to pass on guilt, the judge must instruct as to the possible penalty which the law prescribes.[510] He need not where he himself assesses the penalty as is the usual case.[511] If he does, the jury may use its knowledge of the penalty to adapt its verdict to what it deems adequate punishment for the defendant, thereby exceeding its duty to pass merely on the fact of innocence or guilt.[512] In fact the possibility of compromise verdicts has led some courts to declare instructions as to punishment reversible error.[513]

[506] State v. Nixon, 111 Kan. 601, 207 Pac. 854 (1922).

[507] State v. Brooks, 181 Iowa 874, 165 N.W. 194 (1917).

[508] Hand v. State, 88 Tex. Crim. 422, 227 S.W. 194 (1921). In fact an instruction may be ground for reversal. Hagen v. Commonwealth, 179 Ky. 201, 200 S.W. 336 (1918).

[509] State v. Williams, 185 N.C. 685, 116 S.E. 736 (1923).

[510] People v. Sainz, 162 Calif. 242, 121 Pac. 922 (1912).

[511] Caudill v. Commonwealth, 155 Ky. 578, 159 S.W. 1149 (1913); State v. Inlow, 141 Pac. 530 (Utah 1914), (1915) 15 Col.L.Rev. 188.

[512] Bliss v. State, 117 Wis. 596 (1903); State v. Garrison, 59 Ore. 440 (1911).

[513] Commonwealth v. Switzer, 134 Pa. 383, 19 Atl. 681 (1890).

33. Comment on Evidence

Under the federal practice the trial judge may comment to the jury on the ultimate issue of a case, that is to say, he may express his opinion on the merits.[514] At common law such comment was allowed in both civil and criminal actions.[515] The United States Supreme Court has stated that the constitutional right of trial by jury requires that the judge be empowered to advise on the facts.[516] But in thirty-eight states between 1796 and 1910, constitutional provisions, statutes, or judicial decisions denied this power.[517] Such a rule deprives the jury of the opinion of the only impartial expert present, and tends to debase trial by jury into a contest of skill between opposing counsel.[518] The federal rule results in no hardship to the defendant, since the judge must leave all questions of fact to the jury, must not go outside the testimony, and must not be unduly partisan.[519]

[514] Simmons v. United States, 142 U.S. 148 (1891); 9 Hughes, Federal Practice, Jurisdiction and Procedure (1932) § 7082. The same is true in Canadian practice. Riddell, "Administration of Criminal Law in Canada" (1934) 17 J. Am. Jud. Soc. 141, 144.

[515] Hale, History of the Common Law of England (5th ed.1820) 346; Jessner v. State, 201 Wis. 184, 231 N.W. 634 (1930).

[516] Capital Traction Co. v. Hof, 174 U.S. 1 (1899); see Patton v. United States, 281 U.S. 276, 288 (1930). But cf. People v. Kelly, 347 Ill. 221, 179 N.E. 898 (1931), (1932) 30 Mich.L.Rev. 1303.

[517] Sunderland, "The Problem of Trying Issues," 5 Tex.L.Rev. 18, 32 (1926); Note (1934) 18 Minn.L.Rev. 441. For a complete list of the states, see Note (1932) 30 Mich.L.Rev. 1303, 1307.

[518] (1939) 52 Harv.L.Rev. 698; A.L.I. Code of Crim. Procedure (1930) § 325; Otis, J., "'Governor of the Trial,' or 'Referee at the Game'" (1937) 21 J. Am. Jud. Soc. 105.

[519] Allis v. United States, 155 U.S. 117 (1894). See Note (1934) 18 Minn. L.Rev. 441, 443-450. Out of 3,203 cases appealed in the federal courts between 1924 and 1934, only 28 were reversed because of improper comment by the court in the facts. Otis, J., "Comment to the Jury by the Trial Judge" (1941) 27 A.B.A.J. 749, 753.

Since 1910 there has been a strong movement in the states to return to the common-law rule permitting the judge to comment on the evidence. Illinois,[520] Michigan,[521] and South Dakota [522] have repealed their statutes restricting the right to comment. Colorado,[523] Maine,[524] and Massachusetts,[525] have, by judicial decision, reinstated their original practice. Numerous and vigorous attacks are being made on the rule denying the power to comment.[526]

The constitutionality of statutes forbidding comment by the court on the evidence was raised in a leading Illinois case in 1932.[527] The court held, two justices dissenting, that the statute was constitutional as against claims that

520 This was accomplished by the enactment of the Civil Practice Act. See Fisher, "The Effect of the Civil Practice Act upon Instructing Juries in Criminal Cases" (1933) 28 Ill.L.Rev. 451.

521 Comp. Laws, 1929, § 17322. For cases arising under this statute, see People v. Goldberg, 253 Mich. 83, 234 N.W. 157 (1929); People v. Lewis, 264 Mich. 83, 249 N.W. 451 (1933).

522 Laws, 1919, c.163.

523 Kolkman v. People, 89 Colo. 8, 300 Pac. 595 (1931). See McCormick, "Comment on Kolkman v. People" (1933) 16 J. Am. Jud. Soc. 151.

524 State v. Mathews, 115 Me. 84, 97 Atl. 824 (1916).

525 Hohman v. Hemmen, 280 Mass. 526, 182 N.E. 850 (1932).

526 9 Wigmore, Evidence (3d ed.1940) § 2551; Cartwright, "Present but Taking No Part" (1916) 10 Ill.L.Rev. 537; Storey, Speech on "Protest Against House Bill No. 9354" (1918) 43 A.B.A.Rep. 37; Sunderland, "An Appraisal of English Procedure" (1925) 25 Mich.L.Rev. 109, 119; The Law of Evidence, Some Proposals for Its Reform (1927) 21; Pound, "The American Attitude Towards the Trial Judge" (1928) 2 Dak.L.Rev. 5; Walker, "Judicial Comment on the Evidence in Jury Trials" (1929) 15 A.B.A.J. 647; Hogan, "The Strangled Judge" (1930) 14 J. Am. Jud. Soc. 116; Note (1934) 18 Minn.L.Rev. 441; Fifth Report of the Judicial Council of New York (1939) 185-194; Note (1933) 11 Neb.L.Bull. 463.

527 People v. Kelly, 347 Ill. 221, 179 N.E. 898, 80 A.L.R. 890 (1932), (1933) 23 J.Crim.L. 1035, (1932) 16 J. Am. Jud. Soc. 16, (1932) 30 Mich. L.Rev. 1303, (1932) 6 So.Calif.L.Rev. 56, (1932) 18 Va.L.Rev. 780. Criticizing the power of the legislature to curtail the power of the court to comment of the evidence, see Scott, "Trial by Jury and the Reform of Civil Procedure" (1918) 31 Harv.L.Rev. 669, 680-681.

it violated the right to trial by jury and the separation of powers. The argument as to jury trial by the defendant was that: (1) The jury trial guaranteed was the jury trial as it existed at common law. (2) The right of comment by the judge on the evidence, denied by the statute, was a part of jury trial at common law. (3) Such right was an essential attribute of such trial and not a mere detail of procedure. The majority denied the validity of the third contention, deeming the right a mere procedural detail.

The common law and federal rule allowing the judge to comment on the evidence is laid down in the Institute Code of Criminal Procedure. Section 325 provides: "The court shall instruct the jury regarding the law applicable to the facts of the cause, and may make such comment on the evidence and the testimony and credibility of any witness as in its opinion is necessary for the proper determination of the cause. It shall if requested inform the jury that they are the exclusive judges of all questions of fact and, whether requested or not, the court shall so inform them if it comments on the evidence, the testimony or the credibility of any witness." [528]

34. Comment on Defendant's Failure to Testify

At common law the defendant was not competent to testify. This disqualification has been removed by statute in England in 1898, and in every state in the United States except Georgia, the first state to act being Maine in 1864. Congress allowed the defendant to testify in federal cases in 1872. The question then arose as to whether comment could be made on the failure of the defendant to testify.

[528] Rule 8 of the Model Code of Evidence (1942) of the American Law Institute is substantially to the same effect.

At common law the defendant, being denied the opportunity to testify, might offer his version of the facts in an unsworn statement to the jury.[529] In one state the right to make a statement has been preserved by the same statute which allows him to testify.[530] In the absence of such express provision, the reasons for the ancient privilege seem to have been removed by the modern statutory right of the defendant to testify like any other witness.[531] A contrary doctrine would allow the defendant to introduce evidence not subject to the ordinary limitations on the scope of testimony, of a kind which the prosecution could not offer. He would have no right to make a statement without cross-examination.[532]

There has been but little legislation permitting comment on the failure of the defendant to testify. Six states now permit comment: California, Connecticut, Iowa, New Jersey, Ohio, and Vermont. Massachusetts [533] and South Dakota [534] statutes permitting comment were held unconstitutional. Ohio in 1912 and California in 1934 permitted comment by constitutional amendment. All other states except Iowa [535] and New Jersey have constitutional

[529] 2 Wigmore, Evidence (3d ed.1940) §§ 575-3, 579; cf. Prater v. State, 160 Ga. 138, 127 S.E. 296 (1925) (by statute); 23 C.J.S., Criminal Law, § 1026, p.396.

[530] Anderson v. State, 27 Wyo. 345, 364, 196 Pac. 1047, 1052 (1921).

[531] State v. Townley, 149 Minn. 5, 182 N.W. 773, 17 A.L.A. 253 (1921). *Contra:* Rex v. Sheriff, 20 Cox C.C. 334 (1903); see Commonwealth v. Daskalakis, 246 Mass. 12, 32, 140 N.E. 470, 479 (1923) (capital cases only).

[532] State v. Louviere, 169 La. 109, 124 So. 188 (1929), (1930) 43 Harv. L.Rev. 658.

[533] Opinion of the Justices to the Senate, 300 Mass. 620, 15 N.E. (2d) 662 (1938), (1939) 37 Mich.L.Rev. 777, (1938) 87 U. of Pa.L.Rev. 122.

[534] State v. Wolfe, 64 S.D. 178, 266 N.W. 116 (1936), 50 Harv.L.Rev. 356, (1936) 27 J.Crim.L. 279.

[535] See State v. Ferguson, 226 Iowa 361, 283 N.W. 917 (1939), 18 Neb.L. Bull. 204; Reeder, "Comment upon Failure of Accused to Testify" (1932) 31 Mich.L.Rev. 40, 44.

self incrimination clauses similar to those of Massachusetts and South Dakota. New Jersey recognizes the privilege as part of its common law even though it allows comment by the trial judge.[536] The United States Supreme Court has held that the New Jersey rule does not violate the Federal Constitution.[537] Thus any limitations in state legislation must be found in the state constitutions.

Statutes removing the common-law disability and making the defendant a competent witness to testify, if he desires, generally contain a further provision that failure to take the stand shall not create any presumption against him. A federal statute so provides.[538] The United States Supreme Court has recently held in accord with the weight of authority that such a statute enforces a duty on the trial judge to instruct, when properly requested, that, from the failure of the defendant to testify, the jury shall draw no inference prejudicial to the defendant.[539] Under the usual statute, it is not error to fail to give such an instruction if the defendant has not asked that it be given.[540] Objections to the court's charging on its own motion are without merit and are summarily overruled.[541] A lower federal court has indicated that it is better practice not to give an unrequested instruction, but that if given it will

[536] Parker v. State, 61 N.J.L. 308, 39 Atl. 651 (1898).

[537] Twining v. New Jersey, 211 U.S. 78 (1908).

[538] 28 U.S.C. (1934) § 632.

[539] Bruno v. United States, 308 U.S. 287, 60 Sup.Ct. 198 (1939), 28 Geo. L.J. 417, (1940) 38 Mich.L.Rev. 1323. See also (1939) 33 Ill.L.Rev. 586, (1939) 6 U. of Chi.L.Rev. 494.

[540] People v. Flynn, 73 Cal. 511, 15 Pac. 102 (1887); People v. Warner, 104 Mich. 337, 62 N.W. 405 (1895); Bruntz v. State, 137 Neb. 565, 290 N.W. 420 (1940), 19 Neb.L.Bull. 201.

[541] State v. Comer, 176 Wash. 257, 28 Pac. (2d) 1027 (1934); Helms v. State, 112 Tex. Cr. 203, 17 S.W. (2d) 813 (1929).

not be reversible error unless on the facts the defendant was prejudiced.[542]

As has been seen in almost every state, there are statutes protecting the defendant from any inference from his failure to take the stand.[543] Such privilege has been held to extend to preliminary proceedings, such as an application for bail,[544] a hearing on habeas corpus,[545] or the preliminary hearing before a justice of the peace,[546] as well as to the trial before a jury. It extends throughout the prosecution. Hence the failure of the defendant to testify at an earlier proceeding is not subject to comment in the later proceeding when he remains silent in the latter.[547] But more difficult is the question: What is the rule when the defendant takes the stand in the later proceedings? In most states he is held to have waived his privilege against self incrimination to the extent of being subject to answer all questions relevant to the issue,[548] or to suffer unfavorable comment upon his failure so to answer.[549] But it does not follow that he should be held to have waived his privilege from comment on his failure to take the stand in some earlier proceeding.[550] Pressure

[542] Kahn v. United States, 20 F. (2d) 782 (C.C.A. 6th, 1927).

[543] (1922) 36 Harv.L.Rev. 207; (1939) 30 J.Crim.L. 434; (1928) 37 Yale L.J. 955; 2 Wigmore, Evidence (3d ed.1940) § 488. Some state statutes not only prohibit comment, but require the court to caution the jury against drawing any inference from the silence of the defendant.

[544] Newman v. Commonwealth, 28 Ky. Law 81, 85 S.W. 1089 (1905).

[545] Switley v. State, 73 Tex. Cr. Rep. 619, 166 S.W. 733 (1914).

[546] Bunckley v. State, 77 Miss. 540, 27 So. 638 (1900).

[547] Templeton v. People, 27 Mich. 501 (1873); Parrott v. Commonwealth, 47 S.W. 452 (Ky. 1898).

[548] Carpenter v. State, 193 Ala. 51, 69 So. 531 (1915); People v. Johnston, 228 N.Y. 332, 127 N.E. 186 (1920).

[549] Caminetti v. United States, 242 U.S. 470 (1917).

[550] Note (1923) 36 Harv.L.Rev. 207. *Contra:* People v. Prevost, 219 Mich. 233, 189 N.W. 92 (1922), 36 Harv.L.Rev. 207, 219. The Michi-

should not be employed on the defendant to take the stand from the beginning. Nor should it be imposed on him, so that having once remained silent he will continue silent.

Perhaps the controlling consideration is what the privilege is meant to protect. Authorized comment puts more pressure on the defendant to testify than the jury's independent observation of his silence. Otherwise the statute would be pointless. Against comment it may be argued that this moral coercion is tantamount to compelling the defendant to take the stand. On the other hand, if the privilege is still limited to its historical function of preventing direct, actual compulsion, no constitutional right is impaired.[551] But there has been a tendency to extend the privilege to save the defendant from any possible disadvantage arising out of his failure to testify.[552] Thus there have been dicta that to allow comment is to violate the constitutional guarantee.[553] A different concept of the ends to be attained and a re-examination of the limits of the privilege may produce an opposite result.[554]

In Texas the courts have gone so far as to hold that even the jury's discussion of the failure of the defendant to testify is ground for reversal.[555] The court departs

---

gan case seems to represent a minority view. State v. Bailey, 54 Iowa 414, 6 N.W. 589 (1880); Hare v. State, 56 Tex. Cr. 6, 118 S.W. 544 (1909).

551 8 Wigmore, Evidence (3d ed.1940) § 2250.

552 State v. Ford, 109 Conn. 490, 146 Atl. 828 (1929).

553 Grantello v. United States, 3 F. (2d) 117 (C.C.A. 8th, 1924); Second Report of the Judicial Council of New York (1936) 187, 196-198; Notes (1928) 37 Yale L.J. 955, 964-965, (1917) 15 Mich.L.Rev. 423; 8 Wigmore, Evidence (3d ed.1940) § 2272; Reeder, "Comment upon Failure of Accused to Testify" (1932) 31 Mich.L.Rev. 40.

554 Bruce, "The Right to Comment on the Failure of the Defendant to Testify" (1932) 31 Mich.L.Rev. 226, 233.

555 Harrell v. State, 42 S.W. (2d) 438 (Tex. Cr. App. 1931), (1932) 45 Harv.L.Rev. 746. *Contra:* State v. Dreiling, 95 Kan. 241, 147 Pac. 1108

from the general rule, excluding juror's testimony of their conduct in the jury room. Consideration by the jury of the defendant's failure to testify is so natural that it perhaps cannot be prevented.

In England the judge but not the counsel for the Crown may comment on the failure to testify, while comment by both is prohibited in Scotland, Canada, New Zealand, Bermuda, and New South Wales.[556]

The Minnesota Crime Commission in its report of 1927 recommended that the court and the prosecuting attorney have the right to comment on the failure of the defendant to testify.[557] A similar recommendation was made by the Minnesota Crime Commission of 1934.[558]

Professor Waite proposed that the following rule be adopted as one of the Federal Rules of Criminal Procedure: "If a defendant does not testify in his own behalf, it is permissible for the jury to consider that fact and for the trial judge and the attorneys for the prosecution and the defense to comment upon it; provided, however, that if the accused does take the witness stand he may not be interrogated except by his own attorney concerning any previous alleged criminality."[559] This proposal was not favored by other members of the United States Supreme Court Advisory Committee. The Secretary of the Com-

---

(1915); Williams v. United States, 3 F. (2d) 933 (C.C.A. 6th, 1925). See also (1921) 5 Minn.L.Rev. 235.

556 9 Am. L. Inst. Proc. (1930-1931) 202.

557 Minnesota Crime Commission Report (1927) 32-33. The reason assigned was that the defendant is of necessity well informed yet withholds information and conceals the truth.

558 Report of the Minnesota Crime Commission (1934) 42-43. See also Missouri Crime Survey (1926) 361; Second Report of the Judicial Council of New York (1936) 187-198; Third Report of the Judicial Council of New York (1937) 259-275.

559 Fed. Rules of Crim. Proc., First Preliminary Draft (1943) app. 251-252.

mittee pointed out that experience had not revealed that the present law forbidding comment hampered successful prosecution.[560] Not to subject the defendant if he takes the stand to cross-examination as to his past criminal acts would mislead the jury into thinking him an upright person.

It must be conceded that groups whose opinions command the highest respect have advocated the reform in recent years. In 1931 the American Law Institute by a vote of ninety-one to fifty-three adopted the following rule proposed by the Council of the Institute: "The judge, the prosecuting attorney, and counsel for the defendant may comment on the fact that the defendant did not testify." [561] Rule 201 (3) of the Model Code of Evidence provides: "If an accused in a criminal action does not testify, the judge and counsel may comment upon accused's failure to testify, and the trier of fact may draw all reasonable inferences therefrom." [562] As a protection to the defendant who fails to testify as to a meritorious defense because of fear that his criminal record will be paraded before the jury under the guise of impeachment, it is pro-

560 *Ibid.* Supp. 254-255. See also Note (1915) 5 J.Crim.L. 923; Thompson, J. (1922) 13 J.Crim.L. 296; Pam, J. (1922) 13 J.Crim.L. 297; Moley, Our Criminal Courts (1930) 97; Reeder, "Comment upon Failure of Accused to Testify" (1932) 31 Mich.L.Rev. 40. It is of interest that the Russian criminal code does not require the defendant to testify, and imposes no penalty for a failure to testify. Hazard, "Soviet Criminal Procedure" (1941) 15 Tulane L.Rev. 280, 231.

561 (1931) 9 Am. L. Inst. Proc. 218. This rule was, however, favored by only three of the Advisers and neither of the two Reporters, and the Reporters and Advisers presented six proposed rules to the council. *Ibid.* 202-203. For the discussion by the Institute, see *ibid.* 203-218. See also Millar, "The Modernization of Criminal Procedure" (1920) 11 J.Crim.L. 344, 351.

562 For a discussion of the rule by the Institute, see (1942) 19 Am. L. Inst. Proc. 78-120; (1941) 18 Am. L. Inst. Proc. 245-251.

vided in Rule 106(3) that evidence of a prior conviction shall not be admissible against the defendant unless he first introduces evidence of good character to support credibility.

35. Power of Court to Reopen Case

The trial judge may, in his discretion, on motion of either counsel, permit a case to be reopened at any time before the jury returns a general verdict.[563] It would seem that a judge should be able to do on his own motion what he has discretion to do on the motion of a party.[564] Permitting the judge to reopen saves time, since he could on his own motion order a new trial.[565] Reopening was permitted where, after the evidence was in and both sides had rested, but before argument, the judge on his own motion reopened the case and recalled for further examination a witness who had appeared for the prosecution.[566] It is not the function of a trial judge to serve merely as an umpire in a contest between opposing counsel. He may cross-examine witnesses.[567] He may summon witnesses not called by either party.[568] He may call as the court's witness per-

563 Clancy v. Lord, 87 Cal. 413, 25 Pac. 493 (1891) (after special verdict); Missouri Pac. Ry. v. Oleson, 213 Fed. 329 (C.C.A. 8th, 1914) (after motion for directed verdict); 6 Wigmore, Evidence (3d ed.1940) §§ 1876-1881.

564 Paxson v. Board of Chosen Freeholders, 201 Fed. 656 (C.C.A. 3d, 1912) (after parties had closed); Dunlap v. Seattle Nat. Bank, 93 Wash. 568, 161 Pac. 364 (1916) (during argument of counsel); Rex v. Sullivan (1923) K.B. 47. *Contra:* Hagerle v. Beebe, 123 Iowa 620, 99 N.W. 303 (1904).

565 Schmidt v. Brown, 80 Hun. 183, 30 N.Y.Supp. 68 (1894).

566 State v. Rief, 53 S.D. 438, 221 N.W. 53 (1928), (1929) 42 Harv.L. Rev. 445.

567 State v. Keehn, 85 Kan. 765, 118 Pac. 851 (1911); see (1912) 25 Harv.L.Rev. 394, (1929) 13 Minn.L.Rev. 258, (1933) 23 J.Crim.L. 1043.

568 People v. Rardin, 255 Ill. 9, 99 N.E. 59 (1912); Rex v. Harris, (1927) II K.B. 587. 9 Wigmore, Evidence (3d ed.1940) § 2484. *Contra:* South

sons whom neither party dared to summon because of the rules forbidding the impeachment of one's own witness.[569]

36. Coercion to Secure Verdict

At common law coercion of the jury to secure a verdict was approved by the courts.[570] This is no longer true. Inquiry by the court as to the division of the jury has been held by some courts improper on the ground that it tends to coerce a verdict and that it serves no purpose otherwise unattainable.[571] The practice would seem more objectionable where the court puts the question after recall of the jury than where the jury returns unable to agree.[572] It is to be doubted whether the inquiry has any appreciable coercive effect, and it affords a reasonable method for deciding whether the jury shall be retained for further deliberation.[573] The courts have been supersensitive concerning communications by the court to the jury.[574] Some

---

Covington & Cin. Ry. v. Stroh, 23 Ky. 1807, 66 S.W. 177 (1902). See also Note (1931) 15 Minn.L.Rev. 350.

569 State v. Brown, 91 Fla. 682, 108 So. 842 (1926).

570 Proffatt, Jury Trial (1877) § 475; Winsor v. Queen, 6 B. & S. 143 (1866). It was the settled practice to keep the jury without food, drink, fire, or light until they reached a verdict. 3 Bl. Comm. *414. This practice was early denounced in the United States. People v. Olcott, 2 Johns. Cas. (N.Y.) 301, 1 Am. Dec. 168 (1801). As to the modern English practice, see (1939) 25 A.B.A.J. 533.

571 Eady v. State, 168 Ark. 731, 271 S.W. 338 (1925); Brasfield v. United States, 272 U.S. 448 (1926), (1928) 27 Col.L.Rev. 756; Jordan v. United States, 22 F. (2d) 966 (C.C.A. 9th, 1927), (1928) 41 Harv.L.Rev. 797, (1928) 76 U. of Pa.L.Rev. 622.

572 Cf. Commonwealth v. Anthony, 91 Pa. Super. Ct. 518 (1927).

573 Cf. Montgomery v. State, 19 Okla. Cr. App. 224, 199 Pac. 222 (1921). There seems no coercion where the judge asks for the numerical division and sends the jury back without admonition. State v. Finch, 71 Kan. 793, 81 P. 494 (1905).

574 Lagrone v. State, 84 Cr. App. 609, 615, 209 S.W. 411, 415 (1919); Note (1917) 1 Minn.L.Rev. 277.

courts treat the inquiry as ground for reversal on the theory that the coercive effect is intangible and difficult to prove.[575] Others call for proof of actual prejudice.[576]

37. Conduct of Jury on Submission of Case

Additional evidence should not be presented to the jury when it has retired to the jury room for its deliberations. In fact if, during the deliberations, a juror makes statements to other jurors as of his own knowledge concerning issues in the case which influence the jury arriving at its verdict, the court will usually grant a new trial.[577] In one case after the jury had unanimously agreed that the defendant was guilty, one of the jurors made a statement that the appellant had been previously convicted. The foreman and other jurors at once informed the juror that such statement was improper and could not be discussed. In an extreme decision the defendant obtained a reversal and a new trial.[578]

When the jury after retiring to the jury room desires additional information concerning the testimony or further instructions in law, it should under the common-law rule, return to open court and there state its questions. Most courts take the view that, unless the parties or their counsel consent, there is a right to a new trial.[579] It is not proper for the judge to send a written answer to the questions asked by the jury, or to send papers requested by the

[575] Brasfield v. United States, 272 U.S. 448, 47 Sup.Ct. 135 (1926), (1927) 27 Col.L.Rev. 756.

[576] Montgomery v. State, 19 Okla. Cr. App. 224, 199 Pac. 222 (1921); (1928) 41 Harv.L.Rev. 797; (1928) 76 U. of Pa.L.Rev. 622.

[577] State v. Gaymon, 44 S.C. 333, 22 S.E. 305, 31 L.R.A. 489, 51 A.S.R. 861 (1895). See Note (1918) 19 Col.L.Rev. 416.

[578] Taylor v. State, 274 S.W. 622 (Tex. Cr. App. 1925), 10 Minn.L.Rev. 173.

[579] Note (1915) 15 Col.L.Rev. 539.

jury, or to send oral instructions by the bailiff,[580] or to enter the jury room himself to withdraw an erroneous instruction,[581] even though counsel later agree that the information given was correct. The rule is based on the fact that such communications in the absence of counsel give no opportunity to object, impair the confidence of the public, and permit doing things in a non-public fashion. Sections 331 and 332 of the Institute Code provide adequate safeguards. Under Section 331 if the jurors desire further instructions they shall upon their request be conducted into the courtroom by the officer who has them in charge and there the court shall instruct them. Such instruction may be given only after notice to the counsel for the defendant and the prosecuting attorney. Under Section 332, the court may recall the jurors for additional or corrective instructions, which may be given only after notice to counsel for the defense and to the prosecuting attorney.[582]

38. Jury as Judges of Law

From an early date in English legal history the jury in a criminal case had the right to bring in a general verdict of guilty or not guilty.[583] If it refused to follow the court's instructions and brought in a verdict of not guilty, the defendant was free, and could not be retried.[584] In case of a conviction, however, the defendant might have a new trial. The jury could not be fined for ignoring the instructions of the court.[585] Thus the jury had the power, if not

[580] Quinn v. State, 130 Ind. 340 (1891).

[581] Hall v. State, 8 Ind. 439, 444 (1856).

[582] As to existing law, see (1917) 1 Minn.L.Rev. 277.

[583] Morgan, "A Brief History of Special Verdicts and Special Interrogatories" (1923) 32 Yale L.J. 575, 591.

[584] Farley, "Instructions to Juries—Their Role in the Judicial Process" (1932) 42 Yale L.J. 195, 195-205.

[585] Bushell's Case, Vaughan 135 (C.P.), 6 How. St. Tr. 999 (1670).

the right,[586] to determine for itself what the law might be. It was not until 1895 that the United States Supreme Court conclusively decided that the jury is bound in criminal as in civil cases to follow the judge's instructions on all matters of law.[587] The court based its decision more on principle than on precedent. The Illinois Court only recently adopted the same view.[588]

Statutes attempting to allow the jury to pass on the law as well as the facts may be attacked on constitutional grounds, as well as on grounds of policy.[589] The doctrine of tripartite separation of powers would seem to mean that only judges may declare the law, although it may be argued that the jury is necessarily within the judicial department. It does not seem sound to argue that an essential element of jury trial is abrogated, since the constitutional guarantee has as its purpose the avoidance of encroachment on the powers of the jury and is not aimed at

[586] The right is denied in Thayer, Preliminary Treatise on Evidence (1898) 169, 256. For a criticism of his view, see Howe, "Juries as Judges of Criminal Law" (1939) 52 Harv.L.Rev. 582. See also Warvelle, "The Jurors and the Judge" (1909) 23 Harv.L.Rev. 123; Wade, "Jurors as Judges in Criminal Cases" (1882) 3 Crim.L.Mag. 484.

[587] Sparf and Hansen v. United States, 156 U.S. 51 (1895). There was a majority opinion 55 pages long by Harlan, J. Gray, J., wrote a dissenting opinion 73 pages long, concurred in by Shiras, J.

[588] People v. Bruner, 343 Ill. 146, 175 N.E. 400 (1931), 31 Col.L.Rev. 1042, 15 Minn.L.Rev. 830, 22 J.Crim.L. 430. Today only Maryland and Indiana are contrary. Vogel v. State, 163 Md. 267, 162 Atl. 705, (1932), (1933) 31 Mich.L.Rev. 848, (1937) 1 Md.L.Rev. 175; Trainer v. State, 198 Ind. 502, 154 N.W. 273 (1926), (1927) 11 Minn.L.Rev. 472. For a criticism of the Maryland law, see Dennis, "Maryland's Antique Constitutional Thorn" (1943) 92 U. of Pa.L.Rev. 34.

[589] It should of course be observed that in some situations the distinctions between issues of fact and of law are difficult to draw and that actually the court passes on certain issues of fact. See Thayer, "Law and Fact in Jury Trials" (1890) 4 Harv.L.Rev. 147. According to Thayer, the formula that the court passes on the law and the jury on the facts did not take shape until the sixteenth century.

prohibiting an increase in the powers of the jury. Policy is against the jury's passing on the law since it is contrary to reason and leads to confusion to entrust the interpretation of the law to laymen drawn for occasional and temporary service. The argument that an acquittal is final is not convincing, since such finality is based on the rule against double jeopardy and not on any theory that the jury finally determine the law. The argument that the jury has the right to go wrong is unsound because an improper conviction is not final.

39. Special Verdicts

Special verdicts existed at common law. In order to relieve the jury from the harshness of the attaint, the special verdict was developed.[590] The jury found the facts and the court pronounced judgment on the facts found. But the jury could not be required to render a special verdict if they chose not to do so. As the jury developed in power and standing, the courts sought to eliminate the sweeping power exercised by the jury under a general verdict by requiring them to render a special verdict. But the special verdict was seldom used in criminal cases and even today its use is rare in England.[591] It is probably not much used because the appellate courts have been very strict in requiring the jury to find on all the facts and mental ele-

[590] Morgan, "A Brief History of Special Verdicts and Special Interrogatories" (1923) 32 Yale L.J. 558; Orfield, Criminal Appeals in America (1939) 16-17.

[591] Kenny, Outlines of Criminal Law (15th ed.1942). For a modern instance, see Regina v. Dudley (1884) 14 Q.B.D. 273. As to the details of present English practice, see Archbold, Criminal Pleading, Evidence and Practice (30th ed.1938) 215, 325. But in Continental countries using juries, the usual practice resembles that of special verdicts. Mannheim, "Trial by Jury in Modern Continental Criminal Law" (1937) 53 L.Q.Rev. 99, 106-110.

ments constituting the crime.[592] Often the findings of the jury will be incomplete with the result that the jury will have to reconsider their verdict, or a new trial be granted.[593] Immaterial matters may creep in while material matters may be omitted. The form of the questions put to the jury may be prejudicial or confusing. The conclusions found may be of law, rather than of fact. The argument in favor of special verdicts is that the jurors are not competent to apply the law to the facts, that they are often confused by lengthy instructions as to the law, and that special verdicts will result in fewer errors and therefore fewer reversals.

Something like ten states have statutes providing for special verdicts.[594] It has been used in the federal courts.[595] Rule 49(a) of the Federal Rules of Civil Procedure provides for their use in federal civil cases. Under Section 337 of the Institute Code, the jurors may "in all cases render either a general or a special verdict." Section 341 thus defines a special verdict: "A special verdict is one in which the facts are found by the jurors and the conclusion of law therefrom is left to the court." Under Section 342: "A special verdict shall be in writing. It need not be in any

592 Green, "A New Development in Jury Trial" (1927) 13 A.B.A.J. 715, 716; Notes (1934) 12 Tex.L.Rev. 327, (1942) 21 Neb.L.Rev. 188.

593 For cases holding that the defendant is not entitled to an acquittal upon a special verdict which is defective because it omits a fact essential to constitute the offense charged, but may be again put on trial, see State v. Arthur, 21 Iowa 322 (1866); State v. Ritchie, 3 La. Ann. 511 (1848); Commonwealth v. Call, 21 Pick. 515 (Mass. 1839). *Contra:* State v. Belk, 76 N.C. 10 (1877); State v. Stephanus, 53 Ore. 135, 99 Pac. 428 (1909). See also Note (1934) 12 Tex.L.Rev. 327, 331.

594 A.L.I. Code of Crim. Proc. (1930) commentaries 1000-1001. In some states they are held valid without statute. A single case held that special verdicts violated the right to jury trial. Underwood v. People, 32 Mich., 20 Am. Rep. 633 (1875).

595 Note (1942) 21 Neb.L.Rev. 188.

particular form." Under Section 353, if the jurors in returning a special verdict do not pronounce affirmatively or negatively on the facts necessary for the court to render judgment, the court shall direct the jurors to reconsider their verdict and either to find whether or not such facts existed or to render a general verdict. If the jurors persist in rendering such defective verdict, it shall be received and entered of record as rendered. The Federal Rules of Criminal Procedure are silent, thus leaving the matter in the discretion of the district judges.[596]

40. Sealed Verdict

In a considerable number of states it is held that a jury may, after an agreement during the adjournment of the court, make a sealed verdict and later reassemble and render it in court when the court convenes again.[597] A sealed verdict should require the prior direction of the court, and the consent of the parties.[598] If the jury remains together after the sealing of the verdict, there is no doubt of validity.[599] But the usual situation is sealing followed by separation. It is contended that the jury may be sub-

[596] See (1943) 29 A.B.A.J. 210 for an editorial recommending provisions in the Federal Rules of Criminal Procedure "for special verdicts and special findings in cases where more than a single offense is involved, on the analogy of the Federal Rules of Civil Procedure."

[597] State v. Whittier, 21 Me. (8 Shep.) 341, 38 Am. Dec. 272 (1842); State v. Engles, 13 Ohio 490 (1844); Territory v. Hexter, 3 Mont. 206 (1878); People v. Duffek, 163 Mich. 196, 128 N.W. 245, 31 L.R.A. (N.S.) 1005 (1910); Griess v. State, 121 Neb. 467, 237 N.W. 405 (1931), (1932) 10 Neb.L.Bull. 341. See 43 Am. Dec. 86; 103 A.S.R. 162; 34 A.L.R. 1231; Notes (1936) 70 U.S.L.Rev. 479; (1929) 43 Harv.L.Rev. 139.

[598] Note (1895) 9 Harv.L.Rev. 287, (1898) 12 Harv.L.Rev. 143; Smith v. State, 40 Fla. 203 (1898).

[599] Pounds v. United States, 171 U.S. 35, 18 Sup.Ct. 729, 43 L.Ed. 62 (1897).

jected to undesirable influences in the interval between rendition in open court. But the fact of sealing tends to prevent the operation of wrongful influences. The defendant may poll the jury, and any juror may dissent from the sealed verdict as read. The sealed verdict is not the verdict of the jury; rather the verdict is the oral announcement of the jury, before recording of the verdict. The sealed verdict may not be opened and read in the absence of the jury.[600] In some states it is signed by all the jurors and in others by the foreman. In some states it is delivered to an officer who holds it until the court is again in session; in others, it is retained by the foreman until it is presented in court. In Massachusetts and Pennsylvania an oral verdict is also required, but in Maine the sealed verdict is read aloud by the clerk, who then recites the ancient formula: "Gentlemen of the jury, hearken to your verdict as the court has recorded it." [601] In some states sealed verdicts are not permitted in criminal cases involving either capital punishment or life imprisonment.[602] The courts have been more strict in criminal cases than in civil cases in permitting the amendment of sealed verdicts. A formal defect may be amended, but not a substantial one.[603]

The Federal Rules of Criminal Procedure are silent as to sealed verdicts, thus permitting each district court to determine its own practice. Sections 343 and 344 of the Institute Code make provision for sealed verdicts. Under Section 343 the court may with the consent of the defen-

[600] The presence of a juror may be waived by the defendant. Ex parte Brown, 139 Kan. 614, 32 P. (2d) 507 (1934), 25 J.Crim.L. 629.

[601] State v. McCormick, 84 Me. 566, 24 Atl. 938 (1892).

[602] State v. McCormick, 84 Me. 566, 24 Atl. 938 (1892); Hechter v. State, 94 Md. 429 (1902).

[603] 23 L.R.A. 732; 5 Ann. Cas. 396; 3 L.R.A. (N.S.) 1086; 66 A.L.R. 570.

dant and the prosecuting attorney direct the jurors that if the required number should agree upon a verdict during a temporary adjournment of the court, they may sign it by their foreman, seal it and deliver it to the bailiff, who in turn delivers it to the clerk, after which they may separate until the court next convenes. When the jurors have reassembled, the envelope containing the verdict is to be opened, and the same proceedings had as in the declaring of other verdicts. Under Section 344 the court is to admonish the jurors not to make any disclosure concerning it, nor to speak with other persons concerning the case until the verdict has been rendered in open court.

41. Verdict Where Several Counts Involved

The common law regarded the indictment as entire and the verdict as a nullity unless it found on every point in issue.[604] But today counts are treated in effect as separate indictments.[605] A failure to find on one count is often held to be an acquittal by implication as to such count.[606] This has been held true even where the counts charge separate and distinct crimes.[607] But some authorities then limit the rule and require a finding on each.[608] If the offenses in the separate counts are different, a general verdict of guilty which does not specify on which count or counts the defendant is guilty is invalid.[609] But a general verdict not

[604] King v. Hayes (1728) 2 Ld. Raym. 1519.

[605] Latham v. Regina (1864) 5 B. & S. 635; Selvester v. United States, 170 U.S. 262 (1877).

[606] George v. State, 59 Neb. 163 (1899); Thomas v. People, 113 Ill. 531 (1885).

[607] Hechter v. State, 50 Atl. 1041 (Md. 1902), 2 Col.L.Rev. 259.

[608] Wilson v. State, 20 Ohio 26 (1851); Commonwealth v. Carey, 103 Mass. 213 (1869).

[609] Dozier v. State, 14 Ga. App. 473, 81 S.E. 368 (1914); Scott v. State, 4 Okla. Cr. 70, 109 Pac. 240 (1910).

specifying the count is valid if the different counts merely set forth the same transaction in varying manner.[610] Section 347 of the Institute Code provides: "If different offenses are charged in the indictment or information the jurors shall, if they convict the defendant, make it appear by their verdict on which counts, if the indictment or information is divided into counts, or of which offenses they find him guilty."

42. Recommendation of Leniency

Some states expressly provide by statute for recommendations of leniency by the jury.[611] In the absence of such statutes, recommendations for mercy do not make a verdict of guilty compromised or conditional, but may be treated as surplusage.[612] It has even been held that the court may refuse to receive such a verdict, and may send the jury back for further deliberations,[613] or direct that the verdict be entered without the recommendation.[614] The court is justified in thus treating recommendations voluntarily made by the jury of their own initiative, since the jury should pass only on guilt and not punishment. The problem becomes more complex if the jury, while considering the evidence and before reaching a verdict, inquires of the court whether it can recommend leniency. There is no

[610] Cleveland v. State, 20 Ala. App. 426, 103 So. 707 (1925); Thain v. State, 182 Ind. 345, 106 N.E. 345 (1914).

[611] Notes, 21 Ann. Cas. 244, 245; 17 A.L.R. 1117, 1118-1156; 87 A.L.R. 1362, 1363-1370; (1942) 9 U. of Chi.L.Rev. 497; (1940) 30 J.Crim.L. 782. At common law the jury could not recommend leniency. Note (1931) 29 Mich.L.Rev. 784.

[612] State v. Farnsworth, 41 Idaho 768, 10 P. (2d) 295 (1932).

[613] Coil v. State, 62 Neb. 15, 86 N.W. 925 (1901); People v. Calvert, 93 Cal. App. 568, 269 Pac. 969 (1928).

[614] People v. Lee 17 Cal. 76 (1860).

error if the court refuses to answer such a request.[615] On the other hand, there is no error if the court answers in the affirmative, provided that the court conditions the instruction by adding that it is not bound by the recommendation.[616] But a failure to append such an instruction has been held to be error.[617] Moreover, any statement accompanying the affirmative answer, intimating that the recommendation would be favorably considered in fixing the penalty, is reversible error, since such assurances are very likely to induce jurors to overcome reasonable doubts and convict the defendant.[618] Since it is the general rule that jurors may not impeach their verdicts, it is difficult to determine the effect of an authorization to recommend leniency. Hence any strong probability that the jury was motivated by extraneous factors should invalidate the verdict.

43. Return of Verdict

At common law a verdict had to be rendered in open court in the presence of the judge. Receiving the verdict was considered a judicial function which could not be delegated.[619] The prohibition of any such delegation has been strictly applied in criminal cases, whether the parties have consented or not, probably because the interests of the parties are not waivable and because the consent of the parties cannot turn the clerk into a judge. In civil cases where the parties have consented expressly or im-

[615] Gaines v. Commonwealth, 242 Ky. 237, 46 S.W. (2d) 75 (1932).

[616] State v. Black, 119 N.J.L. 277, 196 Atl. 225 (1938).

[617] People v. Warner, 289 Mich. 516, 286 N. W. 811 (1939), (1940) 24 Minn.L.Rev. 421. *Contra:* State v. Gill, 14 S.C. 410 (1880).

[618] State v. Doucet, 177 La. 63, 147 So. 500, 87 A.L.R. 1356 (1933).

[619] McClure v. State, 77 Ind. 287 (1881).

pliedly, a direction to the clerk to receive the verdict is by the prevalent view a mere irregularity cured by such consent.[620] Possibly a statute is valid permitting the court to order the clerk to receive the verdict in the absence of the judge in a purely ministerial fashion. But it has been held improper even in a civil case for the clerk to send the jury back to bring in a verdict correct in form.[621] Only the court may exercise such power. Rule 31 of the Federal Rules of Criminal Procedure provides that the verdict shall be returned by the jury to the judge in open court.[622]

At the early English common law, a trial judge could always refuse to receive a verdict of acquittal before it had been recorded.[623] This rule is not the law in this country in many states.[624] The old common-law rule seems sounder, since the court should not be compelled to receive the verdict where it is manifestly based on a misunderstanding or disregard of the law of the case as set forth by the court. But where the verdict has been received and recorded, it clearly cannot be set aside.[625]

Ordinarily the court will accept the verdict of the jury. The court has, however, the power in certain circumstances to refuse to accept the verdict just brought in. He

[620] Dubuc v. Lazell, 182 N.Y. 482, 75 N.E. 401 (1905).

[621] Folkner v. Hopkins, 126 Atl. 633 (N.J. 1924), (1925) 25 Col.L.Rev. 508.

[622] Sections 335 and 336 of the Institute Code contemplate the return of the jury to the courtroom and the presence of the judge. Under Sections 350-353 any directions for reconsideration of the verdict are to come from the court.

[623] 2 Hawkins, Pleas of the Crown (8th ed.1924) 623.

[624] People v. Ostrander, 30 Mo. 13 (1860); Register v. State, 10 Ga. App. 623, 74 S.E. 429 (1911); (1926) 40 Harv. Rev. 133.

[625] State v. Craig, 176 N.C. 740, 97 S.E. 400 (1918). Cf. State v. Lee, 65 Conn. 265, 30 Atl. 1110 (1894); State v. Chambliss, 107 So. 200 (Miss. 1926), 40 Harv.L.Rev. 133.

may do this as to verdicts defective in form,[626] insensible and without meaning,[627] or not responsive to the indictment.[628] Such verdicts are invalid and the defendant has not been in jeopardy.[629] But when the crime found is covered in the indictment, though not in the instructions, the verdict is valid and the court must accept it.[630] A refusal to accept the verdict is an invasion of the defendant's right to a verdict found by the jury alone. The Institute Code contains a number of clarifying provisions on reconsideration of verdicts at the direction of the court. Under Section 350, if in the opinion of the court it appears that the jurors have mistaken or misapplied the law, the court may explain to the jurors the reason for that opinion and direct them to reconsider their verdict.[631] If after reconsideration they render the same verdict, it must be entered of record. A verdict of not guilty cannot be reconsidered. If the verdict rendered is neither general nor special, the court may under Section 351 direct a reconsideration. Under Section 352 the court may direct reconsideration of an ambiguous or defective general verdict, and under Section 353 it may direct reconsideration of a defective special verdict.

[626] Grant v. State, 23 L.R.A. 723 (Fla. 1894); see Note (1931) 9 Neb. L.Bull. 345. If the verdict is clear but informal, the court itself should correct the verdict to save time. Note (1927) 27 Col.L.Rev. 476; State v. Anderson, 24 S.C. 109 (1885).

[627] State v. Godwin, 138 N.C. 582 (1905).

[628] Mangham v. State, 87 Ga. 549, 13 S.E. 558 (1891).

[629] Ford v. State, 34 Ark. 649 (1879).

[630] State v. Ostrander, 30 Mo. 13 (1860); Register v. State, 74 S.E. 429 (Ga. 1912), 12 Col.L.Rev. 744.

[631] In England a verdict is not complete until it is accepted by the court, and the court is not bound to receive the first verdict of the jury, but may direct them to reconsider it. Harris and Wilshere, Principles and Practice of the Criminal Law (17th ed.1943) 465.

44. Poll of Jury

While as a general rule jurors may not impeach their verdict, polling the jury is not regarded as an attempt to impeach the verdict. If upon a poll one or more jurors dissent from the verdict as announced by the foreman, in most jurisdictions it is held proper to order the jury to retire for further deliberation.[632] In many states, questions on the poll are limited strictly to the fact of the juror's concurrence in the verdict.[633] In others, even where a juror at first hesitates, if he finally states that he consented to the verdict it will be sustained.[634] On principle it would seem, however, that the better rule would permit a juror to dissent from the verdict as agreed until the time when it is recorded in open court, thereby reducing the danger of intimidation of a majority in the jury room.[635]

The right to poll the jury by asking each individual juror if he assents to the verdict does not exist in Connecticut, Colorado, Maine, and Massachusetts. It exists by statutes or judicial decision in other jurisdictions. Under Section 336 of the Institute Code, polling is pro-

[632] State v. Johnson, 141 La. 775, 75 So. 678 (1917); State v. Waltermath, 162 Wis. 602, 156 N.W. 946 (1916).

[633] Moss v. State, 152 Ala. 30, 44 So. 598 (1907) (improper to ask if juror gave up honest convictions); State v. Hobbs, 294 Mo. 224, 242, S.W. 675 (1922).

[634] State v. Asher, 63 Mont. 302, 206 Pac. 1091 (1922) (juror first replied he concurred only with understanding sentence would be suspended, then agreed it was his verdict); State v. Millroy, 103 Wash. 193, 174 Pac. 10 (1918) (juror answering "it was either that or a hung jury" told to answer "yes" or "no" replied "yes"); State v. Nutter, 99 W.Va. 146, 128 S.E. 142 (1925) (juror declared his assent to verdict based upon jury-room compromise.)

[635] Cf. Devereux v. Champion Cotton Co., 14 S.C. 396 (1880); Weeks v. Hart, 24 Hun. 181 (N.Y. 1881); Sanders v. Charleston Ry., 151 S.E. 438 (S.C. 1930), 39 Yale L.J. 1218.

vided for. If there are dissents from the verdict by any jurors "the court may direct them to reconsider their verdict." It would seem that it could under this discretionary language discharge them. Rule 31(d) of the Federal Rules of Criminal Procedure provides: "When a verdict is returned and before it is recorded the jury shall be polled at the request of any party or upon the court's own motion. If upon the poll there is not unanimous concurrence, the jury may be directed to retire for further deliberations or may be discharged."

45. Unanimous Verdict

Among reforms of the jury often suggested and debated is the abolition of the requirement of unanimity.[636] In favor of the requirement of unanimity it is argued that discussion in the jury room is thereby stimulated. It is also contended that split verdicts, while proper in civil cases, should not be allowed in criminal cases because of the

[636] Burdick, "Criminal Justice in America: Possibility of Improvements by Statutory Changes and Constitutional Amendments Affecting Procedure" (1925) 11 A.B.A.J. 510, 512; Millar, "The Modernization of Criminal Procedure" (1920) 11 J.Crim.L. 345, 355, 357; Sloss, J., "Reform of Criminal Procedure" (1911) 1 J.Crim.L. 705, 711; Lawlor, "Needed Reforms in Criminal Law and Procedure" (1911) 1 J.Crim.L. 877; Note (1932) 23 J.Crim.L. 651; Roberts, J., "Trial Procedure—Past, Present and Future" (1929) 15 A.B.A.J. 667, 669; Wilbur, J., "Shall We Continue to Require a Unanimous Verdict?" (1928) 34 Pa. Bar. Assn. Rep. 333; Willoughby, Principles of Judicial Administration (1929) 505-509; Sixth Report of the Judicial Council of Washington (1939) 13, 30; Attorney General's Conference on Crime (1934) 453; Weinstein, "Trial by Jury and Unanimous Verdicts," (1935) 69 U.S.L. Rev. 513; Rossman, J., "The Judge-Jury Relationship in the State Courts" (1942) 16 (A.B.A. pamphlet); Grace, J., 3 Rep. Proc. Bar Assn. of Arkansas 30, 32-34 (1900); Note, "Proposed Legislation for Jury Reform in New York" (1930) 30 Col.L.Rev. 721, 727-728. In Scotland, majority verdicts may be rendered in all cases. Keedy, "Criminal Procedure in Scotland" (1913) 2 J.Crim.L. 834, 841.

necessity of proving the defendant guilty beyond a reasonable doubt. The unanimity requirement seldom results in mistrial.[637] On the other side, it is argued that it is natural that jurors differ in opinion and that a unanimous verdict is therefore usually due to compromise or choice; that majority rule prevails in appellate courts, legislatures, and boards of directors; that judicial tyranny need not be feared as in the days of the Stuarts; and that the necessity for a unanimous verdict permits one stubborn or corrupted juror to cause a mistrial. Adequate discussion can be secured by permitting a less than unanimous verdict after a period of deliberation, such as twelve hours.

Much delay and expense may be caused by the common-law requirement that the verdict be unanimous.[638] Section 355 of the Institute Code provides: "In capital cases no verdict may be rendered unless all the jurors concur in it. In other cases of felony, a verdict concurred in by five-sixths of the jurors, and in cases of misdemeanor a verdict concurred in by two-thirds of the jurors may be rendered."[639] This provision was one of the four chief parts in the criminal law program of the American Bar Association for 1934.[640] Rule 31(a) of the Federal Rules of

[637] Third Report of the Judicial Council of Massachusetts (1927) 30-32; Second Report of the Judicial Council of Kansas (1928) 8; Eighth Report of the Rhode Island Judicial Council (1934) 15; Note (1937) 22 Corn.L.Q. 415, 417.

[638] Coxe, "The Trials of Jury Trials," (1901) 11 Col.L.Rev. 286, 292. See Notes (1931) 17 Va.L.Rev. 497, (1930) 30 Col.L.Rev. 721, 727, (1934) 18 J. Am. Jud. Soc. 94.

[639] See discussion, 8 Am. L. Inst. Proc. 268-276 (1930).

[640] Harno, "Program on Criminal Law and Its Enforcement" (1934) 20 A.B.A.J. 465, 466-467. The constitutions of Idaho, Louisiana, Montana, Oklahoma, and Texas permit a departure from the rule of unanimity and of these all but Oklahoma have statutes permitting verdicts in some cases by less than a unanimous jury. In Missouri, it has been recommended that the constitution be amended to allow ten jurors to find a verdict

Criminal Procedure restates the common law. Rule 29(a) of the First Preliminary Draft had provided: "A verdict shall be unanimous, but by written stipulation of the parties approved by the court it may be by a stated majority of the jurors." [641] The latter provision was criticized by the bench and the bar as not giving sufficient protection to the defendant.

46. Inconsistent Verdict

Even if verdicts are inconsistent, they may be sustained. In a leading case, the opinion being by Mr. Justice Holmes (his last), the defendant was indicted under the National Prohibition Act on three counts. The first charged maintenance of a nuisance by keeping intoxicating liquor for sale; the second, the unlawful possession of intoxicants; and the third, the unlawful sale of this liquor. Evidence of the purchases of several cases of whiskey was offered to sustain the charges. The defendant was acquitted of possession and sale, but was found guilty of maintenance of a nuisance. The defendant contended that

---

except where the penalty is death or life imprisonment. Missouri Crime Survey (1926) 264, 366-367. In Oregon in 1934, a constitutional amendment was adopted providing for a five-sixths verdict in all but capital cases. See (1934) 25 J.Crim.L. 290. On the Continent unanimity is not required. Mannheim, "Trial by Jury in Modern Continental Criminal Law" (1937) 53 L.Q.Rev. 99, 117.

[641] For recommendations by several federal judges for "utilization . . . of the provisions of existing law which permit . . . the parties to stipulate . . . to accept the verdict of the majority of the jurors," see Report to the Judicial Conference of the Committee on Selection of Jurors (Sept. 1942) 11, Appendix II, 2-3. The provision is recommended also in Proceedings of the Attorney General's Conference on Crime (1934) 172-173, 317, 360, 453. Its validity seems implicit in Patton v. United States, 281 U.S. 276 (1930). See Rottschaefer, Handbook of American Constitutional Law (1939) 789; Note (1941) 40 Mich.L.Rev. 113, 114. See, however, Clark, "Should Verdicts Be Unanimous in Criminal Cases?" (1921) 46 A.B.A. Rep. 591; Illinois Crime Survey (1929) 227.

the inconsistency of the verdict in negativing the possession which constituted a basic element of the nuisance made the conviction reversible. His contention was rejected.[642]

The government contended that the findings were not necessarily inconsistent since, even if the defendant did not have possession, his conviction could be based on an inference that he had knowledge of the business conducted on his premises. But this appears untenable since the trial judge charged that the defendant should be acquitted unless the jury found that he was present at the time of the sale.[643] Mr. Justice Holmes took the broader ground that "consistency in the verdict is not necessary." [644] Such verdicts probably represent the jury's attempt to limit the possible punishment. Federal judges have tended to impose consecutive sentences for the several allied offenses in a single transaction.[645] The defendant seems adequately protected since, if the evidence is insufficient to sustain the conviction, it will be set aside. The likelihood of inconsistent verdicts can be decreased by an instruction that, where several counts present iden-

[642] Dunn v. United States, 284 U.S. 390 (1932), 45 Harv.L.Rev. 931, 41 Yale L.J. 922, 23 J.Crim.L. 489, 18 Va.L.Rev. 553. Conviction of a corporation and acquittal of individual co-indictees as to violation of the Sherman Anti-Trust Act is valid though inconsistent. Note (1940) 40 Col. L.Rev. 554. The state courts are divided, some reversing inconsistent verdicts and others affirming. See Notes (1927) 15 Calif.L.Rev. 415, (1930) 43 Harv.L.Rev. 415, (1940) 40 Col.L.Rev. 554, 556, n.19.

[643] See the dissent by Butler, J. Yet there are a number of cases accepting such tenuous hypotheses. Carrignan v. United States, 290 Fed. 189 (C.C.A. 7th, 1923).

[644] Accord: Steckler v. United States, 7 F. (2d) 59 (C.C.A. 2d, 1925); Browning v. State, 120 Ohio St. 62, 165 N.E. 566 (1929); see (1930) 43 Harv.L.Rev. 657. *Contra:* Kuck v. State, 149 Ga. 191, 99 S.E. 622 (1919).

[645] (1932) 45 Harv.L.Rev. 535.

tical issues of fact, the defendant, if guilty on any count, is so on all.[646]

Failure by the jury to make a finding on some count or counts of the indictment should not be treated as making a verdict inconsistent.[647] It is true that by the weight of authority a failure to make any finding on some counts is an acquittal as to those counts, but only in the sense that the defendant is not convicted and cannot again be put in jeopardy.[648] But it seems improper to infer from this that it is equivalent to an actual finding of not guilty, and can therefore be used to show that the verdict is inconsistent.[649] If the appellate court can see from the record that the failure to make a finding on the first count may have been due to lack of evidence, the risk of an actual inconsistency behind the verdict would allow it to grant a new trial.[650]

47. Impeachment of Verdict

Under the majority view, the testimony of a petit juror as to matters which took place in the jury room cannot be received to impeach the verdict.[651] To allow impeachment would defeat the solemn act of the jurors, would open the

[646] Cf. Horning v. District of Columbia, 254 U.S. 135 (1920); State v. Turck, 5 Pac. (2d) 308 (Wash. 1931).

[647] (1924) 37 Harv.L.Rev. 627.

[648] People v. Weil, 243 Ill. 208, 90 N.E. 731 (1909); State v. Leavitt, 87 Me. 72, 32 Atl. 787 (1894).

[649] *Contra:* Pollock v. State, 97 So. 240 (Ala. 1923), (1924) 37 Harv.L. Rev. 627.

[650] (1924) 37 Harv.L.Rev. 627.

[651] (1917) 1 Minn.L.Rev. 189; (1921) 5 Minn.L.Rev. 235. But the privilege that protects from exposure the arguments and ballots of a juror does not obtain if his place on the jury was fraudulently obtained as by concealment on *voir dire.* Clark v. United States, 289 U.S. 1, 53 Sup.Ct. 314, 77 L.Ed. 993 (1933), 24 J.Crim.L. 446, 31 Mich.L.Rev. 850, 17 Minn.L.Rev 654, 81 U. of Pa.L.Rev. 1000, 8 Wis.L.Rev. 371.

door to tampering with the jury after discharge, and would furnish dissatisfied and corrupt jurors the means of destroying a verdict to which they assented.

At common law, affidavits of jurors were not admissible to impeach their verdicts.[652] In a number of states exceptions have been made to the rule. Under the Ohio rule the conduct of third persons in or out of the jury room, and the conduct of jurors outside of the jury room may be made the subject of jurors' affidavits to impeach the verdict, whereas the conduct of jurors within the jury room is beyond the scope of subsequent inquiry.[653] As to the latter, the primary purpose for exclusion of such evidence is to protect the secrecy of deliberation that is essential to the securing of independent judgment and final unanimity among jurors. There is, however, no good reason why jurors may not, without impairing the secrecy of deliberation, testify as to certain aspects of their own conduct in the jury room. For instance, the use of affidavits to show that the verdict was reached by chance [654] does not defeat secrecy of deliberation, since a chance verdict, instead of being an element of the deliberative function, is a restraint upon it. There are statutes in eight states allowing such procedure as to chance verdicts.

Iowa has a less restrictive rule under which affidavits of jurors are received to show any matter not essentially

[652] Vaise v. DeLaval, 1 T.R. 11 (K.B. 1785). Today in England evidence may not be given by a juror as to discussions in the jury room, but may be given as to the competence of a juror. Kenny, Outlines of Criminal Law (15th ed.1942) 590. As to the Canadian rule, see Note (1934) 12 Can.B.Rev. 309.

[653] Emmert v. State, 127 Ohio St., 235, 187 N.E. 862 (1933), (1935) 44 Yale L.J. 516.

[654] Under Section 364 of the American Law Institute Code of Criminal Procedure, the defendant has an absolute right to a new trial if the jurors decide the verdict by lot.

entering in the verdict.[655] Under this rule, affidavits are admissible to show that the verdict was determined by lot,[656] or to show that the jury considered evidence not produced at the trial.[657] Both are viewed as facts independent of the verdict itself and of the deliberations. On the other hand, affidavits are inadmissible to show that a juror misunderstood the court's instructions, or was unduly influenced by his fellow jurors. Both of these are regarded as integral parts of the deliberative activities of the jury.

Both the Iowa and Ohio rules preserve the privacy of jury deliberations, but suggest two differing attitudes towards a jury verdict. Under the Iowa rule, the process of decision is all important, and the conduct of the jury is carefully supervised by the court. The aim is to make sure that verdicts will be based on ethical and lawful deliberation by the jurors on facts presented at the trial. The rule tends to promote confidence in jury verdicts and to deter jurors from resorting to non-deliberative tactics. The Ohio rule, on the other hand, is more practical and realistic. Evidence showing the conduct of the jury in the jury room is automatically excluded. The process of decision is relegated to a secondary position. But this seems sound

655 Wright v. Telegraph Co., 20 Iowa 195 (1866). See also Harris v. State, 24 Neb. 803, 40 N.W. 317 (1888). The rule is commented on favorably in (1915) 1 Iowa L.Bull. 100, 4 Iowa L.Bull. 130, (1926) 11 Iowa L.Rev. 268, (1914) 14 Col.L.Rev. 248, (1912) 12 Mich.L.Rev. 405, (1925) 23 Mich.L.Rev. 550, (1915) 64 U. of Pa.L.Rev. 86; 8 Wigmore, Evidence (3d ed.1940) § 2353.

656 Capp v. State, 159 S.W. 193 (Ark. 1913), (1914) 14 Col.L.Rev. 248. As to quotient verdicts, see Notes (1922) 6 Minn.L.Rev. 332, (1932) 11 Neb.L.Bull. 214. The authorities are split.

657 State v. Kirk, 168 Iowa 244, 150 N.W. 91 (1914). This is ground for a new trial, if prejudice to the constitutional rights of the defendant is shown, under Section 365 of the American Law Institute Code of Criminal Procedure.

because the jury process of deliberation is subject to so many variables that regulation of the method of reaching verdicts is probably hopeless. Moreover, the Iowa rule results in wholesale reversals and extended litigation.[658]

48. Meaning of Conviction

At common law when the jury found a verdict of guilty it was said that the defendant was convicted.[659] A distinction was taken between conviction by confession or verdict, and attainder by judgment and sentence. Most of the common-law consequences of felony, such as forfeiture, escheat, corruption of blood, followed upon attainder, not conviction. Today the term "conviction" sometimes is used in the older sense and sometimes used in the sense of judgment and sentence.[660] It may have one meaning in connection with a pardon and another in connection with competency as a witness.[661] Under Section 360 of the Institute Code it is thus defined: "The term conviction as used in this Code means the final acceptance of a plea of guilty or the finding by the jury or by the court that the defendant is guilty." [662]

[658] Note (1932) 45 Harv.L.Rev. 746.

[659] Bl. Comm., *262, *336; 3 Co. Inst. 391 a. In appeals in England from a conviction, the term is not used in the same sense. Archbold, Criminal Pleading, Evidence and Practice (30th 1938) 329.

[660] Notes (1908) 8 Col.L.Rev. 584, (1930) 30 Col.L.Rev. 1045, (1939) 18 Neb.L.Bull. 90, (1931) 21 J.Crim.L. 612.

[661] The question also arises: as to added penalties upon conviction of a previous offender, prior conviction of the principal in prosecution of accessory, qualification of voters, removal from public office, disbarment of attorney, forfeiture of medical certificate, rewards upon conviction, suspended sentences, divorce for conviction of a felony, forfeiture of an insurance certificate, etc.

[662] For a similar definition, see A.L.I., Administration of the Criminal Law (1935) Double Jeopardy, § 3.

49. Stenographer

Full protection of the rights of a defendant would seem to call for stenographic reporting of criminal cases.[663] There had been inadequate provision in the federal courts.[664] In January 1944, Congress passed a bill authorizing the appointment of salaried court reporters in the federal district courts.[665] Only two states have failed to make provision for official state court reporters. Such reporters are usually on a salary basis. The new federal statute is based on a careful study of the subject by a committee of the Judicial Conference of Senior Circuit Judges under the chairmanship of Judge John J. Parker.[666] The reporter will be required to record all official proceedings had in open court except when, in civil cases, the

663 "The stenographic reporting of court proceedings is not only a matter to which the public has become accustomed but, under modern methods of administering justice, it is a practical necessity if there is to be an appeal or other review of the proceedings. Even in cases where there is no appeal, a record should be made of proceedings had in open court because of the importance they may have in matters arising in the future. Proceedings even in criminal trials and submissions may be important in subsequent proceedings looking to the parole of the prisoner or the release under writ of habeas corpus." Parker, "The Integration of the Federal Judiciary" (1943) 56 Harv.L.Rev. 563, 573. See also Wigmore, "Lessons from Military Justice" (1920) 4 J. Am. Jud. Soc. 151, 153, (1909) 34 A.B.A. Rep. 578, 585.

664 In one case, a defendant, charged with a violation of the Mann Act, represented that he could not afford to pay the attendance fee of the stenographer, but the government refused to incur any obligation. The trial proceeded for several days, resulting in a verdict of guilty and a sentence of eight years. When the parties undertook the making up of their bills of exception, the court took the position that in the absence of agreement between counsel he could certify no evidence not definitely supported by his own notes, which were fragmentary, or by his positive recollection. See also Holmes v. United States, 155 F. (2d) 528 (C.C.A. 8th, 1940).

665 Comment (1944) 30 A.B.A.J. 59.

666 See Parker, "The Integration of the Federal Judiciary" (1943) 56 Harv.L.Rev. 563, 573.

parties, with the approval of the court, agree to the contrary. He is entitled to transcript fees for transcripts furnished to the parties at rates fixed by each district court with the approval of the Judicial Conference. He is required to transcribe without charge all pleas and proceedings in connection with the imposition of sentence in criminal cases. In criminal cases brought *in forma pauperis,* transcript fees will be paid by the United States.

The importance of having a record of the trial becomes apparent when the defendant takes an appeal. In the absence of a record, it has been held that, even though the defendant may be unable to perfect his appeal, he will not be entitled to a new trial.[667] On principle, a new trial ought to be granted where the defendant is not at fault, as where the court reporter dies before having prepared a transcript of the evidence.

50. Publicity

It has been seen that English trials are conducted with great dignity and freedom from improper publicity. The same is usually true of trials in the federal courts,[668] but abuses in the state courts have been frequent. A special committee of the American Bar Association[669] made the

[667] State v. Ricks, 180 Pac. 257 (Idaho, 1919), criticized (1919) 19 Col. L.Rev. 503, (1919) 29 Yale L.J. 241.

[668] Berge, "The Prosecutor and Crime Publicity" (1943) 29 A.B.A.J. 63.

[669] Hallam, "Some Object Lessons in Publicity in Criminal Trials" (1940) 24 Minn.L.Rev. 453, 477, 507-508; 6 Wigmore, Evidence (3d ed. 1940) § 1836. See also Bellamy, Perry, and Baker, "Cooperation between Press, Radio and Bar" (1938) 28 J.Crim.L. 41; Moley, Our Criminal Courts (1930) 185-206. With respect to Canada, see Wright, "Newspapers and Criminal Trials" (1939) 17 Can.B.Rev. 191; MacLatchy, "Contempt of Court by Newspapers in England and Canada" (1938) 16 Can.B.Rev. 273. The law of Continental Europe is said to be inadequate as to prejudicial newspaper reports before and during trial. Mannheim, "Trial by

following recomendations: (1) that attendance in the courtroom during the progress of a criminal trial be limited to the seating capacity of the room; (2) that the process of subpoena should never be used to secure preferential admission of any person or spectator; (3) that approaches to the courtroom be kept clear so that free access to the courtroom be obtained; (4) that no use of cameras or photographic appliances be permitted in the courtroom, either during the session of the court or otherwise; (5) that no sound registering devices for publicity use be permitted to operate in the courtroom at any time; (6) that the surreptitious procurement of pictures or sound records be punishable as contempt; (7) that during the trial the courtroom and the courthouse be kept free from news distributing devices and equipment; (8) that newspaper accounts be limited to accounts of occurrences in court without argument of the case to the public; (9) that no popular referendum be taken during the pending of the proceedings as to the guilt or innocence of the defendant; (10) that broadcasting of arguments, giving out of argumentative press bulletins, and any other form of argument or discussion addressed to the public, by lawyers in the case during the process of the proceedings be forbidden; (11) that public criticism of the court or jury by lawyers in the case during the progress of the proceedings be not tolerated; (12) that featuring in vaudeville of jurors or other court officers, either during or after the trial be forbidden; (13) that the giving of paid interviews or the writing of paid articles by jurors, either before or during the trial, be forbidden; (14) that public discussions in

---

Jury in Modern Continental Criminal Law" (1937) 53 L.Q.Rev. 338, 397; Wright, "French Criminal Procedure" (1929) 45 L.Q.Rev. 92, 115-116.

speeches, magazine articles, or newspaper interviews, by witnesses during the progress of the proceedings and covering the subject matter thereof be forbidden; and (15) that the atmosphere of the courtroom and adjacent premises be maintained as one of dignity and calm.

The Canons of Judicial Ethics of the American Bar Association provide: "Proceedings in Court should be conducted with fitting dignity and decorum." [670] The bar has long been studying the question.[671] Rule 53 of the Federal Rules of Criminal Procedure provides: "The taking of photographs in the courtroom during the progress of judicial proceedings or radio broadcasting of judicial proceedings from the court room shall not be permitted by the court."

51. Communications by Counsel to Judge

It has been held to be contempt of court for an attorney to present a request for a continuance or for a trial by another judge to the judge ex parte in the privacy of his chambers.[672] Under the Canons of Judicial Ethics of the American Bar Association: "Ordinarily all communications of counsel to the judge intended or calculated to influence action should be made known to opposing counsel." [673] Rule 52 of the Federal Rules of Criminal Pro-

[670] (1937) 62 A.B.A.Rep. 1134, No. 35, adopted in 1924.

[671] (1925) 11 A.B.A.J. 64; (1926) 12 A.B.A.J. 488; (1932) 18 A.B.A.J. 72; Robbins, "The Hauptmann Trial in the Light of English Criminal Procedure" (1935) 21 A.B.A.J. 301, 304; "Report of the Special Committee on Cooperation between Press, Radio and Bar, as to Publicity Interfering with Fair Trial of Judicial and Quasi-Judicial Proceedings" (1937) 62 A.B.A.Rep. 851, 862-865.

[672] Pratt v. United States, 170 Fed. 891 (C.C.A. 9th, 1909). See also Ex parte Cole, 6 Fed. Cas. No. 2,973, 35, 38 (C.C.D. Iowa, 1879).

[673] (1937) 62 A.B.A.Rep. 1128, No. 17.

cedure, as proposed by the Advisory Committee, provided: "Copies of all communications, memoranda and briefs submitted by counsel to a judge and relating to a proceeding pending before him shall be delivered simultaneously to counsel for adverse parties. Counsel shall not confer with a judge regarding the merits of a proceeding pending before him, except in the presence of or with the consent of counsel for adverse parties." The rules, as finally adopted, are silent on the subject.

CHAPTER VIII

MOTIONS AFTER VERDICT

1. Stage in Proceedings

AFTER the defendant has been found guilty, he may attack the proceedings by certain motions after verdict.[1] These motions are in arrest of judgment and for new trial. By a motion in arrest of judgment he may challenge the jurisdiction or the legal sufficiency of the indictment or information, or the regularity of the proceedings on the record. By a motion for new trial, he may attack the regularity of the trial for matters not appearing on the record. In some states all questions may be raised by the latter motion.

2. Benefit of Clergy

Between conviction and judgment the defendant could at common law pray benefit of clergy.[2] After the separation by William the Conqueror of the ecclesiastical from the secular courts, the clergy claimed that persons in holy orders should be exempt from secular jurisdiction. The clergy were accordingly tried in the bishop's courts before a jury of clerks by the oaths of twelve compurgators. This mode of trial usually insured an acquittal. Even if there was a conviction, the court could not sentence to death,

[1] Nat. Com. on Law Obs. and Enf., Rep. on Crim. Proc. (1931) 17-18. See also 23 C.J.S., Criminal Law, §§ 1418-1513, pp.1115-1333; 39 Am. Jur., Criminal Law, §§ 1-218, pp.27-209.

[2] 1 Stephen, A History of the Criminal Law of England (1883) 457-472; 1 Pollock and Maitland, History of English Law (2d ed.1905) 439-457; 3 Holdsworth, History of English Law (3d ed.1923) 293-302; Kenny, Outlines of Criminal Law (15th ed.1942) 573-574; Hall, Theft, Law and Society (1935) 68-70, 72-86.

but could only degrade and imprison him. But about 1300, no accused clergy were surrendered to the bishop until they had been convicted in the secular court, and had thereby forfeited their chattels. Moreover, the clergy had no such benefit in misdemeanors or soon after in treason cases. On the other hand, the benefit was extended to all males who could read. In practice, this came to mean all who could memorize a few words. In 1487 it was enacted that mere layman could have the benefit only once, and should be branded on the thumb to show that they had had it. Under Henry VIII, benefit of clergy was abolished as to "wilful murder of malice aforethought." Under Queen Elizabeth all surrenders to the bishop and all distinctions between clergy and laymen were abolished, and all who obtained the benefit became liable to spend a year in jail. Under William III the benefit was extended to women whether they could read or not. Statutes gradually took away the benefit from the more heinous crimes so that by the time of Blackstone there were one hundred sixty felonies in which it could not be claimed. It was abolished by Parliament in 1827. It survived a little longer in some of the older states in the United States.[3]

3. History of New Trial in England

Although new trials were granted in civil cases as early as the fourteenth century, they were not granted in criminal cases until the latter half of the seventeenth century.[4]

[3] It was successfully claimed in South Carolina as recently as 1855. State v. Bosse, 42 S.C. 276. For an account of it in this country, see Hall, Theft, Law and Society (1935) 94, n.36.

[4] Rex v. Hainis, 2 Keb. 765 (1671); Orfield, Criminal Appeals in America (1939) 17-18; 1 Stephen, A History of the Criminal Law of England (1883) 310-311.

Although there were two cases in 1660 allowing a new trial upon the application of the prosecution, the developing concept of double jeopardy prevented the rule from taking hold. In 1671, the court, being equally divided, refused a new trial after conviction.[5] In 1673 a new trial was granted after a conviction of perjury.[6] Since that date the defendant might apply for a new trial in misdemeanor cases tried by the Court of King's Bench. The grounds for new trial were broad in scope, covering errors in the admission or exclusion of evidence, improper instructions, a verdict against the weight of the evidence, or the furtherance of the ends of justice.[7] No new trial could be granted in felony cases.[8] Application for a new trial was not made before the judges who tried the case but before the King's Bench sitting *en banc*.[9] Under Section 20 of the Criminal Appeal Act, enacted in 1937, the power to grant a new trial was abolished.[10]

Today in England a new trial cannot be ordered even though the defendant appears to be clearly guilty, except

[5] Rex v. Latham, 3 Keb. 143 (1673).

[6] 1 Holdsworth, History of English Law (3d ed.1923) 216; Thayer, A Preliminary Treatise on Evidence at the Common Law (1898) 175-179.

[7] Archbold, Pleading, Evidence and Practice in Criminal Cases (23d ed. 1905) 291.

[8] A single case allowing it, Reg. v. Scaife, 17 Q.B. 238 (1851), was not followed by the Privy Council in Reg. v. Bertrand, L.R. 1 P.C. 520 (1867), and was disapproved by the Queen's Bench Division in Reg. v. Duncan, (1881) 7 Q.B.D. 198, 201.

[9] Riddell, "New Trials at the Common Law" (1916) 26 Yale L.J. 49, 57. No appeal lay from a denial of a motion for new trial.

[10] The practice just before it was abolished is described in Archbold, Pleading, Evidence and Practice in Criminal Cases, (23d ed.1905) 291-294. The defendant might move for an order nisi within eight days after the trial before a divisional court of the King's Bench Division. The court could extend the time in which the motion could be made. The motion was made on the judge's notes of the trial or upon affidavit. The presence of the defendant seems to have been necessary.

after a merely abortive trial.[11] Illustrations of the latter in which a new trial or venire de novo was granted on appeal may be clarifying. In one case, the defendant, during the course of the trial, confessed his guilt and was sentenced without the verdict of the jury being taken. The Court of Criminal Appeal ordered a new trial on the grounds that the trial had been a nullity.[12] Likewise a new trial was ordered where two prisoners separately indicted were tried together.[13] A similar order was made where an unqualified juryman sat on the jury.[14] If a jury cannot agree and is therefore discharged, the defendant may be tried again, but if the second trial results in a disagreement the prisoner is usually discharged.[15]

The English law thus distinguishes between new trial, which is abolished, and venire de novo which is retained. An order for new trial could only be granted in the High Court (King's Bench Division) after a general verdict for the Crown, in the case of indictments or informations for misdemeanor tried in the King's Bench Division, or on a record of the King's Bench Division. A venire de novo may be awarded: (1) before completion of the first trial if the judge thought fit to discharge the first jury; (2) where a special verdict has been returned on which the appellate court could not enter judgment for either party;

[11] Kenny, Outlines of Criminal Law (15th ed.1942) 590; Orfield, Criminal Appeals in America (1939) 18-19. See (1944) 60 L.Q.Rev. 33, 130. In Canada the appellate courts may order new trials, but the trial courts may not. Riddell, New Trial in Present Practice (1918) 27 Yale L.J. 353, 359-360.

[12] Rex v. Hancock, 23 Cr. App. R. 16 (1931).

[13] Crane v. Director of Public Prosecutions, 2 A.C. 299 (1921), 30 Yale L.J. 864.

[14] Rex v. Wakefield (1918) 1 K.B. 216.

[15] Howard, Criminal Justice in England (1931) 373.

(3) by a court of error in cases of mistrial of treason, felony, or misdemeanor.[16]

4. Function of Motion for a New Trial

The function of a motion for a new trial is to call to the attention of the trial court some error which was committed upon the trial or to some newly discovered evidence which was not obtainable at the trial.[17] By means of such a motion it is possible for the trial court to correct errors without subjecting the defendant to the expense, delay, and inconvenience of an appeal.[18] Motion for new trial is one method, perhaps the best, for reviewing a conviction obtained by unfair or unlawful methods.[19] Like the right to appeal, it is not, however, a requirement of due process or other general constitutional guarantees.[20]

[16] Archbold, Criminal Pleading, Evidence and Practice (30th ed.1938) 349-350. See "New Trials in Criminal Cases" (1940) 4 J.Crim.L. (Eng.) 426-431. It is not easy to distinguish mere irregularities in the proceedings resulting in discharge of the defendant and completely null proceedings resulting in another trial. The Court of Criminal Appeal does not always order a new trial even if the proceedings were null.

[17] Broadway & Newport Bridge Co. v. Commonwealth, 173 Ky. 165, 190 S.W. 715 (1917); Territory v. Pettine, 16 N.M. 40, 113 Pac. 843 (1911). See 23 C.J.S., Criminal Law, § 1418, p.1116; 39 Am. Jur., New Trial, § 17, p.42.

[18] People v. Beal, 315 Ill. 71, 145 N.E. 695 (1924); Green v. State, 116 Neb. 635, 218 N.W. 432 (1928).

[19] State ex rel. Kunkel v. Circuit Court of La Porte County, 209 Ind. 682, 200 N.E. 614 (1936).

[20] State v. McCord, 8 Kan. 232, 12 Am. Rep. 469 (1871). Prior to the nineteenth century the legislature often granted new trials by special act. Pound, Criminal Justice in America (1930) 96.

5. On Motion of Defendant

If the defendant has been acquitted in a court not having jurisdiction,[21] or upon an indictment so void or defective that a valid judgment could not be entered upon it,[22] or through his own misconduct, fraud, or collusion,[23] he may be brought to trial again, without the formality of a motion for new trial by the prosecution. In Cleveland the anomaly of granting a new trial after a plea of guilty has frequently occurred.[24] Aside from such cases there can, of course, be no new trial after an acquittal of the defendant.[25] The motion lies after a conviction usually on the application of the defendant, but in some jurisdictions on the motion of the court itself.[26] Section 361 of the Institute Code provides for the granting of a new trial on motion of the defendant or on the court's own motion, pro-

[21] A.L.I., Administration of the Criminal Law (1935) Double Jeopardy, § 8.

[22] *Ibid.* § 9.

[23] *Ibid.* § 11.

[24] Criminal Justice in Cleveland (1922) 335. See Smith, "Cleveland's Crime Survey" (1921) 5 J. Am. Jud. Soc. 68, 75.

[25] State v. Van Horton, 26 Iowa 402 (1868). The only state in which the prosecution may after an acquittal secure a new trial for errors on the first trial prejudicial to the state is Connecticut. State v. Lee, 65 Conn. 265, 30 Atl. 1110, 48 A.S.R. 202, 27 L.R.A. 498 (1894). In United States v. Gibert, 2 Sumn. 19, 47 (1834), the court stated that as to misdemeanors it is still open to inquiry whether the court does not possess the power to grant the prosecution a new trial if it should exercise it. Section 13 of the American Law Institute, Administration of the Criminal Law (1935) Double Jeopardy, provides, however: "Where a person has been acquitted generally, and in the course of the trial a material error has been made to the prejudice of the state, the state shall be entitled to a new trial." See discussion (1932) 10 Am. L. Inst. Proc. 130-135; (1934) 12 Am. L. Inst. Proc. 200-207.

[26] Because of the limited use of new trials in England, America's new trial procedure is regarded as of a statutory character. Hubbard v. State, 72 Neb. 62, 100 N.W. 153 (1904); Riddell, "New Trial in Present Practice" (1918) 27 Yale L.J. 353, 361.

vided that the defendant consents.[27] The Federal Rules of Criminal Procedure allow the court to act on its own motion. The first sentence of Rule 33 provides: "The court may grant a new trial to a defendant if required in the interest of justice."

6. Time

There is no uniform fixed time in which the motion for a new trial may be made in the various states.[28] Under Section 362 of the Institute Code, the motion must normally be made within three days after the verdict or finding of guilt.[29] Rule II(2) of the Criminal Appeals Rules of the United States Supreme Court provided for a similar period. Rule 33 of the Federal Rules of Criminal Procedure increases and makes flexible the time interval permitted. It provides: "A motion for new trial based on any

[27] Accord: Report of the Commission on the Administration of Justice in New York State (1939) § 403, p.147. The cases are divided in this country as to whether the trial court may act of its own motion. Upholding the power is Commonwealth v. Gabor, 209 Pa. 201, 58 Atl. 278 (1904). *Contra:* State v. Williams, 38 La. Ann. 960 (1886); People v. McGrath, 202 N.Y. 445, 96 N.E. 92 (1911). See Note (1921) 30 Yale L.J. 864; 23 C.J.S., Criminal Law, § 1463, pp.1259-1260; 39 Am. Jur., New Trial, § 11, p.38.

[28] The general rule in this country is that it must be made before judgment has been entered. Hogan v. State, 36 Wis. 226 (1874); Willis v. State, 62 Ind. 391 (1878). It should be made at the same term at which the verdict was rendered. State v. Tolla, 73 N.J.L. 249, 63 Atl. 338 (1906); United States v. Mayer, 235 U.S. 55, 35 Sup.Ct. 16, 59 L.Ed. 129 (1914).

[29] "An English critic, accustomed to the procedure of a Court of Assize, might be tempted to regard the three days allowed for one or other motion as unnecessary; it may, at least, cause a definite waste of judicial time on the last day or two of the session." Brunyate, "The American Draft Code of Criminal Procedure, 1930" (1933) 49 L.Q.Rev. 192, 203. In Massachusetts the law has permitted one year in murder cases. See criticism in the Third Report of the Judicial Council of Massachusetts (1927) 39.

other grounds shall be made within 5 days after verdict or finding of guilt or within such further time as the court may fix during the 5-day period."

A leading decision of the United States Supreme Court held that a motion for a new trial, even on the ground of newly discovered evidence, must be made within the term of court.[30] The general rule at common law was that a judgment could not be altered by the court which granted it after the expiration of the term at which it was granted. The law recognized but three exceptions. Clerical errors could be corrected at any time.[31] By a writ of *audita querela,* relief might be obtained against the consequences of a judgment on account of some matter of defense, which had arisen since its rendition, and which could not have been taken advantage of otherwise.[32] Writs of error *coram nobis* were allowed to bring to the attention of the court errors of fact in the procedure not appearing on the record, and which, if known at the time, would have prevented the judgment, such as that a party was dead, an infant, married, or insane.[33] Thus where the ground was newly discovered evidence or partiality of the court, there was no remedy. Modern statutes have often provided prescribed periods to reopen the judgment on such grounds in civil cases. But such statutes often do not cover crimi-

[30] United States v. Mayer, 235 U.S. 55, 35 Sup.Ct. 16, 59 L.Ed. 129 (1914), (1915) 28 Harv.L.Rev. 412, 434; Williston, "Does a Pardon Blot Out Guilt?" (1915) 28 Harv.L.Rev. 647, 659.

[31] Philips v. Smith (1716) 1 Stra. 136. This is not a genuine exception since the record alone is altered to make it conform to the judgment in fact rendered.

[32] 3 Bl. Comm. *405, 406; Avery v. United States, 12 Wall. (U.S.) 304 (1870). See Note (1914) 39 Mich.L.Rev. 963, 970, for a full discussion. See also Moore and Rogers, "Federal Relief from Civil Judgments" (1946) 55 Yale L.J. 623, 659-669.

[33] United States v. Plumer, 3 Cliff. 28, Fed. Cas. No. 16,056 (C.C. Mass. 1859).

nal cases.[34] Equity will not interfere because of the absence of property rights.[35] Thus the defendant has only the inadequate and cumbersome remedy of a pardon, which does not blot out the guilt of the defendant. In civil cases rights of property favor brief times in which to reopen judgments. The same consideration is not present in criminal cases. In England the gap is filled by the power of the Court of Criminal Appeal to allow an appeal at any time on any ground.[36]

Normally motions for new trial come after the verdict and before judgment. But where the ground is newly discovered evidence, it should be possible to move for a new trial even after judgment.[37] Section 362 of the Institute Code allows such a motion to be made within one year after the verdict or the finding of the court "or at a later time if the court for good reason so permits." [38] Rule II(3) of the Criminal Appeals Rules of the United States Supreme Court allowed only sixty days after final judgment, except that in capital cases the motion might be made at any time before final judgment. Rule 35 of the

[34] Klink v. People, 16 Colo. 467 (1891); Howard v. State, 58 Ark 229 (1893).

[35] Notes (1924) 23 Mich.L.Rev. 57, (1927) 40 Harv.L.Rev. 781, (1933) 11 Neb.L.Bull. 421, 424, (1941) 39 Mich.L.Rev. 963, 973-975, (1933) 33 Col.L.Rev. 161.

[36] It has been erroneously stated that a new trial can be allowed. (1915) 28 Harv.L.Rev. 412, 413.

[37] Note (1935) 13 Neb.L.Bull. 305. Three years have been provided in Nebraska since 1935. Note (1940) 19 Neb.L.Bull. 150, 152.

[38] "It may be questioned whether, after judgment and sentence have been passed and recorded, such a reopening of a decided case ought not properly to be brought before the appellate court." Brunyate, "The American Draft Code of Criminal Procedure, 1930" (1933) 49 L.Q.Rev. 192, 203. Such procedure is provided in murder cases in Pennsylvania. Report of the Crimes Survey Committee, Law Association of Philadelphia (1926) 273.

Federal Rules of Criminal Procedure, Second Preliminary Draft, provided the fairest possible rule by abolishing all time limitations as to motions for new trial on the ground of newly discovered evidence as well as on the ground that the defendant has been deprived of a constitutional right.[39] Rule 33 of the Federal Rules of Criminal Procedure allows a two-year period on the ground of newly discovered evidence.

In some states a strict rule is laid down as to the order in which a motion for new trial must be made when the defendant plans to move both for new trial and in arrest of judgment. If the defendant moves first in arrest of judgment, this may preclude him from moving later for a new trial.[40] That is to say, the proper order of motions is, first, motion for new trial and, then, in arrest of judgment. The rule does not seem sensible because a motion in arrest of judgment might result in the discharge of the defendant, while a motion for new trial will not. The defendant may have discovered the ground of a motion for new trial after he had moved in arrest of judgment.[41]

What is the effect of taking an appeal on the right to move for a new trial? The cases are in conflict. The traditional view has been that the perfection of an appeal divests the trial court of jurisdiction to vacate judgment.[42] Even this line of cases concedes that, where the vacation

[39] No time limit is prescribed in Russia, but action is by a higher court. Hazard, "Soviet Criminal Procedure" (1941) 15 Tulane L.Rev. 220, 235.

[40] Bepley v. State, 4 Ind. 264, 58 Am. Dec. 628 (1853); Wharton, Criminal Pleading and Practice (9th ed.1889) § 890, p.628; 23 C.J.S., Criminal Law, § 1467, p.1271, § 1547, p.1353; Abbott, Criminal Trial Practice (4th ed.1939) § 764, p.1416.

[41] 2 Moore, Illinois Criminal Law and Procedure (3d ed.1932) § 1436, p.1074.

[42] Ex parte Johannes, 213 Calif. 125, 1 Pac. (2d) 984 (1931); Fletcher v. State, 128 S.W. (2d) 997 (Ark. 1939), 30 J.Crim.L. 610.

is based on a question other than the one involved in the appeal, the trial court may vacate judgment.[43] The other line of cases holds that the mere fact of appeal does not divest the trial court of its inherent jurisdiction to vacate it under circumstances justifying that relief.[44] Most of these courts recognize an exception after the appellate court has affirmed the judgment, since the judgment is now that of the appellate court.[45]

One ground offered for the traditional view is that of double jeopardy. But that ground is not realistic since the appellate court may remand the case and order a new trial. A second ground is that it would be very confusing for two judicial tribunals to have jurisdiction over the case at the same time.[46] It would permit withdrawal of a case from the scrutiny of the appellate court after it has given study to the fact situation. Moreover, the trial court might become more lax if it could correct errors even after an appeal. The trial court has had ample opportunity to correct its errors before the appeal was taken. For the trial court now to reverse its earlier position makes its action so equivocal as to deserve appellate consideration. The opposing theory is that the trial court retains jurisdiction during the same term and that the trial court is more familiar with the fact situation.

Rule II(3) of the Criminal Appeals Rules of the

[43] State v. DeGrace, 144 Ore. 159, 22 Pac. (2d) 896, 90 A.L.R. 232 (1933).

[44] Chambliss v. Haas, 125 Iowa 484, 101 N.W. 153 (1904). See Tillman v. Commonwealth, 263 Ky. 488, 92 S.W. (2d) 775 (1936).

[45] McArthur v. Dane, 61 Ala. 539 (1878). It was held, however, that a federal district judge might grant a new trial even after affirmance by the circuit court in United States v. Memelo, 152 F. (2d) 759 (C.C.A. 3d, 1946), 60 Harv.L.Rev. 145.

[46] Third Report of the Judicial Council of Massachusetts (1927) 34, 39, reprinted in (1927) 13 Mass.L.Q.

United States Supreme Court provided that a motion for new trial on the ground of newly discovered evidence may be made "unless an appeal has been taken and in that event the trial court may entertain the motion only on remand of the case by the appellate court for that purpose." Rule 33 of the Federal Rules of Criminal Procedure provides that "if an appeal is pending, the court may grant the motion only on remand of the case." Under the former rule a remand of the case must be secured before the motion for a new trial is made in the trial court. Under the latter rule, a motion for new trial could be made without securing a remand. If, however, the trial court grants the motion, a remand will have to be obtained. This will eliminate the need for a remand when the trial court denies the motion.

7. Presence of Defendant

At the present date the presence of the defendant is not necessary at the making of a motion for a new trial.[47] Neither the Institute Code nor the Federal Rules of Criminal Procedure requires it. Section 289 of the Institute Code provides: "In a prosecution for felony or misdemeanor the defendant need not be present during the making, hearing of, or ruling upon a motion or application addressed to the court nor when judgment is rendered."

8. Necessity of Writing

Statutes in many states provide that a motion for new trial shall be in writing. Section 363 of the Institute Code provides: "The motion for a new trial shall be in writing

[47] Wharton, Criminal Pleading and Practice (9th ed.1889) § 548, p.393; 23 C.J.S., § 1504, p.1325.

and shall be filed. It shall state the ground on which it is based. Notice of the motion shall be given to the prosecuting attorney." At times it may be speedier and more convenient to permit the motion to be made orally. There is no requirement in the Federal Rules of Criminal Procedure that it be in writing. Rule 47 dealing with motions in general provides: "An application to the court for an order shall be by motion. A motion other than one made during a trial or hearing shall be in writing unless the court permits it to be made orally. It shall state the grounds upon which it is made and shall set forth the relief or order sought. It may be supported by affidavit."

9. Grounds for New Trial

There is no uniformity among the states as to the proper grounds for new trial.[48] Sections 364 and 365 of the Institute Code set out the grounds in great detail in two broad classes, the first requiring no showing of prejudice to the defendant while the second requires such a showing.[49] Under Section 364 the defendant has an absolute right to a new trial if it is established that the jurors de-

[48] They are listed in the A.L.I. Code of Crim. Proc. (1931) commentaries 1046-1057. See also Wharton, Criminal Pleading and Practice (9th ed.1889) §§ 792-889, pp.559-628. As to the effect of recantation by witnesses for the prosecution, see (1931) 22 J.Crim.L. 599, (1934) 25 J. Crim.L. 285.

[49] Accord: Report of the Commission on the Administration of Justice in New York State (1939) §§ 406-407, pp.148-149; Freeman, "The Draft Code of Criminal Law and Procedure" (1935) 30 Ill.L.Rev. 226, 232; Nat. Com. on Law Obs. and Enf., Rep. on Crim. Proc. (1931) 44. In 1939 the Massachusetts legislature, at the suggestion of the Judicial Council, allowed the Supreme Judicial Court to grant new trials in capital cases "for any reason that justice may require." Fifteenth Report of the Judicial Council of Massachusetts (1939) 8. The trial court was given similar powers. *Ibid.* p.9; see also Fourteenth Report of the Judicial Council of Massachusetts (1938) 38.

cided the verdict by lot, that the verdict is contrary to law or the weight of the evidence, or that new and material evidence that, if introduced at the trial, would probably have changed the verdict or finding of the court, is discovered which the defendant could not with reasonable evidence have discovered and produced upon the trial. Section 365 specifies seven grounds, with respect to which a new trial shall be granted, provided that the substantial rights of the defendant have been prejudiced: (a) that the defendant was not present at any proceeding where his presence is required under the Code; (b) that the jury has received any evidence out of court, other than that resulting from a view of the premises; (c) that the jurors after retiring to deliberate upon the verdict have separated without leave of court; (d) that any of the jurors has been guilty of misconduct; (e) that the prosecuting attorney has been guilty of misconduct; (f) that the court has erred in the decision of any matter of law arising during the course of the trial; and (g) that the court has misdirected the jury on a matter of law or has refused to give a proper instruction which was requested by the defendant. A sweeping final provision of this section provides: "The court shall also grant a new trial when from any other cause not due to his own fault the defendant has not received a fair and impartial trial." To be compared with the detailed Code provisions is the language of Rule 33 of the Federal Rules of Criminal Procedure: "The court may grant a new trial to a defendant if required in the interest of justice."

10. When Motion for New Trial Heard and Decided

Although the defendant usually has but a limited time to move for a new trial, delay may arise from slowness in scheduling the hearing on the motion or in deciding whether to grant the motion. But few statutes endeavor to lay down time limitations.[50] Rule II (1) of the Criminal Appeals Rules of the Supreme Court provided: "Motions after verdict or finding of guilt, or to withdraw a plea of guilty, shall be determined promptly." [51] The Institute Code does not specify any time limit, but provides that where the motion "calls for the decision of any question of fact the court may hear evidence on such motion by affidavit or otherwise."

The Minnesota Crime Commission Report of 1927 recommends that there be provided a definite time for each step in this procedure, giving sufficient time to protect the defendant but preventing unnecessary delay in the final disposition of the case.[52] One of the chief occasions of the delay has been in securing from the court reporter a transcript of the trial proceedings. This defect might be remedied by having such transcripts ordered only if the trial judge finds them necessary to pass on the motion for new trial, and by making provision for prompt action in getting the transcript when one is ordered.

11. Effect of Grant of Motion

When the second trial is held after a new trial is granted, the trial should be conducted as if there had been no prior trial.[53] Section 368 of the Institute Code is clear

[50] A rule of this kind may be hard to enforce. It is not clear that the Criminal Appeals Rule has reduced delay. See Note (1939) 52 Harv.L. Rev. 983, 989-992, Tables II-V.

[51] See 23 C.J.S., § 1498, p.1322; Comment (1911) 2 J.Crim.L. 626.

[52] Minnesota Crime Commission Report (1927) 34-35.

[53] For a suggestion that the entire case need not be retried, see Higgins, "Is This Plan for Abbreviating New Trials Feasible?" (1913) 4 J.Crim.L. 8. The plan would require special verdicts and has not been used in any jurisdiction.

to this effect, providing that "the defendant may be convicted of any offense charged in the indictment or information, irrespective of the verdict or finding on the former trial." Section 14 of the Institute's draft on double jeopardy is to the same effect. The cases are divided upon the question whether, upon a new trial, a defendant may be convicted of a higher degree of the offense than the degree of which he was convicted on a first trial. Many jurisdictions have followed the Institute rule upholding the validity of such convictions.[54] The same question arises where the defendant is granted a new trial after he has been convicted on less than all of several counts in an indictment. The cases are divided. Some courts hold that the new trial reopens the entire case.[55] A majority of the courts favor the view that a new trial may be had only on the counts on which there was a conviction.[56] In this situation there is an even stronger reason for arguing that the defendant does not waive his express or implied acquittal as a bar to prosecutions on the counts for which he was not convicted.[57]

[54] The rule is recommended in Millar, "The Modernization of Criminal Procedure" (1920) 11 J.Crim.L. 344, 362; The Report of the California Commission on the Reform of Criminal Procedure (1929) 24; Report of the Commission on the Administration of Justice in New York State (1939) § 409, p.149; Note (1929) 38 Yale L.J. 978. It is the rule in federal criminal cases. Trono v. United States, 199 U.S. 521, 26 Sup.Ct. 121, 50 L.Ed. 292, 4 Ann. Cas. 773 (1905), (1906) 6 Col.L.Rev. 261. The proposed rule is criticized on the ground that the defendant cannot be regarded as waiving voluntarily a bar to a prosecution for a higher offense. Note (1940) 24 Minn.L.Rev. 522, 537.

[55] State v. Beal, 202 N.C. 266, 162 S.E. 561, 80 A.L.R. 1101 (1932) (distinct offenses).

[56] Bell v. State, 48 Ala. 684, 17 Am. Rep. 40 (1874) (distinct offenses); People v. Dowling, 84 N.Y. 478 (1881) (distinct offenses).

[57] Note (1940) 24 Minn.L.Rev. 522, 537. Section 14 of the American Law Institute, Administration of the Criminal Law (1935) Double Jeop-

12. Right to Reduce Verdict

It is not within the power of the trial court to alter the verdict so as to change it to a conviction for a lesser degree.[58] As a matter of fact American appellate courts usually have no such power either.[59] The English trial courts may not do this, but statutory power is given to the Court of Criminal Appeal to do so on appeal.[60] It would seem that the legislatures might well confer this power on the trial court.[61]

13. Number of Eliminations

The Cleveland Survey of Criminal Justice points out that the stage of motion for new trial offers another possibility of escape from punishment to a defendant. "In the group of Common Pleas cases begun in 1919 there were 292 original convictions for felony before known judges, 95 motions for new trial, of which 41 were allowed by the

---

ardy, is to the opposite effect, providing: "On a new trial the defendant can be convicted of any offense charged in the indictment or any count in the indictment on which the new trial was awarded irrespective of the verdict or finding on the prior trial." Section 368 of the American Law Institute Code of Criminal Procedure is not quite so explicit, making no reference to counts of the indictment.

[58] State v. Howard, 19 Kan. 507 (1878); State v. Symes, 17 Wash. 596, 50 Pac. 487 (1897); Beale, Criminal Pleading and Practice (1899) 357. See, however, United States v. Linnier, 125 Fed. 83 (C.C. Neb. 1903); 24 C.J.S., Criminal Law, § 1579, p.100.

[59] Orfield, Criminal Appeals in America (1939) 105, 191. See (1907) 7 Col.L.Rev. 620; Hall, "Reduction of Criminal Sentences on Appeal: I" (1937) 37 Col.L.Rev. 521, 526.

[60] Orfield, Criminal Appeals in America (1939) 30; Archbold, Criminal Pleading, Evidence and Practice (30th ed.1938) 325. See the Criminal Appeal Act, 1907, 7 Edw. VII, c.23, § 5(2).

[61] Willoughby, Principles of Judicial Administration (1929) 538; Notes (1928) 14 A.B.A.J. 67, 69; (1932) 18 A.B.A.J. 83, 87. California and Nevada have passed statutes.

judges."[62] This meant that fourteen per cent of all convictions were thus set aside, and forty-three per cent of all motions for new trial allowed. Since in most instances the new trial was granted by the trial judge because the verdict was against the weight of the evidence, this indicates poor work by the juries. But in most cases there was no real intention to grant another trial. The verdict was simply set aside in order to make some other adjustment. Only two of the forty-one cases in which new trials were granted actually went to trial.[63] In eighteen cases pleas of guilty to lesser offenses were accepted. Ten cases were "nolled" and one dismissed for want of prosecution. Six defendants received "bench paroles." The large number of motions for new trial seem to indicate poor quality of jurors, befogged instructions by judges to the juries, rearrangements conforming to the consciences of the judges rather than to the law, and yielding to solicitation of the defendant's lawyer or relatives. Since trials are expensive and since it is a difficult matter to prosecute a criminal case through trial, new trials should not be granted indiscriminately.

The Wickersham Commission has pointed out that in many jurisdictions the motion for a new trial became of practical importance, not so much as a means of obtaining a new trial by the action of the lower court as in order to

[62] Criminal Justice in Cleveland (1922) 332. In the last quarter of the nineteenth century "there was a lavish granting of new trials which had become a distinct abuse." Pound, Criminal Justice in America (1930) 162. See also Wigmore, "New Trials for Erroneous Rulings Upon Evidence; A Practical Problem for American Justice" (1903) 3 Col.L.Rev. 433; Nat. Com. on Law Obs. and Enf., Rep. on Crim. Proc. (1931) 30.

[63] Similarly, when the appellate courts reverse and grant new trials, many cases are never brought to trial again. Orfield, Criminal Appeals in America (1939) 193.

serve as the foundation for review by an appellate court. "Any requirement for the latter purpose should be done away with and the motion should be reserved for occasional cases where there is reason for applying to the trial court to correct an error not already canvassed before it instead of taking an appeal." [64] The same question should not repeatedly be raised before the same court.[65] At the same time it may result in expense and delay if the points can be raised only in the appellate court.[66] In England, in

[64] Nat. Com. on Law Obs. and Enf., Rep. on Crim. Proc. (1931) 30-31. See also Note by E. W. Hinton (1931) 26 Ill.L.Rev. 60. The American Law Institute Code of Criminal Procedure has been criticized for permitting the trial court to correct errors already considered by it instead of confining it to errors not canvassed. Brunyate, "The American Draft Code of Criminal Procedure, 1930" (1933) 49 L.Q.Rev. 192, 203. Thus the trial court should not review "errors of the Court in the decisions of points of law arising during the course of the trial and misdirection."

[65] In the earlier practice a motion for new trial and a bill of exceptions were alternative and mutually exclusive. 1 Wigmore, Evidence (3d ed.1940) § 10; 1 Holdsworth, History of English Law (3d ed.1923) 226. It has been pointed out that, where the trial court denies the motion, this is likely to influence the appellate court adversely. Housel and Walser, Defending and Prosecuting Federal Criminal Cases (1938) § 598, p.661-662. This was held true as to a motion for new trial on the ground that the verdict was not supported by the evidence in Peri v. People, 65 Ill. 17, 24 (1872). Compare, however, the opinion of the Missouri Supreme Court as to the function of a motion for new trial. "The purpose of the motion for new trial is to call the attention of the trial court to matters and rulings occurring during the progress of the trial, which the movant contends constitute reversible error, in order to give the trial court an opportunity to correct its own errors, if any there were, and to avoid the necessity of an appeal, as well as to furnish proof to the appellate court that such alleged errors were properly called to the attention of the trial court." State v. Burns, 312 Mo. 673, 678, 280 S.W. 1026, 1027 (1926).

[66] The Third Report of the California Judicial Court recommends a "requirement for submission to the trial court and full disclosure on motion for new trial, of all claimed errors which might be urged on appeal, so as to enable that court to correct the same without delay and avoid the likelihood of reversal, after months of waiting, by reason of vital matters

civil cases new trials must be applied for in the Court of Appeals instead of in the trial court. Because of the large area of American states, the delay, and expense, it seems impractical in criminal cases to require moving in the appellate court. Possibly it would not be too severe a requirement except in rural areas to require that the motion be made to a bench of two or three trial judges.[67]

14. Appeal from Denial or Grant of New Trial

At common law, appeal did not lie for refusal of a new trial.[68] In fourteen states the defendant may appeal from an order denying a new trial.[69] Section 427 of the Institute Code does not provide for such an appeal, allowing the defendant to appeal only from a final judgment of convic-

---

which the trial judge might have corrected." Note (1931) 17 A.B.A.J. 415, 416. See also Book Review (1940) 53 Harv.L.Rev. 898, 899, n.4.

[67] In Philadelphia, Pennsylvania, in capital cases, if a rule to show cause is allowed by the trial judge, the argument must be heard before the trial judge and two other judges, and in other criminal cases it may be so heard. Report of the Crimes Survey Committee, Law Association of Philadelphia (1926) 272. See also Blume, "Motions for New Trials in the Federal Courts" (1941) 25 J. Am. Jud. Soc. 109, 112. Under the Rules of Civil Procedure of the American Judicature Society, Article 40, Section 2, the trial judge "may, if he deems it necessary for the purposes of justice, call in one or more judges to hear it with him." See Bulletin XIV of the American Judicature Society (1919) p.176. "It is a notable feature of French criminal procedure that a new trial cannot be held in the court which originally tried the case. It is thought that the court hearing the cause anew should be one that is able to reach its conclusion in full independence and without predisposition of any kind. Hence it is forbidden for any judge who participated in the earlier judgment to sit in the court at the new hearing." Keedy, "The Preliminary Investigation of Crime in France" (1940) 88 U. of Pa.L.Rev. 385, 399.

[68] Wharton, Criminal Pleading and Practice (9th ed.1889) §§ 779, 902.

[69] A.L.I. Code of Crim. Proc. (1930) commentaries 1202-1203. Appeal in the federal courts lies only for abuse of discretion. 5 Longsdorf, Cyclopedia of Federal Procedure (1929) § 2428, p.757. See urging a freer review, Blume (1941) 25 J. Am. Jud. Soc. 109, 112.

tion or a sentence. In eleven states the prosecution may appeal from an order granting a new trial.[70] Section 428 expressly provides that the prosecution may appeal from such an order.

15. History of Arrest of Judgment in England

The history of arrest of judgment in England appears to be rather incomplete and indistinct. In the words of the Supreme Court of Vermont: "It was early settled at common law that a motion in arrest of judgment could only be for matters apparent on the face of the strict record in the case. See cases in Salkeld and Lord Raymond. We say nothing of 'pleading in arrest of judgment,' the history of which is somewhat obscure, a practice which in a manner survived in the method of praying benefit of clergy and that of taking advantage of a pardon granted before judgment and sentence." [71] Since the statute of jeofails does not apply to indictments, it was held as late as the time of Blackstone that, even in matters of form, "a defective indictment is not aided by a verdict as defective pleadings in civil cases are." [72] Motions in arrest of judgment were thus given a broad scope. They would lie for any defect which could have been attacked by a demurrer.[73] Since, under the earlier law, the defendant was not permitted to see the indictment and only heard it on his arraignment and was not permitted to have counsel, there was inadequate opportunity to move to quash or to demur. "Perhaps for this reason, the courts were very lenient in permitting objections to the indictment to be first raised by the motion in

[70] A.L.I. Code of Crim. Proc. (1930) commentaries 1205.

[71] State v. Shappy, 79 Vt. 306, 65 Atl. 78, 79 (1906).

[72] 4 Bl., Comm. *375.

[73] 4 Bl., Comm. *324. See 3 Holdsworth, History of English Law (3d ed.1923) 618.

arrest of judgment, at which time he might for the first time be advised by counsel." [74]

Today in England, after a defendant has been convicted of felony or treason, he is asked if he has anything to say why the court should not give judgment against him.[75] The inquiry contemplates objections of law only, that is to say, grounds for motion in arrest of judgment. Motion in arrest of judgment is now practically unknown in England.[76] It lies for any objection in law that appears on the face of the record unless it is merely formal.[77] In the case of a felon, as has been stated, he is asked if he raises such objection. The motion may be made at any time between the conviction and sentence but not later.[78] The court may of its own motion arrest the judgment. The effect of arresting judgment is to set aside all proceedings but is not a bar to a new indictment. Appeal will lie from a denial of the motion. The relation of demurrer to arrest of judgment is interesting.[79] In the case of defects in substance apparent on the face of the indictment not cured by verdict, the defendant may plead not guilty instead of demurring. Then if he is convicted he may move

[74] McClintock, "Indictment by a Grand Jury" (1942) 26 Minn.L.Rev. 153, 172.

[75] Archbold, Criminal Pleading, Evidence and Practice (30th ed.1938) 223.

[76] Kenny, Outlines of Criminal Law (15th ed. 1942) 573.

[77] Kenny, Outlines of Criminal Law (15th ed.1942) 586; Archbold, Criminal Pleading, Evidence and Practice (30th ed.1938) 224; Harris and Wilshere, Principles and Practice of the Criminal Law (17th ed.1943) 469.

[78] Rex v. Robinson, 2 Burr. 799 (1759). Before motion for new trial was abolished, normally, though not necessarily, a motion for new trial should be made and heard before a motion in arrest of judgment. Archbold, Criminal Pleading, Evidence and Practice (23d ed.1905) 294.

[79] Archbold, Criminal Pleading, Evidence and Practice (30th ed.1938 143.

in arrest of judgment, thus giving him the same advantage which he could have had upon demurrer, after having had a chance of an acquittal upon his plea of not guilty. The common adoption of this strategy in practice seems to be one of the chief causes for the obsolescence of the demurrer in criminal practice. Holdsworth states of the common-law rule in civil cases: "We have seen that the possibility of thus raising these objections, even at the last stage of the case, can be traced ultimately to the primitive rule that the judges were umpires, set to see that all the rules of law adjective and substantive were observed by the parties; and that, for that reason, they could not give judgment for the plaintiff, if the least defect occurred on the record, which set out the facts to which the law was to be applied." [80]

16. Grounds

In this country a motion in arrest of judgment lies only as to defects appearing in the record.[81] Section 369 of the Institute Code reduces the grounds for arrest of judgment to four: (a) that the indictment or information does not charge an offense; (b) that the court is without jurisdiction of the case; (c) that the verdict is so uncertain that it does not appear therefrom that the jurors intended to convict the defendant of an offense of which he could be convicted under the indictment or information; (d) that the defendant was convicted of an offense of which he could not be convicted under the indictment or information. Rule 34 of the Federal Rules of Criminal

[80] 9 Holdsworth, History of English Law (3d ed.1923) 318.

[81] See Abbott, Criminal Trial Practice (4th ed.1939) § 743, p.1391; Arrest of Judgment, 23 C.J.S., Criminal Law, §§ 1511-1555, pp.1333-1356; 15 Am. Jur., Criminal Law, §§ 434-441, pp.98-102.

Procedure adopts only the first two of the grounds mentioned in the Code rule, as does the Report of the Commission on the Administration of Justice in New York State,[82] and the statutes of about twelve states.[83] In Massachusetts and Rhode Island the only ground available for arrest of judgment is lack of jurisdiction. It has been held that failure of the indictment to charge an offense is not a ground in Maryland,[84] Massachusetts,[85] and Rhode Island.[86] The motion has a considerably wider scope in the eight states which provide by statute that the motion may be founded on any defects in the indictment or information that are grounds for demurrer, unless the objection to the indictment has been waived by a failure to demur; and when the court has no jurisdiction or the indictment or information does not charge a crime, even though no demurrer was filed. In Illinois the motion lies as to defects appearing on the face of the record.[87]

The court should have the power to arrest judgment on its own motion. While the language of the Institute Code

[82] Section 412, p.152. See also Freeman, "The Draft Code of Criminal Law and Procedure" (1935) 30 Ill.L.Rev. 226, 232.

[83] A.L.I. Code of Crim. Proc. (1931) 1071-1072. It has been urged that motion in arrest should be expressly limited "to those objections which have not been waived or cured by the verdict." McClintock, "Indictment by a Grand Jury" (1942) 26 Minn.L.Rev. 153, 173. The Livingston Penal Code of more than a century ago would confine arrest of judgment to cases of failure to allege a crime. Hall, "Edward Livingston and His Louisiana Penal Code" (1936) 22 A.B.A.J. 191, 193. Possibly want of jurisdiction of the person should not be a ground for arrest of judgment on the ground that it may be waived by earlier failure to object.

[84] Cochran v. State, 6 Md. 400 (1854). In accord, see Campbell, "Some Needed Reforms in the Criminal Law" (1903) 6 Rep. Proc. Bar Assoc. of Ark. 53, 68.

[85] Commonwealth v. Monahan, 170 Mass. 460 (1898).

[86] State v. Smith, 29 R.I. 513 (1909).

[87] People v. Goldberg, 287 Ill. 238, 122 N.E. 530 (1919); 2 Moore, Illinois Criminal Law and Procedure (3d ed.1932) § 1431, p.1071; Keigwin, Cases in Criminal Procedure (1939) § 68, p.505.

and the Federal Rules of Criminal Procedure is not specific, they quite clearly contemplate it, as neither speaks of the motion as coming only from the defendant.

17. Time

Under Section 370 of the Institute Code, a motion in arrest of judgment may be made only within three days after a plea of guilty, a verdict of guilty, or a finding of guilty. Rule II(2) of the Criminal Appeals Rules of the United States Supreme Court provided for a similar period, but the rule made no reference to a plea of guilty.[88] Rule 34 of the Federal Rules of Criminal Procedure increases and makes flexible the period permitted. It provides that the motion shall be made "within 5 days after the determination of guilt or within such further time as the court may fix during the 5-day period." Under Section 371 of the Institute Code, the motion shall be in writing, shall be entered of record, and shall specify distinctly the ground on which it is based.[89]

18. Presence of Defendant

By some authority the defendant must be present at the argument of his motion in arrest of judgment.[90] But by

[88] The plea of guilty is included in the Report of the Commission on the Administration of Justice in New York State (1939) § 411, p.152. See also Commonwealth v. Hearsey, 1 Mass. 137 (1804); Klawanski v. People, 218 Ill. 481, 75 N.E. 1028 (1905); Read v. State, 156 So. 650 (Miss. 1934); Keigwin, Cases in Criminal Procedure (1939) § 68, p.506; Clark, Handbook of Criminal Procedure (2d ed. by Mikell, 1918) 431.

[89] The requirement for distinct specification of grounds is perhaps based on the Georgia and North Carolina rule that it is not sufficient that the ground for the motion is specified, but the actual defects in the indictment must be pointed out. Rollin v. State, 70 Ga. 719 (1883); State v. Bryan, 89 N.C. 531 (1883).

[90] Rolls v. State, 52 Miss. 391 (1876).

the weight of authority his presence may be dispensed with,[91] although the court may insist on his presence, if practicable.[92]

19. When Motion in Arrest Heard and Decided

In the case of a motion for new trial the court may be slow in deciding the motion and, as has been seen, the motion may in some cases come after the judgment. Section 372 of the Institute Code provides that the motion in arrest of judgment shall be heard and decided "before judgment is rendered and after reasonable notice has been given to the prosecuting attorney by the defendant." Rule II (1) of the Criminal Appeals Rules of the United States Supreme Court provided: "Motions after verdict or finding of guilty, or to withdraw a plea of guilty, shall be determined promptly."

20. Effect of Grant of Motion

If judgment is arrested, the defendant may be discharged, though this is not true in all cases. Under Section 374 of the Institute Code if there is reason to believe from the evidence that the defendant is guilty of an offense the court may commit him to custody, or, if the defendant is bailable, may admit him to bail, to answer a new indictment or information.[93] On the other hand if no evidence appears affording reason for such belief, he shall

[91] State v. West, 45 La. Ann. 928, 13 So. 173 (1893); State v. Greer, 11 Wash. 244, 39 P. 874 (1895); 23 C.J.S., § 1551, p.1355.

[92] Fleming v. State, 62 Fla. 48, 56 So. 298 (1911).

[93] Accord: Report of the Commission on the Administration of Criminal Justice in New York State (1939) § 414, p.152; Hill v. Nelms, 122 Ga. 572, 50 S.E. 344 (1905); State ex rel. Woods v. Read, 93 W.Va. 150, 116 S.E. 138 (1923); Note (1940) 24 Minn.L.Rev. 522, 534.

if in custody be discharged therefrom, or if he has been released on bail he and his sureties are exonerated.

21. Relation to Demurrer

In the United States, as in England, questions which can be raised by motion in arrest of judgment can also be raised by demurrer, and ought to be so raised though, as a matter of law, they need not be.[94] As one federal court has stated: "We have heretofore expressed our disapproval of the practice of postponing a challenge to the sufficiency of the indictment until after an expensive trial has been had. . . . The better practice is to raise such questions by demurrer in advance of the trial. But, however this may be, no defendant in a criminal case can be found guilty and punished unless the indictment, even if not attacked until by motion in arrest of judgment, states the substance of an offense." [95] It is to be observed that the motion in arrest is not always advantageous to the defendant, since he is forced to go through the harassment and expense of a trial.

22. Appeal from Grant or Denial of Motion in Arrest

In three states, statutes provide that a defendant may appeal from an order denying a motion in arrest of judg-

[94] Housel and Walser, Defending and Prosecuting Federal Criminal Cases (1938) § 574, p.646. Motion in arrest may also lie even though there might have been a motion to quash. Vicente and Dean v. State, 66 Fla. 197, 63 So. 423 (1913). Many matters which are demurrable may be cured through aider by verdict. State v. Carver, 49 Me. 588, 77 Am. Dec. 275 (1862).

[95] Morris v. United States, 168 Fed. 682, 683 (C.C.A. 8th, 1909), cert. denied 214 U.S. 527, 29 Sup.Ct. 704, 53 L.Ed. 1068 (1909).

ment.[96] The Institute Code makes no provision for an appeal. In nineteen states and the federal courts, the prosecution may appeal from an order arresting judgment.[97] Section 428 of the Institute Code allows the prosecution to appeal.

23. Proposals to Abolish

In the opinion of the Wickersham Commission, the motion in arrest of judgment should be eliminated from criminal procedure. It pointed out that this proceeding goes back to the days of mechanical trials when regularity of the record on its face was all that could be inquired into by way of review.[98] Statutes in various states have greatly limited the scope of the motion. Despite the proposed retention of the motion by the Institute Code, the Wickersham Commission would completely abolish it. It should be enough that questions of jurisdiction and of the sufficiency of the indictment may be raised once in the trial court before verdict and once on review. Questions as to the verdict could be raised just as well by motion for new trial.[99] Repeated raising of the same question produces delay and the multiplication of steps in procedure gives the defendant loopholes to which he is not entitled.

96 A.L.I. Code of Crim. Proc. (1930) commentaries 1203. The states are Louisiana, North Dakota, and South Dakota. The federal rule is not clear. That appeal lies, see 5 Longsdorf, Cyclopedia of Federal Procedure (1929) § 2441, p.763. *Contra:* Housel and Walser, Defending and Prosecuting Federal Criminal Cases (1938) § 588, p.653.

97 A.L.I. Code of Crim. Proc. (1930) commentaries 205.

98 Nat. Com. on Law Obs. and Enf., Rep. on Crim. Proc. (1931) 29-30, 47.

99 See also Carr, "Missouri Appellate Practice and Procedure" (1941) 6 Mo.L.Rev. 1, 40. Under the present Missouri statute, motion for new trial supplants motion in arrest of judgment. 23 C.J.S., Criminal Law, § 1514, p.1334.

24. The Writ of Error *Coram Nobis*

The writ of error *coram nobis* is a method of correcting the judgment of the trial court.[100] It differs from an ordinary writ of error or appeal in that it is not an appellate remedy, but is applied for in the trial court.[101] It lay to call up facts which were unknown to the court at the time of the judgment. It lay at any time after judgment, and the issue was determined before a jury. The usual grounds for its issuance were correction of clerical errors, coverture, death, and the appearance of an insane person by attorney and without a guardian. It was abolished in England by the Common Law Procedure Act.

The writ has been expanded in the United States.[102] It has been held to lie where a defendant pleaded guilty because of mob violence,[103] or in ignorance of the meaning of the plea.[104] It lay where a defendant was sentenced too severely in view of his minority.[105] It has been granted where a confession was obtained by duress.[106]

At common law the writ of error *coram nobis* is limited in its scope.[107] It does not lie as to errors of law, such as

[100] (1924) 37 Harv.L.Rev. 744. For the civil procedure, see Orfield, "The Writ of Error Coram Nobis in Civil Practice" (1934) 20 Va.L.Rev. 423; Moore and Rogers, "Federal Relief from Civil Judgments" (1946) 55 Yale L.J. 623, 669-674.

[101] Note (1932) 32 Col.L.Rev. 860, 864, 867. It appears that the federal appellate courts were reluctant to review errors of fact.

[102] See Notes (1932) 10 Neb.L.Bull. 314, (1933) 11 Neb.L.Bull. 421, (1940) 19 Neb.L.Bull. 150, (1946) 26 Neb.L.Rev. 102.

[103] Sanders v. State, 85 Ind. 318 (1882); State v. Calhoun, 50 Kan. 523, 32 Pac. 38 (1893); Nickels v. State, 86 Fla. 208, 98 So. 502 (1923), (1924) 37 Harv.L.Rev. 744, 774.

[104] Dubosky v. State, 183 Ind. 488, 109 N.E. 742 (1915); Ernst v. State 179 Wis. 646, 192 N.W. 65, 193 N.W. 978, 30 A.L.R. 681 (1923).

[105] Ex parte Gray, 77 Mo. 160 (1882).

[106] State v. Ray, 111 Kan. 350, 207 Pac. 192 (1922). *Contra:* State v. Latshaw, 291 Mo. 592, 237 S.W. 770 (1922).

[107] See 31 Am. Jur., Judgments, §§ 798-812, pp. 321-327; 24 C.J.S., Crim-

would warrant a new trial or a writ of error. It lies only as to errors of fact affecting the validity and regularity of the proceedings, when such fact had not been in issue at the trial, and was unknown to the defendant at the time.[108] Most facts will ordinarily have been in issue at the trial or will have been known to the defendant at the time. The error of fact situations in which it will lie are few and do not very often occur, such as death of a party pending the suit and before judgment; infancy, where the party had not been properly represented by a guardian; coverture, where the common-law disability existed; insanity at the time of trial;[109] a plea of guilty induced by fear of mob violence;[110] a confession induced by duress;[111] a plea of guilty in ignorance of the meaning of the plea.[112]

Perhaps it should also lie to vacate a judgment ren-

---

inal Law, §§ 1606-1607, pp.143-157. See Key Number 997, Criminal Law, of the American Digest System for the unceasing flow of decisions.

[108] Asbell v. State, 62 Kan. 209, 215, 61 Pac. 690 (1901); Notes (1924) 24 Col.L.Rev. 797, (1924) 37 Harv.L.Rev. 744, (1931) 26 Ill.L.Rev. 249; Gordon, "Certiorari and the Revival of Error in Fact" (1926) 42 L.Q.Rev. 521, 526. It does not lie as to facts or circumstances arising after judgment. Collins v. State, 66 Kan. 201, 71 Pac. 251, 97 Am. St. Rep. 361 (1903).

[109] Adler v. State, 37 Ark. 517, 37 Am. Rep. 48 (1880) 2 Crim.L.Mag. 198; Note (1921) 10 A.L.R. 214; Weihofen, Insanity as a Defense in Criminal Law (1933) 393-394. A new trial was permitted in Gardner v. State, 82 Tex.Cr. 38, 198 S.W. 312, L.R.A. 1918B, 1144 (Texas 1917), (1918) 27 Yale L.J. 698.

[110] Sanders v. State, 85 Ind. 318, 44 Am. Rep. 29 (1882), (1883) 4 Crim. L.Mag. 371 (1882); Nickels v. State, 86 Fla. 208, 98 So. 497, 98 So. 121 (1923), (1924) 37 Harv.L.Rev. 744; State v. Calhoun, 50 Kan. 523, 32 Pac. 38, 34 Am. St. Rep. 141, 18 L.R.A. 838 (1893). See 24 C.J.S., § 1606, p.150.

[111] State v. Ray, 111 Kan. 350, 207 Pac. 192 (1922). *Contra:* State v. Latshaw, 291 Mo. 592, 237 S.W. 770 (1922). It was allowed because of duress of an officer in Rhodes v. State, 199 Ind. 183, 156 N.E. 389 (1927).

[112] Dubosky v. State, 183 Ind. 488, 109 N.E. 742 (1915); Ernst v. State, 179 Wis. 646, 192 N.W. 65, 193 N.W. 978, 30 A.L.R. 681 (1923).

dered by a judge incapable of acting intelligently because of mental or physical disability.[113] Possibly it should lie where the innocence of the defendant is conclusively proved by newly discovered evidence.[114] Although the cases are contrary,[115] possibly it should lie where the testimony upon which the conviction was based was perjured. Possibly it should lie where fraudulent conduct by the prosecuting attorney prevents the presentation of material facts favoring the defendant.[116] At common law the issuance of the writ was entirely within the discretion of the court rendering judgment, hence no review was possible. But the modern cases tend to allow a review where the discretion has been abused.[117] While the older cases held that affirmance of the judgment in the appellate court precluded subsequent application in the trial court, some modern cases allow such application.[118] Some cases hold that it will not lie where other adequate remedies are available, such as motion in arrest of judgment, new trial, writ of error, motion to vacate the judgment.[119] While

[113] Note (1924) 37 Harv.L.Rev. 744, 747.

[114] Notes (1924) 24 Col.L.Rev. 797, 798, (1932) 10 Neb.L.Bull. 314, 319, (1940) 19 Neb.L.Bull. 150, 154. It was allowed in Indiana in Davis v. State, 200 Ind. 88, 161 N.E. 375 (1928). See also Pemberton, J., dissenting in Humphreys v. State, 129 Wash. 309, 224 Pac. 937, 33 A.L.R. 78 (1924).

[115] Note (1941) 39 Mich.L.Rev. 963, 969. It was allowed in Anderson v. Buchanan, 292 Ky. 810, 168 S.W. (2d) 148 (1943), (1944) 32 Ky.L.J. 296.

[116] Nat. Com. on Law Obs. and Enf., Rep. on Crim. Proc. (1931) 43.

[117] Hodges v. State, 111 Ark. 22, 163 S.W. 506 (1914); Hawie v. State, 121 Miss. 197, 83 So. 158 (1919); Notes (1932) 10 Neb.L.Bull. 314, 316, (1933) 6 Miss.L.J. 143.

[118] Hydrick v. State, 104 Ark. 43, 148 S.W. 541 (1912). See Notes 30 A.L.R. 1416 (1924), (1932) 10 Neb.L.Bull. 314, 316, (1941) 39 Mich.L.Rev. 963, 967, (1933) 6 Miss.L.J. 133, 135.

[119] Stephenson v. State, 205 Ind. 141, 179 N.E. 633, 186 N.E. 293 (1932). It has been held that it does not lie where there may be a motion for new

there are cases suggesting that statutes of limitations do not apply to the writ,[120] others bar it because of laches.[121]

The cases indicate that there is no certain remedy to relieve a defendant unjustly convicted, where the time allowed to move for new trial or for appeal has expired. There appears to be an insoluble conflict between the desire to protect the rights of individual criminal defendants and the desire to obtain finality in judgments.[122] The possible solutions are various. The courts may expand the writ of error *coram nobis*. A statute might be passed expressly giving the trial court or appellate court discretion to intervene in criminal proceedings subsequent to conviction when the circumstances warrant intervention, any statutory limitations to the contrary notwithstanding. The time limit on motions for new trial might be removed. Unless the states adopt remedial processes of this kind, the federal courts will continue to intervene in state criminal procedure by writs of habeas corpus.[123]

---

trial or an appeal, even though the time limit of these remedies has elapsed. People v. Paysen, 123 Calif. App. 346, 11 Pac. (2d) 431 (1932).

120 State v. Calhoun, 50 Kan. 523, 32 Pac. 38, 18 L.R.A. 838 (1893). See Note (1941) 39 Mich.L.Rev. 963, 966-968.

121 Newcomb v. State, 129 Neb. 69, 261 N.W. 348 (1935), (1940) 19 Neb.L.Bull. 150; Lamb v. State, 91 Fla. 396, 107 So. 535 (1926). The Rules of Civil Procedure, Article 39, Section 8, devised by the American Judicature Society, would allow three years after the entry of judgment in civil cases. See Bulletin XIV of the American Judicature Society (1919) 174.

122 Farley, "Coram Nobis—Another View" (1934) 6 Miss.L.J. 327, 336.

123 Note (1941) 39 Mich.L.Rev. 963, 964, 975; Williams, "Federal Habeas Corpus" (1924) 9 St. Louis L.Rev. 250; Dobie, "Habeas Corpus in the Federal Courts" (1927) 13 Va.L.Rev. 433; Note (1935) 35 Col.L. Rev. 404; (1935) 25 J.Crim.L. 943; Holtzoff, "Collateral Review of Convictions in Federal Courts" (1945) 25 B.U.L.Rev. 26.

CHAPTER IX

SENTENCE AND JUDGMENT

1. Stage in Proceedings

THE next step in a criminal proceeding following the motions after verdict is judgment and sentence.[1] After sentence there may be a motion in mitigation of sentence, often leading to modification or diminution of the sentence originally imposed. This stage is the last stage considered in this book. There might be one further step; namely, review in an appellate court. The author has already dealt with that subject in a separate volume.[2]

2. English Procedure

If the defendant is found guilty, the court demands of him, in cases of treason and felony, what he has to say as to why the court should not proceed to judgment against him.[3] This procedure, known as the *allocutus* or allocution, should appear on the record. The procedure is not customary in misdemeanor cases. The defendant must be present when judgment is given in cases of treason or felony.[4] In cases of misdemeanor, his presence is not neces-

[1] Nat. Com. on Law Obs. and Enf., Rep. on Crim. Proc. (1931) 18. See also 4 Bl. Comm. *375. For statements of the existing American law of sentence and judgment, see 15 Am. Jur., Criminal Law, §§ 442-504, pp. 102-154; 24 C.J.S., Criminal Law, §§ 1556-1622, pp.15-205.

[2] Orfield, Criminal Appeals in America (1939).

[3] Archbold, Criminal Pleading, Evidence and Practice, (30th ed.1938) 223. Historically, the purpose was to allow the defendant to move in arrest of judgment, or to plead pardon or benefit of clergy. See (1935) 79 Sol.J. 137; Barrett, "Allocution" (1944) 9 Mo.L.Rev. 115.

[4] See Rex v. Harris (1697) 1 Ld. Raym. 267; Archbold, Criminal Pleading, Evidence and Practice (30th ed.1938) 166, 224; "Power of Court to

sary but is usually required, unless the penalty is a fine or the defendant is too ill or infirm. It is now the practice after verdict to hear evidence of character generally, and of previous convictions not included in the indictment.[5] The court should consider the information given in determining the quantum of the punishment, unless it was challenged by the defendant. If the defendant challenges, the court should either direct proper proof to be given, or ignore the information.

The judgment or sentence is pronounced orally by the presiding judge. Where the trial judge dies before pronouncement of sentence, his successor in office may pronounce it. When pronounced the judgment is minuted on the indictment, and a note thereof is made in the calendar of cases for trial and signed by the judge at the conclusion of the sittings of the court. It is the usual practice to enter up judgment and sentence separately on each count on which the defendant has been convicted, and not on the whole indictment.[6] Then, if on appeal the conviction on one or more counts is quashed, the judgment on good convictions on other counts may stand. The court may at any time during the same assize or sessions vacate the judgment, before it has become a matter of record, and pass another sentence less or even more severe. When the judgment has once been solemnly entered on the record, it cannot be altered; but if any material defect appears on the face of it, it can be reversed or amended on appeal.

Since the sittings of a court of oyer and terminer or

Pass Sentence in Absence of Prisoner" (1933) 97 Justice of the Peace and Local Government Review, 621; Harris and Wilshere, Principles and Practice of the Criminal Law (17th ed.1943), 470.

[5] Rex v. Campbell, 6 Cr. App. R. 131 (1913); Archbold, Criminal Pleading, Evidence and Practice (30th ed.1938) 225.

[6] Archbold, Criminal Pleading, Evidence and Practice (30th ed.1938) 230.

gaol delivery are normally contemplated in law as one day, the sentence runs from the first day of the sittings of the trial court unless otherwise ordered.[7] In the case of quarter sessions or adjourned sessions of the peace, it runs from the day when it is pronounced, unless the court otherwise orders.[8] When a conviction is appealed, the operation of the sentence is suspended until the appeal is heard.[9] When the defendant is convicted of several offenses on different counts of the same indictment or on different indictments at the same assize or sessions, the court may direct that the sentence shall run consecutively or concurrently.[10]

In early times the trial courts found it necessary to exercise rather broad control over their sentences. New trials did not lie as to felony cases, there were no bills of exceptions, and the writ of error was narrow in scope. The courts frequently postponed the imposition of sentence to enable the defendant to apply for a pardon.[11] The courts also asserted the right to suspend for a reasonable period the execution of a sentence which had already been pronounced, in order to permit an inquiry into the insanity or the pregnancy of the defendant.[12] It is not clear that there

[7] Archbold, Criminal Pleading, Evidence and Practice (30th ed.1938) 231.

[8] 21 & 22 Vict. c.73, § 12.

[9] Criminal Appeal Act, 1907 (7 Ed. VII, c.23) § 14(3).

[10] Archbold, Criminal Pleading, Evidence and Practice (30th ed.1938) 232.

[11] Rex v. Rudd, 1 Cowp. 331 (1775). For suggestions of indefinite suspension, see Regina v. Ryan, 7 Cox C.C. 109 (1855); (1874) 9 Am.L.Rev. 600.

[12] 1 Chitty, Criminal Law (2d ed.1826) 757; 2 Hawkins, Pleas of the Crown (8th ed.1924) c.51, § 8; 4 Bl. Comm. *394; 2 Hale, History of the Pleas of the Crown (1778) 412. For suggestion of indefinite suspension, see Barrett, "Executive, Legislative and Judicial Pardon" (1915) 45 Am. L.Rev. 684, 709.

could be delay in other situations as to either imposition or execution of sentence.[13]

When the court postpones sentence until a future date this is known as a "respite." A respite may be granted where the court desires to defer sentence, because of the nature of the offense or the antecedents or physical or mental condition of the defendant.[14] The defendant is usually put under recognizances to come up for judgment when called upon. After the imposition of sentence, execution of the sentence may be suspended for a time. Such suspension is known as a "reprieve," and may be granted by the king or by the court. In two cases the court is bound to grant a reprieve: when a female prisoner is pregnant and when the defendant becomes insane after the pronouncement of judgment against him. In lieu of the right of a pregnant woman to a reprieve, a woman convicted of an offense punishable by death shall be sentenced to penal servitude for life.[15]

Sentence is sometimes postponed, in order that the defendant may move in arrest of judgment or to give the defendant an opportunity to mitigate sentence by making restitution or by giving information.[16] It may be postponed to inflict a certain amount of punishment on the

[13] Note (1912) 12 Col.L.Rev. 543; Bruce, "The Power to Suspend a Criminal Sentence for an Indefinite Period or During Good Behavior" (1922) 6 Minn.L.Rev. 363, 366; (1917) 30 Harv.L.Rev. 369; (1918) 2 Minn.L.Rev. 381, 383.

[14] Archbold, Criminal Pleading, Evidence and Practice (30th ed.1938) 227.

[15] Sentence of Death (Expectant Mothers) Act, 1931, 21 & 22 Geo. V, c.24, § 1.

[16] Kenny, Outlines of Criminal Law (15th ed.1942) 574. Sentence may be pronounced by the judge before whom the verdict was rendered during the sittings or assizes at which the trial took place. Archbold, Criminal Pleading, Evidence and Practice (30th ed.1938) 223.

defendant, when it is the intention to discharge him on recognizance.[17] It has become common for judges, when determining the sentence of the defendant, to be asked to "take into account" other charges of the same kind of crime, on which warrants have been issued against him, and which he now admits to be true and desires to be now dealt with.[18] Cases thus dealt with are then indorsed on the indictment. The total punishment does not ordinarily exceed what would be the maximum for one offense of that class. The defendant thus gets a fresh start on coming out of prison, instead of facing arrest.

There are various penalties which may be imposed on adult offenders: death, penal servitude, imprisonment, whipping, and fine.[19] But instead of imposing any of these, the court may, except in the case of murder, require the defendant to enter into recognizances with or without sureties to come up for judgment when called upon.[20] This procedure may be followed when a case is reserved or an appeal is pending or in cases within the Probation of Offenders Act, or in any other case where the circumstances of the case make such a course desirable in the interests of justice. When no time is specified for coming up for judgment, and it is proposed that the defendant be brought up for judgment, a notice must be given to him and to his bail.

[17] 25 Cr. App. R. 66.

[18] Kenny, Outlines of Criminal Law (15th ed.1942) 581; Archbold, Criminal Pleading, Evidence and Practice (30th ed.1938) 226.

[19] Archbold, Criminal Pleading, Evidence and Practice, (30th ed.1938) 234-248; Jackson, The Machinery of Justice in England (1940) 169-171. As to their history, see 1 Stephen, A History of the Criminal Law of England (1883) 457-492; 11 Holdsworth, History of English Law (3d ed. 1923) 556-580.

[20] Archbold, Criminal Pleading, Evidence and Practice (30th ed.1938) 260-268; Kenny, Outlines of Criminal Law (15th ed.1942) 601-604.

In the King's Bench Division four days' notice must be given.

Probation is now regulated by the Prosecution of Offenders Act, 1907.[21] Under this statute, any court, including both courts of summary and higher jurisdiction, which considers it inexpedient to impose a penalty, may release the defendant on recognizances to be of good behavior and to appear for judgment, within a time not exceeding three years, if called on. The defendant may be ordered to pay damages and costs. The court may attach conditions to the recognizance, such as to restitution, residence, abstinence from intoxicating liquor, entering a farm colony or a refuge or an inebriate's home, or even leaving Great Britain. It may also place him under the supervision of a probation officer, whose duty will be to visit him periodically, report on his behavior, and "advise, assist, and befriend him." If he violates his probation, the recognizance may be forfeited and sentence may be imposed for the original offense. When the defendant is charged with breach of recognizances, he must be given an opportunity to answer the charge.[22] The charge must be proved, but no jury is involved. The Criminal Justice Act, 1925,[23] requires every Petty-Sessional Division to have at least one probation officer and also a probation committee to supervise and remunerate him. The Social Service Committee

[21] 7 Edw. VII, c.17. For a discussion of probation under the English Criminal Justice Bill introduced in 1938, see Note (1940) 40 Col.L.Rev. 105, 116-121; "Symposium on Conviction and Probation" (1941) 19 Can. B.Rev. 500-521; Jackson, The Machinery of Justice in England (1940) 161-168. The English got their system of probation from a study of the Massachusetts system. Radzinowicz and Turner, Penal Reform in England (1940) 31, 114. See also Radzinowicz and Turner, The Modern Approach to Criminal Law (1945) c.8.

[22] Rex v. Pine, 24 Cr. App. R. 10 (1933).

[23] Sections 1(1) and 2(1, 2).

of England has recommended the appointment of full-time salaried probation officers. Under the Criminal Justice Bill introduced in 1938, when the court finds the charge against the offender proved and decides to use probation, a conviction is not entered.[24] While this provision is recognized to be illogical, its proponents desire to protect the probationer against certain disabilities which a recorded conviction may entail despite legislative efforts to remove all disabilities.

After the judgment itself, the court may make certain further orders. After any trial for theft the court may make an order for restitution to the true owner of stolen property which has been identified at the trial.[25] Though at common law there could be no costs in criminal cases,[26] the Costs in Criminal Cases Act, 1908,[27] empowers the courts to order the reasonable costs of the prosecution and of the witnesses for the defense, or of either of them, to be repaid out of public funds, in the case of any indictable offense. Neither side usually receives an allowance for character witnesses. The costs allowed to a prosecutor are said to have averaged about £10. Even this is not enough to recompense a private prosecutor or an innocent defendant. The court may also order the defendant to pay the taxed costs of the prosecution.[28] There are a few excep-

[24] Note (1940) 40 Col.L.Rev. 105, 118. As to existing law, see Radzinowicz and Turner, "Conviction and Probation" (1941) 19 Can.B.Rev. 500.

[25] Kenny, Outlines of Criminal Law (15th ed.1942) 259, 583; Archbold, Criminal Pleading, Evidence and Practice (30th ed.1942) 295-301.

[26] 3 Bl. Comm. *400. The Connecticut Judicial Council has proposed the abolition of costs in criminal cases. Massachusetts so provided in 1890. Eighth Report of the Judicial Council of Connecticut (1942) 7-10.

[27] 8 Edw. VII, c.15, § 1. See Archbold, Criminal Pleading, Evidence and Practice (30th ed.1938) 272-286.

[28] See Archbold, Criminal Pleading, Evidence and Practice (30th ed. 1938) 286-289.

tional cases in which a private prosecutor may be ordered to pay the taxed costs of the defense. At common law there could be no order for damages in criminal proceedings. The Forfeiture Act, 1870,[29] empowers the court in felony cases to order a defendant to pay a sum not over one hundred pounds as compensation for any loss of property suffered by any person through the felony. The act does not cover injuries to the person.

3. Statistics on Sentences

In Missouri from October 1, 1922, to October 1, 1924, there were 7,032 warrants issued for the whole state.[30] Sentence was imposed in 2,680 cases and executed in 2,232 cases. "Only 32% of all warrants issued by the prosecutor in non-liquor felony cases result in punishment." [31] In the middle of the decade from 1920 to 1930, 51 per cent of all felony arrests in Baltimore resulted in punishment, 36 per cent in Milwaukee, 25 per cent in St. Louis, 18 per cent in Cincinnati, 17 per cent in New York City and Kansas City, and 15 per cent in Chicago.[32]

English criminal proceedings are carried on with great celerity. The "interval between the commission of a crime and the verdict and judgment at nisi prius is usually less than a month." [33] At this point it seems well to consider the length of time in court a criminal proceeding in this country takes up to the point of conviction. In Boston it

[29] 33 & 34 Vict., c.23, § 4. See Archbold, Criminal Pleading, Evidence and Practice (30th ed.1938) 292-295.

[30] Missouri Crime Survey (1926) 274.

[31] Thompson, "The Missouri Crime Survey" (1926) 12 A.B.A.J. 616, 629.

[32] Moley, Politics and Criminal Prosecution (1929) 28.

[33] Editorial (1923) 9 A.B.A.J., 640.

takes between 13 and 44 days.[34] For a major offense, the median conviction takes between 36 and 91 days in New York City, 51 days in Chicago, 50 days in St. Louis, 31 days in Kansas City, and 17 days in Milwaukee.[35] In Cleveland the average interval between arrest and disposition, including even cases of plea of guilty, was 67 days, of which 46 days were between indictment and disposition.[36]

The period from arraignment to disposition by the trial court is one of the largest intervals in a criminal proceeding. In Oregon during 1927 and 1928, the median time intervals, for all cases in which the plea on arraignment was not guilty, were 44 as to acquittals, 34 as to convictions, and 93 as to dismissals.[37] In Missouri the median intervals, from the date set for trial to the date of final disposition of the case in the trial court, were 27 as to acquittals, 14 as to sentences, 79 as to nolles prosequis, and 98 as to dispositions on action of the court.[38]

4. Agencies in Sentencing Process

It should be observed that the courts are only one out of five principal agencies which participate in the sentencing process. The legislature usually defines the crime and

[34] Warner and Cabot, Judges and Law Reform (1936) 113.

[35] Nat. Com. on Law Obs. and Enf., Report on Prosecution (1931) Table XXIII, p.214.

[36] Bettman, "Criminal Justice in America: Possibility of Improvement by Administrative and Procedural Reforms in Connection with Criminal Prosecution" (1925) 11 A.B.A.J. 455, 456-457.

[37] Morse and Beattie, Survey of the Administration of Criminal Justice in Oregon (1932) 184.

[38] Missouri Crime Survey (1926) 329. The statistics for a number of cities in various states are set out in National Commission on Law Observance and Enforcement, Report on Prosecution (1931) Table XXVII, p.218.

sets maximum and sometimes minimum limits of punishment. The prosecuting authorities, namely, the complaining witness, the police, and the prosecuting attorney determine whether or not to prosecute, and for what crime, and may advise the court as to the sentence. The parole board may release convicted defendants on parole before the expiration of their sentences. Finally, the executive may grant a pardon or commutation of sentence.

5. Definition of Judgment and Sentence

According to Section 375 of the Institute Code the term "judgment" "means the adjudication by the court that the defendant is guilty or not guilty." A judgment merely stating the penalty would not be valid.[39] It must contain an adjudication by the court that the defendant is guilty or not guilty. According to a writer on judgments, a "judgment of conviction may be said to consist of two parts, to-wit: 1. The facts judicially ascertained, together with the manner of ascertaining them, entered of record; 2. The recorded declaration of the court pronouncing the legal consequences of the facts thus judicially ascertained. Both of these parts are equally necessary in the entry of a judgment of conviction."[40] It has been held, however, that in the absence of a statute it is proper though not necessary that the court should before sentence find as its independent judgment on the facts that the accused is guilty.[41] If the court states the finding of the jury and pronounces

[39] Ellis v. State, 100 Fla. 27, 129 So. 106, 69 A.L.R. 783 (1930).

[40] Freeman, Judgments (5th ed.1925) § 99.

[41] Hoch v. People, 219 Ill. 265, 287, 76 N.E. 356 (1906); Symington v. State, 133 Md. 452, 105 Atl. 541 (1919); 16 C.J., Criminal Law, § 3074, p.1302. See 69 A.L.R. 792; 15 Am. Jur., Criminal Law, § 445, p.106; Abbott, Criminal Trial Practice (4th ed.1939) § 782, p.1438.

sentence thereon, that is a judicial determination of the fact of conviction, and that is all that is required. The Institute Code distinguishes the term "sentence" from "judgment."[42] Under Section 382 the term "sentence" "means the pronouncement by the court of the penalty imposed on the defendant upon the acceptance of a plea of guilty or upon a verdict of guilty or a finding of guilty by the court." Sentence comes later in point of time and fixes the amount of the penalty. There is a sentence only in case of a conviction; there is a judgment in cases of either a conviction or an acquittal.

Under Section 376 of the Institute Code, if the "defendant has been convicted, a judgment of guilty, and if he has been acquitted, a judgment of not guilty, shall be rendered." Under Rule 32(b) of the Federal Rules of Criminal Procedure: "A judgment of conviction shall set forth the plea, the verdict or findings, and the adjudication and sentence. If the defendant is found not guilty or for any other reason is entitled to be discharged, judgment shall be entered accordingly. The judgment shall be signed by the judge and entered by the clerk."

An informal verdict may raise difficulties with respect to judgment, especially a judgment of guilty. Accordingly Section 377 of the Institute Code provides: "If a verdict is recorded from which it can be clearly understood that it is the intention of the jurors to acquit the defendant, judgment of not guilty shall be rendered thereon even

[42] Accord: Report of the Commission on the Administration of Justice in New York State (1939) 154, 157, 159. On the other hand the United States Supreme Court has held that the sentence is the judgment. Berman v. United States, 302 U.S. 211, 58 Sup.Ct. 164, 82 L.Ed. 204 (1937). See, to the same effect, 24 C.J.S., Criminal Law, § 1556, p.15. For the origin of the terms "judgment" and "sentence," see Millar, "The Lineage of Some Procedural Words" (1939) 25 A.B.A.J. 1023, 1029.

though the verdict is defective; but no judgment of guilty shall be rendered on a verdict unless the jurors clearly express in it a finding against the defendant upon the issue or expressly find, in a special verdict, the facts establishing the defendant's guilt."

In an opinion of the United States Supreme Court by Mr. Justice Cardozo, it was held that the term of imprisonment in federal prosecutions is determined by the sentence and judgment.[43] Hence an addition by the clerk to the warrant of commitment that the imprisonment shall continue until payment of a fine also imposed is void. The sentence must of course be responsive to the verdict. Therefore if conviction was for a misdemeanor, sentence could not be for a felony.[44]

6. Fixing by Court or by Jury

In a number of states the jury and not the judge fixes the penalty upon convicted defendants. When the jury can assess the penalty, they may be more likely to convict in a proper case since they need have no fear of a higher penalty fixable by the court. On the other hand, the judges' repeated experience with criminal cases will often fit him better to deal fairly and scientifically with convicted defendants than an ordinary jury.[45]

[43] Hill v. United States, 298 U.S. 460, 56 Sup.Ct. 760, 80 L.Ed. 1283 (1936).

[44] Wilson v. State, 28 Ind. 393 (1867); Kidd v. Territory, 9 Okl. 450, 60 Pac. 114 (1900).

[45] For criticism of vesting discretion as to the penalty in the jury, see Kerr, "A Needed Reform in Criminal Procedure" (1918) 6 Ky.L.J. 107; Note (1938) 24 Va.L.Rev. 462; Fuller, Criminal Justice in Virginia (1931) 133, 161; Report of Committee on Legislation and Law Reform (1937) Proc. Va. State Bar Assoc. 150; Michael and Wechsler, "A Rationale of the Law of Homicide II" (1937) 37 Col.L.Rev. 1261, 1310;

7. Presence of Defendant

The presence of the defendant at sentence is indispensable at least for the more serious crimes.[46] Section 291 of the Institute Code provides: "The defendant shall be present when a sentence of death or imprisonment is pronounced and if such sentence is pronounced in his absence he shall be resentenced when his presence is secured. The defendant need not be present when a sentence of a fine only, or a fine and imprisonment until the fine is paid, is pronounced." His absence is not ground for discharge or new trial, but for resentencing in his presence. Rule 43 of the Federal Rules of Criminal Procedure provides: "The defendant shall be present . . . at the imposition of sentence." The rule permits imposition of sentence in misdemeanor cases in the absence of the defendant if he consents. It should be noted that the requirement of presence has to do with the oral pronouncement of sentence, and not with the writing out of the sentence nor its entry of record.[47]

Leflar, "The Future of Criminal Procedure in Arkansas (1939) Forty-Second Ann. Proc. of Bar Assoc. of Arkansas 291, 299.

[46] State v. Cherry, 154 N.C. 624, 70 S.E. 294 (1911); State v. Bailey, 85 W.Va. 165, 101 S.E. 169 (1919); Miller v. State, 44 S.W. 162 (Tex. Cr. 1898); Price v. Zerbst, 268 F. 72 (N.D., Ga., 1920); Ball v. United States, 140 U.S. 118, 11 Sup.Ct. 761, 35 L.Ed. 377 (1891); Note 6 Ann. Cas. 452 (1907). It has been held that the defendant cannot waive his right to be present at sentence for a felony. Ex parte Lyde, 17 Okl. Cr. 618, 191 Pac. 606 (1920). The following provision is recommended in the Report of the Commission on the Administration of Justice in New York State (1939) 163: "If the conviction is for a felony, the defendant shall be personally present when judgment is rendered or sentence pronounced. If the conviction is for a misdemeanor judgment may be rendered or sentence pronounced in his absence."

[47] 15 Am. Jur., Criminal Law, §§ 454-455, pp.113-114.

8. *Allocutus*

When sentence of death is imposed, the judge must ask in open court whether there is any legal cause why judgment should not be pronounced against him.[48] Resentencing will be sufficient, there being no new trial had.[49] The early English practice of not allowing a defendant accused of felony the benefit of counsel may have made such question essential. The cases are divided as to the necessity of the *allocutus* in felony cases, though a majority do not require it.[50] It is not required in misdemeanor cases.[51]

The Institute Code makes provision for an *allocutus* in all cases when the defendant is present at the pronouncing of sentence.[52] Section 389 provides: "If the defendant is present when sentence is to be pronounced, the court, or the clerk under its direction, shall inform the defendant of the accusation against him and of the judgment and shall ask him whether he has any cause to show why sentence should not be pronounced." [53] Under Section 391 the de-

[48] Ball v. United States, 140 U.S. 118 (1891); People v. Nesce, 201 N.Y. 111, 94 N.E. 655 (1911), 24 Harv.L.Rev. 578, 2 J.Crim.L. 170. *Contra:* Dutton v. State, 123 Md. 373, 91 Atl. 417 (1914), 62 U. of Pa.L.Rev. 741. See (1938) 22 Minn.L.Rev. 733; (1910) 20 Yale L.J., 139.

[49] See (1910) 20 Yale L.J. 139, 141; (1911) 2 J.Crim.L. 170; Rex. v. Geary (1694) 2 Salk. 630, 3 Mod. 265; 1 Chitty, Criminal Law (4th American ed.1841) 700.

[50] Cases holding it necessary are: Croker v. State, 47 Ala. 53 (1872); McCormick v. State, 66 Neb. 337, 92 N.W. 606 (1903); Commonwealth v. Preston, 188 Pa. 429, 41 Atl. 534 (1898). *Contra:* Lamb v. People, 219 Ill. 399, 76 N.E. 576 (1906); State v. Sally, 41 Ore. 366, 70 Pac. 396 (1902).

[51] State v. Bradley, 30 La. 326 (1878); Hancock v. Rogers, 140 Ga. 688, 79 S.E. 558 (1913).

[52] Accord: Report of the Commission on the Administration of Justice in New York State (1939) 159. See Barrett, "Allocution" (1944) 9 Mo.L. Rev. 115, 232.

[53] Failure to conduct the *allocutus* does not result in a new trial, but resentencing with the *allocutus*. See Section 390 of the American Law Institute Code of Criminal Procedure.

fendant may assign only four causes for not pronouncing sentence: (a) that he has become insane since the verdict was rendered; (b) that he has been pardoned of the offense for which he is about to be sentenced; (c) that he is not the person against whom the verdict or judgment was rendered; and (d) if the defendant is a woman, and the sentence is for death, that she is pregnant. Rule 32(a) of the Federal Rules of Criminal Procedure is of a more general and broader character: "Before imposing sentence the court shall afford the defendant an opportunity to make a statement in his own behalf and to present any information in mitigation of punishment." It should be noted that under Section 397 of the Institute Code there may be an inquiry into mitigating or aggravating circumstances upon the suggestion of either party or of the court's own motion.

9. In Open Court

It would appear that judgment and sentence are of such importance that they should occur in open court.[54] Section 379 of the Institute Code provides: "Judgment shall be rendered in open court." Section 384 provides: "Sentence shall be pronounced in open court."[55]

[54] But a judgment and sentence entered by the court in chambers, during a recess, in the presence of court officials, was held valid. O'Neal v. State, 35 Ga. App. 665 (1926). See also McCarty v. Hopkins, 61 Neb. 550, 85 N.W. 540 (1901). A sentence rendered in a room other than the courtroom, used because of an emergency, was held valid in Reed v. State, 147 Ind. 41 (1896).

[55] Accord: Report of the Commission on the Administration of Justice in New York State (1939) 158, 159.

10. Time of Pronouncing Sentence

Because of the possibility that after verdict there may be various motions made requiring decision, such as for new trial or in arrest of judgment, or because there may be a motion to withdraw a plea of guilty, or because a presentence investigation may be necessary or desirable, there is no fixed time for the rendering of judgments of guilty.[56] Judgments of not guilty should be rendered immediately. Section 378 of the Institute Code provides: "If the defendant is acquitted judgment shall be rendered immediately; if the defendant is convicted judgment shall not be rendered until three days after such conviction and only after the overruling of any motion for a new trial or in arrest of judgment. If the defendant expressly waives his right to move in arrest of judgment and for a new trial judgment may be rendered immediately." Thus a time is specified before which judgment cannot be rendered.[57] But no time is specified beyond which it may not be rendered. Under Section 383 when "judgment of guilty has been rendered the court may pronounce sentence." Rule I of

[56] In the absence of statute, the trial court may pronounce sentence before a motion for arrest of judgment and for new trial has been passed upon and before the time allowed for filing such motion has expired. State v. De Grace, 144 Ore. 159, 22 P. (2d) 896, 90 A.L.R 232 (1933). But see 24 C.J.S., Criminal Law, § 1564, p.30. A judgment and sentence rendered on Sunday has been held void with the result that habeas corpus lies. People v. Ramsey, 217 N.Y.Supp. 799 (1926), (1927) 36 Yale L.J. 421. See also Notes (1936) 27 J.Crim.L. 123, (1930), 15 Corn.L.Q. 288. In the absence of an express, statutory provision, such a judgment should be upheld, as no violation of the mores of a community seems involved. In Scotland the court may not impose sentence until the prosecutor moves for sentence, as the case still remains in the control of the prosecution. Keedy, "Criminal Procedure in Scotland" (1913) 3 J.Crim.L. 834, 843.

[57] Imposing sentence earlier than the statute permits, if not then and there objected to, is not necessarily ground for reversal on appeal. State v. Raney, 208 Iowa 1238, 226 N.W. 916 (1929), (1930) 28 Mich.L.Rev. 768.

the Criminal Appeals Rules of the United States Supreme Court provided: "After a plea of guilty, or a verdict of guilty by a jury or finding of guilt by the trial court where a jury is waived, and except as provided in the Act of March 4, 1925, c. 521, 43 Stat. 1259 as amended, 18 U.S.C. paragraphs 724-727 sentence shall be imposed without delay unless (1) a motion for the withdrawal of a plea of guilty, or in arrest of judgment or for a new trial, is pending, or the trial court is of the opinion that there is reasonable ground for such a motion; or (2) the condition or character of the defendant or other pertinent matters, should be investigated in the interest of justice before sentence is imposed." Rule 32(a) of the Federal Rules of Criminal Procedure shortens this to the following statement: "Sentence shall be imposed without unreasonable delay. Pending sentence the court may commit the defendant or continue or alter the bail."

At other stages of a criminal proceeding it has been seen that undue delay often occurs. That is not true with respect to the interval from conviction to sentence. In Massachusetts more than half the defendants are sentenced on the day they plead guilty or are convicted.[58] This stage of the proceedings may therefore be criticized as being too speedy rather than not speedy enough. "Probably in the ordinary felony case only a few days need elapse between conviction and sentence, but in unusual cases there might be an interval of two to three weeks." [59]

11. Weaknesses in Sentencing Process

The chief criticisms of existing sentencing and releasing practices are: (1) Sentencing is too hasty and haphazard;

[58] Warner and Cabot, Judges and Law Reform (1936) 112.

[59] Warner and Cabot, Judges and Law Reform (1936) 114.

although many days may be taken for trial, often only a few minutes are devoted to fixing the sentence. (2) Traditional sentencing practices are not well suited to deal with crimes when these are regarded as behavior problems and when a causal attitude replaces reliance on fear, blameworthiness, and deterrence. (3) Sentencing should therefore be regarded as a somewhat complicated art, requiring the proper balancing of the several purposes of the criminal law, such as retribution, deterrence, prosecution, reform, and social rehabilitation of the defendant; thus presupposing a knowledge by the judge of psychiatry, psychology, sociology, social case work, vocational guidance, and educational techniques. (4) The present administration of criminal justice is not well integrated. The defendant is divided up among the sentencing court, the prison authorities, and the parole board; this division often makes for inconsistent approaches.[60]

12. Presentence Investigation

In 1927 the Minnesota Crime Commission recommended that "before any sentence be suspended, the judge shall have a report of the record, history, and other pertinent matter concerning the person convicted, such report to be had from such offices as may be available, and particularly from the State Bureau of Criminal Identification and Information, or such other central organization as may be established." [61]

The various crime surveys show an increasing recognition of the basic distinction between facts bearing on guilt and facts bearing on the disposition and treatment of the

[60] Glueck, Book Review (1943) 56 Harv.L.Rev. 839, 840.

[61] Minnesota Crime Commission Report (1927) 44.

convicted defendant.[62] Many of the surveys recommend that before granting probation or imposing some other sentence, the court obtain and take account of facts concerning the individual and social history of the offender, his personality, his mental and moral characteristics.[63] The surveys are not very helpful, however, as to the nature of the procedure which should govern the presentation and hearing of the disposition, such as the method of ascertainment and presentation of the evidence relating to the offender; what part the prosecuting attorney should play in the hearing on disposition and what part the defendant and his counsel and witnesses. These and other administrative and procedural questions relating to the disposition, hearing, and decision still call for study, formulation, and development.

Modern criminological research has quite clearly shown the desirability of ample factual data with respect to disposition and treatment before the court pronounces sentence. There can be few things more tragic than concentration on improvement of the guilt-finding process to the exclusion of attention to the proper disposition of the de-

62 It was "not until about twenty years ago that there began a systematic attack on the sentencing practices of the courts and a call for a practical solution involving not so much the redefinition of crimes as the remaking of the procedures following conviction." Glueck, Book Review, (1943) 56 Harv.L.Rev. 839. See also Note (1942) 9 U. of Chi.L.Rev. 715.

63 Nat. Com. on Law Obs. and Enf., Rep. on Crim. Proc. (1931) 135-138; New York State Crime Commission (1928) 68, 184, 272; *ibid.* (1928) 315; *ibid.* (1929) 162 *et seq.;* Illinois Crime Survey (1929) 771; Missouri Crime Survey (1926) 453, 484; Cleveland Crime Survey (1922) 137; Minnesota Crime Commission Report (1927) 44-49, 61; Hadley, "Outline of Code of Criminal Procedure" (1926) 12 A.B.A.J. 690, 693. See Report of the Committee of the Canadian Bar Association on the Administration of Criminal Justice, (1922) 6 J. Am. Jud. Soc. 120, 122. For an excellent discussion of the technique of sentencing in England, see Jackson, The Machinery of Justice in England (1940) 168-184.

fendant.[64] The Federal Rules of Criminal Procedure, Rule 32 (c) (1), strongly implements procedure as to the latter by providing: "The probation service of the court shall make a presentence investigation and report to the court before the imposition of sentence or the granting of probation unless the court otherwise directs." The provision is designed to secure presentence investigation in all cases in which the court does not affirmatively order otherwise.[65] It does this in cases where there will be no probation as well as in probation cases, since such investigation will aid in the imposition of sentence and in correctional treatment. The rule is flexible enough to permit the court to deal with the situation when such investigation would interfere with the work of the probation services in supervising persons on probation or parole. It is a regrettable fact that some courts are not sufficiently staffed to permit of presentence investigation in all cases.

For the guidance of the probation service as well as the court the statute or rule ought to prescribe in detail concerning the report of the presentence investigation. The report should be such as to constitute a thorough social case history of the defendant. The report should be kept confidential, and should be available only to such parties as the attorneys for the parties and prison officials or parole authorities. There are conflicting considerations

[64] For some concrete illustrations see Grimson, J., "Guilty!! Then What?" (1940) 26 A.B.A.J. 397; Schwellenbach, J., "Information vs. Intuition in the Imposition of Sentence" (1943) 27 J. Am. Jud. Soc. 52; Cockrell, J., Successful Justice (1939) 333.

[65] Orfield, "Improving Procedure on Judgment and Appeal in Federal Criminal Cases" (1943) 27 Minn.L.Rev. 169, 171-172. The English Criminal Justice Bill introduced in 1938 stresses the importance of inquiries preliminary to probation. Note (1940) 40 Col.L.Rev. 105, 117-118. Under present English procedure, there is no systematic presentence investigation. Jackson, The Machinery of Justice in England (1940) 172-174.

with respect to making the report available to the defendant or his attorney. On the one hand, making the report available may result in strained and unfriendly relations between the defendant and the probation service.[66] On the other hand, not to make it available might violate due process or be grossly unjust because the amount and character of the sentence is almost as important as the matter of guilt. The defendant should be entitled to know what are the facts which motivate the court in arriving at its sentence.[67] The latter consideration seems to be more important than the former.

Rule 32 (c) (2) of the Federal Rules of Criminal Procedure contains a model clause on the report of the presentence investigation. It provides: "The report of the

[66] See National Probation Association, A State Administered Adult Probation and Parole System (1940) § 26; Cooley, Probation and Delinquency (1928) 328; Ky. Rev. Stat. (1942) §§ 439, 220, 979 b-6; Hall, "Committee on Survey of Crime, Criminal Law and Criminal Procedure" (1938) 29 J.Crim.L. 562, 574-575.

[67] Waite, J., "How Far Can Court Procedure Be Socialized Without Impairing Individual Rights?" (1921) 12 J.Crim.L. 339, 345. "Americans have an ingrained conviction that nothing, however well meant, ought to be forced upon them on the basis of information obtained behind their backs." See also the statement by Governor Henry Horner, "A Bill Affecting Parole in Illinois, The Governor's Veto," (1937) 28 J.Crim.L. 318, 323-324, that if, at the trial, the judge "used a social service history report or gathered facts and circumstances regarding the prisoner that were not admissible as evidence during the trial, and the sentence were based upon this knowledge, it is probable that the case would be reversed for error." See also Stephan v. United States, 133 F. (2d) 87, at 100 (C.C.A. 6th, 1943). An Ohio statute permits the defendant to examine the person making the report. Note (1930) 16 A.B.A.J. 169, 178. In England the defendant may challenge the information given. Harris and Wilshere, Principles and Practice of the Criminal Law (17th ed.1943) 469-470. See Note (1943) 21 Can.B.Rev. 599. For an able presentation of the problem as it has arisen in the German courts, see Grünhut, "The Development of the German Penal System 1920-1932" (1944) 22 Can.B.Rev. 198, 242-243.

presentence investigation shall contain any prior criminal record of the defendant and such information about his characteristics, his financial condition and the circumstances affecting his behavior as may be helpful in imposing sentence or in granting probation or in the correctional treatment of the defendant, and such other information as may be required by the court."

There is a conflict of opinion as to the time when the presentence investigation should be made. Doubtless an investigation before any finding of guilt would permit a more thorough and less hurried study. Because, however, of Anglo-American legal doctrines, such as the presumption of innocence, the defendant should have the right to object to such an investigation's being made before the finding of guilt. No presentence investigation before determination of guilt should be made unless the defendant or his attorney consents in writing that it be made earlier.

13. Opinion on Reasons for Sentence

It does not appear to be the custom for judges to state the sociological, psychological, psychiatric, and any other bases of the sentence which it imposes. Perhaps the most notable exceptions are the opinion of Judge Ulman in the Duker Case[68] and that of Federal Judge Otis in the Pendergast Case.[69] The Pennsylvania Supreme Court requires the trial judge, as soon as he is notified that an appeal has been taken, to file forthwith "at least a brief

[68] Ulman, A Judge Takes the Stand (1933) 211-220. For the opinion in an Ohio state trial court case, see Ohio v. Emonds (1938) 29 J.Crim.L. 427. For the opinion in the Loeb-Leopold Case, see (1924) 15 J.Crim.L. 391. For a Pennsylvania murder case, see Commonwealth v. Ritter, 13 D. & C. 285 (Pa. 1930).

[69] United States v. Pendergast, 281 Supp. 601 (D.C. Mo. 1939).

statement in the form of an opinion of the reasons for the . . . judgment . . . therein referred to." [70] Possibly the systematic writing of opinions might build up a body of scientific sentencing principles.

14. Flexibility in Sentencing

It was thought to be one of the chief glories of the common law that punishment was fixed in character.[71] Penalties were pre-ordained and there was flexibility only as to quantity. Likewise under present statutory systems, the courts are restricted to the penalties and procedures prescribed. The limits,[72] the nature,[73] and the place of execution [74] of the punishment must not differ from those authorized by statute. It follows that non-statutory sentences that the offender abate a nuisance,[75] resign an office,[76] move from the neighborhood,[77] or be deported [78] have been held either void [79] or erroneous.[80] These restric-

[70] Supreme Court of Pennsylvania Rules of Court, Rule 58. The opinion may be very brief. Commonwealth v. Paul, 289 Pa. 542, 137 Atl. 606 (1927). The court does not always insist on compliance. Commonwealth v. Garramore, 307 Pa. 507, 161 Atl. 733 (1932).

[71] 4 Bl. Comm. *378; 1 Chitty, Criminal Law (4th American ed.1841) 701. See Note (1932) 32 Col.L.Rev. 1031.

[72] In re Mills, 135 U.S. 263, 10 Sup.Ct. 762 (1889).

[73] Silversides v. Queen, 2 Gale and Dav. 617 (1842).

[74] In re Bonner, 151 U.S. 412, 14 Sup.Ct. 323 (1894).

[75] Werfel v. Commonwealth, 5 Bin. 65 (Pa. 1812).

[76] State v. Washington, 8 N.J. Misc. 916, 152 Atl. 445 (1930).

[77] People v. Smith, 252 Mich. 4, 232 N.W. 397 (1930).

[78] People v. Lopez, 81 Cal. App. 199, 253 Pac. 169 (1927); cf. People v. Baum, 251 Mich. 187, 231 N.W. 95 (1930); Note (1931) 31 Col.L.Rev. 1013.

[79] In such cases it is said that the court has no jurisdiction and that habeas corpus lies. In re Bonner, 151 U.S. 242, 14 Sup.Ct. 223 (1894); Ex parte Cox, 3 Idaho 530, 32 Pac. 197 (1893).

[80] In several American jurisdictions the sentence must be attacked by

tions have been established by the courts without reference to constitutionality.[81] In addition the penalty must be definite and certain in extent at the time it is pronounced.[82] It follows that the term of imprisonment or the amount of the fine should not depend on a future contingency.[83] The penalty cannot be conditioned to increase if the defendant appeals.[84] The diminution or termination of the sentence may not be conditioned on acts which the court could [85] or could not [86] directly order the convicted defendant to perform.

The restrictions which have just been stated seem to make the sentencing power rather rigid. But this apparent rigidity has been relieved by all sorts of mitigating devices

---

direct appeal. Ex parte Vitali, 153 Mich. 514, 116 N.W. 1066 (1908); 1 Bishop, Criminal Procedure (4th ed.1895) § 930.

81 But exile as a condition of probation was held invalid as violating the constitutional prohibition against cruel and unusual punishment in People v. Baum, 251 Mich. 187, 231 N.W. 95 (1930). This seems an improper construction of that clause; see (1930) 30 Col.L.Rev. 1057, (1931) 26 Ill. L.Rev. 81. But see (1931) 11 B.U.L.Rev. 278.

82 Rex v. Catteral, Fitz. 266 (1730); Rex v. Hall, 1 Cowp. 60 (1774) (imprisonment conditioned on payment of a sum not definitely ascertained). See Note (1913) 61 U. of Pa.L.Rev. 416. As to installment fines, see Note (1940) 30 J.Crim.L. 794.

83 State v. Bennett, 4 Dev. and Bat. 43, 50 (N.C. 1838); Brownbridge v. People, 38 Mich. 751, 754 (1878).

84 Wallace v. State, 126 Ga. 749, 55 S.E. 1042 (1906).

85 Ex parte Baldwin, 60 Calif. 432 (1882). The defendant cannot be sentenced to pay a fine immediately, and in default thereof be imprisoned for a definite term. State v. Perkins, 82 N.C. 681 (1880).

86 The courts have held void or have disregarded as surplusage such conditions in the sentence as: payment of reparation to the injured party, Smith v. Barrows, 21 Ga. App. 650, 94 S.E. 860 (1917); cf. People v. Elliott, 140 Misc. 685, 251 N.Y.Supp. 458 (Gen. Sess. 1931); the giving of a bond, State v. Sturgis, 110 Me. 96, 85 Atl. 474 (1912); the surrender of property, Hudeburgh v. State, 38 Tex. 535 (1873); the execution of conveyances, State v. Bennett, 4 Dev. and Bat. 43 (N.C. 1838); or exile, State v. Baker, 58 S.C. 111, 36 S.E. 501 (1900).

running through the entire course of a criminal proceeding. Some of the trial court practices, such as conditional sentences, are technically illegal and have been condemned as such, quite ineffectively, by the appellate courts.[87] Others are the appropriate use of discretionary procedure much of which has survived from a time when there could be no new trial or an appeal.

In the first place under statutes, as well as at common law, the courts have in most cases a range of discretion as to the amount of the authorized penalty, the exercise of which is not reviewable except in extreme cases of abuse or prejudice.[88] To better exercise its discretion, the court may in all cases accept affidavits from prosecution and defense in aggravation or mitigation of the offense.[89] Although the court may not legally bind itself to sentence the defendant in a certain way or to suspend sentence, the agreement under which the defendant and the prosecution have proceeded will often influence its judgment.[90] While there are many judicial statements that the courts will not permit the use of criminal process to collect private debts, it was the practice at common law,[91] and very likely is even today,[92] for the court to intimate before pronouncing sentence that, if defendant agrees to make restitution to the injured party or do some similar act, the penalty will

[87] Note (1939) 30 J.Crim.L. 138.

[88] Harris v. State, 142 Miss. 342, 107 So. 372 (1926). Orders granting or denying probation are also within the sole discretion of the court. People v. Stover, 317 Ill. 191, 148 N.E. 67 (1925).

[89] United States v. Standard Oil Co., 155 Fed. 305 (N.D. Ill. 1907); State v. Reeder, 79 S.C. 139, 60 S.E. 434 (1907).

[90] Rex v. Lovett, 11 Cox C.C. 602 (1870); cf. In re Grove, 43 Idaho 775, 254 Pac. 519 (1927).

[91] 1 Chitty, Criminal Law (4th American ed.1841) 8, 665, 666; 2 Hawkins, Pleas of the Crown (3d folio ed.1739) 443, c.48, § 2.

[92] Note (1932) 32 Col.L.Rev. 1031, 1034.

take account of his act. If the act of the defendant requires an interval of time, the court may delay the imposition of sentence [93] even until the next term of court,[94] provided that the postponement is unconditional and made without positive indications that an indefinite suspension is intended. In addition to this power, there is a presumption in favor of the validity of its exercise in the absence of facts of record.[95] But all of this would be improper and illegal if it appeared on the record that the defendant's act was induced by coercion, such as threats of an increased penalty.[96] Not many appeals are taken from such sentences, since the reward of a light or suspended sentence is obviously a powerful inducement to the defendant to accede to any suggestion by the court.

In the second place, a substantial minority of cases hold that a court may suspend imposition of sentence indefinitely, and that on breach of the conditions the defendant may at any time be sentenced and committed.[97] A majority of cases have denied the power to suspend imposition of

[93] Headley v. State, 201 Ind. 545, 170 N.E. 433 (1930). Sentence may be delayed in order that the court may ponder its judgment, so as to allow time for appeal or for motions for new trial or in arrest of judgment. See Note (1917) 2 Minn.L.Rev. 381.

[94] Ex parte Dillon, 26 F. (2d) 243 (C.C.A. 9th, 1928).

[95] State v. Powell, 153 Wash. 110, 279 Pac. 573 (1929). See (1930) 30 Col.L.Rev. 120.

[96] The extortion of a change of plea and an agreement not to appeal was reversed on appeal. O'Hara v. People, 41 Mich. 623 (1819). In Heyward v. State, 161 Md. 685, 158 Atl. 897, 902 (Md. 1932), 18 Va.L.Rev. 798, defendant was convicted of operating a lottery. The trial court sought to extract information by intimating that the result of a refusal would be a more severe penalty. No action was taken on appeal because of defendant's failure to take a proper exception below. In Tracy v. State, 46 Neb. 361, 366, 64 N.W. 1069, 1071 (1895), the court held, however, that the defendant might be questioned before sentence, but stated that it did not decide that the court could coerce an answer from the defendant.

[97] State v. Osborne, 79 N.J. Eq. 430, 82 Atl. 424 (1911); Orabona v. Linscott, 49 R.I. 443, 144 Atl. 52 (1928).

sentences indefinitely, some cases holding that as a consequence the court loses jurisdiction to sentence after the expiration of that term of court [98] while others hold that the court retains jurisdiction to sentence.[99] A wide variety of conditions have been imposed; such as that the defendant abate a nuisance,[100] enlist in the Navy,[101] pay excessive costs,[102] compensate the injured party,[103] be of good behavior,[104] leave the county,[105] and surrender at the pleasure of the attorney general.[106] While it is true that the consent of the defendant is necessary for a valid suspension on condition, the defendant has no choice but to acquiesce.[107] In the absence of a statutory check on the procedure, the defendant, who in many states cannot appeal from the order and condition once he has accepted the suspension,[108] is subject to the will of the court.

In the third place, there is an opportunity to influence the defendant's subsequent conduct by alteration of the sentence during the same term, if execution of the sentence has not begun.[109] In fact the Supreme Court of the United

[98] In re Grove, 43 Idaho, 775, 254 Pac. 519 (1927); People v. Allen, 155 Ill. 61, 39 N.E. 568 (1895), 9 Harv.L.Rev. 155.

[99] Ex parte Dunn, 50 S.D. 48, 208 N.W. 224 (1926); Hoggett v. State, 101 Miss. 269, 57 So. 811 (1911).

[100] State v. Addy, 43 N.J.L. 113 (1881).

[101] People v. Patrick, 118 Calif. 332, 50 Pac. 425 (1897).

[102] State v. Crook, 115 N.C. 760, 20 S.E. 513 (1894).

[103] State v. Hilton, 151 N.C. 687, 692, 65 S.E. 1011, 1013 (1909).

[104] State v. Hardin, 183 N.C. 815, 112 S.E. 593 (1922).

[105] Hoggett v. State, 101 Miss. 269, 57 So. 811 (1911).

[106] Orabona v. Linscott, 49 R.I. 443, 144 Atl. 52 (1928).

[107] State v. Burgess, 192 N.C. 669, 135 S.E. 771 (1926); State v. Osborne, 79 N.J. Eq. 430, 445, 82 Atl. 424 (1911).

[108] This is on the theory that suspension of sentence is not a final judgment. But the defendant could test the legality of the sentence by refusing to comply with its provisions.

[109] State v. Daugherty, 70 Iowa 539, 30 N.W. 685 (1886); State ex rel. Nelson v. Smith, 114 Neb. 653, 209 N.W. 328 (1926).

States has held that even after execution of sentence has commenced the trial court may during the same term reduce the punishment,[110] though an increase under similar circumstances is not proper since it is said to involve double jeopardy.[111] After the expiration of the term [112] or after the taking of an appeal,[113] the sentence may not be altered, unless it was wholly void in the first place.[114] Just as in the case of the initial power to impose sentence, the power to increase or decrease rests wholly in the discretion of the court. Thus the trial court has been sustained even when it clearly appears that the trial court increased the penalty because the defendant had given notice of appeal.[115]

In the fourth place, the trial court is universally regarded as having an inherent power to stay execution of sentence in the interest of justice,[116] or to enable the convicted defendant to pay a fine,[117] or for other reasonable ends. But the stay can be only temporary and for a definite period. Suspension of execution indefinitely and on condition is generally viewed as illegal. Difficulty arises as to the effect of such suspension where the defendant is arrested for breach of the condition during a subsequent term of court or at a time beyond the running of the term

110 United States v. Benz, 282 U.S. 304, 51 Sup.Ct. 113, 75 L.Ed. 354 (1930), 44 Harv.L.Rev. 967. Accord: In the Matter of Brittain, 93 N.C. 587 (1885). See (1922) 7 Minn.L.Rev. 349; (1930) 15 Minn.L.Rev. 828.

111 Ex parte Lange, 85 U.S. 163 (1873).

112 Ex parte Courson, 17 Ala. App. 243, 84 So. 411 (1919); State v. Carlson, 178 Minn. 626, 228 N.W. 173 (1929).

113 In re Griffin, 98 N.C. 225, 3 S.E. 515 (1887). *Contra:* People ex rel. Woodin v. Ottaway, 247 N.Y. 493, 161 N.E. 157 (1928).

114 Ex parte Gunther, 193 Ala. 486, 69 So. 442 (1915); McCormick v. State, 71 Neb. 505, 99 N.W. 237 (1904).

115 State v. Sudderth, 184 N.C. 753, 114 S.E. 828 (1922). See, however, Meaders v. State, 96 Ga. 299, 303, 22 S.E. 527, 528 (1895).

116 In re Brahm, 98 Cal. App. 731, 277 Pac. 895 (1929).

117 Gouvia, for Writ of Habeas Corpus, 45 R.I. 254, 121 Atl. 389 (1923).

of imprisonment imposed by the sentence. One group of cases holds that the court has lost jurisdiction to enforce the sentence.[118] But what appears to be a majority of jurisdictions regard the original sentence as being in effect and requiring satisfaction.[119] The result of the latter approach is that the defendant who has been recommitted is given only the satisfaction of knowing that he was illegally released in the first instance. It makes no difference that the condition was oppressive or that the defendant in good faith performed any number of acts in conformity with the conditional order of suspension.[120] Considering the actual choice open to the defendant, it is not realistic to assert, as the courts do, that he is estopped from complaining since he did not see fit to demand originally that he be punished in a lawful manner. In these states the defendant is far worse off than the defendant in the few states where trial courts are held to have inherent powers to suspend execution of sentence indefinitely and on condition. In the latter group of states, not only is the consent of the defendant necessary,[121] but his liberty is secure so long as he observes the conditions imposed.[122]

[118] Ex parte United States, 242 U.S. 27, 37 Sup.Ct. 72 (1915); State v. Sapp, 87 Kan. 740, 125 Pac. 78 (1912). See (1922) 36 Harv.L.Rev. 342; (1923) 37 Harv.L.Rev. 913.

[119] Holden v. State, 156 Ark. 521, 247 S.W. 768 (1923); Ex parte Fisher, 95 W.Va. 397, 121 S.E. 287 (1924). As in cases of suspension of imposition of sentence, the courts rely on two theories: (1) that the courts never had the power to grant more than a temporary delay; (2) that indefinite suspension is an unconstitutional encroachment on the pardoning power of the governor. See Notes (1912) 12 Col.L.Rev. 543, (1916) 30 Harv.L. Rev. 369, (1917) 2 Minn.L.Rev. 381.

[120] Thus the condition is viewed as mere "surplusage," State v. Abbott, 87 S.C. 466, 70 S.E. 6 (1910); or is treated as a nullity, Ex parte Thornberry, 300 Mo. 661, 254 S.W. 1087 (1923); or is not even mentioned.

[121] See Notes (1922) 1 N.C.L. Rev. 116, (1929) 8 N.C.L. Rev. 465.

[122] State v. Smith, 196 N.C. 438, 146 S.E. 73 (1929). See Notes (1917)

It has thus been seen that the sanctions once regarded as confined to a single purpose, retribution, are being used by the trial courts to cut through old distinctions between the executive and judicial branches of government, as well as those between civil and criminal cases. The use of such devices by courts and governors [123] is an informal effort to approximate the aims of criminologists in recent years. Assuming the desirability of such practices, the problem becomes one of devising suitable machinery. One of these is probation which enables the courts, as to less serious offenses, to suspend either imposition or execution of sentence or both. Most of the probation acts leave a wide discretion to the courts, both in granting probation and in imposing conditions. About the only limitation not permitted is exile. This freedom from limitations on conditions is probably due to the inability of the defendant to appeal from a probation order which is not ordinarily deemed a final judgment.[124]

Flexibility can best be obtained through statutes. Most statutes permit suspension of sentence for only definite and limited periods. Statutes restrict probation to misdemeanants and less dangerous felons who have not been previously convicted. The supervision provided under most probation statutes insures some restraint as well as

---

3 Corn.L.Q. 298, (1926) 40 Harv.L.Rev. 133. The defendant is held to be barred from attacking the agreement on which he obtained the suspension, hence there has been no attempt to limit the variety of conditions. Note (1932) 32 Col.L.Rev. 1031, 1040.

123 Pardons have been granted on such conditions as exile from the United States, abstention from liquor, payment of costs of trial, restitution to the injured party, exile from the state, supervision by a probation officer, and lawful conduct. See Notes (1925) 39 Harv.L.Rev. 111, (1932) 32 Col.L.Rev. 1031, 1041.

124 Walther v. State, 179 Ind. 565, 101 N.E. 1005 (1913); Renado v. Lummus, 205 Mass. 155, 91 N.E. 144 (1910).

aid to the released offender. It is regrettable that some courts hold that probation statutes do not derogate from the common-law power to suspend sentence.[125]

About the only condition of probation held invalid is leaving the state. It has been regarded as constituting cruel and unusual punishment.[126] Granted that being forced to leave the state is unusual, it does not seem cruel as by cruelty is meant physical torture.[127] Historically, to be invalid the punishment must be both cruel and unusual.[128] Public policy does not appear to be violated as the most serious criminals are not placed on probation, and thus sent into other states. Moreover the governor may pardon criminal defendants on condition they leave the state.[129] It may well be that rehabilitation may be greatly facilitated by the criminal defendant's having to leave the scene of his criminal activity. If a statute permits banishment, that may make it easier to uphold the sentence.[130]

15. Indeterminate Sentence

In recent years the theory determining the consequences of convictions of crime has shifted from punishment to fit the crime to punishment suitable to the criminal defen-

[125] State v. Osborne, 79 N.J.Eq. 430, 82 Atl. 424 (1911); People v. Flynn, 55 Misc. 639, 106 N.Y.Supp. 125 (Sup.Ct. 1907). *Contra:* Commonwealth ex rel. Wilhelm v. Morgan, 278 Pa. 395, 123 Atl. 337 (1924).

[126] People v. Baum, 251 Mich. 187, 231 N.W. 95 (1930), 30 Col.L.Rev. 1057, (1931) 35 Dick.L.Rev. 167, (1931) 26 Ill.L.Rev. 81, (1931) 22 J. Crim.L. 121, (1931) 16 St. Louis L.Rev. 254. Accord: State v. Baker, 58 S.C. 111. 36 S.E. 501 (1900).

[127] State v. Feilen, 70 Wash. 65, 120 Pac. 75 (1912).

[128] In re Kemmler, 136 U.S. 436, 446, 10 Sup.Ct. 930, 933 (1889).

[129] Ex parte Hawkins, 61 Ark. 321, 33 S.W. 106 (1895); Commonwealth v. Haggerty, 4 Brewst. 326 (Pa. 1869); see 60 A.L.R. 1415.

[130] Note (1931) 26 Ill.L.Rev. 81.

dant. It followed that instead of rigidly fixing the penalty by statute considerable discretion was left to the judges. For instance in Illinois, one found guilty of murder may be sentenced to anything from fourteen years' imprisonment up to life imprisonment, or to capital punishment. In Indiana, the court may impose a penalty of from ten to twenty-five years' imprisonment for burglary; from one to ten years for larceny of goods over twenty-five dollars in value; from one day to five years for larceny of goods of less than twenty-five dollars in value.[131]

Studies of the sentencing process show that there is no uniformity of approach among trial judges.[132] Some tend to give the maximum penalty and some the minimum. Some penalize certain types of crime severely while others may do the opposite. Some place many defendants on probation while others seldom provide for probation. Some judges penalize certain races and nationalities severely while others may be overlenient with the same groups. Individual judges often have no consistent policy of their own as to the cases they pass on. Often there is no thorough and scientific analysis of the behavior problems of

[131] Wood and Waite, Crime and Its Treatment (1941) 436.

[132] Lawes, Life and Death in Sing Sing (1928) 10-11; Sutherland, Criminology (1924) 278; Cantor, Crime, Criminals and Criminal Justice (1932) 275-276; Morse and Beattie, Survey of the Administration of Criminal Justice in Oregon (1932) 151-169; Report of the Crimes Survey Committee, Law Association of Philadelphia (1926) 380; Wood and Waite, Crime and Its Treatment (1941) 436-437; Gaudet, "Individual Differences in the Sentencing Tendencies of Judges" (1938) Archives of Psychology, No. 230; Coghlan, Thomsen, and Ussing, "Studies in Criminal Sentencing" (1903) 19 L.Q.Rev. 136; Emerson, "The Human Element in Justice" (1919) 10 J.Crim.L. 90; Gaudet, Harris, and St. John, "Individual Differences in the Sentencing Tendencies of Judges" (1933) 23. J. Crim.L. 811; Exner, Studien über die Strafzumessungs—Praxis der Deutschen Gerichte (1931); Hall, "Reduction of Criminal Sentences on Appeal: I" (1937) 37 Col.L.Rev. 521, 553.

individual offenders. Judges are often pressed for time and receive little assistance from social workers and probation officers.

But since judges, though vested with wide discretion, have not applied consistent policies in sentencing and for various other reasons, the legislatures began to take the determination out of the hands of judges, and to place it in the hands of parole boards.[133] Under the new laws the actual length of individual imprisonment is left up to parole boards, departments of correction, or other administrative boards. The notion is that these boards have an opportunity to study a prisoner carefully; hence can act more wisely than the judge can act in advance. Roscoe Pound points out that "the current of modern legislation is reducing the sentence of the court in all important prosecutions to a mere form, and is committing determination of the actual nature and duration of penal treatment of offenders to boards of probation and parole." [134]

In connection with parole and parole boards the indeterminate sentence has developed. An indeterminate sentence is a sentence to imprisonment either for a wholly indefinite term, or for an indefinite term not less than the minimum period or more than the maximum period fixed by the judge pursuant to statutory authorization. The first type of indeterminate sentence is not employed in any American jurisdiction for any crime. The second type is employed in thirty-nine jurisdictions, including the District of Columbia and the Territory of Hawaii.[135]

133 Wood and Waite, Crime and Its Treatment (1941) 437-438; Minnesota Crime Commission Report (1927) 44-49, 61.

134 Pound, "The Future of the Criminal Law" (1921) 21 Col.L.Rev. 1.

135 Notes (1937) 50 Harv.L.Rev. 677, (1944) 53 Yale L.J. 773, 783. See also Lindsey, "Historical Sketch of the Indeterminate Sentence and the Parole System" (1925) 16 J.Crim.L. 9; "A Brief Comparative Study of

In every state the maximum period of incarceration under an indeterminate sentence is the maximum prescribed by law for the offense.[136] Doubtless there are some hardened criminal defendants who ought to be held even longer. But the defendant is entitled to protection against capricious and erroneous judgment, and a maximum sentence offers a rough solution. Yet habitual offender laws go very far in curtailing individual liberty and apply inflexible standards in doing so. Thirty-five jurisdictions provide for varying minimum terms of imprisonment under an indeterminate sentence. In twenty-five the minimum term is either the minimum period prescribed by law for the offense, or is fixed by the court or jury at not less than the statutory minimum. In four states there are minimum terms fixed at not less than a definite period of years. In five jurisdictions there are minimum terms to be fixed by the court or parole board without reference to the statutory minimum or a definite period of years. Only two states provide no minimum sentence to the state prison and also allow parole after commitment at any time. The arbitrary provisions in most states seem hard to justify. A possible argument is that those offenders who should not serve a fixed minimum term may be placed on probation. But a short term less than the minimum set by law may be the best treatment for certain offenders. Furthermore, the scope of probation is limited in many jurisdictions by the age of the offender or the type of crime. The real explana-

---

Indeterminate Sentence and the Parole Statutes" (1925) 16 J.Crim.L. 70; Glueck, "Indeterminate Sentence and Parole in the Federal System" (1941) 21 B.U.L.Rev. 20; separate articles by Glueck, Holtzoff, J., Coleman, J., and Nordbye, J. (Jan.-March, 1941) Federal Probation, No. 1.

[136] For a recent survey, see Beattie and Tolman, "State Sentencing Practices and Penal Systems," contained in Report to the Judicial Conference of the Committee on Punishment for Crime (1941) 81-126.

tion for the requirement of minimum terms seems to lie in the legislative unwillingness to break away from the attitude that criminal defendants should suffer for their wrong, irrespective of the good to society accomplished.

Thirteen jurisdictions authorize the judge and one the jury to fix the minimum and maximum terms of the sentence within the minimum and maximum limits prescribed by law for the offense. Six states give the parole board unrestricted authority to fix the period of incarceration between such statutory limits. It is a regrettable fact that judges sometimes defeat the purpose of indeterminate sentence laws by fixing the minimum term at slightly less than the maximum. Three states have therefore required a certain interval between judge-made limits.

In fifteen states indeterminate sentences may be imposed only in felony cases. Twelve states limit such sentences to crimes punishable by imprisonment in the state prison. No such sentences are needed as to misdemeanors as the maximum period of custody is short, and incarceration is in jails and houses of correction. In six states the indeterminate sentence is not extended to second offenders. In seventeen states certain crimes, such as treason, murder, and rape, are specifically exempted from the application of the indeterminate sentence laws. In seven states it is discretionary with the court whether the sentence shall be definite or indefinite. This seems undesirable, as it is hard to ascertain what offenders will not respond to treatment until after a reasonable period of incarceration.

There are at least five major considerations in favor of the indeterminate sentence.[137] First, there is a stronger deterrent force arising out of the uncertainty of incarceration for an unknown period than that arising out of a

[137] Note (1937) 50 Harv.L.Rev. 677, 684-685.

definite sentence. In the second place, the offender is given an incentive to self-betterment through the realization that the length of his incarceration depends largely on his showing of improved moral and industrial qualities. Thirdly, individual deterioration is averted by release as soon as the defendant can safely be released. In the fourth place, if a parolee commits an offense while in legal custody, he may be returned to prison without the formality of a court trial. Finally, parole oversight is much less costly than imprisonment.

By the great weight of authority, indeterminate sentence statutes have been held constitutional.[138] The principal constitutional objections to this type of statute have been that it is a cruel and unusual punishment, and an unlawful delegation of legislative power to an administrative body, and an interference with the pardoning power of the governor.[139]

The question of the power of an administrative body to alter the sentence of the trial court is neatly raised in a recent Illinois case. The defendant was convicted of assault with intent to murder. The trial judge sentenced him to the penitentiary. In accordance with the provisions of a 1941 amendment to the Illinois Parole Act,[140] the court recommended a term of ten to fourteen years. The recommendation was subject to change by the vote of four of the five members of the Division of Correction.[141] Before the date of the amendment, the court had power only to

[138] People v. Joyce, 246 Ill. 124, 92 N.E. 607 (1910), (1911) 24 Harv.L. Rev. 236; Miller v. State, 149 Ind. 607, 49 N.E. 894, 40 L.R.A. 109 (1898), 7 Yale L.J. 367.

[139] See Lindsey, "Historical Sketch of the Indeterminate Sentence and Parole System" (1925) 16 J.Crim.L. 9.

[140] Ill. Rev. Stat. (1941) c.38, § 802.

[141] Ill. Rev. Stat. (1941) c.38, § 803a.

pronounce a general sentence which could be absolutely terminated by the Department of Public Welfare before the defendant had served the statutory maximum. The Illinois Supreme Court held that the 1941 amendment was an invalid attempt to sanction interference by an administrative body with the judicial power to pronounce final sentence.[142]

The great weight of authority upholds the validity of indeterminate sentence statutes as not impairing the independence of the judiciary. But the Illinois Court adopted the view that a statute permitting an administrative body to modify a recommendation embodied in a judicial sentence is a more serious encroachment upon judicial authority than is a statute, like the earlier amended statute, preventing the court from making any recommendation as to the length of imprisonment. A general sentence by the court under an indeterminate sentence statute is usually regarded as one for the maximum term imposed by law for the specific crime.[143] Nevertheless, statutes authorizing administrative boards to determine the length of imprisonment after general sentence by the court have been upheld.[144]

The authority of parole boards to grant absolute releases to prisoners before their maximum terms have expired has been recognized in a number of states.[145] Where

[142] People v. Montana, 380 Ill. 596, 44 N.E. (2d) 569 (1942), (1943) 43 Col.L.Rev. 385.

[143] Commonwealth v. Kalck, 239 Pa. 533, 87 Atl. 61 (1913).

[144] State v. Mulcare, 189 Wash. 625, 66 Pac. (2d) 360 (1937); People v. Hayes, 9 Cal. App. (2d) 157, 49 Pac. (2d) 288 (1935).

[145] Miller v. State, 149 Ind. 607, 49 N.E. 894 (1898); Wilson v. Commonwealth, 141 Ky. 341, 132 S.W. 557 (1910); see People ex rel. Haupt v. Lasch, 122 Misc. 223, 227, 202 N.Y.Supp. 416, 419 (1924). *Contra:* People v. Cummings, 88 Mich. 249, 50 N.W. 310 (1891); Commonwealth v. Cain, 28 Atl. (2d) 897 (Pa. 1942).

the indeterminate sentence law requires the court expressly to limit the term to the maximum prescribed by the specific statute, the appellate courts find no difficulty in permitting the prison board to regulate the conditions of confinement and parole.[146] Likewise, whether the sentence is absolute or indeterminate, statutes providing for deductions for good behavior according to rules established by prison authorities are often upheld.[147]

The cases reveal that most courts are impressed by the merits of the administrative determination of problems inherent in the sentencing and paroling of offenders. They have therefore not been so insistent upon the need for upholding the exclusive power of the judiciary in this field as in others. The Illinois case shows a hesitancy to allow the pronouncement of an opinion which may be nullified by another department of government, somewhat akin to the judicial hostility to requests for advisory opinions.

The matter of sentence and punishment for crime in the federal courts has given the Judicial Conference of Senior Circuit Judges much concern.[148] It is now realized that the

[146] People v. Adams, 176 N.Y. 351, 68 N.E. 636 (1903). A breach of the conditions of parole may result in the surveillance of a parolee over a longer period of time than originally contemplated by the imposed sentence. Anderson v. Corall, 263 U.S. 193 (1923).

[147] Woodward v. Murdock, 124 Ind. 439. 24 N.E. 1047 (1890). *Contra:* Commonwealth ex rel. Johnson v. Holloway, 42 Pa. 446 (1862). The transfer by administrative officials of a defendant sentenced from one institution to another which will provide more suitable treatment is valid. In re Murphy, 62 Kan. 422, 63 Pac. 428 (1901); Sheehan, Petitioner, 254 Mass. 342, 150 N.E. 231 (1926). See (1913) 13 Col.L.Rev. 256.

[148] Parker, J., "The Integration of the Federal Judiciary" (1943) 56 Harv.L.Rev. 563, 574. The same problem arises in the case of the Youth Correction Authority Act of the American Law Institute. The Act is criticized by Hall, "The Youth Correction Authority Act, Progress or Menace" (1942) 28 A.B.A.J. 317, 319; and defended by Lewis, "The Youth Correction Authority Act" (1942) 28 A.B.A.J. 322, 323. See also Phillips, J., "The Criminal Youth Problem" (1942) 28 A.B.A.J. 581.

methods of the federal courts are not in line with modern criminological or sociological thought. In 1940 the Conference recommended to Congress the passage of an indeterminate sentence act, largely based on the California statute. But a number of circuit conferences objected to the law with the result that the Conference of Senior Judges recommended further study of the subject. A committee of federal circuit and district judges made a thorough study culminating in a report [149] reserving to the trial judge ultimate power in the matter of sentencing.[150] The report is based on the concepts that the sentencing power is judicial in character and that the administrative agencies should by all means be subject to judicial review to the end that fundamental rights of the individual may not be impaired.[151] Specifically the chief recommendations of the report are as follows: "(1) Retain in the trial judge full power to fix the length of all sentences and to admit to probation. (2) When the sentence, in the opinion of the judge, should be for more than one year, require that a sentence for the maximum term be initially imposed, with power in the judge to modify the sentence later. (3) Pro-

[149] Report to the Judicial Conference of the Committee on Punishment for Crime (1942). See (1942) 28 A.B.A.J. 556. See Phillips, "Should a Board Be Created to Advise District Judges What Their Sentence Should Be?" (1944) 30 A.B.A.J. 69; Blanton, "The Proposed Federal Correction Acts: A Reply" (1944) 30 A.B.A.J. 73.

[150] It is arguable that the power to suspend sentence and release on probation should be left with the judge, because segregation in a temporary classification institution is likely to carry with it a certain stigma and to have a definite psychological effect on the offender. Gausewitz, "Considerations Basic to a New Penal Code" (1936) 11 Wis.L.Rev. 480, 485-486. The dignity of the judicial office should not be reduced; and judges can develop uniform treatment policies. Michael and Wechsler, "A Rationale of the Law of Homicide" (1937) 37 Col.L.Rev. 1261, 1311-1313.

[151] See also Otis, J., "Proposed Federal Indeterminate Sentence Act" (1941) 25 J. Am. Jud. Soc. 102.

vide a Board of Corrections with power to make recommendations to the judges as to sentence in cases where sentence is for more than a year, but with power in the judge to fix the sentence notwithstanding the recommendation of the Board. (4) Provide, in the case of offenders under 24 years of age, that the judge in his discretion, instead of imposing an ordinary sentence of imprisonment on them, may commit them to the custody of the Youth Authority Division of the Board of Corrections for correctional treatment."

16. Judicial Finality of Sentence

There are frequent statements that a court may alter its sentence only before the commitment of the prisoner and during the same term of court at which it was pronounced.[152] Largely as a consequence of their early inability to grant new trials or to allow a review of the verdict by appeal, the courts availed themselves of this power and have continued to exercise it.[153] Where, however, the sentence has been partly executed, there are many decisions holding that the doctrine of the separation of powers causes a loss of jurisdiction.[154] The constitutional pro-

[152] Bradford v. People, 22 Colo. 157, 43 Pac. 1013 (1896); State v. Municipal Court, 179 Wis. 195, 190 N.W. 121 (1922); 2 Bishop, New Criminal Procedure (4th ed.1895) § 1298. While an appeal is pending, the court may not alter its judgment. State v. Municipal Court, 179 Wis. 195, 190 N.W. 121 (1922).

[153] People v. Court of Sessions, 141 N.Y. 288, 36 N.E. 386 (1894); (1917) 30 Harv.L.Rev. 369.

[154] United States v. Murray, 275 U.S. 347 (1928) (probation), (1928) 37 Yale L.J. 825; Emerson v. Boyles, 170 Ark. 621, 280 S.W. 1005 (1926) (suspension); Tracy v. State, 24 Okla. Cr. 144, 216 Pac. 941 (1923) (modification). In some states this objection is fatal the moment a sentence unconditional in form is pronounced. Neal v. State, 104 Ga. 509, 30

hibition against double jeopardy has been considered a further restriction.

Traditional doctrines were challenged in a decision of the United States Supreme Court upholding a reduction of sentence even after commitment.[155] With respect to the separation of powers, the argument against jurisdiction is twofold. In the first place, and of primary importance, is the surrender of the custody of the defendant by the court to the executive. In the second place, there seems to be a usurpation of the pardoning power of the executive. But logically both grounds are unsound. The assumption that partial execution invariably places the defendant in the hands of the executive is valid only if at such time the court's jurisdiction over him has terminated, which is the very question in dispute. The action of the executive in pardoning is predicated on the validity of the judicial act, while the action of the court overturns the act itself.[156] Even if suspension or modification were conceded to be a species of pardon, it should be remembered that the doctrine of separation of powers has not barred the courts from doing acts which in their nature are not clearly judicial.

As might be expected, attempts by a court to increase the sentence even during the same term, whether for good

---

S.E. 858 (1898) (suspension); State v. Ensign, 38 Idaho 539, 223 Pac. 230 (1924) (annulment); People v. Meservey, 76 Mich. 223, 42 N.W. 1133 (1889) (increase). See Bruce, "Power to Suspend a Criminal Sentence" (1922) 6 Minn.L.Rev. 363, 364.

155 United States v. Benz, 282 U.S. 304 51 Sup.Ct. 113, 75 L.Ed. 192 (1931), 19 Geo.L.J. 365, 44 Harv.L.Rev. 967, (1931) 15 Minn.L.Rev. 828. But the power to resentence one convicted as a fourth felony offender, when it develops that the third offense was a misdemeanor, was denied in In re Cedar, 265 N.Y. 620, 193 N.E. 414 (1935), 35 Col.L.Rev. 448.

156 State v. District Court, 73 Mont. 541, 237 Pac. 525 (1925); (1917) 30 Harv.L.Rev. 369, 371.

cause[157] or not[158] have been met by the additional objection of double jeopardy.[159] The result has been that the defendant has sometimes got off very lightly. The United States Supreme Court has stated that the double jeopardy provision is aimed not only to avoid repeated trials, but also to prevent two punishments for the same offense.[160] But the conclusion that an increase in the penalty after partial execution is jeopardy does not necessarily follow. Whether or not there is jeopardy depends upon the time at which the first jeopardy has expired.[161] If the power to alter the sentence exists, it follows that the first jeopardy has not expired until the end of the period during which the change may be made. Thus the objection assumes the very question in controversy. It may be thought that the jeopardy argument is of no weight because it does not stand in the way of a sentence being decreased. However, the obvious answer is that defendant in asking for a lower sentence has waived any possible jeopardy.

Where the original sentence should be altered in view of the facts pertaining to the trial itself, the court in reviewing is exercising a proper judicial function. But some practical limitations on the power are necessary. For procedural reasons the power was historically confined to

[157] Ex parte Lange, 18 Wall. 163 (U.S. 1873); People v. Simon, 284 Ill. 28, 119 N.E. 940 (1918); In re Jones, 35 Neb. 499, 53 N.W. 468 (1892). *Contra:* Jobe v. State, 28 Ga. 235 (1859); People v. Kaiser, 230 App. Div. 646, 246 N.Y.Supp. 309 (1930).

[158] But cf. State v. Sudderth, 184 N.C. 753, 114 S.E. 828 (1922), (1923) 7 Minn.L.Rev. 349 (upholding sentence increased because defendant appealed).

[159] Ex parte Lange, 18 Wall. 163, 193, 193 (U.S. 1873); In re Jones, 35 Neb. 499, 53 N.W. 468 (1892).

[160] Ex parte Lange, 18 Wall. 163, 173 (U.S. 1873).

[161] Holmes, J., dissenting in Kepner v. United States, 195 U.S. 100, 134 (1904).

the term of court in which the original sentence was imposed.[162]

As has been seen, when a sentence has not been executed, the court may alter the sentence at any time during the same term of court. But if it has been executed even in part it may not be altered.[163] After the expiration of the term of court its power is gone. There are various exceptions to these rules in a number of cases. In one case in which the defendant had been sentenced to imprisonment and fine, he had a physical encounter with the woman from whom he had stolen after the sentence. It was held that the trial court could modify the judgment during the same term by imposing an additional prison sentence, even though the fine imposed under the original sentence had been paid.[164] In a leading case[165] decided in 1930, the

162 People v. Weinstein, 298 Ill. 264, 131 N.E. 631 (1921); Auldridge v. Womble, 157 Ga. 64, 120 S.E. 620 (1923). The theory was that until the end of the term all judgments are in the "breast of the court." See Goddard v. Ordway, 101 U.S. 745, 752 (1879); 1 Bacon, Abridgement (7th ed.1832) 192.

163 Thus where a three to five year term was at first imposed, the defendant served for 43 days, the court could not at that point increase to 20 years, although that was the proper penalty for the crime. Hickman v. Fenton, 120 Neb. 66, 231 N.W. 510, 70 A.L.R. 819 (1930), (1931) 9 Neb.L.Bull. 343. See Emerson v. Boyles, 170 Ark. 621, 280 S.W. 1005, 44 A.L.R. 1193 (1926), 35 Yale L.J. 1012. In People v. Turney, 273 Ill. 546, 553-554, 113 N.E. 105 (1916), the court stated: "Under the practice in this state it is customary, upon the completion of a criminal trial wherein a verdict of guilty is returned, to enter judgment at once, to pass sentence upon the defendant and to issue a warrant or mittimus to the proper officer where imprisonment is a part of the sentence. When the cause has been thus concluded and the prisoner has been committed to the custody of the proper officer of the penitentiary or reformatory the jurisdiction of the trial court ceases first, because the defendant has entered upon the execution of his sentence; and second, because the court has lost jurisdiction of the person of the defendant."

164 State v. Godwin, 210 N.C. 447, 187 S.E. 560 (1936), (1937) 71 U.S.L. Rev. 11. See Note (1939) 30 J.Crim.L. 146. *Contra:* State v. Cannon, 11

United States Supreme Court held that a federal district court has power during the same term to amend sentence to *shorten* the terms of imprisonment, although the defendant has been committed and has entered on the service of sentence.[166] Likewise it has been held that a federal district court has the power after the expiration of the term to grant probation when the defendant has not begun service of sentence.[167] When a federal district court at the time of sentencing reserved jurisdiction of the case, it could order release on probation although the defendant had served portions of his sentence.[168] If the original judgment was void and not merely voidable, there is jurisdiction even after the term has expired.[169]

Neither the Institute Code nor the Criminal Appeals Rules of the United States Supreme Court deals with the problem of reduction or correction of sentence. It would seem desirable that a motion to correct an illegal sentence should lie at any time. But a motion in the trial court to reduce a legally correct but criminologically excessive sentence should be limited to some fairly short period such as sixty days after sentence.[170] The abuse in the federal

---

Ore. 312, 2 Pac. 191 (1884); In re Sullivan, 3 Calif. App. 193, 84 Pac. 781 (1906); State v. Addy, 43 N.J.L. 113 (1881).

165 United States v. Benz, 282 U.S., 304, 51 Sup.Ct. 113, 75 L.Ed. 354 (1930). Accord: State v. O'Connor, 154 Minn. 45, 191 N.W. 50 (1922); Re Brittain, 93 N.C. 587 (1885); Ammon v. Johnson, 2 Ohio C.D. 149, 3 Ohio C.C. 263 (1888). *Contra:* Auldridge v. Womble, 157 Ga. 64, 120 S.E. 620 (1923); State v. Ensign, 38 Idaho 539, 223 Pac. 230 (1924); People ex rel Swanson v. Williams, 352 Ill. 227, 185 N.E. 598 (1933).

166 See 44 A.L.R. 1211, 70 A.L.R. 823.

167 In re Edelson, 15 F.Supp. 1086 (D. Pa. 1936).

168 United States v. Wittmeyer, (1936) 16 F.Supp. 1000, (1937) 28 J. Crim.L. 141, (1937) 35 Mich.L.Rev. 1009.

169 DeBenque v. United States, 85 F. (2d) 202, 205-206, 100 A.L.R. 839, 843-844 (D.C. Ct. of App. 1936).

170 Orfield, "Improving Procedure on Judgment and Appeal in Federal

courts, at least, has been that trial judges by entry of orders from time to time have extended for the purposes of a particular case the term of court at which a sentence was imposed for periods of years, and have granted motions for reduction a long time after the sentence was imposed. This has been done on the theory that reduction of sentence is always permissible during the same term of court.[171] In one notorious case a federal judge, after imposing a ten-year sentence, which the defendant began to serve, extended the court term for three successive years, and then, on motion of the defendant, modified the judgment by reducing the sentence to the time already served. It might fairly be argued that such action amounted to an encroachment upon the executive power to pardon.

The above suggestions are incorporated in Rule 35 of the Federal Rules of Criminal Procedure: "The court may correct an illegal sentence at any time. The court may reduce a sentence within 60 days after the sentence is imposed, or within 60 days after receipt by the court of a mandate issued upon affirmance of the judgment or dismissal of the appeal, or within 60 days after receipt of an order of the Supreme Court denying an application for a writ of certiorari." The question seems unsettled whether or not the defendant is entitled to be present at the correction of a sentence.[172]

Criminal Cases" (1943) 27 Minn.L.Rev. 169, 173. See Smith, "Cleveland's Crime Survey" (1922) 5 J. Am. Jud. Soc. 68, 75; Criminal Justice in Cleveland (1922) 285-286.

[171] United States v. Benz, 282 U.S. 304, 51 Sup.Ct. 113, 75 L.Ed. 354 (1931). See 15 Am.Jur., Criminal Law, § 473, p.128.

[172] An English case seems to hold that he is entitled to be present. Rex v. Casey (1932) 23 Cr. App. Rep. 193; "Power of Court to Pass Sentence in Absence of Prisoner" (1933) 97 Justice of the Peace and Local Government Review (1933), 621. Under Rule 43, Fed. Rules Crim. Proc., he need not be present at reduction.

Clerical mistakes in judgments or orders should be subject to correction at any time.[173] The same rule ought to apply to errors arising from oversight or omission. The past rule of the federal courts has permitted such errors to be corrected during the term, at least if the effect is to reduce the penalty.[174] Rule 36 of the Federal Rules of Criminal Procedure provides: "Clerical mistakes in judgments, orders or other parts of the record and errors in the record arising from oversight or omission may be corrected by the court at any time and after such notice, if any, as the court orders."

17. When Sentence Is Void or Voidable

The authorities are in conflict as to whether an excessive sentence or a sentence to the wrong place is void[175] or merely voidable.[176] If it is regarded as void, habeas corpus will lie.[177] But the discharge is from custody and not from the legal penalty and further proceedings.[178] Where the sentence is regarded as merely voidable, relief

[173] That has been the rule in federal criminal cases. Rupinski v. United States, 4 F. (2d) 17 (C.C.A. 6th, 1925). It is the rule in federal civil cases. Federal Rules Civ. Proc., Rule 60(a). See 15 Am. Jur., Criminal Law, § 478, p.133; Note (1918) 18 Col.L.Rev. 485.

[174] See Ex parte Lange, 18 Wall. 163 (U.S. 1873); United States v. Benz, 282 U.S. 304 (1931). As to *nunc pro tunc* corrections in the record, see Note (1918) 18 Col.L.Rev. 485.

[175] Ex parte Cox, 3 Idaho 530 (1893). See (1914) 14 Col.L.Rev. 86.

[176] Sennott's Case, 146 Mass. 489 (1888); Ex parte Tani, 29 Nev. 385, 91 Pac. 137, 13 L.R.A. (N.S.) 518 (1907). See (1919) 28 Yale L.J. 292.

[177] (1914) 14 Col.L.Rev. 86. In Ex parte Burden, 92 Miss. 14, 45 So. 1, 131 Am. St. Rep. 511 (1907), when the verdict was for a misdemeanor and sentence for a felony, the sentence was held wholly void, and habeas corpus granted.

[178] In re Bonner, 151 U.S. 242 (1894); cf. Michaelson v. Beemer, 72 Neb. 761 (1904).

may be had by appeal.[179] Under the earlier law, reversal of an erroneous sentence resulted in the complete discharge of the defendant. Under the present law he is resentenced.[180] When a defendant is resentenced after having served under a void sentence, credit should be given for service under the void sentence.[181]

18. When Sentence Commences

According to the great weight of authority, if there is no statute providing otherwise, delay in taking the defendant into custody after conviction and sentence in no way releases the defendant from serving the full sentence.[182] Sentence commences at the date when the defendant is taken into custody or offers to surrender himself.[183] Arguably, however, if the delay is unreasonable, the court should lose jurisdiction.[184] The serving of another sentence for a crime committed while the defendant was out on bond pending proceedings in error would not affect a prior sentence not served at all, although a delay of three years was involved.[185] The theory is that the time fixed for

[179] Note (1895) 9 Harv.L.Rev. 220, 287.

[180] Note (1895) 9 Harv.L.Rev. 220.

[181] Note (1939) 29 J.Crim.L. 738.

[182] Volker v. McDonald, 120 Neb. 508, 233 N.W. 890, 72 A.L.R. 1267 (1931), (1932) 10 Neb.L.Bull. 334. For the Canadian practice, see Note (1927) 5 Can.B.Rev. 145.

[183] Riggs v. Sutton, 113 Neb. 556, 203 N.W. 999 (1925), (1926) 10 Minn. L.Rev. 166.

[184] (1930) 30 Col.L.Rev. 120; (1938) 28 J.Crim.L. 765; (1924) 34 Yale L.J. 203. If the defendant is prematurely discharged by mistake, over his objection, so that he is virtually ejected from prison, he should be given credit for the time spent at large prior to a later recommitment. White v. Pearlman, 42 F. (2d) 788 (C.C.A. 10th, 1930), (1931) 25 Ill.L.Rev. 827, (1931) 4 So.Calif.L.Rev. 243.

[185] Brott v. Fenton, 120 Neb. 792, 235 N.W. 449 (1931). See, however, In re Jennings, 118 Fed. 479 (C.C. Mo. 1902), (1903) 16 Harv.L.Rev. 450.

the commencement of execution of sentence is not one of the important elements of the sentence.[186] The essential part of the sentence is the punishment, including the kind and the amount thereof. If the statute and the sentence are silent as to commencement, the sentence will commence at incarceration. Even though the sentence fixes a time for commencement, this may be construed as directory.[187] Section 401 of the Institute Code provides: "When the sentence imposes imprisonment it need not state the date at which the imprisonment is to begin or end." Upon unreasonable delay in execution, the prisoner should seek habeas corpus and move to have his sentence carried out immediately, rather than wait until the end of his sentence to raise the objection.[188]

19. Effect of Parole Violation on Duration

By the weight of authority where there is a violation of parole, whether the condition be imposed by statute or by the terms of the parole itself, the defendant is placed in the same position in which he was prior to the parole and the time he was at large cannot be deemed a part of the sentence.[189] One theory is that a violation of the conditions, either precedent or subsequent, renders the parole void.[190] A second theory is that the parole merely stops

[186] (1934) 34 Yale L.J. 203.

[187] Bernstein v. United States, 254 Fed. 967, 3 A.L.R. 1569 (C.C.A. 4th, 1919), cert. denied 249 U.S. 604, 39 Sup.Ct. 260, 63 L.Ed. 798 (1919).

[188] Gorovitz v. Sartain, 1 F. (2d) 602 (D. Ga. 1924); Note (1938) 28 J.Crim.L. 765, 767.

[189] Ex parte Alvarez, 50 Fla. 24, 39 So. 481, 7 Ann. Cas. 88, 111 A.S.R. 102 (1905); Anderson, Warden v. Corall, 263 U.S. 193, 44 Sup.Ct. 43, 68 L.Ed. 247 (1923), (1924) 8 Minn.L.Rev. 256. See Notes 16 L.R.A. (N.S.) 304, 10 Ann. Cas. 203, 28 A.L.R. 947. The same is true as to a violation of probation. Kaplan v. Hecht, 24 F. (2d) 664 (C.C.A. 2d, 1928).

[190] State v. Wolfer, 53 Miss. 135, 138, 54 N.W. 1065, 19 L.R.A. 783, 39 A.S.R. 582 (1893).

the execution of the sentence for the time and the sentence continues *in fieri.*[191] Many state jurisdictions, however, hold that a defendant cannot be required to remain in prison beyond the expiration of the original sentence and that the time he was out on parole is to be reckoned in computing the sentence.[192] The theories of this approach are that a defendant on parole, being subject to the supervision of the warden and the conditions of parole, is not a free man; and that a defendant cannot extend the terms of his imprisonment by contract any more than he could have become a prisoner in the first instance by contract.[193]

20. Effect of Escape on Duration

An escape interrupts the running of a term of imprisonment.[194] Punishment is the essential element, and the commencement and expiration of the sentence are mere formalities of execution.[195] The defendant should not be allowed to take advantage of his own wrong.[196] This has been extended by analogy to paroled prisoners who remain at large after revocation of their parole.[197] A similar

[191] Fuller v. State, 122 Ala. 32, 26 So. 146, 45 L.R.A. 502, 82 A.S.R. 17 (1898).

[192] In re Prout, 12 Idaho 494, 86 Pac. 275, 5 L.R.A. (N.S.) 1064, 10 Ann. Cas. 199 (1906); Woodward v. Murdock, 124 Ind. 439, 24 N.E. 1047 (1890); Scott v. Chichester, 107 Va. 933, 60 S.E. 95, 16 L.R.A. (N.S.) 304 (1908).

[193] White, "Some Legal Aspects of Parole" (1942) 32 J.Crim.L. 600, 612.

[194] In re McCauley, 123 Wis. 31, 100 N.W. 1031 (1904); Ex parte Moody, 121 Miss. 313, 83 So. 529 (1920). *Contra:* Wilson v. Attorney-General, N.Z.L.R. 496 (C.A.) (1938), (1939) 52 Harv.L.Rev. 526.

[195] Petition of Moebus, 73 N.H. 350, 62 Atl. 170 (1905).

[196] Cleek v. Commonwealth, 21 Gratt. 777 (Va. 1871).

[197] Anderson v. Corall, 263 U.S. 193 (1923); People ex rel. Patterson v. Bockel, 270 N.Y. 76, 200 N.E. 586 (1936).

theory has been applied where an official improperly releases a prisoner.[198]

21. Sentence on Several Counts

Difficulty and confusion may arise with respect to sentences imposed on an indictment or information containing several counts. In one case a general verdict was entered on an indictment containing several counts. After sentence some of the counts were found bad. The sentence did not exceed what might properly have been imposed on the good counts. Such a sentence was treated as valid.[199] But where the total of the sentences imposed exceeds the sentence which may be imposed under any count, the court should state separately the sentence which it is imposing for each count.[200]

One of the knottiest questions of criminal procedure is how to tell when sentences are concurrent and when they are consecutive.[201] Early cases centered about the question as to the court's power to impose cumulative sentences in the absence of statutory authority. The weight of authority was to the effect that it had such a power.[202] The

198 Massey v. Cunningham, 169 Ark. 410, 275 S.W. 737 (1925) (sheriff); Hopkins v. North, 151 Md. 553, 135 Atl. 367 (1926) (magistrate and sheriff). But cf. Ex parte Eley, 9 Okla. Cr. 76, 130 Pac. 821 (1913) (county attorney, county judge, and sheriff); White v. Pearlman, 42 F. (2d) 788 (C.C.A. 10th, 1930) (warden).

199 Haynes v. United States, 101 Fed. 817 (C.C.A. 8th, 1900), 14 Harv. L.Rev. 229.

200 Orfield, "Improving Procedure on Judgment and Appeal in Federal Criminal Cases" (1943) 27 Minn.L.Rev. 169, 172-173. In England the practice usually is to enter judgment and sentence separately on each count on which the defendant has been indicted. Archbold, Criminal Pleading, Evidence and Practice (30th ed.1938) 230.

201 See (1928) 11 Minn.L.Rev. 72; (1932) 22 J.Crim.L. 902; (1932) 11 Neb.L.Bull. 204; (1925) 25 Col.L.Rev. 671.

202 Wallace v. State, 41 Fla. 547 (1899); In re Walsh, 37 Neb. 454

United States Supreme Court has stated: "Where sentences are imposed on verdicts of guilty, or pleas of guilty, on several counts or on several indictments consolidated for trial, it is the rule, that the sentences so imposed run concurrently, in the absence of specific and definite provision therein that they be made to run consecutively by specifying the order of sequence. If the order in which the terms of imprisonment for the different offenses is to be served is not clearly designated, the terms are to be served concurrently, and the defendant cannot be held in further confinement under the sentence after the expiration of the longest term imposed. Cumulative sentences are permissible, and in some cases appropriate, but when imposed on different counts or indictments there must be certainty in the order of sequence." [203]

It is the prevailing rule that when it is not stated in either of two or more sentences imposed at the same time that the imprisonment under one is to begin at the expiration of the others, the sentences will run concurrently.[204] The same rule has been applied where the sentences are imposed at different times,[205] including different terms,[206] or by different courts where served at the same place of confinement.[207] The sentences have been held to be con-

---

(1893); (1928) 13 Minn.L.Rev. 63; (1928) 37 Yale L.J. 385. In England a sentence beginning at the end of the defendant's previous imprisonment was held valid as early as 1770. Wilkes' Case, 19 Howell St. Tr. 1075, 1135. A statute confirmed this rule as to felonies. (1827) 7 & 8 Geo. IV, c.28, § 10.

203 United States v. Daugherty, 269 U.S. 360, 46 Sup.Ct. 156, 70 L.Ed. 309 (1926).

204 Breton, Petitioner, 93 Me. 39, 44 Atl. 125, 74 A.S.R. 335 (1899).

205 Ex parte Gafford, 25 Nev. 101, 57 Pac. 484, 83 A.S.R. 568 (1899).

206 In re Black, 162 N.C. 457, 78 S.E. 273 (1913).

207 Dickerson v. Perkins, 182 Iowa 871, 166 N.W. 293, 5 A.L.R. 374 (1918); Zerbst v. Lyman, 255 Fed. 609, 5 A.L.R. 377 (C.C.A. 5th, 1919);

secutive despite the absence of specific directions to that effect when they were under separate charges and to be served at different places.[208] Since the question is often a matter of the discretion of the court, and not fixed by statute as it might be, the court may consider in mitigation the fact that several offenses occurred in what was substantially one transaction.[209]

Under Section 402 of the Institute Code the test is whether or not the offenses are charged in the same indictment: "When the defendant has been convicted of two or more offenses charged in the same indictment or information the terms of imprisonment shall be served concurrently unless the court expressly directs that they or some of them be served consecutively. Sentences of imprisonment for offenses not charged in the same indictment or information shall be served consecutively unless the court expressly directs that they or some of them be served concurrently." [210]

When a prisoner commits a crime while on parole and is convicted and sentenced, the parole statute ordinarily provides that the prior unexpired sentence is separate and shall be served first, or it provides that the second sentence shall state whether it be served consecutively or concurrently with the first.[211] In the absence of express pro-

---

Note 53 A.L.R. 625. *Contra:* Hightower v. Hollis, 121 Ga. 159, 48 S.E. 492 (1904).

[208] United States v. Remus, 12 Fed. (2d) 239 (C.C.A. 6th, 1926), 11 Minn.L.Rev. 72.

[209] See (1932) 22 J.Crim.L. 902; (1932) 45 Harv.L.Rev. 535.

[210] But a federal court has held that the fact that the sentences are in two separate causes and not on separate counts of the same indictment is not controlling. Boyd v. Archer, 42 F. (2d) 43, 70 A.L.R. 1507 (C.C.A. 9th, 1930).

[211] White, "Some Legal Aspects of Parole" (1942) 32 J.Crim.L. 600, 614-615, 621-622. See 5 A.L.R. 380 (1919); 53 A.L.R. 625 (1927).

vision, the sentences are concurrent. In the federal courts, the Supreme Court has held that the parole statute meant the sentences to be consecutive.[212]

The federal courts have held that probation may be allowed for one count, although imprisonment is ordered for another count of the same indictment.[213] Yet the Supreme Court interpreted the Federal Probation Act, enacted in 1925, to mean that probation must be granted before the defendant begins to serve his sentence.[214] The court pointed out that the purpose of the statute was to provide for a means of rehabilitation by an immediate suspension of sentence during good behavior rather than to create judicial powers resembling the executive power of parole and pardon. On this theory, a probation order granted after imprisonment had begun was reversed, even though the trial court had specifically reserved jurisdiction.[215] Likewise, the imposition of a term of imprisonment as a condition to probation has been condemned.[216] Another group of cases have forsaken the rationale of the Murray Case, have held that each count is capable of having a separate sentence, and have allowed probation under one count of an indictment while ordering imprisonment under another.[217] Moreover, a court which disallowed

[212] Zerbst v. Kidwell, 304 U.S. 359, 58 Sup.Ct. 872, 83 L.Ed. 1399 (1938), 24 Iowa L.Rev. 165.

[213] Weber v. Squier, 124 F. (2d) 618 (C.C.A. 9th, 1941), (1942) 55 Harv.L.Rev. 1210.

[214] United States v. Murray, 275 U.S. 347, 48 Sup.Ct. 146, 72 L.Ed. 309 (1928).

[215] United States v. La Shagway, 95 F. (2d) 200 (C.C.A. 9th, 1938). *Contra:* United States v. Wittmeyer, 16 F. Supp. 1000. (D. Nev. 1936), appeal dismissed, 89 F. (2d) 660 (C.C.A. 9th, 1937), 35 Mich.L.Rev. 1009.

[216] Watkins v. Merry, 106 F. (2d) 360 (C.C.A. 10th, 1939).

[217] White v. Steigleder, 37 F. (2d) 858 (C.C.A. 10th, 1930); United States v. Pendergast, 28 F. Supp. 601 (D. Mo. 1938), (1939) 28 Geo.L.J.

mixed sentences when there were two counts in one indictment reached the opposite result where two indictments were involved.[218] But perhaps the basic question is whether the defendant can better be reformed and rehabilitated by probation or by parole. For the court to order imprisonment and probation seems both logically and criminologically inconsistent.[219] When the defendant once is incarcerated, the parole act provides the method for his rehabilitation. Probation is not meant to be a substitute for parole. In construing the probation statute, the word "sentence" should include several sentences on different counts of one indictment or on separate indictments arising out of one wrong.[220]

22. Habitual Offenders

Under the statutes of many states habitual offenders are punished more severely than other offenders. Occasionally defendants are sentenced without the court's knowing of the previous convictions. In New York it was once held that a defendant could not be given an increased sentence as a subsequent offender unless the indictment and plea so specified.[221] To avoid this a new statute provided that a person may be punished as a subsequent offender, even though he was not indicted or convicted as such.[222] Any time after conviction or sentence as a first offender, a person may be resentenced and given a cumula-

---

420. *Contra:* United States v. Greenhaus, 85 F. (2d) 116, 107 A.L.R. 630 (C.C.A. 2d, 1936), cert. denied 299 U.S. 396 (1937).

218 See Kelly v. United States ex rel. Frad, 89 F. (2d) 866 (C.C.A. 2d, 1937), affirmed sub. nom. Frad v. Kelly, 302 U.S. 312 (1937).

219 Chappell, "The Courts Interpret the Federal Probation Act" (1939) 29 J.Crim.L. 708, 713-714; Note (1942) 55 Harv.L.Rev. 1210.

220 Cf. Mouse v. United States, 14 F. (2d) 202 (D. Kan. 1926).

221 People v. Rosen, 208 N.Y. 169, 101 N.E. 595 (1913).

222 Notes (1926) 26 Col.L.Rev. 752, 754, (1926) 12 A.B.A.J. 386, 387.

tive sentence as a second or fourth offender if found to be such by his own admission or by a jury. The previous sentence is vacated with deductions from the new sentence of all time actually served under the second conviction before resentencing. The United States Supreme Court has held that a similar West Virginia statute is constitutional.[223] Section 403 of the Institute Code prescribes a procedure relative to sentencing for second or subsequent offenses. The proceedings must be taken at some time prior to complete execution of sentence. The defendant is given the right to counsel. If the defendant does not admit the fact of prior conviction the court determines the issue without resort to a jury. It is made the duty of prison wardens, probation, parole, and peace officers to report prior convictions to the prosecuting attorney, as soon as they acquire knowledge of prior convictions.

There is a sharp division of authority as to whether or not a pardoned conviction may be made the basis for increased punishment under habitual criminal statutes.[224] Some courts have held that it may be made the basis for the enhanced penalty.[225] Almost an equal number hold contrary.[226] The latter view is based on the theory that a

[223] Graham v. West Virginia, 224 U.S. 616, 32 Sup.Ct. 583 (1911). See also People v. Gowasky, 244 N.Y. 451, 155 N.E. 737, 58 A.L.R. 9 (1927), 11 Minn.L.Rev. 561; Notes (1937) 51 Harv.L.Rev. 345, (1934) 9 Ind.L.J. 534, 58 A.L.R. 20; McCuaig, "Modern Tendencies in Habitual Criminal Legislation" (1929) 15 Corn.L.Q. 62.

[224] Note (1930) 14 Minn.L.Rev. 293.

[225] People v. Carlesi, 154 App. Div. 481, 139 N.Y.S. 309 (1913), aff'd 208 N.Y. 547, 101 N.E. 1114, aff'd 233 U.S. 51, 34 Sup.Ct. 576, 58 L.Ed. 843 (1914), (1913) 26 Harv.L.Rev. 644; State v. Edelstein, 146 Wash. 221, 262 Pac. 622 (1927); Groseclose v. Plummer, 106 F. (2d) 311 (C.C.A. 9th, 1939), (1940) 30 J.Crim.L. 778.

[226] Edwards v. Commonwealth, 78 Va. 39, 49 Am. Rep. 377 (1883); State v. Martin, 59 Ohio St. 212, 52 N.E. 188, 43 L.R.A. 94, 69 A.S.R. 762

pardon blots out guilt, removes the penalties and disabilities consequent upon conviction, and gives new credit and capacity. A pardon does not, however, remove all the consequences of crime. The former line of cases adopts the theory that the punishment under the statute is not a punishment for the first offense, but one solely for the second offense—which is aggravated by reason of repetition. This view is the ground upon which habitual offender statutes have been held constitutional.[227] In actual fact one becomes a habitual criminal by repetition of offenses whether or not a prior conviction has been pardoned. Of course injustice might result where the defendant was in fact innocent of the prior offense of which he had been pardoned. In such a case he should be allowed to show the reason for the pardon to avoid the increased penalty.[228] The Iowa statutes expressly provide that convictions pardoned for innocence should not be considered under habitual offender laws.[229] If no other remedy exists, the governor should reduce the sentence.

23. Suspension of Sentence and Probation

One group of states has held that the court may suspend the imposition of sentence for a reasonable time for a proper purpose, such as to enable it to examine the facts and circumstances upon which the penalty is to be based, but in the absence of statutory authority an indefinite suspension is improper. Thus when the defendant was

---

(1898); Scribner v. State, 20 S.W. (2d) 416 (Tex. Cr. App. 1929), (1930) 14 Minn.L.Rev. 293. See also (1931) 22 J.Crim.L. 122.

[227] McDonald v. Massachusetts, 180 U.S. 311, 21 Sup.Ct. 389, 45 L.Ed. 542 (1901). See (1927) 11 Minn.L.Rev. 561.

[228] He was not, however, permitted to do so in the first case raising the question. People ex rel. Prisament v. Brophy, 38 N.E. (2d) 468 (N.Y. 1941), (1942) 51 Yale L.J. 699.

[229] Iowa Code (Reichmann, 1939) § 13402.

brought up three and a half years after his conviction for imposition of sentence, the sentence then rendered was held invalid, and habeas corpus lay to discharge the defendant.[230] A majority of jurisdictions hold that imposition of sentence may not be indefinitely postponed.[231] It is argued that such suspension encroaches on the power of the executive to pardon. Suspension for an indefinite time is viewed as a discharge upon which the defendant is entitled to rely.[232] The fate of the defendant should not be left indefinitely in the hands of the judge who tried the case.

A number of cases have asserted that judicial power to suspend execution of sentence is inherent in courts at common law.[233] But the weight of authority denies such power as an infringement on the executive prerogative of pardon.[234] A separate question is as to the power to enforce the sentence after its period would have elapsed but for its suspension. Where suspension is permitted, later commitments have been held proper, the trial court still retaining jurisdiction to act.[235] Likewise where the suspen-

[230] In re Grove, 43 Idaho 775, 254 Pac. 519 (1927). See also State ex rel. Dawson v. Sapp, 87 Kan. 740, 742, 125 Pac. 78, 79 (1912).

[231] 15 Am. Jur., Criminal Law, § 480, p. 136. See 24 C.J.S., Criminal Law, § 1571, p.47. See Notes (1912) 12 Col.L.Rev. 543, (1932) 32 Col.L. Rev. 1031, (1934) 12 Neb.L.Bull. 408, (1895) 9 Harv.L.Rev. 155.

[232] Note (1912) 12 Col.L.Rev. 543.

[233] Weber v. State, 58 Ohio St. 616, 51 N.E. 116 (1896); State v. Buckley, 75 N.H. 402, 74 Atl. 875 (1909). See 15 Am. Jur., Criminal Law, § 492, p.142; 24 C.J.S., § 1618, p.170.

[234] Ex parte United States, 242 U.S. 27, 42, 37 Sup.Ct. 72, 61 L.Ed. 129 (1916), (1917) 30 Harv.L.Rev. 369, (1918) 2 Minn.L.Rev. 381; State v. Abbott, 87 S.C. 466, 70 S.E. 6 (1911); State ex rel. Payne v. Anderson, 43 S.D. 630, 181 N.W. 839 (1921); Bruce, "The Power to Suspend a Criminal Sentence for an Indefinite Period During Good Behavior" (1922) 6 Minn.L.Rev. 363; Note (1931) 29 Mich.L.Rev. 637.

[235] Matter of Collins, 6 Cal. App. 803, 97 Pac. 188 (1908); Fuller v.

sion is illegal, the commitment has been allowed.[236] But whether the suspension is valid or not, there is a disadvantage in allowing later imprisonment. A sentence may be kept hanging over a defendant's head indefinitely. The defendant should be given the option of completing the sentence or accepting the terms of the suspension.[237]

In jurisdictions not permitting an indefinite suspension of imposition of sentence, there is authority that illegal delay in imposing sentence deprives the court of its jurisdiction to pronounce sentence.[238] Some courts have given like effect to illegal postponement of execution of sentence.[239] But the reasoning is weaker there because, a valid sentence having been imposed, the defendant is illegally at large.[240]

The Minnesota Crime Commission in its report of 1927 recommended that, whenever a sentence is sus-

---

State, 100 Miss. 811, 57 So. 6 (1912); Ex parte Harris, 49 N.D. 7, 187 N.W. 140 (1921), (1923) 36 Harv.L.Rev. 342. *Contra:* Ex parte Clendenning, 22 Okla. 188, 97 Pac. 650 (1928); People v. Shattuck, 274 Ill. 491, 113 N.E. 921 (1916).

[236] Neal v. State, 104 Ga. 509, 30 S.E. 858 (1898); In re Lujan, 18 N.M. 310, 137 Pac. 587 (1913). *Contra:* In re Webb, 89 Wis. 354, 62 N.W. 177 (1895); Tuttle v. Long, 100 Me. 123, 60 Atl. 892 (1905). See Note (1912) 12 Col.L.Rev. 543, 545, pointing out that after all a valid judgment has been rendered.

[237] Ex parte Taggert, 12 Okla. Cr. 439, 158 Pac. 288 (1916).

[238] People v. Barrett, 202 Ill. 287, 67 N.E. 23 (1903), 3 Col.L.Rev. 589; Mackelprang v. Walker, 277 Pac. 401 (Utah 1929), (1930) 30 Col.L.Rev. 120; United States v. Wilson, 46 Fed. 748 (D. Idaho 1891). See 15 Am. Jur., Criminal Law, § 486, p.139; 24 C.J.S., Criminal Law, § 1564, p.29.

[239] In re Webb, 89 Wis. 354, 62 N.W. 177 (1895); Ex parte Clendenning, 1 Okla. Cr. 227, 97 Pac. 650 (1928). *Contra:* State v. Abbott, 87 S.C. 466, 70 S.E. 6 (1911), 24 Harv.L.Rev. 579; Ex parte Lujan, 18 N.Mex. 310, 137 Pac. 587 (1913), (1914) 27 Harv.L.Rev. 590. See 15 Am. Jur., Criminal Law, § 497, p.148.

[240] (1914) 27 Harv.L.Rev. 590; (1912) 12 Col.L.Rev. 543; (1931) 29 Mich.L.Rev. 637; (1934) 12 Neb.L.Bull. 408.

pended by a court, a written record should be made of the reasons therefor.[241]

Even in states permitting indefinite suspension of the imposition of sentence, such rules may be superseded by probation statutes. If the court then endeavors to sentence after the period fixed by the probation statutes, the defendant will be entitled to release on habeas corpus.[242] The defendant must be discharged when the probationary period has lapsed without any breach of the conditions of probation.

Probation is a procedure under which a defendant, after conviction or plea of guilty, may be released under the supervision of a trained probation officer on good behavior, subject to return to custody and punishment.[243] It is an outgrowth of the older suspended sentence. But the latter was generally based on inadequate investigation and followed by no supervision. Probation in its proper form is based on a careful presentence investigation and careful supervision under definitely prescribed conditions of behavior.

When a trial court has pronounced sentence and then suspended execution and placed the defendant on probation, the cases are clear that there is a final judgment,

241 Minnesota Crime Commission Report (1927) 31-32.

242 Commonwealth ex rel. Wilhelm v. Morgan, 278 Pa. 395, 123 Atl. 337 (1924). See also People ex rel. Decker v. Page, 211 N.Y.S. 401, 125 Misc. 538 (1925), holding that the probation statute does not affect the court's common-law right to suspend sentence indefinitely; 24 C.J.S., Criminal Law, § 1618, p.174.

243 Orfield, "Improving Probation in Nebraska" (1946) 26 Neb.L.Rev. 69. For a discussion of the Federal Probation Act, see Chappell, "The Courts Interpret the Federal Probation Act" (1939) 29 J.Crim.L. 708. As to the history of probation, see Grinnell, "The Common Law History of Probation" (1941) 32 J.Crim.L. 15. As to the legal aspects of probation, see the chapter "Some Legal Problems Raised by Probation," by Warner in Probation and Criminal Justice (1933).

from which an appeal may be taken.[244] But where imposition of sentence itself is suspended, there has been much doubt concerning the finality.[245] In 1943, the Supreme Court held that the judgment was final and that probation is equivalent to a judgment.[246] This view seems desirable. Probationary supervision is the same whether sentence is imposed or not. The defendant is subject to specific restrictions placed on him by the court, and is under the supervision of a probation officer who must report to the court about his activities. At any time during the probationary period, the defendant may be called in and sentence imposed upon him. It would be unfair to the defendant not to allow him to appeal.

In federal criminal cases there may be no probation after execution of sentence has commenced, even though only a day has been served.[247] It has been held that the interference by a judge with a sentence after incarceration is close to an exercise of the pardoning power lodged in the executive and not in the court.[248] The shame and stigma of imprisonment which the Probation Act seeks to avoid in proper cases will already have been accom-

[244] Berman v. United States, 302 U.S. 211, 58 Sup.Ct. 164, 82 L.Ed. 204 (1937).

[245] Holding that there is no finality, see Miller v. Aderhold, 288 U.S. 206, 53 Sup.Ct. 325, 77 L.Ed. 702 (1933); Ex parte Marquez, 3 Cal. (2d) 625, 45 Pac. (2d) 342 (1935); Commonwealth v. Carelli, 90 Pa. Super. 416 (1917); Birnbaum v. United States, 107 F. (2d) 885, 126 A.L.R. 207 (1939). See Note (1940) 31 J.Crim.L. 310. *Contra:* Nix. v. United States, 131 F. (2d) 857 (1942); Wimbish v. Reece, 170 Ga. 64 (1930); State v. Liliopoulos, 165 Wash. 197, 5 Pac. (2d) 319 (1931).

[246] Korematsu v. United States, 319 U.S. 432, 63 Sup.Ct. 1124, 87 L.Ed. 1497 (U.S. 1943), (1944) 29 Iowa L.Rev. 508. See Note (1940) 31 J.Crim.L. 310.

[247] United States v. Murray, 275 U.S. 347, 48 Sup.Ct. 146, 72 L.Ed. 309 (1928), 76 U. of Pa.L.Rev.875, (1928) 37 Yale L.J. 825, (1928) 23 Ill.L. Rev. 166, (1928) 12 Marq.L.Rev. 168, (1928) 76 U. of Pa.L.Rev. 875.

[248] Davis v. United States, 15 F. (2d) 697 (D.C. 1926).

plished.[249] The Parole Act does not protect the defendant adequately, as the defendant must have served one third of his sentence before parole. This is scarcely adequate protection to juveniles, first offenders, and others who by reason of infirmity or other circumstances should not be imprisoned.[250] On principle, probation should be possible even after commencement of execution of sentence. Not to allow probation seems to be based on the false assumption that the purpose of imprisonment is punitive and overlooks the stimulus to good behavior arising out of the hope of an early release. On the other hand, to allow probation after execution would doubtless burden the trial courts with petitions for probation.

Several cases have held that a defendant, released under a suspended sentence, is entitled to notice and a hearing on the issue whether he has broken the conditions of the suspension, before the suspension may be revoked.[251] Under the Federal Probation Act there must be a hearing.[252] But this is based on statute and not on any constitutional right. Cases not requiring notice and a hearing argue that suspension is a matter of grace, hence may be revoked at will.[253] The contrary contention is that, while the defendant is still under control of the court, he has been granted a certain measure of liberty, which is a

249 Archer v. Snook, 10 F. (2d) 567, 568 (D. Ga. 1926).

250 See (1927) 36 Yale L.J. 420.

251 Ex parte Lucero, 23 N.M. 433, 168 Pac. 713, L.R.A. 1918 C, 549 (1917); State v. Zolantakis, 70 Utah, 296, 259 Pac. 1044, 54 A.L.R. 1463 (1927), (1928) 12 Minn.L.Rev. 413; 15 Am. Jur., Criminal Law, § 500, p.151; 24 C.J.S., Criminal Law, § 1618, p.193; 54 A.L.R. 1471. See (1924) 37 Harv.L.Rev. 913; Hall, "Committee on Survey of Crime, Criminal Law and Criminal Procedure" (1938) 29 J.Crim.L. 562, 573.

252 Escoe v. Zerbst, 295 U.S. 490, 55 Sup.Ct. 818 (1935), (1936) 11 Wis. L.Rev. 291.

253 People v. Goodrich, 149 N.Y.Supp. 406 (1914); People v. Dudley, 173 Mich. 389, 138 N.W. 1044 (1912).

valuable right not to be taken away without due process of law. Accordingly, this view requires, before revocation and recommitment, notice and opportunity to be heard,[254] a hearing in open court with the right to be represented by counsel,[255] but not a jury trial, since the issue is not that of guilt but of violation of probation.[256] In the analogous situation of a conditional pardon, the better view is that the defendant is entitled to a hearing as to whether he has violated the condition.[257] There are cases holding that a parole may be revoked summarily and without a hearing.[258]

An interesting case concerning the power of the federal trial court to modify its sentence after revocation of probation was recently decided by the United States Supreme Court.[259] It was held that the trial court, which had imposed and then suspended a sentence and placed the defendant on probation, could not, on revoking the proba-

[254] Ex parte Lucero, 23 N.M. 433, 168 Pac. 713, L.R.A. 1918 C 549 (1917).

[255] State v. Burnette, 173 N.C. 734, 91 S.E. 364 (1917).

[256] State v. Everett, 164 N.C. 399, 79 S.E. 274, 47 L.R.A. (N.S.) 848 (1913). *Contra:* State v. Renew, 136 S.C. 302, 132 S.E. 613 (1926).

[257] State ex rel. O'Connor v. Wolfer, 53 Minn. 135, 54 N.W. 1065, 19 L.R.A. 783, 39 A.S.R. 582 (1893); Fleenor v. Hammond, 116 F. (2d) 982 (C.C.A. 6th, 1941), (1940) 24 Minn.L.Rev. 584, (1941) 8 U. of Chi.L.Rev. 771. It should be noted, however, that while a pardon condones the crime and takes away civil disabilities, a suspension of sentence does not. People v. Court of Sessions, 141 N.Y. 288, 36 N.E. 386, 23 L.R.A. 856 (1894).

[258] Ex parte Sparks, 907 Tex. Cr. 190, 234 S.W. 393 (1921); (1908) 67 Cent.L.J. 188; (1923) 32 Yale L.J. 850. But see White, "Some Legal Aspects of Parole" (1942) 32 J.Crim.L. 600, 610. Favoring a hearing in cases of revocation of probation, parole, or pardon as a constitutional right as well as good practice, see Weihofen, "Revoking Probation, Parole or Pardon Without a Hearing" (1942) 32 J.Crim.L. 531.

[259] Roberts v. United States, 320 U.S. 464, 64 Sup.Ct. 113, 88 L.Ed. 41 (1943), three justices dissenting. The case is noted in (1944) 12 Geo. Wash.L.Rev. 240; (1944) 11 U. of Chi.L.Rev. 286.

tion, impose a new and more severe sentence. Only the original sentence could be imposed. The statute provides that "the court may revoke the probation or the suspension of sentence, and may impose any sentence which might originally have been imposed." [260] In the original proceedings, the defendant might have been sentenced to a three year prison term; instead he received a two year term, but was placed on probation. Prior to the statute, two different approaches to the probation problem were recognized. Under one approach the defendant should be confronted with a fixed and specific threat which may not be modified, if he should later violate his probation. The second approach favored flexibility both at the trial and when probation was revoked. It appears that Congress was aware of these two approaches. The language of the statute would seem to indicate that it chose the latter approach. It is true that there have been cases where the power to impose lesser punishment has been upheld by the lower federal courts.[261] The Supreme Court confined itself to an attempt at increase in punishment, and might thus possibly uphold a reduction.

The decision may also be questioned as a matter of policy. The policy considerations favoring the decision are, first, that a definite prison term is a more effective deterrent of violation of probation than a prison sentence, the length of which has not been irrevocably determined; and, second, that imposition of sentence prior to probation is more efficient and speedier since the original sentence may be imposed, in case of violation of probation, without consideration of anything except the fact of viola-

[260] U.S.C., title 18, § 725, 18 U.S.C.A., § 725 (1940).

[261] United States v. Antinori, 59 F (2d) 171 (C.C.A. 5th, 1932); Scalia v. United States, 62 F. (2d) 220 (C.C.A. 1st, 1932).

tion. The opposing contentions are that the second approach leaves the court free to utilize all available knowledge regarding the offender at the time of the new sentence, including knowledge gained while he was on probation; and that the method appears to be just as effective a deterrent against violation of probation.[262] The result of the decision may be that trial judges will place defendants on probation without any tentative sentence. The few state court decisions do not accord with the decision.[263]

24. Effect of Repeal of Statute

After a defendant has commenced serving his sentence, the repeal of the constitutional amendment or statute under which the prosecution was had does not invalidate the sentence, unless there be language of a retrospective character in the amendment or statute.[264] It is enough that there has been no appeal or other proceedings and that the judgment became final before the repeal.[265] Final judgment serves as insulation from inquiry into the causes

[262] Puttkammer, "The Trial Court's Freedom of Discretion in Sentencing After Revocation of Probation" (1944) 11 U. of Chi.L.Rev. 286.

[263] In People v. Stone, 25 N.Y.Supp. (2d) 94 (1940), the court held that the original sentence could be decreased or increased. In Ex parte Goetz, 117 Pac. (2d) 47 (D.C. App., Calif. 1941) there is a dictum that, where probation is granted after sentence, the sentence may be modified or set aside.

[264] Rives v. O'Hearne, 64 App. D.C. 48, 73 F. (2d) 984 (1934). See also United States ex rel. Voorhees v. Hill, 6 F.Supp. 922 (1934), (1935) 3 Geo.Wash.L.Rev. 247. For a criticism of the law as to repeal, see Levitt, "Repeal of Penal Statutes and Effect on Pending Prosecutions" (1923) 9 A.B.A.J. 715; Notes (1934) 1 U. of Chi.L.Rev. 808, (1934) 82 U. of Pa.L. Rev. 398.

[265] United States v. Chambers, 291 U.S. 217, 54 Sup.Ct. 434, 78 L.Ed. 763 (1934), 2 Geo.Wash.L.Rev. 395, (1934) 34 Col.L.Rev. 557, (1934) 18 Minn.L.Rev. 738, (1934) 1 U. of Chi.L.Rev. 808, (1934) 32 Mich.L.Rev. 700, (1934) 7 So.Calif.L.Rev. 481.

of detention. The criminal statute must be in existence on each of three occasions: (1) when the alleged offenses occurred; (2) at the time of the trial; and (3) when final judgment is rendered. It is required at the time of the commission of the crime so that the defendant may have notice that such conduct is objectionable. It is required at the time of trial and of final judgment so that the court may have jurisdiction to try and dispose of the case.[266]

25. Injunction Against Execution of Sentence

A court of equity will not enjoin the execution of a sentence even though the penalty is death.[267] No irreparable injury to property is threatened.[268] Equity will not protect liberty or life simply as such. Multiplicity of suits might perhaps be urged as a ground of equity jurisdiction. The fact that infliction of the penalty might itself be a crime is not a ground for equity jurisdiction since equity seldom enjoins criminal acts as such.

26. Indemnity to Persons Wrongfully Convicted

An act of Congress approved May 24, 1938, provides that any person convicted of a federal crime who, having served all or part of the sentence imposed, shall hereafter, upon appeal or a new trial or rehearing, be found not guilty of the crime of which he was convicted or shall hereafter receive a pardon on the ground of innocence, may

[266] Lunning v. State, 9 Ind. 309 (1857).

[267] Ferguson v. Martineau, 115 Ark. 317, 171 S.W. 472, Ann. Cas. 1916 E, 421 (1914); People v. Superior Court, 190 Cal. 624, 213 Pac. 945 (1923), (1924) 23 Mich.L.Rev. 57; State v. Lowe, 54 N.D. 637, 210 N.W. 501, (1926). But see Gore v. Humphries, 162 Ga. 653, 135 S.E. 481, (1926), (1927) 40 Harv.L.Rev. 781; (1933) 11 Neb.L.Bull. 421, 424.

[268] But none was required in a sterilization case. Mickle v. Henrichs, 262 Fed. 687 (D. Nev. 1918).

maintain suit against the United States in the Court of Claims for damages sustained as a result of such conviction and imprisonment.[269] It must appear that the plaintiff did not commit any of the acts charged or that his conduct in connection with such charge did not constitute a crime against the United States or territory, and that he did not contribute to the bringing about of his arrest or conviction intentionally or by willful misconduct or negligence. The amount of damages awarded shall not exceed $5,000.

The earliest progenitor of such a statute was a Prussian statute sponsored by Frederick the Great in 1766. Today many Continental countries have such a statute.[270] In only four states in this country is there any remedy other than by special legislative grant for erroneous conviction and imprisonment.[271]

Two main theories support compensation as against the doctrine that the state can do no wrong. The first is analogous to that governing eminent domain; namely, that the owner of private property taken for a public use should be compensated. In the case of a criminal proceeding private liberty has been taken. The second theory is that which supports workmen's compensation. Just as there are bound to be accidents in industry, so there are mistakes made in the administration of the criminal law.

[269] 52 Stat. 438, 18 U.S.C. ¶¶ 729, 732 (1940), (1938) 52 Harv.L.Rev. 333; Borchard, "State Indemnity for Errors of Criminal Justice" (1941) 21 B.U.L.Rev. 201.

[270] Borchard, "Convicting the Innocent" (1932) 380 *et seq.;* Borchard, "European Systems of State Indemnity for Errors of Criminal Justice" (1913) 3 J.Crim.L. 684.

[271] Cal. Gen. Laws (Deering, 1937) Act 1681; N.Y. Laws, 1946, c.10; N.D. Comp. Laws Ann. (Supp. 1925) § 11269(b); Wis. Stat. 1945, c.285.05. The New York statute is discussed in (1946) 21 N.Y.U.L.Q. Rev. 422.

Two classes of injustice to a defendant in a criminal proceeding should be distinguished. The first is the detention of a person erroneously accused extending up to his acquittal. The second is that of conviction followed by sentence and imprisonment. The latter injustice is the more flagrant and should be remedied first, although most European countries indemnify in both cases.

The right to recover should be limited to prevent abuse. In the first place, the alleged victim must be required to prove his innocence of the crime charged against him and that he did not commit any other crime. He must show either that he did not commit the crime or that no crime was committed. In the second place, recovery should be limited to his pecuniary injury, such as loss of income, costs of defense, and for securing his ultimate acquittal or pardon. The highest recovery possible should be $5,000. Moreover, the accused must not have caused his prosecution by his own censurable conduct, such as the concealment of evidence. A special court of claims should handle claims of indemnity.

INDEX